GEORGE ELIOT: THE CRITICAL HERITAGE

THE CRITICAL HERITAGE SERIES

General Editor: B. C. Southam

The Critical Heritage series collects together a large body of criticism on major figures in literature. Each volume presents the contemporary responses to a particular writer, enabling the student to follow the formation of critical attitudes to the writer's work and its place within a literary tradition.

The carefully selected sources range from landmark essays in the history of criticism to fragments of contemporary opinion and little published documentary material, such as letters and diaries.

Significant pieces of criticism from later periods are also included in order to demonstrate fluctuations in reputation following the writer's death.

GEORGE ELIOT

THE CRITICAL HERITAGE

Edited by

DAVID CARROLL

London and New York

MILSTEIN
PR
4688
.C3
1971b

First Published in 1971
Reprinted 1995, 2000

2 Park Square, Milton Park,
Abingdon, Oxon, OX14 4RN
&
270 Madison Ave, New York,
NY10016

Transferred to Digital Printing 2005

Routledge is an imprint of the Taylor & Francis Group

Printed and bound in Great Britain by
T.J.I. Digital, Padstow, Cornwall

British Library Cataloguing in Publication Data

ISBN 0–415–13462–5

General Editor's Preface

The reception given to a writer by his contemporaries and near-contemporaries is evidence of considerable value to the student of literature. On one side we learn a great deal about the state of criticism at large and in particular about the development of critical attitudes towards a single writer; at the same time, through private comments in letters, journals or marginalia, we gain an insight upon the tastes and literary thought of individual readers of the period. Evidence of this kind helps us to understand the writer's historical situation, the nature of his immediate reading-public, and his response to these pressures.

The separate volumes in the *Critical Heritage Series* present a record of this early criticism. Clearly, for many of the highly productive and lengthily reviewed nineteenth- and twentieth-century writers, there exists an enormous body of material; and in these cases the volume editors have made a selection of the most important views, significant for their intrinsic critical worth or for their representative quality—perhaps even registering incomprehension!

For earlier writers, notably pre-eighteenth century, the materials are much scarcer and the historical period has been extended, sometimes far beyond the writer's lifetime, in order to show the inception and growth of critical views which were initially slow to appear.

In each volume the documents are headed by an Introduction, discussing the material assembled and relating the early stages of the author's reception to what we have come to identify as the critical tradition. The volumes will make available much material which would otherwise be difficult of access and it is hoped that the modern reader will be thereby helped towards an informed understanding of the ways in which literature has been read and judged.

B.C.S.

To
My Parents

Contents

Silas Marner (1861)

Romola (1862–3)

Felix Holt (1866)

CONTENTS

xi

CONTENTS

Preface

Almost all the sixty-nine items in this collection are English or American reviews written shortly after George Eliot's novels were first published. I have also included some obituary comment and two reviews of Cross's *Life* (1885); here the Victorian critics had an opportunity of looking back and commenting on the novelist's career as a whole. Some of George Eliot's reactions to criticism are also given in order to suggest the nature of the relationship between herself and the reviewers. The material is arranged for the most part in chronological order, and anonymous authors have been identified whenever possible. The text is invariably taken from the first edition; titles of books have, however, been standardized, typographical errors silently corrected, and I have supplied the titles to all items except No. 58.

My aim has not been comprehensiveness. The reviews collected here are merely a fraction of the contemporary criticism of the novels. The only way to achieve a semblance of completeness would have been to print excerpts from a great number of reviews. But this would simply indicate who was for and who against the novels, and the purpose of this volume is not to record and count votes. More interesting are the reasons the reviewers give for their reactions. This is the basis on which these sixty-nine items have been selected and the reason why they have generally been reproduced in full: the critic may then record his responses and develop his argument at his own speed, and reveal fully his critical assumptions and values. Within these limits I have tried to include as many varied points of view as possible. These selected reviews and comments are placed in broader perspective in the Introduction. There I seek to describe the critical trends which become apparent from reading very many more reviews of George Eliot's novels than are reprinted here.

Acknowledgments

I would like to thank the following: the Trustees of the National Library of Scotland for permission to reproduce Bulwer-Lytton's letter to John Blackwood, and the Assistant Keeper of Manuscripts, Mr Alan S. Bell, for his assistance; Mrs G. A. Morley for permission to reprint John Morley's review of *Felix Holt*; Oxford University Press for permission to reprint Anthony Trollope's letter to George Eliot from *The Letters of Anthony Trollope*, ed. Bradford A. Booth (1951); and Yale University Press for permission to reprint passages from *The George Eliot Letters*, ed. Gordon S. Haight (1954–5). In the preparation of this volume, I am indebted to Professor Haight's edition of the letters.

Introduction

I

One is taken aback at first simply by the number of contemporary reviews of George Eliot's novels. In a way unprecedented today, tens of thousands of words—in the daily newspapers, the weekly reviews, the monthly and quarterly journals—were devoted to each work as it appeared. The second surprise is the sustained sense of urgency these anonymous reviewers bring to their task. They are not interested in using the work under review as a pretext for literary gossip or self-display. They want to know if the particular novel is a true picture of reality and whether its effect is beneficial or pernicious. On these grounds they assess its worth. The urgency of their discussion springs from the unquestioned assumption that art presses closely upon life, both emotionally and intellectually, and that it is the critic's task to confront literary works with his own values and beliefs. Sometimes, one feels, these beliefs come between the critic and the novel; they are either too conventional or inflexible to respond to the challenge. But these writers never pretend that their task is anything but serious and important. They keep their eyes on the novel they are reviewing and give as true an account of it as possible. They are unwilling to analyse in any detail and, if tempted to do so, usually apologize for presuming to instruct the reader. Indeed, pages of the longer essays were often filled with very generous quotations, on the principle that it is simpler to pass the bottle than to describe the wine.

After the success of *Adam Bede* (1859), George Eliot received un-flagging attention from these critics until the end of her career. Everything she wrote, even *Impressions of Theophrastus Such* (1879), even the poetry, became the subject of lengthy discussion and debate in the periodicals. But the admiration which this indicates was not of a steady growth. The graph of her reputation had some steep and, to the twentieth-century reader, unexpected ups and downs. The evolution of a writer's career only appears inevitable in the simplified perspective of later generations. Posterity has the advantage of hindsight, possesses most of the facts—the letters, the notebooks, the cancelled drafts—and its premise is pattern and growth. The contemporary reviewer, on the other hand, writes out of the confused, disordered situation which is the literary period as it happens. To him each novel is a new challenge to be linked as expeditiously as possible to the most convenient fixed point of reference. In this local perspective, which has its own advantages, George Eliot's career was anything but predictable.

In one sense, the widespread popularity of *Adam Bede* misled her readers and critics for years. They waited long and patiently for her to repeat this success, but she never did. When *Romola* (1862–3) appeared they realized it was necessary to adjust to the new reality; bucolic charm was a thing of the past. George Eliot's refusal to reproduce her early success might have been an impressive sign of her integrity if that success had been free of deception. But when her pseudonym was lifted shortly after her first novel many readers felt they had been badly deceived: the clerical gentleman who stressed so impressively the demands of duty in his vivid picture of a Christian society turned out to be a female atheist living with another woman's husband. This contradiction—I have stated it in an extreme form—became with all its implications the focus of the Victorian criticism of the novels. Could the kind of humanism which George Eliot expressed with growing explicitness in her novels be the basis of a realistic picture of life?

This was a question of more than academic interest. It brought together in an explosive mixture the two most pronounced characteristics of the Victorian reader—an insatiable interest in fictional characters and a commitment to the Christian religion. The reading-public followed the fortunes of George Eliot's characters as if they were real people, measuring their consistency against standards which were in the last resort religious. The question, asked with surprising intensity, was: given this character in these circumstances would he have acted in this way? The explosion occurred when Maggie Tulliver became infatuated with Stephen Guest in the third volume of *The Mill on the Floss* (1860). The reviewers were enraged that a theory of life which they found unacceptable had been allowed to falsify a character they accepted without reservation. But George Eliot could not be summarily dismissed as a novelist. One reviewer shrewdly observed that she 'was already accepted as a great artist; her teaching had been dubbed clerical, and it was too late in the day to turn upon her and call her an atheist' (No. 38).

For the rest of her lifetime the critics addressed themselves to this problem. When they confront its paradoxes honestly and openly we see criticism of a high order. Stretching their moral and aesthetic categories to the limit, they seek to contain works of art which are radically new and disturbing. Sometimes, in order to account for the novels, they discover there a direct conflict between artist and philosopher, between dramatist and commentator. This could lead to the dismemberment of the novels, so infuriating to their author. Alternatively, the critics refuse any simple solution and seek to define in all its complexity the relationship between a creative power they consider awe-inspiring and a religion of humanity they find limiting and melancholy. When they write in this way—and it is a skill not restricted to the better-known figures—then they produce criticism which is both exciting and important.

George Eliot stood apart from this critical debate which continued throughout her writing career. Or at least so it appeared. Lewes went to enormous pains to shield her from the slightest breath of criticism, opening and censoring all her letters, snipping reviews out of the newspapers, surreptitiously adding cautionary postscripts to letters to their friends. They agreed on this policy after the publication of *Adam Bede* when, Lewes told Sara Hennell, George Eliot had 'felt deeply the evil influences of talking and allowing others to talk to her about her writing. We resolved therefore to exclude everything as far as we could. No one speaks about her books to her, but me; she sees not criticisms.'[1] He remained to the end constantly aware of what he called 'her terrible diffidence'.[2] But the censorship was either relaxed or Lewes became careless, for it is clear from George Eliot's letters that she knew at first or secondhand many of the contemporary assessments of her work, and not all of these were friendly. John Blackwood confirms this in a letter he wrote to his brother William after a visit to the Priory in 1876. 'She was looking a little worn and I think Lewes fidgets her in his anxiety both about her and her work and himself. She says she never reads any review, but she certainly hears plentifully all that is said or written in London on the subject of *Deronda*.'[3] It is a revealing glimpse of both George Eliot and her solicitous guardian; after almost twenty years as censor Lewes is still protecting the novelist against the criticism to which she clearly has access.

George Eliot certainly disliked and disapproved of what she heard and read. Adverse judgment had an immediately debilitating effect upon her writing, increasing her natural self-doubt to the proportions of neurosis. Perhaps this was one of the reasons she came to see the reviewers as a serious barrier between her novels and their rightful audience. In her letters and occasional writings she attacks them repeatedly for their quick judgments, their self-esteem, their sheep-like conformity. Occasionally, as in this comment in 1860, she mixes a little sympathy with her censure. 'We must have mercy on critics who are obliged to make a figure in printed pages. They must by all means say striking things.' But her own experiences with the *Westminster Review* seem on the whole to have increased her mistrust. She continues: 'Either we should not read printed criticisms at all, (*I don't*) or we should read them with the constant remembrance that they are a fugitive kind of work which, in the present stage of human nature, can rarely engage a very high grade of conscience or ability.'[4]

In her own reviews, before she became a novelist, she repeatedly warns writers against those false friends, the reviewers, whose commendation is guaranteed to mislead. In 1856 she cautions the Silly Lady Novelists she has just briskly castigated: 'By a peculiar thermometric adjustment, when a woman's talent is at zero, journalistic approbation is at the boiling pitch; when she attains mediocrity, it is already at no more than summer heat; and if ever she reaches excellence, critical enthusiasm drops to the freezing point.'[5] One of her own frequent critical strategies is to acknowledge the complaints of the carping reviewers, promptly dissociate herself from them, and declare her allegiance to the reading-public. Harriet Beecher Stowe's novel *Dred* has some deficiencies, she admits in her review of 1856, and no doubt the critics will display them to the full. But, in the meantime, the novel 'will be devoured by the million, who carry no critical talisman against the enchantment of genius. We confess ourselves to be among the million, and quite unfit to rank with the sage minority of Fadladeens.'[6]

The last sentence, both in tone and sentiment, carries us straight into the world of George Eliot's early novels, which she began writing a few months later. There her fictional persona uses the same rhetorical device to express the morality of shared humanity. Both are protests against the detached, critical state of mind which forgets that people, in novels or out of them, are human beings like ourselves. And from the novels one could compile without difficulty a manual of criticism for the guidance of the reviewers she so mistrusted. It is interesting to see how they respond to a writer who tells them how to do their job. Later in her life she came to see their role as inevitably injurious; by 1877 the proliferation of criticism in the periodicals was 'a chief curse of our time'.[7] The reason is obvious. The reading of criticism, she had written in 1871, 'accustoms men and women to formulate opinions instead of receiving deep impressions, and to receive deep impressions is the foundation of all true mental power'.[8] This theoretical basis for her objection must have been strengthened by the growing awareness that after *Adam Bede*, certainly after *Silas Marner* (1861), she was not going to repeat the early rapturous and unconditional success. Her letters show her turning this way and that for reassurance that her novels have been appreciated. If the reviewers are hostile she turns to the reading-public; if sales are disappointing she has the consolation of enthusiastic letters from individual readers. She is delighted when the cognoscenti reassure her about the greatness of *Romola*, and Jews confirm the reality of *Daniel Deronda* (1876).

Her pseudonym complicated relations with the reading-public. While it was still effective, speculation was mainly confined to George Eliot's sex and the reviewers combed through her work for evidence. Would a woman quote Greek? Could anyone but a clergyman know so much about clerical life? Except perhaps a clergyman's wife? When the pseudonym was lifted and her private life revealed, then came the equally tiresome post-mortems. 'It was certain,' she said in 1860, 'that in the notices of my first book after the removal of my incognito there would be much *ex post facto* wisdom, which could hardly profit me, since I certainly knew who I was beforehand, and knew also that no one else knew, who had not been told.'[9] Meanwhile the works themselves, George Eliot felt, were being obscured by biographical speculation and the wisdom of hindsight. There is, however, surprisingly little gossip and scandal in the reviews; only the growing uneasy awareness that the novels, despite their considerable charm, are the work of the translator of Strauss and Feuerbach. The reviewers are on the alert for any sign of unorthodoxy—the sectarian journals in particular are lynx-eyed—and when they find it they challenge it directly.

This kind of interest may bring an urgency to the discussion of the novels, but it may also further distort the symmetry already disturbed by the critics' obsessive interest in character. And here one sympathizes with George Eliot's complaints. The majority of reviewers never treated the unity of her novels with the seriousness she intended. Her well-known *cri de cœur* over the dissection of *Daniel Deronda*[10] by readers who were only interested in Gwendolen was not an isolated case; her letter of thanks to R. H. Hutton (No. 35) for his review of

Romola shows how anxious she was for each novel to be read as a complex, unified whole. Here, if anywhere, George Eliot is most clearly in advance of her critics. In her critical writings and, of course, in the novels themselves, she reveals a concept of organic form far more subtle and sophisticated than any but the most astute of her reviewers expect to find in fiction. They, for the most part, were distracted from these more formal considerations by the immediate challenge of the novels.

George Eliot's final comment on the 'sheeplike flock' of critics was published posthumously in 1884. It is a harsh judgment written in her most abstract, sibylline manner. These writers, she says, are incapable of making a genuine assessment of a living writer. They have developed only one quality, 'a susceptibility to their own reputation for passing the right judgment, not the susceptibility to qualities in the object of judgment'.[11] As a further indication of George Eliot's mistrust of the reviewers this is significant, but as a true assessment of the critical treatment she received during her lifetime it is, as I think this volume shows, unfair.

II

Scenes of Clerical Life

The criticism of George Eliot began before she had written her first story. In her journal for 1856 she describes how, dozing in bed one morning at Tenby, she imagined she was writing a story entitled 'The Sad Fortunes of the Reverend Amos Barton'. George Henry Lewes, immediately enthusiastic, considered it 'a capital title'. Eventually it became her first story, but, as her journal records, the criticism began before it was written.

George used to say, 'It may be a failure—it may be that you are unable to write fiction. Or perhaps, it may be just good enough to warrant your trying again.' Again, 'You may write a chef-d'œuvre at once—there's no telling.' But his prevalent impression was that though I could hardly write a *poor* novel, my novel would want the highest quality of fiction—dramatic presentation.

Lewes' doubts began to disappear when he heard the first part of 'Amos Barton'. The scene at Cross Farm convinced him she could write dialogue. Yet he was cautious. 'There still remained the question whether I could command any pathos; and that was to be decided by the mode in which I treated Milly's death.' Lewes went up to town to give her a quiet evening at home. When he returned, she read the scene to him. 'We both cried over it, and then he came up to me and kissed me, saying "I think your pathos is better than your fun." '12

Lewes no doubt felt he could put George Eliot through her literary paces with a certain amount of authority. He had written fiction himself and was already one of the most versatile of the established reviewers in the 1850s. His enthusiasm however wasn't catching. The brief notices which did appear were moderately encouraging. Dickens praised the 'exquisite truth and delicacy' of the stories in thanking George Eliot for his presentation copy,13 and The Times found itself 'impressed' (No. 2). Other critics began to shape those definitions of the author's domestic realism which are to recur so frequently during the next few years. They praise her combination of pathos and humour, the absence of exaggeration, and the prosaic homeliness of this fictional world without ideal heroes and heroines which they associate with Crabbe, Goldsmith, and the paintings of Wilkie. They accept George Eliot's realism without demur. One critic takes its everyday quality so much to heart that he would prefer to omit the melodrama of Tryan's purple past from 'Janet's Repentance' (No. 5).

The only unpleasant noises had come earlier from John Blackwood in Edinburgh. He was the publisher and friend of Lewes to whom 'Amos Barton' had been sent; eventually he was to publish all George Eliot's novels, with the exception of Romola, and become one of her closest friends. She described him in these early days with prophetic insight as 'my editor, who seems to have been created in pre-established harmony with the organization of a susceptible contributor'.14 But the new relationship had several uneasy moments during the publication in 1857 of Scenes of Clerical Life in eleven instalments in Blackwood's Magazine. The letters included here (No. 1) show George Eliot, Lewes and Blackwood only gradually settling into the comfortable and successful partnership which was to last for twenty years. From the first, Blackwood was apprehensive about the effect of George Eliot's frank realism upon his readers. Certain details he found too specific and in need of 'softening'; certain characters were too reproachable and needed rehabilitating. Admittedly the stories were powerful, but couldn't the next one be a little more cheerful? The next one turned out to be 'Janet's Repentance' (which even Henry James found 'scabreux' nine years later)15 and his concern comes to a head. He finds

7

the opening scene 'rather a staggerer', and confesses that he feels she is becoming more and more committed to a 'harsher Thackerayan view of human nature'.

This time, despite Lewes' repeated warnings, Blackwood had gone too far. George Eliot's annoyance had been growing with Blackwood's concern. His informal, colloquial comments had been weighed carefully by the new author and his objections answered in a thoughtful, measured style. But he would persist in re-writing the stories to his own satisfaction, and with this there could be no compromise. He must make a choice. 'There is nothing to be done with the story, but either to let Dempster and Janet and the rest be as I *see* them, or to renounce it as too painful.' Her ultimatum, Blackwood confesses in his open way, gave him 'quite a turn'. Of course he will publish the story as it stands, and she must not take his comments too seriously. His cheerful and accommodating frankness had saved the day, but there had been some prickly moments. It is a fascinating episode. On the one hand, there is the experienced publisher, aware that he has found a genuine new talent, and yet sensitive to the demands of his readers; on the other, the anonymous and unknown novelist firmly meeting all criticisms with the tenets of her carefully formulated realism, and finally, with the confidence of her untried genius, refusing any compromise. It is a paradigm of George Eliot's relations with her readers for the rest of her career. And one mustn't forget the crucial role of Lewes, the intermediary between publisher and author, cautioning one, encouraging the other, and bringing into existence the novelist whose reputation so quickly eclipsed his own.

III

Adam Bede

George Eliot made her reputation soon after the publication of *Adam Bede* on 1 February 1859. On 12 February there was a brief dismissive notice in the *Spectator*. On 26 February the *Athenaeum* and the *Saturday Review* published favourable reviews. The *Westminster Review* in its April number quoted the novel extensively and praised it warmly. Then, to confirm the growing enthusiasm, *The Times* began its review on 12 April with the words: 'There can be no mistake about *Adam Bede*. It is a first-rate novel, and its author takes rank at once among the masters of the art' (No. 8). And virtually everyone agreed. Mrs

Poyser, in particular, was seized upon with cries of delight; she was quoted in Parliament; she was as great as the glorious Sam Weller. It looked as if Dickens' early success was about to be repeated.

Three thousand copies were sold in the first three months, and by March 1860 the novel had been translated into Hungarian, German, Dutch and French. Lewes wrote to one of his sons in 1860 that *Adam Bede* 'has had greater success than any novel since Scott (except Dickens)'. Then he brings his delight under control: 'I do not mean has *sold* more—for *Uncle Tom's Cabin* and *Les Mystères de Paris* surpass all novels in sale; but in its *influence*, and in obtaining the suffrages of the highest and wisest as well as of the ordinary novel reader, nothing equals *Adam Bede*.'[16] This puts the success of the novel in perspective. More than 300,000 copies of Harriet Beecher Stowe's novel had been sold during its first year of publication, while the sale of *Adam Bede*, although it continued steadily for many years, numbered 16,000 in 1859. But George Eliot had found a wide audience and she was delighted. After Dickens' generous letter (No. 9), it seemed that *Adam Bede* had all the marks of a popular success. The final doubtful accolade came in October when, to the intense annoyance of Lewes, the publisher Newby announced a new novel entitled *Adam Bede, Junior. A Sequel.*

George Eliot had been sure that her novel was 'too quiet and too unflattering to dominant fashions ever to be very popular'.[17] But these were the very qualities hailed by the reviewers. In the words of *The Times*, the characters were 'so true, and so natural, and so racy' that many readers insisted they were recorded rather than invented. This was fine, if naïve testimony to George Eliot's realism; it only became annoying when it gave support to the bizarre claims of the impostor Liggins. The major characters were not only real, they also seemed detachable from each other and the milieu in which they were presented. Consequently, contemporary readers could indulge their fascination in them without inhibition. Similarly, as the reviewers demonstrated, set pieces of description could be removed from the novel and enjoyed, like Mrs Poyser's sayings, for their own sake.

The more perceptive reviewers went beyond the realism to the skill which it concealed. The critic of the *Saturday Review* knew that it was not simply a question of observation. When creating a character, an author must first have an idea, something like a scientific hypothesis, around which the details are to be grouped, 'something that comes from the observer, not the observed—a general key to the character which the drawer of the character assumes at first, and then proves by elaborating it' (No. 7). But it was generally agreed that behind all literary skills was the author's imaginative sympathy which asserts that we all share a common humanity. This, however, creates its own problems for the novelist. It is much easier to draw a character by stressing points of difference and contrast, as the critic of *The Times* shrewdly observes, than it is 'to dwell mainly on those traits which we have all in common, and, which, therefore, are anything but salient'. It was recognized that George Eliot overcame this problem by the way she explored the inner lives of her characters. External differences which define characters are balanced against the profound similarities which unite them. This technique encourages charity, says the critic of *Bentley's Quarterly Review* in the most thorough of all the discussions of the novel; if the author explores her characters deeply enough, 'there is quite sure to be something in the process with which we can sympathise' (No. 10). But the corollary, this reviewer maintains, is not as cosy as *The Times* would have us believe. *Adam Bede* does not show that we are all alike, only that we are all exposed to similar temptations. How we react depends upon our individual consciences.

Regardless of the finer points of morality, the reviewers acknowledged with some excitement that George Eliot had reclaimed a large area of human experience from obscurity. Her picture of rural life in the Midlands at the turn of the century was another victory for the nineteenth-century novel against what George Eliot called, in her fine oxymoron, 'the vulgarity of exclusiveness'.[18] There were, of course, less high-minded reasons for their interest. As a critic in *Blackwood's Magazine* reminds us, readers want stories to be as remote from their everyday lives as possible. 'If you wish [the costermonger] to weep, it must be over the sorrows of a baroness at the very least: he hears of his neighbour the dustman hammering his wife—a creature of ordinary clay—without any particular excitement of his sensibilities.' The educated classes too enjoy the occasional safari into novels of working-class life in search of something different. But writers who seek to exploit this demand, this critic warns, have a difficult task.

They are writing about things with which they can have but a very imperfect acquaintance. Even the very best of such stories, in spite of their cleverness and popularity, give us but a stage view, after all, of the life and feelings of the lower classes. And as to most attempts of the kind, the characters are about as real as the shepherds and milkmaids of the *Trianon*. But in the volumes before us we think we have the genuine article. . . .[19]

There were some reservations about the novel. It was agreed that the plot was no more than adequate as a means of displaying character. The *Athenaeum* and the *Saturday Review* went further. They felt that George Eliot lost control of her novel with the incidents of the seduction, the execution, and the reprieve. They objected for two reasons. First, they regretted that she betrayed her own aesthetic theory by switching from the everyday world of lifelike carpenters where she was strong to the world of melodrama and last-minute rescues where she was weak. The second objection was to the aesthetic itself. At the end of the novel, complains the *Athenaeum*, 'the brutal facts are not softened to fit them for their place in a work of Art'.[20] We all know that milkmaids are seduced but that is no reason for introducing the reader of a pastoral novel to 'the startling horrors of rustic reality' (No. 7). Certainly, if readers ignored George Eliot's elaborate pattern of consequences, it might seem as if she were mixing two species of fiction which they clearly wish to keep separate.

Rustic reality contained the account of Hetty's seduction and pregnancy, and this raised many eyebrows. The *Examiner* felt bound to protest against the 'almost obstetric accuracy of detail',[21] while the *Saturday Review* appealed to a more discreet tradition: 'Let us copy the old masters of the art, who, if they gave us a baby, gave it us all at once' (No. 7). Several years later, one reviewer was to point to George Eliot's presentation of Hetty as the first indication of that 'vein of perilous voluptuousness running through her works'.[22] The more perceptive critics saw that she was the most original part of the novel. Other novelists in particular realized that George Eliot had caught with marvellous accuracy a fluid, indeterminate character with no foundation of belief or personality. Dickens' adjectives are carefully chosen; he knew of nothing 'so skilful, determined, and uncompromising'. And in 1866 Henry James still found her 'on the whole, I think, the most successful' of all George Eliot's female figures.[23]

Surprisingly, there had been no serious objection to the treatment of religion in the novel. The *Eclectic Review* even enjoyed 'the high Christian morality of the work'.[24] *The Times* noticed that *Adam Bede* was a 'secular rendering of the deepest sentiment of Christianity', but it found nothing to make it uneasy. Only the critic of the radical *Westminster Review* in an otherwise unexceptional article suspected that George Eliot's strict theory of consequences with its denial of redemption was at all unorthodox. With considerable perception he goes further and suggests that George Eliot is so widely tolerant of religion only because she 'regards the numerous theological creeds, about which the clerical mind has so long disputed, as being only shells of different shape and colour, enclosing the fruit of the religious spirit common to the human race, or as so many mental structures which in less successive metamorphoses man forms and afterwards casts off'.[25] This was a lonely voice, but it was a foretaste of things to come when the reviewers began to write their appraisals of *The Mill on the Floss*. By then, of course, they knew that George Eliot was, among other things, the translator of Strauss and Feuerbach. Henry Crabb Robinson's disturbed reaction to the rumour in July 1859 was representative. 'Such a fact destroys all comfortable notions of right and wrong, true and false, as they make the writer quite independent of personal character.'[26]

IV

The Mill on the Floss

The Mill on the Floss was published on 4 April 1860 and 6,000 copies were sold in the first seven weeks. After the success of *Adam Bede* this was to be expected. The critics, however, were not to repeat their earlier raptures. At the beginning of May, Lewes acknowledged that the reception was 'less favourable than it was about *Adam*', and he suggested two reasons: 'The disclosure of the authorship would have much influence in that direction, which would be increased by the fact of the book being a "second book".' Then to his journal he confided a third: 'Moreover I doubt whether it is intrinsically so interesting as *Adam*. Neither the story nor the characters take so profound a hold of the sympathies.'[27] As far as Blackwood and Sons were concerned, his pessimism was justified. The two-volume second edition of 1860 was in their terms 'certainly a failure',[28] while the one-volume third edition of 1862, of which 1,400 copies were printed, lasted until 1866.

Several ingredients were missing from the previous successful mixture. Most of the rural charm had evaporated and the critics did not feel much sympathy for what was left—the vulgarity which, says the reviewer of *Blackwood's Magazine* uncompromisingly, 'we are bound to say finds its most natural home in the breast of the thriving British tradesman'.[29] Mrs Poyser's pungency has turned rancid in Aunt Glegg. Even the sympathetic critic of *The Times* found most of the characters 'prosaic, selfish, nasty', while for the hostile *Dublin University Magazine* the novel is 'a series of photographic studies, of which a good deal is provokingly commonplace, and a good deal more is tiresomely repellant' (No. 20). For him it is final proof of the barrenness of George Eliot's realism. This reviewer also notices another omission: the 'religious flavour which helped the sale of *Adam Bede* has been left out of its successor'. Without this the true nature of George Eliot's beliefs was far more apparent.

It would, however, be misleading to suggest that George Eliot's popularity was lost as rapidly as it had been won. Several reviewers remind their readers that this author has opened up a new field of human experience and to complain about her commonplace subject-matter is absurd. *The Mill on the Floss* is a 'silk purse', says *The Times*, 'produced out of materials that appear to be singularly barren of silk' (No. 17). And she has lost none of her old skill in delineating character. These connoisseurs of fictional portraiture are particularly impressed by the way in which George Eliot balances individual traits against family likeness within the extended clan of the Tullivers and Dodsons. The perceptive critic of the *Guardian* goes further. He sees in this novel a definite move beyond the two or three types of character in *Adam Bede* to 'greater freedom in the treatment, greater confidence in the effect of what seems casual and accidental in conveying the image clearly' (No. 16). Such enthusiasm centred, of course, on the portrayal of the children, and the author's uncanny ability to enter into their minds. Dickens has given powerful pictures of odd children 'with a certain naturalness in the oddity', the *Spectator* acknowledges, but George Eliot 'reminds us of what nearly all children are' (No. 12). She has broken through the literary stereotype of childhood and the reviewers pay their supreme compliment: the boundary between art and life has disappeared. 'Why is it so delightful', asks *Blackwood's* reviewer, 'to read what we have all known and felt so well already?'[30]

The third volume of the novel was another matter. This aroused the most indignant and sustained opposition George Eliot had to face in her entire career. The reviewers felt both shocked and betrayed. After being taken at a leisurely pace through two volumes of apparently commonplace life at Dorlcote Mill they were suddenly plunged into the terrible conflicts of passion and conscience in volume three. With Maggie's infatuation for Stephen Guest, the Charlotte Brontë in George Eliot had taken over from the Jane Austen with a vengeance. This sudden disruption, many of them felt, destroyed any possible aesthetic harmony. For the critic of the *National Review*, the novel disintegrates into 'a masterly fragment of fictitious biography in two volumes, followed by a second-rate one-volume novel'.[31] And they all agree that the fault is to be found in the presentation of Maggie. The *Saturday Review* sums it up: 'the young woman with the overmastering passion is very slightly connected with the little Maggie of the Mill' (No. 13).

The reasons the critics give for their objections differ widely. Some blame George Eliot for being too realistic. We all know, acknowledges the *Westminster Review*, that the 'influence exercised by the sexes over each other is quite incalculable' but that is nature not art (No. 19). The 'actual course of human things', agrees the *Guardian*, 'is not necessarily the pattern for a work of art' (No. 16). The assumption here, very different from George Eliot's own, is that art refines and elevates inexplicable human relations. Bulwer-Lytton's letter (No. 14) with its classical analogies and appeal to the Becoming takes this a step further. He is not concerned with *how* a character acts; Maggie's infatuation may be 'quite natural'. But she should not have been placed in 'a position at variance with all that had before been Heroic about her'. George Eliot's brisk dismissal of his criticism (No. 15) underlines very vividly the extent to which her fiction is based upon the psychological delineation of mixed human beings.

The second group of critics accused George Eliot not of bad art but of bad psychology. The Maggie they know and love would not have fallen in love with Stephen Guest. They are especially disturbed by her helplessness in the grip of what the *National Review* calls 'physiological law'.[32] The *Dublin University Magazine* finds it so improbable that its only purpose must be to parade George Eliot's 'faith in the philosophy put forth by the author of *Elective Affinities*'. Who could do it better, is the implication, than the woman living with the biographer of Goethe. Englishmen, fortunately, will reject this out of hand for they 'have not yet come to believe in the triumph—speaking vulgarly— of matter over mind' (No. 20). These critics vent their well-bred anger upon the luckless Stephen Guest, that second-rate dandy, that under-bred coxcomb, who makes Swinburne almost apoplectic (No. 23), and who should have been made to feel not only the beauty of Maggie's arm, but also, in the words of the *Quarterly Review*, 'its weight'.[33] They feel betrayed because the heroine with whom they have unreservedly identified themselves suddenly begins to act reprehensibly. It clearly came as a great surprise. They have been following Maggie's adventures, not tracing the pattern created by the interaction of the human organism and its environment. They protest that the heroine's free-will has been arbitrarily compromised at a moment of severe crisis.

Unfortunately, it was too late to disentangle themselves. They have been inveigled by their sympathies into a situation where right and wrong can no longer be clearly demarcated. *Macmillan's Magazine* doubts whether any author is 'justified in leading his readers into a labyrinth, the way out of which he does not first, see clearly himself'. Here we are getting to the centre of the storm. This critic continues: 'there is a picturesque piteousness which somehow confuses one's sense of right and wrong' (No. 21). The Victorian reader's sympathies have been turned against his moral judgment and he feels aggrieved. George Eliot should have been delighted. A few years earlier she had invoked the name of Goethe to denounce the line clearly separating the virtuous from the vicious as 'an immoral fiction'.[34] *The Times* half-agreed. Honesty is always honesty, it said, but 'now and then it is well that motives should be tested' (No. 17). Several journals emphatically disagreed, and it was here that opposition to the novel finally crystallized. They found George Eliot's appeal to the casuists over the heads of the men of maxims dangerous in the extreme. '[W]e have', she had said, 'no master-key that will fit all cases'; and therefore moral judgments must be constantly referred 'to the special circumstances that mark the individual lot'.[35] This they refuse to accept. The *Eclectic Review* spoke on behalf of many readers when it riposted: 'There *is* a "master-key" which may be safely and successfully applied to all the puzzles of life.'[36] It recommends faith and prayer to George Eliot.

The reviewers now begin to see the vivid and detailed rendering of Maggie's upbringing as a devious means of mitigating her guilt, and the attack upon George Eliot's morality becomes inseparable from doubts about her realistic technique. By placing characters in the complex web of heredity, physiology, and environment, George Eliot reduces the importance of actions and distracts attention from their simple rightness and wrongness. Their significance is pushed back into motives and forwards into consequences, and finally left to the mercy of circumstances. The freedom of the will is fatally undermined and we are left, in the words of *Macmillan's Magazine*, with the 'dreary creed of overpowering circumstances'. And yet it was this same circumstantial rendering of milieu that captured the reader's belief and sympathy. Perhaps the review in the *Guardian* (No. 16) epitomizes best the kind of response *The Mill on the Floss* elicited from a disturbed reading-public. This critic, as his impressionistic style suggests, is writing while still under the powerful influence of the novel. But he resists its spell ('Perhaps cooler reflection may modify this judgment') for he knows that his own values are being challenged by this 'work in which undeniable imaginative power takes new and very mixed shapes'. He cannot resolve the conflict and he has the honesty to say so.

V

Silas Marner

Silas Marner was published a year after *The Mill on the Floss* on 2 April 1861. Before publication the subscription totalled 5,500; by the end of the year 8,000 copies were sold and the novel had earned George Eliot £1,760. Sighs of relief were mingled with the paeans of praise. The reviewers were delighted that George Eliot had returned from the insoluble dilemmas of *The Mill on the Floss* to what they see as the orthodoxy of *Adam Bede*. This is what the *Athenaeum* implies when it announces that 'the interest is true and wholesome, not in the least morbid or questionable'.[37] The *Westminster Review* similarly commends George Eliot for purging from her genius 'all impurities and foreign substances' (No. 30). Reassured by the happy ending of this story, they are prepared to forget the unfortunate third volume of *The Mill on the Floss*.

The praise of her sympathetic and homely realism is couched in the usual terms. 'The author touches and treats all the characters from their own point of view,' says the *Athenaeum*, 'and with something of the tender love with which everybody regards himself.'[38] The critic of the *Saturday Review* is particularly impressed by George Eliot's refusal to see the poorer classes as 'a distinct race' who exist 'in order to take tracts and broth' from the rich (No. 27). This, of course, was the kind of praise they had lavished on *Adam Bede*; none of them see George Eliot's 'legendary tale' as a new departure. The critic of *The Times* is convinced in fact that she intended to write another *Adam Bede* but for some reason suddenly stopped short. There is a gap of sixteen years, the story winds up and he feels cheated: 'The first part, forming more than two-thirds of the volume, is thus a magnificent portico to the second part, which is a pretty little cottage, hidden behind a mass of more stately architecture' (No. 29). Similarly he considers that Silas, 'a singularly unaccountable being', is a most unsuitable hero for the carefully consequential world of George Eliot's novels. These remarks have little to do with *Silas Marner* but they indicate the power of the earlier works. They suggest how quickly a novelist creates her readers and how stubbornly they seek to assimilate the new to the old. Perhaps this is what the *Saturday Review* is demonstrating when it says: 'It is as good as *Adam Bede*, except that it is shorter.'

If these critics welcomed the new novel as a piece of the old Dutch realism with some careless brushwork, its opponents saw it as a further step down the slippery slope of photographic literalism. It is simply a question of which premise the critic chooses. In its characteristic way the *Revue des deux Mondes* substitutes its own aesthetic for George Eliot's: 'we definitely prefer those writers who wish to satisfy that desire for the great and the beautiful which is not only one of the needs of human nature, but also one of its glories'. By these criteria *Silas Marner* is judged a resounding failure. George Eliot's realism must result in a shapeless muddle: 'If the true process of art is the minute reproduction of reality, then all details are equally important and demand to be treated with the same attention.'[39] The *Dublin University Magazine* also peers myopically at George Eliot's moral fable and wonders at the point of such literalism: 'Even a photograph, to bear inspection, must be taken with more or less regard for artistic effect' (No. 31). Then the critic changes his ground. Even this 'slavishly literal rendering' turns out to be a false picture.

The extreme opposition between these two groups of critics is crystallized in their response to the brilliantly rendered scene at the Rainbow. Each reviewer, seeking final proof of his high or low estimate of the novel, turns to chapter six and out come the rustics smoking their pipes and drinking their beer. For the larger group of critics it is the perfection of Dutch realism in an English setting, for the smaller it is literal, boorish twaddle. They like it or dislike it for the same reason: it is so real. Between the two views there is no middle ground, for neither George Eliot's defenders nor her detractors go beyond verisimilitude to the larger meaning of the story. Only R. H. Hutton, one of George Eliot's most perceptive contemporary critics, examines the purpose of her graphic realism in his review in the *Economist* (No. 28). He is struck by the contrast between this picture of 'unintellectual social life' and the 'strong intellectual impress' it has been given. He begins to discern the themes around which the novel is organized and to discuss the techniques by which they are defined.

Then he too comes to the obligatory Rainbow scene. For him it is neither a Dutch interior nor a bad photograph. The rustic discussion, he notices, contains 'a faint shadow of the intellectual phases of "modern thought" ', and from here he moves outwards to other aspects of the story, and finally to the significance of the divided structure. Generally, however, *Silas Marner* was too well constructed for many readers to glimpse between subject-matter and technique any trace of George Eliot's unorthodoxy. What a school edition of the novel in 1903 called its 'tender religious charm'[40] would ensure its success for many years to come.

VI

Romola

On the strength of her previous success, George Smith offered George Eliot £10,000 in May 1862 for her new novel, *Romola*. The successful serialization of Trollope's *Framley Parsonage* was coming to an end in the *Cornhill* and Smith needed some popular fiction to boost the sales of his magazine. Lewes described this enthusiastically as 'the most magnificent offer ever yet made for a novel',[41] but George Eliot was not to be rushed. Her work wasn't far enough advanced for early publication, and she didn't like the idea of dismembering her carefully contrived artefact into sixteen monthly parts. After some misgivings, she finally accepted £7,000 for publication in twelve monthly parts—this was later increased to fourteen—and the copyright was to revert to herself after six years. *Romola*, with illustrations by Frederic Leighton, began to appear in July 1862.

It was, of course, a far more learned piece of work than any of her previous fiction. Enormous labour went into the reconstruction of fifteenth-century Florence; in Henry James' opinion it was in this 'splendid mausoleum'[42] that George Eliot buried her simplicity. Lewes became worried while it was being written. A surreptitious footnote in a letter to John Blackwood shows his concern: 'This between ourselves. When you see her, mind your care is to discountenance the idea of a Romance being the product of an Encyclopaedia.'[43] But for George Eliot the agony of creation indicated a new development of her art, and readers would have to accommodate themselves accordingly. In a letter of July 1862 she insisted on the 'freedom to write out one's own varying unfolding self, and not be a machine

18

always grinding out the same material or spinning the same sort of web'. The connoisseurs of Dutch realism were clearly going to have their loyalty tested. 'Of necessity,' she says, 'the book is addressed to fewer readers than my previous works, and I myself have never expected—I might rather say *intended*—that the book should be as "popular" in the same sense as the others.'[44] George Smith, who had been forewarned, decided to take a risk, and lost heavily.

Several years later Lewes was to refer to the early reception of the novel as 'a universal howl of discontent',[45] but reassurance came in the form of 'wonderful eulogies' from the more select audience of 'learned Florentines, and Englishmen of high culture (F. Maurice, Bulwer, Anthony Trollope etc.). . . .'[46] These 'immense big-wigs',[47] as George Eliot called them, were, however, a very different audience from the people they had overheard talking about *Adam Bede* in the remotest parts of North Wales in 1859.[48] In this sense *Romola* is an important turning-point in George Eliot's career: it divided her reading-public into those who welcomed the latest unfolding of her genius and those who persisted until the very end in their nostalgia for the world of the early novels.

The critics were caught awkwardly between the two. They belonged for the most part to the first audience, but they were writing for the second, and this is reflected in their reviews. Invariably they begin by regretting the novel's lack of popular appeal; Florence with its Piagnoni is a poor substitute for Loamshire and Mrs Poyser. They can't see the point of the remote setting for it is clear that George Eliot is dealing with the same moral problems as before. All it achieves, as far as the *Westminster Review* is concerned, is the exacerbation of the faults of her genius. Since George Eliot's forte is the exploration of the inner life, she ought to let experience—not imagination—provide the externals of plot and setting (No. 37). Only R. H. Hutton in his masterly account of the interlocking themes of the novel justifies its location in Renaissance Italy, in that 'strange era, which has so many points of resemblance with the present' (No. 34). But the more fully he comes to understand the organic form of the work the more fully he shares the common dislike of its serialization.

Virtually all agree that the purely historical portraits do not come alive. The English critics invoke the name of Scott, that far less scrupulous historian, for purposes of contrast, while the *Revue des deux Mondes* advises George Eliot to take a few lessons from Stendhal.[49] It is her 'instructive antiquarianism' (No. 36) which annoys them most. Some years later Mrs Oliphant was to remind her readers that *Romola* was a superb guide-book of Florence 'not to be equalled by any Murray known to man'.[50] But they were looking for a romance and would have welcomed a few inaccuracies.

When the critics had disposed of the historical stage-sets, they found themselves for the first time face to face with George Eliot's stern morality. It is an instructive confrontation. No longer distracted by the familiar realism they suddenly begin to grasp the depth and range of her mind; before long they too are awe-struck members of the new select audience. But they find this George Eliot a less comfortable writer than the earlier one, and a reading of *Romola* begins to sound like an ascetic exercise. 'It will be scarcely possible,' says the *Athenaeum*, 'to rise from the perusal . . . without feeling a desire to cease from a life of self-pleasing' (No. 33). They are universally impressed by George Eliot's ability to define so clearly a character like Tito who, in the words of the *Spectator*, is 'full of soft fluid selfishness'. But they are at the same time intimidated by the remorseless way in which she destroys her creation. It was only in later years that doubts about Tito's character began to be expressed; in 1888 Leslie Stephen praised him ambiguously as 'one of her finest feminine characters'.[51]

Romola certainly made George Eliot's readers look with fresh eyes at the bucolic charm of the earlier works. But however many devout English ladies copied passages from the novel into their New Testaments,[52] it was never a popular success. The *Saturday Review* summed up its reception in one sentence: 'No reader of *Romola* will lay it down without admiration, and few without regret' (No. 36).

VII

During the 1860s, general assessments of George Eliot's work began to appear in the periodicals. These often repeat earlier judgments, but now the critics make more explicit the values by which they praise or condemn. There is still a powerful conservative lobby which finds the subject-matter of the novels unacceptable. In 1860 the *Quarterly Review* wondered why George Eliot should force upon us 'uninteresting and tiresome people in all their interminable tediousness'. 'The idea that fiction should contain something to soothe, to elevate, or to purify,' sighs this reviewer, 'seems to be extinct.'[53] In 1866 the *North British Review* also disputes George Eliot's aesthetic, finding her 'tragedy of every-day life' a contradiction in terms. But this critic develops a more careful definition of her central weakness. This is to be found in her delineation of character. He is not suggesting, he says, that she should make all her characters immaculate, or even some entirely good and some entirely bad. This would be absurd. But, 'on the other hand, to show noble natures yielding to temptations unworthy of them, or influenced by motives over which they should have easy command, is to make light of the distinction between right and wrong. . . .'[54] He finds it distasteful to see noble characters associated with impure motives.

To George Eliot's advocates it is, of course, this picture of mixed, commonplace characters influenced by contradictory motives which gives the novels their universal significance. Perhaps the crucial issue dividing the two groups may be suggested by referring to the favour-able assessment in the *National Review* in 1860. This critic—it is R. H. Hutton—agrees with the *North British Review* on the absurdity of a rigid separation of good and bad characters. He is also aware of the opposite danger, shown by 'our modern satirists' who consider it impossible to discriminate between good and evil. Between the two extremes he finds the valid method:

The only moral in a fictitious story which can properly be demanded of writers of genius is,—*not* to shape their tale this way or that, which they may justly decline to do on artistic grounds,—but to discriminate clearly the relative nobility of the characters they do conceive; in other words, to give us light enough in their pictures to let it be clearly seen where the shadows are intended to lie.[55]

This kind of discrimination shifts the reader's attention from the dramatic action to motives and consequences; now, noble characters are not always required to triumph. In 1860, George Eliot stated con-cisely the difference between this view, which is her own, and the view of her opponents. She is amazed, she says, at all those critics who com-plain '*not* because my representations are untruthful but because they are impartial—because I don't *load* my dice so as to make their side win'.[56] It is the difference between realistic and idealistic criteria, or in George Henry Lewes's terms, between Realism and Falsism.[57]

However uneasy the critics may feel about the moral purpose of the novels, they very rarely discuss openly the author's religious beliefs. The *North British Review*, despite its earlier reservations, even congratu-lates George Eliot on her wide religious sympathies. The *Quarterly* wonders if she is, as appears, a member of the Broad Church party. The suspicion of her accepting Dr Strauss's myths is a 'distressing question' which is shelved almost as quickly as it is raised.[58] In 1867 the *British Quarterly Review* is perturbed by a similar rumour. If it is true, declares this critic, that 'George Eliot has no serious regard for Christianity, except in her capacity as artist, the spectacle presented by her works in this point of view is, in our opinion, the most melancholy, the most appalling, to be met with in literature'.[59] The question is left open; the critics do not turn to the novels for proof; they would rather not talk about it.

There was one writer who refused to treat George Eliot's beliefs in this gingerly fashion. That fine but neglected Victorian critic, Richard Simpson, goes directly and with easy authority to the foundations of her ethical beliefs in Strauss, Feuerbach, Comte, and Goethe, and produces in 1863 the most incisive analysis of her early novels in the nineteenth century (No. 38). George Eliot knows, he argues, that her positivist belief in 'the pure emanation of feeling' is incompatible with any system of religion. But she realizes that religious doctrines are still necessary to enable people to convert their feelings into energies—'for energy results from the union of belief and feeling'. Consequently in her fiction she sympathizes with a variety of religious forms which she herself rejects. This is only a temporary expedient: in time the shell of Christianity will fall away and reveal the true inner substance, the feeling which it has been safeguarding. Her advocacy of this belief is for Simpson the remarkable achievement of the novels: 'It is no small victory to show that the godless humanitarianism of Strauss and Feuerbach can be made to appear the living centre of all the popular religions.'

And this is the danger. For Simpson, a Liberal Catholic, is a hostile critic of a strategy he finds dishonest. It is wrong he feels to reassure people and undermine their beliefs at the same time. The novelist has first separated belief and feeling in order to show that they are not necessarily interdependent. Then she has put them together again so cunningly in the novels that only the most perceptive and mistrustful of readers would suspect they had ever been disconnected. But they have, irrevocably. And Simpson proceeds in his axiomatic, antithetical style to explore sensitively the structure of the novels, their language, their characters, returning constantly to test his findings against his initial thesis. It is a masterly presentation of George Eliot as the anthropologist of Christianity. It is an explanation both of the novels and of their contemporary reception. It should make the twentieth-century reader examine afresh George Eliot's urgent need 'to make', as she repeatedly said, 'matter and form an inseparable truthfulness'.[60] In Simpson's terms, the matter is so radical that it has to be concealed in a conventional form. But the irony, he feels, is that she has been in one sense too successful. 'There is a limit,' he concludes, 'beyond which this process defeats itself; the philosopher grows too cunning to be understood, and the disguise is more wholesome than the well-concealed purpose is deleterious.'

Simpson's ability to stand back from the novels and assess their wider implications was, of course, not typical of the time. Most critics were more concerned with the truth of George Eliot's surface realism and how far this corresponded with their own experience. There was, however, one group of reviewers debarred from this perennial concern. American critics of the novels acknowledge repeatedly that they are not qualified to test the truth of George Eliot's descriptions from their own experience. They have to rely on less empirical evidence. In a review of *Felix Holt* in 1866 a writer in the *North American Review* admits that 'In America we know little of the England of thirty-five years ago, but we see enough of the fidelity of the author to nature to know that we may trust her.'[61] Writing in the same year, Henry James was more cautious: 'an American, in treating of her books, must be satisfied not to touch upon the question of their accuracy and fidelity as pictures of manners and customs'. He agrees that the 'rich density of detail' of the novels is 'strong internal evidence of truthfulness', but wonders if they are rather 'too redolent of peace and abundance'.[62] This critical tentativeness gave way to a more self-confident attitude as the kind of realism George Eliot represented in North America began to pass out of favour. In 1873, for example, one American critic refused to consider his unfamiliarity with English society a handicap. On the contrary, he felt it enabled him to place in proper critical perspective the naïve literalism which had captivated so many English readers of the novels. His distance from the world of *Middlemarch* allows him to 'stand in the position of posterity, for whom much will be obscure that is now familiar'. And he forecasts that the novel's popularity is only local and contemporary: 'If an exact imitation of certain special modes of life is the chief claim to merit of a great part of the story, if the reader is not able to appreciate the truth he will find the interest of the delineation lacking.'[63]

Clearly, the local felicities of George Eliot's Dutch realism were less compelling on the other side of the Atlantic. Perhaps this was a major reason for the novels' lack of popular success in North America. In 1869, the Irish novelist and critic, Justin McCarthy was struck after a six-month visit by the fact that while Dickens and Charles Reade were more popular in New York than in London, in George Eliot's case the reverse was true. He seeks to remedy the situation, first, by pointing out to his American readers that in England 'educated public opinion' ranked her works 'higher than the novels of any other living author', and secondly, by assuring them of the reality of unfamiliar fictional characters. 'Mrs Poyser lives, and I have met aunt Glegg often.'[64] But already, a journal like the influential *Atlantic Monthly* felt that George Eliot displayed 'a somewhat excessive regard for the appearances of realness in and for itself'.[65] More aesthetic criteria are in vogue and Turgenev is now the representative of genuine realism. It is the Russian novelist, according to the American critic G. P. Lathrop in 1874, who maintains 'the aesthetic balance between idea and fact' which George Eliot has lost. Her novels, by contrast, read 'too much like treatises on human nature, anecdotically illustrated'.[66]

´ VIII

Felix Holt

With *Felix Holt*, published on 15 June 1866, George Eliot returned to John Blackwood, and her readers to the familiar Loamshire. The reviewers may chide those people who had been incapable of appreciating George Eliot's genius in Florence, but they too return to the old haunts with relief. Their expectations, however, have changed. After the rigours of *Romola* it was no longer possible to wander at ease through the portrait gallery of George Eliot's fiction. But what new aesthetic standards were to replace the old form of enjoyment? The contemporary criticism of *Felix Holt* suggests that most of the critics had no satisfactory answer.

The reviewer in the *Westminster Review* strikes the characteristic note in his first sentence: 'George Eliot's novels are not novels in the ordinary sense of the term.' Apparently, they are dramas in the sense in which *Hamlet* and the *Agamemnon* are dramas, because their 'interest centres always in the solution of some moral problem'.[67] Similarly, the *North American Review* begins by suspecting that both in *Romola* and *Felix Holt* the author 'had a definite dramatic aim'. Certain episodes 'are easier to account for on the supposition of a design to heighten the unity and interest of the plot by contrast, than on the ground of a purely naturalistic development of the story'.[68] Discriminations are clearly being made. But having shifted into this higher critical gear, both writers suddenly lose direction. The critic of the *Westminster Review* makes a sketchy definition of the moral problem presented in the novel and then guiltily samples a few of its beauties in the old familiar way. The critic of the *North American Review* experiences a similar loss of nerve after his opening statement. George Eliot has never *said* she had a definite dramatic aim, 'and as it is possible to explain everything in her books in another way, it is much better to look at such excellent novels from the simplest point of view, and to leave to the French the aesthetic discussion of her works'.[69]

Their dilemma is a symptom of a more general change. The earlier view of fiction as a loose, amorphous predator aggrandizing itself at the expense of the more genteel genres is giving way in the 1860s to a more austere view of the novel based on a demand for an Aristotelian unity of action. Indeed, comparisons with the drama became so widespread that in 1862 Bulwer-Lytton protested against the attempt to curtail the freedom of fiction with irrelevant restrictions. 'To prose fiction,' he said in *Blackwood's*, 'there must always be conceded an immense variety in the modes of treatment—a bold licence of loose capricious adaptation of infinite materials to some harmonious unity of interest, which even the most liberal construction of dramatic licence cannot afford to the drama.'[70] But many of the critics of *Felix Holt* insisted on applying dramatic criteria. They were prompted to some extent by George Eliot's references to classical drama, by the fact that half of the novel at least is a Greek tragedy in modern dress, and they may even have heard the rumour that the author had put aside her poetic drama, *The Spanish Gypsy*, to write this novel. But, whatever the reason, they were to be disappointed. Between the divided structure of *Felix Holt* on the one hand and the incredibly complicated legal plot on the other, they did not find the dramatic unity they were looking for.

The most severe in its judgments is the *Edinburgh Review*. 'The story', it finds, 'has the defect of running in two parallel lines with only an occasional and arbitrary connexion' (No. 44). This critic shares with the *Spectator* the view that too many episodes are inorganic excrescences obscuring the clear contours of the novel. He reminds George Eliot

peremptorily that 'art compensates for its inability to copy the multiplicity of Nature by deliberate attention to unity'. Henry James, too,
in the first of his several reviews of the novels, finds that *Felix Holt*
lacks 'the essential simplicity' of a masterpiece. He acknowledges that
the separate parts are 'vigorous' but the effect of the whole is 'meagre'
(No. 43).

The novel, in other words, falls apart in their hands. Felix is blamed
primarily for lacking the stature which might have unified the discrete
parts. For the *Spectator* (No. 40) he is a 'mutilated statue', 'a grand
stump of a character', while for James he is 'a fragment' insufficiently
heroic for his task. They find him equally unreal as a nineteenth-century
social reformer. This demagogue who wears a cloth cap and discusses
Ciceronian figures of speech is for the *Edinburgh Review* as convincing
'as a shepherd at the opera'. The *North British Review* is even more
brusque in its dismissal of George Eliot the social historian: 'the date
of the tale might as well have been 1732, and the title Felix Holt the
Mahometan'.[71] The labyrinthine plot, worked out with the help of
Frederic Harrison and Blackstone's *Commentaries*, fails to placate them.
For the *Saturday Review* (No. 39) it seems irrelevant to the concerns
of the main characters, the two 'jar and clang together', while the
London Quarterly Review feels it is degrading to interweave a mystery
story into a serious work of fiction.[72] Even the superbly restrained
delineation of Mrs Transome's tragedy is unappreciated. Not only
does she 'outrage decency', in the words of the *Contemporary Review*,
but her tragedy is really irrelevant to the drama: 'The story, in all its
main features, would remain the same, if the dark blot on Mrs Transome's character had never occurred.'[73] Even James finds her 'a superfluous figure' (No. 43).

The curious thing is that however much the critics attack the novel
they remain convinced that it is an important and impressive work. It
is a form of critical schizophrenia. Perhaps they know they are applying
criteria which are, as Bulwer-Lytton said, irrelevant. And he, in fact,
had suggested an approach far more fitting to an understanding of
Felix Holt. The 'interest of a novel may be very gentle, very irregular',
he maintained, provided that everything finally refers to 'the ulterior
idea for which the action is invented'.[74] The critics who adopt this
more flexible approach find much more to praise. *The Times* echoes
Bulwer-Lytton in its rejection of unrealistic standards; this kind of
cavilling 'reminds one rather vividly of the old paltry squabbles about
the unities' (No. 41). Instead, Dallas interprets the novel intelligently

in terms of a broad thematic contrast 'between feeling as it flows from the heart and feeling as it is moulded by custom'. Within the unity created by comparison and contrast, this smaller group of critics has freedom to enjoy the novel. Mrs Transome comes in for her rightful praise, and Felix is found less inadequate now that he is not required to carry the burden of the novel singlehanded. The *Saturday Review* even admires this latter-day Savonarola. No doubt it was both exciting and reassuring to sympathize with a Radical who spent a good deal of his time castigating the workers. As John Blackwood cannily observed to his London manager when justifying the £5,000 he had paid for *Felix Holt*: 'Her politics are excellent and will attract all parties.'[75] And five weeks after publication he was delighted: 'I do not know that I ever saw a Novel received with a more universal acclaim.'[76] But then the reservations so many critics had expressed began to make their mark. By December 1866 the sales were proving disappointing, and by the time *Felix Holt* was included in the Cabinet Edition twelve years later only 7,300 copies of the novel had been printed. Blackwood must have lost heavily.

IX

Middlemarch

Blackwood had been irritated by the discrepancy between the original reception of *Felix Holt* and its subsequent meagre sales. He blamed the library system. It fostered the production of mediocre three-volume novels—'but of a really good book each copy is made to do duty some hundred times over'.[77] In his view, people had got out of the habit of buying books. He told George Eliot in 1866 that they must experiment with a new form of publication. Lewes was delighted. For several years he had been badgering Blackwood to make a fortune for all of them by issuing the novels in part numbers like Dickens'. They decided to publish the new novel in eight 5/- parts at two-monthly intervals, before its appearance in four volumes at two guineas. The first part was published in December 1871 and the last part in December 1872, the final three numbers having been published monthly to meet the final crescendo of interest.

'No former book of mine,' recorded George Eliot in her journal in 1873, 'has been received with more enthusiasm—not even *Adam Bede*. . . .'[78] Lewes, however, was at first disappointed; he had hoped to sell 10,000 copies of each part and sales were averaging just under 5,000. But striking evidence of the novel's popularity came later with the appearance of the cheap edition in May 1874. Up to then, the parts, the first edition, and the library edition had sold altogether 8,500 copies. In its first six months, to Blackwood's astonishment, the cheap edition at 7/6 sold over 10,000 copies. By the end of 1878, almost 31,000 copies of the edition had been sold.

In 1919 Virginia Woolf declared, and it has been repeated many times during the last twenty years, that Middlemarch 'is one of the few English novels written for grown-up people'.[79] Yet its contemporary reception was not by any means the universal shout of approval which recent critical orthodoxy might lead us to expect. The Victorian reviewers still found Adam Bede more enjoyable. They were, of course, impressed as they had been before by a picture of society on such a panoramic scale. 'The social formation of Middlemarch,' said The Times, '. . . is laid bare in a complete section cut clean from summit to base of its ancient stratifications.'[80] And they revelled in the wealth of characters, major and minor, with an immediacy of enjoyment which the twentieth century finds naïve and undisciplined. This is a phenomenon difficult to record in an account of this kind. But it should be stated and repeated that in the reviews not only of Middlemarch but of all the novels, with the exception of Romola, a catalogue of characters was one of the most regular features. It was the best way, the reviewers obviously found, of sharing an enjoyment in the variety, the idiosyncrasy, and the truthfulness of human nature in the novels.

In Middlemarch many readers came to feel they could not enjoy these things in the old uninhibited way. The Times acknowledges this: 'As a novel proper it is inferior to the earlier work; its plot is not exciting; it has not the liveliness, variety, and picturesqueness of its great predecessor [Adam Bede].' In place of these qualities, Middlemarch has 'a philosophical power'.[81] But when they begin to examine this larger power the critics frequently become profoundly uncomfortable. One way of expressing this discomfort is to say that they are not sure what the novel is about. The reviewer of the Atlantic Monthly says that some critics consider it a study of the effects of provincial life upon character, while others insist the novel is the story of Dorothea's struggle against surrounding obstacles. He doesn't believe it is either.[82] The modern reader immediately says it is both because they are inseparable. The Victorians, however, were less ready to merge character and environment in this facile way. As we have seen, they frequently complain that in the densely specified worlds of the novels the rightness of actions is too easily obscured in the pursuit of motives and consequences. And this uncertainty is particularly disturbing in *Middlemarch* which is —and all the reviewers agree on this—a profoundly melancholy study of failure and disillusionment. They want to know who is to blame for the failure. Is the novel a study of Dorothea's and Lydgate's inadequacies, or a critique of provincial life?

When they turn to the novel they find George Eliot's answers wilfully confusing. As far as the *Nation* (No. 50) can see, *Middlemarch* was written both to illustrate and deny the dictum of Novalis that character is destiny. There is an ambiguity here which the reviewers mistrust. What they prefer and expect is an area of freedom around each fictional character in which he can act and be judged. This freedom, they feel, is being denied. And in the presentation of Dorothea, they are convinced, George Eliot is not simply ambiguous but contradictory. In her final comment on her heroine on the last page of the novel, George Eliot had said: 'Among the many remarks passed on her mistakes, it was never said in the neighbourhood of Middlemarch that such mistakes could not have happened if the society into which she was born had not smiled on propositions of marriage from a sickly man to a girl less than half his own age—on modes of education which make a woman's knowledge another name for motley ignorance—on rules of conduct which are in flat contradiction with its own loudly-asserted beliefs.' This, they felt, was too much. The uproar was similar to that which greeted the attempt to exonerate Maggie at the end of *The Mill on the Floss*. Reviewer after reviewer seized upon this passage and demanded to know why George Eliot should seek to shift the blame on to Middlemarch society in this way. 'What more could Dorothea's friends have done,' asks one irate Canadian critic, 'unless they had put strychnine in Casaubon's tea?'[83] It is unfair both on provincial society and on the character whose freedom and responsibility are diminished. George Eliot removed the offending sentence from the 1874 edition of the novel.

What were George Eliot's motives for this misrepresentation? The *British Quarterly Review* suggested that she exaggerated the sins of society in order to protect those characters who embodied her own positivist values: 'It is only profound belief in God which prevents us from indulging a certain amount of moral superstition about our human ideals. . . .'[84] This makes explicit something which is implied in the whole debate—the absence, the wilful denial of any spiritual dimension to Middlemarch society. One American reviewer tried to bring this home to his readers by recalling the incident of 'a thoughtful and sensitive young man, who rose from the perusal of *Middlemarch* with his eyes suffused with tears, exclaiming: "My God! and is that all?" '[85] In this secular society the paradox of free-will and determinism cannot be resolved in the orthodox Christian way, and this is why so many readers are unable to accept the novel as a true account of life. The alternative, which they refuse to consider, is expressed by the *Atlantic Monthly*: man neither controls nor is controlled by, but is himself a part of nature.[86]

It was felt that George Eliot was not only unfair to Middlemarch society in general but also to several characters, like Rosamond and Celia, who were closely identified with its values. This charge of bias by the author against one of her own characters had occurred earlier with regard to Tom Tulliver. Her reply (No. 22b)—which raises as many questions as it answers—was to ask who made Tom sympathetic in the first place? This is a characteristic appeal by George Eliot to the organic unity of the novel—or rather to the undeniable fact that she wrote all of it. But the critic of the *Spectator* insists, and he is not alone, that we are forced to object because George Eliot 'has a speculative philosophy of character that always runs on in a parallel stream with her picture of character', and the two are frequently at odds (No. 45e). This is why the *Saturday Review* objects to the far too lenient treatment of Ladislaw in the author's commentary. This form of criticism can be seen as a backhanded compliment. It means, says the *Spectator*, that 'George Eliot's imagination is too powerful to let her paint these young people exactly as she would (from her own partisan point of view) be inclined to do' (45c). In revenge, the philosopher in George Eliot keeps stabbing the artist in the back. This is why the minor characters are the most consistent ones. They exist almost entirely in the world of the critical commentary and so are not victims of the author's dissociated sensibility. Edward Dowden's famous distinction (No. 47) which he drew in 1872 between George Eliot's primary, historical self and her 'second self' which lives and speaks through her novels is an attempt to meet this criticism. He is seeking to mitigate the direct confrontation between the author and her characters by reminding readers that both are part of the same novel.

For the first time a majority of critics seem to have become aware of the wide gap separating George Eliot's own beliefs from the beliefs of the world she is presenting. They have been alerted by the persistent irony of the commentary. The *Fortnightly Review* expresses it most forcibly: 'To the old world belong the elements of her experience, to the new world the elements of her reflection on experience' (No. 49). This, some critics feel, betrays her into several anachronisms, the most serious of which is the way she belittles the part played by Christian belief in Middlemarch. The *London Quarterly Review* cannot allow that 'Dorothea, not illustrating a Positivist thesis in 1876, but living her life more than a generation ago, in 1830 . . .'[87] would not have been a devout Christian. Now, instead of attributing this inconsistency to an oversight, the critics blame George Eliot's thesis for distorting the reality of her fictional world.

This conflict of interests was also blamed for what the critics saw as the fragmentary structure of the novel. George Eliot had clearly not been able to decide which to create, a diagram or a picture, and so she had done neither. Her solution, said *The Nation* (No. 50), should have been obvious. When it became clear to her that Dorothea and Lydgate were not to be romantically entangled, she ought to have published the novel as three separate tales, in the same way as *Scenes of Clerical Life*. James too was unhappy over the structure. He rubs his hands over Dorothea, 'that perfect flower of conception', but regrets that she isn't the undisputed central consciousness of the novel. But he swallows his disappointment ('When was a panorama compact?'), and proceeds to describe very suggestively the peculiar power of the novel as expressed through Dorothea and Lydgate, the 'two suns in the firmament of the novel, each with its independent solar system' (No. 51). But this kind of ranging exploration, discerning similarity of theme behind difference of circumstance, was rare.

The final impression is that the critics realized new and difficult demands were being made upon them by *Middlemarch*. George Eliot's own account of what she was intending in the novel had been disarmingly simple—'to show the gradual action of ordinary causes rather than exceptional'.[88] But this carried profound aesthetic and moral implications. The minute study of human motives and actions on this scale, unrelieved by what the *North American Review* called 'the belief in the existence of something better than what we see' is, it believed, 'terrible in its realism'.[89] The more perceptive reviewers realized that no conventional fictional form could have accommodated this intention. 'In consequence of the very aim of the tale,' said the *British Quarterly Review*, 'it could hardly be a satisfying imaginative whole, either tragic or otherwise.'[90] But in the last resort they felt this was irrelevant. It would be presumptuous, said the *Fortnightly Review*, to judge a work of this magnitude purely on aesthetic grounds. This is the final Victorian testimony to the greatness of *Middlemarch*. So much life has been incorporated into its pages that conventional requirements of artistic form have become outdated. The *Quarterly* was prompted to write an obituary of the English novel,[91] and James agreed it was certainly the end of an epoch. 'If we write novels so, how shall we write History?'

X

Daniel Deronda

James's question had been echoed by the other reviewers of *Middle-march*. However brilliant the performance, many of them saw it as a *cul-de-sac* of realism and despair. They speculated on where George Eliot could turn next, and their hopes and fears are expressed by the critic of *St. Paul's Magazine* at the end of his review of the novel. 'Humanity, in all its stern reality, endeavour, and failure, she realizes with amazing truthfulness and power; but for the humanity which, we hope, is to be, she has not enough of a New Gospel to communicate. The old truths she has illuminated with vivid and matchless skill; but she does not advance a new evangel.'[92] *Daniel Deronda* was George Eliot's answer. It made the required transition from the realities of provincial life to the uncertainties of the future. But when the critics saw what the New Gospel was to be, they hesitated, and in the main decided they preferred the old certainties.

Despite their disappointment, they show great respect, for as Leslie Stephen said, 'She was now alone among novelists as a representative of first-rate literary ability, having survived all her greatest contemporaries.'[93] The *Edinburgh Review* aptly expresses the combination of reverence and reservation: ' "Nobody except George Eliot could have written it, but—," has become the formula with which even the boldest preface their faltering disapproval.'[94] The critics express their disappointment in their customary way. They trim the novel to suit their tastes. Just as they had jettisoned the final volume of *The Mill on the Floss*, the historical background of *Romola*, and the tendentious commentary of *Middlemarch*, so now they dismiss the Jewish half of *Daniel Deronda*. George Eliot's anger at this kind of treatment is well known, and here she was to complain of 'the laudation of readers who cut the book into scraps and talk of nothing in it but Gwendolen. I meant everything in the book to be related to everything else there.'[95] And yet one can sympathize with the reviewers too. The unity they are accustomed to is not a web-like interrelatedness, but a unity of dramatic action. This novel, as the *International Review* said, 'oscillates between two plots, neither of which can be considered a sub-plot' (No. 63), with the apparent intention of arousing and then frustrating the reader's romantic interest. Gwendolen is not allowed to marry Deronda just as Dorothea was wilfully prevented from rescuing Lydgate. James's Pulcheria sums it up in her waspish way: 'A silly young girl and a heavy, overwise young man who *don't* fall in love with her! That is the *donnée* of eight monthly volumes' (No. 62). Rejecting the challenge of the discontinuous action, these readers take from the novel the parts they find appealing. For them it was already conveniently dismembered.

By removing the Jewish half they could make *Daniel Deronda* conform to their expectations of what a novel should be. They are ecstatic over Gwendolen, that fascinating mixture of Dorothea and Rosamond, and absorbed in the opening question of the novel. Why, asks the *Saturday Review*, should they also be expected to show interest in the alien life of the other half of the novel, 'this subsidence into Jewish hopes and aims'? (No. 57). It was exactly at this kind of reader that George Eliot had aimed the novel. But it was going to be more difficult than she had anticipated 'to widen the English vision a little'[96] in the direction, not of Midland rustics or prosaic clergymen, but of Jews in contemporary London. As her journal shows (No. 54), she only gradually became aware of the extent of the opposition as the monthly parts were being published during 1876. Some critics began to wonder if the mysticism of race and nation had sufficient human interest to be the subject of fiction. This, in a sense, is the question posed by the novel, and the purpose of Deronda's education is to answer it finally in the affirmative. But the process is a lengthy one and most readers were not prepared to tolerate in the interim what Saintsbury called the 'bottled moonshine of Mordecai's mysteries' (No. 56).

The critics blame Deronda for allowing the business of race and heredity to interfere with a very acceptable marriage to a vital, if wayward, English girl. They abuse his bloodlessness in no uncertain terms. One critic finds him 'intolerably dreadful',[97] another 'a transient and embarrassed phantom',[98] while Robert Louis Stevenson entitled him 'the Prince of Prigs'.[99] The *Spectator* diagnosed as well as abused him, and suggested that Deronda turns into a 'wreath of moral mist' because

George Eliot's philosophy 'has parted with all the old lines of principle, except the keen sympathy with every noble sentiment which she always betrays, and imported nothing new and definite in their places. . . .'[100] When this sympathy is raised to heroic proportions as in Deronda, the character begins to lose definition as he becomes assimilated into other people's demands which are his only criteria. The *Academy's* shrewd *caveat* (No. 52) on the subject of George Eliot's moral premises is also aimed at the absence of any moral principles in the novels by which characters could be more clearly and traditionally defined. In the absence of these, the author has to rely upon commentary which, they feel, is becoming increasingly abstract, philosophical, and scientific. Several critics felt the strain. The *Spectator* suspects there is always something else George Eliot wanted to say, and 'had not been able quite to find the right word'.[101] The critic in the *Nation* (No. 59) finds the same discrepancy he noticed in *Middlemarch* between the way the author responds to her characters in her commentary and the way we respond. The *British Quarterly Review* agrees and yet feels the commentary is necessary for without it Deronda's conduct is inexplicable: 'We require the explanation, but yet we grumble at its necessity.'[102]

This, however, was not the only response. At the other extreme there was a small group of readers who were delighted with the novel. 'Had not learned Jews and impassioned Jewesses written to her,' Lewes confided to Edward Dowden in 1877, 'from Germany, Poland, France, as well as England and America, assuring her that she had really touched and set vibrating a deep chord, Mrs. Lewes would have been very despondent. . . .'[103] These readers were overjoyed that George Eliot had subtilized the stereotype of the Jew by occupying the middle ground between Sidonia and Fagin. They show their gratitude by insisting that the Jewish half of the novel is not, as James said, 'at bottom cold', but vibratingly alive and real. They appeal from the fiction to reality, from Mordecai to Isaac Disraeli and Emanuel Deutsch, to prove that the former is, in the words of *Macmillan's Magazine*, 'no inert scarecrow of abstractions, but a warm living reality'.[104] Historically and culturally, these critics insist, Mordecai is a plausible figure; the sceptical Victorian reader might have replied that in *Romola* the street names of Florence were also recorded correctly.

An exclusive focus on either half of the novel clearly misrepresents *Daniel Deronda*. It becomes either a conventional love story with a bungled ending, or a treatise on the political future of the Jews with some romantic colouring. There is, surprisingly at this stage of George Eliot's career, a third group committed to neither half and prepared to find everything related to everything else. Their premise is that *Daniel Deronda* is different not only in degree but also in kind from the other novels. 'It is practically a first book by a new author,' says the reviewer in the *Gentleman's Magazine*, 'and must be judged accordingly' (No. 58). Edward Dowden uses a similar strategy when he draws an extreme contrast between *Middlemarch* and *Daniel Deronda*: one is critical and realistic, the other constructive and ideal. This leads the reviewers to redefine their critical terms. George Eliot is still true to experience, they find, but whereas in the earlier fiction the facts were 'taken more in the gross', in *Daniel Deronda* 'there is a passionate selection of those facts that are representative of the highest (and also of the lowest) things' (No. 64). The criteria of Dutch realism are now quite irrelevant. George Eliot has invaded the territory of the Romance which her earlier success had helped to discredit.

When the critics view the novel as a world of the possible rather than of the exclusively probable, they achieve a detachment which brings both Mordecai's ideal world and Gwendolen's 'attempt to see beyond the edge of her gown'[105] into focus. Now their interpretations become more abstract and allegorical. For one reviewer, Deronda and Grandcourt are the angel and fiend playing at chess for Gwendolen's soul as it struggles into existence (No. 58). The same triangle represents for the *International Review* the extreme polarization of the two forces, character and circumstance, which have been so inextricably enmeshed in George Eliot's previous novels. The form of the Romance enables her to present them now in extreme opposition (No. 63).

This group of critics has allowed the form of the novel to suggest a new synthesis in which both the English upper classes and the Jews have a proper but subordinate place. They are prepared to forego many of the conventional satisfactions of fiction in order to respond to this final challenging phase of George Eliot's career.

XI

Daniel Deronda to Cross's *Life* (1885)

During the last few years of George Eliot's life and on her death in 1880 many general appraisals of the novels appeared. These inevitably contain a great deal of conventional eulogy. We are reminded more than once that her birthplace was only twenty miles from Shakespeare's. But they also contain serious reservations. For when these writers step back from the particular scenes and characters which had delighted them earlier and try to define in general, usually ethical, terms the nature of George Eliot's achievement, they find themselves forced to take a gloomy view of her religion of humanity which clearly pervades the novels. They find it, in varying degrees, inadequate, misleading, or pernicious.

As early as 1874, *Scribner's Monthly* was warning its readers that her novels, contrary to appearances, were not really suitable for the Sunday School library,[106] while in 1877 the hostile *London Quarterly Review* debunked the 'optical delusion' that George Eliot was depicting the Christian religion sympathetically from the inside.[107] The publication of *Impressions of Theophrastus Such* (1879) provided further indisputable evidence. The *Spectator*, for example, used this volume of essays to make explicit and condemn George Eliot's 'sociological morality' which it finds increasingly dominant in her writings. 'If you care to try morality not by what it is, but by the cohesion it lends, or fails to lend, to the social system,—you must, to a great extent, be guided by the *quantity* of the effect, by the number of links whose hold on each other is strengthened or relaxed. . . .'[108] W. H. Mallock is also dubious about the effectiveness of this social calculus, but in his essay in the *Edinburgh Review* (No. 65) he is anxious that George Eliot's true originality should be recognized. She is, he declares, 'the first great *godless* writer of fiction that has appeared in England'.

This view of George Eliot as the stern and sombre sage, deprived of Christian hope, teaching her substitute religion, is later distilled by F. W. H. Myers in his obituary reminiscences in the *Century Magazine*. This is the paragraph which was to become so well known:

I remember how, at Cambridge, I walked with her once in the Fellows' Garden of Trinity, on an evening of rainy May; and she, stirred somewhat beyond her wont, and taking as her text the three words which have been used so often as the inspiring trumpet-calls of men,—the words *God, Immortality, Duty*,— pronounced, with terrible earnestness, how inconceivable was the *first*, how unbelievable the *second*, and yet how peremptory and absolute the *third*. Never perhaps, have sterner accents affirmed the sovereignty of impersonal and unrecompensing Law. I listened, and night fell; her grave, majestic countenance turned toward me like a sibyl's in the gloom; it was as though she withdrew from my grasp, one by one, the two scrolls of promise, and left me the third scroll only, awful with inevitable fates. And when we stood at length and parted,

amid that columnar circuit of the forest-trees, beneath the last twilight of
starless skies, I seemed to be gazing, like Titus at Jerusalem, on vacant seats and
empty halls,—on a sanctuary with no Presence to hallow it, and heaven left
lonely of a God.[109]

It is a suggestive incident narrated in such a way as to endorse a contemporary conviction. By modulating from George Eliot's forthright
statement to the surrounding darkness of the garden, Myers conveys
a feeling of sadness and nostalgia. The novelist becomes another Mrs
Transome regretting too late her earlier apostasy. She must, the
reviewers feel, have had second thoughts. Isn't the sage conducting
services at the Priory, asks one critic, 'a *fallen* prophetess . . . so intoxicated by some dreadful poison as to grow dull to the vision of consoling
good which once had seemed her familiar grace?'[110] These aspersions
may seem irrelevant to George Eliot's fiction, yet they have a profound
bearing upon the second major concern of the critics at this time.

Unanimously, they agree, the early novels are infinitely superior to
the later ones. The latter lack the 'charm' and the 'magic' which,
Virginia Woolf was to suggest, male reviewers expect to find in their
womenfolk. The critics support their conviction with a few, repeated
clichés. When she is relying on her own early experiences, George Eliot
is able to create concrete, living characters; when she has to rely
increasingly upon her own imagination and theory, then the characters
are painstakingly constructed. The decline of her genius represents the
victory of the philosopher over the artist. Leslie Stephen's obituary
essay (No. 67) expresses this point of view, and he agrees with Mallock
that Maggie Tulliver, 'a composite product of both of the author's
methods', is the crucial test-case. After Maggie has been compromised
by George Eliot's thesis, the battle is lost and, despite *Silas Marner*, the
best that can be expected is the unsatisfactory settlement between the
conflicting sides of her genius in *Daniel Deronda*.

It was not simply the philosopher in George Eliot which triumphed
over the artist. It was an atheist philosopher. Whereas, in the early
novels, the artist is relying upon her own childhood experiences—
when she was still a Christian—for the material out of which to create
vital and opaque characters, in her later novels as the philosopher
becomes more polemical she has to fabricate a reality to fit the demands
of her thesis. The result—the argument continues—is the lifeless robots
of *Romola* and *Daniel Deronda* which we are encouraged to dismantle
and put together again. One critic feels it is improper, even immoral,
to dissect characters in this way. 'Have we not constantly the feeling

of knowing too much about them? There is in all men . . . a spark of soul, of individuality, of the unforeseen, that eludes all our research.'[111] The idea of George Eliot as Frankenstein seems rather alarmist, but it indicates the widespread aversion to the idea of the philosopher clumsily tampering with the creations of the artist on the instructions of a preconceived theory.

The conclusion of this argument is that George Eliot was a successful novelist despite her radical intellect to which she finally succumbed. This is certainly one way of dealing with her heterodoxy. Her strengths are associated with her earlier, orthodox self, her weaknesses with her growing atheism. The critic of the *Dublin Review* doesn't waste words: 'as anti-Christian feeling grows into a fixed habit with her, George Eliot's books lose their charm'.[112] And this was a very common point of view in the 1880s. It is made up of several overlapping prejudices and arguments but they all have one thing in common. They are based upon extreme and ingenuous divisions—between the early novels and the later ones, between the artist and the philosopher, between the dramatization of character and its analysis, and between George Eliot the lapsed Christian and George Eliot the rampant atheist.

John Walter Cross's *Life* appeared in 1885 and immediately undermined the simple dualities upon which this account of the writer in conflict with herself was based. The reviewers were amazed by the rigour and application of her intellectual training. Lord Acton suspected that her acquirements 'might not have satisfied University tests',[113] but for virtually everyone else she stood revealed as one of the most powerful intellects of the time. 'Before she wrote a tale at all,' said Frederic Harrison, 'George Eliot in mental equipment, stood side by side with Mill, Spencer, Lewes, and Carlyle.'[114] Several critics began, at this point, to treat the native woodnotes of the early fiction more sceptically.

Even more surprising was the consistency of her thought and belief. Previously it had been assumed that the changes of direction in George Eliot's fiction were the manifest signs of her inner conflicts. Now the critics discover that her thought has a developing consistency which transcends any of the sudden changes which they had postulated. Frederic Harrison expresses the general surprise: 'It is most striking that in all this history of mental progress there is no perceptible break. One phrase grows out of the other without storm or interruption; and throughout the same religious earnestness remains and deepens, even whilst the bases of belief are changed.'[115] The critics are now forced to face the facts which disprove the earlier theories: George Eliot was an intellectual through and through from an early age, and she lost her religious faith irrevocably before she became a novelist. In his review of the biography, the critic of *The Times* frankly acknowledges his previous error:

There are literary surprises besides, which have all the excitement of sensation. We fancied we had traced the growth and development of her mind in the tone and fashion of her fiction. It seemed natural that she should have begun with the sweet and simple realism of her *Clerical Tales* and her *Adam Bede*—somewhat pedantic as the phraseology occasionally is, even in these—that after rising to the more cosmopolitan culture of *Romola*, and passing through the political speculations of *Felix Holt*, she should have ended in the colder sparkle of her *Middlemarch*, or the more mystical philosophy of *Daniel Deronda*. We find in reality that her latest style might more naturally have been her earliest; that the tone and thought of the *Daniel Deronda* and the *Middlemarch* are in harmony with the letters of the girl of nineteen; that the *Adam Bede*, and the other books which have most fascinated us, are rather happy interludes in the course of her intellectual career than an essential growth to it.[116]

The novels which had previously provided the plan of George Eliot's life for the reading public now take their place in the larger perspective of her intellectual career which is presided over by the forbidding and humourless sage called into existence by Cross's anxious editing of the letters. The conflicts and tensions which enlivened the earlier accounts of her life have been replaced by an almost oppressive consistency of thought and purpose. This single-mindedness was made possible, the reviewers of the biography realized, by George Eliot's progressive and melancholy withdrawal from the life around her into the seclusion of what John Morley called a 'moral and intellectual hothouse'.[117] The growing earnestness, abstractness, and despondency is, for Saintsbury, part of 'the Nemesis of the *liaison* with Lewes'.[118] Perhaps, speculates the *Saturday Review*, this hothouse treatment was the only kind of training which would have enabled George Eliot 'to win the Novel Stakes time after time as she did'. Without it she would have written fewer books, but they would have probably been 'healthier'.[119] James too expresses regret at her 'sequestration' and sums up concisely what several critics were implying: 'If her relations with the world had been easier, in a word, her books would have been less difficult.'[120]

Earlier, the novels had been used to substantiate the obscure story of George Eliot's life; now the life becomes a limiting judgment on

the novels. The critics obviously feel that the picture of George Eliot
in the *Life* is not what they expect of a novelist. She is too intellectual,
too consistent, perhaps too hardworking. 'Is this the woman who wrote
Adam Bede?' asks an incredulous Mrs Oliphant.[121] Imperceptibly, the
adjectives shift from the life to the work. It is here, in the discussions
of the biography, that one can see George Eliot's reputation being
determined for the next twenty or thirty years. The retreat from the
hard clarity of the individual novels to the general assessments of the
author's work, now culminates in Cross's lifeless silhouette. This was to
intervene stubbornly between the novels and the reading-public for
many years. George Eliot's contemporaries had been surprised to find
that the novels they knew were written by this woman; later generations assumed that this woman could not have written anything for
them.

As the decline of George Eliot's reputation is getting under way in
England in these years following her death, there is a sudden awakening
of interest in France. During her lifetime she had been received
apathetically or ignored. François D'Albert Durade, her old friend in
Geneva, had translated five of the novels into French—*Adam Bede*
(1861), *The Mill on the Floss* (1863), *Silas Marner* (1863), *Romola* (1878),
Scenes of Clerical Life (1884)—but the sales were minimal and they
aroused little enthusiasm.[122] The criticism of the novels in French
periodicals is invariably unsympathetic, if not actively hostile, and
makes dismal reading. Most critics writing from classical premises
are outraged at the aesthetic expressed in the novels. It is for them the
wilful denial of both art and morality. The meaningless photographic
realism, the confused moral standards, the bizarre structure of the
novels—their anger mounts with their incomprehension. They had
one way of moderating the worst of George Eliot's excesses. The most
popular method of presenting fiction in the periodicals was by *réductions
critiques*, lengthy summaries interspersed with quotations; here the
most extreme irregularities of the novels could be smoothed out.

Two critics, Edmond Scherer and Émile Montégut, did approach
the novels more sympathetically during her lifetime.[123] Less doctrinaire
and conservative than their contemporaries, they sought to understand
this alien form of realism by relating it to George Eliot's morality.
Montégut evolved a theory which linked the realism to her Protestant
background and thereby tried to explain both its peculiar quality and
the hostility with which it was received in France. But even here, in the
writings of these two critics, attractively rounded generalizations are

the substitute for analysis and insight. The more significant awakening of interest dates from Ferdinand Brunetière's influential article on George Eliot in the *Revue Bleue* in 1881.[124]

Brunetière was anxious to repel the scornful attacks which the Naturalists were mounting against all forms of idealism and morality in art—Zola's *Le Roman Expérimental* had appeared in 1880—and George Eliot was a convenient ally. With the assistance of her novels, he could not only denounce the logic of Flaubert and Zola, but present an alternative to their extreme solution. He could show that George Eliot was like them a realist, but that this did not necessarily entail the rejection of all traditional moral values. She, he felt, was pointing the way towards the synthesis of traditional values and the new scientific ideas while avoiding Zola's mechanistic determinism. The crucial quality which enabled her to achieve this was her deep sympathy for her prosaic characters. This is the secret of English Naturalism. 'French Naturalism, on the contrary, expresses only disdain and contempt for its Bouvards and Pécuchets.' It must learn that education, intelligence, and beauty are not the only criteria; the inner life has its own values. And only when French writers have acquired this sympathy will they begin to create once more credible, rounded characters. He attributes the difference between the two countries to three centuries of Protestantism on the one hand, and the French language on the other. The latter is too 'aristocratic' to describe commonplace people and events in a familiar way, and this reinforces the French tendency to see man as the material of art, rather than to see art as something made for man. 'The theory of art for art's sake,' he concludes, 'is essentially Latin.' The English version of the theory, however, was soon helping to undermine George Eliot's reputation in her own country.

XII

After 1885

'I am afraid,' says Constantius in James's conversation on *Daniel Deronda* in 1876, 'that Pulcheria is sadly aesthetic.' But it was her thorough boredom with George Eliot which was to triumph over both the judiciousness of Constantius and the worship of Theodora in the years to come. At the end of the century the critics are in revolt against the novel-with-a-purpose, and in particular against the purely

ethical terms in which George Eliot's life and work had been assessed
since her death. A reviewer in the *Atlantic Monthly* in 1889 enlists the
support of Oscar Wilde and Vernon Lee in order to insist more forcibly
that fiction must not be allowed into the pulpit, and then quotes with
delight a parody of George Eliot the moralist in action. The novelist
is addressing Falstaff:

For really, Sir John, you have no excuse whatever. If you were a poor devil who
had never had any but bad examples before your eyes!—but you have had all
the advantages which destiny can give to man on his way through life. Are
you not born of a good family? Have you not had at Oxford the best education
England is able to give to her children? Have you not had the highest connections? And, nevertheless, how low you have fallen! Do you know why? I have
warned my Tito over and over again against it: because you have always done
that only which was agreeable to you, and have shunned everything that was
unpleasant.[125]

The heavy-handedness of the parody indicates how anxious the
critics were to debunk the stereotype of the Victorian sage which had
been respectfully bequeathed to them. Frequently they resort to personal abuse. W. E. Henley, a male apostate as he calls himself, seeks to
ridicule George Eliot in 1890 with a series of epigrams. She is, among
other things, 'An Apotheosis of Pupil-Teachery', 'Pallas with prejudices
and a corset', and 'the fruit of a caprice of Apollo for the Differential
Calculus'.[126] Her reticence about sex becomes in the emancipated
nineties the index of her blinkered earnestness. She might have persuaded earlier readers of her breadth of vision but to Henley she is
an absurdly learned and rather squeamish woman ('George Sand *plus*
Science and *minus* Sex') whom he denounces with virile boisterousness.
Six years later Arnold Bennett became similarly annoyed, both as man
and writer, when people called George Eliot's style masculine: 'On
the contrary it is transparently feminine—feminine in its lack of
restraint, its wordiness, and the utter absence of feeling for form which
characterizes it.' He has just dipped into *Adam Bede* and he records in
his journal the certainty that she 'will never be among the classical
writers'.[127]

The general feeling is that George Eliot's fictional world is very
restricted, well-disciplined, and controlled far too easily by a doubtful
morality. Saintsbury defined its limited range in 1891 by suggesting
that George Eliot showed 'an insufficient devotion to the great god
Nonsense, whether in his Avatar of Frivolity or in his Avatar of
Passion'.[128] By 1895 in his *Corrected Impressions*, he was convinced that

both coterie admiration and popular support had been dead for several years. Though she may still be read, George Eliot 'has more or less passed out of contemporary critical appreciation'.[129]

Leslie Stephen's authoritative study in the 'English Men of Letters' series in 1902 rekindled some serious critical interest. It is however noticeable that Stephen, although he shares many of George Eliot's beliefs, has serious doubts about her ultimate status. 'Certain speculative doctrines', he feels, limit and distort the reality of the novels in a debilitating way. Even her psychological originality, W. C. Brownell argues at this time, has been devalued in the general reaction, led by Robert Louis Stevenson, against the scientific invasion of literature.[130]

The *Cambridge History of English Literature* embalmed George Eliot in 1916 with high but chilling praise: 'Of no greater woman of letters is the name recorded in English annals. . . .' But while Thackeray and Dickens are given separate chapters, George Eliot is relegated to the company of Disraeli, Kingsley, and Mrs Gaskell in a discussion of 'The Political and Social Novel'. The centenary in 1919 aroused some interest over and above the conventional reflex action, but it is important primarily for Virginia Woolf's essay in *The Times Literary Supplement*.[131] A little ashamed of how, 'half consciously and partly maliciously, one had accepted the late Victorian version of a deluded woman who held phantom sway over subjects even more deluded than herself', Virginia Woolf goes back to the novels and writes her moving tribute. Most significantly, she sees in the works a pattern of vital growth, how the 'large grasp' of George Eliot's mind could not remain content with the rustic novels of reminiscence but had to assume a more personal standpoint. The 'disconcerting and stimulating fact remained that she was compelled by the very power of her genius to step forth in person upon the quiet bucolic scene'. And, unlike her father (No. 67), Virginia Woolf does not believe that this entails a diminution of George Eliot's power—'for, to our thinking, it is at its highest in the mature *Middlemarch*, the magnificent book which with all its imperfections is one of the few English novels written for grownup people'. The well-known sentence anticipated George Eliot's return to favour by means of her later work, but when it was written it was far from representative.

More characteristic of the period between the wars are the assessments of Oliver Elton in 1920 and Lord David Cecil in 1934. Both accept the conventional division of her powers into the spontaneously creative and the artificially intellectual. Praise of the first is quickly modified by censure of the second, which is seen as curtailing and finally preventing artistic fulfilment. 'While exhaustively describing life,' Elton concludes, 'she is apt to miss the spirit of life itself,'[132] and Cecil regrets that her 'tidy little compartments of right and wrong' leave out too much that is complex and mysterious.[133]

These were the kind of judgments castigated by F. R. Leavis in his important *Scrutiny* articles on George Eliot in 1945–6 which later formed part of *The Great Tradition* (1948). He follows the lead of Virginia Woolf in trying to put George Eliot together again. He questions the antithesis which had bedevilled her reputation for decades. Her intellectual and moral preoccupations do not create 'patches, say, of tough or drily abstract thinking undigested by her art;'[134] these preoccupations are an integral part of her vital and inclusive vision. Leavis introduces his own discriminations, of course, but George Eliot remains for him a central figure in the great tradition of the English novel, beside whom Meredith is a 'shallow exhibitionist' and Hardy 'a provincial manufacturer of gauche and heavy fictions'. The most fitting adjective to describe her is the charismatic 'Tolstoyan': 'George Eliot, of course, is not as transcendently great as Tolstoy, but she *is* great, and great in the same way.'[135]

Two other studies at the same time—by Gerald Bullett (1947) and Joan Bennett (1948)—signalled the rescue of George Eliot's reputation, and since then criticism of the novels in a variety of forms has proliferated. Her carefully constructed works have fulfilled so generously the needs of the academic critic that her greatness is now rarely questioned. It has been further implicitly confirmed by Gordon S. Haight's impeccable edition of the letters (1954–5) where George Eliot is rescued from Cross's editing and appears both as the woman who went off to Weimar with George Henry Lewes in 1854 and as the novelist who wrote *Adam Bede* and *Daniel Deronda*.

NOTES

1 *The George Eliot Letters* (1954–5), ed. Gordon S. Haight, iv, 58.
2 *Letters*, iv, 405.
3 *Letters*, vi, 253.
4 *Letters*, iii, 322.
5 *Essays of George Eliot* (1963), ed. Thomas Pinney, p. 322.

6 *Essays*, pp. 325–6. Fadladeen was the Chamberlain of the Harem to Aurungzebe in Moore's *Lalla Rookh*, and 'a judge of everything'.

7 *Letters*, vi, 418.

8 *Letters*, v, 155.

9 *Letters*, iii, 324.

10 See Introduction, pp. 32–3.

11 *Essays*, p. 443.

12 *Letters*, ii, 407–8.

13 *Letters*, ii, 423.

14 *Letters*, ii, 335.

15 *Atlantic Monthly* (October 1866), xviii, 48.

16 *Letters*, iii, 275. *Les Mystères de Paris* by Eugène Sue was published in 10 volumes, 1842–3.

17 *Letters*, iii, 191.

18 *Essays*, p. 270.

19 *Blackwood's Magazine* (April 1859), lxxxv, 490–1. [W. Lucas Collins.]

20 *Athenaeum* (26 February 1859), p. 284. [Geraldine Jewsbury.]

21 *Examiner* (5 March 1859), p. 149.

22 *British Quarterly Review* (January 1867), xlv, 164.

23 *Atlantic Monthly* (October 1866), xviii, 487.

24 *Eclectic Review* (March 1859), cix, 333.

25 *Westminster Review* (April 1859), lxxi, 502.

26 *Henry Crabb Robinson on Books and Their Writers* (1938), ed. E. J. Morley, ii, 787.

27 *Letters*, iii, 291–2.

28 *Letters*, iv, 318.

29 *Blackwood's Magazine* (May 1860), lxxxvii, 612. [W. Lucas Collins.]

30 *Ibid.*, p. 615.

31 *National Review* (July 1860), xi, 214. [R. H. Hutton.]

32 *Ibid.*, p. 217.

33 *Quarterly Review* (October 1860), cviii, 495. [James Craigie Robertson.]

34 *Essays*, p. 147.

35 *The Mill on the Floss*, VII, ii.

36 *Eclectic Review* (August 1860), cxii, 224.

37 *Athenaeum* (6 April 1861), pp. 464–5.

38 *Ibid.*

39 *Revue des deux Mondes* (1 September 1861), xxxv, 195–7. [P. A. Cucheval-Clarigny.]

40 *Silas Marner*, ed. Annie Matheson (1903), p. 232.

41 *Letters*, iv, 17–18.

42 *Galaxy* (March 1873), xv, 428.

43 *Letters*, iii, 474.

44 *Letters*, iv, 49.

45 *Letters*, vi, 312.
46 *Letters*, iv, 58.
47 *Letters*, iv, 75.
48 *Letters*, iii, 152.
49 *Revue des deux Mondes* (15 December 1863), xlviii, 967. [E-D. Forgues.]
50 *Blackwood's Magazine* (July 1874), cxvi, 82.
51 *Dictionary of National Biography*, xiii (1888).
52 *Letters*, v, 276.
53 *Quarterly Review* (October 1860), cviii, 484, 498.
54 *North British Review* (September 1866), xlv, 225. [H. H. Lancaster.]
55 *National Review* (July 1860), xi, 213. [R. H. Hutton.]
56 *Letters*, iii, 356.
57 'Realism in Art: Recent German Fiction', *Westminster Review* (October 1858), lxx, 493.
58 *Quarterly Review* (October 1860), cviii, 498.
59 *British Quarterly Review* (January 1867), xlv, 159.
60 *Letters*, v, 374.
61 *North American Review* (October 1866), ciii, 558.
62 'The Novels of George Eliot', *Atlantic Monthly* (October 1866), xviii, 480-1.
63 *North American Review* (April 1873), cxvi, 439. [T. S. Perry.]
64 *Galaxy* (June 1869), vii, 804-5.
65 *Atlantic Monthly* (September 1874), xxiv, 322.
66 *Ibid.*, p. 323.
67 *Westminster Review* (July 1866), lxxxvi, 200.
68 *North American Review* (October 1866), ciii, 557. [A. G. Sedgwick.]
69 *Ibid.*
70 *Blackwood's Magazine* (May 1863), xciii, 558.
71 *North British Review* (September 1866), xlv, 210.
72 *London Quarterly Review* (October 1866), xxvii, 103.
73 *Contemporary Review* (September 1866), iii, 58. [Henry Alford.]
74 *Blackwood's Magazine* (May 1863), xciii, 558.
75 *Letters*, iv, 247.
76 *Letters*, iv, 289.
77 *Letters*, iv, 352.
78 *Letters*, v, 357.
79 *The Times Literary Supplement* (20 November 1919), pp. 657-8.
80 *The Times*, 7 March 1873, p. 3.
81 *Ibid.*, p. 4.
82 *Atlantic Monthly* (April 1873), xxxi, 494. [A. G. Sedgwick.]
83 *Canadian Monthly* (June 1873), iii, 550.
84 *British Quarterly Review* (April 1873), lvii, 414. [R. H. Hutton.]
85 *Scribner's Monthly* (March 1881), xxi, 791.
86 *Atlantic Monthly* (April 1873), xxxi, 491.

87 *London Quarterly Review* (January 1877), xlvii, 453.

88 *Letters*, v, 168.

89 *North American Review* (April 1873), cxvi, 439. [T. S. Perry.]

90 *British Quarterly Review* (April 1873), lvii, 408. [R. H. Hutton.]

91 *Quarterly Review* (April 1873), cxxxiv, 359. [Robert Laing.]

92 *St. Paul's Magazine* (May 1873), xii, 616. [George Barnett Smith.]

93 *Dictionary of National Biography*, xiii (1888).

94 *Edinburgh Review* (October 1876), cxliv, 468.

95 *Letters*, vi, 290.

96 *Letters*, vi, 304.

97 *Academy* (9 September 1876), x, 253. [George Saintsbury.]

98 *Progress* (June 1883), i, 382. [J. Robertson.]

99 *Letters of Robert Louis Stevenson* (1911), ed. Sidney Colvin, i, 220.

100 *Spectator* (10 June 1876), xlix, 734. [R. H. Hutton.]

101 *Ibid.*

102 *British Quarterly Review* (October 1876), lxiv, 475.

103 *Letters*, vi, 336.

104 *Macmillan's Magazine* (June 1877), xxxvi, 105. [Joseph Jacobs.]

105 *Gentleman's Magazine* (October 1876), xvii, 422.

106 *Scribner's Monthly* (October 1874), viii, 698. [W. C. Wilkinson.]

107 *London Quarterly Review* (January 1877), xlvii, 462.

108 *Spectator* (14 June 1879), lii, 752. [R. H. Hutton.]

109 *Century Magazine* (November 1881), xxiii, 62.

110 *Dublin Review* (October 1881), vi, 459. [William Barry.]

111 *London Quarterly Review* (January 1877), xlvii, 460.

112 *Dublin Review* (October 1881), vi, 463.

113 *Nineteenth Century* (March 1885), xvii, 471.

114 *Fortnightly Review* (1 March 1885), xxxvii, 314.

115 *Ibid.*, p. 319.

116 *The Times*, 27 January 1885, p. 4.

117 *Macmillan's Magazine* (February 1885), li, 247.

118 *Corrected Impressions: Essays on Victorian Writers* (1895), p. 172.

119 *Saturday Review* (7 February 1885), lix, 181.

120 *Atlantic Monthly* (May 1885), lv, 671.

121 *Edinburgh Review* (April 1885), clxi, 519.

122 *Scenes of Clerical Life* had been translated first into French in 1863 by Emmanuel Leon Pasquet. *Daniel Deronda* was translated in 1881 by Ernest David, while *Middlemarch* had to wait until 1890 (by M.-J. M.). See Couch, pp. 174–83. The German translators acted more promptly. By January 1864 George Eliot believed that all her novels, with the exception of *Romola*, were translated into German (*Letters*, iv, 130). Dr Emil Lehmann later translated both *Felix Holt* (1867) and *Middlemarch* (1872–3), while *Daniel Deronda* was translated by Adolf Strodtmann in 1876.

123 See Edmond Scherer, *Études critiques de la littérature contemporaine*, i (1863), 17–27; v (1878), 287–304; viii (1885), 187–242. Émile Montégut, *Revue des deux Mondes* (15 June 1859), xxi, 867–97; (1 March 1883), lvi, 77–99; (15 March 1883), lvi, 305–46.

124 *Revue Bleue* (17 September 1881), xxvii, 353–63. Reprinted in *Le Roman naturaliste* (1897).

125 *Atlantic Monthly* (October 1889), lxiv, 533. [Agnes Repplier.] The parody is by the German critic and historian, Karl Hillebrand (1829–84).

126 *Views and Reviews: Essays in Appreciation* (1890), p. 132.

127 *The Journals of Arnold Bennett* (1932), ed. Newman Flower, i, 6.

128 Edmond Scherer, *Essays on English Literature* (1891), trans. George Saintsbury, p. xxiii.

129 *Corrected Impressions: Essays on Victorian Writers* (1895), p. 172.

130 *Victorian Prose Masters* (1901), pp. 99–100.

131 *The Times Literary Supplement* (20 November 1919), pp. 657–8.

132 *A Survey of English Literature, 1830–1880* (1920), ii, 260.

133 *Early Victorian Novelists: Essays in Revaluation* (1934), 319.

134 *The Great Tradition* (1948), p. 32.

135 *Ibid.*, p. 124.

SCENES OF CLERICAL LIFE

January–November 1857

1. John Blackwood discovers a new author

Extracts from the correspondence between the publisher John Blackwood, George Henry Lewes, and George Eliot (see Introduction, pp. 7–8). All page references are to *The George Eliot Letters*, ed. Gordon S. Haight (1954–5).

(a) George Henry Lewes to John Blackwood

6 November 1856

Meanwhile I trouble you with a m.s. of *Sketches of Clerical Life* which was submitted to me by a friend who desired my good offices with you. It goes by this post.

I confess that before reading the m.s. I had considerable doubts of my friend's power as a writer of fiction; but after reading it those doubts were changed into very high admiration. I don't know what you will think of the story, but according to my judgement such humour, pathos, vivid presentation and nice observation have not been exhibited (in this style) since the *Vicar of Wakefield*—and in consequence of that opinion I feel quite pleased in negotiating the matter with you.

This is what I am commissioned to say to you about the proposed series. It will consist of tales and sketches illustrative of the actual life of our country clergy about a quarter of a century ago; but solely in its *human* and *not at all* in its *theological* aspect; the object being to do what has never yet been done in our Literature, for we have had abundant religious stories polemical and doctrinal, but since the *Vicar* and Miss Austen, no stories representing the clergy like any other class with the humours, sorrows, and troubles of other men. He begged me

particularly to add that—as the specimen sent will sufficiently prove
—the tone throughout will be sympathetic and not at all antagonistic
(ii, 269).

(b) John Blackwood to George Henry Lewes

12 November 1856

I am happy to say that I think your friend's reminiscences of Clerical
Life will do. If there is any more of the series written I should like to
see it, as until I saw more I could not make any decided proposition
for the publication of the Tales in whole or in part in the Magazine.
This first specimen 'Amos Barton' is unquestionably very pleasant
reading. Perhaps the author falls into the error of trying too much to
explain the characters of his actors by descriptions instead of allowing
them to evolve in the action of the story; but the descriptions are very
humorous and good. The death of Milly is powerfully done and affected
me much. I am not sure whether he does not spoil it a little by specify-
ing so minutely the different children and their names.

The windup is perhaps the lamest part of the story and there too I
think the defect is caused by the specifications as to the fortunes of
parties of whom the reader has no previous knowledge and cannot
consequently feel much interest. At first I was afraid that in the amusing
reminiscences of childhood in church there was a want of some softening touch as the remembrance of a father or mother lends in after
years to what was at the time considerable penance.

I hate anything of a sneer at real religious feeling as cordially as I
despise anything like cant, and I should think this author is of the same
way of thinking although his clergymen with one exception are not
very attractive specimens of the body. The revulsion of feeling towards
poor Amos is capitally drawn although the asinine stupidity of his
conduct about the Countess had disposed one to kick him.

I daresay I shall have a more decided opinion as to the merits of the
Story when I have looked at it again and thought over it, but in the
meantime I am sure that there is a happy turn of expression throughout,
also much humour and pathos. If the author is a new writer I beg to
congratulate him on being worthy of the honours of print and pay. I
shall be very glad to hear from you or him soon (ii, 272).

(c) George Henry Lewes to John Blackwood

15 November 1856

I have communicated your letter to my clerical friend, who, though somewhat discouraged by it, has taken my advice and will submit the second story to you when it is written. At present he has only written what he sent you. His avocations, he informs me, will prevent his setting to work for the next three weeks or so; but as soon as he is at liberty he will begin.

I rate the story much higher than you appear to do from certain expressions in your note, though you too appreciate the humour and pathos and the happy turn of expression. It struck me as being fresher than any story I have read for a long while, and as exhibiting in a high degree that faculty which I find to be the rarest of all, viz. the dramatic ventriloquism. At the same time I told him that I perfectly understood your editorial caution in not accepting from an unknown hand a series on the strength of one specimen (ii, 273-4).

(d) John Blackwood to George Henry Lewes

18 November 1856

I was very far from intending that my letter should convey anything like disappointment to your friend. On the contrary I thought the Tale very good and intended to convey as much. But I daresay I expressed myself coolly enough. Criticism would assume a much soberer tone were critics compelled *seriously to act* whenever they expressed an opinion. Although not much given to hesitate about anything I always think twice before I put the decisive mark 'In type for the Magazine' on any M.S. from a stranger. Fancy the intense annoyance (to say nothing of more serious considerations) of publishing month after month a series about which the conviction gradually forces itself on you that you have made a total blunder.

I am sorry that the author has no more written but if he cares much about a speedy appearance I have so high an opinion of this first Tale that I will waive my objections and publish it without seeing more; not, of course committing myself to go on with the other Tales of the series unless I approved of them. I am very sanguine that I will approve as in addition to the other merits of 'Amos' I agree with you that there is great freshness of style. If you think also that it would stimulate the author to go on with the other Tales with more spirit I will publish 'Amos' at once. He would divide into two parts. I am blocked up for December but I could start him in January.

I am glad to hear that your friend is as I supposed a Clergyman. Such a subject is best in clerical hands and some of the pleasantest and least prejudiced correspondents I have ever had are English Clergymen (ii, 275).

(e) George Henry Lewes to John Blackwood

22 November 1856

Your letter has greatly restored the shaken confidence of my friend, who is unusually sensitive, and unlike most writers is more anxious about *excellence* than about appearing in print—as his waiting so long before taking the venture proves. He is consequently afraid of failure though not afraid of obscurity; and by failure he would understand that which I suspect most writers would be apt to consider as success—so high is his ambition.

I tell you this that you may understand the sort of shy, shrinking, ambitious nature you have to deal with. I tried to persuade him that you really *did* appreciate his story, but were only hesitating about committing yourself to a *series* and your last letter has proved me to have been right. Although, as he never contemplated binding you to the publication of any portion of the series to which you might object, he could not at first see your position in its true light. All is, however, clear now. He will be gratified if you publish 'Amos Barton' in January, as it will give him ample time to get the second story ready, so as to appear when 'Barton' is finished, should you wish it. He is anxious, however, that you should publish the general title of *Scenes of Clerical Life*—and I think you may do this with perfect safety, since it is quite clear that the writer of 'Amos Barton' is capable of writing at least one more story suitable to Maga, and two would suffice to justify the general title.

Let me not forget to add that when I referred to 'my clerical friend' I meant to designate the writer of the clerical stories, not that he was a clericus. I am not at liberty to remove the veil of anonymity—even as regards social position. Be pleased therefore to keep the whole secret —and not even mention *my* negotiation or in any way lead guessers—

(should any one trouble himself with such a guess—*not* very likely) to jump from me to my friend (ii, 276-7).

(f) John Blackwood to George Eliot

29 December 1856

Along with this I send a copy of the January number of the Magazine in which you will find the first part of 'Amos Barton'. It gives me very great pleasure to begin the number with 'Amos' and I put him in that position because his merits will entitle him to it and also because it is a vital point to attract public attention to the *first* part of a Series, to which end being the first article of the first number of the year may contribute.

I have already expressed to our friend Mr. Lewes the very high opinion I entertain of 'Amos' and the expectations I have formed of the Series should his successors prove equal to him, which I fully anticipate.

It is a long time since I have read anything so fresh so humorous and so touching. The style is capital, conveying so much in so few words.

Those who have seen the Tale here are chiefly members of my own family and they are all enthusiastic in praise.

You may recollect that I expressed a fear that in the affecting and highly wrought scene of poor Milly's death the attempt to individualise the children by reiterating their names weakened the effect, as the reader had not been prepared to care for them individually but simply as a group—the children of Milly and the sorrow stricken Curate. My brother says no—'Do not advise the author to touch anything so exquisite'—Of course you are the best judge.

I now send proof of the conclusion of 'Amos' in acknowledgment of which and of the first part I have the pleasure of making a cheque £52-10/—Fifty Guineas.

If the Series goes on as I anticipate there is every prospect that a republication as a separate book at some time or other will be advisable. We would look upon such republication as a joint property and would either give you a sum for your interest in it or publish on the Terms of one half of the clear profits to be divided between author and publisher, as might be most agreeable to you (ii, 283).

(g) John Blackwood to George Eliot

30 January 1857

The public is a very curious animal and those who are most accustomed to feel its pulse know best how difficult it is to tell what will hit the bull's eye, but I shall be much astonished if the death of Milly does not go to the hearts of all readers. It is a most touching death bed scene.

Critics are a good deal divided about the first part of 'Amos', but they generally are about anything of real merit. Some of my friends praise it very much; others condemn. I was rather startled by two of my familiars—about the best men going—declaring dead against 'Amos'. They have rather modified their opinions now and I think may probably end by agreeing with me. They were the first men who had seen the Magazine after it was published and finding two such lads against me it required all the self reliance, without which an Editor would be the most miserable dog alive, to make me feel quite easy and satisfied that I was right. With one of them, Colonel Hamley, I do not recollect of ever differing in opinion before. He thought the Author very possibly a *man of Science* but not a practised writer. The idea of a man of Science had occurred to me before from some of the illustrations.

I forget whether I told you or Lewes that I had shown part of the M.S. to Thackeray. He was staying with me and, having been out at dinner, came in about eleven o'clock when I had just finished your M.S. and was busy talking about it to Mrs. Blackwood. I said to him 'Do you know I think I have lighted upon a new Author who is uncommonly like a first class passenger.' I showed him a page or two, I think the passage where the Curate returns home and Milly is first introduced. He would not pronounce whether it came up to my ideas but remarked afterwards that he would have liked to have read more, which I thought a good sign. The Newspapers generally have I think been very favourable, but I do not attach very much weight to what they say until they catch the general echo (ii, 290–1).

(h) George Eliot to John Blackwood's brother, William

4 February 1857

Thank you for your last kind letter, fulfilling your promise to let me know something of the criticisms passed on my story. I have a very moderate respect for 'opinions of the press,' but the private opinions of intelligent people may be valuable to me.

In reference to artistic presentation, much adverse opinion will of course arise from a dislike to the *order* of art rather than from a critical estimate of the execution. Any one who detests the Dutch school in general will hardly appreciate fairly the merits of a particular Dutch painting. And against this sort of condemnation, one must steel oneself as one best can. But objections which point out to me any vice of manner or any failure in producing an intended effect will be really profitable. For example, I suppose my scientific illustrations must be a fault, since they seem to have obtruded themselves disagreeably on ~~some~~ one of my readers. But if it be a sin to be at once a man of science and a writer of fiction, I can declare my perfect innocence on that head, my scientific knowledge being as superficial as that of the most 'practised writers' (ii, 291–2).

(i) John Blackwood to George Eliot

16 February 1857

I inclose proof of the first part of 'Mr. Gilfil' with which I am very greatly delighted. The proof fully confirms the impression made by the M.S. The first eight pages in particular are bright, lifelike, and witty as may be. Many men write well and tell a story well, but few possess the art of giving individuality to their characters so happily and easily as you in both these stories. I think 'Mr. Gilfil' is likely to be more generally popular than 'Amos' and I have no qualms in starting him without seeing the conclusion.

On the proof I have made some marks in regard to which I shall be very glad if you agree with me. The last marks affect ~~rather seriously~~ the plot of the story but I think my objections may be obviated without any serious alteration of the plan. It is not a pleasant picture to see a good fellow loving on when the lady's heart is *openly* devoted to a Jackanapes, and I am a little puzzled as to how you are to bring the excellent Gilfil out ~~unless~~ without making him too abjectly devoted a lover for a man of character. I think the objection would be readily met by making Caterina a little less openly devoted to Wybrow and giving a little more dignity to her character. Understand that I by no means object to her; on the contrary I think that she promises to be most interesting and I look with great anxiety for the picture of her half-broken heart turning to Gilfil. I hope she finally rejects the insufferable Wybrow—but I must not speculate upon your plot, and if I am wrong in my opinions about the demeanour of Caterina with Wybrow recollect that I write to some extent in the dark. (ii, 297).

(j) George Eliot to John Blackwood

18 February 1857

You will see that I have availed myself of your suggestions on points of language. I quite recognize the justice of your criticism on the French phrases. They are not in keeping with my story.

But I am unable to alter anything in relation to the delineation or development of character, as my stories always grow out of my psychological conception of the dramatis personæ. For example the behaviour of Caterina in the gallery is essential to my conception of her nature and to the development of that nature in the plot. My artistic bent is directed not at all to the presentation of eminently irreproachable characters, but to the presentation of mixed human beings in such a way as to call forth tolerant judgment, pity, and sympathy. And I cannot stir a step aside from what I *feel* to be *true* in character. If anything strikes you as untrue to human nature in my delineations, I shall be very glad if you will point it out to me, that I may reconsider the matter. But alas! inconsistencies and weaknesses are not untrue (ii, 298-9).

(k) John Blackwood to George Eliot

8 June 1857

The first part of 'Janet's Repentance' of which I inclose proof rather puzzles me. It is exceedingly clever and some of the hits and descriptions of character are first rate, but I should have liked a pleasanter picture. Surely the colours are rather harsh for a sketch of English County Town life only 25 years ago. The glimpse at the end of the part shows that a powerful and pathetic story is coming and I rather wish you had plunged sooner into it instead of expending so much humour in the delineation of characters who do not seem likely to assist materially in the movement of the Story and who are not in themselves interesting.

The first scene especially I think you should shorten. It is deuced good but rather a staggerer in an opening scene of a *Story of Clerical Life*. Dempster is rather too barefaced a brute and I am sorry that the poor wife's sufferings should have driven her to so unsentimental a resource as beer. Still it is true to nature. The case is but too common, and I have no right to pass any opinion on this part of the story until I see more of it. I shall be very glad if in returning the proof you can send me a further portion of M.S. as I feel very confident that what is coming will more than dissipate the slight doubts I feel about the popular qualities of this first part.

I greatly regret not being able to give applause altogether unqualified, but I may mention a capital sign that both my brother and I liked it better on the second reading than on the first. For the meantime I feel certain that I am right in advising you to *soften* your picture as much as you can. Your sketches this time are all written in the harsher Thackerayan view of human nature, and I should have liked to have seen some of the good which at page 10 you so neatly indicate as existing at Milby. When are you going to give us a really good active working clergyman, neither absurdly evangelical nor absurdly High Church? (ii, 344-5).

(l) George Eliot to John Blackwood

11 June 1857

I am not much surprized, and not at all hurt by your letter received today with the proof. It is a great satisfaction—in fact my only satisfaction, that you should give me your judgment with perfect frankness. I am able, I think, to enter into an editor's doubts and difficulties, and to see my stories in some degree from your point of view as well as my own. My answer is written after considering the question as far as possible on all sides, and as I feel that I shall not be able to make any other than *superficial* alterations in the proof, I will, first of all, say what I can in explanation of the spirit and future course of the present story.

The collision in the drama is not at all between 'bigotted churchmanship' and evangelicalism, but between *ir*religion and religion. Religion in this case happens to be represented by evangelicalism, and the story so far as regards the *persecution*, is a real bit in the religious history of England that happened about eight-and-twenty years ago. I thought I had made it apparent in my sketch of Milby feelings on the advent of Mr. Tryan that the conflict lay between immorality and morality—irreligion and religion. Mr. Tryan will carry the reader's sympathy. It is through him that Janet is brought to repentance. Dempster's vices have their natural evolution in deeper and deeper moral deterioration (though not without softening touches) and death from intemperance. Everything is softened from the fact, so far as art is permitted to soften and yet to remain essentially true. The real town was more vicious than my Milby; the real Dempster was far more disgusting than mine; the real Janet alas! had a far sadder end than mine, who will melt away from the reader's sight in purity, happiness and beauty.

My sketches both of churchmen and dissenters, with whom I am almost equally acquainted, are drawn from close observation of them in real life, and not at all from hearsay or from the descriptions of novelists. Dempster is no more like a dissenter than Jonathan Oldbuck is like Davie Deans.[1] If I were to undertake to alter Dempster's language or character, I should be attempting to represent some vague conception of what may possibly exist in other people's minds, but has no existence in my own. Such of your marginal objections as relate to a mere detail I can meet without difficulty by alteration; but as an artist I should be utterly powerless if I departed from my own conceptions of life and character. There is nothing to be done with the story, but either to let Dempster and Janet and the rest be as I *see* them, or to renounce it as too painful. I am keenly alive, at once to the scruples and alarms an editor may feel, and to my own utter inability to write under any cramping influence, and on this double ground I should like you to consider whether it will not be better to close the series for the Magazine *now*. I daresay you will feel no difficulty about publishing a volume containing the story of 'Janet's Repentance,' though you may not like to hazard its insertion in the Magazine, and I shall accept that plan with no other feeling than that you have been to me the most liberal and agreeable of editors and are the man of all others I would choose for a publisher.

My irony, so far as I understand myself, is not directed against opinions—against any class of religious views—but against the vices and weaknesses that belong to human nature in every sort of clothing. But it is possible that I may not affect other minds as I intend and wish to affect them, and you are a better judge than I can be of the degree

---

[1] Characters from Scott's *The Antiquary* (1816) and *The Heart of Midlothian* (1818) respectively.

in which I may occasionally be offensive. I should like *not* to be offensive—I should like to touch every heart among my readers with nothing but loving humour, with tenderness, with belief in goodness. But I may have failed in this case of Janet, at least so far as to have made you feel its publication in the Magazine a disagreeable risk. If so, there will be no harm done by closing the series with No. 2, as I have suggested. If, however, I take your objections to be deeper than they really are—if you prefer inserting the story in spite of your partial dissatisfaction, I shall of course be happy to appear under Maga's wing still.

When I remember what have been the successes in fiction even as republications from Maga I can hardly believe that the public will regard my pictures as exceptionally coarse. But in any case there are too many prolific writers who devote themselves to the production of pleasing pictures, to the exclusion of all disagreeable truths for me to desire to add one to their number. In this respect, at least, I may have some resemblance to Thackeray, though I am not conscious of being in any way a disciple of his, unless it constitute discipleship to think him, as I suppose the majority of people with any intellect do, on the whole the most powerful of living novelists (ii, 347–8).

(m) John Blackwood to George Eliot

14 June 1857

Your long and interesting letter of the 11th affords me much pleasure as it gives me great confidence that in spite of my objections to this first part of 'Janet's Repentance' the Tale as it goes on will prove one of your best. Indeed the glimpse of what was coming in the last pages left this impression on my mind at first.

I do not fall in with George Eliots every day and the idea of stopping the Series as suggested in your letter gave me 'quite a turn' to use one of Thackeray's favourite phrases. There is nothing in the part that can make me 'afraid' to publish it. On the contrary no one can read it without being impressed by the ability and truth of the individual pictures, and I only wished to convey my fear that you are wasting power in sketching in so many figures who would not help on or add to the popularity of your story.

From the tone of this first part I do not think that it will be much liked, but you know what groundwork you require, and when I have not seen the whole of your M.S. you must always take my remarks as those of one writing to some extent in the dark. I wish much now that I had the rest of your M.S. as I feel sure that it would enable me to write and heartily congratulate you upon a new success. . . .

In continuing to write for the Magazine I beg of all things that you will not consider yourself hampered in any way. Of course I will say when I think you are failing to produce the effect you intend or otherwise missing the mark, but unless you write entirely from the bent of your own genius or knowledge or observation it would not be worth my while to make any comments at all.

The cordial tone of your letters gives me great pleasure, and after reading your last I should have liked very much to have shaken hands with you and expressed the hope which I now write that there are many years of happy friendly and literary intercourse before us (ii, 352-3).

(n) John Blackwood to George Eliot

7 July 1857

Your Bishop is doubtless a true sketch, but I wish he had been a better sample of the cloth. Some allusion to the solemn and affecting sight that a confirmation ought to be would not lessen the effect of your quaint and amusing picture of the scene at Milby thirty years ago and would destroy the chance of any accusation of irreverence or wish to make the ceremony ridiculous (ii, 360).

(o) George Eliot to John Blackwood

12 July 1857

My own impression on rereading very carefully the account of the confirmation is, that readers will perceive, what is the fact—that I am not in the least occupying myself with confirmation in general, or with Bishops in general, but with a particular confirmation, and a particular Bishop.

Art must be either real and concrete, or ideal and eclectic. Both are good and true in their way, but my stories are of the former kind. I undertake to exhibit nothing as it should be; I only try to exhibit some things as they have been or are, seen through such a medium as my own nature gives me. The moral effect of the stories of course depends on my power of seeing truly and feeling justly; and as I am not con-

scious of looking at things through the medium of cynicism or irreverence, I can't help hoping that there is no tendency in what I write to
produce those miserable mental states (ii, 362).

(p) George Henry Lewes to John Blackwood

12 July 1857

Entre nous let me hint that unless you have any *serious* objection to
make to Eliot's stories, *don't* make any. He is so easily discouraged, so
diffident of himself, that not being prompted by necessity to write, he
will close the series in the belief that his writing is not relished. I laugh
at him for his diffidence and tell him it's a proof he is *not* an author.
But he has passed the middle of life without writing at all, and will
easily be made to give it up. *Don't allude to this hint of mine.* He wouldn't
like my interfering (ii, 363–4).

2. Samuel Lucas, unsigned review, *The Times*

2 January 1858, p. 9

Samuel Lucas (1818–68), journalist, biographer, was a frequent
contributor to *The Times*, and edited the poems of Thomas
Hood (1867) (see No. 3 for George Eliot's reaction).

Of the other recent fictions we have been most impressed with the
series of *Scenes from Clerical Life*, which have been just reprinted from
Blackwood's Magazine, and which are now claimed by Mr. George
Eliot—a name unknown to us. It is quite possible that this may be a
mere *nom de plume*, and we are not curious to inquire at all upon this
point. But we should be greatly surprised to hear that the real writer
was previously known under any other appellation, for, like others

who have speculated on his identity while these tales were publishing, we cannot assign his peculiarities to any living novelist. Were these the early days of Galt or Lockhart,[1] or could even Crabbe come back from the grave in a softer mood and with a resolve to discard versification for prose, we should have some basis for conjecture; but now we have none. We lay no particular stress on the parochial limits of the scene and the parochial relations of its occupants. We observe only that the sources of interest are chiefly domestic and homely, and that there is a careful study of familiar types, and an absence of exaggeration in their treatment which recall the productions of a school of fiction akin to that of Wilkie in pictorial art. A sobriety which is shown to be compatible with strength, clear and simple descriptions, and a combination of humour with pathos in depicting ordinary situations, are characteristics of this school, and are evinced by Mr. Eliot.

Of the three stories comprised in these clerical scenes, we prefer the 'Rev. Mr. Gilfil's Love Story' to 'the Sad Fortunes of the Rev. Amos Barton,' or to 'Janet's Repentance.' It has the peculiarity of being a retrospect commencing from Mr. Gilfil's death, and we are drawn into it from an intimation of what the hero became in the decline of life, when his wound was cicatrized, and love had given place to softened regret. The picture of Mr. Gilfil at this latter stage is charmingly painted with firm and effective touches, and, as Sir Walter Scott said of the Wakefield Vicar, though each touch serves to show that he is made of mortal mould and is full of human frailties, the effect of the whole is to reconcile us to human nature. The charm, too, is sustained by an adherence to probability and by the allowance for influences which the incidents alone do not involve, but which we know to make up a large proportion of every man's life. The artificial elements of the story are thus kept within bounds, the tendency to sacrifice to their exigencies is compensated by a reference to the actual results of experience, and a closer resemblance than usual is thus established between the conceptions of fiction and the realities of the world.

The story itself is sufficiently simple, though highly romantic. . . .

[summary of the story with long excerpts follows]

The opening chapter gives the portrait which we so much admire of Mr. Gilfil towards the close of his long widowhood. Here the author

---

[1] John Galt (1779-1839) is best known for his historical novels and studies of country life in Scotland; John Gibson Lockhart (1794-1854), author of the famous *Life of Sir Walter Scott* (1837), was also a poet and novelist.

rejects the conventional usage of representing a bereaved hero as unhappy ever after. There is a closed chamber at the vicarage into which as the sanctuary of his dearest recollections Mr. Gilfil occasionally enters, but apart from which he takes an interest not only in the duties but in the pleasures of life which still remain to him. In his parish he is rather exemplary than over-zealous; he is social and pleasant with the farmers, acceptable to the gentry, considerate to the poor, and an especial favourite with children, which latter peculiarity, with his liking for a pipe and gin-and-water, more particularly distinguish him from the ordinary heroes of romance in similar circumstances. . . .

[quotes scene beginning 'Thus in Shepperton . . .' in ch. 1]

A writer who can work out his simple theme thus quietly and effectively needs no further commendation or exhibition on our part.

3. George Eliot's Journal

2 January 1858

The George Eliot Letters, ii, 415–16.

Jan. 2. George has returned this evening from a week's visit at Vernon Hill. On coming upstairs he said, 'I have some very pretty news for you—something in my pocket!' I was at a loss to conjecture, and thought confusedly of possible opinions from admiring readers, when he drew the *Times* from his pocket,—today's number, containing a review of the *Scenes of Clerical Life.* He had happened to ask a gentleman in the railway carriage coming up to London to allow him to look at the *Times,* and felt quite agitated and tremulous when his eyes alighted on the review. Finding he had time to go into town before the train started, he bought a copy there. It is a highly favourable notice, and as far as it goes, appreciatory.

When G. went into town he called at Nutt's, and Mrs. Nutt said to him 'I think you don't know our curate. *He* says the author of *Clerical Scenes* is a High Churchman; for though Mr. Tryan is said to be Low Church, his *feelings* and *actions* are those of a High Churchman.' (The curate himself being, of course, High C.) There were some pleasant scraps of admiration also gathered for me at Vernon Hill. Doyle[1] happening to mention the treatment of children in the stories, Helps[2] said, 'O, he is a great writer!'

I wonder how I shall feel about these little details ten years hence, if I am *alive*. At present I value them as grounds for hoping that my writing may succeed and so give value to my life—as indications that I can touch the hearts of my fellow men, and so sprinkle some precious grain as the result of the long years in which I have been inert and suffering. But at present fear and trembling still predominate over hope.

4. Unsigned review, *Atlantic Monthly*

May 1858, i, 890–2

Fiction represents the character of the age to which it belongs, not merely by actual delineations of its times, like those of *Tom Jones* and *The Newcomes*, but also in an indirect, though scarcely less positive manner, by its exhibition of the influence of the times upon its own form and general direction, whatever the scene or period it may have chosen for itself. The story of *Hypatia*[3] is laid in Alexandria almost two thousand years ago, but the book reflects the crudities of modern English thought; and even Mr. Thackeray, the greatest living master of costume, succeeds in making his *Esmond* only a joint-production of the Addisonian age and our own. Thus the novels of the last few years

[1] Richard Doyle (1824–83), illustrator and caricaturist.
[2] Arthur Helps (1813–75), historian, civil servant, and close friend of Lewes.
[3] By Charles Kingsley, 1851.

exhibit very clearly the spirit that characterizes the period of regard for men and women as men and women, without reference to rank, beauty, fortune, or privilege. Novelists recognize that Nature is a better romance-maker than the fancy, and the public is learning that men and women are better than heroes and heroines, not only to live with, but also to read of. Now and then, therefore, we get a novel, like these *Scenes of Clerical Life*, in which the fictitious element is securely based upon a broad groundwork of actual truth, truth as well in detail as in general.

It is not often, however, even yet, that we find a writer wholly unembarrassed by and in revolt against the old theory of the necessity of perfection in some one at least of the characters of his story. 'Neither Luther nor John Bunyan,' says the author of this book, 'would have satisfied the modern demand for an ideal hero, who believes nothing but what is true, feels nothing but what is excellent, and does nothing but what is graceful.'

Sometimes, indeed, a daring romance-writer ventures, during the earlier chapters of his story, to represent a heroine without beauty and without wealth, or a hero with some mortal blemish. But after a time his resolution fails;—each new chapter gives a new charm to the ordinary face; the eyes grow 'liquid' and 'lustrous,' always having been 'large'; the nose, 'naturally delicate,' exhibits its 'fine-cut lines'; the mouth acquires an indescribable expression of loveliness; and the reader's hoped-for Fright is transformed by Folly or Miss Pickering[1] into a commonplace, tiresome, *novelesque* Beauty. Even Miss Brontë relented toward Jane Eyre; and weaker novelists are continually repeating, but with the omission of the moral, the story of the *Ugly Duck*. Unquestionably, there is the excuse to be made for this great error, that it betrays the seeking after an Ideal. Dangerous word! The ideal standard of excellence is, to be sure, fortunately changing, and the unreal ideal will soon be confined to the second-rate writers for second-rate readers. But all the great novelists of the two last generations indulged themselves and their readers in these unrealities. It is vastly easier to invent a consistent character than to represent an inconsistent one;—a hero is easier to make (so all historians have found) than a man.

Suppose, however, novelists could be placed in a society made up of their favorite characters,—forced into real, lifelike intercourse with them;—Richardson, for instance, with his Harriet Byron or Clarissa,

[1] Ellen Pickering (d. 1843), popular romantic novelist.

attended by Sir Charles; Miss Burney with Lord Orville and Evelina; Miss Edgeworth with Caroline Percy, and that marvellous hero, Count Altenburg; Scott with the automatons that he called Waverley and Flora McIvor. Suppose they were brought together to share the comforts (cold comforts they would be) of life, to pass days together, to meet every morning at breakfast; with what a ludicrous sense of relief, at the close of this purgatorial period, would not the unhappy novelists have fled from these deserted heroes and heroines, and the precious proprieties of their romance, to the very driest and mustiest of human bores,—gratefully rejoicing that the world was not filled with such creatures as they themselves had set before it as *ideals!*

To copy Nature faithfully and heartily is certainly not less needful when stories are presented in words than when they are told on canvas or in marble. In the *Scenes from Clerical Life* we have a happy example of such copying. The three stories embraced under this title are written vigorously, with a just appreciation of the romance of reality, and with honest adherence to truth of representation in the sombre as well as the brighter portions of life. It demands not only a large intellect, but a large heart, to gain such a candid and inclusive appreciation of life and character as they display. The greater part of each story reads like a reminiscence of real life, and the personages introduced show little sign of being 'rubbed down' or 'touched up and varnished' for effect. The narrative is easy and direct, full of humor and pathos; and the descriptions of simple life in a country village are often charming from their freshness, vivacity, and sweetness. More than this, these stories give proof of that wide range of experience which does not so much depend on an extended or varied acquaintance with the world, as upon an intelligent and comprehensive sympathy, which makes each new person with whom one is connected a new illustration of the unsolved problems of life and a new link in the unending chain of human development.

The book is one that deserves a more elegant form than that which the Messrs. Harper have given it in their reprint.

5. Unsigned review, *Saturday Review*

29 May 1858, v, 566–7

The readers of *Blackwood's Magazine* during the past year were set speculating as to the authorship of the *Scenes of Clerical Life*, which were obviously the production of a peculiar and remarkable writer, whose style showed little or no family resemblances with that of any living author. The republication of these stories in two volumes, with the name of George Eliot attached, has done little towards satisfying curiosity, since the suspicion is pretty general that George Eliot is an assumed name, screening that of some studious clergyman, a Cantab, who lives, or has lived the greater part of his life in the country, who is the father of a family, of High Church tendencies, and exceedingly fond of children, Greek dramatists, and dogs. Thus much internal evidence suggests. For ourselves, we are indifferent as to the rest. It is enough for us that George Eliot is a new novelist, who to rare culture adds rare faculty, who can paint homely every-day life and ordinary characters with great humour and pathos, and is content to rely on the truth of his pictures for effect. Considering how unfamiliar most of us are with life in its romantic and adventurous forms, and with men and women of colossal proportions, it is strange that writers rarely have the courage or the talent to depict the characters and experiences which they and we know so well, but fly off at a tangent of improbability as soon as their pens touch paper. George Eliot has the courage and the talent to paint what he knows, and only what he knows. As he says:—

At least eighty out of a hundred of your adult male fellow-Britons returned in the last census, are neither extraordinarily silly, nor extraordinarily wicked, nor extraordinarily wise; their eyes are neither deep and liquid with sentiment, nor sparkling with suppressed witticisms; they have probably had no hairbreadth escapes or thrilling adventures; their brains are certainly not pregnant with genius, and their passions have not manifested themselves at all after the fashion of a volcano. They are simply men of complexions more or less muddy, whose conversation is more or less bald and disjointed. Yet these commonplace people—many of them—bear a conscience, and have felt the sublime prompting to do the painful right; they have their unspoken sorrows, and their sacred joys;

their hearts have perhaps gone out towards their first-born, and they have mourned over the irreclaimable dead. Nay, is there not a pathos in their very insignificance—in our comparison of their dim and narrow existence with the glorious possibilities of that human nature which they share?

Depend upon it, you would gain unspeakably if you would learn with me to see some of the poetry and the pathos, the tragedy and the comedy, lying in the experience of a human soul that looks out through dull grey eyes, and that speaks in a voice of quite ordinary tones.

He has made us weep over this pathos, and laugh over this comedy; and he has done so with a quiet truth which we find in few of his contemporaries. We read the *Clerical Scenes* as they appeared, month by month, and we have re-read them in these volumes with ever fresh admiration. But instead of forestalling the reader's enjoyment by sketching a meagre outline of the stories, we shall offer a few remarks on their style and treatment.

'The Sad Fortunes of the Rev. Amos Barton' gives us the picture of a curate who, on eighty pounds a year, has to support a wife and six children in decency, and to minister to the spiritual wants of a congregation. Here is a subject thoroughly commonplace. The man himself is wholly commonplace. Yet the story is not only interesting, but perfectly fresh and original—the character is not only a distinct individuality, but one which appeals to and wins our deepest sympathy. We do not admire Barton; indeed we rather laugh at him; yet the laughter is tempered by sympathy, and we like him for the same reasons that we like many other commonplace people—because of his charming wife, his charming children, his misfortunes, and his position. He is not handsome, he is not wise, he is not even nobly virtuous:—

[quotes descriptions of Amos Barton and his wife]

To make a hero out of such a curate required steadfast faith in the power of truth, and disregard of conventions. The same disregard of circulating-library principles is seen in the portrait of the Rev. Mr. Gilfil, whose love story forms the second of these sketches. We are introduced to Mr. Gilfil when he is old; his romance has been lived; he has loved and suffered; but instead of our being called upon to weep over a wasted life, and to pity a noble ruin, we are forced to love and admire a quite ordinary mortal, caustic, benevolent, active, somewhat miserly, and given to the evening solace of a pipe and gin-and-water. George Eliot knows that many refined lady readers may be offended by this termination of Mr. Gilfil's romance:—

But in the first place, dear ladies, allow me to plead that gin-and-water, like obesity, or baldness, or the gout, does not exclude a vast amount of antecedent romance, any more than the neatly executed 'fronts' which you may some day wear, will exclude your present possession of less expensive braids. . . .

Once more is the boldness of this writer shown in his choice of 'Janet's Repentance'—the third and finest of these *Clerical Scenes*. He calls upon us to accept as a heroine a woman driven by ill-treatment and misery to that unpoetical, but unhappily too real, refuge—wine! This tragic sin is dealt with at once delicately and boldly; and the story of her repentance and victory is one of the most pathetic scenes we know. A beautiful, impulsive, loving woman is shown us in her sin and in her rescue; and the influence exerted over her mind by the sympathetic earnestness of the Rev. Mr. Tryan—whose persecutions and sorrows also form an important element in the story—is represented in a style so truthful that we seem to be reading an actual biography.

While commending the truthfulness of the characters and incidents, we must make one exception. The episode of Mr. Tryan's early love and sorrow is a great mistake. It is one of the incidents hackneyed in fiction; and we are surprised to find it among incidents so fresh as those of the *Clerical Scenes*. Another objection we must urge, although it is purely technical. In 'Mr. Gilfil's Love Story' a great mistake in art is made in the construction—there are no less than three retrospects in it. One is enough, in all conscience. When the story fairly commences, it proceeds with due rapidity.

As might have been expected, a writer who selects topics so unlike those of other novelists, and who disregards conventions in conception, will not be likely to fall into the slipslop and conventions of expression which make the generality of novels difficult to read twice. In no page of these volumes have we noticed writing for writing's sake, or phrases flung out at hazard. The language always expresses distinct ideas, and the epithets are chosen because they are fitting. Indeed, so far from care-lessness being the fault of the style, we should rather urge the objection of a too-constant elaboration, especially in the earlier pages, where almost every sentence seems finished into an epigram or an aphorism. The pudding is often too profuse in plums—too scanty in connective dough. Instead of simply referring to the village organist, he refers to 'a collector of small rents, differentiated by the force of circumstances into an organist;' the curate's hat 'shows no symptom of taking to the hideous doctrine of expediency, and shaping itself according to circum-stances;' and 'the human animal of the male sex was understood to be perpetually athirst, and "something to drink" was as necessary a "condition of thought" as Time and Space.' Casual phrases like these betray a mind of philosophic culture, but they mar the simplicity of the style. When the author is describing scenery, which he does with poetic felicity, or in his emotional and reflective passages, the style has none of these *literary* betrayals.

[quotes examples of descriptive and reflective passages]

We know not whether George Eliot has most power over tears or laughter; but as humour is a rarer quality than pathos, we are disposed to admire his humour most. It is very genuine, and not only plays like lambent flame amid the descriptions, but animates the dialogues with dramatic life. And this leads us to notice another merit in these stories —the characters are not only true portraits, but they are living beings. Their feelings and motives are seen to be part and parcel of their natures and conditions, their talk is individual, belongs strictly to *them*, and not to the author. Hence even the little scraps of village gossip, or kitchen talk, introduced to carry on the story, have an independent life-like value. Whether the dialect is correctly or incorrectly given, we cannot say, but we are quite certain that the language is that of peasants, farmers, and servants, not the language of fiction.

[quotes examples of dialect]

We have abstained from giving any hint of the conduct of the stories, lest the reader's pleasure should be diminished; and we have confined ourselves to a very few salient points. The extracts have sufficed to show that George Eliot is a new writer—or, if a writer already known, one who has adopted a decidedly new style. The work has satire, but the satire is loving; it has pathos, but the tears make human nature more beautiful; it is homely in its pictures, but they are connected with our most impassioned sensibilities and our daily duties; it is religious, without cant or intolerance; and as Ruskin says of a good book, 'It may contain firm assertion or stern satire, but it never sneers coldly, nor asserts haughtily; and it always leads you to love or reverence something with your whole heart.'[1]

[1] *The Elements of Drawing*, 1857 (*Works*, XV, 226).

ADAM BEDE

February 1859

6. Jane Welsh Carlyle to George Eliot

20 February 1859

The George Eliot Letters, iii, 17–19. On receiving this letter, George Eliot declared that 'the sort of effect she declares herself to have felt from *Adam Bede* is just what I desire to produce—gentle thoughts and happy remembrances . . .' (*Letters*, iii, 24).

Dear Sir

I must again offer you my heartiest thanks. Since I received your *Scenes of Clerical Life* nothing has fallen from the skies to me so welcome as *Adam Bede, all to myself,* 'from the author.'

My Husband had just read an advertisement of it aloud to me, adding; '*Scenes of Clerical Life? That* was *your* Book wasn't it?' {The '*your*' being in the sense not of possession but of predilection} 'Yes,' I had said, 'and I am so glad that he has written another! *Will* he send me this one, I wonder?'—thereby bringing on myself an utterly disregarded admonition about 'the tendency of the Female Mind to run into unreasonable expectations'; when up rattled the Parcel Delivery cart, and, a startling double-rap having transacted itself, a Book-parcel was brought me. 'There it is!' I said, with a little air of injured innocence triumphant!—'There is *what*, my Dear?'—'Why, *Adam Bede* to be sure!'—'How do you know?' {I had not yet opened the parcel} 'By d*i*vination.'—'Oh! —Well!—I hope you also *divine* that *Adam Bede* will justify your enthusiasm now you have got it!'—'As to *that*' {snappishly} 'I ~~don't~~ needn't have recourse to divination, only to natural logic!'——Now; if it had turned out *not Adam Bede* after all; where *was* my 'diminished head'[1] going to have hidden itself?—But Fortune favours the Brave!

[1] *Paradise Lost*, iv, 35.

71

I had foretold aright, on both points! The Book was actually *Adam Bede*, and *Adam Bede* 'justified my enthusiasm'; to say the least!

Oh yes! It was as good as *going into the country for one's health*, the reading of that Book was!—Like a visit to Scotland *minus* the fatigues of the long journey, and the grief of seeing friends grown old, and Places that knew me knowing me no more! I could fancy in reading it, to be seeing and hearing once again a crystal-clear, musical, Scotch stream, such as I long to lie down beside and—*cry* at (!) for gladness and sadness; after long stifling sojourn in the South; where there [is] no *water* but what is stagnant or muddy!

In truth, it is a beautiful most *human* Book! Every *Dog* in it, not to say every man woman and child in it, is brought home to one's 'business and bosom,'[1] an individual fellow-creature! I found myself in charity with the whole human race when I laid it down—the *canine* race I had *always* appreciated—'not wisely but too well!'[2]—the *human*, however,—Ach!—*that* has troubled me—as badly at times as 'twenty gallons of milk on one's mind'![3] For the rest; why you are so good to *me* is still a *mystery*, with every appearance of remaining so! . . .

Now, Heaven knows if such a long letter to read be not illustrating for *you* also 'the tendency of the female mind to run into unreasonable expectations'! But just consider! Is it possible that, with my opportunities, I should not know perfectly well, what a 'distinguished author' *does* with letters of compliment *that bore him*; either by their length or their stupidity? He lights his pipe with them or he makes them into spills; or he crushes them into a ball, and pitches them in the fire or waste-paper basket; does anything with them *except read them!* So I needn't take fright about having *bored* you; since, long before it came to that, I should have, or shall have been slit up into spills, or done good service in lighting your pipe! It is lawful for *Clergymen* to smoke, I hope,—for their own sakes? The newspaper critics have decided you are a Clergyman, but I don't believe it the least in the world. You understand the duties and uses of a Clergyman too well, for *being* one! An old Lord, who did not know my Husband, came up to him once at a Public meeting where he had been summoned to give his 'views' {not *having* any} on the 'Distressed Needle Women,' and asked; 'pray Sir, may I inquire, are *you* a Stock-Broker?'—'A Stock-Broker! certainly not!'—'Humph! Well I thought you *must* be a Stock-Broker; because, Sir, you go to the root of the matter.'—If that be the signal

[1] Francis Bacon, *Essays*, dedication of 1625 ed.   [2] *Othello*, V, ii, 343.
[3] Mrs. Poyser's worry in ch. 32 of the novel.

of a Stock-Broker I should say you must certainly be a *Stock-Broker*, and must certainly *not* be a *Clergyman!*

Respectfully and affectionately yours, whatever you be,

Jane W. Carlyle.

7. Unsigned review, *Saturday Review*

26 February 1859, vii, 250–1

See Introduction, pp. 9–11.

It is not often that it is safe to praise a novel, for although a little over-tenderness may not only be acceptable, but even useful, to an author whose promise is better than his performance, and may guide the regular novel-reader to a book that is better than usual, it has the bad effect of making persons waste their time who do not wish to read novels unless they are really good. But *Adam Bede* is a novel that we can have no remorse in speaking well of. Persons who only read one novel a year—and it is seldom that more than one really good novel is published in a year—may venture to make their selection, and read *Adam Bede*. Whatever faults they may discover in it, they will also find that it contains things which stamp it as a book by itself, leaving new impressions and awakening new feelings. The author has got into an original field of observation, and as he has very great powers of observing, and a happy method of making his detached points of observation into a connected whole, he gives us something we have not had before. He is evidently a country clergyman, and the object of his observation has been the rustic life of a village in one of the central counties—a very unpromising object of observing to most men, but most men are not observers. We all know that a country carpenter may have a history and a character—plans, hopes, and regrets—which, if unfolded before us, would interest us as much as the revelation of the secrets of a richer man. But between the educated man and the country carpenter there is generally an impassable barrier. It is easy to ascertain that he wears a flannel-jacket, that he is civil and not drunk; but to go a step further, to guess even whether he thinks you civil and not drunk, is by no means so easy. Every now and then, however, the carpenter comes across the path of a gentleman who has a natural gift for understanding him, and then, if this gentleman will take the trouble not only to exercise his faculty, but to record the result, we arrive at some sort of knowledge of the carpenter. This is what the author of *Adam Bede* has done. Adam Bede is a carpenter, and his acquaintances are farmers and blacksmiths. It is a real credit for a writer to have made such characters realities, and not have made them, as most novelists who attempt the thing do, mere lay figures on which the authors hang their old shooting-jackets, while they walk round in an evening dress smirking and pointing out how jolly and genial they are with their own old clothes.

We see the process by which the book has attained its excellence when we examine the sketches of characters that are entirely subordinate. Sometimes we have capital sketches, even when the character is introduced once, and is evidently introduced only that the sketch may be given. We have, for instance, a description of an adult nightschool, the only object of which is to introduce sketches of three of the scholars. They were rustics whom the author had studied, and these studies are brought in to fill up a corner of the larger picture. In these sketches, slight as they are, there is great merit; and it may be remarked that mere observation is never enough to make even a slight sketch good. There must be something more than the faculty of noting distinct, telling, characteristic points—there must be a central idea of the subject of the sketch around which minutiæ are to be grouped. There must be something that answers to the hypothesis in experimental inquiry—something that comes from the observer, not the observed—a general key to the character which the drawer of the character assumes at first, and then proves by elaborating it. In its widest and highest form, the power of adding to observation the element of the observer's own thought is humour, and no one can doubt that in *Adam Bede* there is real humour of a rare and genuine kind. Mrs. Poyser, a farmer's wife, is a really humorous creation, and she is humorous with the humour of truth, and not of exaggeration. The Hall Farm is like a farm with a real dairy to be kept clean, and real maids to be scolded, not a mere theatrical farm, intended to display the powers of the first and second rustic clown. And yet every sentence that Mrs. Poyser says has something entertaining in it. She is so consistent, so busy and practical, so warm-hearted, and so very sharp with her tongue.

The continuity of character is so well kept up, not only in Mrs. Poyser, but in Adam Bede and in Mrs. Poyser's two nieces, with whom Adam successively falls in love, that it would be unfair to speak of the tale as a series of disconnected sketches; but the continuity is wholly in the characters, and the story, as a story, breaks down. Probably the author found it difficult to hit on any very dramatic and stirring incident in rustic life to make the turning point of his novel; but whatever his difficulties may have been, his choice has been very unfortunate. The story turns on the seduction of one of Mrs. Poyser's nieces by a neighbouring squire. In the early days of the squire's love-making there are some well-imagined scenes, and although we think Hetty in danger, we are not much frightened or shocked. Adam will be rather jealous, but that is all. At the end of the second volume, however, we are plunged into a sea of horrors. Poor Hetty is deserted by her lover, and agrees to marry Adam Bede; but she cannot make up her mind finally to deceive him or herself. She leaves her uncle's house, and sets off southward in quest of her lover. Finally, she bears a child, murders it, is tried for the murder, and sentenced to death. The rope is almost round her neck, when her old lover dashes up to the scaffold bearing a commutation of her sentence into transportation. This series of events takes the author from ground where he is strong to ground where he is weak. He knows and cares nothing about trials, scaffolds, and pardons. He only brings them in because he conceives that a certain allowance of melodrama is a necessary ingredient. The consequence is, that the third volume is weak, poor, and superficial, compared with the other two. We are taken away from the new region of lifelike carpenters and dairymaids into the hackneyed region of sham legal excitement. The degree of horror and painfulness is also out of keeping with the calm simplicity of rural life. Of course, every one knows that every sin under heaven is committed freely in agricultural villages, and if any one chooses to insist that pretty dairymaids are in danger of being seduced, he at least keeps within the bounds of fact. But that is no reason why a picture of village character and village humour should be made so painful as it is by the introduction into the foreground of the startling horrors of rustic reality. We do not expect that we are to pass from the discreet love of a well-to-do carpenter to child-murder and executions, and the shock which the author inflicts on us seems as

GEORGE ELIOT

superfluous as it is arbitrary. There is also another feature in this part
of the story on which we cannot refrain from making a passing
remark. The author of *Adam Bede* has given in his adhesion to a very
curious practice that is now becoming common among novelists, and it
is a practice that we consider most objectionable. It is that of dating and
discussing the several stages that precede the birth of a child. We seem
to be threatened with a literature of pregnancy. We have had *White
Lies* and *Sylvan Holt's Daughter*,[1] and now we have *Adam Bede*. Hetty's
feelings and changes are indicated with a punctual sequence that makes
the account of her misfortunes read like the rough notes of a man-
midwife's conversations with a bride. This is intolerable. Let us copy
the old masters of the art, who, if they gave us a baby, gave it us all
at once. A decent author and a decent public may surely take the
premonitory symptoms for granted.

There is also some fault to be found with the manner in which the
author intrudes himself in the book. Original as he is in all that depends
on his own personal observation, he falls, as almost all men fall, under
the influences of his age in his general views of life and duty. Evidently
he has sat at the feet of Mr. Kingsley, and Mr. Kingsley may in many
points be proud of his follower. He is tolerant, large-hearted, sensible,
and discreet. But he follows the custom of his school in a direction
where that school is very apt to err. He makes a great deal too much of
a very slight novelty of opinion at which he has himself arrived, and
he puts the merit of holding this opinion on much too grand a footing.
The story of *Adam Bede* is supposed to have taken place fifty years ago,
and one of the characters is a good, easy-going rector. That such a
man, though not fervent in doctrinal controversies, and given to a
little quiet sporting, might really be a good and useful man seems a
very simple truth, and one that might be advanced without the slightest
danger of affronting public opinion at this day. But the author of *Adam
Bede* makes what he calls a pause in the story, and, in the language of
Mause Headrigg,[2] declares himself willing to 'bear testimony in the
Grassmarket,' and undergo any reasonable sort of martyrdom, while
all that he really does is to emit the most harmless and inoffensive
proposition. But these are only incidental blemishes in a very meri-
torious work. After all that can be said against it, *Adam Bede* remains a
novel that is rarely rivalled even in these days of abundant fiction
writing.

[1] By Charles Reade, 1857, and Holme Lee [Harriet Parr], 1858, respectively.
[2] Character in Scott's *Old Mortality* (1816).

76

8. E. S. Dallas, unsigned review, *The Times*

12 April 1859, p. 5

Eneas Sweetland Dallas (1828–79), reviewer and critic on the staff
of *The Times*, is best known for his book, *The Gay Science* (1866),
in which he attempted to apply the ideas of psychology to the
analysis of aesthetic effects. This review firmly established George
Eliot's reputation (see Introduction, pp. 8–11).

There can be no mistake about *Adam Bede*. It is a first-rate novel, and
its author takes rank at once among the masters of the art. Hitherto
known but as the writer of certain tales to which he gave the modest
title of *Scenes*, and which displayed only the buds of what we have
here in full blossom, he has produced a work which, after making
every allowance for certain crudities of execution, impresses us with a
sense of the novelist's maturity of thought and feeling. Very seldom
are so much freshness of style and warmth of emotion seen combined
with so much solid sense and ripened observation. We have a pleasant
feeling of security in either laughing or crying with such a companion.
Our laughter shall not be trifling, and our tears shall not be maudlin.
We need not fear to yield ourselves entirely to all the enchantments
of the wizard whose first article of belief is the truism which very few
of us comprehend until it has been knocked into us by years of experience—that we are all alike—that the human heart is one. All the
novelists and all the dramatists that have ever lived have set themselves
to exhibit the differences between man and man. Here, they seem to
say, are circumstances precisely similar, and yet mark how various are
the characters which grow out of these circumstances. The Pharisee in
the Temple felt that he was different from other men, thanking his
God for it; and which of us, in the immaturity of experience, is not
forced chiefly to consider the differences between ourselves and other
men, often utterly forgetting the grand fact of an underlying unity?
Here we see monsters, and there we see angels, alien faces and inaccessible natures. It is only after much beating about, long intercourse with

society, and many strange discoveries and detections, that the truism
which we never doubted becomes a great reality to us, and we feel
that man is like to man even as face answers to face in a glass. It is in
the enunciation of this difficult truism that Mr. Thackeray differs from
all previous novelists. It is the supreme motive of all that he has written,
and the key to all the criticism that has been poured upon him. There
is not a page of his works in which we do not hear the author exclaiming, 'You see all these people that appear to be so different; I tell you
they are all alike. You despise that wretch;—thou art the man. See
what a monster I have painted;—I am that monster. Good friends, let
us all shake hands; external differences are very well and very amusing,
but I beseech of you to think less of the external differences than of the
prevailing identity. We shall have less of laughing at each other and
tearing each other to pieces when we come to recognize that there is
no inherent distinction between Tyburn Jack and the Lord Mayor,
between Sally, the cook, who looks after the dripping and thinks
tenderly of the policeman, and the great lady intent upon pin-money
and wondering whether Arthur is going to offer his arm to the supper-
room. People are bad, no doubt, but they are no worse than we are;
we think kindly of ourselves—we give fine names to our own faults,
we find excuses for our errors. Pray let us give the fine names all round;
let us think kindly of others; let us excuse our neighbours; let us not
condemn the world wholesale.' With regard to which philosophy two
things are to be noted,—the first that, whether true or false, it is the
reverse of uncharitable; it is the expression of a warm human sympathy.
In point of fact, it is but a secular rendering of the deepest sentiment of
Christianity—the sense of personal unworthiness in the presence of
God, which teaches us the weakness of our nature and how near the
very best of us are of kin to the chief of sinners and the most degraded
of beings. The second, that a novelist, writing in accordance with this
philosophy, has a most difficult task to perform. It is comparatively
easy to draw a character so long as we dwell mainly on points of
difference and contrast. But when the object is to touch lightly on
mere peculiarities, and to dwell mainly on those traits which we have
all in common, and, which, therefore, are anything but salient, the
difficulty of the task is enormously increased.

We do not mean for one moment to detract from Mr. George
Elliot's originality when we say that after his own fashion he follows
this difficult path in which Mr. Thackeray leads the way. He has fully
reached that idea which it is so easy to confess in words, but so hard to

admit into the secret heart, that we are all alike, that our natures are the same, and that there is not the mighty difference which is usually assumed between high and low, rich and poor, the fool and the sage, the best of us and the worst of us. In general, it is only matured minds that reach this state of feeling—minds that have gone through a good deal and seen through a good deal; and our author has precisely this broad sympathy and large tolerance, combined with ripe reflection and finished style, which we admire in Mr. Thackeray. Here the comparison ends. Mr. Elliot differs so widely from Mr. Thackeray in his mode of working out the philosophy which is common to both that some of our readers may wonder how we could ever see a resemblance between him and the great painter of human vanities and weakness. Whereas Mr. Thackeray is, to the great disgust of many young ladies, continually asserting that we have all got an evil corner in our hearts, and little deceitful ways of working, Mr. Elliot is good enough to tell us that we have all a remnant of Eden in us, that people are not so bad as is commonly supposed, and that every one has affectionate fibres in his nature—fine, loveable traits, in his character. The novel before us is crowded with characters, but they are loveable. It is true that one individual is guilty of seduction, that another is guilty of murder, and that a third is a greedy old miser, but the author finds good in them all and lets them off easy, not only with pardon, but in the two former cases loaded with affectionate sympathy. If in this way he has gone to an extreme, it is a fault which most persons will readily forgive, since it enables them to think better of poor fallen human nature. How kindly he excuses that selfish old Squire who has not a thought for one human being apparently! 'I believe,' says his grandson and heir, 'if I were to break my neck he would feel it the greatest misfortune that could befall him, and yet it seems a pleasure to him to make my life a series of petty annoyances.' Then says the parson, with his kindly philosophy, and with a phrase which puts a fine gloss on all manner of selfishness, 'Ah, my boy, it is not only woman's love that is ἀπέρωτος ἔρως, as old Æschylus calls it. There's plenty of "unloving love" in the world of a masculine kind.' The ingenuity with which the kindhearted Squire is thus made to fit into a new and improved edition of human nature, gilt-edged, is characteristic. Mr. Thackeray, on the contrary, would have made us unwilling to condemn the man by showing us that we, too, have our selfish fits, and that especially the grandson who makes the complaint is longing for the death of the useless old Fogie. But, although tending to such opposite results, the principle upon which both novelists work is the same. Here is a sentence which Thackeray himself might have written:—'Before you despise Adam as deficient in penetration, pray ask yourself if you were ever predisposed to believe evil of any pretty woman—if you ever could, without hard headbreaking demonstration, believe evil of the one supremely pretty woman who has bewitched you. No; people who love downy peaches are apt not to think of the stone, and sometimes jar their teeth terribly against it.' We might quote a long passage to a similar effect from the first chapter of the second volume, but it will be sufficient to give one sentence in which the author represents human affection as triumphing over every obstacle of mental deficiency and personal appearance. After mentioning the ugly fellows with squat figures, ill-shapen nostrils, and dingy complexions, whose miniatures are kissed in secret by motherly lips, he says:—'And I believe there have been plenty of young heroes, of middle stature and feeble beards, who have felt quite sure they could never love anything more insignificant than a Diana, and yet have found themselves in middle life happily settled with a wife who waddles.'

The story is simple enough, and, as far as the mere skeleton is concerned, soon told. For the sake of introducing a fair young Methodist who has the gift of preaching, the date of the incidents is thrown to the end of last century, but the time is not strictly observed, and we are not very much surprised to be informed that Bartle Massey 'lighted a match furiously on the hob,' which is far from being the only anachronism in the tale. Mrs. Poyser, the chatty wife of a well-to-do farmer, is the pivot on which the plot revolves. She is the chorus who is continually intervening with her opinions. As far as conversation goes, it might be important to mention that she has a husband, and that her husband has a father; but the story is not affected by such trivial circumstances. She has two nieces, however, Hetty and Dinah, who are of the utmost importance, for they supply the motives of all the action in the novel.

[summary of plot follows]

There is not much of a story it will be seen. The great charm of the novel is rather in the characters introduced than in the action which they carry on. All the characters are so true, and so natural, and so racy that we love to hear them talk for the sake of talking. They are so full of strange humours and funny pretty sayings that we entirely overlook the want of movement in the story. Besides which, when the dialogue ceases, the author's reflections are so pointed, and his descriptions are so vivid, that we naturally think more of what we have than of what we have not. There is not a character in the novel which is not well drawn, and even if the portrait is but a sketch still it is a true one. We have not mentioned the name of Mr. Irwine, the parson, who is very carefully drawn, nor of his mother, who is touched off in a more rapid manner; and yet the former is a very important personage in the dialogue, and is a fine moral influence throughout the tale. He is a very favourable specimen of the moral preachers of the close of last century, and the author has placed him in contrast to the more Scriptural style of which Dinah Morris, the young Methodist, is the representative. He sympathizes strongly with both, but leans most to the side of those moral teachers who have been somewhat harshly judged he thinks. Comparing Mr. Irwine with the curate of an 'evangelical' turn who succeeded him, he makes Mr. Poyser pronounce this judgment:—'Mr. Irwine was like a good meal o' victual; *you are the better for him without thinking on it*; but Mr. Ryde is like a dose o' physic; he gripes you and worrets you, and after all he leaves you much the same.' Irwine is a noble man, with a fine presence and a kindly, catholic nature. He was a silent influence, who did not trouble his parish much with theological 'notions,' but gave them the example of a kind heart, and demanded from them the reward of honest lives. 'It's summat like to see such a man as that i' the desk of a Sunday,' says that rattling Mrs. Poyser. 'As I say to Poyser, it's like looking at a full crop o' wheat, or a pasture with a fine dairy o' cows in it; it makes you think the world's comfortable-like.' The tolerance with which an author who is able to conceive the character of Dinah Morris, and to sympathize with her religious views, is thus pleased to regard a very opposite type of the religious character—a type which many worthy people, no doubt, would be disposed to brand as utterly irreligious, is one of the finest things in the novel, and affords a very good illustration of the tendency of the author to beat down all external differences, and bring into the light the grand points of genuine resemblance. You fancy that there can be nothing in nature more diverse than the spiritually-minded, praying, and preaching Dinah Morris, and the carnally-minded, easy, gentlemanly Mr. Irwine. I tell you, again and again, says Mr. Elliot, that there is no difference between them.

It will be evident that in order to establish the identity of man with man an author must travel a good deal into the region of latent thoughts, and unconscious or but semi-conscious feelings. There is infinite variety in what we express; there is a wonderful monotony in that great world of life which never comes into the light, but moves within us like the beating of the heart and the breathing of the lungs—a constant, though unobserved influence. It is in this twilight of the human soul that our novelist most delights to make his observations. Old Lisbeth Bede says of her son Adam, who is continually visiting the Poysers with the object (unknown even to himself) of seeing Dinah Morris:— 'Eh, donna tell me what thee't sure on; thee know'st nought about it. What's he allays going to the Poysers' for, if he didna want t'see her? He goes twice where he used t' go once. Happen he knows na as he wants t' see her; *he knows na as I put salt in's broth, but he'd miss it pretty quick if it warna there.*' It is to the world of thoughts indicated in Mrs. Bede's very homely remark that the author has turned his chief attention. Like Mr. Thackeray, he takes a peculiar pleasure in showing the contrariety between thought and speech, the heart within and the mask without, which we call a face. He is always showing that we are better than we seem, greater than we know, nearer to each other than, perhaps, we would wish. It is a fertile theme of immense interest, and through the three volumes the author has handled it with rare skill. His dissection of all the motives at work in Arthur Donnithorne's mind when he is pleased to trifle with the affections of Hetty is very masterly —how he was tempted, how he struggled with the temptation, and what a strange under-current of feeling was carrying him on to his purpose, while he took note only of the feeble ripple on the surface. In the case of poor Hetty we have a similar analysis, but one still more difficult, owing to the utterly thoughtless character of the girl. She, perhaps, might be accepted as a fair example of the truth of Pope's very unjust saying, 'Most women have no characters at all.' Not that she is unreal—she is drawn to the life; but she is one of those who are so much less than they seem to be, whose most significant acts mean so little, that it is not easy to fix upon any central principle in their nature, any strong point of thought, or word, or act which belongs to them.

[Gives examples of actions unconsciously motivated.]

The gem of the novel is Mrs. Poyser, who, for that combination of shrewd remark and homely wit with genuine kindliness and racy style which is so taking in Mr. Samuel Weller, is likely to outvie all the characters of recent fiction, with the single exception of the hero we have named. Mrs. Poyser, in her way, is as amusing as either Mrs.

Gamp or Mrs. Nickleby, and much more sensible. Wife of a rough and ready farmer, she is a great woman. She is the firstling of the author's mind, which he is not likely to surpass, even as that glorious Sam Weller, the firstling of Mr. Dickens's pen, has not been outshone by any successor. Mrs. Poyser pervades the novel. Her wisdom is always coming out either spoken by herself, or quoted by somebody else, or mentioned by the author. On one occasion, the author, unable to express himself in his own words, introduces Adam Bede to express the thought in his words, and Adam Bede, finding his own language inadequate, is obliged to fall back upon the expressions used by Mrs. Poyser, whom accordingly he quotes. 'You're mighty fond o' Craig,' says Mrs. Poyser to her husband, speaking of a certain Scotch gardener; 'but for my part, I think he's welly like a cock as thinks the sun's rose o' purpose to hear him crow.' This is the Poyser style, a good pungent style, remarkably effective when it is necessary to scold her husband, to subdue her nieces, or to lash the maids. It is a fine thing to hear her out of the goodness of her heart and the fulness of her wisdom abuse her whole household. One poor maid breaks a jug. How they all catch it, as if there never happened such an event before! In the midst of her storming, she herself breaks a jug, and instantly we are entertained with the philosophy of jug-breaking, from which it is to be gathered that there is a fatality in jugs, and that they fly out of one's hands with a determination to be broken, no matter how tight they are held. Her style runs into proverbs.

[examples of sayings by Mr and Mrs Poyser, and by Lisbeth Bede]

We might go on quoting these speeches until at last we transfer half the novel to our columns. The hero of the work, Adam Bede, is not so remarkable for his speeches as for what he does. He speaks out in a strong, manly way, but not very often with that sharp epigrammatic force which is so characteristic of Mrs. Poyser, Lisbeth Bede, and the schoolmaster, Bartle Massey, who, by the way, has met with a disappointment in early life, and has ever since been a womanhater, as will be seen in the following profound remark:—'Nonsense! it's the silliest lie a sensible man like you ever believed, to say a woman makes a house comfortable. It's a story got up, because the women are there, and something must be found for 'em to do. I tell you there isn't a thing under the sun that needs to be done at all, but what a man can do better than a woman, unless it's bearing children, and they do that in a poor make-shift way; it had better ha' been left to the men—it had better ha' been left to the men.' The speeches of Seth Bede and of Dinah Morris, though excellent as illustrations of character, are, like those of Adam, not of the epigrammatic sort. Dinah's sermon is very fine, and she herself is a most beautiful piece of portraiture—a perfect chrysolite. The minor sketches are superabundant; they crowd the canvass. We have not here one great and real character in the midst of a mob of lay figures. The subordinate personages are in their way quite as well pictured as the leading ones. The whole work, indeed, leaves upon us the impression of something highly finished and well matured, and we close the volumes wondering whether the author is to do better in his next novel,—curious, also, to know who the author really is. Nobody seems to know who is Mr. George Eliot, and when his previous work appeared it was even surmised that he must be a lady, since none but a woman's hand could have painted those touching scenes of clerical life. Now, the question will be raised, can this be a young author? Is all this mature thought, finished portraiture, and crowd of characters the product of a 'prentice hand and of callow genius. If it is, the hand must have an extraordinary cunning, and the genius must be of the highest order.

9. Charles Dickens, letter to George Eliot

10 July 1859

The George Eliot Letters, iii, 114–15. Dickens was anxious to get George Eliot to write for *All the Year Round*.

. . . Believe me, when I wrote to you on the subject of the *Scenes of Clerical Life*, I did nothing but relieve my mind, very inadequately, of the strong feelings of admiration with which you had filled it. Wherever I went, I said the same things. It was a rare and genuine delight to me, to become acquainted in the spirit with so noble a writer;

and it would have been hardly less difficult to me to repress myself for good and all, than to repress my admiration of such genius. . . .

Adam Bede has taken its place among the actual experiences and endurances of my life. Every high quality that was in the former book, is in that, with a World of Power added thereunto. The conception of Hetty's character is so extraordinarily subtle and true, that I laid the book down fifty times, to shut my eyes and think about it. I know nothing so skilful, determined, and uncompromising. The whole country life that the story is set in, is so real, and so droll and genuine, and yet so selected and polished by art, that I cannot praise it enough to you. And that part of the book which follows Hetty's trial (and which I have observed to be not as widely understood as the rest), affected me far more than any other, and exalted my sympathy with the writer to its utmost height. You must not suppose that I am writing this to *you*. I have been saying it over and over again, here and elsewhere, until I feel in a ludicrously apologetic state for repeating myself on this paper.

I cannot close this note without touching on two heads. Firstly (Blackwood not now being the medium of communication), if you should ever have the freedom and inclination to be a fellow labourer with me, it would yield me a pleasure that I have never known yet and can never know otherwise; and no channel that even you could command, should be so profitable as to yourself. Secondly, I hope you will let me come to see you when we are all in or near London again, and tell you—as a curiosity—my reasons for the faith that was in me that you were a woman, and for the absolute and never-doubting confidence with which I have waved all men away from *Adam Bede*, and nailed my colors to the Mast with 'Eve' upon them.

A word of remembrance and regard to Lewes—and of congratulation—that I know he will feel and understand as I do. . . .

GEORGE ELIOT

10. Anne Mozley, unsigned review, *Bentley's Quarterly Review*

July 1859, i, 433–56

Anne Mozley (1809–91), essayist and reviewer for several periodicals, edited *The Letters and Correspondence of Cardinal Newman* (1891). She is identified as the author of this enthusiastic, yet balanced article in *DNB* (see Introduction, p. 10).

The reign of romance is an extending one. It gains ground in spite of the perpetual protests of utilitarianism, useful knowledge, and Puritanism. The number of those who 'never read novels' diminishes season by season, or those who make the complacent profession have to qualify it by an ever-increasing list of exceptions; for, in fact, every man's own favourite field of thought falls by turns under the illuminating ray of the magician. Fancy and invention grow bold in their experiments, taught by success that there are very few scenes in the world which skill cannot turn into a good picture: so one by one the strongholds of commonplace, actual life yield to their invasion. Having long expatiated in flights of heroism, startling incidents, violent contrasts, and all extremes of character and fortune till their legitimate vein is exhausted, they have sought a fresh one, and found themselves as potent in extracting interest and wonder out of the every-day externally uniform life which the many must lead, as they were of old in the exceptional careers and incidents to which we still attach the title of romance, which fall to the lot of few indeed, and which have delighted because of their strangeness and the novelty of the ideas and impressions they awake in us. There is a grave class of minds who cannot give their sympathy but through their experience: to such the efforts of imagination, and the description of scenes and modes of life of which they have no personal knowledge, will tell nothing, will be slighted as frivolities beneath the regard of men engaged in the actual business of life. But let one of this class be a real observer, and find his immediate field of speculation illustrated by a keener observation and clearer insight than his own, and he will no longer be insensible to the charm of invention. All that goes to a good novel will not be thrown away upon him, and to his surprise he will feel himself stirred by as keen an interest in fancied sorrows, as engrossed in the fortunes of imaginary persons and mere shadows, as any novel-reader he ever despised.

In this way, one by one, they fall into the train. Thus persons who had resisted Walter Scott, because they had no old-world sympathies, were subdued by Sam Weller and Mrs. Gamp; those who could not condescend to these vulgar wits found *Vanity Fair* to reproduce what they knew of the world; the harsh, unattractive, but vivid nature of *Jane Eyre* and *Shirley* caught some not to be snared by smoother blandishments. Mrs. Gaskell's pictures of mechanic life, amid whirling wheels and smoking chimneys, were accepted by others as an embodiment, for which they could vouch, of the mode of existence of the masses; so utilizing fiction, elsewhere a barren, unprofitable pleasure. The *Heir of Redclyffe*[1] brought to their allegiance many who never fancied before that they could get through a novel. The *Caxtons*[2] won a more precise class, who had pronounced all previous romance vain and demoralizing; and Mr. Kingsley's amusing doubt and dramatized paradox struck others who rejoiced in a freedom from prejudice, and found their favourite calling of propounding knotty questions all the pleasanter, and not less puzzling for being wrapped in a seductive veil of allegory: and now, in contrast with all these, we conclude our brief enumeration with *Adam Bede*, a story which we believe has found its way into hands indifferent to all previous fiction, to readers who welcome it as the voice of their own experience in a sense no other book has ever been.

Certainly *Adam Bede* has a voice of its own which chimes in a telling, because natural and simple way, with associations and thoughts which have been lying half developed and struggling for expression in many minds. It is remarkable, too, for a steady protest against exclusiveness, a characteristic of our time, as prevalent in our literature as in society, and as marked in the high-toned religious fiction of the day as in its more natural home, the fashionable novel; but from which a large number must always revolt, either from personal feelings or a sense of injury to the claims and rights of humanity. In another point the notices of the press show an undesigned coincidence of response—and that is the tone of the author on religious matters; orthodox and serious, but viewed rather in their moral than doctrinal aspect, as more within the

[1] By Charlotte Yonge, 1853.   [2] By Bulwer-Lytton, 1849.

scope of his subject and turn of thought. It strikes us that the laity, unconsciously to themselves, recognise a champion: here is a religious utterance which somehow differs a good deal from the general tone of the pulpit utterances we have been used to. Conscience takes a higher stand than has been sometimes found compatible with the war of doctrine waged in this polemical age. With all the force of wit, humour, common sense, and pathos, some home questions have been put which sermon-hearers think it will not be easy for their pastors to answer; and, above all, Mrs. Poyser's immortal illustration has avenged much irritation, discontent, and weariness, which the sufferer did not know before could be defended and justified. Do any two people ever talk three minutes over this story without quoting, with a particularly sly relish, the definition of Mr. Ryde's style of preaching, as though it met some case very near home, which, out of respect or delicacy, they will not further indicate? No names may be mentioned, the subject may be treated as a general one, but not the less does it go home to each individual's business and bosom; and the next time he hears a cold, harsh, controversial sermon—which may very likely be next Sunday—not only does the joke soothe at the time, answering to the marbles the Master Poysers carried to church, with the prospect of 'handling them a little secretly during the sermon,' but he feels armed with a reason for his repugnance which before seemed to need an apology; for whatever views this writer expresses, they are clearly arrived at by a process of thought; the weight of calm conviction gives value to every sentiment whether we agree or not; and we feel that in this story we have the experience of a life.

Adam Bede has the difficulty, as it is commonly considered, of a prominent moral, too often an impediment to the natural development of a story; but owing to its simplicity and breadth, and its appeal to universal assent and sympathy, in this instance it gains a support, as assisting to develop character, and to work out and give verisimilitude to the plot, if the simple structure of incidents can be so denominated. Its moral is, that the past cannot be blotted out, that evil cannot be undone. This conviction is expressed with a strength and persistency that turns into a sort of inspiration the author's motive for the labour of composition; which, if a delight, is assuredly in this case also a labour, from the conscientious adherence to truth, or what seems to him truth, which marks the whole. This, we feel, is no young genius writing from a teeming imagination full of airy shapes, but one who has learnt from experience, and, we must believe, real contact with trouble; not through sympathy only—the school of young writers whose sensibility is quickly stirred to create pictures out of every feeling or emotion brought before them—but, together with sympathy, by actual participation in the emotions and sorrows portrayed. Though new as an author, it is not possible that this writer can be new to life; there is no guess-work here, but hard-won knowledge, with ample space to look back upon the conflict, to mature thought out of transient pain. And space, too, for retrospect, not only of pain and sorrow, but of joy—space to live over again in the memory a peaceful happy existence—so peaceful amid such gentle excitements that the happiness was perhaps not realized till it was over. For this is another indirect, but not less valuable moral of the book, to teach us that our real happiness consists in the less excited and agitated period of our lives, in a tenor of quiet days amid simple natural scenes. It teaches us to value these while we have them, proving, by the gentle pathos of a yearning memory, that it is the peaceful pleasures that wind the closest round the heart, which form the habits, mould the mind, satisfy the unconscious desires and needs of our nature, raise that structure of thoughts, fancies, habits, and ways, which make up ourself, and which, except in the wounding of the most intimate affections, cause the widest, most irreparable breach when we lose them. There are country scenes in *Adam Bede* looked back upon with an almost passionate tenderness, as though the senses ached for the genial old home.

What connection the writer may have had with country life we do not know. A close participation in its cares and business is not compatible with the indications of a thorough education; but some sort of constant familiar intercourse with its details is evident, and forces us into speculations as to the real authorship of this remarkable work. Here is a picture of life of rare power, of close adherence to nature. Where has this knowledge been learnt? through what processes has the author acquired his skill? He at once stands on a different footing with us from the ordinary novelist, whose versatility enables him to make so much out of a little fact, such showy fabrics out of small suggestions. Somehow we never find ourselves attributing invention to this writer. Whether true or not, we believe that it is all real as far as the emotions of the actors are concerned; that what is so vividly reported is taken from life; that the author has witnessed, perhaps experienced, all the deeper, more powerful feelings so truthfully portrayed. And here we will commit ourselves to an opinion on this disputed question with the diffidence that people must feel who know that any day may test their discernment; but we feel ourselves incapable of entering upon a discussion of *Adam Bede* with our readers without expressing our suspicion that it is from a female pen. There are, it is true, many passages and whole scenes which do not support the view, but the impression comes back in spite of them. The time is past for any felicity, force, or freedom of expression to divert our suspicions on this head; if women will write under certain conditions, perhaps more imperatively required from them than from men, as well as more difficult of attainment, it is proved that a wide range of human nature lies open to their comprehension; so that if things in this novel seem to be observed from a woman's point of view, we need not discard the notion because it is well and ably done. While we make this concession, we wish it to be understood that we still hold our own conviction, that there are subjects and passions which will always continue man's inalienable field of inquiry; but on this region we do not think the author of *Adam Bede* trenches. Genius, to be sure, is of no sex, nor can we pretend to set limits to the insight of the imagination into every possible human scene or contingency; and this shall be our answer if 'George Eliot' proves to be no *nom de guerre*, or if Mr. Anders[1] is right and the author *is* Mr. Joseph Liggins after all, as he persists in declaring himself; or, as others say, a very young man, son of a small town tradesman, who has dug into other memories, and knows nothing of what he writes but through the fancy. But until the fact is proved against us we shall continue to think that the knowledge of female nature is feminine, not only in its details, which might be borrowed from other eyes, but in its whole tone of feeling; that so is the full, close scrutiny of observation exercised in scanning every feature of a bounded field of inquiry; that the acquaintance with farm life in its minute particulars, and the secure ground on which the author always stands in matters of domestic housewifery, is another indication; that the position of the writer towards every point in discussion is a woman's position, that is, from a stand of observation rather than more active participation. Then, as every supposition seems to us more probable than that *Adam Bede* should prove to be a clergyman's work, and yet it is full of knowledge of clerical doings, this is to us another sign; for woman are by nature and circumstances the great clerical sympathisers; and often the politics of a parish, its leaders and party divisions, the most stirring bit of public life that comes under their immediate eye. Lastly, there is the moral: women are known dearly to love a 'well-

[1] Clergyman supporter of the impostor Liggins.

directed moral.' We will not multiply reasons, because, after all, impressions arise for which it is difficult to assign a cause. So having thus satisfied our candour, we will not further invade the reserve the author seems determined to maintain in spite of all attacks made on it by 'Times,' correspondents, but continue to apply such personal pronouns as *he* would have us use.

The influence of association is strongest on minds which, by nature active and observant, have always had leisure to allow congenial impressions to work into the inner being; which are not too busy to disregard any circumstances of their position; minds which people every familiar scene with a pleasant, leisurely crowd of thoughts and fancies, till each salient point is hung and garlanded with these memorials, and haunted, as it were, by a summer hum of reverie. We all have scenes sacred by this influence, spots to which habit has so closely allied us that we see ourselves reflected in them; we belong to them, and they to us; in which every shadow has its secret, and every yearly returning sunbeam its especial affinity with ourselves; where every form, every face, every voice, is charged with a significance beyond what meets the eye or ear. It is in such moments that we feel our whole being; the past, the present are one; a sense of harmony pervades us; every gentle feeling is in the ascendant. When gifted minds come to describe scenes and persons with whom they hold these associations, they unconsciously fulfil the precept of charity, for they love their subject as they love themselves, and feel towards them as towards parts of themselves. And herein lies the difference of one talent for description with another, whether it be of an inanimate scene or a character. There is a power of description, graphic, lifelike, truthful, which engages and entertains us for a while, and then, we know not why, palls upon us. We cannot account for the fact, that, in spite of our testimony to its success, our attention is not chained, our sympathy flags. We do not doubt the reason to be, because the author has not felt in the process, he has merely observed: there is no other connection between him and his subject. There are others who seem, by the same process, by the same words, to infuse a life and virtue into their work, as though a warm south wind breathed around them; and this is the genial influence of association connecting them closely with their subject. After all there is something cold-blooded in mere portrait-painting, in giving features, touch by touch, just as we see them, however correctly it is done; and we soon begin to feel this without thinking of the reason. But where the heart is concerned the perception is immediately quickened; all things group themselves harmoniously; instinct leads to the points which really tell upon other minds; trifles are trifles no longer, when the light of love glorifies them; and it is through association, far more than through the inherent merits or beauties of any particular subject, that this love is generated. We love the scenes and people about us as we love our children, not because they are better or prettier than other places or other children, but because the good and beauty in them have spoken to us, are incorporated with our nature till we are blended in an absolute union.

We believe it is the power of association which gives the charm to the *Vicar of Wakefield*. Goldsmith, through the wilful vagabondism of his career, looked back upon its one stationary period—to the rustic parsonage where life, hope, poetry, and wit first stirred and glowed within him; to that home, peopled, as it must have been, by tempers that could not be seriously ruffled, since his provocations never alienated them from himself. This retrospect we look upon as the source of the exquisite repose which constitutes that tale the most soothing and harmonious of fictions. No one can call this delightful book a correct picture of society and manners as they ever were or will be: there is little truth of fact about it; and sometimes, in our craving for this quality elsewhere, we muse over our own inconsistency in being more than content with such a travesty of actual life as it gives us. But it was real to him. He was not expatiating in mere fancies. We do not doubt that as he looked back his home did seem to him that Arcadian mixture of homeliness and refinement, of labour and leisure, of wisdom and folly, of knowledge and ignorance. If it portrayed no one else it pictures himself in all these points, and so, under the quaint veil of anomalies, is true at bottom. Nor do we doubt that all the more prominent scenes of humour had their counterpart, in fact even to the bargain of the green spectacles; since, for the edification of mankind, the author was invested with the somewhat contradictory powers of enacting absurdities in good faith, and afterwards so keenly appreciating his own blunders as to turn them into everlasting lessons for mankind.

And a certain homeliness is necessary to the full growth of associations: they must have, in some sense, to do with the business of life as well as its repose, with the happiness and dignity of work. The elegancies of the fashionable world, the domain of rigid proprieties, have no power of creating them: in the one, the mind is too feverishly engrossed with the present; in the other, under too much restraint. In *Adam Bede* we recognise their sway in every page,—in the description of the village church, in Joshua Rann's mysteriously sonorous reading, in the damp sequestered coolness of Mrs. Poyser's dairy. How every sense recalls its pleasantness! All summer, with its sights and sounds and delicious labours seem to surround us as we read—

Ah! I think I taste that whey now—with a flavour so delicate that one can hardly distinguish it from an odour; and with that soft gliding warmth that fills one's imagination with a still, happy dreaminess. And the light music of the dropping whey is in my ears, mingling with the twittering of a bird outside the wire net-work window—the window overlooking the garden, and shaded by tall guelder roses.

Our own age, as we have said, differs from its predecessors in its gradual reclaiming large tracts of existence from the obscurity of an utter removal from all that interests the fancy. This can only be done by degrees, as some warm heart perceives in its own surroundings, in the life in which its own sympathies expand, a capability of being so delineated as to awake similar sympathies in others. It requires genius to awake to the fact that the people we live amongst are just as full of interest as those whom other people have made famous—that it is only dull people who see nothing to care for in their own society and immediate neighbourhood. To prove this, the author, turning the tables on those fastidious tempers who sigh for ideal excellence, favours us with the supercilious experiences of the publican, Mr. Gedge, who, wherever he lived, found his neighbours—'and they were all the people he knew—"a poor lot, sir," big and little, a poor lot,' for his own part frankly avowing that

The way in which I have come to the conclusion that human nature is love-able—the way I have learnt something of its deep pathos and its sublime mysteries has been by living a great deal among people more or less commonplace and vulgar.

To delineate such nature does, as he says, need very exact truth, and it is this recognition of its difficulty which constitutes much of his strength.

Dreading nothing, indeed, but falsity, which, in spite of one's best efforts, there is still reason to dread. Falsehood is so easy, truth so difficult. Examine your words well, and you will find that even when you have no motive to be false, it is a very hard thing to say the exact truth, even about your own immediate feelings; much harder than to say something fine about them which is not the exact truth.

93

This author's intense desire to be true is often a check upon his scenes, and throws him rather on investigating motives than giving their results in words. It sometimes looks as if he would venture on no expression until he had traced it to its source, and, consequently, we find that some of the characters who occupy us most speak very little; we follow their turns of thought, we see the desires that most actuate them, and do not know that they never betray themselves in words. In every crisis he gives us the gradual growth of a thought, or impulse, from its first unconscious stirring in the kindred nature to its maturity in speech and action. This habit, no doubt, conduces to charity: a deed done, or even a word spoken, is an act over which we can sit in judgment; but how that word came to be spoken, the temptation which led to it, the human nature which yielded—there is quite sure to be something in the process with which we can sympathise; enough for pity and fellow feeling to mingle with our virtuous indignation, and divest it of some of its harshness. Even Hetty, vain and hard as she is, into whose inner life we are so carefully initiated, who speaks so few words, and yet whom we feel to know so well, she is less repulsive to us than if we did not see the workings of her mind and the imperviousness to external influences for good which her narrow self-concentration has produced.

In consequence of this system of tracing effects to their causes, it has been said that the author of *Adam Bede* represents people as all alike, comparing him, in this respect, with Mr. Thackeray.[1] With that gentleman's works we are not now concerned; but the fact of showing all people as equally exposed to temptation, and liable to err, has nothing to do with proving them all alike—which can only be done by showing that all people alike *yield* to temptation. This is contrary, not only to the professed teaching, but to the whole bearing of the story—which enforces that men need not do wrong unless they like; that they have a voice within which distinctly forbids evil actions, and a power under certain conditions of resistance. To us the aim, and more than the aim, the real effect of it is, to press upon us the mighty difference that conscience, and a fixed principle of action, makes in the same human natures. Ordinary novelists are prone to allow so much to human weakness, its passions and temptations, that conscience is shoved out of its place as a *part* of our nature, and made, as it were, an external power which we have to obey, not an inward voice, quite as much a part of us as our appetites, and as urgent in asserting its rights. Here there is no

---

[1] See review of *Adam Bede* in *The Times* (No. 8).

fatality, no inevitable sin, but free will and awful responsibility. It is a fact that the most absorbing and original novel we have had for many a year is also the most sternly moral. The story admits us into three consciences, in the various degrees of efficiency which the habit of attending to their dictates will produce, round which the words and acts of the rest of the characters group themselves and on which rule they work.

[The characters of Adam, Arthur, and Hetty are described]

Where a Methodist preacher is heroine, the question of religion must be more predominant than it is usually permitted to be in a novel; but *Adam Bede* is an embodiment of the author's whole experience, and he has taken his own line of what is eligible and suitable. Dinah, then, represents the religious principle as Adam does conscience, and, as far as general acceptance goes, is a success: but for ourselves she wants the weight of that reality which distinguishes the rest. She is a spirit amongst bodies of flesh and blood. As the saying now is—we do not believe in her. It is not that she is too good. There are women as self-denying, as humble, as sympathising, as gracious, as full of all womanly and housewifely accomplishments, but we do not think they preach. We are not here entering into the question of their right to preach; but the woman who is impelled to such utterances is absorbed by them; her mind will be diverted into one channel; her strictly feminine duties will be a work of principle not of congenial, natural occupation. The author labours to make Dinah one of the group, and represents her—what such a woman would not be,—at *home* amongst them. She would be more so if her character were more tinctured by her opinions. Of course a young woman enthusiastic enough to *preach* would be witnessing and testifying in private life, and either converting or making herself intolerable to the people about her; but though she uses some Methodist phrases, she has little of the animus of that sect in her: she is liberal, eclectic, enlightened, independent, and therefore unreal. Something is wanting to make us understand how such very natural people can be at their ease in that restrained demure presence. Except for the subtle delight old Lisbeth found in tormenting her younger son, we don't follow her pertinacious determination to get her for Adam. Mrs. Poyser's coruscations of splenetic humour play round her; but they don't fit, they neither amuse, rouse, nor irritate her. Mrs. Poyser, to be sure, is one of those who can speak their minds without the necessity for sympathy; and her opinions are too decided to need support from without. She would be awed by Dinah no more than by the old squire. Her view of Methodism was a fixed idea, of which she liked to deliver herself. The eccentricities of spiritual natures could find no opening to her cold common sense.

'Direction!' she exclaims; 'when there's a bigger maggot than usual in your head you call it direction, and then nothing can stir you. You're like the statty i' the outside o' Treddles'on Church, a starin' and a smilin' whether it's fair weather or foul.'

But all strictness found something akin to her nature; so we understand her respecting the rigid attire and abjuring of recreation; and there is a touch of quaint humility, not foreign to the practical before the spiritual mind, in her estimate of a pure presence.

An' she makes one feel safer when she's i' the house, for she's like the driven snow, anybody might sin for two as had her at their elbow.

We do not deny that Dinah is a beautiful creation, but the other inmates of Hayslope are something too genuine for such complimentary holiday terms. Then Dinah's sermon, eloquent and good in itself, does not strike us as probable under the circumstances—not what a woman would preach, though very like what the author would work out in his closet. Its plan is the result of reasoning, not impulse; what a person would write who had studied the line taken by St. Paul in his sermon to the Athenians. A woman of Dinah's class and views would have begun at once to assert some leading truth of the gospel, not have led up to it by the gradual process of proving God's providential care and our inborn consciousness of the being of a God. And so in the very beautiful prayer in Hetty's cell, the author's own method of reasoning (as in the apostrophe, 'She cries to me, thy weak creature! Saviour, it is a blind cry to thee,') is more apparent than the actual train of thought likely to direct Dinah.

[Seth Bede and the Rev. Irwine, and their religions, are discussed]

The state of religious intelligence in a rural population must have been subject for speculation to so keen an observer. His conclusions would not satisfy the abstract requirements of a theologian, but he carries his reader along with him in his charitable solutions of a difficulty: showing light where the form may be indefinite, and putting a pious interpretation on many an ignorant heterodoxy; as where Lisbeth at her husband's funeral

Had a vague belief that the psalm was doing him good; it was part of that decent burial which she would have thought it a greater wrong to withhold from him, than to have caused him many unhappy days while he was living. The more there was said about her husband, the more there was done for him; surely the safer he would be. It was poor Lisbeth's blind way of feeling that human love and pity are a ground of faith in some other love.

Or in Bess Cranage's ritualistic view of her deficiencies—

She had always been considered a naughty girl. She was conscious of it. If it was necessary to be very good, she must be in a bad way. She couldn't find her places at church as Sally Rann could; she had often been tittering when she curcheyed to Mr. Irwine.

And Joshua Rann's church principles pass without a protest from his pastor because he knew that something deeper remained unexpressed.

I like a pint wi' my pipe an' a neighbourly chat at Mester Casson's now an' then, for I was brought up i' the church, thank God! and ha' been parish clerk this two an' thirty year. I should know what the church religion is.

Even Adam's love for the church service is not allowed to be the consent of his reason after study and reflection, for here association comes in—'The secret of our emotions never lies on the bare object but on its subtle relations to our own past'—a sentiment which throws light on the author's entire views on such things.

We do not know whether our literature anywhere possesses such a closely true picture of purely rural life as *Adam Bede* presents. Every class that makes up a village community has its representative; and not only is the dialect of the locality accurately given but the distinct inflection of each order. The field labourer's rude utterance, 'as incapable of an under tone as a cow or a stag,' receives a touch of cultivation when it is used by the mechanic; and these two, again, are varied in the farmhouse; while each individual has appropriate peculiarities which give a distinct truth of portraiture. No person, we apprehend, can be an adept in minute observation of character, or, at least, in delineating it, without a correct ear and a good verbal memory. When we have a distinct idea of the words people will use, we are led to a clearer notion of the range of their ideas; accuracy in expression secures an amount of accuracy of thought. And well does the midland county dialect come out in this its first appearance, as far as we know, as a written language: how faithfully it expresses both pathos, common sense, and humour! On Adam's lips how forcible, on Mrs. Poyser's

tongue how pungent, in old Lisbeth how querulous! All these niceties
of observation show themselves in the differences of intellect and cultivation which each calling develops. What a stride there is between the
village mechanic and the village labourer! How sharp, intelligent, and
ready does the former become under the constant demand on his
resources! for it is well known that a really clever rustic workman is
the best and most inventive man in his trade; the most equal to all its
demands, the most capable of profiting by new advantages. Adam is a
picture of a good country carpenter as well as of a good man. And
what truth in the various labourers, influenced as each is by his calling!
Alick the foreman, to whom we are first introduced eating cold beans
with his pocket-knife with so much relish: a saturnine character with
a 'ventral laugh;' whose honest parsimony made him feed the poultry
with small handfuls because large ones affected him painfully with a
sense of profusion; who spent his life in a kind of dull rivalry with his
kind, and especially with 'Tim', the two who lived together, and yet,
as labourers only can, rarely spoke to each other, and never looked at
each other even over their dish of cold potatoes; and who was of
opinion

That church, like other luxuries, was not to be indulged in often by a foreman
who had the weather and the ewes on his mind. 'Church! nay, I'n gotten summat
else to think on,' was an answer he often uttered in a tone of bitter significance
that silenced further question.

Old Kester Bale, who knew the 'natur' of all farming work, and used to
worship his own skill in his curtseying survey of well-thatched ricks
every Sunday morning. Ben Tholoway, the one pilferer that infests
all farms, whose master did wisely to be lenient, for 'Ben's views of
depredation were narrow; the house of correction might have enlarged
them.' With what truth and humour is the harvest-supper described,
with how strong a sympathy for the occasion! Hot roast beef we are
made to feel as sublime a thing as these men must feel it, who, every
day in the year except Sunday, eat their dinner cold under a hedge.
And the silence! the real business of the occasion too serious for a
divided attention, 'even if these farm labourers had anything to say,
which they had not.' The harvest song, and the thumping, and the
subsequent slow unthawing under the influence of the ale! The first
vain efforts for a song! The 'Come, Tim' to the bashful minstrel seized
by the company as a 'conversational opportunity,' and echoed all
round the table: for everybody could say 'Come, Tim!' Tim's surly

sheepishness, and next the whole party very much in earnest to hear David's song till it was clear the lyrism of the evening was as yet in the cellar! Its final release from that confinement, Tim and David singing at once, till—

Old Kester, with an entirely unmoved and immoveable aspect, suddenly set up a quavering treble, as if he had been an alarum, and the time was come for him to go off.

The whole picture is real in every detail, and in its place inappreciable, relieving the reader after the too-painful scenes which precede it.

There is a dance, too, in another part of the story with which we sympathise: of course a country dance, so dear to memory—a 'glorious country dance, best of all dances'—the dance bewailed in many a tender elegy, which, if the pen of genius could be allowed a voice, would again be in the ascendant. 'Pity it was not a boarded floor, then the rhythmic stamping of the thick shoes would have been better than drums.' That merry stamping, that gracious nodding of the head, that waving bestowal of the hand, where can we see them now?

But all the author's humour centres in Mrs. Poyser, a new development of an old type. Mrs. Poyser never tries to amuse: she is the veriest utilitarian in her profession, and takes too business-like a view of life for smiles in her own person, or for any sanction of them in others. We almost apologise to her for finding mere diversion in so much cool, caustic, good sense. Indeed, her power lies in denuding everything of adventitious distinction, of its merely ornamental character, and reducing it to its first principles. Hetty's beauty is a constant mark for her analysis: 'she is no better nor a cherry wi' a hard stone inside.' Her pretty tasteful finery is 'rags.' 'It's what *rag* she can get to stick on her as she's thinking on from morning till night.' Whatever is not useful is worthless in her eyes, as she objects to lap-dogs because they are good neither for 'butchers' meat nor barking.' She is perpetually tracing things to their causes—to that *inside* which no fair exterior can divert from her thoughts. No dignity can live through the licence of her tongue: some apt but derogatory comparison will surely drag it through the mire. She is more than equal, she is mistress of every occasion, superior to every antagonist: her tongue is always trenchant, inexorable, always conqueror. We begin by pitying her maids, that 'Molly,' whose first hiring and widowed mother are perpetually cast up at her; that 'poor two-fisted thing' whose 'equils for awkwardness her mistress niver knew;' for whom she has a running lecture, which she takes up where she left it off like a tune on a barrel-organ. But we soon learn that she is no coward oppressor of the weak, and, moreover, that there is honour in furnishing a subject and matter for her inexhaustible powers of illustration. Besides, Molly is avenged: the author gives her and the reader this satisfaction in the scene of broken crockery. Mrs. Poyser may speak her mind to all the world, even to the powerful and malignant old squire, unscathed, but Molly stands on another footing. For as the exponent of certain virtues in their humblest development she is a favourite: her ready 'Lawk' in response to the children's demands for wonder and sympathy contrasts genially with Hetty's indifference to their pleasures. She is a bit of warm-hearted humanity, and on the whole valued as such. Mrs. Poyser's especial work is taking down pretension and resisting encroachment: she is merciful where her rights are acknowledged. Her husband knows this, and has an easy life of it—shaking with silent laughter at her sallies, winking to his allies when she arouses to action, and enjoying her successes, even when they risk his interests. Now and then she sets him down, but he takes it meekly, as when he ventures to hint, 'Thee 'dst be as angry as could be wi' me if I said a word against anything she did;' and she replies, 'Because you'd very like be finding fault wi'out reason. But there's reason i' what I say else I should na say it.' Many a good thing does she pour into his ear in compensation for his forbearance. If she despises all mankind she despises him least: he is slow of speech to be sure, 'but what he says he'll stand by'; and as for slowness, 'the men are mostly so tongue-tied that you're forced partly to guess what they mean like the dumb animals.' Her line is never complimentary, but her husband must appreciate the implied homage in her question—'Where's the use of a woman having brains of her own, if she's tackled to a geck as everybody's a laughing at? She might as well dress herself fine and sit back'ards on a donkey.' Herself a pattern of stability, subversion of natural order is her type of weakness. 'The right end up'ards' is strength and prosperity; a foolish wife is 'your head in a bog, and when it's there, your heels (in the shape of unprofitable short horns) may as well go after it.' And the excuse of bad managers, who say the weather's in fault, is dismissed with 'as there's folks 'ud stand on their heads, and then say the fault was in their boots.'

Mrs. Poyser's readiness at illustration is too much a peculiarity of the author's own for us to suppose it borrowed from another. All his characters are rich in this gift, but he has done well to show it in its efflorescence, where the vigour and independence of a farmer's wife's position gives it a natural home and affords it such an infinite variety of material. A woman has no better field than a dairy farm for the exercise of her own especial gifts, and may develop into anything when, as Mrs. Poyser says, she earns half and saves half the rent; while the consciousness of usefulness in the great primitive occupation of mankind gives a certain dignity which no other calling imparts. She controls the fate and destiny of so many animate and inanimate things, and is always face to face with the productive powers of nature. And how well the sense of responsibility is conveyed! We quite understand what it must be to lie awake with twenty gallons of milk on the mind; and when her keen forethought raises the picture of 'Bethel with his horse and cart coming about the back places, and making love to both the gells at once,' we see it all, and agree with her 'that if we are to go to ruin it shanna be wi' having our back kitchen turned into a public.' And after all, in spite of the rough rind, how genial she is! with her mother's love for Totty, that perfect type of farmhouse infancy; with her wifely pleasure in setting out her plentiful table for her husband, his father, and his friends; with her calm satisfaction watching the cattle in that cheery scene, the farmyard, so dear to this author, whose keen observation has been busy many a time taking in the meaning and causes of its seeming hubbub and confusion, and tracing effects to their causes just as keenly as though a human heart were depicted. We see Mrs. Poyser serenely knitting at her door as the evening bustle begins, the patient beasts running confusedly into the wrong places; for the alarming din of the bull-dog was mingled with more distant sounds, the tremendous crack of the waggoner's whip which the timid feminine creatures, with pardonable superstition, imagined to have some relation to their own movements; the silly 'calves;' the ducks drinking dirty water, to get a drink with as much body in it as possible; the strong-minded donkey; Marty wickedly provoking the gander by hissing at him;—every stroke of the picture is by a sure and loving hand, and gives an intense reality to the human life it surrounds. The scenes of Sunday peace in village and farmhouse are as feelingly true in the days of old Sunday leisure thus commemorated—

Surely all leisure is hurry, compared with a sunny walk through the fields from 'afternoon church,' as such walks used to be in those old leisurely times, when the boat, gliding sleepily along the canal, was the newest locomotive power; when Sunday books had most of them old brown leather covers, and opened with remarkable precision always in one place.

The blacksmith's Sunday clean face is recorded, which always made his little grand-daughter cry at him as a stranger; and 'Timothy's Bess' standing at her own door nursing her baby, while others went to church, 'feeling, as women do in that position, that nothing else can be expected of them;' and indoors where the clock is ticking in a peaceful Sunday manner, and the very stones and tubs seemed quieter than usual, and the water gently dripping from the pump is distinctly heard. Queen and controller of such a world, Mrs. Poyser, in spite of the weight on her shoulders and the hard work on her hands, ought to be and is a happy woman. That she is an arrogant one, confident first in the superiority of the female sex, and next in her supremacy over all other females, is perhaps true; but conceit in her case is imposing: the author elsewhere, and on other subjects, shows the petty side of this quality; for which he has an agreeable, sly appreciation in every phase and aspect, from the pragmatical parade of knowledge in the Scotch gardener, to the condescension which led Arthur to put on his uniform to please the tenants (we are told 'he had not the least objection to gratify them in this way, as the uniform was very advantageous to his figure'), and the act of generous forethought of Joshua Rann, who had 'provided himself with his fiddle in case any one should have a sufficiently pure taste to prefer dancing to a solo on that instrument.' Not that we are allowed to laugh superciliously at *his* rustic vanities, for Joshua has an ear both for reading and music, and the author is not more aristocratic than nature herself.

This may seem a strange mode of speaking about the reading of a parish clerk, a man in rusty spectacles, with stubbly hair, a large occiput, and a prominent crown; but that is nature's way. She will allow a gentleman with a splendid physiognomy and poetic aspirations to sing wofully out of tune, and not give him the slightest hint of it, and takes care that some narrow-browed fellow trolling a ballad in the corner of a pot-house shall be as true to his intervals as a bird.

We have assumed in our readers a knowledge of the plot, for it is too late to introduce this popular tale to their attention; our part has rather been to look for the source of its interest and the qualities and aims of its author. Though the story sometimes flags, and the plot has its weak points, it is effective for its purpose of delineating character; and we have few scenes more telling, few situations more original and striking in the conception than the battle in the wood between Adam and Arthur—the real scene of Arthur's punishment and humiliation—in which the author satisfies his demand for justice; for as for his sub-

sequent years of expatriation and repentance, our experience of life
tells us that such expiations are not undertaken by the Arthurs of real
life; but the battle, the blow, the vengeance, might be and are facts to
our apprehension and consent; so fully is all worked out; the transitions
of feelings; the conflicts between new and old sensations; the alternation
of rage on the first discovery of the lovers, with Adam's horror when
he thought he had killed his rival; the concentration in the present
as he feebly recovers; the affectionate tender attentions; the inevitable
walk arm-in-arm; the returning memory and mistrust. Two persons
are seldom brought together in a more striking and critical situation;
the reader's sympathy alternates between the actors with the liveliest
curiosity; events, and the emotions consequent on them, succeed one
another in what we feel a natural order; we read with a growing
confidence in the author's mastery of the position he has imagined. And
Adam's passionate appeals for justice, when the terrible truth is forced
upon him, are of equal power, and have a real weight on the reader.
To how many cases are they not applicable? 'Is he to go free while
they lay all the punishment upon her, so weak and young? I'll go to
him; I'll bring him back; I'll make him look at her in her misery. He
shall look at her till he can't forget it: it shall follow him night and day—
as long as he lives it shall follow him; he shan't escape wi' lies this time!'
Hetty's wanderings, too, the fascination of her dreaded home, her
confession, are all-engrossing; and all the author's pity and tenderness
are lavished on Adam, in the prostration of strong and generous nature
under an overwhelming calamity. There is courage as well as truth to
nature in allowing him to recover from such a blow. It is the pleasure
of ordinary romance to represent the finer clay of humanity as so
susceptible of sorrow that a blow to the tenderer affections is final—
there is no rising again from it; the victim lives, perhaps, but is never
suffered again to enjoy life. No second morn may light up the heaven
of heroes and heroines. All our experience tells us it is not so; all of us
have witnessed and blessed the inherent power of reaction in a healthy
nature; and the author of *Adam Bede*, because he knows it to be so, has
not only restored Adam to serenity, but has made him happy in a second
attachment, concluding some very tender and just thoughts on the
work sorrow is designed to achieve, with the counsel which may be
received as the watchword and motive of his story. 'Let us rather be
thankful that our sorrow lives as an indestructible force, only changing
its form as forces do, passing from pain to sympathy, the one poor
word which includes all our best insight and our best love.'

11. Unsigned review, *London Quarterly Review*

July 1861, xvi, 301–7

This review, which appeared in a Methodist periodical more than two years after the publication of *Adam Bede*, is typical of the attacks on George Eliot's irreligion which developed after her pseudonym was lifted (see Introduction, pp. 2–3).

Next on our list follows a bold conception: a novel half immoral, half Dissenting; a tale of seduction, relieved by Methodist sermons and prayers! The popularity of *Adam Bede* has been immense. 'Particular' ladies have placed it on their drawing-room tables; sober people have declared that all young men ought to read it; nay, to our excessive astonishment, we have heard it called a religious novel. Let us glance at the plot of the story. Arthur Donithorne, the generous, honourable, kind-hearted young squire, falls in love with the farmer's niece, pretty Hetty Sorrel; and blindly, and almost unresistingly, abandons himself to the impulses which are certain to bring disgrace on himself and ruin on his victim. We say, unresistingly, for we count it no resistance to make resolutions which are never put in practice. In the course of three months, (for this is no gradual fall!) he is represented as pursuing his object almost without a struggle, lying to disguise it without a blush, and then leaving his victim, with very insufficient precautions to save her from the worst consequences of their mutual wrong-doing. Then Hetty, without the smallest demur, accepts Adam Bede as an affianced lover, and prepares to marry him; until, overwhelmed by the certainty of her disgrace, she takes to flight, murders her baby in a fit of lightheadedness, is tried, and condemned to die,—Arthur only becoming aware of her situation in time to exert his utmost efforts to change the sentence of death into transportation. Then both become penitent, and are put out of sight for some years, after which Arthur returns home, and Hetty dies.

What is it that makes a novel of which such a plot is the centre, a favourite among thoughtful and religious people? First, the exceeding literary merit of the book, and the artistic skill which hides its evil beneath its good. We doubt if one reader in twenty has ever placed these facts fairly before his own judgment, or given them their right names,—so skilfully are they veiled under inference and silence, so skilfully alternated with the better parts of the story. Also there is great merit in the charm and ease of the dialogue, in the spirit and correctness with which most of the characters are sketched, and in the real wit and wisdom embodied in Mrs. Poyser and Adam Bede himself. Probably, also, the amount of religious talk has found favour with religious people; as if mere words could constitute religion in a book any more than in a life. That which its speakers put forward as their truest convictions, that which is inculcated in the passing reflections of the author, that good or evil which is held up to be followed, tolerated, or avoided,—*that* is the religion of the book.

[quotes speeches on the question of individual responsibility from chs. 16 and 17]

From these quotations it would seem that our strength to resist evil consists in a natural power to act on foreseen consequences. Those who, like Adam, have this power, are fortunate; those who, like Arthur, have it not, will be ruled by their 'moods,'—the moods which are part of that nature which no man can act against. The strength which all mankind may possess by virtue of that light 'which lighteth every man that cometh into the world'—the strength to choose right as right, and to resist wrong as wrong, apart from all consequences, is not recognised in *Adam Bede*. On the contrary, the whole book is a vivid picture of the irretrievable *effects* of wrong doing, and its only morality is to impress self-restraint by a clearer view of those effects. At first sight this may seem moral and religious; but it is an immorality and an irreligion to preach only the consequences of sin, whilst the guilt of yielding to it is ignored. Look at the history of Arthur's fall in connexion with the passages we have quoted: the folly and the evil results are drawn by a master-hand; but the coarseness, baseness, and guiltiness of his whole conduct are so skilfully thrown into the shade, that we do not believe any reader would guess the extent of the wrong he has done, until it comes to light in the interview between Arthur and Adam. Then, as it would seem, for the first time, 'all screening self-excuse forsook him for an instant, and he stood face to face with the first great irrevocable evil he had ever committed'—Then?—not till then!—then?—only for an instant! Though he had to lie to Adam 'as a necessity', though, 'while it jarred with his habitual feelings,' he could remember that 'he had to be judicious and not truthful;' even after all this, the young man, who is represented as an honourable, high-minded gentleman, instead of feeling himself disgraced for ever, 'would gladly have persuaded himself that he had done no harm! And if no one had told him the contrary, he could have persuaded himself so much better. Nemesis can seldom forge a sword for herself out of our conscience; . . . out of the suffering we feel in the suffering we may have caused: there is rarely metal enough there to make an effective weapon.' And when he thought of Hetty, compunctious and anxious as he was, he could argue with himself that 'it was an unfortunate business altogether, but there was no use in making it worse than it was, by imaginary exaggerations and forebodings of evil that might never come. The temporary sadness, to Hetty, was the worse consequence: he resolutely turned away his eyes from any bad consequence that was not demonstrably inevitable. But—but Hetty might have had the trouble in some other way, if not in this. And perhaps hereafter he might be able to do a great deal for her, and make up to her for all the tears she would shed about him. She would owe the advantage of his care for her in future years to the sorrow she had incurred now. *So* good comes out of evil. Such is the beautiful arrangements of things!' Is this a kind, generous, high-principled gentleman?—rather, as Adam calls him, 'a selfish, light-minded scoundrel.' Our author moralizes on the woful deterioration of two months, and on the slavery exercised over us by our own deeds; but a soliloquy like this is the expression of long-formed character, not of two months' degeneracy. Doubtless there are many Arthurs in the world, but they are *not* generous, high-principled gentlemen. He who can with open eyes walk first into temptation, and then into vice; he who can shamefully deceive the man who trusts him, and seduce the woman who loves him, yet whose first thought throughout is to excuse himself, may be an easy-tempered, open-handed fellow, but he can never have been noble-minded or high-principled; had he bee so, his sins would have been torture to him. But then, you see, we were not all born heroes; we all have not strength to abstain in sight of future consequences; we are governed by 'moods' which lie in our nature— the nature against which we can never be at variance. Therefore, instead of harshly condemning others less strongly built than ourselves, we must have patience and charity towards our stumbling, falling companions. We must get our heart-strings bound round the weak and erring, so that we may share their inward suffering. Human nature is loveable in itself, and even in common-place and vulgar people we shall find deep pathos and sublime mysteries. This is the religion of *Adam Bede*.

Look at it carefully in the extracts we have given at large. What is the meaning of this strong assertion of the vulgar and common-place against the ideal heroic? The words are true enough in themselves, but what is their import taken in connexion with the story? Mr. Irwine and Captain Donithorne are not common-place, nor do they stand in opposition to any false heroic, but to the true and simple rule of right. In this loud demand for sympathy with them, for charity and patience towards them, is there no fear that we may forget that rule?—especially when we are urged to compassion by love and sympathy alone. Is it by suffering in their sufferings that we are to learn forbearance? Not so, lest pity for the suffering make us forget the sin. It is by high conscience of the rule of right, and by the sense of our own transgression and God's free forgiveness, that we are to learn the only true and safe ground for gentleness towards others. 'Be ye kind one to another, tender-hearted, forgiving one another, even as God for Christ's sake hath forgiven you.'[1] Conscientiousness without humility is harsh and cold, but charity without righteousness is lax and low. We are *not* to let go our hold of God's high standard; we are not to lose sight of the baseness of sin and the darkness of guilt; we are not to forget that by God's help we *can* seek good and avoid evil, against our own 'moods' and against the force of temptation. George Eliot's religion is of a different kind. By the skill of an accomplished author he puts guilt and responsibility out of sight, raises from circumstances an extenuating plea, invests natural character with excusing force, makes the consequences of wrongdoing more prominent than wrongdoing, the sufferings of sin more prominent than sin, and then demands leniency for offenders, not because we too have fallen, but because they could scarcely choose but fall. Well may they hope for leniency in judgment who drag down the standard that alone condemns them: their religion is the religion of 'I could not help it,' and the plea that excuses others excuses themselves. We are far from saying that this is ever put forward in express words; such a masterly writer does not need to do so; but he always contrives to present to the mind of his readers the idea of our helplessness to resist evil.

The literary machinery by which this is effected, consists of a minute

[1] *Ephesians*, iv, 32.

unhealthy analysis of feelings and impulses, to which the action of the will is made subordinate. A mind at crosspurposes with itself is laid bare before us; a mind resolving on good, and satisfying itself with the resolution, only to cling the closer to evil; content to fail, wishing and longing to fail, even while it resolves. We see the whole process of self-debate and self-deceit; we see the low motives lurking behind the higher ones, and secretly swaying the mind against its better convictions; we see the course of temptation and hesitation, and the final surrender to deceit, dishonour, and guilt. But to what purpose is this morbid analysis? The Lacedæmonians bade their children see the loathsomeness of drunkenness in their besotted Helots,[1] but they never bade them contemplate or study the alluring process of temptation, or the gradual progress of degradation. He who bids us do this, forgets the aid which the play of imagination lends to evil. Why do the horrors of war and shipwreck continually tempt boys into the army and navy? Why does one semi-madman's shooting at the Queen, or jumping off the Monument, incline others to the same insanity? Simply, because the imagination is strong to stamp pictorial representations on the mind, and weak to register the prudential or moral motives which serve to counteract them. In *Adam Bede* the process of temptation is so skilfully managed, so veiled by silence, so entangled by metaphysical analysis, that while the sin and guilt come out plain in the consequences, we are merely left to infer some excusing weakness in the fall.

[then the reviewer extends his criticism to *The Mill on the Floss*]

[1] Plutarch, *Lycurgus*, xxviii.

THE MILL ON THE FLOSS

April 1860

12. Unsigned review, *Spectator*

7 April 1860, xxxiii, 330–1

The new story by the author of *Adam Bede* is full of power—a vague
word to use, but, as far as any one word can stamp a whole work of
art, it is the only word with any approach to fitness in it. The story
is in the main the record of the struggle of a young girl towards a
noble life—a life she can intensely feel to be alone worthy of a woman,
but which she has not the simple strength of will and act to realize at
once in its directness. Few persons in the novel-dramas which make so
much of our literature now-a-days are so distinctly embodied and
vividly coloured as the Maggie Tulliver who has just been introduced
as a new guest in so many thousand English homes. Her love for her
brother—clinging, exacting in its excess of lovingness, but still thoughtlessly unselfish, is painted with wonderful minuteness. Very few writers
can enter into the thoughts of children, can follow out their little trains
of half-reasonings, and detect the ways and methods by which they
arrive at conclusions: and of those few, George Eliot seems to us, in the
present day, to possess in the highest degree the gift of knowing the
child-soul in those things which are common to all children. Charles
Dickens has given portraits of odd children, very touching in their
manner, and with a certain naturalness in the oddity, that, without
knowing enough of the few exceptional originals, makes us feel that
the pictures are true portraits. But George Eliot reminds us of what
nearly all children are. Her children are healthy with flesh-and-blood
rosiness, not sickly or queer. You seem to look into their blue eyes,
pat their little heads, 'sunning over with curls,' or hear their voices
saying such things as any bright-eyed little four-year old will say to the
first comer. In 'Mr. Gilfil's Love Story' and *Adam Bede* there were a
few touches giving hints what the author could do in this way, but

such delightful hints that we could not wish to know more; we were thankful that for us these little people were *not* 'characters,' would not grow up, would ever remain children, and that the little 'flaxen-headed two-year-old' who, 'with admirable directness and simplicity,' said to Mr. Gilfil, 'What zoo dot in zoo pottet?' would never be reported as speaking better English.

In the new story, the author describes Maggie Tulliver from her childhood upwards, and traces the influence of all the home associations on the young girl's mind. Her active mind, her spirit sensitive to all things, her heart with a hunger and thirst to be loved, are analyzed with a wondrous instinctive knowledge of the inner workings of a child's mind. All the persons around her leave some kind of impression on her. Her father is a man of narrow culture, with that consciousness of its narrowness which indicates the power of a nature much broader, and which is shown most in his love for 'his little wench'—the wayward child he clings to half-blindly, not understanding her mind but understanding that he loves her. His love for her keeps alive in her a most wholesome and healthy tenderness. But the very native limits of his mind still leave much of the depths of her feeling unsounded. Towards her brother, she is imperatively attracted. His boyhood is also drawn; the lines are few, the touches seem but mere accidental tints left by the pencil, but the character is painted to the very life. The plain practical turn of the boy's mind, his involuntary contempt for imperfections he does not share, his passive bewilderment as to things he cannot learn, and his quiet undemonstrative energy in going through with the work before him; are the main characteristics of the portrait. The manner in which he meets his sister's love—frank and sincere in his amount of love when he shows it, equally frank and sincere, when, by withholding it, he awards her what he considers deserved punishment—but which to her mind, morbidly sensitive, is an abyss of pain he can never by any possibility realize to his narrow solid mind—is a curious instance of the power the author has of tracing, with rare insight, not alone the inner workings of two very different natures, but the effect the two natures have upon one another. There is not much depth or variety in the brother's character, but the truth with which it is done indicates the richness of the artist's power who, in her second-rate characters, follows the firm outline her cunning hand has traced as conscientiously as in fulfilling the more gracious task of working out the leading figures of the great design.

The next influence on Maggie's character brings into light new revelations of the spirit within her. Philip Wakem, a deformed young man, son of her father's bitter enemy, a hard-griping solicitor, has been partially known to her from childhood. He, thoughtful and perceptive, has watched her and been won by the strange beauty of her character, not inaptly expressed by deep wild eyes, with wondrous power of expressing all her beauty and all her weakness—all her deep heart-wish to be noble, all her fitfulness in striving to fulfil the high ideal she can so quickly conceive. He can see in her a beauty of soul not visible to herself. He can interpret her thoughts, better than she can, and detect in her intermittent asceticism a mere stunting of emotions that ought to have full play. The awakening of the girl's higher faculties under the influence of a mind of wider range and finer tone than her own is indicated, and the effect of the circumstances of her childhood and youth on her manners, speech, and actions, is shown so naturally, that one for a time quite forgets the artist and her art. Maggie is no exceptional girl in any way; far, far removed from the 'faultless monster' of the old romance, and still as far from the pale, clever, and sharp-spoken young woman whom *Jane Eyre* made fashionable for a time. A woman's natural impulses; all the wild fancies and self-torturing thoughts of a young girl vivid in imagination, but not strong in any mental exercise, and obliged to live a life at first very narrow, and then very mean—are described exactly as they might happen, as they do happen, in thousands of English homes. The novelty and interest lie in the fact that in very few works of fiction has the interior of the mind been so keenly analyzed. We had such an analysis in *Jane Eyre*, powerful and distinct for evermore to all who read that great story; but Jane Eyre was no ordinary young woman; she was exceptional in circumstances, exceptional in her own nature. Maggie Tulliver is not exceptional; the wayward little child, 'naughty' to the last degree, quick in her 'ways,' is natural enough, and the growth of her characteristics bears all the impress of the facts around her. Her mental conflicts are not alone analyzed in her childhood and youth and in relation to all her home ties. As life advances, two kinds of love contend for mastery within her; she remembers her first awakening to higher things at the dawn of womanhood, and her first lover keeps a place in her thoughts which he never forfeits. It is almost impossible to those who have not read the book to describe how delicately and clearly the author brings before us the distinction between Maggie loving Philip Wakem and Maggie loving Stephen Guest. The contending thoughts are so natural; they seem inevitable, and through every weak word, every unconscious betrayal, bringing complication and suffering into the story—keenly as one feels them, as if they were painful scenes we saw acted before our eyes—we still have an instinctive sense that they are unavoidable, that they could not be left unspoken, or undone. There are parts of the story where the style gives a kind of consciousness of reality, as if you heard the words spoken by a voice shaken with the emotions so well described; there are passages of dialogue where the love between men and women is expressed more naturally and powerfully, we think, than in any novel we ever read. Rising fresh from the perusal, we may overrate the power of these passages, and attribute to style or words what may be due to situations the interest of which is prepared by skilful construction; but we think there can be no mistaking the wondrous human passion that animates the scenes between the two lovers—bound to others in honour, yet clinging together with such appealing love.

Some parts of the story are likely to be misunderstood at first reading; some passages appeared to us out of harmony and some incidents forced, until the very last pages threw a light over the whole. It is the epic of a human soul, traced through childhood, development, and temptation. The sordid scenes at Dorlcote Mill—described with photographic truth and minute manner-painting worthy of Miss Austen—are still interesting only in their effect on Maggie; her impatience is more natural, and her impetuous aspiration after something higher than her home-surroundings stands out more distinctly. The character of Mrs. Tulliver and her three sisters,—with all their family fretfulness and peculiarities, their idolatry of the 'proprieties,'—supply not only a background dull and mean enough for the bright, bold, dark-eyed girl, but furnish an excuse for much that is erring in her 'ways.' You feel that, in such a home, a child like Maggie would inevitably grow up into a woman such as Maggie Tulliver is. Her native glow of love and sense of beauty lead her perforce into the path traced out. In this novel, therefore, we have reproduced the old grand element of interest which the Greek drama possessed, the effect of circumstances upon man; but you have, in addition, that analysis of the inner mind, of which *Hamlet* stands in literature the greatest example. In the case of Maggie, we have a career regarded both from the inside and from the outside; we feel the throbbing of her heart at each new sensation, and we see, as it were, from our own stand-point, the outward facts that awaken her to new life. On sweeps the river of life and of destiny; the flood resistless, the waters strong: men and homes, and old associations of outer life, are swept away for miles, or engulphed; all around drifts from its moorings; and, as spectators, we watch the roll of the resistless tide. On comes one young girl, alone upon a raft, hardly saved from the flood; she strives against the current, but is still swept along, and now we are made conscious of her thoughts and feelings. We see not alone the river of life, with its hard facts floated away, and its merciless waters, but we are conscious of every thought of the victim. We follow back to the heart the retreating blood that has left the cheek pale; we know every gleam of hope and pang of despair that runs through mind and soul, as the familiar landmarks are passed, and she is drifted down with the flood. We do not remember any novel where the interest so clearly centres round the one character, where every fact—the smallest—is read with deep attention, because it may affect her—as in real life the very name of a town or street, or even shop, remembered in connexion with some one person much beloved, has at once a new vivid life. Not that Maggie is made actually powerful in her influence on the other persons; but that everything she does, or anything done to her, is of interest, and thus the whole story takes a noble unity.

Sterne eulogized critics who were pleased 'they knew not why, and cared not wherefore.'[1] In the present day, we are perhaps unhappily too critical to be satisfied with that simple and gracious reception of great works of art. We cannot help analyzing the mechanism of this great story. It seems to us that the first idea was simply what we have indicated—the onward 'storm and stress' of the soul, the outward rush and plash of the river of life on which it is swept along. It is with great joy that we recognize the consummate art with which this idea is worked out. The smallest details worked in help to make the idea real. There is even in the material facts a half-hidden symbolism indicating the idea of the story. When Maggie tells Philip Wakem why she loves her brother, she thinks that it was holding his hand she first saw the rushing water of the Floss. The quarrel about the water privileges affects her whole life. She is carried away by the flood out to sea with the man she loves and must not love, and where her physical danger and her moral peril are brought close together. Finally, the catastrophe comes as the river of life overwhelms her, and the symbolism is complete. The beauty of this under-current of symbolism is that it is unexpressed, but the mere material facts of the river playing such a great part in Maggie's life give one the feeling that she is swept along by a current of circumstances she can neither resist nor control.

[1] *Tristram Shandy* (1760-7), III, xii.

We might dwell on minor beauties; but we have lingered too long over our task. Inferior to *Adam Bede* in the varied interest of three or four good characters, it is superior as a work of art; with a higher aim and that aim more artistically worked out.

13. Unsigned review, *Saturday Review*

14 April 1860, ix, 470–1

This review represents the kind of objection many readers felt to George Eliot's presentation of spiritual conflict and passionate love in *The Mill on the Floss*: 'There are emotions over which we ought to throw a veil'.

A year ago, most readers who had just finished *Adam Bede* would have been greatly surprised to hear two things which we now know to be true. It would have been very strange news that *Adam Bede* was written by a woman, and it would have been equally surprising to learn that within a twelvemonth the authoress would produce another tale quite worthy to rank beside its predecessor. Now that we are wise after the event, we can detect many subtle signs of female authorship in *Adam Bede*; but at the time it was generally accepted as the work of a man. To speak the simple truth, without affectation of politeness, it was thought to be too good for a woman's story. It turns out that a woman was not only able to write it, but that she did not write it by any lucky accident. The *Mill on the Floss* may not, perhaps, be so popular as *Adam Bede*, but it shows no falling off nor any exhaustion of power. We may think ourselves very fortunate to have a third female novelist not inferior to Miss Austen and Miss Brontë; and it so happens that there is much in the works of this new writer that reminds us of these two well-known novelists without anything like copying. George Eliot has a minuteness of painting and a certain archness of style that are quite after the manner of Miss Austen, while the wide scope of her remarks, and her delight in depicting strong and wayward feelings, show that she belongs to the generation of Currer Bell, and not to that of the quiet authoress of *Emma*. Where all excel, it is of no use to draw up a sort of literary class-list, and pronounce an opinion as to the comparative merits of these three writers; but no one can now doubt that the lady who, with the usual pretty affectation of her sex, likes to look on paper as much like a man as possible, and so calls herself George Eliot, has established her place in the first rank of our female novelists.

She has done us all one great kindness, for she has opened up a field that is perfectly new. She has, for the first time in fiction, invented or disclosed the family life of the English farmer, and the class to which he belongs. She paints farmers and their wives and children, and their equals in the little villages and towns around them, and brings before us their settled opinions, convictions, and humours. Both in her present novel and in *Adam Bede* she throws the date of her story back a few years, and paints the farmers of a past generation. Perhaps the type is altering now, and is too much mixed up with other forms of English social life to present salient peculiarities to the eye of the novelist. But George Eliot not only draws the farmer of other days and his wife, but she multiplies the shapes which she makes these people assume. In the *Mill on the Floss* there is a whole volume devoted to depicting the ways and doings of persons in the rank of Mr. and Mrs. Poyser. It is scarcely possible that new friends of this sort in novels should please us quite as much as the old ones, for we have no longer the sensation of pleased surprise that any one can describe such people. But if Mrs. Poyser remains unequalled, the great variety of characters, all distinct and yet all hitherto unanticipated, who figure in the first volume of the *Mill on the Floss*, show that the range of the writer's observation goes far beyond one or two specimens. The most conspicuous of these characters are three sisters who belong to the family of Dodson, and are possessed with an immovable belief in the innate superiority of everything Dodson. These sisters have married three men dissimilar enough in taste and temper to have each an individual and distinct existence, and yet with a general resemblance in the cast and level of their minds which stamps them as belonging to the same class and the same generation. There is nothing in which George Eliot succeeds more conspicuously than in this very nice art of making her characters like real people, and yet shading them off into the large group which she is describing. Some notion of what it requires to make a good novelist may be obtained by reflecting on all that is implied in the delineation of three farmer's daughters and their husbands, with separate and probable characters, and in allotting them suitable conversation, and following the turns and shifts of their minds within the narrow limits of the matters that may be supposed to interest them. It is this profusion of delineative power that marks the *Mill on the Floss*, and the delineations are given both by minute touches of description and by dialogues. To write dialogue is much harder than merely to describe, and George Eliot trusts greatly to the talk of her farmers' wives in order to make her conception of these sisters come vividly before us. Both in the description and in the dialogue there are exhibited a neatness of finish, a comprehensiveness of detail, and a relish for subdued comedy that constantly bring back to our recollection the best productions of Miss Austen's genius. Like Miss Austen, too, George Eliot possesses the art of taking the reader into her confidence. We seem to share with the authoress the fun of the play she is showing us. She joins us in laughing at her characters, and yet this is done so lightly and with such tact that the continuity of the story is not broken. Every one must remember the consummate skill with which Miss Austen manages this, and if we do not quite like to acknowledge that our old favourite has been equalled, we must allow that George Eliot performs the same neat stroke of art with a success that is little inferior.

Portraiture, however, and the description of farmers and their wives, only occupies one portion of George Eliot's thoughts. There is a side of her mind which is entirely unlike that of Miss Austen, and which brings her much closer to Charlotte Brontë. She is full of meditation on some of the most difficult problems of life. She occupies herself with the destinies, the possibilities, and the religious position of all the people of whom she cares to think. Especially she seems haunted with the thought of the amazing discrepancy between what she calls 'the emmet-life' of these British farmers, and the ideal of Christianity. She dwells on the pettiness, the narrowness, the paganism of their character. She even takes a pleasure in making the contrast as strong as she can. In her stern determination to paint what she conceives to be the truth, to soften nothing and not to exalt and elevate where she profoundly believes all to be poor and low, she shocks us with traits of character that are exceptional, however possible. In the *Mill on the Floss* an old miller is ruined, and the fault, as he thinks, lies at the door of a roguish lawyer. When he finds his ruin is accomplished, he solemnly takes the family Bible, and in the fly-leaf records a curse against his enemy. Usually, however, the proceedings of the Dodsons and their set are much milder. It is the gossip, the stinginess, the total absence of all spirituality in the farmer circles that weigh upon George Eliot. She has set herself to imagine how such influences would tell upon an exception to the set, in a lively, imaginative, impulsive girl, the daughter of the Dodson married to the miller. The history of this girl is taken up when she is seven years old, and is continued until she has been for some time a young woman. She goes through great outward trials, in addition to the perpetual suffering inflicted on her by relations who entirely misunderstand her. She has a period in which fiction is everything to her, and she consoles herself for all that reality imposes on her by the delightful dreams of the imagination. When her suffering becomes too intense, she takes refuge in mystical religion. Later on, she seems to accept the doctrine inculcated by one of her lovers, that resignation cannot be the highest end of human life, as it is merely negative. She then passes into a stage where she is absorbed in the fierce moral conflicts awakened by a passion to which she thinks it wrong to yield. All this is entirely in the vein of Charlotte Brontë, and the *Mill on the Floss* shows that George Eliot has thought as keenly and profoundly as the authoress of *Jane Eyre* on the peculiar difficulties and sorrows encountered by a girl of quick feeling and high aspirations under adverse outward circumstances. But the objection which we feel to difficult moral problems being handled in fiction is certainly not removed by the writings of either of these gifted women. What does it all come to except that human life is inexplicable, and that women who feel this find the feeling painful? It is true that a girl like the heroine of the *Mill on the Floss* is not an improbable character. Many a girl in the obscurity of an uncongenial home has first taken to ascetic and mystical religion, and then had doubts forced on her whether such a religion could give her peace. But because they really occur, it does not follow that spiritual doubts and conflicts are a proper subject for a novelist. Fiction has, in such matters, the great defect that it encourages both the writer and the reader to treat the most solemn problems of human life as things that are to be started, discussed, and laid aside at pleasure. The conduct of the story always affords an opening to escape from the responsibility of definite thought. It does even more than afford an opening—it forces the mind to escape from reflection into the study of outward life. The subjects started are, therefore, always too large for the manner in which they are handled. When women like George Eliot and Currer

Bell are writing, we are perhaps too interested in their style, in the freshness of their thoughts, and in the story they are telling, to care much for the abandonment of the moral difficulties that have been raised. But no one who considers how much harm the light, trifling, and inadequate discussion of great subjects does in the present day, can have much pleasure in finding that a novelist powerful enough to become the example and excuse of lesser writers exhibits ascetic religion as a temporary phase in a young woman's career.

Passion, and especially the passion of love, is so avowedly the chief subject of the modern novel that we can scarcely quarrel with a novelist because the passion she chooses to describe is of a very intense kind. We all know that love is neither a smooth-going nor a strictly decorous and prudential affair, and there are many emotions in female breasts, even when the sufferer is judged by her acquaintance to be an ordinary sort of person, which would shock friends and critics if put down in black and white. But there is a kind of love-making which seems to possess a strange fascination for the modern female novelist. Currer Bell and George Eliot, and we may add George Sand, all like to dwell on love as a strange overmastering force which, through the senses, captivates and enthrals the soul. They linger on the description of the physical sensations that accompany the meeting of hearts in love. Curiously, too, they all like to describe these sensations as they conceive them to exist in men. We are bound to say that their conceptions are true and adequate. But we are not sure that it is quite consistent with feminine delicacy to lay so much stress on the bodily feelings of the other sex. No one could be less open to the charge of thinking lightly of purity than George Eliot. She proclaims in every page the infinite gain of virtue. In her new novel she has set herself to describe the triumph of principle over feeling, as in *Adam Bede* she described the dreadful results of giving feeling the victory. But she lets her fancy run on things which are not wrong, but are better omitted from the scope of female meditation. The heroine, for example, is in love with a man who passionately loves her, but as each is pre-engaged, they are separated by duty and honour. All goes on very well until one day the lover, when alone with the heroine, takes to watching her arm. Its beauties are minutely described, as well as the effect gradually produced on him. At last, in a transport of passion, he rushes forward, seizes on the lovely arm, and covers it with kisses. There is nothing wrong in writing about such an act, and it is the sort of thing that does sometimes happen in real life; but we cannot think that the conflict of sensation and principle raised in a man's mind by gazing at a woman's arm is a theme that a female novelist can touch on without leaving behind a feeling of hesitation, if not repulsion, in the reader. In points like these, it may be observed that men are more delicate than women. There are very few men who would not shrink from putting into words what they might imagine to be the physical effects of love in a woman. Perhaps we may go further, and say that the whole delineation of passionate love, as painted by modern female novelists, is open to very serious criticism. There are emotions over which we ought to throw a veil; and no one can say that, in order to portray an ardent and tender love, it is necessary to describe the conquest of a beautiful arm over honour and principle. As it seems to us, the defect of the *Mill on the Floss* is that there is too much that is painful in it. And the authoress is so far led away by her reflections on moral problems and her interest in the phases of triumphant passion, that she sacrifices her story. We have such entire changes of circumstances, and the characters are exhibited under such totally different conditions of age and mental development, that we get to care nothing for them. The third volume seems to belong to quite a new story. The Dodsons have faded away, and the young woman with the overmastering passion is very slightly connected with the little Maggie of the Mill who makes her appearance at the beginning of the novel. As in *Adam Bede*, the interest fades off towards the end; and we are not sorry when the tremendous machinery of a flood is called in to drown off two of the principal characters. We hope that some time George Eliot will give us a tale less painful and less discursive. There is something in the world and in the quiet walks of English lower life besides fierce mental struggles and wild love. We do not see why we should not be treated to a story that would do justice to George Eliot's powers, and yet form a pleasing and consistent whole.

14. Sir Edward Bulwer-Lytton to John Blackwood

14 April 1860

MS: National Library of Scotland. Extracts published in *The George Eliot Letters*, iii, 314–15, 317, and in *The Mill on the Floss*, ed. Gordon S. Haight, Boston, 1961, pp. x, xv.
The first Baron Lytton (1803–73) was secretary for the colonies in 1858–9 and a prolific novelist, the author of *Pelham* (1828), *Eugene Aram* (1832), *The Last Days of Pompeii* (1834), *Ernest Maltravers* (1837), *The Last of the Barons* (1843), etc. His aesthetic premises, as this letter indicates, were very different from George Eliot's. See her reply (No. 15) and Introduction, p. 14.

Knebworth. 14 April 1860

My dear Sir,

I have just finished *The Mill on the Floss*, and can assure you of my very high opinion of its many beauties. That rare and minute knowledge of the female heart which struck me so forcibly in *Adam Bede* is here brought out with more variety, and in more richness of humour. All the Dodson Sisters are wonderful. I feel it a great relief to get rid of the Provincial Dialect and the language of Dialogue in the rural characters is extremely natural without vulgarity and full of point and playfulness. The only criticism I should here make is that now and then there is a little unconscious imitation of Dickens; not more so perhaps than so fascinating and popular a genius as his would inevitably cause in persons writing somewhat after him and resorting to somewhat the same classes of Society for characters. Putting that aside the general style is admirable.

In the 1st volume as to construction and position I did not see a fault. Tom and Maggie as children are most beautifully drawn.

Towards the later part of the 2nd volume I began to fear that there might be the same fault, (as *I* think it) which I found in *Adam Bede*. Viz: the want of clear perception and close study of what I call 'position' in Narrative. There is position in Narrative as well as Drama, and it can never be neglected without more or less injury to the story. In fact, it comprises much of what the ancient critics meant by 'the Becoming.' No character should be placed in a position that does not become the conceptions already formed of that character, and it is vain to reply that there is no violation of his Natural in such a position. The Natural that belongs to the Individual Character *is* violated. There is nothing for instance of the 'unbecoming' or 'false position' in the beating of Thersites; it becomes him to be beaten. But if Achilles had thrashed Agamemnon for taking away Briseis,[1] it might be quite natural in Achilles to do so but it would have been 'unbecoming' so far as Agamemnon was concerned, and it would have been difficult afterwards to respect him as the King of Men.

Now when Tom and Maggie go to meet Philip, Maggie is put into a false position as regards the previous description of her hasty generous impulsive character to stand by and listen with so little interruption to her brother's coarse abuse of Philip and her natural fear must have been first [sic] that Philip should think she had brought Tom there, and it was a sort of treachery; and her irresistible impulse must have been to burst out with passionate sympathy for Philip. She is brought there, as it is, for no sufficient cause in the plot—merely to witness her lover's humiliation—and the situation is untrue to the courage of her character. Hence she loses somewhat in interest after that scene.

But this is unimportant compared to the error, as I think, of the whole position towards Stephen. It may be quite natural that she should take that liking to him, but it is a position at variance with all that had before been Heroic about her. The *indulgence* of such a sentiment for the affianced of a friend under whose roof she was, was a treachery and a meanness according to the Ethics of Art, and nothing can afterwards lift the character into the same hold on us. The refusal to marry Stephen fails to do so.

This brings me to another view of a fault in the same direction. In studying plot or incident, this very remarkable writer does not enough weigh what is Agreeable or Disagreeable. Now the Disagreeable should be carefully avoided. You may have the painful, the terrible, the horrible, even; but the *disagreeable* should be shunned. For instance: It is a disagreeable and unworthy position for Philip to treat so lightly *the blows his father had received from the father of the woman he wants to marry*, and Philip sinks in dignity on account of it. Lastly: The Tragic should

[1] Daughter of Briseus and the cause of the feud between the two heroes.

be prepared for and seem to come step by step as if unavoidable. But that is not the case here.

One feels from the time that Maggie's father *dies* in consequence of his meeting with Philip's father, that the end cannot be happy, but the steps that lead towards an end so gloomy are not sufficiently marked and solemn, and when the Drowning comes at last, it fails accordingly in the pathos and terror it would otherwise excite; and there has not been even sufficient care taken to make that final reconciliation in death of brother and sister as touching as it should be. Tom indeed has been by that time set so far apart from his sister, that he can't be jerked back into the old boyish love of a sudden, and we don't see why he should be drowned at all.

These are to my mind defects that belong to the same class of defects as those in *Adam Bede*, but they are not so marked, and those defects did not prevent or even injure the great popularity of *Adam Bede*. Neither will they, in this case; I even doubt whether they will be visible to most readers. Where such defects really tell, (even supposing I am right which I may not be) is 10 or 20 years hence in the *duration* of a work. They scarcely touch its first sale or the author's immediate reputation. I have been thus lengthy in dwelling on faults, real or supposed, because I measure the author by a very high standard. I know no female author with such grasp of character, such deep cuts into secret recesses of the heart, such ease and power of language, such charming combination of unaffected pathos and delicate, affluent humour. And on the whole I like the Book even better than *Adam Bede* which is indeed saying a great deal.

E.B.L.

15. George Eliot to John Blackwood

9 July 1860

The George Eliot Letters, iii, 317–18. John Blackwood had for-warded Bulwer-Lytton's letter (No. 14) on 4 July 1860. He assumes she will disagree with the criticism of her novel, but he considers the letter 'a very good one and gratifying, as the tone of consideration in which the *big fellow* writes shows how thoroughly he feels that he is speaking about another very *big fellow*' (*Letters*, iii, 315).

Holly Lodge. July 9. 60.

My dear Sir

I return Sir Edward's critical letter, which I have read with much interest. On two points I recognize the justice of his criticism. First, that Maggie is made to appear too passive in the scene of quarrel in the Red Deeps. If my book were still in MS, I should—now that the defect is suggested to me—alter, or rather expand that scene. Secondly, that the tragedy is not adequately prepared. This is a defect which I felt even while writing the third volume, and have felt ever since the MS. left me. The '*epische Breite*'[1] into which I was beguiled by love of my subject in the two first volumes, caused a want of proportionate fullness in the treatment of the third, which I shall always regret.

The other chief point of criticism—Maggie's position towards Stephen—is too vital a part of my whole conception and purpose for me to be converted to the condemnation of it. If I am wrong there—if I did not really know what my heroine would feel and do under the circumstances in which I deliberately placed her, I ought not to have written this book at all, but quite a different book, if any. If the ethics of art do not admit the truthful presentation of a character essentially noble but liable to great error—error that is anguish to its own noble-ness—*then*, it seems to me, the ethics of art are too narrow, and must be widened to correspond with a widening psychology.

---

[1] Epic breadth.

But it is good for me to know how my tendencies as a writer clash with the conclusions of a highly accomplished mind, that I may be warned into examining well whether my discordancy with those conclusions may not arise rather from an idiosyncrasy of mine, than from a conviction which is argumentatively justifiable.

I hope you will thank Sir Edward on my behalf for the trouble he has taken to put his criticism into a form specific enough to be useful. I feel his taking such trouble to be at once a tribute and a kindness. If printed criticisms were usually written with only half the same warrant of knowledge, and with an equal sincerity of intention, I should read them without fear of fruitless annoyance. I remain, my dear Sir,

Always yours truly
Marian Evans Lewes.

16. Unsigned review, *Guardian*

25 April 1860, pp. 377–8

See Introduction, pp. 15–16.

The impressions of a reader of this book will probably vary in the progress of his reading. At first, the feeling will possibly be one of disappointment. With a full recognition of the keen observation and consummate exhibition of character, displayed in bringing out in living distinctness a set of well-to-do persons of the retired tradesman or higher farmer class, and their peculiar ideas about the duties and claims of relationship, there comes also the doubt whether all this was worth the painting, especially as they are all of them more or less disagreeable —persons whom we only like to read about, if we have the accompanying consciousness that we have nothing to do with any like them. But as the chapters go on, we begin to see that there is something more in view than a mere introduction to the domestic life, contrasts, and

bickerings at Dorlcote Mill and Garum Firs. Greater interests—
misfortune, disappointment, the sickness that lays low the ruined
strong man, mingle with the details, still most completely and powerfully painted, of every-day life, shed their awful lights on what is weak
and commonplace, give a touching interest to the distresses of trivial
minds unable to rise to the height of their sorrow, and bring out in
various new aspects the people whom we have only known in frugal
and monotonous prosperity. We begin to feel the vigour of the narrator: we begin to feel that we have not been tempted, by the fame of
Adam Bede, to what is but a mere curious and genial study of the still
life, which goes on in the comfortable homes of the substantial population of the provinces. If we are a little disappointed that we have met
with no one to delight in like Mrs. Poyser, we cannot help being
sensible of a great variety of persons, quite new, and yet very familiar
to us, with the most distinct marks of individuality in everything they
say and do, whose action on one another's happiness and characters
is followed out into all its complications, and all its results, touching
and sad, as well as grotesquely comic. The story gains upon us in
interest, not so much with reference as to what it is to end in, but
because of the interweaving of the tragic elements, of human vicissi-
tudes, and human ways of behaving under them, with what so undeni-
ably belongs to the most homespun and unimaginative forms of English
life. But we read on, and a remarkable change meets us. We have
entered on entirely different scenery. We have left behind us the quiet
country stream in its summer softness, or dull wintry chilliness, with
its dipping willows and rumbling mill-wheel, and the modest and tidy
and rather lifeless square houses beside it: and we are in a wide open
estuary, with a wild sea rising and a lowering sky, broken by passing
gleams and bursts of glorious sunset light, but with night coming on,
and the dim and mysterious horizon of tossing water before us, and
lines of white breakers not far off. We pass from the petty collisions
and narrow thoughts of most ordinary farmers and tradesmen,
delicately described, with an intense zest and humour in the process, to
scenes where our interest is concentrated on struggles and conflicts
of passion, faith and right, analysed with a glance which nothing
escapes, and described with unsurpassed and terrible power. We pass
from what amuses us with the oddities of life, and delights us still
more by the skill which reproduces them so faithfully, to what awes us
with a glimpse into the deepest questions, and the most tremendous
realities of life, questions and realities about our temptations, our sins,

and our destiny. With whatever reserves we may have to make, both as to the conduct and the substance of the story, our impulse at this concluding stage of it is to say that it is one of the grandest and most subduing, as it is one of the boldest pictures ever attempted, of the way in which the soul makes trials for itself, and of the unexplored depths of weakness and of strength, which temptation, as it becomes more intense and decisive, brings to light.

Perhaps cooler reflection may modify this judgment. The truth is, that any one who respects himself and the exact reality of his own judgments, will in most cases hesitate a good deal to pronounce from a first reading an ultimate verdict on a work in which undeniable imaginative power takes new and very mixed shapes. It is easy to put on a self-deceiving, perhaps an inwardly disavowed, confidence in criticising. But to speak honestly, some time must elapse before we could be certain of what we really thought of a story like this. We naturally compare it with *Adam Bede*. There is less than in *Adam Bede* to attract us towards any of the characters; there is more of unrelieved and uncompensated painfulness in the course and end of the story. And say what we will, manifest power and much accompanying beauty will not reconcile most of us to the continued strain on our feelings, when tragedy is represented, not among heroes whose loftiness seems to make them fit for it, but among ordinary people of our own mould and time. It is too near the truth which we are familiar with to be agreeable even in fiction. But apart from this, the new story will fully stand comparison with the former one. There is less concentration of power in the latter one than there is on those two or three types of character to which *Adam Bede* has given a permanent and familiar existence among us. But there is greater copiousness and variety in the persons introduced, greater freedom in the treatment, greater confidence in the effect of what seems casual and accidental in conveying the image clearly, less apparent elaboration and effort in impressing it on our minds, greater boldness and versatility in the play and contrast of the characters. The story, of course, has its hero and heroine, but neither they nor any one else take up a disproportionate share of our attention, from the combined result of the action and influence of all. We are struck, not merely by the brilliant handling of one or two pieces in the game, but by the diffused power over all, of however unequal value and different nature, and over all the board. There is the same deep and subtle insight into the strange secrets of living character; the same recognition if not reconciliation of its seeming contradictions; the same unsatisfied and outspoken and yet elastic and unperturbed searchings out of the perplexities of human life; the same apt and ready and tell-tale dialogue, letting us learn for ourselves, and yet making us welcome explanation and description when they come; the same cunning knowledge of the effects of a touch of familiar home-liness or of an allusion to more recondite learning; the same quaint half-smile, and sly taking for granted of the reader's thoughts, and effecting a communication of sentiment between his greater shrewdness and the narrator's humbler and more simple views of things; the same profound irony without a shade—or with only a doubtful one—of bitterness. In another point, too, we are reminded of *Adam Bede*. The authoress is like a painter or a musician who gets tired after the great effort of his work. She does not know how to bring her story to a natural end. When once the point is past to which the whole has been tending, and in which all her strength and intensity have been put forth, she does not care much what becomes of her people. She marries them, or she drowns them, it does not much matter which. But there is an exhaustion, a dim and unfinished appearance, about her last chapters, which contrasts more than it ought to do with the vehemence and vividness to which her penultimate ones have gradually mounted up.

The story is one of the development of character, from childhood to the spring of life; and the principal influence, which is represented as acting on it from without, is that of kindred. Maggie Tulliver grows up—from a raw untaught girl, full of fire, enthusiastic, impulsive, yearning for sympathy and love, liable to great mistakes, and capable of great reparations, into the dark tall queenly beauty, early called to meet fierce temptation—the centre of a crowd of relations, of the most varied natures, all playing full on her growing character, but all more or less antagonistic to her own, and by whose very different influences combined, she is thrown on herself, to find her own way in the world, and frame her own law of life. We are for a moment reminded of the real girlhood of Charlotte Brontë and her sisters in their uncongenial home. In the social machinery employed there is something which recalls Galt's novel of the *Entail*. The same class furnishes the charac-ters: the Lairds of Grippy, with their cares divided, and their ideas moulded, as well by the counters and warehouses of Glasgow as by the still more congenial ancestral fields, are the Scotch representatives of the Tullivers and Dodsons, the Gleggs and Pullets and Deanes, the respectable and self-respecting farmer families, who appear as millers and small squires in the neighbourhood of the mercantile Lincolnshire town of St. Ogg's; or as traders, retired or active ones, from its wharves and shops. And, as in the *Entail*, there is the same close and minute following out of the action and reaction of the various members of a kindred; the same exhibition of their homely and not always very attractive relations to one another; and in both stories they speak in the same idiomatic dialect, and with the same naked plainness, whether of vigorous sense or coarse self-assertion or unconscious triviality. With a hard, energetic, but not ungenerous or unaffectionate father, very litigious, very full of perplexity at the success of 'raskills,' and hating and admiring at once the lawyer's art of 'wrapping things up in a lot of unreasonable words as arn't a bit like them,' and of being able 'to let a man know what you think of him without paying for it'— with a weak, soft mother, blond, dull, and proud of being a Dodson, whom her father married because she was not clever;—Maggie's living hopes and love are centred on her brother Tom—in boyhood as in youth, when misfortune, and success arising out of misfortune stoutly and manfully encountered, had annealed him, a stern lover of right so far as he could see it, but self-confiding, narrow, inexorable, and inconsiderate, not inclined to spare himself, but still less forgiving to others, whose difficulties he could not or would not take the trouble to understand. Sister and brother grow up, the sister clinging to the brother, and hungering after love and interest from him, tormented and provoked but not repelled by his harsh justice or stinging disregard; the brother, claiming a right of influence over her, attached to her more than he is aware of, yet outwardly caring for her most as his father's daughter—but necessarily, in the end, without either of them quite realising it, shaking off the allegiance which it was her dream in life to give him, and leaving her to walk alone. Other even less congenial relations do their part in snubbing and keeping down Maggie's soaring and passionate spirit. Heavy misfortunes, brought on by her father's obstinate love of lawsuits, darken the world to her, and develop, in still more unamiable lights, the various qualities of those with whom she is connected. She seeks, and for a time finds, relief in self-renunciation, in the thoughts awakened by the *Imitation of Christ*, in the soothing melodies of the *Christian Year*. But this is broken in upon. She comes across an old childish acquaintance, a schoolfellow of her brother's, but also the son of the lawyer to whom her father ascribes his ruin, and against whom he has written a vow of revenge, and made his son also sign it, in the family Bible. In Philip Wakem she finds something of what she wanted to find in her brother—something, but not all; he is accomplished and full of worth; he does not conceal his love for her, but he is deformed and painfully sensitive of his deformity, and her feelings towards him are for a long time simply those of pity and interest in his conversation. But their acquaintance, in spite of great impediments, ripens at last into an engagement. But now comes her trial. She goes to stay with her cousin Lucy, and there meets her cousin's accepted lover, Stephen Guest. Stephen is fascinated by Maggie's loftier beauty; and she, by degrees, yields to the force of a different feeling towards him than she ever felt towards Philip. The struggle, on both sides, against the force of passion, and the shame of double treachery, the rises and falls, the almost escapes, and the fatal accidents which again open the door to temptation, are painted with the most powerful and most unpitying truth. Except the one element of overwhelming fascination, not a word is urged in palliation. It ends in their drifting—literally on the current of the Floss, as well as metaphorically, into a flight together. Then at the last moment, when the disgrace of the elopement was irretrievable, when worldly prudence as well as the temptation itself combined to urge the one step further into the wrong, her strength awakens and returns. Before she is lost, her eyes are opened; she leaves Stephen, and comes back to face the inevitable shame in the place where she is known, and where every house, faster than all her brother Tom's, is closed against her. This is the leading feature of the book: the wonderful skill with which such a conflict, and then such a reaction of moral strength in the very jaws of destruction, is made not only endurable, but in the last degree solemn and affecting. It hardly adds to the deep tragedy of the book, after the first keen trials are described, brought on her deservedly, yet as much by her final victory over evil, as by her long dallying on its edge, that she perishes in a flood on the river, with her brother, whom she had attempted to save.

Two faults strike us at once in this remarkable work. One is of structure. Nobody who reads it can, we should think, avoid the feeling that in the last volume he passes into a new book. There is a clear dislocation in the story, between Maggie's girlhood and Maggie's great temptation. It is perfectly true that it may be the same in real life. There was very likely a tranquil childhood previous to deeds or sufferings which have made the world ring. The commonplace trivialities and unmeaning events of life go on in their most unexciting course to the very eve and verge of the frightful catastrophe—the sudden death, the downfall of prosperity, the hopeless wreck of character and hope. But the actual course of human things is not necessarily the pattern for a work of art. A poem or a novel calls forth a certain group of feelings which seem to become its appropriate atmosphere; we read *Winter's Tale*, or the *Tempest* in a different attitude of mind, with different associations of ideas, with different expectations as to the strings which are to be touched within us, from those with which we read *Hamlet* or *Othello*. We do not expect, and it is hardly pleasant, to be called in the same work from one set of thoughts, and, still more, one set of feelings, to another; to have them suddenly strained and screwed up; so that we hardly realise the scenes we were among a few chapters back. Nor is this incongruity avoided by the early interspersing of auguries and warnings of coming fate, which a second reading discovers, but which, if they were not passed unheeded, were certainly ineffectual in preparing us for what was to come, and for harmonising the two portions of the story.

Our other objection is a different one. Passion is one of the legitimate materials of the novelist. But he incurs deep responsibility by the way in which he treats it. And we cannot think that he does good service by bringing into clear and powerful light its perverted and unwholesome growths; by making seem probable a development of it which, on the data given us, is an improbable one. It goes against our sense of likelihood that Maggie, being what she is represented, could have been so fascinated by Stephen; certainly nothing is shown us in Stephen, except his own admiration for her, to account for it; and again, we must say that it is most improbable that if Maggie had strength to break her chain at the last and most difficult moment, she should not have had strength to break it before. Moral improbabilities are not atoned for by the power which softens them down and disguises them. But, however this be, the picture of passion gradually stealing like a frightful and incurable poison over not merely principle and self-respect, but even over the faith and honour to the unsuspecting and confiding which the very opinion of the world helps us to hold sacred—of the 'limed soul which, struggling to be free, is more engaged,' is one which had better never have been set before us with so much plainness. We will say at once that the writer never for an instant loses sight of the sin and the shame which she is describing. There may be a passage here and there which show how dangerous the subject is to meddle with. But there is nothing but warning in the result; the loss and the brave penitence, the incurable wound and the generous and humble acceptance of necessary chastisement, are more moving than many sermons. But fully allowing all this, we still hold that there are temptations which it is of itself a temptation to scrutinise too closely; conflicts in the conscience, which it only hardens us to contemplate, much more to do so in our idle hours—wrong doing and wrong feeling, which we are safer and happier in knowing only at a distance—

Non raggioniam di lor, ma guarda e passa.[1]

And in this story, the boldness and power with which ultimate victory and recovery are held up before us are, practically, not a compensation for the equal power and boldness with which, secure of the final triumph of good, the writer has displayed in all its strength the force of evil, changing itself into ever new shapes, penetrating into the most unexpected recesses of the heart, starting up afresh after it seemed conquered, and sweeping two helpless souls before it, like an irresistible fate, up to the last and most improbable moment of rescue.

17. E. S. Dallas, unsigned review, *The Times*

19 May 1860, pp. 10–11

For Dallas see headnote to No. 8; for George Eliot's reaction to this review see No. 18.

'George Eliot' is as great as ever. She has produced a second novel, equal to her first in power, although not in interest. As far as interest is concerned, indeed, it would have been exceedingly difficult to repeat the triumph of *Adam Bede*, in which the author contrived to paint the lily and to gild refined gold by adding the charm of a delightful philosophy to the pleasure of a good story. The reader will at once remember that he could not help liking all the characters in that history. The

[1] Virgil's advice to Dante: 'Let us not speak of them, but look and pass by' (*Inferno*, iii, 51).

general influence of the book was to reconcile us to human nature, to make us think better of our fellow men, to make us feel that in the weakest there is something to be admired, in the worst something to be loved, to draw us nearer to each other by showing how completely we are one, and so to give us not only the temporary delight of listening to a pleasant tale, but also the permanent good of an increased sympathy with our kind. It was comparatively easy to excite our interest in the doings of persons towards whom we were led to entertain such friendly feelings. We treasured all their sayings, we watched eagerly all their movements, we were curious as to all their thoughts. The author, apparently afraid of repeating herself, and determined to avoid the imputation of representing the world as too good and sugary, now introduces us to a very different set of personages. A majority of the characters brought together in these three volumes are unpleasant companions—prosaic, selfish, nasty. We are launched into a world of pride, vain-glory, and hypocrisy, envy, hatred and malice, and all uncharitableness. Everybody is quarrelling with everybody in a small mean way; and we have the petty gossip and malignant slander of village worthies painted to the life. These are not promising materials, but the authoress has impressed her genius on them, and, relying on her marvellous powers of delineation, has felt that by the mere force of truth she could command our attention and compel applause. We doubt, indeed, whether Miss Lydia Languish[1] will care much for this novel, and we are almost afraid to dwell on the nature of the theme which 'George Eliot' has chosen, lest the timid reader should be repulsed, and we should suggest an allusion to the supposed impossibility of making a silk purse out of a sow's ear. As to the fact that here we have the silk purse there can be no mistake, but it would require the genius of 'George Eliot' to describe by what magic it is produced out of materials that appear to be singularly barren of silk.

We can only indicate what lies on the surface, and we must attribute a great part of 'George Eliot's' triumph to the charm of her style. She plays with her subject; there is no appearance of effort; even when she is most serious she is half sportive; even when she has reached her climaxes she is entirely at her ease. This pervading humour is very pleasant, and takes the reader unawares. It does not much matter what is the subject with which such a mind as 'George Eliot's' plays; the result is sure to be amusing. One of our poets has declared, that in the meanest flowers he found thoughts that were too deep for tears; he

[1] The romantic heroine of Sheridan's play *The Rivals* (1775).

might have added, too deep for anybody to care about them. It is not every topic that spontaneously yields the elements of tears and tragedy. The elements of comedy are much more universal, and 'George Eliot' manages to make us smile through her novel, and to be tickled by incongruities that in less skilful hands would be as thorns and briars to vex the reader. In the three volumes there is not a dull page. The style is singularly apt and rich, and its felicities are not the result of tricks. Onward it flows and bears us along with a resistless force, and before we can get tired of the sometimes prosy interlocutors of the drama, the author steps in and rouses our attention with a wise remark or a pleasant reflection that shows the wideness of her reading, the closeness of her observation, and the maturity of her thought. It seems, too, not less easy for her to make her characters speak than to speak herself. As if her descriptions were not vivid enough, she prefers to make her characters speak for themselves, and the dialogue is sustained with marvellous ability—the slightest shades of difference between the personages being rendered with great subtlety. This is remarkably displayed in the representation of the odious Dodson family, in which the family likeness is strictly preserved, while the individual traits are not lost. Relying on her imitative power in this respect, and on the fascination which a truthful picture exerts over every mind, 'George Eliot' has invited our attention to the hard realities of a life in which none but a true genius could find the elements of a successful novel.

The two leading characteristics of almost all the personages to whom we are introduced are honesty and pugnacity, and these flow from one and the same source. A strong character, such as is here described, that feels its own strength, delights in it, and is proud of it—is honest, because dishonesty is a weakness, not because it is an injury to others. The Dodson family are stingy, selfish wretches, who give no sympathy and require none, who would let a neighbour starve, and let a brother be bankrupt when a very little assistance would save him from the disgrace; but they would not touch a penny that is not theirs, there is no legal obligation which they would not discharge, they would scorn the approach of a lie. They would be truthful and honest, not as a social duty, but as a personal pride—because nobody should have it in his or her power to say that they were weak enough to neglect a manifest obligation. From the same source of self-satisfied strength comes pugnacity in all its forms of rivalry and contradiction, jealousies and criticisms, lawsuits, and slanders, and blows. Everybody in this tale is repelling everybody, and life is in the strictest sense a battle. Even the good angel of the story, that little Maggie, who is full of affection, and whose affection is continually leading her into blunders and misfortunes, is first of all introduced to us while she is indulging an unnatural ferocity towards her doll, whose head she is punching—driving a nail into it as Jael drove one into the temples of Sisera.[1] Her brother Tom, who is the next important personage in the little community, is chiefly remarkable for self-assertion and hard-headed resistance of fate—his strong wrestling with adversity, and his anxiety to punish the slightest offence. Her father, Mr. Tulliver, is the incarnation of pugnacity. Her uncles and aunts are nothing if not critical, and after bickering among themselves for days together, and crowing over each other in the pride of imaginary conquest, look out upon their little parish with somewhat of the dissatisfaction which made the most renowned of victors lament that there were no more worlds to conquer. Two of the most remarkable scenes in the book are quite characteristic.

[describes the registering of the curse in the Tulliver family Bible and the death of Mr Tulliver]

This life of proud self-assertion that on the bad side presents itself in an incessant bickering, and on the best side appears as a devotion to justice and truth for selfish ends, may become interesting by being made heroic. The Brontës—both Charlotte and Emily—were fond of depicting this character, and by their account, by the account of Mrs. Gaskell, and by that of 'George Eliot,' it is a character that abounds in the northern counties. But when Charlotte or Emily Brontë dealt with such a nature, they ennobled or, at least, magnified it. In their pages we looked on men essentially selfish and unsociable—men encased in armour of proof against all encroachment—men who wronged nobody and who vowed that nobody should wrong them. But the selfish isolation of such characters was lit up with passion, was justified or expiated by long suffering from some overwhelming wrong, was idealized by being joined to the possession of great intellectual powers. 'George Eliot' has attempted a more difficult task. She takes these characters as we find them in real life—in all their intrinsic littleness. She paints them as she finds them—snapping at each other over the tea-table; eyeing each other enviously at church; privately plotting how to astonish each other by some extraordinary display; putting the worst construction on every word and act; officiously proffering advice

[1] *Judges*, iv, 21.

and predicting calamity; living with perfect content their sordid life of vulgar respectability. The first half of the novel is devoted to the exhibition of this degraded species of existence, which is dissected with a masterly hand. Although it is the least exciting part of the work, it is the part of which the reader will carry away the most vivid recollection. The Dodson family will live for ever, and they inspire the work. With a self-denial which we cannot but admire, the author has resolutely set herself the task of delineating, without exaggeration, without extenuation, with minute accuracy, the sort of life which thousands upon thousands of our countrymen lead—a life that outwardly is most respectable, but inherently is most degraded—so degraded, indeed, that the very virtues which adorn it are scarcely to be distinguished from vices. We may be told that honesty is always honesty, and that if people arrive at true results we should not investigate too curiously their devious roads and their stumbling gait in travelling to the desired end. That is the practical philosophy of society, but now and then it is well that motives should be tested, and that we should see how much nearer than the Pharisee the publican and the sinner are to the kingdom of Heaven—how easily treachery may lurk in a kiss, and how naturally honesty may be as mean and detestable as a lie.

When 'George Eliot' got exactly half through her work she foresaw the criticisms which a novel based on such a foundation would certainly provoke, and she commenced her fourth book . . . by uttering against her story all that the most savage critic can have it in his heart to say.

[summarizes the opening of book four]

Without attending to the clue thus furnished by the author, her object will be overlooked and full justice will not be done to her work. We must point out, however, that the object which the author has set herself of painting in all its nakedness, hideousness, and littleness the life of respectable brutishness which so many persons lead, illumined by not one ray of spiritual influence, by no suspicion of a higher life, of another world, of a surrounding divinity,—lifts the present work out of the category of ordinary novels. The author is attempting not merely to amuse us as a novelist, but, as a preacher, to make us think and feel. The riddle of life as it is here expounded is more like a Greek tragedy than a modern novel. In form we have the modern novel, with its every-day incidents and its humorous descriptions, but in spirit we have the Greek play with its mysterious allusions and its

serious import. In the highest sense we might call this a religious novel,
only that description is liable to be misunderstood, and especially as
religion is chiefly 'conspicuous by its absence.' We read on, wondering
what is the meaning of the story, wondering why these mean, prosaic
people, the Dodsons ever live; wondering why a brilliant novelist asks
us to make their acquaintance and to become interested in their paltry
existence, when suddenly the author breaks in upon us with the
criticism to which we have already referred, and which we have partly
quoted. She says in effect:—'You, reader, are oppressed by all this
meanness—disgusted at all this hardness—perplexed that I should think
it worthy of your notice. I perfectly agree with you; but such is life,
and it is in the midst of such a life, the most marked quality of which is
the utter absence of poetry or religion, that many of us grow up—it
was in the midst of such a desert that my little heroine, Maggie,
bloomed into beauty. It is well that these things should be impressed
upon us, and that we should lay them to heart.'

In fulfilling this portion of her task, which occupies exactly the first
half of the novel, the author has very cleverly helped herself out of a
difficulty. It is difficult to describe adults leading a purely bestial life
of vulgar respectability without rendering the picture simply repulsive.
But the life of children is essentially an animal life—a life, therefore,
that to a certain extent accords with the brutish habits of maturer
personages; with this great difference, however,—that what is repulsive
in the mature is amusing in the young. We do not expect boys and girls
to have a strong sense of invisible things,—to be very spiritual in their
aims—to make any striking display of poetry, sentiment, or religion.
We wink at their enormities in sweets, we laugh at their savage
tyrannies, and we take them for what they are—dear little animals,
and nothing more. 'George Eliot' relieves the repulsiveness of the insect
life which she has exhibited in the Dodson family by making her bigger
insects all revolve around these two little creatures, Maggie and Tom
Tulliver. Her description of the childlife is unique. No one has yet
ventured to paint the childlife in all its prosaic reality. It is true that we
have long since got out of the Mrs. Barbauld[1] and Miss Edgworth
groove, in which we had contrasted pictures of the good boy and the
bad boy, the girl who was lazy and the girl who was active. Then
succeeded more careful studies of the child nature, and we do not know
that in this respect the productions of Mr. Disraeli, both in *Venetia*,
where he gives the youth of Lord Byron, and in *Coningsby*, have ever

[1] Mrs Anna Letitia Barbauld (1743-1825), poet, essayist, and writer of children's books.

been surpassed. But in his writings and those of other novelists there is not a little of that poetical colouring which is natural to us in looking back on our childhood. 'George Eliot', in approaching the subject, determined, as best agreeing with the general scope of her novel, to paint reality; and she has pictured the boy and girl life with the most amusing fidelity. We see all the little squabbling and domineering that goes on among children; we see them disgracefully intent on raspberry tart; we see the boy, after he has eaten up his share, mysteriously survey-ing his sister's, and wondering whether she will spare him a bit; we see the pleasure which they take in first tickling a toad, and then smashing it with a stone; we see all the envies, and cruelties, and glut-tonies that in men would be revolting, but are only grotesque in these funny little animals.

[Maggie's history described at length]

But again we say that for the full appreciation of the present novel the object of it must not be forgotten; and that object is, to establish the contrast between a life of utter respectability and a life of stumbling and dubious, but still honest and noble, aspiration. Err as she may, sin as she may, the very faults of Maggie are more to be respected and loved than the hard consistency of her brother Tom and the Pharisaical rigidity of the Dodson family. One must not press the maxim too far, and we protest by anticipation against the novels that are sure to be written on the model of the present one, showing that it is a grand thing to lead a Bohemian life, and that respectability and the payment of one's debts is necessarily mean and uninteresting. In its own place, however, it contains a truth which ought to be attended to, and which a writer so sober as 'George Eliot' is not likely to overstrain.

18. George Eliot to William Blackwood

27 May 1860

The George Eliot Letters, iii, 299.

The *Times* article arrived on Sunday. It is written in a generous spirit, and with so high a degree of intelligence, that I am rather alarmed lest the misapprehensions it exhibits should be due to my defective presentation, rather than to any failure on the part of the critic. I have certainly fulfilled my intention very badly if I have made the Dodson honesty appear 'mean and uninteresting,' or made the payment of one's debts appear a contemptible virtue in comparison with any sort of 'Bohemian' qualities. So far as my own feeling and intention are concerned, no one class of persons or form of character is held up to reprobation or to exclusive admiration. Tom is painted with as much love and pity as Maggie, and I am so far from hating the Dodsons myself, that I am rather aghast to find them ticketed with such very ugly adjectives.

19. Unsigned review, *Westminster Review*

July 1860, lxxiv, 24–32

This critic begins by congratulating himself on being the first to guess the sex of the author of *Adam Bede*. He then contrasts George Eliot with Charlotte Brontë, a genius 'who pours forth her feelings . . . without premeditation'.

We do not think that *The Mill on the Floss* will increase the author's popularity, but it fully sustains her reputation. *Adam Bede* was far from structural perfection; but *The Mill on the Floss* is still more defective in this particular. Its development is languid and straggling beyond expression; it affects us like the spring in which it appeared with a weary longing and suspense that is too forcibly contrasted with the rapid movement of the conclusion of the story; the slow, placid, and somewhat turbid stream too suddenly changes to a rushing waterfall; the canal ends in a cascade: this destroys the harmonious impression that every work of art ought to leave upon our minds. It is in vain to reply that this is a true transcript of nature, that the gradual accumulation of moral motive often ends in a sudden breaking through barriers which appeared to be too firmly fixed to be moved. This defence might perhaps be set up if Maggie had been more decidedly the central figure of the early portion of the tale; but, being lost in the early crowd, she is too suddenly and exclusively brought forward in the latter scenes; she engrosses too much attention compared with the effect she produces in her youth. The moral unity of the book is disturbed by a too brilliant and purely local light.

Passion will no doubt thus burst through the routine of daily life, and break to pieces the rules on which that life reposes; but as a work of art, it is not enough to be merely true to nature, an external probability and an internal harmony must be arrived at; and although we are sufficiently well acquainted with Maggie's nature to realize the full force of the temptation to which she is exposed, we are not prepared for the qualified consent with which she yields to it. The greatest fault, however, is not that her conduct is insufficiently grounded in her character,

—for few will deny the careful preparation of the reader's mind for some such catastrophe,—so much as in the inordinate disproportion between the parts she plays at different periods of the story. It is not—far from it—that she is too insignificant to be made the supporter of that great struggle, but that the struggle itself is out of harmony, not with her, but with two-thirds of the tale itself. It is a very striking fact that the author compromises her heroine, but does not commit her to the breach of any of those positive social rules for which it is still evident she has but a small esteem. A man writing such a story would have made Maggie transgressing but loveable, would not have taken such care to be yet on the right side of rules declaimed against. We cannot help loving Maggie; indeed, she is almost the only loveable person in the tale; but there is something in the development of her mind that affects us painfully.

[summary of Maggie's history]

This history is very natural, but very sad. Why did she love Guest? we say. What was there about the man to attract her when there was so much to forbid her thinking of him?

George Eliot will no doubt say, why does any one love another? what reason can the lover give for his passion that will not seem absurd to him who asks for one? The influence exercised by the sexes over each other is quite incalculable, is determined by no rules, is what the Germans call *dæmonisch*, and beyond the sphere of reason. This is true enough in life, beneath whose surface we can penetrate to so small a depth, but in books we look for some indication of the affinities of choice; in this consists the distinction between art and nature, and on this point we think that George Eliot has sacrificed too much to her beloved realism. That realism, which is so triumphantly in place in all the prosaic relations of the Tullivers and Dodsons, seems here inadequate; we revolt at Maggie's weakness, and take up arms against the author in spite of a truth we cannot controvert.

Maggie is the representative, after all, of the poetical temperament, and stands out throughout the book a protest against the obscure and emmet-like lives of all who belong to her. When boors are to be painted, we rejoice in Jan Steen,[1] and recognise humanity though in most unlovely forms; the narrow-minded Gleggs, Pullets, and Tullivers, we accept with all their coarseness, but the shortcomings of those who

[1] Seventeenth-century Dutch painter.

long for and aspire after a better and higher life afflict us: we shrink from the failures of those we love, with a feeling too closely allied to pain to admit of our drawing any satisfaction from the truthfulness with which they are delineated.

As with Donnithorne so here with Stephen Guest, the hero escapes with but a qualified reprobation; his dishonourable abduction of Maggie is treated as the quite natural result of his passion for her; in George Eliot's eyes he is evidently not disgraced by conduct that would cause any honourable man to turn his back on him, conduct that cannot have left him a moment's peace of mind to enjoy that colourless marriage to which the author at last consigns him. The treatment of Stephen Guest is the result of that fascination which men exercise over women even when most intoxicated by them, and affords a cardinal test and patent demonstration, if it were still needed, of George Eliot's sex. On this topic, however, enough has perhaps been said. The separate beauties of the *Mill on the Floss* are numberless. You seem to be wandering down a long gallery filled with the masterpieces of Dutch cabinet paintings; it is true there is Rubens and his fires looming in the distance, but at present we have only to concern ourselves with the quiet beauty of the scenes before us. You can hardly stop before a single frame without finding food for the day's thought and feeling, and yet the pictures are so numerous that their minute beauties escape: the colour and tone are so uniform that we are a little weary; but how natural, how tender, how delicate are the subjects of these sweet domestic scenes, how faithful these half-boorish family quarrels. In all English literature there is nothing, in our opinion, so true and so affecting as the love of old Tulliver for his 'little wench,' his 'Magsie,' the only one in the family who could sympathize with that father in whose veins flowed the blood of an ancestor capable of ruining himself for a genial extravagance, blood so hostile to the prosaic, prudent Dodsons, who never did a foolish thing and hardly ever a wise one. The manner in which Maggie grows up, leaning on that somewhat lonely father, the mutual and yet inarticulate understanding which exists between them, is one of the finest conceptions anywhere to be met with, and as finely delineated as it is delicately conceived.

The beauty of the early pictures of mill life, the children among the pigeons, the chickens and the calves, have all the natural truth of Landseer's works without their somewhat affected prettiness. The quarrels between the children, their misunderstandings, and Maggie's ambition —the great ambition of girls—to be the associate of her brother's amusements, show a closeness of observation, a wonderful power of seizing on the most representative topics, and are given with a true homeliness of expression that will make many a mother's heart leap. These scenes are lovely, why should they end in all that ruin? We cannot reconcile ourselves to it; but the author is here our providence, and we must submit. When we first alight among these pastoral localities, we feel that there is a hostile influence in the air; we are soon oppressed by the overshadowing influence of indebtedness, and at last cower under the drenching storm of the lost lawsuit. It is impossible to deny the art with which everything is introduced, supported, and developed up to the time of Tulliver's death. We cannot help forming a theory, which is perhaps an indiscretion. It seems to us that up to this period in the tale, the author has drawn her materials from events and men that have passed under her immediate observation; there is a reality and local colour that we imagine to be otherwise unobtainable. At Tulliver's death the groundwork of fact disappears, and the problem of Maggie's nature alone occupies the author's attention. This has to be worked out in fictitious circumstances; at least, there is not that breath of truth and reality about the events of her stay with her cousin which we seem to inhale with the tale of Maggie's youth, as though the apple-blossoms and cowslips round the mill were in perpetual bloom.

What can be compared to the profoundly-studied and perfectly-executed picture of the whole group of Tullivers and Dodsons; indeed, the Dodsons are typical characters, full of the deepest significance to those who wisely read their history. These Christian pagans, narrow, contracted, ignorant, full of prejudice, and ready to anger, are yet governed by a code of traditionary morality, with a completeness that does not admit of their questioning anything that has been customary in their family, which has for generations been respectable, after their notions of respectability. They are a picture in little of nine-tenths of the world we live in: that overwhelming self-esteem which is so ridiculous when compared with the qualities on which they pride themselves, yet lies at the root of all the good qualities they possess. Self-esteem has not in vain been called by the 'wisest of mankind' the next thing to religion; indeed, with the Dodsons it completely usurps its place. As an effectual motive power it no doubt does so now in many quarters that would repel the accusation as the highest insult; but it is too often the real vital force which since the period of religious revivals has only been clothed by a set of religious expressions, without in any degree losing its predominating influence in the ultimate formation of character.

It is a profound touch of Nature and an instance of the insight of true genius which makes Mrs. Glegg, who had always declared that Maggie would come to no good, yet offer her a home when all the world had turned their backs upon her, on the ground that those who spoke ill of the Dodson blood had better be well advised before they brought their remarks to her door.

George Eliot, like Maggie, hungers and thirsts after a higher life, and cannot reconcile herself to these pitiful limitations. In her book, which, could she have confined herself to what she has seen and known, would have been homogeneous and *sui generis* in its unsurpassed and, we think, inimitable reproduction of Nature, she relinquishes the lofty calm of critical insight for a region of questions to which no complete answer can be given. All aspiration is subjective and consequently delusive; we seek in others what we desire to be ourselves, without sufficiently considering how far we have advanced and what chance we have of finding in others those qualities we so much desire, without reflecting that our imaginations will surely mislead us—that a day of sad awakening must arise when we shall have to mourn over the ruin of our dreams.

It is true those realist canons which have governed George Eliot in her early volumes are not forsaken in the last, but how sad the result. What can we think? Must so many Maggies die before the Dodson rules are a little enlarged? We are afraid that there is no consolation to be found, if this indeed is 'the fate of loveliness on earth.'

[gives examples of George Eliot's humour]

We have spoken of what we consider the defective moral grouping of the *Mill on the Floss*; it has also, in our opinion, defects in its external structure in the sequence of its events; the *dénouement* is altogether melodramatic; indeed, there is a tendency to and taste for startling events in George Eliot, which seems to crop out of the rich culture of her mind, like the primitive rocks of an earlier world. The flood in the mill, and the rescue of Hetty in *Adam Bede*, are instances of what we mean; they are vestiges of a Titanic time, before the reign of the peaceful gods commenced; devices condescended to as external escapes from moral difficulties, always to be deprecated, and we hope soon to be thrown aside by one so well able to dispense with every artifice as George Eliot.

We cannot like Tom Tulliver; as a boy he is natural, and his character is brought out with exquisite skill; he is as much a Dodson as a Tulliver can be, and has all the virtues of the Dodsons, on a somewhat higher lever of character; his manly endeavours to succour his father, the crowning triumph of that day, when chiefly from his savings all the creditors are paid, is the true glory of a Dodson; but after his father's death he retrogrades, he becomes preternaturally hard (it is true his vanity is wounded, and vanity is the most ruthless of our passions, for passion it often becomes); and he is unnaturally blind to his sister's love. His mercantile adventures with Bob Jakin will make many a City man smile, and wish they had so judicious a pedlar to regulate their investments. A money question is a trying one with George Eliot; the rate of profit of the most thriving young speculator; the morality, we mean business morality, of burning a bill of exchange from sentimental motives, and the general possibility of a man's saving out of thirty shillings a week, when he has a wife and child to support who have been brought up in comparative affluence, are all points in which her insight, because the area of experience, fails her. Bob is in our opinion the least successful of all the characters in the book. He approaches too near the farcical in his amusing interview with that female dragon Mrs. Glegg, and he is far from being the first who has entertained a dog-like love for a woman out of his reach.

Philip Wakem is a carefully drawn figure, but seems to us to lack vitality, though nothing can be finer than his recovery from the blow he sank under at Maggie's disappearance, his letter to her, or his conversation with his father when he declares his love. We have not thought it necessary to give an analysis of the plot; it is too well known by all who are likely to take up this Review; neither have we thought it desirable to give a collection of the quaint humorisms that abound in the two first volumes, or to make a catena of the profound and far-reaching remarks which abound throughout the book; this would neither be fair to the author nor agreeable to our readers. These beauties are for the most part so organic, that to withdraw them from their context would be to dislocate them from that vital nexus which gives them their highest charm. We have confined ourselves to a few words of welcome, and fewer still of warning, to one whose works will henceforth be looked forward to with an ardour of expectation that has had no equal for many years.

20. Unsigned review, *Dublin University Magazine*

February 1861, lvii, 192–200

This is the most hostile contemporary review of the novel. Rejecting entirely George Eliot's prosaic realism, it appeals to 'that highest realism' which discovers 'a wealth of ideal grace and music amid all the discords and deformities of life'. (See Introduction, pp. 13, 14.)

[Introductory comments on *Adam Bede*].

The *Mill on the Floss*, though perhaps less popular than *Adam Bede*, is, on the whole, an improved edition of its elder sister. Of course, it is built on the same faulty principles, and reproduces the same or very similar faults of detail. There is quite as much of the old wearisome twaddle, of the old photographic pettiness, mingled with a larger vein of sententious satire, and set off by a certain amount of picturesque animalism. Of unpleasant characters and superfluous scenes there is no lack. Perhaps, indeed, they abound more than ever. The greater part of the first volume is taken up with the early childhood of Tom and Maggie Tulliver, whose aunts and uncles could hardly be matched in real life, let alone fiction, for foolish notions and disagreeable ways. Mr. Riley is drawn for us in one chapter, with such tedious carefulness that we wonder the more at never seeing him again. Chapter after chapter paints the growth of a blind, earthy passion, strong enough to drown the most urgent calls of duty, honour, kind feeling—to sweep away the stoutest barriers of social decency and rational self-control. Mrs. Tulliver and her sister, Pullet, are less tolerable than Mrs. Poyser, or even Mrs. Bede. The religious flavour which helped the sale of *Adam Bede*, has been left out of its successor. Instead of Dinah Morris, with her mild sermons, saintlike speeches, and apostolic yearnings, we have only a quiet, ladylike, tender-hearted Lucy Deane. Dr. Kenn is rather a faded copy of Mr. Irwine. Still, after all deductions, we own to liking the new work better. It is more artistic, has more of sustained interest, than the other. In poor, weak, loving Maggie, the writer has given us a nobler heroine than Hetty of the rounded form and shrivelled heart. Both the Tullivers, father and son, are drawn with a firmer and bolder hand than either of the brothers Bede. Bob Jakin, farcical as he may be deemed by many, comes in as an agreeable relief to the darker aspects of the story, and keeps the last strands of our faith in human goodness from snapping in twain for ever. Philip Wakem is not badly outlined, although his latter years miss the promise of his boyhood. Instead of a downright seduction, the guilty courtship is allowed to end in Maggie's penitent refusal even to marry the selfish lover, who leaves her no choice between such a step and the scandal sure to assail her, innocent as she may be, on her return home. The interest, mild as it is throughout, keeps rising towards the close; and the catastrophe, if it were really inevitable, lacks none of that touching power and startling clearness which mark off the genuine artist from workmen of the stamp of Mr. Wilkie Collins.

The story itself is slight, spun out, and disappointing at the last.

[summary of the plot]

Here was matter for a good homely tale, in one volume, large or small. In the hands of Goldsmith, Fielding, or Miss Austen, such a conception would have been carried out gracefully and quietly, with no waste of words, no heaping-up of meaningless details. In the hands of George Eliot, it begins at the beginning of all things, and stops short at the end of her third volume. Could a fourth have been added, probably Maggie and Tom would have been allowed to survive the flood. As it is, we have three volumes, one of which is wholly superfluous, while the others might have been cut down one-half. When will modern novelists learn that the half is sometimes greater than the whole? Why should we go back to Maggie's earliest years to get an insight into what she afterwards becomes? At any rate, a few explanatory touches would surely have told us all we cared to know. The author of Lavinia[1] would have described as clearly in a few pages what this authoress spreads over a whole volume. We ask for meat, and she gives us pap—for a history, and she gives us sermons. Maggie's childish troubles, her impulsive ways, her April temperament—the private talk she holds with her wooden Fetish—her craving for the love of her stern, unsympathetic brother—Tom's alternate fondness and contempt for

[1] By G. D. Ruffini, 1860.

146

her—his boyish quarrel with Bob Jakin, because that youth would not toss him fair—his efforts after Latin and Euclid, under Mr. Stelling, are drawn with great truthfulness and some telling humour. But what, after all, was the use of provoking us to confess how strongly we are reminded of our childish pleasure in the works of Miss Edgeworth? Are we children, that a whole volume should be taken up, not only with scenes of child-life, but even with moral reflections on the same? If novelists will write about children, let them write for children only, or write books in which the story shall end with the heroine's descent from the nursery to the drawing-room. In novels, as in real life, manhood must have, at least, as many claims to our respect as childhood. Whatever else may be said of him, the author of *Tom Brown's Schooldays* showed much good sense in drawing the curtain on his hero at the moment of his entrance into college life. The general reader has lately been somewhat surfeited with childish stories, but it was left for George Eliot to give him childish lectures as well.

Let any one carefully read the first volume of her last work, and then ask himself for what conceivable purpose it was written. Mr. Tulliver takes a chapter to inform his wife of his intention to ask Riley about a school for his son, Tom. In another chapter Mr. Riley gives his opinion on the subject, and the author winds up with a long statement of his motives for the advice so given. Then we have two chapters of very small description, that read like a smartened version of *Frank*,[1] fitly capped by two paragraphs of sentiment that seems meant to pass off with the weaker brethren for new. Another chapter continues the history of Tom's and Maggie's childhood, relieved by an introductory sketch of the Dodson family, with whom in the next, we form a closer acquaintance round the dinner-table of Mrs. Tulliver. For those who like Dutch painting, and are curious about the habits of a class whose vanities and meannesses reflect their own, as it were, in a cracked and tarnished mirror, the account of this meeting will offer a charm unsurpassed in any other passage from the same author. Let us, too, give whatever praise may be justly due to a masterpiece of photographic realism little less humorous and far more truth-like than aught conceived by Mr. Dickens. If the painting a party of very stupid or very unpleasant people, without curtailing a word of the conversation or slurring the smallest trifle that any one present might have felt, seen, or done, be in itself a great achievement, the author's triumph is here complete. Only we should fancy that a truer artist would have dwelt

[1] *The Autobiography of Frank, the happiest little dog that ever lived* (1861), by A. M. Grey.

rather less fondly on Mrs. Pullet's wearisome twaddle, on Mrs. Glegg's eternal scoldings and squabbles with all about her, on Maggie's wretchedness after she has wilfully cut off her long shaggy hair. Then comes a long detailed account of Mrs. Tulliver's visit, with her children and niece, to her sister Mrs. Pullet, whose love of physic and tenderness about furniture are brought out with a tiresome faithfulness hardly improved by a varnish of funny writing about Mrs. Pullet's new bonnet or Tom's love for animals. In two more chapters, we are told of Maggie's revenge on Lucy for Tom's unkindness to herself, followed by her flight in quest of the gipsies, who only send her home again instead of making her their queen. Then follows a faithfully coarse, unpleasant, and wholly needless picture of Mr. and Mrs. Glegg quarrelling over the breakfast-table. Worse still than aught before, in its tiresome minuteness and pedantic trifling, is the long chapter devoted to Tom's 'first half' under the roof of Mr. and Mrs. Stelling. Here, if anywhere, the woman's hand is unmistakably shown, and the lack of true perspective becomes most palpable. A few lines would have said more than enough about Tom's broadchested tutor, and the failure of his system when tried on such a pupil. Nor was the writer expected to decide for us whether the brain be an intellectual stomach, a sheet of white paper, or a field awaiting the plough, any more than she was justified in making us hear Tom and Maggie blunder over the Latin lesson which Tom is saying aloud to his kind-hearted little helpmate. Nearly all the rest of this volume is taken up with further descriptions of Tom's school-life, his gradual intimacy with the new school-fellow, Philip Wakem, and the friendship formed by Maggie with the lawyer's pale-looking, deformed, but clever and fine-natured son.

In this way does the novel drag its heavy length along. Instead of a well-drawn, harmonious picture, we get a series of photographic studies, of which a good deal is provokingly commonplace, and a good deal more is tiresomely repellant. A life of pervading selfishness, ill-nature, stupidity, narrow culture, lit by stray and few gleams of high or holy feeling, is the poor result of this microscopic inquiry, this pretentious striving after truth. Even if this were art, is the writer of it, after all, true to her experience of mankind at large? For whose profit or entertainment does she work out effects so darkly displeasing with a brush so mercilessly fine? To give half views of life is the besetting sin of our modern realists, but here the worst side is kept turned to us of set purpose, without any of the saving pretences elsewhere offered. Mr. Thackeray, at least, is too good a workman to draw his characters mostly without a heart. But in these volumes there are few touches of that better nature which makes the whole world kin. In the first, especially, we escape from scenes of pure childishness only to breathe an air heavy with moral firedamp or intellectual fog. Throughout them all we grope our way amid broad shadows, relieved by a few flickering rays of cheap candle-light, and nothing more. In their moral effects, they seem to remind us of some faded old picture, bearing the name, but hardly sustaining the credit of Rembrandt or Salvator Rosa.[1] If George Eliot really finds human life, for the most part, as 'narrow, ugly, and grovelling' as she has drawn it here, we neither envy her experiences nor care to see them detailed in print. Other, larger eyes than hers have usually traced out a very different kind of doctrine; and even if the mass of men had no more to recommend them than the Tullivers and Dodsons, through whose lives she cooly bid us wade, there would still remain the fact, that neither human art nor human morals can be refined or ennobled by examples taken exclusively or even frequently from the meanest, poorest, and grossest types of human character. A book of this sort tends neither to purge our passions nor to tickle us into wholesome laughter. The strongest feelings it leaves behind are those of scorn or dislike for most of the people drawn, and of wonderment at the author's taste in drawing them as she has done.

In the second volume the story moves a little faster; there is somewhat less redundancy of small details, and a little more food for human interest. Maggie's earlier attempts at self-culture are described with some power and feeling, nor are we unpleasantly surprised at Bob Jakin's kindly remembrance of olden favours rather than recent grudges. But the reaction caused in Maggie's heart by the reappearance and eloquent sophistries of Philip Wakem draws us back with her into the mire of that low animal life from which she, for one, had so nearly struggled out. Under the guise of profitable intercourse with an old friend, she indulges in frequent stolen meetings with a young man whose only aim is to beguile her into returning a love as selfish on his side as it is long unsuspected by her. One manly word from Philip would have saved Maggie from that weary struggle between a rational sense of duty and a blind yearning for fancied friendship, which ended, after a twelvemonth, as such conflicts under such conditions are always likely enough to end.

But a yet worse fall awaits the heroine in the third volume. The stolen meetings had been brought to a sudden close, but Maggie had

[1] Seventeenth-century Italian landscape-painter.

pledged her love to Philip, and repeated that pledge to him before her angry brother, even while she promised never to see him again without her brother's leave. Yet a new admirer no sooner opens his spells upon her—an admirer already bespoken by her cousin Lucy—than she falls slowly but surely into the snare, her eyes still open, her moral sense by no means overpowered. The course of this strange magnetic union is traced through a large part of the last volume; with what purpose, save to show George Eliot's faith in the philosophy put forth by the author of *Elective Affinities*,[1] we cannot say. The lengthened treatment of a mystery so full of doubt and danger, by an Englishwoman writing for readers of both sexes, speaks as poorly for her good taste as the readiness wherewith a large-hearted girl yields up all her noblest scruples, her tenderest sympathies, to the paltry fear of seeming cruel in the eyes of a weak, unworthy tempter, speaks, in our opinion, for her knowledge of human character. Surely, no woman of Maggie's sort would have let herself be wholly drawn away from her love for the deformed and suffering Philip by a mere outside fancy for the good-looking, sweet-voiced coxcomb, Stephen Guest. Nor could any moral or artistic end be furthered by a close relation of the circumstances which made her so unaccountably false both to her old lover and the cousin with whom she had been staying. We are not for picking needless holes, and do not care to cry out with prudish horror at the notion of an ardent lover rushing to kiss a handsome girl's beautiful round arm. It is not for showing up a conventional fallacy, however respectable, that George Eliot deserves our blame. But in her hatred of things conventional, she goes too often to the opposite extreme. The development of a gross passion much more akin to lust than love, takes up far too many pages of a work not specially written for students of modern French literature or the disciples of M. Comte. Englishmen have not yet come to believe in the triumph—speaking vulgarly—of matter over mind. With all due allowance for the power of circumstances, they cling the more reverently to their old faith in a sound heart and a steady will. In the love passages between Stephen and Maggie, they find only a detailed unlikely picture of animal feelings, far less suited to ordinary readers than the superficial coarseness of Joseph Andrews. A little more reticence on a subject so perplexing to the largest minds would have saved the writer much waste of time, and satisfied the requirements of an art that has little to do with scientific problems or exceptional phases of life.

1. By Goethe, 1808.

It is true that Maggie does at last regain her moral balance, but by that time the volume is nearly come to an end, while the story itself has still apparently some way to run. At the eleventh hour the heroine is allowed to put forth that firm will which was conveniently kept in the background when the right use of it would have come much more easily, and saved all concerned from much needless suffering. The two lovers having reached York together, might have been condemned to go on to Scotland, wed each other, and live unhappily ever after; but then we should have lost the neighbourly greeting that awaited our strong-minded penitent on her return to St Ogg's, while Lucy would have been driven to keep her spirits up by accepting the love which Tom Tulliver was dying to present her. On the other hand, Stephen might have been punished by the loss of both his sweethearts, and Lucy in time allowed to pair off with honest, faithful Tom; Maggie, meanwhile, being left to work out her allotted penance before returning chastened and made whole to the arms of her first and truest lover. Had George Eliot made better use of her materials, she would have found more room for a fit conclusion. As things are, the story is suddenly carried off its legs in the flood that drowns poor Maggie; and the remaining characters are hustled from the stage at once stroke, as if author and readers were alike glad to be rid of them on any terms.

We shall not imitate a certain reviewer by asking what George Eliot's religious views may be. As a novelist, she has faults enough to amend, without being unfairly hit by an utterly needless reference to her translation of Strauss. A theological novel may be a fit subject for criticism on theological grounds, but in the case of a novel like *The Mill on the Floss* we have no more right to challenge the author's private leanings on religious questions, than we have to charge her with all the meannesses of the Dodson family, or the heartless sensualism of Hetty Sorel. By its own merits the work must stand or fall. Its moral bearings, however, present a fair mark for critical arrows; and some of us may honestly demur to the strong sway which outward circumstances seem, in these novels, habitually to wield over innate strength of character and clearness of moral insight. Unlike the Greek dramatists and our own Shakespeare, George Eliot seems too fond of showing fate triumphant not only against human happiness, but still more against human virtue. 'The good that we would, we do not; the evil that we would not, that we do,'[1] is a text which she never tires of illustrating, to the loss of artistic contrast, and the weakening of her

[1] *Romans*, vii, 19.

hold on human sympathies. In our highest moments we feel her pictures to be less and lower than the truth, and lament that one who can write with such clear force and true feeling, should have taken so much delight in drawing the meaner instead of the nobler aspects of human life; the ruined huts on the Rhone, instead of the ruined castles on the Rhine.

George Eliot has much both to learn and to unlearn before she can take the place which her friends would claim for her among the novelists of our day. Her clear, racy, nervous English, heightened by gleams of quiet humour and thrills of calm pathos, lends rather a perilous charm to passages teeming with the worst luxuriance of that petty realism which passes with careless critics for art of the first order. Even these are less intolerable than those other passages of laboured irony and didactic commonplace, which read like bits of private note-books foisted into their present places, on much the same principle that leads a clever schoolboy to astonish his friends at home with easy lectures on things not generally unknown. Where Thackeray himself cannot always tread with safety, George Eliot can only succeed in falling. Her interjectional remarks are seldom very wise or very pertinent. In nine cases out of ten they only interrupt the story, without offering a fair sop to the reader's impatience. Utterly lacking the tender illustrative beauty of like halting-places in *The Newcomes* and *Vanity Fair*, they often jar upon our feelings with signs of imperfect knowledge hidden beneath a great show of philosophic sarcasm and a sound of idle complaining. With the peevish fretfulness of a camel in the act of loading, our authoress keeps groaning out her tiresome tirades against evils for the most part of her own imagining. Only a woman or Mr. Charles Reade would have called our attention to the startling fact that a boy of thirteen really took pride in wearing a real sword, or that he had 'no distinct idea how there came to be such a thing as Latin on this earth.' She sneers and rails like a sort of womanly Carlyle at an unreal monster, called by her 'good society,' which gets all its religion and science done to order, and knows nothing of any high belief or saving enthusiasm. Sometimes another Emerson seems to be telling us, in large and poetic phrases, that boys will feel like boys, and that old associations make life pleasant. Of these tendencies some will doubtless cure themselves with the enlarged experience of the coming years, while others flow from the inherent faultiness of those art principles which George Eliot has hitherto followed. With better principles, the work done by such a writer would bring more credit to herself, and give more pleasure to thoughtful readers. When she shall have learned the difference between painting and photography, between the poetic and the prosaic sides of human life, between careful selection and careless accumulation of small details, between that larger insight and sterner self-control, which go to the making of a first-rate novel, and the microscopic cleverness that evolves a series of faithful but disjointed sketches; when her eyes shall have been opened to the truths of that highest realism which reflects the 'soul of goodness in things evil,'[1] painting the bloom upon the cheek, the light in the eye of Nature, and discovering a wealth of ideal grace and music amid all the discords and deformities of life; then, indeed, but not before, will she find herself on the road to a higher and more lasting success than aught she can otherwise hope to achieve.

[1] *Henry V*, IV, i, 4.

21. Dinah Mulock, unsigned review, *Macmillan's Magazine*

April 1861, iii, 441–8

Dinah Maria Mulock (1826–87), later Mrs C. L. Craik, was a prolific, popular novelist, author of *John Halifax, Gentleman* (1857). In a letter to a friend in 1860, George Eliot refused to consider herself 'a rival of Miss Mulock—a writer who is read only by novel readers, pure and simple, never by people of high culture' (*Letters*, iii, 302). Miss Mulock begins her review by affirming that it is the high responsibility of the novelist to interpret the divine pattern of the universe; George Eliot is then assessed in these terms (see No. 22 for George Eliot's reaction, and Introduction, p. 15).

Of *The Mill on the Floss*, in a literary point of view, there can be but one opinion—that, as a work of art, it is as perfect as the novel can well be made: superior even to *Adam Bede*. For the impression it gives of *power*, evenly cultivated and clear sighted,—the power of creation, amalgamating real materials into a fore-planned ideal scheme; the power of selection, able to distinguish at once the fit and the unfit, choosing the one and rejecting the other, so as to make every part not only complete as to itself, but as to its relation with a well-balanced whole—the *Mill on the Floss* is one of the finest imaginative works in our language. In its diction, too: how magnificently rolls on that noble Saxon English—terse and clear, yet infinitely harmonious, keeping in its most simple common-place flow a certain majesty and solemnity which reminds one involuntarily of the deep waters of the Floss. The fatal Floss, which runs through the whole story like a Greek fate or a Gothic destiny—ay, from the very second chapter, when

'Maggie, Maggie,' continued the mother, in a tone of half-coaxing fretfulness, as this small mistake of nature entered the room, 'where's the use o' my telling you to keep away from the water? You'll tumble in and be drownded some day, an' then you'll be sorry you didn't do as mother told you.'

This is a mere chance specimen of the care over small things—the exquisite polish of each part, that yet never interferes with the breadth of the whole—which marks this writer as one of the truest *artists*, in the highest sense, of our or any other age.

Another impression made strongly by the first work of 'George Eliot,' and repeated by 'his' (we prefer to respect the pseudonym) second, is the earnestness, sincerity, and heart-nobility of the author. Though few books are freer from that morbid intrusion of self in which many writers of fiction indulge, no one can lay down *The Mill on the Floss* without a feeling of having held commune with a mind of rare individuality, with a judgment active and clear, and with a moral nature, conscientious, generous, religious, and pure. It is to this moral nature, this noblest half of all literary perfectness, in our author, as in all other authors, that we now make appeal.

'George Eliot,' or any other conscientious novelist, needs not to be told that he who appropriates this strange phantasmagoria of human life, to repaint and re-arrange by the light of his own imagination, takes materials not his own, nor yet his reader's. He deals with mysteries which, in their entirety, belong alone to the Maker of the universe. By the force of his intellect, the quick sympathies of his heart, he may pierce into them a little way—farther, perhaps, than most people— but at best only a little way. He will be continually stopped by things he cannot understand—matters too hard for him, which make him feel, the more deeply and humbly as he grows more wise, how we are, at best,

> Like infants crying in the dark,
> And with no language but a cry.[1]

If by his dimly-beheld, one-sided, fragmentary representations, which mimic untruly the great picture of life, this cry, either in his own voice, or in the involuntary utterance of his readers, rises into an accusation against God, how awful is his responsibility, how tremendous the evil that he may originate!

We doubt not, the author of the *Mill on the Floss* would shudder at the suspicion of this sort of involuntary blasphemy, and yet such is the tendency of the book and its story.

A very simple story. A girl of remarkable gifts—mentally, physically, and morally: born, like thousands more, of parents far inferior to herself

---

[1] Misquotation from Tennyson's *In Memoriam*, liv, st. 5.

—struggles through a repressed childhood, a hopeless youth: brought suddenly out of this darkness into the glow of a first passion for a man who, ignoble as he may be, is passionately in earnest with regard to her: she is tempted to treachery, and sinks into a great error, her extrication out of which, without involving certain misery and certain wrong to most or all around her, is simply an impossibility. The author cuts the Gordian knot by creating a flood on the Floss, which wafts this poor child out of her troubles and difficulties into the other world.

Artistically speaking, this end is very fine. Towards it the tale has gradually climaxed. From such a childhood as that of *Tom* and *Maggie Tulliver*, nothing could have come but the youth *Tom* and the girl *Maggie*, as we find them throughout that marvellous third volume: changed indeed, but still keeping the childish images of little *Tom* and little *Maggie*, of Dorlcote Mill. Ay, even to the hour, when with that sense of the terrible exalted into the sublime, which only genius can make us feel—we see them go down to the deeps of the Floss 'in an embrace never to be parted: living through again, in one supreme moment, the days when they had clasped their little hands in love, and roamed through the daisied fields together.'

So far as exquisite literary skill, informed and vivified by the highest order of imaginative power, can go, this story is perfect. But take it from another point of view. Ask, what good will it do?—whether it will lighten any burdened heart, help any perplexed spirit, comfort the sorrowful, succour the tempted, or bring back the erring into the way of peace; and what is the answer? Silence.

Let us reconsider the story, not artistically, but morally.

Here is a human being, placed during her whole brief life—her hapless nineteen years—under circumstances the hardest and most fatal that could befal one of her temperament. She has all the involuntary egotism and selfishness of a nature that, while eagerly craving for love, loves ardently and imaginatively rather than devotedly; and the only love that might have at once humbled and raised her, by showing her how far nobler it was than her own—Philip's—is taken from her in early girlhood. Her instincts of right, true as they are, have never risen into principles; her temptations to vanity, and many other faults, are wild and fierce; yet no human help ever comes near her to strengthen the one or subdue the other. This *may* be true to nature, and yet we think it is not. Few of us, calmly reviewing our past, can feel that we have ever been left so long and so utterly without either outward aid, or the inner voice—never silent in a heart like poor *Maggie's*. It is, in any case, a perilous doctrine to preach—the doctrine of overpowering circumstances.

Again, notwithstanding the author's evident yearning over *Maggie*, and disdain for *Tom*, we cannot but feel that if people are to be judged by the only fair human judgment, of how far they act up to what they believe in, *Tom*, so far as his light goes, is a finer character than his sister. He alone has the self-denial to do what he does not like, for the sake of doing right; he alone has the self-command to smother his hopeless love, and live on, a brave, hard-working life; he, except in his injustice to poor *Maggie*, has at least the merit of having made no one else miserable. Perfectly true is what he says, though he says it in a Pharisaical way, 'Yes, *I* have had feelings to struggle with, but I conquered them. I have had a harder life than you have had, but I have found *my* comfort in doing my duty.' Nay, though perhaps scarcely intended, Bob Jakin's picture of the solitary lad, 'as close as an iron biler,' who 'sits by himself so glumpish, a-knittin' his brow, an' a-lookin' at the fire of a night,' is in its way as pathetic as *Maggie's* helpless cry to Dr. Kenn, at the bazaar, 'O, I must go.'

In the whole history of this fascinating *Maggie* there is a picturesque piteousness which somehow confuses one's sense of right and wrong. Yet what—we cannot help asking—what is to become of the hundreds of clever girls, born of uncongenial parents, hemmed in with unsympathising kindred of the Dodson sort, blest with no lover on whom to bestow their strong affections, no friend to whom to cling for guidance and support? They must fight their way, heaven help them! alone and unaided, through cloud and darkness, to the light. And, thank heaven, hundreds of them do, and live to hold out a helping hand afterwards to thousands more. 'The middle-aged' (says 'George Eliot,' in this very book), 'who have lived through their strongest emotions, but are yet in the time when memory is still half-passionate and not merely contemplative, should surely be a sort of natural priesthood, whom life has disciplined and consecrated to be the refuge and rescue of early stumblers and victims of self-despair.'

Will it help these—such a picture as *Maggie*, who, with all her high aspirations and generous qualities, is, throughout her poor young life, a stay and comfort to no human being, but, on the contrary, a source of grief and injury to every one connected with her? If we are to judge character by results—not by grand imperfect essays, but by humbler fulfilments—of how much more use in the world were even fond, shallow *Lucy*, and narrow-minded *Tom*, than this poor *Maggie*, who seems only just to have caught hold of the true meaning and beauty of existence in that last pathetic prayer, 'If my life is to be long, let me live to bless and comfort,' when she is swept away out of our sight and love for ever.

True this is, as we have said, a magnificent ending for the book; but is it for the life—the one human life which this author has created so vividly and powerfully, that we argue concerning it as if we had actually known it? Will it influence for good any other real lives—this passionately written presentment of temptation never conquered, or just so far that we see its worst struggle as but beginning; of sorrows which teach nothing, or teach only bitterness; of love in its most delicious, most deadly phase; love blind, selfish, paramount, seeing no future but possession, and, that hope gone, no alternative but death—death, welcomed as the solution of all difficulties, the escape from all pain?

Is this right? Is it a creed worthy of an author who has pre-eminently what all novelists should have, 'the brain of a man and the heart of a woman,'[1] united with what we may call a sexless intelligence, clear and calm, able to observe, and reason, and guide mortal passions, as those may, who have come out of the turmoil of the flesh into the region of ministering spirits, 'αγγελοι,' messengers between God and man? What if the messenger testify falsely? What if the celestial trumpet give forth an uncertain sound?

Yet let us be just. There are those who argue that this—perhaps the finest ending, artistically, of any modern novel, is equally fine in a moral sense: that the death of *Maggie* and *Tom* is a glorious Euthanasia, showing that when even at the eleventh hour, temptation is conquered, error atoned, and love reconciled, the life is complete: its lesson has been learnt, its work done; there is nothing more needed but the *vade in pacem* to an immediate heaven. This, if the author so meant it, was an idea grand, noble, Christian: as Christian (be it said with reverence) as the doctrine preached by the Divine Pardoner of all sinners to the sinner beside whom He died—'To-day shalt thou be with me in paradise.'[2] But the conception ought to have been worked out so plainly that no reader could mistake it. We should not have been left to feel, as we do feel, undecided whether this death was a translation or an escape: whether if they had not died, *Maggie* would not have been again the same *Maggie*, always sinning and always repenting; and *Tom* the same *Tom*, hard and narrow-minded, though the least ray of love and happiness cast over his gloomy life, might have softened and made

[1] Elizabeth Barrett Browning, 'To George Sand: A Desire' (1844).   [2] *Luke*, xxiii, 43.

a thoroughly good man of him. The author ought to have satisfied us entirely as to the radical change in both; else we fall back upon the same dreary creed of overpowering circumstances: of human beings struggling for ever in a great quagmire of unconquerable temptations, inevitable and hopeless woe. A creed more fatal to every noble effort, and brave self-restraint—above all to that humble faith in the superior Will which alone should govern ours—can hardly be conceived. It is true that there occur sometimes in life positions so complex and over-whelming, that plain right and wrong become confused; until the most righteous and religious man is hardly able to judge clearly or act fairly. But to meet such positions is one thing, to *invent* them is another. It becomes a serious question whether any author—who, great as his genius may be, sees no farther than mortal intelligence can—is justified in leading his readers into a labyrinth, the way out of which he does not, first, see clearly himself, and next, is able to make clear to them, so as to leave them mentally and morally at rest, free from all perplexity and uncertainty.

Now, uncertainty is the prevailing impression with which we close the *Mill on the Floss.* We are never quite satisfied in our detestation of the *Dodson* family, the more odious because so dreadfully natural that we feel we all are haunted by some of the race, could name them among our own connections, perhaps have even received kindnesses from a *Mrs. Pullet*, a *Mrs. Glegg*, or a *Mrs. Tulliver.* We are vexed with ourselves for being so angry with stern, honest, upright, business-like *Tom*—so contemptuously indifferent to gentle unsuspicious *Lucy*, with her universal kindness, extending from 'the more familiar rodents' to her silly *aunt Tulliver.* We question much whether such a generous girl as *Maggie* would have fallen in love with *Stephen* at all; whether she would not from the first have regarded him simply as her cousin's lover, and if his passion won anything from her, it would but have been the half-angry half-sorrowful disdain which a high-minded woman could not help feeling towards a man who forgot duty and honour in selfish love, even though the love were for herself. And, last and chief perplexity of all, we feel that, granting the case as our author puts it, the mischief done, the mutual passion mutually confessed, *Stephen's* piteous arguments have some justice on their side. The wrong done to him in *Maggie's* forsaking him was almost as great as the wrong previously done to *Philip* and *Lucy*:—whom no self-sacrifice on her part or *Stephen's* could ever have made happy again.

And, to test the matter, what reader will not confess, with a vague

sensation of uneasy surprise, to have taken far less interest in all the
good injured personages of the story, than in this mad *Stephen* and
treacherous *Maggie*? Who that is capable of understanding—as a thing
which has been or is, or may one day be—the master-passion that
furnishes the key to so many lives, will not start to find how vividly
this book revives it, or wakens it, or places it before him as a future
possibility? Who does not think with a horribly delicious feeling, of
such a crisis, when right and wrong, bliss and bale, justice and conscience, seem swept from their boundaries, and a whole existence of
Dodsons, *Lucys*, and *Tom Tullivers*, appears worth nothing compared
to the ecstacy of that 'one kiss—the last' between *Stephen* and *Maggie*
in the lane?

Is this right? The spell once broken—broken with the closing of the
book—every high and pure and religious instinct within us answers
unhesitatingly—'No.'

It is *not* right to paint *Maggie* only as she is in her strong, unsatisfied,
erring youth—and leave her there, her doubts unresolved, her passions
unregulated, her faults unatoned and unforgiven: to cut her off
ignobly and accidentally, leaving two acts, one her recoil of conscience
with regard to *Stephen*, and the other her instinctive self-devotion in
going to rescue *Tom*, as the sole noble landmarks of a life that had in it
every capability for good with which a woman could be blessed. It is
not right to carry us on through these three marvellous volumes, and
leave us at the last standing by the grave of the brother and sister, ready
to lift up an accusatory cry, less to a beneficent Deity than to the
humanly-invented Arimanes[1] of the universe.—'Why should such
things be? Why hast Thou made us thus?'

But it may be urged, that fiction has its counterpart, and worse, in
daily truth. How many perplexing histories do we not know of young
lives blighted, apparently by no fault of their own; of blameless lives
dragged into irresistible temptations; of high natures so meshed in by
circumstances that they, as well as we, judging them from without, can
hardly distinguish right from wrong, guilt from innocence; of living
and loveable beings so broken down by unmerited afflictions, that
when at last they come to an end, we look on the poor dead face with
a sense of thankfulness that there at least,

> There is no other thing expressed
> But long disquiet merged in rest.

---

[1] The commander of the forces of evil in Zoroastrianism.

All this is most true, *so far as we see*. But we never can see, not even the wisest and greatest of us, anything like *the whole* of even the meanest and briefest human life. We never can know through what fiery trial of temptation, nay, even sin,—for sin itself appears sometimes in the wonderful alchemy of the universe to be used as an agent for good,— a strong soul is being educated into a saintly minister to millions of weaker souls: coming to them with the authority of one whom suffering has taught how to heal suffering; nay, whom the very fact of having sinned once, has made more deeply to pity, so as more easily to rescue sinners. And, lastly, we never can comprehend, unless by experience, that exceeding peace—the 'peace which passeth all understanding,' which is oftentimes seen in those most heavily and hopelessly afflicted: those who have lost all, and gained their own souls: whereof they possess themselves in patience: waiting until the 'supreme moment' of which our author speaks, but which is to them not an escape from the miseries of this world, but a joyful entrance into the world everlasting.

Ay, thank heaven, though the highest human intellect may fail to hear it, there are millions of human hearts yet living and throbbing, or mouldering quietly into dust, who have felt, all through the turmoil or silence of existence, though lasting for threescore years and ten, a continual still small voice, following them to the end: 'Fear not: for I am thy GOD.'[1]

Would that in some future book, as powerful as *The Mill on the Floss*, the author might become a true 'Αγγελος,' [messenger] and teach us this!

[1] *Isaiah*, xli, 10.

22. George Eliot replies to a critic

1861

These are George Eliot's comments on No. 21. Page references are to *The George Eliot Letters*.

(a) George Eliot to John Blackwood

30 March 1861

There is an article on the *Mill* in McMillan's Mag. which is worth reading. I cannot of course agree with the writer in all his regrets: if I could have done so, I should not have written the book I did write, but quite another. Still it is a comfort to me to read any criticism which recognizes the high responsibilities of literature that undertakes to represent life. The ordinary tone about art is, that the artist may do what he will provided he pleases the public (iii, 394).

(b) George Eliot to John Blackwood

4 April 1861

And letters drop in from time to time giving me words of strong encouragement—especially about the *Mill*; so that I have reason to be cheerful, and to believe that where one has a large public, one's words must hit their mark. If it were not for that, special cases of misinterpretation might paralyze me. For example, when you read McMillan, pray notice how my critic attributes to me a disdain for Tom: as if it were not *my* respect for Tom which infused itself into my reader— as if he could have respected Tom, if I had not painted him with respect; the exhibition of the *right* on both sides being the very soul of my intention in the story. However, I ought to be satisfied if I have roused the feeling that does justice to both sides (iii, 397).

23. Swinburne: 'the hideous transformation'

1877

From Algernon Charles Swinburne, *A Note on Charlotte Brontë*.

Swinburne uses *The Mill on the Floss* to prove Charlotte Brontë's superiority; it indicates 'the difference which divides pure genius from mere intellect'.

And now we must regretfully and respectfully consider of what quality and what kind may be the faults which deform the best and ripest work of Charlotte Brontë's chosen rival. Few or none, I should suppose, of her most passionate and intelligent admirers would refuse to accept *The Mill on the Floss* as on the whole at once the highest and the purest and the fullest example of her magnificent and matchless powers—for matchless altogether, as I have already insisted, they undoubtedly are in their own wide and fruitful field of work. The first two-thirds of the book suffice to compose perhaps the very noblest of tragic as well as of humorous prose idyls in the language; comprising, as they likewise do, one of the sweetest as well as saddest and tenderest as well as subtlest examples of dramatic analysis—a study in that kind as soft and true as Rousseau's, as keen and true as Browning's, as full as either's of the fine and bitter sweetness of a pungent and fiery fidelity. But who can forget the horror of inward collapse, the sickness of spiritual reaction, the reluctant incredulous rage of disenchantment and disgust, with which he first came upon the thrice unhappy third part? The two first volumes have all the intensity and all the perfection of George Sand's best work, tempered by all the simple purity and interfused with all the stainless pathos of Mrs. Gaskell's; they carry such affluent weight of thought and shine with such warm radiance of humour as invigorates and illuminates the work of no other famous woman; they have the fiery clarity of crystal or of lightning; they go near to prove a higher claim and attest a clearer right on the part of their author than that of George Sand herself to the crowning crown of praise conferred on her by the hand of a woman even greater and more glorious than either in her sovereign gift of lyric genius, to the salutation given as by an angel indeed from heaven, of 'large-brained woman and large-hearted man.'[1] And the fuller and deeper tone of colour combined with greater sharpness and precision of outline may be allowed to excuse the apparent amount of obligation—though we may hardly see how this can be admitted to explain the remarkable reticence which reserves all acknowledgment and dissembles all consciousness of that sufficiently palpable and weighty and direct obligation—to Mrs. Gaskell's beautiful story of *The Moorland Cottage*; in which not the identity of name alone, nor only their common single-ness of heart and simplicity of spirit, must naturally recall the gentler memory of the less high-thoughted and high-reaching heroine to the warmest and the worthiest admirers of the later-born and loftier-minded Maggie; though the hardness and brutality of the baser brother through whom she suffers be the outcome in manhood as in childhood of mere greedy instinct and vulgar egotism, while the full eventful efflorescence of the same gracious qualities in Tom Tulliver is tracked with incomparable skill and unquestionable certitude of touch to the far other root of sharp narrow self-devotion and honest harsh self-reliance.

'So far, all honour'; as Phraxanor says of Joseph in the noble poem of Mr. Wells.[2] But what shall any one say of the upshot? If we are really to take it on trust, to confront it as a contingent or conceivable possibility, resting our reluctant faith on the authority of so great a female writer, that a woman of Maggie Tulliver's kind can be moved to any sense but that of bitter disgust and sickening disdain by a thing—I will not write, a man—of Stephen Guest's; if we are to accept as truth and fact, however astonishing and revolting, so shameful an avowal, so vile a revelation as this; in that ugly and lamentable case, our only remark, as our only comfort, must be that now at least the last word of realism has surely been spoken, the last abyss of cynicism has surely been sounded and laid bare. The three master cynics of French romance are eclipsed and distanced and extinguished, passed over and run down and snuffed out on their own boards. To the rosy innocence of Laclos, to the cordial optimism of Stendhal, to the trustful tenderness of Mérimée, no such degradation of female character seems ever to have suggested itself as imaginable. Iago never flung such an imputation on

---

[1] Elizabeth Barrett Browning's sonnet, 'To George Sand: A Desire' (1844).
[2] 'Joseph and his Brethren: a dramatic poem' (1824), by Charles Jeremiah Wells (1800–79).

all womanhood; Madame de Merteuil[1] would never have believed it. For a higher view and a more cheering aspect of the sex, we must turn back to these gentler teachers, these more flattering painters of our own; we must take up *La Double Méprise*—or *Le Rouge et le Noir*—or *Les Liaisons Dangereuses*.[2]

But I for one am not prepared or willing to embrace a belief so much too degrading and depressing for the conception of those pure and childlike souls. My faith will not digest at once the first two volumes and the third volume of *The Mill on the Floss*; my conscience or credulity has not gorge enough for such a gulp. Whatever capacity for belief is in me I find here impaled once more as on the horns of that old divine's dilemma between the irreconcilable attributes of goodness and omnipotence in the supposed Creator of suffering and of sin. If the one quality be predicable, the other quality cannot be predicable of the same subject. . . . The hideous transformation by which Maggie is debased—were it but for an hour—into the willing or yielding companion of Stephen's flight would probably and deservedly have been resented as a brutal and vulgar outrage on the part of a male novelist. But the man never lived, I do believe, who could have done such a thing as this: as the man, I should suppose, does not exist who could make for the first time the acquaintance of Mr. Stephen Guest with no incipient sense of a twitching in his fingers and a tingling in his toes at the notion of any contact between Maggie Tulliver and a cur so far beneath the chance of promotion to the notice of his horsewhip, or elevation to the level of his boot.

Here then is the patent flaw, here too plainly is the flagrant blemish, which defaces and degrades the very crown and flower of George Eliot's wonderful and most noble work; no rent or splash on the raiment, no speck or scar on the skin of it, but a cancer in the very bosom, a gangrene in the very flesh. It is a radical and mortal plague-spot, corrosive and incurable; in the apt and accurate phrase of Rabelais, 'an enormous solution of continuity.' The book is not the same before it and after. No washing or trimming, no pruning or purging, could eradicate or efface it; it could only be removable by amputation and remediable by cautery.

[1] Character from *Les Liaisons Dangereuses.*
[2] A story by Mérimée, 1833, and novels by Stendhal, 1831, and Laclos, 1782, respectively.

24. Ruskin: 'the sweepings out of a Pentonville omnibus'

1880–1

These are two extracts from Ruskin's *Fiction, Fair and Foul* which appeared originally as five articles in the *Nineteenth Century*. The first extract is taken from *Nineteenth Century* (June 1880), vii, 941–63, the second from (October 1881), x, 516–31. In August 1881 Ruskin confided to a friend that he would like to write about George Eliot 'because now [she] was in Heaven, I could write her Epitaph without any chance of meeting her afterwards' (*Works*, ed. E. T. Cook and A. Wedderburn, 1909, xxxvii, 372).

(a) It is quite curious how often the catastrophe, or the leading interest, of a modern novel, turns upon the want, both in maid and bachelor, of the common self-command which was taught to their grandmothers and grandfathers as the first element of ordinarily decent behaviour. Rashly inquiring the other day the plot of a modern story from a female friend, I elicited, after some hesitation, that it hinged mainly on the young people's 'forgetting themselves in a boat'; and I perceive it to be accepted as nearly an axiom in the code of modern civic chivalry that the strength of amiable sentiment is proved by our incapacity on proper occasions to express, and on improper ones to control it. The pride of a gentleman of the old school used to be in his power of saying what he meant, and being silent when he ought (not to speak of the higher nobleness which bestowed love where it was honourable, and reverence where it was due); but the automatic amours and involuntary proposals of recent romance acknowledge little further law of morality than the instinct of an insect, or the effervescence of a chemical mixture.

(b) All healthy and helpful literature sets simple bars between right and wrong; assumes the possibility, in men and women, of having healthy minds in healthy bodies, and loses no time in the diagnosis of fever or dyspepsia in either; least of all in the particular kind of fever which signifies the ungoverned excess of any appetite or passion. The 'dulness' which many modern readers inevitably feel, and some modern blockheads think it creditable to allege, in Scott, consists not a little in his absolute purity from every loathsome element or excitement of the lower passions; so that people who live habitually in Satyric or hircine conditions of thought find him as insipid as they would a picture of Angelico's. The accurate and trenchant separation between him and the common railroad-station novelist is that, in his total method of conception, only lofty character is worth describing at all; and it becomes interesting, not by its faults, but by the difficulties and accidents of the fortune through which it passes, while, in the railway novel, interest is obtained with the vulgar reader for the vilest character, because the author describes carefully to his recognition the blotches, burrs and pimples in which the paltry nature resembles his own. *The Mill on the Floss* is perhaps the most striking instance extant of this study of cutaneous disease. There is not a single person in the book of the smallest importance to anybody in the world but themselves, or whose qualities deserved so much as a line of printer's type in their description. There is no girl alive, fairly clever, half educated, and unluckily related, whose life has not at least as much in it as Maggie's, to be described and to be pitied. Tom is a clumsy and cruel lout, with the making of better things in him (and the same may be said of nearly every Englishman at present smoking and elbowing his way through the ugly world his blunders have contributed to the making of); while the rest of the characters are simply the sweepings out of a Pentonville omnibus.

And it is very necessary that we should distinguish this essentially Cockney literature,—developed only in the London suburbs, and feeding the demands of the rows of similar brick houses, which branch in devouring cancer round every manufacturing town,—from the really romantic literature of France. Georges Sand is often immoral; but she is always beautiful. . . . But in the English Cockney school, which consummates itself in George Eliot, the personages are picked up from behind the counter and out of the gutter; and the landscape, by excursion train to Gravesend, with return ticket for the City-road.

SILAS MARNER

April 1861

25. John Blackwood to George Eliot

19 February 1861

The George Eliot Letters, iii, 379–80

My Dear Madam

I have read the M.S. you have sent of *Silas Marner* with the greatest admiration. The first 100 pages are very sad, almost oppressive, but relieved by the most exquisite touches of nature and natural feelings hit off in the fewest and most happily chosen words. I wish the picture had been a more cheery one and embraced higher specimens of humanity, but you paint so naturally that in your hands the veriest earth-worms become most interesting perfect studies in fact.

The child found on the hearth replacing the poor weaver's lost treasure is a beautiful idea and is I hope to be the medium of restoring the unfortunate Silas to a more Christian frame of mind. How perfectly you paint the poor creature quite at sea when his simple faith was cut from under his feet.

The conclave at the Rainbow is beyond price and no one but yourself could have done Mrs. Winthrop. She is perfect. Nancy Lammeter is very good and her toilette in presence of the Miss Gunns is screaming, but Priscilla is my favourite; she promises to be a truly rich bit of character. I cannot help feeling sorry that you have done for the only one of the Cass family who had anything about him to redeem the breed.

My only objection to the story is the want of brighter lights and some characters of whom one can think with pleasure as fellow creatures, but this may come in the sequel of the story and in the meantime the touches of nature, the humour, and the power and precision are as wonderful as in anything you have ever written. Are you sure you will be able to wind up in the space you allot to yourself? I should almost doubt it.

Shall we calculate upon a post 8° volume to sell at 12/- and make a proposition upon that basis, or is there any chance of your matter extending to what would make two smaller volumes? We can get the whole into type in a very few days.

Congratulating you upon your unfailing powers, which seem as inexhaustible as ever, believe me

always yours truly
John Blackwood.

26. George Eliot to John Blackwood

24 February 1861

The George Eliot Letters, iii, 382–3. *Silas Marner* was published in one volume at 12s. Blackwood offered her £800 for an edition of 4,000 copies, i.e. a royalty of 33 per cent.

My dear Sir

It is not possible, I think, that *Silas* will make more than one volume; and I hope you will have the entire M.S. in your hands in ten days. Is it wise (you, of course, are the best judge) to charge more than 10/6? Though, certainly, the volume is likely to be rather larger than one volume of a three-volumed novel.

I don't wonder at your finding my story, as far as you have read it, rather sombre: indeed, I should not have believed that any one would have been interested in it but myself (since William Wordsworth is dead) if Mr. Lewes had not been strongly arrested by it. But I hope you will not find it at all a sad story, as a whole, since it sets—or is intended to set—in a strong light the remedial influences of pure, natural human relations. The Nemesis is a very mild one. I have felt all through as if the story would have lent itself best to metrical rather than prose fiction, especially in all that relates to the psychology of Silas; except that, under that treatment, there could not be an equal play of humour. It came to me first of all, quite suddenly, as a sort of legendary tale, suggested by my recollection of having once, in early childhood, seen a linen-weaver with a bag on his back; but, as my mind dwelt on the subject, I became inclined to a more realistic treatment.

My chief reason for wishing to publish the story now, is, that I like my writings to appear in the order in which they are written, because they belong to successive mental phases, and when they are a year behind me, I can no longer feel that thorough identification with them which gives zest to the sense of authorship. I generally like them better at that distance, but then, I feel as if they might just as well have been written by somebody else.

It would have been a great pleasure to me if Major Blackwood could have read my story. Have you advertised it in the next Maga?

Ever yours truly
M. E. Lewes.

27. Unsigned review, *Saturday Review*

13 April 1861, xi, 369–70 (See headnote to No. 39)

The highest tribute that can be paid to this book may be paid it very readily. It is as good as *Adam Bede*, except that it is shorter. And that an author should be able to produce a series of works so good in so very peculiar a style, is as remarkable as anything that has occurred in the history of English literature in this century. The plot of *Silas Marner* is good, and the delineation of character is excellent. But other writers who have the power of story-telling compose plots as interesting, and perhaps sketch characters as well. It is in the portraiture of the poor, and of what it is now fashionable to call 'the lower middle class,' that this writer is without a rival, and no phase of life could be harder to draw. A person with observation and humour might give a sketch of one or two sets of poor people, and of village farmers and carpenters, but the sketches he could give would be limited by his personal observation. George Eliot alone moves among this unknown, and to most people unknowable, section of society as if quite at home there, and can let imagination run loose and disport itself in a field that, we think, has been only very partially opened even to the best writers. Sir Walter Scott drew a few pictures of humble Scotch life, and none of his creations won him more deserved reputation than the characters of Andrew Fairservice and Caleb Balderstone,[1] and the scenes among the poor fishing population in the *Antiquary*. But, good as these sketches were, they were very limited. We soon got to an end of them; but in *Silas Marner*, the whole book, or nearly the whole book, is made up of such scenes. The writer can picture what uneducated villagers think and say, and can reproduce on paper the picture which imagination has suggested. The gift is so special, the difficulty is so great, the success is so complete, that the works of George Eliot come on us as a new revelation of what society in quiet English parishes really is and has been. How hard it is to draw the poor may easily be seen if we turn to the ordinary tales of country life that are written in such abundance by ladies. There the poor are always looked at from the point of view of the rich. They are so many subjects for experimenting on, for reclaiming, improving, being anxious about, and relieving. They have no existence apart from the presence of a curate and a district visitor. They live in order to take tracts and broth. This is a very natural, and in some degree a very proper view for the well-intentioned rich to take of the poor. It is right that those who have spiritual and temporal blessings should care for the souls and bodies of those around them. But the poor remain, during the process and in its description, as a distinct race. What they think of and do when they are not being improved and helped, remains a blank. Those, too, who are above the reach of occasional destitution are entirely omitted from these portraitures of village life. Every one is agreed that it would be impertinent to improve a man who gets anything like a pound a week. When, therefore, George Eliot describes the whole of a village, from the simple squire down to the wheelwright and his wife, the ground thus occupied is virgin soil.

[1] In *Rob Roy* (1817) and *The Bride of Lammermoor* (1819).

There are two chapters in *Silas Marner* describing the conversation of a coterie at a public-house, and what they did and said on a man appearing before them to announce a robbery, which are perfectly wonderful. It is not, perhaps, saying much to say that an intelligent reader who knew beforehand that such a scene was to be described would be utterly puzzled to think of any one thing that such people could satisfactorily be represented as remarking or doing. But some notion of what George Eliot can do may be obtained by comparing what the best writers of the day are in the habit of doing when they attempt scenes of this sort. Sir Edward Lytton and Mr. Dickens would venture to try such a scene if it came in their way. Sir Edward Lytton would only go so far as to put some very marked character or some very important personage of the story in the centre of the group, and put everything into relation and connexion with him. This is really the good ladies' novel view of the poor in another shape. The poor cluster round some one superior to them, and the only reason of the superiority which Sir Edward Lytton can claim, so far as he can claim any at all, arises from the poor being supposed to be in a position of greater naturalness and simplicity. They are represented as taking their ease in their inn, and not as being talked to by their anxious-minded betters. Mr. Dickens sets himself to draw the poor and the uneducated much more thoroughly, but his mode is to invest each person with one distinguishing peculiarity. This gives a distinctness to each picture, but it makes the whole group artificial and mechanical. He always, or almost always, keeps us in the region of external peculiarities. We are made to notice the teeth, the hair, the noses, the buttons of the people described, or some oddity of manner that marks them. The sentiment of the poor is often caught in Mr. Dickens's works with great happiness, and the chance observations that they might make under particular circumstances are well conceived; but George Eliot goes far beyond this. The people in the public-house in *Silas Marner* proclaim in a few words each a distinct and probable character, and sustain it. The things they say are perfectly natural, and yet show at once what the sayers are like. We know that these poor are like real poor people, just as we know that the characters in Shakespeare are like real men and women. The humour of the author, of course, pervades the representation, just as it does in the comic parts of Shakspeare. Our enjoyment in a large measure depends on the enjoyment of the writer; nor is it probable that any group at a pothouse would really say so many things on any one evening that, if recorded, would amuse us so much. But this is one of the exigencies of art. In order not to waste space, that which is characteristic must be placed closely together. Were it not for this absence of dilution, the history of the village group of Raveloe, the village in which the scenes of *Silas Marner* are laid, might be a mere record of an actual evening passed at a country public. It is a kind of unpermissible audacity in England to say that anything is as good as Shakspeare, and we will not therefore say that this public-house scene is worthy of the hand that drew Falstaff and Poins; but we may safely say that, however much less in degree, the humour of George Eliot in such passages is of the same kind as that displayed in the comic passages of Shakspeare's historical plays.

There are two points especially with regard to the poor which George Eliot has mastered, and the mastery of which lends a lifelike reality to *Silas Marner*. These are the frankness of the poor and their religion. The villagers in *Silas Marner* speak out. They say what they have to say, and do not mince matters. This is the rudeness of persons who do not mean to be rude; for they do not dream of the rules which a consideration for the feelings of others teaches those who are more refined. When Silas Marner, the hero of the story, a poor weaver, loses his money, he is visited by a Job's comforter in the person of the parish clerk. This comforter comes in the dignity of a parish official and a parish wit, and with really kind intentions, to say a kind thing to a man whom he dislikes and despises, but yet respects a little, and pities a great deal.

[describes in detail this episode from ch. 10]

This is only one specimen of the direct, and, as rich people would think, insulting language which George Eliot, with the happiest effect, puts into the mouth of the poor. But the author knows the class described too well to show them long together without the intervention of deep feeling of some sort. The Job's comforter is succeeded by a real comforter—by a motherly, patient, humble-minded woman. Dolly Winthrop, with her quaint kindness, her simple piety, and her good sense, is as touching and at the same time as amusing a character as George Eliot has drawn.

[describes Dolly Winthrop's visit to Silas in ch. 10]

The difference, so far as truthfulness of description and insight into the poor go, between George Eliot and the usual lady-novelist, cannot be better estimated than by contrasting Dolly and her I.H.S. cakes, her reverent belief in 'Them,' and her views of this world and the next, with the model cottager's wife of domestic fiction. The one is a living woman, the other is an improveable puppet.

We wish to avoid telling the story of Silas Marner to those who have not read the book, and it fortunately happens that there is nothing in the story that calls for observation. There does not appear to us to be a fault in the plot or in the working of it out. The errors that marred the *Mill on the Floss* have been entirely avoided. The classes which the author can draw, and those alone, have been drawn. There is nothing like the inanity of Stephen Guest or the spiritual conflicts of Maggie. On the other hand, the plot secures the writer from the danger of trespassing on unknown ground which was the origin of some weaknesses in *Adam Bede*. The trial and the reprieve of Hetty were incomparably the worst parts of the story, for the simple reason that the writer evidently knew nothing about trials and reprieves. There is, again, nothing painful in *Silas Marner*. The secret is one that it is not distressing either to have concealed or to find out, and the misery of those who are miserable is not of a very intense kind. We are left unembarrased to enjoy those pictures of humble life which have constituted the great merit of George Eliot's works, and which appear in this new volume with as much freshness, novelty, and humour as ever. All that can be said against *Silas Marner*, as compared with its predecessors, is that it is shorter, and therefore slighter. The author has less ground to cover, and has not been obliged to fill up space with improbable incidents or painful scenes. The work has therefore been easier. The characters have had to be sustained for a shorter time, and the delineation of mental conflicts and emotions has been more in outline. If we take into consideration all the difficulties encountered and surmounted, *Adam Bede* still remains perhaps the author's greatest production. But, within its limits, *Silas Marner* is quite equal to either of its predecessors, and, in combining the display of the author's characteristic excellences with freedom from blemishes and defects, is perhaps superior.

28. R. H. Hutton, unsigned review, *Economist*

27 April 1861, pp. 455–7

Richard Holt Hutton (1826–97) was a versatile journalist, theologian, and man of letters. He was editor of the unitarian journal, the *Inquirer* (1851–3), and in 1855 became the joint-editor with Bagehot of the new *National Review* from which he retired in 1864. He was also Professor of Mathematics at Bedford College, London (1856–65), and joint-editor of the *Spectator* (1861–97) in which position he defended Christianity against agnosticism and rationalism. Eventually he became an Anglican and devoted his later years to theological writing. He reviewed George Eliot's novels widely and, as this perceptive essay shows, was far more aware of their philosophical implications than most of his contemporaries (see Introduction, pp. 17–18, and Nos. 34, 40, 45, 55).

This tale is a permanent and no trifling addition to the wealth of English literature. There is no element of power wanting to make it more impressive, and no element of beauty wanting to make it more attractive. The conception is as fine as the execution is marvellous. It does not approach in tragic power some parts of *Adam Bede*, because the scope of the narrative will not admit of it,—but it is a more perfect whole; and a more unique and subtle, though not so deep an interest constitutes the plot. No book that we have ever read combines so completely the broadest masculine power with the most delicate feminine insight and finish. Nor is there, as far as we have noticed, a single cynical Thackerayism about the book like those which so often disfigure the introductory discussion-paragraphs to the various chapters in *Adam Bede*,—unless, indeed, we except a single word which we have italicised in the following characteristic sentence:—

The prevarication and white lies which a mind that keeps itself *ambitiously* pure is as uneasy under as a great artist under the false touches that no eye detects but his own, are worn as lightly as mere trimmings when once the actions have become a lie.

Why should the word 'ambitiously' have been inserted there? It is, we believe, the only cynicism in the book.

One of the most striking features in this striking tale is the strong intellectual impress which the author contrives to give to a story of which the main elements are altogether unintellectual, without the smallest injury to the verisimilitude of the tale. There is no character delineated through whose mouth the author could express a subtle thought without impropriety;—and she herself indulges very sparingly in the descriptive comment which formed so large an element in *The Mill on the Floss* and *Adam Bede*. Yet not the less is the tale a most intellectual as well as graphic picture of the most unintellectual social life which has been known in England during the last fifty years. This is managed in various ways. From the outset the eye of the reader is fixed on the psychological facts which the story is intended to illustrate, though there is no attempt to analyse or discuss their metaphysical origin. Again, the intellectual effect is throughout produced by the *kind* of humour shown in the selection of the traits of life delineated. The turn given to the conversation of the peasants, though never untrue or unreal in them, has almost always a distinct relation to the intellectual forms of the same questions as discussed in modern times by the educated classes,—and hence there is a subtle undercurrent of humour which betrays the mind of the writer even in her most happy delineations of the rural peasantry whom she portrays. Indeed, where this is not the case,—where the conversation of the villagers is not studied, as it usually is, with explicit relation to the corresponding classes of thoughts that occupy more cultivated minds,—the principle of selection is intellectual contrast, instead of intellectual similarity. Sometimes, as in the beginning of the inimitable dialogue in the Rainbow, the theme taken up has no subtle references at all, but is simply and solely one to excite a butcher's and farrier's fervour. But the pungency is given by the grotesqueness of the contrast between the professional interests of the lower and middle classes, and by that additional flavour of professionality which every descent in the scale of education certainly ensures.

[long quotation from the beginning of ch. 6]

Nor does the conversation remain long in this phase. As soon as Mr. Macey, the parish clerk and tailor, enters into it, a faint shadow of the

intellectual phases of 'modern thought,'—just sufficient to remind the
reader of the form which they take in the present day, without in any
way marring the truth of the picture,—begins to fall on the discussion.
Mr. Macey has fallen upon some appropriate form of the difficulty of
distinguishing between the 'subjective' and the 'objective.' He it is who
tells us that 'there's allays two 'pinions; there's the 'pinion a man has of
himsen, and there's the 'pinion other folks have on him. There'd be
two 'pinions about a cracked bell if the bell could hear itself.' And
further, in discussing the error of a bride and bridegroom who had
interchanged their respective responses in the marriage service, he
throws up the difficult question as to the relation between 'substance'
and 'form.' ' "Is it the meanin' or the words as makes folks fast i'
wedlock?" For the parson meant right, and the bride and bridegroom
meant right. But then, when I come to think on it, meanin' goes but
a little way i' most things, for you may mean to stick things together
and your glue may be bad, and then where are you? And so I say to
mysen, "It isn't the meanin', it's the glue." And I was worreted as if I'd
got three bells to pull at once . . . But where's the use o' talking?—you
can't think what goes on in a 'cute man's inside.'

Nor is it only from the quaint traces of connection between the
cultivated and the uncultivated classes, that this tale derives its intellectual impress. The whole structure of it is cast in an intellectual mould.
Its motto is taken from Wordsworth:—

> A child, more than all other gifts
> That earth can offer to declining man,
> Brings hope with it, and forward-looking thoughts.[1]

And the idea of the tale is to contrast the withering effects of a mild,
innocent love of gold growing upon a contracted and timid mind that
had early received a shock both to its faith and human trust, with the
influence of the affection for a little child which replaces the lost gold,—
the former constantly narrowing the connection between the miser
and the social life around him, the latter constantly widening and
deepening it. The art and originality of the story lies in the completely
innocent cast given to the miserliness of the old weaver, his almost
entire freedom from any touch of moral responsibility for the growth
of this passion, and in the complete and unresisted revulsion of feeling
caused by the loss of his gold and the substitution of a living interest
in its place. Silas Marner's character is no common conception. The

[1] 'Michael', 146-8.

absolute sway of blind association over it would commonly be considered inconsistent with any distinct picture at all. Yet is is a most distinct and marvellous picture throughout.

[quotes descriptions of Silas under the influence of gold (ch. 2) and Eppie (ch. 14)]

The subtle intellectual character of the tale is given also in great part by the character of its 'poetical justice.' Instead of finding the ordinary kind of retribution for the weakness and cowardice of the principal hero of it, Godfrey Cass, the authoress gives that gentleman what he himself considers an unusual run of good fortune, and then shows him regretting this good fortune in later life. The story in this respect is very finely contrived. The mere external good fortune seems to fall where it is little deserved,—but this is only in order to show how inevitably ill-deserved fortune will be embittered by the very elements out of which it is constituted. It is easy to see that the author has studied closely the 'poetical justice' of real life. She does not visit any one with the *kind* of condign punishment in which novelists usually delight. The evil character of the piece, betrayed into the theft of the weaver's money, does him the greatest real service instead of injury, by disburdening him of this petrifying treasure. But as he, staggering under his stolen wealth, disappears with it into the night, never again to return to the scene, he steps, as we afterwards learn, into one of the stone-pits near the weaver's cottage, and is drowned by his own booty. The gold remains there for 16 years, and is discovered just in time to serve as the marriage portion of the weaver's adopted child. Thus all the incidents of the tale work together for good to the poor weaver, and restore gradually his broken trust in man and God. There is nothing much more beautiful, humorous, and pathetic in fiction than the conversations in which Dame Winthrop gropes her way towards some solution of poor Silas Marner's early difficulties, and leads him to the conclusion that he is not abandoned by 'Them above,' but that on the contrary, as the weaver expresses his trust in Providence, 'There's dealings with us, there's dealings.' There is no more delicate and powerful writing in this delicately-written and powerful book than Dame Winthrop's mode of presenting the inference, from her own compassion and love for her poor neighbours, to the still greater compassion and love of 'Them above.' But this we must leave to our readers to read for themselves.

29. E. S. Dallas, unsigned review, *The Times*

29 April 1861, p. 12

See Introduction, pp. 16–17, and headnote to No. 8.

To George Eliot belongs this praise—that not only is every one of her tales a masterpiece, but also they may be opened at almost any page, and the eye is certain to light upon something worth reading—some curious dialogue or vivid description, some pregnant thought or happy phrase. *Silas Marner* is, like the rest of her fictions, full of matter and delightful in manner. It is a picture of secluded village life in the midland counties in the early part of the present century, and we owe not a little gratitude to the author for the good which she has done, as well as for the amusement which she has imparted by means of such pictures. She has given dignity to the life of boors and peasants in some of our bucolic districts, and this not by any concealment of their ignorance, follies, and frailties, nor by false colouring, bombastic sentiment, and exceptional events, but by a plain statement of the everyday life of the people. The charm of George Eliot's novels lies in their truthfulness. Nothing is extenuated nor aught set down in malice. We see the people amid all their grovelling cares, with all their coarseness, ignorance, and prejudice—poor, paltry, stupid, wretched, well-nigh despicable. This mean existence George Eliot raises into dignity by endowing it with conscience and with kindliness. There is nothing glittering about it. Here we have no mock heroics. There is not the slightest attempt to represent the boor as a village Hampden, nor the passing pedler as a poet wanting the accomplishment of verse. The personages of the tale are common, very common people, but they are good and kind, hardworking and dutiful. It is very wonderful to see how their lives are ennobled and beautified by their sense of duty, and by their sympathy with each other. It is the grandest of all lessons—the only true philosophy—the most consoling of creeds—that real greatness is within reach of the poorest and meanest of mankind. Wealth, glory, the pride of intellect, and the advantages of personal

179

form—these are rare gifts, which seem to be scattered at random among the good and the bad; and in this ambitious age, when we see every one hastening to be rich and covetous of distinction, it is pleasant to be reminded that the honest man is the noblest work of God. George Eliot reminds us of it in her own genial way—transporting us into the midst of these stupid, common-place inhabitants of Raveloe—making them move before us and speak as if they lived, and making us feel a warm interest in all their petty concerns and humble endeavours. Such a novelist, while she amuses, teaches us. We open her volumes confident of most brilliant entertainment, and we close them wondering at the art of a writer who manages to reverse a time-honoured phrase and to render us, not sadder and better, but merrier and better.

While this is the general effect of all George Eliot's tales, it is most marked in what is still her greatest work—*Adam Bede*. The present tale, which is complete in one volume, has for its hero a sort of Seth Bede, and this statement will indicate to most persons the excellences and defects of the novel. A novel of which a Seth Bede is the hero must, of necessity, be less absorbing, and ought to be shorter, than one which could boast such a hero as Adam. Silas Marner is, like Seth, a simple-hearted and not very clear-headed Methodist, who, after going through a great deal of trouble, and having his life embittered by disappointment, slander, and ingratitude, comes at last to see an over-ruling justice in human affairs, and to put trust in his fellow men. In a world so full as this is of sin and suffering, it is difficult for the victims to believe in the benignant order of the universe. There could not be a more unfortunate victim than poor Silas Marner. He is cheated of his good name and branded as a thief through the instrumentality of his dearest friend; his betrothed, on whom he had set his heart, leaves him to marry this ingrate; afterwards he is suddenly robbed of all his hardwon savings, and he finds himself without means, and all alone in the world. The good and kind but weak-minded man curses his destiny, and cries aloud in his despair that there is no God, but only a devil on the earth. He is petrified; all the springs of his life are dried up; he withdraws from the society of his fellow men; all trust is gone, and he has neither physical nor intellectual energy enough to work his way back. How is this man to be recovered? It is to the moralist a most tempting question—to the novelist a most difficult one. It is easy according to the more common theories to suppose a man preached into contentment, or suddenly 'revived' by a spiritual convulsion. We are not aware, however, that Job ever got much good from the preaching of his friends, and it must be confessed that spiritual revivals and convulsions are not the ordinary means of reformation. Reformation of character and change of views are generally the result of long discipline, and we gather from the motto on the title-page of the present work—

> A child more than all other gifts,
> That earth can offer to declining man,
> Brings hope with it, and forward-looking thoughts,[1]

that George Eliot meant to exhibit the unconscious influence of a child in gradually redeeming and reviving what may be almost described as a lost soul. The author appears, however, to have stopped short of her design, and to have satisfied herself with stating the result instead of detailing the process. In two-thirds of the volume we have Silas Marner before us in his hopeless, helpless estrangement from his fellow men. The picture of his silent misery is filled in so carefully, the canvas is spread so large, and we are introduced to so many of his neighbours, that when, at the 240th page, we find the weaver of Raveloe adopting little Eppie as his own child we feel that the story is about to commence. Still more do we feel this when, a few pages further on, just as the first part of the tale is about to close, and while the motto on the title-page is ringing in our memories, we read that though now there are no white-winged angels to lead men from the city of destruction, still a hand is often put into theirs to lead them gently into a calm and pleasant land, that such a hand is to lead Silas Marner into the light, and that the hand is a little child's. But we are left to imagine the process, for the second part of the tale commences after a supposed lapse of 16 years, in which the great change has been effected in the mind of Silas Marner. He comes out a new man; he gets a sudden turn of good fortune; and the story winds up. The first part, forming more than two-thirds of the volume, is thus a magnificent portico to the second part, which is a pretty little cottage, hidden behind a mass of more stately architecture. There are critics who will regard this objection to the story more seriously than we can. It amounts to this, that George Eliot laid out the plan of a great epic, found that she was overstepping the limits of a novel, and ruthlessly curtailed her design. The result is, that here we have, it is true, a fragment, but it is a fragment of George Eliot's most ambitious work. It is not finished like *Adam Bede*, but in passages it is grander and deeper.

[1] Wordsworth's 'Michael', 146–8.

That George Eliot should have shrunk from the completion of her task as she appears to have at first planned it is not surprising. Her efforts as a writer were strained to the uttermost, but for many reasons the increase of effort on her part could not be followed by any increase of effect on the reader. Here we might repeat a good deal of the criticism suggested by the *Mill on the Floss*, in which the writer employed her great powers on materials so unpromising that none but a novelist of the highest class could have turned them to account. It was strange to see how, by the force of her genius, George Eliot made a brilliant story out of the little sayings and doings of the mean, prosaic, odious Dodson family. In her new novel she has undertaken a task still more difficult, for the centre of interest in it is a half-witted man. Silas Marner is at his best but a poor creature—a kindly, godly simpleton, much troubled with fits; but after his disaster he is not half the man he was. He is in a maze; there is no saying what he is or what he will do, and the catalepsy or trances to which he is subject must render him a singularly unaccountable being. But the pleasure of fiction depends mainly on our being able to count upon the elements of human character and to calculate results. When even among the subordinate characters of a story an imbecile is brought forward it involves the introduction of chance and uncertainty into a tissue of events the interest of which depends on their antecedent probability. This is so clearly the case that everybody must have felt a diminution of interest in any tale in which the production of the leading incidents depends on those passions that reduce the mind to a state of imbecility. Take drunkenness, for example; it is always unsatisfactory to hear of a catastrophe brought on by a man deprived of his senses through drink. Or, take jealousy, the most imbecile of the passions; though Lord Macaulay says that every English audience feels most sympathy with the Moor, while any Italian audience would most enjoy the subtleties of Iago,[1] it may be doubted whether any intelligent Englishman takes much interest in Othello, and, at all events, the stupidity to which his passion degraded him renders his conduct so unreasonable that in watching it we are met with continual disappointment. In all such cases of imbecility, whether it is natural and permanent or superinduced for the moment, we are out of our reckoning, we know not what to anticipate, and we are robbed of that expectancy which enters so largely into the pleasure afforded by fiction. It follows, therefore, that the Dodson family, with all their earthiness, are in one sense at least more fit for

---

[1] 'Machiavelli', *Edinburgh Review* (March 1827), xlv, 272-3.

the purposes of story than a half-witted Silas Marner with all his glimpses of the spiritual. Mean as the Dodson family are, yet, having the elements of their character before us, we see that they are calculable elements, and we can forecast their legitimate results. But what can we anticipate in the play of events for a man who, whatever be his moral elevation, is of weak mind and is subject to fits which for the time render his existence a blank? There are novels in which such a character might not be out of place even as the leading personage of the tale. In Mr. Wilkie Collins's last novel[1] the chief interest centres around two half-witted women in succession. Events occur which by no possibility could have happened had these women been in full possession of their senses. But in a novel which claims our attention chiefly for the intricacy of its plot, and slightly for the evolution of its characters, we almost forget the blank unsatisfactory nature of the leading personages in thinking of the startling incidents that crowd upon our notice. The interest of George Eliot's tales resting upon a different foundation, does not admit of such handling. In her stories, the characters are all in all; the incidents are of secondary importance, and grow out of the characters; a hero whose mind is nearly a blank, and whose life is represented as the sport of chance, is at variance with the spirit of her books. This will be evident if we state what are the two critical incidents in the life of Silas Marner. He was a young man of exemplary life and ardent faith, and belonged to a little flock of Methodists, assembling in a small back street, who regarded him with peculiar interest 'ever since he had fallen at a prayer meeting into a mysterious rigidity and suspension of consciousness, which, lasting for an hour or more, had been mistaken for death.' One night, while he was watching by the side of a dying deacon, he fell into one of these fits, and during his unconsciousness the deacon not only died, but also was robbed. Here is the first introduction of chance into the story. The weaver is accused of the robbery, and his Methodist friends determine to find out the guilty man, not by investigation, but by the drawing of lots. Chance upon chance—the lot fell upon Silas Marner, who goes forth and settles in the parish of Raveloe, a blighted being. At Raveloe he lives a lonely life for 15 years, at the end of which he falls into one of his trances, and on recovering his consciousness finds a little golden-haired child sleeping on his hearth. This is the second great chance of his life. As in one fit of unconsciousness he lost his all, so in another fit of unconsciousness he obtained a recompense. In either case he was helpless, had nothing to

[1] *The Woman in White* (1860).

do with his own fate, and was a mere feather in the wind of chance. From this point forward in the tale, however, there is no more chance —all is work and reward, cause and effect, the intelligent mind shaping its own destiny. The honest man bestows kindness upon the child, and reaps the benefit of it in his own increasing happiness, quickened intelligence, and social position. Only this is but a very small portion of the tale, so small that, seeing the importance of it, remembering the prominence which is given to it by means of the motto on the title-page, and knowing that the spirit of it more accords with George Eliot's artistic genius than that portion of the volume which occupies the greater number of pages, we have been forced to the conjecture that the story is not what the author originally intended it to be, but is huddled up at the end.

It is one of the evils of criticism that we cannot take any exception to a great work of art without suggesting that it is a failure. But to associate *Silas Marner* with any idea of failure is the very opposite of our intention. Criticize it as we may, the worst we can have to say of it is, that in aim it transcends the field of ordinary novels, and that in accomplished result it suggests too high a standard of measurement. Taking it as it is, and with all its faults, we really could not name another woman capable of producing a greater work, and it may be doubted whether, with the same materials, any man could have done better. As for the writing, it contains some of George Eliot's best composition, though at the same time it should be added that, as there is less of dialogue and more of narrative in the present work than is usual in the novels of this author, she appears to have felt the necessity of elaborating her own remarks to the uttermost. What her sentences in this way gain in force they lose in freedom; but with her rich vein of humour it will readily be understood that even when her writing is most laboured, the loss of freedom is not considerable. Her vein of humour, combined as it is with a peculiar seriousness and sense of the mystery of human life, is very fine, and gives an inexpressible charm to her descriptions of stupid, poverty-stricken boors. An author who manages to make us laugh at them and with them has gone far to make us forget the repulsiveness of their habits, and to prepare us for real sympathy in their struggles. The volume before us is full of those little touches which give vividness and humour to the most homely pictures. We open it at random and come upon a scene in the village public-house where the parochial worthies are drinking their beer, smoking their long pipes, and discussing their little affairs.

[quotes examples from chs. 6 and 7, and then Dolly Winthrop's 'theology' from ch. 16]

This is the burden of the book expressed in comical fashion. The weaver of Raveloe is very much in the position of the man of Uz. He is surrounded with comforters, most of whom are even less sympathizing than the comforters of Job, and he sinks into a deeper despair than that of the most patient of men, for, as we have said, he cursed and denied God in his affliction. The picture of his misery and the discipline of his repentance are but a homely, human version of the older and diviner drama. Instead of supernatural incidents and divine colloquies, we have ordinary accidents and village prattle. Instead of the Deity coming forth to justify his afflicted creature and to teach him better, a little child proves to the world the good qualities of his heart, and gives light and liberty to his understanding. It is a noble lesson, beautifully taught, though in saying thus much we run a risk of conveying the impression that George Eliot belongs to the class of religious or moralizing novelists who have rendered hateful the very idea of serious purpose in a novel. This is not the case, however. Hers is a very spiritual nature, and she cannot choose but regard life from a very lofty point of view. But her novels are true novels, not sermons done into dialogue. The moral purpose which is evident in her writing is mostly an unconscious purpose. It is that sort of moral meaning which belongs to every great work of art, and which no elevated mind can get rid of. She tells a simple story without the least idea of inculcating any copy-book lesson, but by merely elevating the reader to her mount of observation she cannot fail to suggest to the mind some profound reflections.

30. Unsigned review, *Westminster Review*

July 1861, lxxvi, 280–2

It is a great gain, because full of promise to her readers, that the last of George's Eliot's works is undoubtedly the finest, the stream of thought runs clearer, the structure of the story is more compact, while the philosophical insight is deeper and more penetrating than in any of her former productions. It has been said that *Silas Marner* is deficient in interest, but the only element of interest in which it can be called wanting, is that which is supplied by the vulgar excitement of exceptional circumstances or of abnormal characters. In *Silas Marner*, the dead level and dry bones of English country life fifty years since, are illumined and vivified by a power of sympathetic insight which is one of the rarest of intellectual gifts. There is nothing so difficult to a cultivated intellect as to enter into the mental states of the ignorant and uninformed, it is an accomplishment of genius alone, the minutest analysis, and the most comprehensive inductions are but tools and helps in such a task. In the progress towards clear conceptions of any kind, the vestiges of the confused notions they replace are trodden out, the memory of our first feeble intellectual life is as irrecoverable and obscure as that of our physical birth. Insight into the past conditions even of our own minds, is one of the rarest acquisitions of reflection; and the difficulty of attaining such insight when times and men foreign to ourselves are concerned is so great, that it is only within the last generation that even history has aspired to do more than chronicle the events of each succeeding year.

Heretofore novelists have either relied on an interesting and well-constructed tale, or on the gradual and skilful development of a well-considered plot, or on unexpected solutions of prepared difficulties; and when this has been the case the study of character has generally been weak and incomplete; or they have seized upon some particular type of character the growth of which they wish to display, and in this case the circumstances in which the hero or heroine is placed are generally forced and unnatural, being neglected as subordinate to the main purpose of the author. The most remarkable peculiarity and distinguishing excellence of *Silas Marner*, is the complete correlation between the characters and their circumstances; the actors in this story come before us like the flowers of their own fields, native to the soil and varying with each constituent of the earth from which they spring, with every difference that is implied in defective or excessive nutriment, but yet no more the creatures of blind chance, each asserting his own individuality after his kind, and none over-stepping the possibilities of culture furnished by such a world-forgotten village as Raveloe. It is impossible to dissociate any of the characters from the village in which they were born and bred—they form an organic whole with Raveloe; they are not connected with it by any external, or even humorous bands, but by vital threads that will not bear disruption. The stranger Silas is at last assimilated by the little society, and only truly lives when the process has been completed. Nothing can be more profound than this picture of the manner in which all human beings are influenced by their environment, the consequence of this most wonderful fitness between the characters and the scene of their life, is that on laying down the book we do not dwell upon Silas Marner or Godfrey Cass or Dolly Winthrop, or any particular character, but are forced to embrace them all with all their restricted country life; nothing short of all Raveloe satisfies the memory; there is no episode that can be detached from the story, no character that can be spared, much less conceived other than it shows itself; there is about them all a certain absoluteness like that which characterizes the works of nature.

In her former works the author has taken a more or less critical position over against society; in the present one, though criticism cannot sleep in such an intellect, she appreciates more fully the strange compensations which accompany incomplete states of development, and brings out, without express statement, that conclusion which has so often stood at the commencement of many a feeble sermon, that there is but little connexion after all between a high moral character and clear conceptions of morality.

The profound insight with which the seed of retribution is shown shrouded in every act, and the intimate fitness which this retribution assumes in her hands is beyond praise; truth calls not for praise, but demands acknowledgment. Novels claim to illustrate the instructiveness of life; but this instructiveness, however, is in direct proportion to the truth of the picture, and the light thrown on it by the author. Mostly it is the case that where the reflections are true and just, the situations are exceptional, or where the circumstances are those of every-day life, the remarks on them are weak, trivial, or obvious. Of

Silas Marner it is impossible to say which is most admirable, the vivid painting of life itself, or the profound remarks on the progress of that life; nor is this all, the kindly humour which glows through every judgment is as conciliating as the verdict is convincing, and the more so as the author shows no foregone purpose in the construction of the fable, but leaves it to bear its own fruit. It not so much directly instructs as adds to the experience of its readers, and like life itself adds to it in proportion to their power of understanding the results it offers. There is no single feature of this novel which will surprise those who are acquainted with the former works of the author, their greatest beauties are to be found in this; the objections which have been taken to the incompleteness and insufficiency of Captain Donnithorne and Stephen Guest, are here met by the best of all possible answers in the full and masterly treatment of the character of Godfrey Cass; the profound truth and delicate discrimination evinced in the delineation of this character are but too apt to be overlooked; it is one of those portraits which gain upon you the more you look at it, and which you leave with the feeling that no art could improve. A somewhat objectionable use of physiological images which certainly disfigured some few pages of the *Mill on the Floss*, is no longer recognisable, but the author's talent, like some fine crystal, assuming its definite form, has here, purged out of its symmetrical structure all impurities and foreign substances.

31. Unsigned review, *Dublin University Magazine*

April 1862, lix, 396–401

This hostile review is very similar to the same journal's abuse of *The Mill on the Floss* (No. 20) (see Introduction, p. 17). The reviewer prefaces his discussion of *Silas Marner* with some condescending remarks on the poor quality of contemporary novels.

The general character of last year's novels bears out, we dare think, the general tenor of these latter remarks. We had one or two perhaps of very high excellence; several more were very good in their way; but the great bulk follow the descending scale of merit, from the middling down to the very weak and the utterly worthless. Of course our estimate is framed partly at second hand, for what reader past his teens would have either the wish or the time to wade through half the new works of fiction which publishers are wont to advertise as ranking among the best novels of the year? We can but judge of the many by what we know of the few. If the better class of readers set much store by *Framley Parsonage* and *Silas Marner*, we can easily guess what floods of fiction and water are turned on for the use of that larger crowd to whom George Eliot and Mr. Trollope are names of little meaning. Dearly loving a good story, and feeling the mighty magic wielded by a Scott or a Fielding, we are often shy of opening a new novel written by never so masterly a hand, lest nothing should come of our venture but vanity and vexation of spirit. That, whether for our ultimate gain or loss, the shyness has sometimes been overcome, the following pages will show; but only a boarding-school miss, whose time hung heavy on her hands, would think of dooming us to the fearful penance of exploring the various works in which her untutored soul beheld daily some new heaven.

We have alluded to George Eliot; and *Silas Marner* is just one of those books which a discerning novel-reader will fear equally to take up and to leave unread. There was enough of promise in *Adam Bede* and *The Mill on the Floss* to make one hopeful of yet better things to come, while the faults which marred those other works were serious enough to suggest the fear of their being repeated on a larger scale in the next. We are sorry to say that the fear has proved a surer prophet than the hope. A duller book it has seldom been our lot to read through; and, but for a strong wish to deal fairly by an author whose art principles are utterly at variance with our old-fashioned views, we should never have surmounted the first half of it. George Eliot is not lively at the best of times, but here the very spirit of wilful dulness seems to have claimed her for its own. Her characters were never remarkable for pleasantness, but here they make themselves more than usually disagreeable. Mean, boorish, heavy-witted, most of them fail alike to touch our hearts and to amuse our fancies. The story itself beats all its forerunners for want of strength, coherence, and completeness; reflecting as it were throughout its few hundred pages the very spirit of its half-dazed, weak-bodied, passive-minded hero. Her philosophy, seldom deep or original before, seems here to roam delighted over a dead level of the tritest commonplace. It is amusing to hear her bringing out as new discoveries in the world of feeling a class of truths which most people have taken in with their mother's milk. Like persons slowly recovering the use of some long-lost bodily sense, she delights in pointing out each old-world experience as it flashes for the first time across her newly awakened soul. When the author of *St. Leon* finds out the use and beauty of those homely affections which the author of *Political Justice* had wholly banished from his new code of morals, we are struck with awe, not at the depth of wisdom displayed in Godwin's amended theory, but only at the saddening tokens of a clever man's original blindness to the truths that lay immediately before his feet. A like feeling comes over us as we listen to George Eliot's sententious prosing about the worship of chance, or watch the gradual unfolding of Silas Marner's long arrested sympathies under the quickening presence of his adopted foundling.

A stupid hero may form the meet centre of a dull story; but the two together make up a heavy tax on the reader's patience. It is useless to say that the life here drawn could not be otherwise than dull, if it were drawn faithfully. A novelist's duty is, above all things, to entertain. A skilful artist will select the most taking point of view for his work. Without sacrificing truth to effect, he will turn out a picture full of life and colour, and aerial bloom; not a mere colourless photograph where the horizon presses close upon the foreground, and the main figure lacks all the peculiar grace and even the just proportion of its living model. If George Eliot has a special taste for low life, she might surely pick out scenes better worth recording than most of those which here greet us. What good can any one gain by reading page after page of the boorish twaddle kept up by the folk who spend their evenings, with the help of pipes and beer, in the 'Rainbow' parlour? It may be very like the ordinary talk of such people; but life in a novel is short, and a little of that rubbish goes a long way with all who have any hankering after something better than pothouse gossip, very slightly flavoured with pothouse jokes; and there is hardly any thing better than this throughout the book. Even the account of Squire Cass's Christmas party hangs fire; and the sudden appearance of Silas, with his babyish treasure-trove in his arms, affords a welcome relief to the Squire's dull jokes, Mrs. Crackenthorp's feeble attempts to smile, and Godfrey's mild manœuvres for getting a quiet talk with Miss Nancy. Let any one calmly compare such scenes as these with the descriptions in *Elsie Venner*,[1] of Colonel Sprowle's ball and Widow Rowens's tea-party, and he will hardly hesitate which to prefer, even if he thinks more highly of our country-woman's genius than we do of either hers or the American's. Mr. Holmes succeeds where George Eliot fails, less by reason of his greater natural gifts, than because of his larger experience and finer tact.

These dull clowns, who talk at best like thin dilutions of Mrs. Poyser, whose ideas and imagery seldom rise above the level of their native dunghills, whose highest faith in the powers above falls far below that of a good Mahommedan or an educated Hindoo, are they the only kind of people one is like to meet with in the far-off country-side? Do such as these form even the staple of our English country folk, in any class above the very lowest? We think that most of those who have had more than a passing glimpse of life in the rural districts, would agree with us in answering—No! Of boors and beasts there are enough in all classes. Farmers are not proverbial for refined manners or comprehensive wits. The 'bold peasantry, their country's pride,' are sometimes given over to superstitions almost as dark as spirit-rapping, revivalism, and the creed of M. Comte. But a truthful picture of the masses should embrace other samples than the worst; and a truthful picture this of George Eliot's certainly is not. English nature cannot on the whole, be much altered from what it was during the great war with France; and we dare avow that, in these days, there are few country

[1] By Oliver Wendell Holmes, 1861.

parishes on which the life and manners portrayed in *Silas Marner* would not be accounted a pure libel. Which of us has not heard fall from many an humble mouth words whose wisdom, kindliness, or Christian meaning, not many persons of higher birth and rarer breeding could easily surpass? Have the virtues which grace so many an English hut and homestead of to-day sprung up like mushrooms in a single night, that so few traces of them were to be found among the Raveloe parishioners of fifty years ago? That strong religious faith, that unquestioning delight in Biblical lore, which crops out nowadays in the life and language of many an unlearned Englishman, were they so little known to the bulk of our grandfathers, that even good, tender-hearted Dolly Winthrop could find no better words for comforting the bewildered Silas than such as, after repeated ponderings, presented themselves to her unaided ignorance? In telling him that 'all as we've got to do is to trusten,—to do the right thing, as fur as we know, and to trusten,' she certainly stumbles into pure good sense and sound religion; but had George Eliot known more of her poor Christian countryfolk, the advice so given would have been offered sooner, and in language more directly borrowed from Scriptural sources.

If these life-pictures are not essentially true, what sufficient reason may we discover for the book containing them? Tastes differ; and the life herein painted may to many seem worth examining, simply because it is low and mainly heathenish. Modern readers will devour any thing, if only it has a look of being true, or bears a name already endeared to their eyes. Yet surely the gentle dulness of *Silas Marner* must pall on those who liked the novelty of it when taken, with due disguises, in *Adam Bede* and *The Mill on the Floss*. Even persons of the Poyser pattern grow wearisome after many pages; and Maggie inspired a much stronger interest than Nancy Lammeter or Silas himself can possibly do. Even a photograph, to bear inspection, must be taken with more or less regard for artistic effect. It is not improving to live for ever in close contemplation of pigstyes and refuse-heaps. If 'the short and simple annals of the poor' contained nothing pleasanter than what George Eliot can show, it were best to explore them no further. Silas Marner is certainly a most original hero, and his character is drawn with a good deal of original power; but after all said and done, he seems, to our thinking, a poor creature whom one may pity, but cannot care for overmuch. A curious pathological study is the only name we can give to this sketch of a poor daft body whose soul, even to the last, never quite wakes out of the moral catalepsy into which it fell, after the cruel treachery of that dear friend with whom he 'had gone out and in for ten year and more' had lost him not only a sweetheart and a fair name among his fellows, but, worst of all, his whole faith in a God who could join, as then it seemed to him, in bearing witness against the innocent. It seems to us that neither in this, nor in most of her other characters, can George Eliot succeed in winning the reader's active sympathies. A more genial artist would have made all hearts yearn with compassion towards the lonely, blighted, hope-forsaken outcast, who, for so many years, shrank from all fellowship with his new neighbours, working by day at his weaver's loom, and nightly digging out of their hiding-place the pieces of gold accumulated from week to week by his successful toil; but this author's cold, hard style serves only to rob her subject of that ideal charm which so often, for the time being, clothes the victim of any great misfortune. It is with a very languid kind of interest we learn the abstraction of Marner's cherished gold, and watch the growth of his affection for the golden-haired foundling, who seemed sent by a pitying fate as if on purpose to make good his loss. Somewhat livelier is the interest we take in little Eppie's childish frolics, and the pleasant troubles they cause her adoptive father; for George Eliot is thoroughly at home in describing children; and the ways of very young children, if faithfully recorded, cannot fail to amuse. But with Eppie grown up, the reign of dulness returns, and her timely wedding permits us to feel only too thankful that the book is done.

The one other character for whom we have any thing like a personal regard, is Dolly Winthrop, the wife of a burly, beer-loving, wheelwright in Raveloe village, a tender, large-hearted, long-suffering, housemother, who helps poor Silas equally to look after his new-found treasure, and to regain somewhat of his better mind. Her shrewd, kindly sayings, fall here and there about the story like patches of sunshine down a gloomy lane. Of the remaining personages there is not much to say. Nancy Lammeter looks a fair sample of her sex and class; but neither her husband nor the other males of the Cass family are drawn with the strength and clearness of a master hand. Like most of the author's male figures, they are but shadows and nothing more. If the story is simple, and the actors mostly dull, the leading incidents are startling enough. Dunstan Cass, for instance, having stolen the weaver's money, disappears from the scene for sixteen years, no one knowing of his crime or caring to know of his whereabout. At last it turns out that he had never lived to enjoy his plunder, for the skeleton and the money are found together in a pit near Marner's cottage. As a set-off, we suppose, to this piece of melodramatic justice, nothing is ever told us about the false friend who robbed Marner of his sweetheart and his early trust alike in God and man, although, for moral and artistic purposes, it would have been both safe and easy to let the poor weaver have some kind of token that such wrongdoing did not always prosper, even in this world. As it is, there is no sufficient ending to a disjointed story. Silas gets back the gold for which he had ceased to care; but the cloud upon his heart and intellect still remains, lightened somewhat by stray beams of hope and comfort, but as far as ever from being torn aside. So may it often be in real life; but art has higher ends than a slavishly literal rendering of chance facts.

ROMOLA

July 1862–August 1863

---

32. Anthony Trollope to George Eliot

28 June 1862

The Letters of Anthony Trollope, ed. Bradford A. Booth, 1951, pp. 115–16. During the writing of *Romola*, George Eliot had been helped in matters Florentine by Trollope's brother, Thomas Adolphus Trollope, who had been very impressed by 'the minuteness of her care to reproduce the form and pressure of the time of which she was writing' (*The George Eliot Letters*, iii, 432).

My dear Mrs. Lewes,

I have just read the first number of *Romola* and I cannot refrain from congratulating you. If you can, or have, kept it up to the end you will have done a great work. Adam Bede, Mrs. Poyser, and Marner have been very dear to me; but excellent as they are, I am now compelled to see that you can soar above even their heads. The description of Florence,—little bits of Florence down to a close nail, and great facts of Florence up to the very of life among those full living nobles,—are wonderful in their energy and in their accuracy. The character of Romola is artistically beautiful,—a picture exceeded by none that I know of any girl in any novel. It is the perfection of pen painting,—and you have been nobly aided by your artist. I take it for granted that it is Leighton.[1] The father also of Romola is excellent.

Do not fire too much over the heads of your readers. You have to write to tens of thousands, and not to single thousands. I say this, not because I would have you alter ought of your purpose. That were not

---

[1] Frederic Leighton (1830–96), later 1st Baron Leighton of Stretton, distinguished painter, and President of the Royal Academy, 1878.

worth your while, even though the great numbers were to find your
words too hard. But because you may make your full purpose compatible with their taste—

I wonder at the toil you must have endured in getting up your work,
—wonder and envy. But I should never envy your success, or the great
appreciation of what you have done that will certainly come,—
probably today, but if not, then tomorrow.

Yours very heartily
Anthony Trollope

33. Unsigned review, *Athenaeum*

11 July 1863, p. 46

Those who have read *Romola* in its monthly course should begin the
story afresh, now that it is complete and appears in a connected form;
otherwise, they may be unable to recognize the many rare merits and
beauties which it contains. As a serial story *Romola* was not attractive;
readers found their patience wearied by the minuteness with which they
were required to follow the transitions of popular feeling in Florence;
the intrigues and political parish business of that wonderful Italian
republic, from the death of Lorenzo de' Medici, in the year of grace
1492, until the people killed their apostle, prophet and reformer,
Savonarola, in 1498. Old political struggles, even in our own times
cannot obtain listeners to their details after the personal interests which
magnified their importance have been set at rest by the event; and to
have the demagogues and actors of the concentred interests and
intrigues of one jealous Italian city reproduced, however vividly, is
more curious than interesting. It is like attempting to feast on the bread
and wine found in the ruins of Pompeii. But, read as a consecutive
whole, these scenes take their due place as the framework and background for the human characters, whose struggles and hopes and fears
have a perennial interest, and which are in *Romola* as vivid as if they

concerned English men and women of 1863. The amount of reading that the author must have achieved to get up the minute details of time, place, circumstance and costume, down even to the old proverbs, jokes and squibs of the passing moment,—to say nothing of the skill with which the aspect of the political questions of the period are grasped and presented to the reader, as they would have appeared to the eyes of those concerned in them, is marvellous;—a monument of patience and easy walking in heavy fetters, which commands the reader's wonder. But, then, the jokes are dried; the appearance of vitality given to politics and pageants long since dead and passed away is remarkable; but neither the politics nor the people are really alive,—they are only well dried, preserved and coloured, and the reader feels as though he were ungrateful, in not being better entertained by all that has cost so much time and labour. There is a theatrical element in the studied accuracy of dress, scenery and detail. Read, however, as a whole, this framework is less oppressive, whilst the human interest takes its due place and proportions. There are noble things to be found in *Romola*, which will make the reader's heart burn within him. It will be scarcely possible to rise from the perusal without being penetrated by 'the joy of elevated thoughts,' without feeling a desire to cease from a life of self-pleasing, and to embody in action that sense of obligation, of obedience to duty, which is, indeed, the crowning distinction that has been bestowed on man, the high gift in which all others culminate. This is high praise; and a work that can produce this effect, if only on a single reader, has not been written in vain.

The character of Savonarola is the gem of the book; it has been grasped and delineated with a wonderful force and truth, that commends itself instinctively as a real presentment of the man. It is an historical study, given with subtle insight and delicate shadowing: the influence of his surroundings, the peculiar nature of the human and political elements among which he worked, their influence upon him, and the aspect they bore to him, are all taken into consideration. When Savonarola is in question, the reader is glad to have had impressed upon him the details of public and private Italian life at that period which alone can throw light on the character of the Saint. The scene between Romola and Savonarola, when she is flying from her husband, is noble, and puts an end to all inclination to criticize or complain.

The character of Tito Melemo, the husband of Romola, is not successful; with all that is said of his grace, his beauty, his fascination, he remains vague in image, and there is a certain weariness in his

sayings and doings. The poor old Baldassene, with his brain bewildered
by the enormity of Tito's ingratitude, his fierce desire for vengeance,
and the flicker of his intelligence gradually becoming extinguished
under the sense of injustice and misery, is very clever; but his feebleness
is painful, and the constant failure of all his efforts to assert his own
cause, or even to utter his accusation, is too long drawn out; the sympathy of the reader is fatigued, and his final death-clutch upon Tito
does not make itself clear to the reader. The men are so nearly dead,
one from starvation, and the other from drowning, that the scene,
though sufficiently sombre, is not effectual. As a novel *Romola* cannot
be called entertaining: it requires sustained attention, and it is by no
means light reading; but those who do not seek the mere amusement
of an exciting story will find noble things in *Romola*—eloquent and
beautiful pages—subtle utterances and lovely thoughts. It has not the
powerful interest that is to be found in the author's former novels; but
there are indications of much higher powers of mind. The winding up
of the book is very well managed, and is quite satisfactory. Romola is
left in the possession of a far better life than if all her early hopes had
been fulfilled.

34. R. H. Hutton, unsigned review, *Spectator*

18 July 1863, xxxvi, 2265-7

The most understanding of the reviews of *Romola*, as George
Eliot confirms (No. 35). (See headnote to No. 28 and Introduction, p. 19.)

It was easy to be mistaken in the first chapters of this book, and it is
pleasant to acknowledge that we were mistaken, and had not the insight
to see the first faint signs of one of the greatest works of modern
fiction. It is from no desire to vindicate that mistake that we regret
that *Romola* should have been published in fragments. That it was not in

any way affected by this mode of publication,—that it was not written in fragments, but was created by a continuous artistic effort, is clear enough. Still, perhaps, that is one reason for the inadequacy of the first impression. George Eliot's drawings all require a certain space, like Raffael's Cartoons, and are not of that kind which produce their effect by the reiteration of scenes each complete in itself. You have to unroll a large surface of the picture before even the smallest *unit* of its effect is attained. And this is far more true of this, probably the author's greatest work, than of her English tales. In the latter, the constant and striking delineation of social features with which we are all familiar, satisfies the mind in the detail almost as much as in the complete whole. It takes a considerable space to get a full view of Hetty or Dinah in *Adam Bede,* and a still greater space to understand the characters of Adam, or of Arthur Donnithorne. But, in the meantime, the vivid detail, the dry humour, the English pictures with which we are all so familiar, fascinate and satisfy us even before we have gained this clear view of the whole characters. This cannot be so when even greater power is shown in mastering the life of a foreign nation in a past age. We do not care about the light Florentine buzz with which so great a part of the first volume is filled. Its allusions are half riddles, and its liveliness a blank to us. Small local colours depend for their charm on the familiarity of small local knowledge. Then, again, George Eliot is— we will not say much greater as an imaginative painter of characters than as an imaginative painter of action, for action, also, she paints with marvellous power,—but much more inclined for the one than the other. What her characters *do* is always subordinate with her to what they *are.* This is the highest artistic power, but it carries its inconveniences with it. She does not carry her readers *away,* as it is called; it is generally easy to stop reading her; she satisfies you for the moment, and does not make you look forward to the end. She has Sir Walter Scott's art for revivifying the past,—but not Scott's dynamical force in making you plunge into it with as headlong an interest as into the present. For this she compensates by a deeper and wider intellectual grasp,—but still it is easy enough to understand why half-developed characters, sketched in with unfamiliar local colours on a background of history that has long melted away, should have looked strange and uninviting, especially when not carried off by any exciting current of event, to the ordinary reader's eyes. It is marvellous that, in spite of these disadvantages, the wide and calm imaginative power of the writer should have produced a work which is likely to be permanently identified with English literature,—in which Italy and England may feel a common pride.

The great artistic purpose of the story is to trace out the conflict between liberal culture and the more passionate form of the Christian faith in that strange era, which has so many points of resemblance with the present, when the two in their most characteristic forms struggled for pre-eminence over Florentines who had been educated into the half-pedantic and half-idealistic scholarship of Lorenzo de Medici, who faintly shared the new scientific impulses of the age of Columbus and Copernicus, and whose hearts and consciences were stirred by the preaching, political as well as spiritual, of one of the very greatest as well as earliest of the reformers—the Dominican friar Savonarola. No period could be found when mingling faith and culture effervesced with more curious result. In some great and noble minds the new Learning, clearing away the petty rubbish of Romanist superstition, and revealing the mighty simplicities of the great age of Greece, grew into a feeling that supplied all the stimulus of fever, if not the rest of faith, and of these the author has drawn a very fine picture of the blind Florentine scholar, Romola's father, Bardo, who, with a restless fire in his heart, 'hung over the books and lived with the shadows' all his life. Nothing is more striking and masterly in the story than the subtle skill with which the dominant influence of this scholarship over the imagination of the elder generation of that time,—the generation which saw the first revival of learning, is delineated in the pictures of Bardo and Baldassarre. In the former you get something like a glimpse of the stately passion for learning which, in a later age (though England was then naturally behind Italy), took so vital a hold of the intellect of Milton, and overlaid his powerful imagination with all its rich fretwork of elaborate classical allusion. In the latter character,—Baldassarre, the same impression is conveyed in a still more subtle and striking form, because by painting the intermittent flashes of intellectual power in a scholar's failing memory, and its alternations with an almost animal passion of revenge, we gain not only a more distinct knowledge of the relative value in which scholarship was there and then held as compared with other human capacities, but a novel sense of sympathy which, in an age of diffused culture like this, it is not very easy to attain with the extravagance, as we should now think, of the price set upon it. There are few passages of subtler literary grandeur in English romance than that which paints the electrifying effect of a thrill of vindictive passion on Baldassarre's paralyzed memory, in recalling once more his full command of Greek learning, and the sense of power which thus returned to him:—

[quotes incident in ch. 38]

This passage, taken with those which lead up to it, whether they refer to Bardo or Baldassarre, has the effect of reproducing one great feature in the age of the revival of learning with the finest effect—that sense of large *human* power which the mastery over a great ancient language, itself the key to a magnificent literature, gave, and which made scholarship then a *passion*, while with us it has almost relapsed into an antiquarian dryasdust pursuit. We realize again, in reading about Bardo and Baldassarre, how, for these times, the first sentence of St. John, 'In the beginning was the Word,' had regained all its force, to the exclusion, perhaps, of the further assertion that the Word was with God and was God. That sense of the great *power* of language, of which we have now so little, which, indeed, it is the tendency of the present day to depreciate, was in that day full of a new vigour, and to some extent contested with the mysteries of the Gospel the control of great men's souls. This is the picture which Romola makes so living for us. We find here the strife between the keen definite knowledge of the reviving Greek learning, and the turbid visionary mysticism of the reviving Dominican piety. We find a younger generation, represented by Romola, and Dino, and Tito, that has inherited this scholarship, and finds it wholly inadequate for its wants, looking upon that almost as dry bones which the older generation felt to be stimulating nourishment,—and either turning from it, like Dino, to the rapture of mystical asceticism, or using it, like Tito, as a useful sharp-edged tool in the battle of Florentine politics, or trying, like Romola, to turn it to its true purpose, viz., that of clarifying and sifting the false from the true elements in the great mysterious faith presented to her conscience by Savonarola. The pride of laborious farseeing scholarship, gazing with clear scornful eyes at the inarticulate convulsive ecstasies of faith—all the powers of language rebelling passionately, as it were, against the deep and fervent passions which transcend the containing powers of language, and boil over its edges, in religious, or even in the opposite animal raptures,—this is a picture wonderfully painted, and which produces all the more impression, that the minute vivid ripple of the light gossip of the Florentine market-place gives a ground-tone to the book.

This fundamental conflict between the Greek scholarship and the

mystical Christian faith which runs through the book, is made even
more striking by the treacherous character of the man who represents
the Greek culture cut adrift from all vestige of moral or religious faith.
The fine gradations of social dissimulation, so characteristic of Florence
in the Medicean era, ranging from the one politic insincerity of
Savonarola, which raises so grand a struggle in his mind, down to the
easy-sliding treachery of Tito, bring up before us in another shape the
characteristic contrasts of the age between that earnest spirit which
revived the old culture, because it was *truer* than the degraded current
superstitions,—that pliant worldliness which adopted, and adapted
itself to it, because it was an instrument of finer edge and wider utility,
—and lastly, that fervent faith which despised it as substituting the
study of a dead past for the great conflict of a living present. Tito's
smooth dissimulation is all the more striking a picture, because it comes
out as the natural fruit of a mind almost incapable of either strong
conviction or strong personal fidelity, gliding about in an age when
strong convictions were coming to the birth, and among a race barely
redeemed from that spirit of political falsehood which was just going
to be called Machiavellian by a proud sense of loyalty to personal and
party ties. Tito is pictured, as the Greeks of that time perhaps deserved
to be pictured, not as originally false, but as naturally pleasure-loving,
and swerving aside before every unpleasant obstacle in the straight path,
at the instance of a quick intelligence and a keen dislike both to personal
collisions and to personal sacrifices. His character is, to use a mathe-
matical term, the osculating curve which touches that of each of the
others at the surface, and nowhere else—Savonarola's at the point of
his external political policy, Romola's in her love of beauty and hatred
of the turbid malarious exhalations of visionary excitement, and the
scholarly enthusiasm of Bardo only in the apt classical knowledge, by
no means in the ardour of his love for it. On Tito's very first entrance
on to the stage, the Florentine artist of the story, Piero di Cosimo, is
eager to paint him as a Sinon, not that there is treachery in his face, but
that there is in it the softness and suppleness, and gliding ease of movement, and nimbleness of intellect, which, in a time of political passion,
seem likely to lead to treachery, because, first, they qualify, both
intellectually and morally, for the traitor's part, and, next, they serve
to mask his play. From this first scene, when the fatal ease of the man's
manner is first suggested, to the noble scene at the conclusion, in which
he sounds, and sounds successfully, Savonarola's too eager statesman-
ship, with intent to betray him to the Duke of Milan and the Pope,

you see Tito's character grow into the foulest treachery, simply from its consistent desire to compass every pleasant end which suggests itself to him as feasible, without openly facing, if he can help it, any one's severe displeasure. Nor is anything drawn more finely than the peculiar species of fear which is an essential part of this character,— a fear which, in the last resort, spurs the keen intellect of the man into a certain desperate energy, but which usually remains too cowardly even to understand itself, and lurks on in the character as a kind of unconscious resentment against those who wring from him the exercise of such an energy. A character essentially treacherous only because it is full of soft *fluid* selfishness is one of the most difficult to paint. But whether when locking up the crucifix, which Romola received from her dying brother's hands, in the little temple crowned with the figures of Ariadne and Bacchus, and fondly calling her 'Regina mia,' which somehow conveys that he less *loves* the woman than passionately admires her—or buying his 'garment of fear,' the coat of light chain armour, from the armour-smith,—or thoughtlessly deceiving the poor little contadina Tessa by the mock marriage at the carnival—or shrinking before Romola's indignation into that frigid tone of empty affectionateness which is the clearest sign of a contracted heart—or interpreting the Latin proclamation to the people with a veil of good-nature over his treacherous purpose—or crowned in the feast at the Rucellai Gardens, and paling suddenly beneath Baldassarre's vindictive glance—or petting Tessa and her children in his hiding-place on the hill—the same wonderful power is maintained throughout, of stamping on our imagination with the full force of a master hand a character which seems naturally too fluent for the artist's purpose. There is not a more wonderful piece of painting in English romance than this figure of Tito.

Of Romola it is less easy to say whether one is absolutely satisfied or not. The *soupçon* of hardness of which one is conscious as somewhat detracting from her power, the skill with which the author has prepared us for a mental struggle exactly similar, even in its minutest features, to what might occur today between the claims of a sublime faith appealing to the conscience, and a distaste for miracle or vision in its prophet, the striking contrast with Tessa, the ignorant 'pretty little pigeon,' who thinks every one who is kind to her a saint,—all render it a little difficult to say whether we know her intimately, or whether we have only a very artistic idea of what she is *not*, and what she *is* only by inference and contrast. Our own feeling is that Romola is the least perfect figure in the book, though a fine one,—that she is a shade more modernized than the others, several shades less individual, and, after all, though the pivot of her character turns, as it were, on faith, that she does not distinctly show any faith except the faith in rigid honour, in human pity, and partially also in Savonarola's personal greatness and power. We do not say the character is not natural,—we only say it is half-revealed and more suggested than fully painted, though these harder feminine characters always seem to ask to be outlined more strongly than any others.

But the great and concentrated interest of the book—at least, after the wonderful development of Tito's character—is the portrait of Savonarola, which it is almost impossible not to feel as faithful as history, as it is great as romance. You see the same large human-hearted Italian Luther, narrower than Luther on some sides, owing to the thin Medicean culture against which he led the reaction, but with a far more statesmanlike and political purpose, and far more fiery imagi-nation, the same, in fact, whom Mr. Maurice has delineated intellec-tually with so much delicate fidelity in his history of modern philo-sophy,[1] and who impresses himself upon us in almost everything he wrote, but yet never before presented clearly to the eye. His portrait evinces almost as great a graphic power, and far more scrupulous care than Sir Walter Scott used in those pictures of the various Stewarts which will certainly outlive the very different originals. Nothing can be finer and more impressive—nothing more difficult to make fine and impressive—than Savonarola's exhortation to Romola to return to the home from which she was flying. You see in every word the man's profound trust in God as the author of all human ties, and of all social and political ties, breaking through the fetters of his Dominican order, and asserting the divine order *in* nature rather than the divine order *out of* nature. This, however, is not the finest picture given of him. The finest is contained in the profoundly pathetic scene in which Savonarola, having in the fervour of his eloquence committed God to working him a miracle at the right moment, is brought to book both by his enemies and friends on the question of the trial by fire, and kneels in prayer that in fact refuses to be prayer, but rises into a political debate within him-self as to the policy of seeming to take a step which he knows he must somehow evade. 'While his lips were uttering audibly *cor mundum crea in me*, his mind was still filled with the images of the snare his enemies had prepared for him, still busy with the arguments by which

[1] J. F. D. Maurice, *Modern Philosophy* (1862), ch. 3.

he could justify himself against their taunts and accusations.' But the scene is too long and too fine for us to spoil it by snatching it from the context, and is, indeed, closely bound up with the noble picture of the encounter with Tito which follows. Our author rejects apparently the authenticity of the last great words attributed to Savonarola as he is dying on the scaffold, which Mr. Maurice accepts. 'The voice of the Papal emissary,' says the historian of philosophy, 'was heard proclaiming that Savonarola was cut off from the Church militant and triumphant: Another voice was heard saying, "No, not from the Church triumphant, they cannot shut me out of that." ' It is a pity that George Eliot rejects, as we suppose she does, the evidence for these words. They would have formed a far higher artistic ending to her story than the somewhat feeble and womanish chapter with which it concludes,—the only blot on the book. Large and genial as is the sympathy with Savonarola, there is, perhaps, no wish to represent his faith altogether as a triumphant faith. Yet Romola's faith in goodness and self-sacrifice, and in little children and 'the eternal marriage of love and duty,' and so forth, which the proem tells us is ever to last, would be an idle dream for the world, without a Christ in whose eternal nature all these realities live and grow.

But the defects, if they are defects, in this book, and the certainly somewhat unfortunate amplification of Florentine gossip in the first volume, before the reader is drawn into that rushing tide of Savonarola's revolution round the skirts of which Tito's treacherous destiny hovers, like a bird of prey over a raging battle, are blemishes too slight to do more than distinguish still more vividly the high purpose and calm imaginative serenity of this great romance. It will never be George Eliot's most popular book,—it seems to us, however, much the greatest she has yet produced.

35. George Eliot to R. H. Hutton

8 August 1863

The George Eliot Letters, iv, 96–7 (see No. 34).

After reading your article on *Romola*, with careful reference to the questions you put to me in your letter, I can answer sincerely that I find nothing fanciful in your interpretation. On the contrary, I am confirmed in the satisfaction I felt when I first listened to the article, at finding that certain chief elements of my intention have impressed themselves so strongly on your mind, notwithstanding the imperfect degree in which I have been able to give form to my ideas. Of course if I had been called on to expound my own book, there are other things that I should want to say, or things that I should say somewhat otherwise; but I can point to nothing in your exposition of which my consciousness tells me that it is erroneous, in the sense of saying something which I neither thought nor felt. You have seized with a fulness which I had hardly hoped that my book could suggest, what it was my effort to express in the presentation of Bardo and Baldassarre; and also the relation of the Florentine political life to the development of Tito's nature. Perhaps even a judge so discerning as yourself could not infer from the imperfect result how strict a self-control and selection were exercised in the presentation of details. I believe there is scarcely a phrase, an incident, an allusion, that did not gather its value to me from its supposed subservience to my main artistic objects. But it is likely enough that my mental constitution would always render the issue of my labour something excessive—wanting due proportion.

It is the habit of my imagination to strive after as full a vision of the medium in which a character moves as of the character itself. The psychological causes which prompted me to give such details of Florentine life and history as I have given, are precisely the same as those which determined me in giving the details of English village life in *Silas Marner*, or the 'Dodson' life, out of which were developed the destinies of poor Tom and Maggie. But you have correctly pointed out the reason why my tendency to excess in this effort after artistic vision makes the impression of a fault in *Romola* much more perceptibly than in my previous books. And I am not surprised at your dissatisfaction with Romola herself. I can well believe that the many difficulties belonging to the treatment of such a character have not been overcome, and that I have failed to bring out my conception with adequate fulness. I am sorry she has attracted you so little; for the great problem of her life, which essentially coincides with a chief problem in Savonarola's, is one that readers need helping to understand. But with regard to that and to my whole book, my predominant feeling is,—not that I have achieved anything, but—that great, great facts have struggled to find a voice through me, and have only been able to speak brokenly. That consciousness makes me cherish the more any proof that my work has been seen to have some true significance by minds prepared not simply by instruction, but by that religious and moral sympathy with the historical life of man which is the larger half of culture.

36. Unsigned review, *Saturday Review*

25 July 1863, xvi, 124–5

This review is probably by John Morley (see headnote to No. 39).

No reader of *Romola* will lay it down without admiration, and few without regret. Great as is the power displayed in it, and varied as is the interest awakened in it, there is still the general impression produced by it that the authoress has been tempted into a field where, indeed, she is not less than she has been, but where her merits are obscured, and their effect impaired. She has left the description and study of English life, and has attempted to overcome the difficulties of the historical novel. Nothing can exceed the diligence with which she has applied

herself to her task. She has set herself to paint Florence at the end of the
fifteenth century, and to present the chief scenes of a decade of Florentine history. And if a sketch of Florence were her main object, she
has selected a good time, and has mastered every detail that could give
reality and picturesqueness to her representation. The period she has
chosen enables her to bring on the canvas Macchiavelli and Savonarola,
the exile of the Medici, the triumphant entry of Charles VIII. of France,
and countless intrigues of one Florentine party against another. It
enables her to depict the popular feeling about the Church, the wavering of opinion that preceded the Reformation, and the scholarly quarrels of the literary heroes of the *Renaissance*. Florentine life, also, both in
the past and the present, is full of salient curiosities which catch and
delight a studious English eye. To note these and to understand them,
and to store them up and bring them out at last as children bring out
of their baskets the shells and stones they have worked hard to collect,
is a great pleasure. But it seems a pity that these things should be done
by the authoress of *Adam Bede*. A lesser hand might have been employed to collect these simple treasures. However instructive it may
be, it is not without a tax on our patience that we read long accounts
of Florentine antiquities, and translations of sermons by Savonarola,
and extracts from chronicles of processions. Sometimes the antiquarian
quite drowns the novelist, and we are startled at lighting on one of those
artless contrivances by which, in Becker's *Charicles* or *Gallus*,[1] a casual
remark or passing fancy of the hero introduces a description that
admirably illustrates all the hard bits in a satire of Horace or Juvenal.
It is not without a pang that we come to passages in *Romola* such as that
where an authoress known and respected as one of the first living writers
of fiction actually goes off like Becker, or G. P. R. James,[2] on the *Wars
of the Jews*,[3] and having first thrown out a preliminary ' "Fediddio,"
exclaimed Francesco Cei, "that is a well tanned Giovanni," ' proceeds
to say that 'to make clear this exclamation of Cei, it must be understood that the car of the Zecca or Mint was originally,' &c. &c., and so
on for two pages of cram. Nor is this instructive antiquarianism relieved
by any success of historical portraiture. Most of the Italians introduced
are mere names to us—some few of them, like Politian, old names, but
most of them new names—the names of men about whom we know

[1] Wilhelm Adolf Becker (1796–1846), classical archaeologist, published his two historical
novels in 1840 and 1838 respectively.
[2] G. P. R. James (1799–1860) wrote many historical novels.
[3] Immanuel Bekker (1785–1871) edited Josephus in six volumes (1855–6).

nothing and care nothing, even when the most indefatigable and ingenious antiquarian has tried to teach us and to interest us. Macchiavelli
is, indeed, a man whose fame, and opinions, and influence are familiar
to us. But historical accuracy forbids the novelist to make Macchiavelli
act in the period selected. He is merely a young man allowed occasionally to talk in as smart and cynical a manner as the skill of the authoress
can manage. Savonarola alone affords scope for effective historical
painting. The conception of the character of Savonarola which is here
given is profound, subtle, and probably true. It would be difficult to
convey more vividly the strange union of deception and noble truthfulness which was prominent in him. But there is little life in the scenes
where he is introduced. He is merely a study, clever, original, and
faithful. He does not fascinate and engross us with that semblance of a
real man which, with so much less apparent effort of thought and art,
Scott knew how to give to those creations of his imagination to which
he attached great historical names.

But it must be remembered that readers can only have what authors
can give them, and that authors cannot always give what readers
would most like. The authoress of *Romola* has already published four
tales of English life, and four tales of English life are quite enough to
use up the experience and exhaust the reflections even of a mind so
acute, so observant, and so meditative. She has only to look at her
contemporaries and notice with dismay the effects of continuing to
write after the well of thought has run dry, and when the same water
has to be pumped backwards and forwards if the fountain is to play at
the bidding of publishers. The minds of men gifted with great creative
power can, indeed, turn from one set of subjects and one set of characters
to another. Shakespeare, and Scott, and Goethe are, within certain
limits, inexhaustible. But there is another order of minds, which is
really creative and original, but which is always driven into the same
groove, and works within bounds which have been probably assigned
by the actual experience of life. The authoress of *Adam Bede* has a
mind of this sort. With all its humour, and feeling, and philosophical
and pictorial power, it is centred upon a few elements of character, and
is controlled as if by the inevitable presence of certain familiar incidents.
Stripped of their Florentine covering, and divested of those touches of
variety which the genius of the writer imparts to them, several of the
characters of *Romola*, and some of the chief events, are old—not in the
sense that they are mere repetitions, or that the authoress ever shows
poverty of invention, but that they involve the same moral problems,

and cause or encounter the same difficulties in life. Especially the authoress seems to be haunted with the consequences that flow from the weakness of men. It is not because men are bad, or cruel, or lustful, so much as because they are weak, and get into little scrapes, which make them lie, that women are miserable. These weak men, liking comfort, prone to lie, hoping in a foolish sanguine way for the best, go tottering to their ruin, and drag down women with them. They drag down the pretty childish ones with babyish ways and a thirst for innocent animal delight, and if they do not quite drag down the nobler natures, the proud, and unselfish, and highminded, they make their lives a weariness and a bitterness, and rob them of the high joys for which heaven fitted them. This is the sight in human life which has wrung the soul and stirred the spirit of the authoress of *Romola*; and it is this that has supplied her with a base for that kind of philosophical meditation which derives its strength from indignation, and its subtlety from the analysis of weak no less than of powerful characters.

In *Romola*, this weak, wavering man, his own victim and the victim of the circumstances he creates, assumes a shape which affords room for so elaborate a delineation as almost to conceal his similarity to the types of the same character in the earlier works of the authoress. If she has got nothing else out of her Florentine researches, and out of her selection of an historical, remote, and uninteresting period, she has at least got the possibility of drawing such a character as Tito—a Greek and an Italian at once, beautiful, refined, flexible, mean, cowardly, and yet charming and kind, and not very bad. In the latter part of the tale the subtle drawing of his character is swallowed up by the sad necessities of the Florentine story. His personal history and his personal character are lost in a dreary network of Medicean and anti-Medicean intrigues. We know that he is somehow very cunning, but what he wants, or how he hopes to get it, and why he should or should not get it, is a mystery. At last he is killed, but the tragedy of his death is impaired by our anxiety to get him out of the embroglio of Piagnoni, and Campagnacci, and Arrabbiati somehow or other—if in no other way, by being flung into the Arno and then strangled by a private enemy—but, at any rate, somehow. But in the earlier part of the story his character is worked out with an infinite vividness, and among much simpler elements. He burns to get on in the world; he sincerely loves Romola; he likes to play and trifle with the rural Tessa; and he is haunted day and night by the fear of Baldassere, the old man who has been a father to him, but whom he has deserted, and robbed, and denied. In the midst of these conflicting feelings and circumstances of his life he moves, instinct with life and beauty, and so profoundly averse to pain that he wishes to spare pain to others no less than to himself. It would be impossible to conceive the weak man, doomed to ruin himself and his attendant women, noble and simple, under conditions demanding more skill to depict and to control them. The authoress has been equal to the task she has set herself; and if at last all these Medicean intrigues make him flit before us like a wicked bloodless ghost shrouded in a veil, he leaves behind him the memory of the powerful pictures which the authoress has associated with him. There is, first, the picture of a man falling into falsehood, and made positively, though gradually, worse, not only by the contact with evil, but by the companionship of unrelenting truth and purity, which perpetually reminds him of the barrier between himself and innocence which he has built up. And there is the picture of a life passed in perpetual fear, and of the terrible burden which the undying vengeance of the half-witted old man he has wronged imposes on him in his greatest prosperity.

Romola, however, is the central character of the work which bears her name, and the interest attaching to her increases as the book goes on. Fortunately, as she is a woman, and a good woman, she is not thought suited to the Medicean intrigues, and only suffers in a remote and readable way from them. At first, she seems cut on a bigger scale than there is any occasion for. She is too much of a goddess to make it fair play for such a weak mortal as Tito to have to love her. It is only when she discovers his baseness, and gets into great moral difficulties, and has to settle how to deal with many conflicting claims of duty, that we see she was not shaped as a goddess for nothing. Then all the nobleness of her character, and all the originality and skill of the authoress who created her, begin to appear. Nothing in her behaviour seems to us more admirably conceived than her conduct to Tessa. Romola is married to Tito, and separated from him on account of his political sins and his ingratitude to her dearest friends, when she finds that Tito has another wife, the victim of a mock marriage—a silly, innocent peasant girl, with two children. Romola is too unhappy, too profoundly shocked at her husband's baseness, to feel much indignation at his infidelity, or to visit his sins on his children, and on the poor, confiding, simple girl who has loved him. She is very kind to Tessa, and learns to love the children, and in fact, after his death, has Tessa and the children to live with her. There is, perhaps, a little exaggeration of romance in this, but her general treatment of Tessa gives us her measure. She has too deep and large a nature for jealousy. Scarcely less interesting is the account of the weakness and the concessions to which her circumstances force her. She revolts with her whole soul against the meanness of her husband, and wants to fly from him; but she is brought back into the paths of duty by Savonarola, and consents to hold the position of a wife, and to occupy her time in good works. The grateful, meek earnestness with which she takes up the task imposed on her, and uses it as an escape from her own feelings, gives her character that air of softness which it would otherwise want.

Romola is saved by Savonarola from despair, and thenceforth is thrown into close relations with him. It is through Romola that the authoress gives her judgment on Savonarola, and all that is effective in the description of this unsuccessful reformer is connected with Romola's history. We cannot, therefore, separate the relations of Romola and Savonarola from the general mode in which the authoress deals with the questions which Savonarola raised, and with the nature and value of a religious enthusiasm like his. It is here that the peculiar power of her mind shows itself. Nothing in the mere portraiture of character, or in the contrivance of incident, equals the general impression of greatness of mind which her mode of treating such subjects awakens. She makes us feel that we are in the hands of a thinker who has thought far down into the depths of the religious mind, and who has seriously and anxiously desired to ascertain what is the place of religious thought in the facts of life. Romola, at the end, stands aloof from Savonarola, loving him, burning with the recollections of his nobleness and zeal, well aware that enthusiasm does not alter the iron course of things, alive to the deceptions in which the desire for the religious improvement of the world involved him, determined herself not to pretend to be more certain of religious truths than she is, and concentrated in the discharge of daily duty and the offices of love. This is the character which the authoress depicts as surviving in a noble soul the contact with a pure and visionary enthusiasm. It would be difficult to say that, under such circumstances, there is any wisdom wiser than that which Romola displays, and which the authoress has the strength and courage to depict.

37. Unsigned review, *Westminster Review*

October 1863, lxxx, 344–52

It cannot be denied that *Romola* is less popular than its predecessors, but we do not hesitate to say that it is its author's greatest work. We hope we shall be able, in the course of the following observations, in some degree to explain this apparent contradiction. In the minds of a great majority of her readers George Eliot's name is indissolubly connected with the remembrance of Mrs. Poyser, the Dodsons, and Dolly Winthrop, and they cannot dispense with the pleasure they have heretofore derived from such quaint and original humour; it is not sufficient that there are passages in *Romola* full of refined wit and as deeply humorous as any to be found in *Adam Bede, The Mill on the Floss*, or in *Silas Marner*; they are not, indeed, set in a homely *entourage* which demands no thought, but rather call for habits of reflection but little cultivated by most novel-readers. Indeed, we have seen it insinuated that the circle of the author's powers had been already filled, and that the recourse to a foreign background for her fable was a sign of weakness and exhaustion. This is an inexcusable criticism; the critic must be himself weak indeed who fancies he can discern any sign of failing powers in *Romola*. It is quite another question whether the selection of a foreign and historical background was judicious. This point is doubtless open to debate, and in our opinion is the only one worth discussion. The strong hold which George Eliot lays on the intellectual and ethical side of all that comes before her mind, and the predominant critical tendency of her mode of thought, make it more necessary with her than with other authors that she should have the direct support of personal experience for the external circumstances in which she places her characters. Her imagination has a strong bias towards moral conceptions rather than towards sensuous, much less passionate ones; with her passion and direct action lie strangled in thought, and deeds present themselves to her rather as problems than as facts. In those dramatic conceptions which give force, unity, and rapid action to a tale she is comparatively deficient. The keenness of her mind urges her on to results, and thought and feeling have so much the upper hand that the lower and more picturesque qualities of our nature have but little attraction for her. The moral progress of mankind is a far higher thing to her than the finest poetry, which is but an instrument in that progress. This bias leads her to treat the events by which she develops the characters of her stories with too great an arbitrariness, and to disregard their natural sequence in a manner which strongly contrasts with the inexorable consecutiveness of every step in the development of the characters themselves. In the minute analysis of moral growth she has no equal; no one has so fully seized the great truth that we can none of us escape the consequences of our conduct, that each action has not only a character of its own, but also an influence on the character of the actor from which there is no escape; 'our deeds are like children that are born to us; they live and act apart from our own will. Nay, children may be strangled, but deeds never: they have an indestructible life, both in and out of our consciousness.' The strength with which this truth is here expressed shows the deep feeling from which it arises. To this deep moral maxim George Eliot constantly recurs, not in *Romola* only, but in *Romola* it forms the central idea to which all else is made subservient; the external machinery of the tale is but the means by which it shall be set in an adequate light, considerations of probability are comparatively small matters, and the most fortuitous coincidences are accepted without a pang so that they do but aid in the display of that which is of more importance to the author than any superficial likelihood. If it were possible for her to consider the external circumstances in which she places her hero, apart from the influence those circumstances are intended to exercise on him, and as governed by laws of their own, she would be the first to recognise how remarkable an accumulation of improbable coincidences she heaps on Tito's head. But this is the greatness of George Eliot, that where others are feeble she is strong, and it is only to be regretted that she is too regardless of that much less difficult accomplishment which is within the reach of any one with one tenth her genius. On this account we think it is to be regretted that *Romola* is an Italian story, and a story of the fifteenth century. By departing so far from the life around her she enters into a more full command of her whole material, which forces her to rely upon her imagination for those parts of her fable which the character of her mind strongly leads her to neglect. It would have been more difficult had Romola lived among us to arrange with such facile opportuneness the incidents of Tito's downward course. It is true the remembrance of similar features in Silas Marner forces us to allow that even in that case they might have had much of this character, but the greater familiarity of the incidents would have afforded some disguise. The beneficial influence of such a direct study from nature is manifest in the first two volumes of the *Mill on the Floss* the complete harmony between the Tullivers and Dodsons and the external circumstances in which they are placed, affords the best illustration of our meaning, unless, indeed, that wonderful scene at the Rainbow, in *Silas Marner*, be not a more striking example. No care and labour have been spared to give an objective character to the portraiture of ancient Florence, but this care has resulted only in an accumulation of details. The three great parties which divided the state at the close of the fifteenth century are displayed rather in their thoughts than in their actions, their violent passions and unscrupulous deeds are so treated in the light of their results that they are sicklied over with the pale cast of thought, and lose a great part of their local colour. All the minute details of Florentine life with which the canvas is crowded do not produce a lasting and enduring impression. The picture contains too much of the substance of the author's studies, and is brightened rather by the deep and profound general views which they suggested to her than by those living characteristic touches which make a departed age to live before the reader. There is to our feeling a most characteristic difference between the impression produced by the pictures of Italian life and by those which she draws of the personal conflicts in the minds of the characters which are really hers; in these her reflections drop from her like ripe fruit come to its fullest maturity, there is a spontaneousness about them that has an irresistible charm, but in all that concerns the surroundings of her characters there is an evident sign of labour, not indeed upon the surface, but at too short a distance beneath it. The fullest knowledge is insufficient where the mind resists, or does not go forward without effort. This difference is difficult to seize and perhaps impossible fully to analyse; but it resembles that which is always found between a fine original picture and a copy by another artist, however able. The two shall be identical, line for line, and yet no one is deceived by the copy; there is a something wanting, which can only be described as the result of perfect freedom of movement.

Again, we do not recognise the truth of detail in a description of public life so remote from us as we should the features of our own time, and the author has not the power to carry us away with the description she gives. This historical background, too, somewhat oppresses the human interest of the tale, and in its ultimate impression affects us like a mediæval painted window, in which the action has to be disentangled from the blaze of colour and overwhelming accessories. To this source may be traced much of that want of appreciation with which the book has met. The general novel-reader is impatient at such details as those of the entry of Charles VIII., and of the Auto-da-fé of Vanities, and longs to hear more of that struggle between Romola and her husband which comes home to his business and bosom. There is another reason why *Romola* is not popular with the crowd. George Eliot's deep insight into the self-questioning human mind places her among those 'neutrals who alone can see the finer shades of fact which soften the antithesis of virtue and vice, who are not distressed to discern some folly in martyrs and some judiciousness in those who burn them.' The lofty superiority from which she draws the inspiration of that neutrality meets with no answering voice in the souls of the multitude. How few in these questions are not in some sense partisans, and where will they find a weapon to their hands in the pages of *Romola*? There is another result of this scientific insight, which, from the point of view of art, exercises a hostile influence over the power of the author's best scenes: they are so philosophically treated, and so full of the subtlest analysis of the varying motives which struggle for the mastery in the actors, that we are in constant danger of being more attracted by the treatment of the moral question than interested by its bearing on the fate of those whom it affects. We have heard many say that they cannot interest themselves in Tito and Romola, but we never heard any one who was capable of entering into the special purpose of this history who thought himself fully able to express his admiration either of the deep insight displayed in it or of the delicate beauty of the distinctions and qualifications by which it is preserved from any excess or exaggeration. If it is said of any book that it offers in every page some food for thought or some rare beauty of expression, it is not generally found to conduce to its immediate perusal. Festus' more convenient season[1] is time enough for such things. How then shall a book which touches on the finest chords of the human heart with a delicacy that proclaims the last results of modern culture be heard among the coarse appeals to curiosity or passion which occupy the public ear?

We cannot but think, however, that this long and elaborate disquisition on the relations between the sexes as a moral question is set forth by George Eliot too much in the colours of the nineteenth century. The conception of the marriage tie which underlies the whole story seems to us antedated by the whole interval which separates the

[1] *Acts*, xxiv, 25. The phrase is used by Felix not Festus.

age of Alexander VI. from our own. We think it would be very difficult to produce any evidence of claims to the kind of union to which Romola aspired as existing in the minds of the women of the fifteenth century, much more to prove them so universal as to be within the immediate appreciation of a man merely clever and self-seeking like Tito; and here again we find another reason for wishing that Romola had been a modern Englishwoman, she having so much more the character of one than that of an Italian lady of four centuries since. It is an insufficient excuse to plead that the great features of human life and character are determined by conditions too permanent to offer any radical distinctions between their manifestations from century to century. The hills indeed are, as George Eliot says, where they were of old, and the rivers flow in their accustomed beds; but many and great are the changes which four hundred years produce in these great features of physical nature, and greater far the differences which such a lapse of time brings with it in the form of the moral questions which are offered to each generation of mankind. We cannot escape from the feeling that the chief interest of *Romola* reposes on ideas of moral duty and of right which are of very modern growth, and that they would have been more appropriately displayed on a modern stage. The lovely and noble Romola would even now be more admired than loved, and surely we have not retrograded in devotion to all that is good and beautiful. It is not yet given to every one to love a Romola. Tito, too, seems to us to smack more of the intellectual strength and moral weakness of the nineteenth century than of the strong faith and equally strong passions of the age of Cæsar Borgia and Machiavelli. Nothing can surpass the skill with which he is displayed, gradually entangled in the web of his own subtleties; but he would have cut short his trials with steel or poison in the age in which he is represented as enduring them. Instead of being content with frightening a wife he no longer loved when she threatened him with exposure and ruin, he would have relieved himself from that fear in a very different way within twenty-four hours. But he is a child of the nineteenth century, and shrinks from the more practical procedure of the fifteenth. He is Hetty, but a man, and not a fool. Indeed, the deepest and most powerful conception of the whole book is this of Tito—amiable, with great abilities and no vices, but living in other men's regards, and shunning every form of personal discomfort; weak, but not naturally wicked. How sad the view of life which at last leads such a man to commit some of the basest deeds, and yet who can say one feature of this wonderful portrait is at

all exaggerated? Where was there ever a moral more forcibly set forth?
Let no man sport with his existence. *Ernst ist das Leben.*[1] No wonder
a doctrine that calls on every one to take heed unto his ways is not
universally popular. The novel-reader who takes up a volume to
escape from or fill up the void of thought, may well exclaim when he
meets with such a lion in his path, that he does not find in *Romola* the
amusement of which he was in search; the terrible earnestness of what
really comes home to him, is as little welcome as the learning which he
either does not appreciate or prefers to seek elsewhere. No! *Romola* is
not likely to be generally popular; it is too great both in mind and
heart.

There are few things requiring a more delicate touch than such
stories as that of Tessa and her little ones; yet what an air of idyllic
beauty is thrown over the whole episode by her ignorance and their
innocence. George Eliot is always charming in her treatment of
children; they have not yet become the theatre of those conflicts which
she hates, and she loves them without distrust or remorse. How
admirably this episode is made to show that a man may be a villain
and yet have soft affections, and a noble woman be jealous of something higher than mere personal fidelity to herself. In her treatment
of Baldassare the author displays all the qualities on which we have
remarked. His remorseless vindictiveness and thirst for blood seems to
her so near an approach to lunacy, that she makes him mad whenever
he has a chance of action. It might be insinuated that this is done in
order that the avenging sword may hang a little longer over Tito's
head, and that it is but an artifice to prolong the effect of the hovering
Nemesis of his hate. But there are no artifices in George Eliot's art.
The true reason is, that she does not sufficiently sympathize with such
depths of passion to give them adequate expression; they are so repug-
nant to her that she hardly compassionates the wronged old man, and
certainly does not sufficiently display those features of his character
which caused him to be successively forsaken by the woman he loved
and by the boy he had adopted and tenderly cared for. How was it
that he who so longed to be loved was denied all answer to his yearnings
where he had set his heart? It can only be because his vindictive hate
had so debased him, even in the mind that conceived his character,
that no room was left for sympathy; and the savage animalism of his
passions lowering him to the brutes made George Eliot less than
humane to one who had put off what alone interests her as distinctively

[1] 'Life is earnest' (Schiller, *Wallensteins Lager* (1798), Prolog 138).

human. This concentration of self in the reckless pursuit of a personal gratification is the strongest expression of that tendency in our race which is uniformly decried throughout *Romola*, whether it shows itself in the luxurious self-indulgence of Tito or in the noble Romola when she essays to throw off the trammels of a life that no longer answers to her ideal. The same idea is prolonged into the treatment of Savonarola, whose personal aims and longings for the glory that he thought his due are made to be his ruin, and to furnish the road to his defeat and death. That this is a true view of his character is in accordance with all we know of him, and connects him in a peculiar way with the ethical basis of the tale. His influence on its progress is but slight; the power which he exerted for a time over the imagination of Romola was not so much personal as the effect of the new views of duty which he brought before her; Christian morality could have found its way to an intellect like hers without the necessity of an intermediate human idol, and would not then have so failed her when she could no longer lean on his character for support. We do not mean that there is not much profound psychological insight displayed in the treatment of their mutual relations, but that all else in the story which is concerned with Savonarola leaves the reader but slightly moved and but feebly interested; it sinks down into that picture of ancient Florence which is so full of learned detail, and which stands in such grievous need of a central light which shall harmonize the whole.

The conclusion of the story is its weakest part, because here, if anywhere, there was need of action. Few, we think, can be fully satisfied with the manner of Tito's death. It may be said that he fell a victim to a popular tumult which had been indirectly brought about by his own treachery; that he was swept from the scene of his plottings by a side wind of the storm he had called forth by his betrayal of Savonarola; but this conclusion is hardly led up to with sufficient clearness. Rather does it seem to us that the author wishes to indicate how impossible it is for the cleverest schemer to be prepared for every contingency to which his wiles expose him; that all his ingenuity was insufficient to guard him against the low cunning of a Ceccone and a chance opportunity. That he should escape the infuriated mob to fall helpless into the hands of his powerless enemy is so painfully improbable that few have read it without some shock to their feelings. Here, again, we may observe the tendency in George Eliot to avoid all violent action; Tito is too exhausted to resist his murderer, and has only strength enough to recognise the retributive avenger before he dies. Romola's

GEORGE ELIOT

history after her second flight is strangely disconnected with the rest of the tale. The pestilential village and its call upon her sympathies is another of those extravagantly fortuitous circumstances of which the author makes such free use. All sense of probability is here sacrificed for a moral effect, which yet jars upon us like an isolated light that does not harmonize with the rest of the picture. But any road is welcome that leads us to the lovely Epilogue, and to that eloquent summary of the whole purpose of the book with which Romola warns her husband's son against the faults of him he knew not was his father:—

[quotes speech beginning, 'It is not easy, my Lill. . . .']

38. Richard Simpson on George Eliot

October 1863

Unsigned article, 'George Eliot's Novels', *Home and Foreign Review* (October 1863), iii, 522–49.

Richard Simpson (1820–76) was a versatile journalist, Shakespearian scholar, historian, and writer on Roman Catholic affairs. Ordained in the Church of England, he was converted to Roman Catholicism and became closely associated with Lord Acton and the Liberal Catholic movement. He was assistant editor and editor of the *Rambler* in 1856–9, and later with Acton started the short-lived *Home and Foreign Review* (1862–4). As a writer on religious matters he was radical, contentious, and sincere; as a literary critic he is judicious, philosophical, and incisive. Despite its hostility, this article is an outstanding interpretation and reassessment of George Eliot's novels (see Introduction, pp. 22–3).

George Eliot did not burst upon us like a flood, but trickled into fame through the channel of a monthly magazine. Readers who in 1858 took up the *Scenes of Clerical Life*, reprinted from *Blackwood's Magazine*, with the languid inexpectancy with which the first writings of new novelists are received, were astonished that, instead of an author, they had found a man,—and a man uniting the characteristics of Montesquieu's two classes, those who think for us, and those who amuse us. He was apparently a young clergyman, whose piety was mitigated by irony, who had carefully formed a style on the best models, and who had stored his mind with the results of an intelligent and sympathetic observation of common life. People were struck with his power of putting before them the sorrows of the 'breaking heart that will not break' in Amos Barton, the shut soul's hypocrisy in young Wybrow, and the strength of stormy pity in 'Janet's Repentance'. The only exception the most orthodox found to make to him was for a liberality, scarcely edifying, in approving indiscriminately every school of religious opinion; but then it was remarked that his object was to bring into vivid light the fundamental agreement underlying all these differences. His liberality was clearly far removed from indifference. Had he not the deepest scorn for sensual hypocrisy, and for the 'dingy infidelity' which he happily compared to 'the rinsings of Tom Paine in ditchwater'? Obviously here was an author on whom the eye of expectation was to be kept open.

George Eliot knew how apt is long watching to end in slumber, and so made haste to provide the expected supply before the eye had time to close. Within a year a second appearance was put in, this time with a decisive stroke. Though the virtue of *Adam Bede* was in its characters, its dialogue, and its pathos, yet there was also a religious purpose in it,—a genial, all-embracing charity, that won golden opinions for its author. 'He is evidently a country clergyman,' said the oracle of the hour. 'Evidently he has sat at the feet of Mr. Kingsley, and Mr. Kingsley may in many points be proud of his follower.'[1] One distinguished critic pronounced him to be 'a gentleman of High-Church tendencies.'[2] Another reviewer was struck with the 'depth of the teaching' and the 'loveliness of the lesson,' which furnished such an excellent argument for foundling hospitals on the French system.[3] The critic of the *Westminster Review*,[4] however, after maturely considering the internal evidence, hazarded a conjecture that George Eliot was a woman, but doubted, after all, whether it was a real person, or an entity uniting 'the best qualities of the masculine and feminine mind.' This critic differed from the rest in thinking that the true moral of the story was what they would call irreligious. 'Strictly speaking,' he made it say, 'no sin can be atoned for;' when once the freedom has been sold by the criminal act, there is no redemption; the consequences are inevitable. He hazarded another remark, viz. that George Eliot apparently regarded creeds 'as being only shells of different shape and colour, enclosing the fruit of the religious spirit common to the human race; or as so many mental structures, which in his successive metamorphoses man forms and afterwards casts off.' The theory of the *Westminster Review* was not much regarded, but it was true.

The pseudonym of George Eliot had not been assumed in vain. It would have been difficult even for so able a writer to gain the public

---

[1] *Saturday Review* (No. 7 above).   [2] *Saturday Review* (No. 5 above).
[3] *Dublin Review* (September 1859), xlvii, 39.
[4] *Westminster Review* (April 1859), lxxi, 486–512.

ear as a professedly religious and even clerical author, if the same name had been signed to the *Clerical Scenes* in 1858 and to *Adam Bede* in 1859, as had been signed to translations of Strauss's *Life of Jesus* in 1846, and of Feuerbach's *Essence of Christianity* in 1853. Besides these translations, Marian Evans had also contributed to the *Westminster Review* sundry articles of the same theological principles. She was known, moreover, to be a literary fellow-labourer of Mr. Lewes, who is credited with some share in all her novels, and whose literary history, therefore, should be remembered in discussing them. He began by writing a novel, *Ranthorpe*, which he kept by him five years, and then compressed and published in 1845. He must have been conscious that it was a failure, in spite of some sharp analyses of character in the style of La Rochefoucauld. Its jerky plot, full of moral monstrosities, and the absence of natural dialogue, and of all self-development of character, show it to be destitute of the essential elements of a good novel. Besides publishing another novel, he devoted himself, between 1845 and 1857, to history, chiefly with the view of forming a criticism upon philosophy and art. He published a life of Robespierre, an essay on the Spanish drama of Vega and Calderon, some arguments about the colouring of Greek architecture, an exposition of Comte's positive philosophy, a biographical history of philosophy, and a life of Göthe. The two last are his most important works. The one contains his judgment on philosophical questions; the other on art. Since 1857 he has devoted himself to science. He has edited Johnson's *Chemistry of Common Life*, and published the *Physiology of Common Life*, *Sea-Side Studies*, and *Studies in Animal Life*.

There is an organic unity in the career of these two authors, which allows us to consider them as a double mouthpiece of a single brain. The first production was a novel that failed, not because it was a silly book, but because it was not a good novel; its materials, though meagre, were good; but its form was tohu and bohu.[1] A period of study followed, when philosophy, art, and religion were critically examined, and the positivism of Comte, the art-canons of Göthe, and the religious system of Strauss and Feuerbach, were adopted. Next came the period of creation, in which the empire of positive philosophy was extended in the sphere of physiology on the one hand, and in the sphere of sociology on the other. This period dates from 1858, and is marked by the physiological books of Mr. Lewes, and the novels of George Eliot.

[1] Hebrew phrase from *Genesis* i, 2: 'without form, and void'.

The founder of positivism felt that his system was not complete without a religion to match it. In arranging this religion, Comte fell into two mistakes natural to a Frenchman. As a revolutionist, he despised Christianity, and sought to build his system on the non-historical basis of St.-Simon. As a systematiser, he could not resist the temptation of making religion into a system, and seated himself on a high stool at a desk to be the timekeeper of an impalpable world of feeling and emotion, which is not subject to the sound of the clock. George Eliot, in attempting the same task, avoided these two rocks. Sympathising with Göthe and the historical method of the Germans, rather than with the Frenchman's revolutionary negation of the past, and knowing that Christianity had been the religion of the last eighteen centuries, she felt that, if the religion of positivism was to have any solid foundations, and not to be a mere castle in the air,—if it was destined to be the next phase in the development of our race,—it must claim to be founded on Christianity; it must be exhibited as the inner substance, which, having ever existed as a germ within the shell of Christianity, will be displayed in all its fresh ripeness when the dead husk drops away. She felt also that religion, the pure emanation of the feelings, was essentially incompatible with system, or even with maxims. She avoided, therefore, both the scholastic and the aphoristic methods, and adopted the apologue and the parable as the vehicles of her teaching, which requires not an understanding to argue, but a character to persuade.

This is why, though she has no belief in Christianity, she can yet, without dishonesty, speak as if she had faith. In reality, the positivist believes in no religion whatever. Belief implies doctrine. To the positivist, however, religious doctrines are only impressions on the imagination, which, though they do not correspond with any reality in the universe, are yet necessary to enable man to turn his feelings into energies—for energy results from the union of belief and feeling. But the imagination is not free; it cannot, without the consciousness of fiction, imagine that to be which it knows not to be. A few generations back, says the positivist, it was easy to believe that the world was created 6000 years ago by a Being who inhabits the blue heavens. Astronomy and geology have rendered that belief impossible now to all who know those sciences; the educated man who pretends to possess it must be a fanatic or hypocrite. But in past ages, and in the uneducated classes of the present, the belief may be perfectly honest and natural; it may enter into legitimate union with the feelings, and produce the most virtuous energy. Thus the positivist, who disbelieves all dogma, may have a hearty sympathy with the orthodoxy of the uneducated, or, what comes to the same thing, of past generations of educated men. The Tübingen historians, however unfair to modern churchmen, can be quite chivalrous in their defence of the old; and George Eliot, who probably despises either the intellect or the honesty of a man who remains a Christian in the full glare of modern philosophy and science, can enter with the most loving interest into the religious feelings of the 'clown unread, and half-read gentleman;'[1] of clergymen of the last generation, carefully nurtured in the current orthodoxy; and of medieval Florentines, lay and clerical, whom no education then attainable could have raised to the sublime knowledge of the modern positivist. She knows that the master of superstition is the people, and that here wise men must follow fools; and that it is only by sympathy, and by entering into other people's minds, that we can gradually reconcile their thoughts to our own; while, on the other hand, if we wish to secure a lasting existence to our own thought, we must make it popular. It is no small victory to show that the godless humanitarianism of Strauss and Feuerbach can be made to appear the living centre of all the popular religions.

When the pseudonym was discovered, it had already served its purpose. George Eliot was already accepted as a great artist; her teaching had been dubbed clerical, and it was too late in the day to turn upon her and call her an atheist. Either novel-readers did not care if she was so; or they doubted the watchmen who, not for the first time, were raising a false alarm of wolf; or they found in her books internal evidence to refute all that was said against her. Under these circumstances, in 1860, after the lapse of a year, she published the *Mill on the Floss*—a novel which the critics, having their eyes anointed with the revelation of the author's name, treated, on moral grounds, more severely than they had treated *Adam Bede*, while they owned that the work maintained the writer's high credit as an artist. We must presume on our readers' knowledge of the plots of these works, since it is manifestly impossible to analyse and criticise them all in a single article. At present we are only giving an account of their reception. One reviewer, guessing that something was wrong, but not exactly knowing what, went to buffets about a passage where the author, after remarking that milk and mildness are equally apt to turn sour, wonders whether the placid early Madonnas of Raffaelle did not grow peevish

[1] Dryden, *The Hind and the Panther* (1687), iii, 409.

as their strong-limbed boys grew troublesome.[1] The Madonnas here clearly stand for the women whose portraits they are. But if it were not so, if the jest were interpreted in its most ribald sense, even then it would be no sign of unbelief in a person like George Eliot, of whom the saying would be true, that she never really believes a creed that she cannot afford to jest about. It is hard to love those before whom we dare not play the fool. There are tempers which can scarcely show respect where they feel affection. A second critic, on the other hand, erred by neglecting the biographical clue to George Eliot's purpose, and dwelt upon the testimony she unconsciously bore to the truth of Catholicism, and on the way in which she brought home to the conscience the doctrine of the Personality of God[2]—the one doctrine which, of all others, she most thoroughly denies. An able writer in another review, overlooking the explanation derivable from the author's purpose, supposed that she chose a world where all is direct, outspoken, and non-reticent, because she felt that she had not the capacity for catching the undertones and allusive complexity of draw-ing-room conversation.[3] The novel which she published the next year (1861) did not refute this idea. *Silas Marner* moved among peasants and rustic squires, doctors, farmers, and parsons. Its moral and even religious tendency appeared unexceptionable; and the interest of the story was concentrated in a wonderful way in the psychological change of the weaver from superstition, through infidelity, to faith. The artistic merits of the book were even more remarkable, and extorted admiration for

> The fertile head that every year
> Could such a crop of wonders bear.

In 1862 the publication of *Romola* commenced in the *Cornhill Magazine*. The choice of the subject was a direct defiance to those who supposed George Eliot to be incapable of painting refined and educated society. The scholars and artists of the Renaissance, the enthusiastic devotees of Savonarola, the whole population and movement of Florence in the fifteenth century, are there exhibited with as much sympathy and graphic power as the religion of various English sects, and the life of our rural population, in her other novels. She had completely changed her scene, but had kept her old power, her old idea of art, and her old purpose.

[1] *Quarterly Review* (October 1860), cviii, 492.
[2] *Blackwood's Magazine* (May 1860), lxxxvii, 622-3.
[3] *National Review* (July 1860), xi, 194.

There is a very just prejudice against novels with a purpose. They are generally religious; and their chief characteristic is the ludicrous contrast between their pretension and their power. Didactic novels are generally written by persons who cannot teach, and have no story to tell. But, on the other hand, no great work can be written without a purpose—religious, political, philosophical, or artistic. Cervantes intended to quiz the pseudo-chivalry of Spain, and Voltaire to mock Leibniz. The purpose of most of our present novelists seems to be to find some unworked vein; they would be discoverers, like geographers or gold-diggers. The purpose of George Eliot is clear enough, as we shall show after we have examined the machinery of her novels.

The elements of a novel are three—the plot, the development by description and dialogue, and the characters. In the best specimens the three elements are in more or less perfect equilibrium; but excellent works have been written in which one of them has complete preponderance. Some of Calderon's dramas are all plot, without dialogue or characters to speak of; *Hudibras* has neither plot nor characters, but has wonderful merit in its dialogue and description; Richardson's novels develope character, but have no merit in their plots or their dialogue. Novels whose virtue is in their plot are tales of intrigue or incident. Those which depend on their dialogue are either studies of wit, of repartee, and brilliant ideas, like some of Mr. Dickens'; or they are pictures of manners, like Mr. Thackeray's lighter sketches. Novels of character are those where the psychological analysis is the aim of the author. This analysis may be conducted by the writer himself, speaking in his proper person, as in *Ranthorpe*; or by the interlocutors themselves, who gradually unfold their characters in conversation, as in a drama of Shakespeare; or in the plot itself, when the incidents do not happen fortuitously, but are actions such as the given characters would naturally perform, or the natural consequences of such actions. Congruity requires that in a novel of character there should be as little accidental as may be, and that whatever there is should be probable; and that the plot should be endogenous, in which the main incidents are acts naturally growing out of the characters represented. The exhibition of character requires that man should be the architect, not the plaything of circumstance,—like the statesman of whom Dryden says that he 'some circumstances finds, but more he makes.'[1] Accident, especially improbable accident, though it adds to the excitement of the novel of incident, and makes the novel of wit or manners more amusing, is

[1] *Absalom and Achitophel* (1681), 209.

painfully incongruous in the novel of character, where the opportune coincidences of pre-arranged casualties have often quite a ludicrous effect, which requires a touch of comedy to justify it—as the preposterous story of Hamlet's return from his English voyage is varnished over by the grim Fridolin-like[1] comicality of his sending Rosencrantz and Guildenstern to be massacred in his stead. In plots of character accidents ought only to be admitted when they belong to a known legend, or when they are occasions of exhibiting new traits. Mr. Fechter[2] admirably explained and justified the awkward change of foils in the last scene of *Hamlet* by a brief access of ungovernable fury after his wound, which made him close with his antagonist and wrench the foil from his hand. It thus became an incident which threw a new light on the character.

The plots of all George Eliot's stories except the two last are good specimens of the characteristic self-developing kind. The clerical scenes are simple stories, requiring no extraneous incident to explain them. In *Adam Bede* the opportune death of the old squire is an arbitrary arrangement for increasing the pathos, by raising Arthur as high as possible just at the moment when he is to be brought so low. His gallop with the reprieve in his pocket is a stock incident of melodrama, and therefore, at first sight, ludicrous; but it is perfectly justifiable on grounds of internal probability and consistency. In the *Mill on the Floss* all the actions flow naturally from the characters described, till we come to the flood at the end,—a violent means of cutting the tangled knot of Maggie's destiny. The author clearly felt the incongruity of the incident, and did her best to prepare her readers for it by almost personifying the Floss, and making it the pivot of a secondary plot in which natural forces are the agents. We are carefully prepared, from the very first, for the treacherous character of the river, and are led ever to suspect some shrewd turn from it. But all the preparation is insufficient to justify a catastrophe perfectly apposite for a plot of intrigue and incident, but out of place in a plot of character. The author probably felt, and wished us to feel, that Tom and Maggie had woven a web round their lives which only the iron hand of death could unravel, and that high art required their destruction,—just as it does that of Macbeth and his wife, Romeo and Juliet, Lear and his daughter,—because, though they had not eaten their share at life's feast, they had poisoned their cup, and deposited within their souls a memory the stirred

---

[1] See Schiller's ballad 'Der Gang nach dem Eisenhammer' (1798).
[2] The actor Charles Albert Fechter (1824–79) first played Hamlet in March 1861.

precipitate of which would embitter all their days. Those, however, who do not attribute to feelings and emotions so high and sacred a character as George Eliot does, cannot think the wounds incurable, and therefore protest against the gratuitous tragedy, where a comic end would be more to the purpose.

The secondary plot, which remains in quite elemental and zoophytic form in the *Mill on the Floss*, becomes more highly organised in *Silas Marner*. It is necessary, for the development of the weaver's character, that he should become a miser, lose his gold, recover somewhat of his neighbours' good-will by misfortune, find a child, and be restored to social life by love. It was congruous, too, that he should find his gold again at last. Now to make all these accidents happen just in the nick of time only because they were wanted, would be feeble in the extreme; but if a secondary plot is introduced, out of which they naturally grow, they lose their arbitrary character, and are felt to be in place. Hence the secondary hero, Godfrey Cass, is introduced, as the centre of a plot which naturally bears fruit in the theft of Marner's gold, in throwing the child on his hands, and in restoring his hoard when it has been supplanted by a living idol as the object of his devotion. George Eliot surrounds herself with a mystic Egyptian darkness, and we approach her temple through an avenue of sphinxes; but it is not impossible to discover the irony of making Marner's conversion depend altogether on human sympathies and love, while he, simple fellow, fails to see the action of the general law of humanity, and attributes every thing to the 'dealings' which regulate the accidents. *Silas Marner* contains an apology for Providence arbitrary and petitionary as the silliest of religious novels, and an apology for the special doctrines of Feuerbach's humanitarianism worked up with the utmost dialectic and psychological ability. There is great ingenuity in this method of planting opinions which one wishes to eradicate, and of hiding a subtle argument for error under a specious defence of the truth.

The plot of *Romola* is a great advance upon the compound plan of *Silas Marner*. In it George Eliot develops an element of strength which she had exhibited from the first. In her earliest tales she had sketched the social scenery amid which the action was carried on as carefully as other writers paint the physical landscape. She had the gift of putting before us Shepperton, and Milby, and Hayslope, and St. Ogg's, and Raveloe, not only as sunny villages or busy towns, but as living communities, with a public opinion and parish politics of their own. At first these sketches were only backgrounds—living rings in which the

posy of the story was set—a sort of chorus to comment on the play, and
sometimes to furnish motives for the action, but taking no active part
in the development of the plot. But after she had made her physical
scenery take, as it were, a personal part in the catastrophe of Tom and
Maggie, it was an easy step to bring her moral scenery into action. In
Romola the population of Florence is not only made the setting and
background of the tale, but it takes a prominent part in the conduct
of the story. Its religious movement is represented by Savonarola; and
its political movement, which has plenty of representatives, has its
main bearing on the chief characters in the person of Romola's god-
father, Bernardo. The psychological interest of the tale turns upon the
development of the characters of Romola and her husband Tito;—
Romola gradually improved by the influence of Savonarola, who
turns her noble but ill-directed impulses into the channel of duty, and
Tito gradually growing more selfish and unprincipled as his popularity
and political influence increase. The rest of the plot adheres with more or
less fidelity to the political and religious history of Florence at the close
of the fifteenth century, and arranges itself round the dramatic career
of Tito the Greek adventurer. The figure of Savonarola, which is only
of relative importance in the plot, is worked out with great vividness,
so as to dispute the preëminence with the regular hero and heroine.
The various political parties are all duly represented; and the shop
of the Florentine Figaro, Nello, affords a good opportunity for grouping their principal figures, and bringing them into relation with Tito.
This shop, the Duomo, and the Via de' Bardi, are the three centres of
the story. Its perpetual bustle, and the multitude of characters introduced, preclude the possibility of making the plot one of mere character. Of the fortuitous incidents introduced into it, some are justified by
history, others are purely arbitrary; and these arbitrary accidents are
not always happily accounted for. M. Victor Hugo has consecrated
the license of giving a sort of ubiquity to the characters, and making
them always pounce accidentally on the very person, and at the very
time, that the exigencies of the plot require. George Eliot has availed
herself of the privilege, and we must not quarrel with the ubiquitous
Bratti or with the omniscient Nello. But such a rencounter as that of
Fra Girolamo and Romola in chapter xl, where the Frate reads her
very thoughts, shows an intimate acquaintance with her closest secrets,
and assumes an air of undoubting confidence in her obedience, ground-
ing his claim on a special revelation made to him, is so palpably
monstrous that we cannot help asking the object of it. Fra Girolamo

tells Romola more about herself than our Lord told the Samaritan woman, and Romola accordingly believes him implicitly. But at the end of the story we find that the Frate's claim to prophetic insight was an imposture. What is to be said of this chapter, then? Is he falsely alleging that to be a revelation which he has skilfully learned through spies and other sources of information? Or are we to be referred to the fancied powers of mediums and magnetisers? Or, because his end was excellent, is he to be justified in using falsehood to compass it? 'The end I seek,' he is made to say in chapter lix., 'is one to which minor respects must be sacrificed.' If this is a fair representation of Fra Giro-lamo's character,—Villari[1] gives but little basis for it,—he deserves to be execrated. But George Eliot sets him forth as an example, for the very reason that by such means he strove 'to turn beliefs into ener-gies' for the very highest end. Now here is a dishonesty inseparable from positivist religion, in which religious belief does not correspond to objective truth, but is only an impression on the imagination, useful to excite, direct, and give energy to the feelings. It is necessarily tran-sient and unstable; here to-day, gone to-morrow. Yet the religious teacher of men must pretend that his own faith is firm, or he will not confirm that of his hearers. 'It is the lot of every man who has to speak for the satisfaction of the crowd, that he must speak in virtue of yesterday's faith, hoping it will come back to-morrow' (chap. lxii.); just as George Eliot preaches yesterday's Christianity, but without the corresponding hope. It is the misery of religion, she says, that it should have so much of superstition and conscious imposture at its roots (chap. lii.); that it should be at once necessary, and founded upon falsehood. And this, we may add, is the condemnation of positivist religion, that it justifies falsehood and imposture, by making them the necessary roots of a religious energy, which, again, is necessary for the moral advancement of mankind. It founds morality on falsehood, and roots up honour from the religious mind. And the part of Fra Girolamo in *Romola* is well contrived to teach this lesson. The catas-trophe of *Romola*, though little less improbable than that of the *Mill on the Floss*, yet so naturally flows from the previous incidents and the character of Baldassarre, that the improbability is scarcely felt; while the judgment assents to the measure dealt out both to Tito and Romola as perfectly congruous with their deserts.

Such are the plots of George Eliot's novels; social, characteristic, and endogenous, rather than individual, incidental, and developed by

[1] Refers presumably to *Storia di Savonarola* (1860) by Pasquale Villari (1826–1917).

external accident. They remind one of a group of detached figures in front of a crowded bas-relief;—or of a *concerto* where the melody is taken up first by one and then by another solo instrument, the orchestra playing the accompaniment. It is only in *Romola* that the author's plot has attained its full symphonic form, in which the orchestral parts become as important as the solos; she is not yet, however, a perfect contrapuntist, nor is she always successful in preparing her dissonances, or giving a natural *entrata* to her subjects.

In the conduct of the dialogue and description George Eliot distributes her personages into three great divisions: those whose conversation and acts develope the plot; those who have little else to do than to comment upon it; and the author herself commenting, as it were, upon these comments, and awarding her final judgment. She gives great importance to the commentors; in almost all her tales she has one or more shrewd, plain, sensible, uneducated persons, who put forward the popular view, and speak in proverbs and racy phrase. She uses them as a kind of chorus to describe that which is not acted, and to expound so much of the antecedents of the story and the characters as it is necessary for the reader to know. Her greatest gift is the wonderful truth of these representations of popular ideas, and the idiomatic vigour which she throws into her dialogue. In 'Amos Barton' Mrs. Hackit and Mrs. Patten, in 'Janet's Repentance' the male and female representatives of the public opinion of Milby, gave a promise which was more than realised in the brilliant creations of *Adam Bede*, Mrs. Poyser, Lisbeth, and Bartle Massey. In the *Mill on the Floss* the representation of public opinion is more narrow, being confined to that of the Dodson family; but it gains in directness and comicality as much as it loses in more general truth. In *Silas Marner*, again, we have the inimitable discussion at the Rainbow, moderated by the landlord, an eclectic philosopher or intellectual tactician, trimming to all opinions and uniting all suffrages. In *Romola* we have Nello, the shrewd barber, with his head frizzled and crisped by his continual brushes with the Florentine wits. Besides these speculative characters, George Eliot is fond of giving us a practical one or two of the same class, native wits, overflowing with helpful common sense, who become confidants of the chief actors, and are able to lend important aid in the development of the plot. Such are Nancy, Amos Barton's maid-of-all-work, the gardener and coachman in 'Mr. Gilfil's Love-Story,' Bob Jakin the pedlar in the *Mill on the Floss*, Dolly Winthrop in *Silas Marner*, and Bratti in *Romola*. In the male characters of this stamp, notwithstanding their raciness of speech, George Eliot is apt to become commonplace and theatrical, and to give us copies, more or less servile, of the well-known type of Dickens's John Brodie. All these portraits have this in common, that it is their dialogue, and not the delineation of their characters, which gives them their value.

In *Romola* we have a powerful picture of refined and educated society, very different from that of the rude communities of the other novels; but there is no attempt to redress the failure of Mr. Deane's drawing-room at St. Ogg's in the *Mill on the Floss*. The author has succeeded in giving us the conversation of Machiavelli, and the wits, the scholars, and the politicians of Florence, but has not ventured upon their *salons*. There is a banquet, but it is a political one, not one where leisure is the ruling divinity of the day. George Eliot has no right notions of leisure. It is gone, she says; the steam-engine, instead of propagating it, has only created a vacuum for eager thought to rush in. Even idleness is eager now. Old Leisure was an indolent, rustic, self-indulgent person-age, 'undiseased by hypothesis,' to whom life was not a task, but a sinecure. She has no conception of the *blasé* leisure of the modern drawing-room. Her *salon* is that of Madame de Staël; it is a kind of Athenian agora, filled with very clever men all anxious for something new. The regions cultivated with such success by Victor Hugo, Mr. Thackeray, and Mr. Trollope, remain a *terra incognita* to her.

She talks a good deal about epigrams, and never mentions proverbs; but she makes excellent proverbs, and poor epigrams. Like most artists, she seems to value her productions by their cost, and not by their substance. She is not without wit; but her wit is not of that refined, *malin*, and careless kind which befits the drawing-room. It is more the wit of the wine-party or club, or of the professed joker whose facetiousness is manufactured by rule and line. One of the easiest forms of joke is the adroit substitution of a privative for an expected positive result. It is a form of which George Eliot seems especially fond: her young ladies refuse the most ineligible offers out of devotion to their aunts; her young gentlemen have all the arduous inacquaintance with Latin which their education requires; her parsons' sermons are the most edifying that ever remained unheard by a church-going population; her groups of sisters have a proper family unlikeness; her Christians are well stocked with saving ignorance; her apothecaries spend all their income on starving their one horse. Such jokes occur in clusters. Some-times she ventures on a pun; she tells us that beans were, in more than one sense, the political pulse of Florence. One who has so deep a fund of humour ought not to need reminding of the laborious ineffectiveness of this kind of wit.

Thoroughly possessed with the devil of exposition, she cannot be a drawing-room dialectician. She has not the trifling, fanciful, tricksy reflectiveness, indolent and careless of improvement, which plays only with feelings and thoughts too superficial to shock. She is more like a preacher, improving each occasion, moralising on every incident, and summing up her conclusions in proverbs, aphorisms, or apologues, which she either distributes among her commentating characters, such as Mrs. Poyser, or else reserves for herself. For she maintains a running exposition on her own drama, and illustrates it with a copious supply of maxims, ethical, psychological, and physiological, enough to furnish forth a 'just volume' of *ana*. Thus she notices that to emotional natures, whose thoughts are shadows cast by feeling, words are facts, and even when known to be false have a mastery over smiles and tears; that susceptible persons are more affected by a change of tone than by unexpected words; that we all have a superstitious feeling, that if we expect evil very strongly it is less likely to come; and that 'a proud woman who has once learned to submit carries all her pride to the reinforcement of her submission, and looks down with severe superiority on all feminine assumption as "unbecoming." '

This last maxim looks as if it was a note on Catherine's last speech in the *Taming of the Shrew*. It suggests an enquiry whether the wisdom stored up in George Eliot's pages comes from a wide experience of life, or from a laborious analysis of books. Some of her sayings are simply decanted out of newspapers. 'Before I said "sniff," ' says Mr. Macey, 'I took care to know as she'd say "snaff." ' The original of this is to be found in one of the Swinfen trials.[1] If George Eliot consents to look at the world through the eyes of casual witnesses and reporters, we may easily conceive with how much more industry she consults the pictures which great artists have already painted, not only for the purpose of imitating their style or copying their details, but to generalise their instances into aphorisms capable of begetting a generation of incidents after their kind. Her expository spirit is not always proof against the temptation of appending the aphorism to the imitated incident, thus as it were killing the goose that lays the golden eggs, by anatomising its ovary. For instance, whereas, in Dickens, the Jew on his trial wonders who will mend the broken rail of the dock,[2] so, in

---

[1] A law-case which lasted from 1856 to 1861, arising out of the disputed will of Samuel Swinfen (d. 1854).   [2] Fagin in *Oliver Twist* (1837-8), ch. 52.

George Eliot, Adam Bede, in the midst of his agonising suspense about Hetty, watches the hands and listens to the ticking of the clock, as if he had a reason for doing so. Then follows the general maxim: 'In our times of bitter suffering there are almost always these pauses, when our consciousness is benumbed to every thing but some trivial perception or sensation. It is as if semi-idiotcy came to give us rest from the memory and the dread which refuse to leave us in our sleep.' Are we wrong in attributing to Mr. Lewes not only the multitude of similar physiological observations' in which George Eliot's novels abound, such as the interminable references to 'atavism,' but also the curiously symptomatic treatment of poor Hetty's malady, and the psychologico-medical study of Baldassarre in *Romola*,—a powerful portrait of febrile impotence dominated by a master passion, like a corpse possessed by a spirit; of a poor wreck of humanity helplessly gathering up the shattered fragments of memory in the arms of a tremulous purpose, and failing at the decisive moment, but still persevering even in despair? It is rather the physician than the artist who speaks here. Not that we object to medical information, even in a novel, provided there is not too open a display of the forceps and the dissecting-knife.

But George Eliot seems to have laid painters under contribution even more than physicians, novelists, and poets. She has an eminently pictorial mind, and loves to look at nature through the glasses of Watteau, or the Dutch painters, or Piero di Cosimo. She tries to fix in her readers' minds the scenes she has so vividly conceived in her own, even if she has to use ungrammatical and affected forms of language for the purpose. She seems to feel that a sentence has a more pictorial effect when it stands for a simple apprehension, than when it signifies a judgment. Simple apprehension regards the thing, judgment the process. The one gives the picture to the sense, the other unfolds its generation to the reason. There is, then, something to be said for leaving out verbs, and for writing sentences like this: 'An upper room in a dull Stoniton street with two beds in it—one laid on the floor;' or this, the opening sentence of the *Mill on the Floss*: 'A wide plain, where the broadening Floss hurries on between its green banks.' Although George Eliot has left off this grammatical affectation, still she always begins her stories with an elaborate picture; so elaborate indeed in *Romola*, that it is a real relief when the paint-pot is emptied and the inkstand comes into requisition again. We are persuaded that the study of pictures has helped her as much as the study of living models. We should not be surprised if the famous scene at the Rainbow in *Silas Marner*—a scene compared

by competent critics to Shakespeare's scenes at the Boar's Head—
turned out to be one the like of which she has never witnessed except
on the canvas of Teniers, seen through an atmosphere of Dickens, or of
her own deep knowledge of rustic life. 'The pipes began to be puffed
in a silence which had the air of severity; the more important customers,
who drank spirits and sat nearest the fire, staring at each other as if
a bet were depending on the first man who winked; while the beer-
drinkers, chiefly men in fustian jackets and smock-frocks, kept their
eyelids down and rubbed their hands across their mouths, as if their
draughts of beer were a funereal duty attended with embarrassing
sadness.' Almost all this may be seen in Teniers.[1] The ethical interpretations of the tipplers' attitudes are common-places of the art-criticism
of the day. Their way of talking, their long pauses, their 'unflinching
frankness' in addressing each other, and the characteristic differences
between the interlocutors, may all be learned elsewhere than in the
public-house parlour. When Teniers has once given the picture, the
rest of the scene is such as might be worked out on general principles
of human nature, which are fundamentally the same whether dressed
for the drawing-room or the plough-tail. When Mr. Macey says of Mr.
Lammeter, 'He came from a bit north'ard, so far as ever I could ever
make out; but there's nobody rightly knows about those parts,' he
only puts into the dialect of Warwickshire the same placid ignorance
which Lord Dundreary[2] drawls out in the dialect of the drawing-room.

The great merit of George Eliot's dialogue is its proverbial raciness.
The proverb—a conclusion of long experience, a general truth of
ethics expressed in a figurative form—is a kind of saying that cannot be
manufactured by line and rule, like jokes and epigrams. But its figurative form allows it to be imitated; and one illustration will often suggest
another equally applicable. Mr. Lewes singles out for special commendation a passage in Göthe's *Elective Affinities*, where Edward, hearing
that his flute-playing has been criticised, 'at once feels himself free from
every obligation of duty.' George Eliot clearly imitates this when she
describes Dr. Kimble turning up 'a mean trump-card with an air of
ineffable disgust, as if, in a world where such things could happen, one
might as well enter on a course of reckless profligacy.' In these instances
the figurative way of expressing the first angry feeling of disappointment is quite proverbial. It is almost an intimation that not all Mrs.
Poyser's sayings are original, when Mr. Irwine is made to say of her that

[1] David Teniers the elder (1582–1649), Flemish genre painter.
[2] Character in the play *Our American Cousin* (1858) by Tom Taylor (1817–80).

she is one of the untaught wits that help to stock a country with proverbs, and that her comparison of a Scottish gardener to the cock who thought the sun had risen to hear him crow, was an Æsop's fable in a sentence. An author would scarcely thus commend her own creations. But whencesoever derived, George Eliot has made these proverbs her own by adapting them almost as skilfully as Cervantes appropriated the old stores of Spanish proverbial wisdom to his Sancho Panza. Those of her proverbial expressions the virtue of which consists in the truth of the observation used as a *simile*, are probably original: 'Looking as silly as a tumbler when he has been upside down and has got on his heels again,' embodies a physiological observation which we recommend our readers to verify the next time they assist at a performance of acrobats.

In dialogue by which character is developed George Eliot is no great artist. If it were not for her own copious comments, the text would often be obscure. She lacks invention, and she lacks subtlety. She can explain how speakers only half reveal their real thought, but she cannot exhibit the process; she is soon obliged to pass from dialogue to commentary.

The last and most important element of the novel is the characters. When well exhibited, they make up for want of plot, as in Miss Austen; and for want of dialogue, as in Richardson. Since Scott, each personage of a novel is expected to display himself in dialogue, as in a drama, in which the author acts as scene-shifter and chorus. The first requisite in a character is a distinct individuality—not an external consistency which makes a gardener talk of flowers, and a dairy-woman of cheeses; nor an arbitrary signalment which distinguishes him by an outward badge, like a habit of sniffing, or of saying '*for* to do' a thing; but an internal consistency, which represents the person as the endogenous growth of a central life, putting forth its own natural fruit under the stimulating or depressing influence of circumstance. To make circumstance into the power which determines the character is to mould the man from without. To deny to circumstance its influence over the character is to isolate man in society and in the world, and to render the novel impossible. Character builds up a life out of circumstance, using circumstances as its materials, and, by its use of them, testing the plastic power of its intellect and will. Philip Wakem, however he may wish to be as other men, cannot help having both his intellect and his heart impressed by the circumstance of his deformity.

When novels contain true pictures of character,—when they hold up a true mirror to man's nature,—they become tolerable glasses for readers to see themselves by. It is easy to read any novel frivolously— for its adventures, its intrigue, its hurried action, or its emotional power; or to read it for its literary merits only—for its brilliancy, its wit, or its artistic unity. But novels which paint character truly lead, through self-examination, to self-knowledge. George Eliot searches her readers' hearts when she describes the culpable irresolution, weakness, self-deception, and insincerity of Arthur Donnithorne, or Godfrey Cass, or Tito. Mr. Thackeray's *Snob Papers* have made many men doubt whether they were gentlemen or pretenders; and this is perhaps a reason why the author of them is regarded by some as Socrates was at Athens, when he bored the young men with his lessons of self-knowledge. George Eliot avoids this cause of unpopularity by cutting deeper; she knows that, in our moral as well as our physical nature, the skin is the most sensitive part. You may call your friend a devil with impunity; but beware of telling him that he is a bore. Men, though they say 'What a fool I am!' more readily than 'What a knave I am!' had rather be wicked than ridiculous; and so it is safer to gird at their vices than their follies. For vice is secret, and folly walks in the sun; men are therefore less offended with general satires on vice, which, if they bite, bite in secret, than those on folly, which, as it were, pull their noses in public. It is less offensive to be whipped in one's cell than at the cart's tail in the market-place. But George Eliot does not whip even vice very severely; she probes the conscience tenderly, and 'pleasant is her absolution.'[1] Nobody is very good, she says, and nobody very bad; there are no ideal characters in real life. If your general aim is good, and you work hard for it, we will not look too closely at your means. There is Fra Girolamo, a man by no means truthful to a fault, one who sought his own glory, but who is a model for imitation because he sought it by labouring for the very highest end,—the moral regeneration of our race. Crime is misfortune following upon weakness. Fiendish malice is unknown outside melodrama. 'Plotting covetousness, and deliberate contrivance, in order to compass a selfish end, are nowhere abundant but in the world of the dramatist; they demand too intense a mental action. . . . It is easy enough to spoil the lives of neighbours without taking so much trouble: we can do it by lazy acquiescence and lazy omission; by trivial falsities for which we hardly know a reason; by small frauds neutralised by small extravagances; by maladroit flatteries, and clumsily improvised insinuations.'

[1] *The Canterbury Tales*, 'General Prologue', 222.

George Eliot, we see, is a searching but indulgent moralist. She admits neither saints nor devils, but mixed natures,—heroes with a leaven of villany, and villains with a spice of heroism. Deep down in every one, she teaches, there is the same human nature; the deeper we go, and the more thoroughly we strip off the bark, the more plainly we discover the ultimate unity. The world wags by universal laws, not by policy or by plotting, and especially gives no encouragement to the small finesse of fools baiting mouse-traps to catch elephants.

In probing the depths of human nature, George Eliot comes to the critical question of the relations between passion and duty, reason and feeling, man and mankind, the soul and God. The antithesis of passion and duty figures itself to her mind as a kind of sexual distinction; so that if woman could be defecated from all male fibres, she would be all passion, as man, purged of all feminine qualities, would be all hard duty. Adam Bede before he is softened by sorrow, and Tom Tulliver, are instances of males nearly pure; but George Eliot, averse from ideals, cannot give so abstract a symbol of hard virility as M. Victor Hugo's Javert.[1] On the other hand, woman, as woman, is in her system all emotional; in its highest form it is a being with black hair and large dark eyes, and is a mass of yearnings, passions, and feelings; it makes love and lovers too; it feels, and is the cause of feeling in men—like Falstaff, who was not only witty himself, but also the cause why wit should be in others. Tina, in 'Mr. Gilfil's Love-Story,' is the most idealised representative woman that George Eliot draws; but Milly, and Beatrice, and Janet, and Hetty and Dinah, and Maggie and Lucy, and Eppie and Nancy, and Romola and Tessa, must all be studied if we would complete the idea. According to this idea, the influence which woman exerts over man is twofold. One is 'the soothing, unspeakable charm of gentle womanhood,' mastering by its simple presence, by the 'serene dignity of being.' This kind is blond and blue-eyed, a sleepy Venus, like Dudu.[2] The other is the active influence, which makes man's blood boil, and awakes in him the slumbering fires of passion and feeling. This is the dark-eyed kind. It is the hearth at which the strong man's feelings are kindled, and where they become gradually purified, like Adam Bede's in the crucible of Hetty's little heart. It raises the storm which the other kind calms. This is why they go in pairs in George Eliot's novels; why Tina and Beatrice exert a joint and successive influence on Captain Wybrow, Hetty and Dinah

[1] In Les Misérables (1862).
[2] Byron, Don Juan, VI, xlii, I.

on Bede, Lucy and Maggie on Stephen Guest, Molly and Nancy Lammeter on Godfrey Cass, Romola and Tessa on Tito.

This influence of woman is not of necessity in proportion to her intrinsic worth. The inward grace may be entirely incommensurate with the visible means. The little-hearted Hetty can kindle the conflagration which proves the pure gold of Adam's large soul. But in itself woman's love is always pure; it may be barked over with vulgarity, frivolity, vanity, and giddiness, but when the shell is broken and cleared away, the central fire is found to be burning brightly. Even from the most sterile and frivolous of female hearts, George Eliot shows that suffering may bring out tones more pathetic than could be drawn from nobler women, because in them the deep fundamental pathos of our common nature shows itself without the complications of adventitious distinctions. The sphere which George Eliot claims as specially her own is the pathos of human nature stripped of all acquired and accidental trappings of education, rank, and intelligence.

In the relation she gives to the sexes we see something of the old Teuton veneration for women, and something of the worship of mother, wife, and daughter enjoined by Comte. This possibly may account for Mr. Lewes's complicity in her doctrine. Woman, in her books, walks as a superior being. Milly is firmer than Amos; Tina is irresistible; Janet, when she is rescued by Tryan, soon shows her superiority to him; Dinah leads Adam as she chooses, though she respects his manliness; Mrs. Poyser is the dominant spirit at the Hall Farm; and Mr. Hackitt rides behind his wife. Maggie has a much larger soul than the inflexible Tom; and though Lucy and Stephen are equally colourless, Lucy at least has principles and moral strength. Nancy is altogether firmer than Godfrey Cass, and Eppie wiser than Marner. Dolly Winthrop views the stronger sex in the light of animals naturally troublesome, like bulls and turkey-cocks: 'The men are awk'ard and contrairy mostly, God help 'em; but when the drink's out of 'em they aren't unsensible, though they're bad for leeching and bandaging—so fiery and unpatient.' Romola is infinitely stronger than Tito, or Fra Girolamo himself, though she owes every thing to his opportune influence; Tessa is a foolometer, showing how little womanhood is wanted to balance all the manly intelligence and will of Tito.

But in the picture which George Eliot gives of woman in herself we see simply the defilement of her sex. It is natural that the female novelist should exaggerate the importance of the woman's relations to man, but not that she should degrade her nature. 'They tell me,' said

Talleyrand to Madame de Staël, 'that you and I are both in *Corinne*,[1] disguised as women.' It is natural that the authoress should make her women act male parts, and give her men something of a feminine character. Though she ought to be able to draw woman in herself, for the simple reason that she is a woman, yet she may be too far separated from the ordinary life of her sex to be a good judge of its relations. The direct power and the celebrity of authorship may obscure and replace the indirect influence and calm happiness of domestic feminine life. For admiration and affection do not easily combine. Celebrity isolates the authoress, and closes her heart; it places her where experience of the ordinary relations of the sex is impossible, and where she is tempted to supply by theory what is lacking in experience. She gives us her view of woman's vocation, and paints things as they ought to be, not as they are. Women work more by influence than by force, by example than reasoning, by silence than speech: the authoress grasps at direct power through reasoning and speech. Having thus taken up the male position, the male ideal becomes hers,—the ideal of power,— which, interpreted by her feminine heart and intellect, means the supremacy of passion in the affairs of the world.

Thus the misconception of relations leads directly to an error in the essence of things. The supremacy of passion in human affairs, though it leaves conduct subject to the law of the inevitable consequences of actions, does not leave it subject to the law of honour and delicacy. Indeed, a supreme passion is inconsistent with honour and delicacy either in men or women; and both the male and female characters of female novelists are liable to this defect. It is an hallucination in Miss Kavanagh[2] to suppose that we owe to these writers the importation of delicacy into English romance. On the contrary, they generally saturate their female characters with passion and sensuality. Mrs. Aphra Behn, Mrs. Centlivre, Madame de Staël, George Sand, the Countess Hahn-Hahn, Mrs. Inchbald, Currer Bell, Mrs. Norton,[3] and George Eliot, simply misuse their sex. The female writers who avoid this profanation are those who, like Miss Edgeworth, refuse to believe in the mysterious involuntary force of love, and shun passion as dangerous to the moral

[1] By Madame de Staël, 1807.
[2] Julia Kavanagh (1824–77), novelist and critic. See her *English Women of Letters: Biographical Sketches* (1863).
[3] Mrs Aphra Behn (1640–89), novelist and dramatist; Mrs Susannah Centlivre (1670–1723), actress and dramatist; Countess Hahn-Hahn (1805–80), German novelist; Mrs Elizabeth Inchbald (1753–1821), novelist, dramatist, and actress; Mrs Caroline Norton (1808–77), poet and novelist.

equilibrium. But George Eliot deifies passion,—her feminine passion of love, and her male passion of justice. Human emotion is the only supernatural sphere which the positive philosophy recognises as the one wherein it has no currency. Passion, love or hate, it acknowledges as the mysterious involuntary power, which admits of no superior in man's intellect or will. Of itself this passion is pure and right in its tendencies; it goes wrong through the admixture of unworthy motives. Hetty falls, not through passion, but through a deficiency of passion; she sacrilegiously places her vanity and frivolity upon the pedestal which belongs to love, and she is deservedly smitten by the outraged divinity. Maggie is the example of passion unmixed with frivolity, walking on the brink of the abyss—*Dominæ cupiditatis ad nutum*[1]—but not toppling over; giving passionate kisses to the declared lover of her dearest friend, drifting away with him along the river, blistering her good name, but refusing at the last moment to be his wife, and thus to consummate the cruellest wrong and treachery to others with infamy to herself. This, then, is the divine principle, the lack of which alone prevents a Javert or Tom Tulliver being the highest type of humanity, —the green-sickness of youth in the guise of a fierce and ignoble desire, governed by the moon, feeding itself on delicious poison which it knows to be deadly, swallowing up honour, duty, humanity, and the most sacred ties, working all the effects of hatred, and calling itself love. As a feeling, this love is put before us as a thing too sacred to be suppressed; but to yield to it, and to act upon it, may sometimes bring us into collision with the inevitable law of consequences. In such cases it must be renounced; dwelt upon in the memory, but rejected in practice, it will be the material for the sacrifice upon which all true nobility is founded. Hence the eagerness after forbidden dainties is to be encouraged, on the ground that the present coveting after unfit things is the best way of ensuring future self-denial.

As pendants to her two classes of females, George Eliot provides us with two classes of males, each class being further broken into two divisions. In the first class will predominates; in the second, intelligence. The first comprehends those hard, stern, strong-willed characters in whom retributive justice is a passion which often congeals into the principle of duty. Of these some are more or less amenable to the feminine influences, like Adam Bede, Sir Christopher Cheverell, and Tom Tulliver; the others, in default of being so influenced, remain or become brutes; such persons are the lawyers Dempster and Wakem,

[1] 'at the nod of their mistress desire' (Lactantius, *Institutes*, VII, i, 19).

Dunsey Cass and Dolfo Spini, and in a measure old Tulliver and Baldassarre. The second class comprehends those who have little strength of will, but much imagination and versatility. Of these, some, in spite of their vacillations and worship of chance, become, through the influence of women, or under the pressure of sorrow, capable of renunciation and self-sacrifice, like Arthur Donnithorne and Godfrey Cass; in others selfishness is predominant to the last, as in Captain Wybrow, Tito, and the fatted calf Stephen Guest. George Eliot does not pretend to represent these characters in ideal simplicity, nor even to maintain a consistent manliness in them. Arthur's conduct under Adam Bede's assaults illustrates the text which says that 'the churning of milk bringeth forth butter,' but violates the common rule of characters like his,—to depress whom you have injured, and to destroy whom you have depressed. Adam himself, the model of manly strength, breaks out into childish and impotent threats against Arthur; as if resolute men let the world know their resolution, instead of doing first and talking afterwards, or keeping in view the difference between the loquacity of wishing, and the laconic energy of willing.

Between these two classes we have a third or epicene division. They are generally men whose negative qualities have become positive through feminine influence, transient or lasting. Women are like the conductors of an electric machine; men, like the little pith-balls that rush to embrace the conductor, till, after being filled with the new influence, they begin to feel a repulsion, and fly off again. For men of this sort the only harvest-time is in spring. In the first access of love, or in the first years of marriage, they drink in a sufficiency of feminine influence; and then the wife dies, or becomes the object of friendship instead of passion, and the man, fully charged with feminine electricity, feels no more drawn towards the flame. He remains a widower, cherishing a memory which is a source of strength to his soul, like Barton, or Gilfil, or Philip Wakem. Even those who have no cause to cherish the memory, like Bartle Massey, or Adam Bede after his passion for Hetty, find themselves changed beings, and trace some of their best gifts to the feminine influence. George Eliot's widowers owe a great debt to their wives; not so her widows. Janet Dempster and Romola had husbands who only improved them by making their life a sacrifice. Woman is put before us as the treasury of the divine gift; and man has very little to give to her, but much to accept from her. The only male fibre which men can contribute to woman's nature is precision and regularity of thought. The want of this is the distinguishing

243

characteristic of the female mind. Men live by diagrams; but 'a woman will bake you a pie every week of her life, and never come to see that the hotter the oven the shorter the time.' Priscilla Lammeter, the only old maid whom George Eliot attempts to describe, exhibits the manly character of her mind precisely in this: 'My pork pies,' she says, 'don't turn out well by chance.'

If the character of Savonarola does not fall into any of the divisions we have referred to, it is because he is drawn not from theory, but from history. Therefore he protrudes from the stratified plains of George Eliot's novels like a vast mass of primitive fiery rock upheaved by other forces, and standing like a stranger amid the fields and woods which it fertilises by the streams that roll from its sides.

George Eliot repeats herself in her plots and situations, and still more in her characters. Her mind is pictorial and tenacious, and can scarcely let go a thought once engraved there. In her successive books she gives us the same characters, the same situations, the same arguments; but disguised in different dresses, and surrounded with different circumstances. She forces into circulation that special coinage the genuineness of which has been most questioned. If Bob the pedlar's chaffering with Mrs. Glegg is called farcical, she will make Bratti repeat it in *Romola*; if the deathless hate of old Tulliver is called incredible, then she will force us to believe the terrible *vendetta* of Baldassarre; if Maggie's floating away is rejected, we must have Romola's drifting away instead. Tito, with his difficulties about his two wives, is a highly elaborate reproduction of Godfrey Cass. The moral conception of the versatile and accomplished Greek is the same as that of the heavy and half-educated squire; the same type had already done duty in Arthur Donnithorne, and was first indicated in Captain Wybrow. The same passionate, craving, yearning, emotional brunette nature shines forth in Tina, Janet, and Maggie, and is reproduced, tempered by education and refinement, and by a dash of blond steadiness and blue-eyed principle, in Romola. George Eliot is not prolific in types. She does not see that there are as many forms of mind as figures of body; her difficulty is in invention. She is a musician who cannot compose new tunes, but is continually resetting, developing, and adorning her old melodies with variations and counterpoint; and her successive developments do not fit on one to the other, so as to form a succession of novels in which the same persons might figure, like those of Mr. Trollope and Mr. Thackeray. In each she begins *de novo*, and develops the fundamental idea in a distinct direction. For she knows that every force can produce more than one change, every cause more than one effect, and every type a whole family of species and varieties.

We will not discuss the amount of truth which may lie hid in her idea of women having almost the monopoly of the emotional nature—of the passions, which are the elements of life; a bubbling and fermenting source of power, whose impulses seem like the acts of external force, instinctive, indefinite, vague, involuntary, but rich and mighty, like a divine energy within us. Perhaps she does not think that women possess it more really than men, but that in the woman it is not over-laid with all the unreasonable products of manly reason; with our logical feats, and our honeycombed brain with its thousand cells, one containing reason, another understanding, a third bad wit, and a fourth nothing at all—that is to say, the idea. In women, perhaps, we get to the bottom more quickly, without having to pioneer our way through this tangled growth; and we find the central volcanic fire, with its hot lava, its scoriæ, its smoke, its lurid flames, and its consuming heat, unscreened by veils, uncoloured by glassy mediums. Her women, perhaps, are so much alike, because her idea of woman is so one-sided and so simple.

We have now to say a few words about the purpose of George Eliot's novels. However improper it may be to assume a knowledge of a man's ordinary intentions, it is different when the work criticised is one of speculation and intellect; for then the rule holds good that the practical purpose is identical with the speculative principle. Now the speculative principles on which George Eliot's novels are built up are plain. In her ideas of art and philosophy she identifies herself with Mr. Lewes; and Mr. Lewes has spoken plainly: Göthe is his master in art, including views of life, morals, and religion; and Comte is his master in science. For him Göthe is the *vates sacer* of the modern era, as Dante was of the middle ages. All who would speak intelligibly to modern ears must accept Göthe's principles and views. He has taught us, in his *Hermann and Dorothea*, the pathos that is to be found in common life, and in ordinary men and women. He has taught us in all his works that art paints what is, and does not run after the ideal of what ought to be. In *Faust* he gives an example of that vital force which brings together and keeps united things in themselves most opposite, and exhibits a living combination of refinement with horrors, of reflection with tumult, of high and delicate poetry with broad and palpable effects. In *Faust* he also teaches the value of prodigality—of touching upon and illustrating, in the same work, a great number of typical aspects of life. In *Faust*, moreover, he teaches us how to use legends, and how the most improbable situations may be justified by a traditionary story. He teaches us to distrust logic, to hunger for realities, and not to be satisfied with maxims and definitions. These principles, taken almost at random from Mr. Lewes's life of Göthe, are clearly the guiding stars of George Eliot. She not only seeks her pathos in common life, but expounds the whole doctrine on the subject in almost all her novels. She abjures the ideal, she hates impossible virtues and improbable vices, and strives to paint facts with all the roughnesses of reality. She tries to exhibit the vital force which unites contradictory things in one life, the hospitality of the mind which admits all opinions, the liberalism of the soul which is vicious while it is virtuous and virtuous while it is vicious. She gives the greatest possible variety to her books by the multiplicity of her characters, the composite nature of each, the richness of her social backgrounds, and the brief glimpses which she gives us of all kinds of life. In her way of dealing with a religion which she does not believe, she follows Göthe's rule of treating the legendary as if true, of throwing her whole mind into the position of the actors in her drama, and of speaking not as she would speak, but as they would have spoken. She also holds that 'the mysterious complexity of our life is not to be embraced by maxims, and that to lace up ourselves in formulas of that sort is to repress all the divine promptings and inspirations that spring from growing insight and sympathy.' The very story of *Adam Bede* is only a modification of *Faust*; and the relish with which Dolly Winthrop's paraphrase for God, and the Italian *Messer Domeneddio* are employed, as well as the remark upon Raffaelle's Madonnas, remind one of the spirit which dictated the second prologue of Göthe's play.

The moral and religious principles of Göthe are also those of Mr. Lewes and George Eliot. Göthe was a man 'of deep religious sentiments, with complete scepticism on most religious doctrines.'[1] The famous confession of faith in *Faust* is a pantheism which ends by declaring that Feeling is God, and that dogma is all smoke. Grander, deeper, holier thoughts, says Mr. Lewes, are not to be found in poetry;[2] this confession is the same in substance with what the priest teaches in somewhat different language; and yet 'to make feeling the essence of religion,' says Feuerbach, 'is nothing else than to make feeling the essence of God.'[3] The moral teaching of *Faust* is, first, a warning against sacrificing

[1] G. H. Lewes, *The Life and Works of Goethe* (1855), VII, v.   [2] *Ibid.*, VI, vii.
[3] *Das Wesen des Christenthums* (1841), i, 2.

the future to the present; against the blindness to consequences caused by the imperiousness of desire; and against the recklessness with which inevitable results are braved in perfect consciousness of their being inevitable, provided a temporary pleasure can be obtained. The moral of the second part is positive. It shows how the toiling soul, after trying in vain the various directions of individual effort and individual gratification, and finding therein no peace, is finally conducted to the recognition of the vital truth that man lives for man, and that only in as far as he is working for humanity can his efforts bring permanent happiness. All this moral doctrine is summed up in the one word, Renunciation; we must content ourselves with the knowable and attainable; we must renounce ideal and absolute happiness. We are only capable of a kind of relative content, which comes with weariness; in labour there is a stimulus which gives energy to life; and the thought that our labour tends in some way to the benefit of others makes the rolling years endurable. The surest way to reap all the enjoyment we can out of life is to take a kind of sentimental pleasure in sorrow and suffering, as giving a mysterious grandeur to the soul.

Such are the moral and religious lessons which Mr. Lewes learns from Göthe. They are taught also by George Eliot. With her, doctrines are but names for sentiments, beliefs are only useful to turn feelings into energies, and faith is an 'illusion.' To her mind, the substance of every religion is the same; there is the same meaning at the bottom of all Christian sects, and that one meaning is, love to man—a tender, self-sacrificing love, which embraces a life of labour and sorrow for no other reason than to comfort the sorrowful and to aid those who are in want. Like Göthe, she desires to expose the deep misery of the vacillating purpose, and the inevitable wretchedness that follows not vice only, but even imprudence; to preach the doctrine of renunciation; to hold up the labour which works for man as our highest occupation; and to exhibit the mighty effects of the sacrament of sorrow. All these doctrines are not only indicated symbolically as in *Faust*, but are preached in clear aphorism, *more suo*, by George Eliot.

That which gives the religious charm to George Eliot's novels is the way in which she handles the doctrine of renunciation and self-sacrifice for the benefit of others. In this she speaks as a Christian, even as a Catholic; for as the atheistical Buddhism is the most moral, spiritual, and pietistic of all the religions of paganism, so is the atheistical religion of the positivists the most like Christianity. It is indeed a Christian anthropology, without the basis of Christian theology. We may illustrate this by the persevering way in which George Eliot inculcates confession. Confession to a clergyman is the crisis in the psychological development of Tina in 'Gilfil,' and of Janet in the third tale. In *Adam Bede* the whole chain of sin and shame fails of prevention, because Arthur fails in his resolution to confess to the vicar; a weakness which the author attributes to the fact that he attempted to do so at the breakfast-table instead of in a confessional. In the next tale the confession of Maggie to Dr. Kenn has not the same organic relation to the story; its introduction, therefore, shows how important the author considered it for the moral development of her heroine. In *Silas Marner* and *Romola* the moral lesson is the evil of concealment, the brood of sins which a guilty secret generates in the soul, and the doctrine that 'the contaminating effect of deeds often lies less in the commission than in the consequent adjustment of our desires—the enlistment of our self-interest on the side of falsity; as, on the other hand, the purifying influence of public confession springs from the fact that by it the hope in lies is for ever swept away, and the soul recovers the noble attitude of simplicity.' However indulgent George Eliot is to falsehood for a good purpose, she has no pardon for lies told to conceal a crime.

But though she is attracted to Catholicism by its moral side—probably for Feuerbach's reason, because it attaches itself to the sufferings of Christ through sympathy, while Protestantism attaches itself to His merits, and merely rejoices over instead of compassionating His sufferings—she has no faith in any one of its dogmas. She delights to show how these dogmas, whatever power they have at certain times over the feelings, are evanescent in their influence, and how faith, instead of being unchangeable, is a most variable and fanciful illusion. She quizzes religion by the irony with which she makes the self-sacrificing resolution of Tryan gradually, in the last weeks of his life, soften before the dark eyes of Janet, and the nunlike devotion of Dinah find an appropriate consummation in matrimony. Marner loses his faith simply by a trust in a special providence, and becomes an infidel when the lots go against him. The final disgrace of Fra Girolamo springs from his rash acceptance of a miraculous ordeal which he shirks. The moral is, that he who expects a natural law to be set aside in order to vindicate any cause, however holy and however religious, embraces a degrading superstition, exciting hopes the inevitable disappointment of which leads men into desperation and atheism. The principle implied is, when absolutely stated, inconsistent with a religion founded on miracle, with the belief in a personal Providence, or in any other God than the system of the Universe.

There is no doubt that the humanitarianism so eloquently and warily inculcated by George Eliot responds to a feeling of modern days. Our forefathers thought that the first duty of man was to vindicate God, to put the perjurer and blasphemer to death. We leave God to take care of Himself; and we feel, if we do not say, with the poet,

But I, I sympathise with man, not God.

They tolerated vice if it were covered with the robe of religion, and forgave the 'mœurs souterraines' of a novel on the strength of its 'opinions supercélestes.'[1] We, on the other hand, tolerate pantheism, and atheism itself, if it comes to us in the garb of self-sacrifice, renunciation, and universal charity. We forget that such an unnatural union cannot last long; that the real object of all perversions of religion is to find a substitute for a violated morality; that, in the long-run, the denial of God and the soul, and the indifference to the next world, must make us luxurious in this, insensible to honour, and incapable of any great effort; that to substitute the temporal future of the race for our own eternal future as the motive of virtue, is a folly, because we cannot care much more for our remote posterity than for our remote ancestors.

But it does not follow, because the purpose of George Eliot is bad, that her books are altogether so. The best books, says Chamfort, do almost as much harm as good;[2] conversely, the worst books may do some good as well as harm. Next to those who form the national taste and fix the national character, the greatest geniuses are those who corrupt them. For if they choose their side like fanatics, they are apt to defend it like philosophers; and the worse their cause is, the better must their reasons be. Again, there are well-disguised wickednesses, as there are well-dressed wicked men; and the more monstrous the wickedness the philosopher has to recommend, the more impervious will be the disguise in which he wraps it up. There is a limit beyond which this process defeats itself; the philosopher grows too cunning to be understood, and the disguise is more wholesome than the well-concealed purpose is deleterious. Thus it is with George Eliot's novels. The positive good of her sensible ethics outweighs the negative evil of her atheistic

[1] Montaigne, *Essais* III, xiii ('De L'Expérience').
[2] *Maximes et Pensées* (1795), no. 3.

GEORGE ELIOT

theology; and her books may be read not only with pleasure and profit, but—unless the reader is possessed by squint suspicion—without a conception of the hidden meaning which lies under their plot, their dialogue, and their characters.

FELIX HOLT

June 1866

39. John Morley, unsigned review, *Saturday Review*

16 June 1866, xxi, 722–4

John, 1st Viscount Morley (1838–1923) was a journalist, biographer, Radical politician, and statesman. As well as being the editor of both the *Fortnightly Review* (1867–82) and the *Pall Mall Gazette* (1880–3), he also edited the 'English Men of Letters' series, for which he wrote the volume on Burke (1867). He was a successful Irish secretary and secretary for India, and a supporter of Gladstone of whom he wrote his famous *Life* (1903). It is probable that Morley also wrote the *Saturday Review* articles on *Silas Marner* and *Romola* (Nos. 27 and 36). See M. M. Bevington, *The Saturday Review*, New York, 1941, p. 182.

The opening lines of *Felix Holt* affect the reader like the first notes of the prelude to an old familiar melody. We find ourselves once more among the Midland homesteads, the hedgerows, 'liberal homes of unmarketable beauty,' and the great corn-stacks in the rick-yard, while here too, as in the old Loamshire of *Adam Bede*, 'the busy scenes of the shuttle and the wheel, of the roaring furnace, of the shaft and the pulley' lie 'in the midst of the large-spaced, slow-moving life of homesteads and far-away cottages and oak-sheltered parks.' Everybody recognises the charm of the old touch in the picture of 'the neat or handsome parsonage and grey church set in the midst; there was the pleasant tinkle of the blacksmith's anvil, the patient cart-horses waiting at his door; the basket-maker peeling his willow wands in the sunshine; the wheelwright putting the last touch to a blue cart with red wheels; here and there a cottage with bright transparent windows showing pots full of blooming balsams or geraniums, and little gardens in front all double daisies or dark wall-flowers; at the well clean and comely women carrying yoked buckets, and towards the free school small Britons dawdling on and handling their marbles in the pockets of unpatched corduroys adorned with brass buttons.' And in contrast with these are the dirty children and languid mothers of the grimy towns—'pious Dissenting women, perhaps, who took life patiently and thought that salvation depended chiefly on predestination and not at all on cleanliness.' There was a great deal of nonsense talked about *Romola*, and foolish persons kept on cavilling at that wonderful book, because the authoress had left what they styled her own ground. As if she had not made Florence in the fifteenth century as much her own ground as Loamshire in the nineteenth, and as if, moreover, a writer of genius could always be ready to give the public just what it happens to want, instead of what she happens to be able to give. The authoress of *Felix Holt* probably had her eyes half turned upon these too captious admirers when she says of the parson who benefited his curate by pointing out how he could best defeat a Dissenting controversialist, that he had all 'those sensibilities to the odour of authorship which belong to almost everybody who is not expected to be a writer—and especially to that form of authorship which is called suggestion, and consists in telling another man that he might do a great deal with a given subject by bringing a sufficient amount of knowledge, reasoning, and wit to bear upon it.' But though it was extremely absurd to persist in disliking Romola because she was not a Warwickshire dairymaid, and still more absurd to persist that the authoress had no business to shift her scenes or change her characters, we may still rejoice that she has again come back to those studies of English life, so humorous, so picturesque, and so philosophical, which at once raised her into the very first rank among English novelists.

The popular notion about the excellence and brilliancy of the style of George Eliot's novels is that it is simply the excellence of a painter like Teniers. People talk of *Silas Marner* as if there were nothing in it except Nancy Lammeter and the famous meeting in the parlour of the inn; of the *Mill on the Floss*, as if it were only a rural chronicle of Gleigs and Dodsons and Tullivers; of *Adam Bede*, as if it contained no more than a photographic reproduction of the life of midland dairies and farm-houses and apple-orchards. No doubt the same kind of remarks will be made about the latest, and in some points the best, of the writer's stories. And there is no lack of material even for the limited appreciation involved in such criticism as this. The talk of the miners over their ale; of the respectable farmers and shopkeepers over their three-and-sixpenny ordinary in the country market-town; of the upper servants in the butler's pantry of an old manor-house, is as witty and as truthful, and in its own way as artistically admirable, as anything that the writer has ever done. And the variety is much greater among these quaint-speaking souls, with narrow slow-moving lives, and only the dimmest and haziest outlook, and the most heavily-clogged sensibilities. Instead of the one or two who have hitherto sufficed to furnish a background for the graver and more tragic action of the story, in *Felix Holt* there are a dozen. There is the Dissenting minister's old servant who is always being severely 'exercised' in spirit, who, if remonstrated with for boiling the eggs too hard, would sigh that 'there's hearts as are harder,' and who, in reply to anything like a joke, would exclaim, 'Dear me, don't you be so light, Miss; we may all be dead before night;' and the good-humoured pitman who says that he's 'been aforced to give my wife a black eye to hinder her from going to the preachin'; Lors-a-massy, she thinks she knows better nor me.' There is the little old waiting-woman who looks on life as she looks on her evening game of whist, 'I don't enjoy the game much, but I like to play my cards well, and see what will be the end of it.' And there is Mrs. Holt, the groaning member of the church assembled in Malthouse Yard, who, though full of humble professions, avows, 'I've done *my* duty and more if anybody comes to that; for I've gone without my bit of meat to make broth for a sick neighbour; and if there's any of the church members say they've done the same, I'd ask them if they had the sinking at the stomach as I have.' These are only three or four out of a much greater number of similar characters, all fully and clearly drawn, and each thoroughly different from the other, except in the one point of leading a dull uncultured life. For though they all say good things, what they say is not all good in the same way, but because it is in each case the natural style of a distinct character which has been keenly observed and fully conceived. But to see nothing in this or any other novel by the same writer but these droll, stupid, quaint beings, with their odd humours and rude conceits, is as bad as to see nothing in *Hamlet* except the gravediggers, nothing in *Romeo and Juliet* except the nurse and the friar and the apothecary, nothing in the *Midsummer's Night's Dream* but Bottom and Snug, Snout and Quince. It is natural that George Eliot's brilliant comedy should be most talked about, because everybody in the world feels bound to like humour, and no man does not think he understands it. And, besides, the authoress's view of life is always brought out with so much mellowness, with such artistic delicacy and finish, with an air of such even tranquillity, that the incautious reader commonly overlooks the profound pathos which lies under the surface of nearly every book she has written. If she allowed herself to take the reader aside and pour deliberately into his ear a stream of general moralizing, or if she borrowed an artificial impressiveness from an abrupt *staccato* style as so many French writers, even writers of eminence, are fond of doing, the half-tragic moral and point of almost all her work would be forced upon the least reflective kind of reader. But her sense of what is due to art, or, in other words, her fine and comprehensive discernment of the proportion between the different elements of human life, and her consciousness of the unnumbered tints and shades which colour its various faces, are enough to prevent her from narrowing and concentrating all her strength upon a single effect, or throwing over her whole picture one single over-whelming colour or light. One living novelist, and an accurate observer of life too, feels only the superficial joys, the fainter pains, by which mortals are affected. Another, who has watched the doings and sufferings of men from loftier and more poetic heights, is roused to declaim like Prometheus against the selfish malignity or cold indiffer-ence with which the gods regard the sons of men. In the hands of the first, we are entertained, but we never rise from the ground. In the hands of the other, life is no longer the life of men, but of furious Titans and beneficent demi-gods. The authoress of *Felix Holt* and of *Romola* is wider and maturer in her philosophy than either. She looks out upon the world with the most entire enjoyment of all the good that there is in it to enjoy, and with an enlarged compassion for all the ill that there is in it to pity. But she never either whimpers over the sorrowful lot of man, or snarls and chuckles over his follies and littlenesses and impotence. For example, in *Felix Holt* there is an odd little Dissenting minister, one of the most exquisitely perfect and pleasing characters ever drawn. In an interview with a Radical candidate seeking his vote and interest, he does his best to modify the candidate's views about the ballot. A cynical sprite might have made himself merry, the authoress says, 'at the illusions of the little minister, who brought so much conscience to bear on the production of so slight an effect.' 'I never smiled at Mr. Lyon's trustful energy,' she goes on, 'without falling to penitence and veneration immediately after; for what we call illusions are often, in truth, a wider vision of past and present realities—a willing movement of a man's soul with the larger sweep of the world's forces —a movement towards a more assured end than the chances of a single life.' This complete perception of the fatal effects of looking at men and women and conduct through a philosophy which dwarfs us into a swarming tribe of tiny ants bustling to and fro with bits of straw and pigmy crumbs over our hill, is one illustration of the benign, elevated, and calm spirit which breathes through the authoress's style. And this is the more remarkable because of the fulness with which every chapter shows the writer's consciousness of the puzzle which surrounds human existence. If life in her books is never made too small by comparing it with some imaginary standard fit for gods and giants, neither is all excluded that cannot be satisfactorily measured by the stupid little two-inch rule of those who have become optimists with shut-up minds, either out of sheer self-conceit and vanity, or else because a too narrow religion or philosophy has made them so.

One of the puzzles, which runs pathetically through *Felix Holt* as through *Romola* and the *Mill on the Floss*, is the evil usage which women receive at the hands of men. Mrs. Transome, in the novel before us, is perhaps a stronger illustration than either Maggie Tulliver or Romola of the curse which a man can be to a woman. And it is not designed for a mere outburst of impotent anger and misery when she exclaims, partly crushed, partly defiant, that 'God was cruel when he made women.' She gives a reason for her seemingly impious accusation, and her own history and position supplied an extenuating condition, or else an argument in its support. 'A woman's love,' she said, 'is always freezing into fear; she wants everything, she is secure of nothing. . . . What is the use of a woman's will? if she tries, she doesn't get it, and she ceases to be loved.' Fate had been unkind to the unhappy woman. 'After sharing the common dream that when a beautiful man-child was born to her, her cup of happiness would be full, she had travelled through long years apart from that child to find herself at last in the presence of a son of whom she was afraid, and to whose sentiment in any given case she possessed no key.' This is a picture of which men would have seen more, and thought more, if they had been less ready to avoid pitying women in the right place by a willingness to pity them in the wrong place, where they don't either merit or want pity. Mrs. Transome has other causes than a rather cold and self-reliant son to exclaim, 'I would not lose the misery of being a woman, now I see what can be the baseness of a man.' 'One must be a man—first to tell a woman that her love has made her your debtor, and then ask her to pay you by breaking the last poor threads between her and her son.' The whole chapter descriptive of the interview in which a man tries to save himself from disagreeable things by inducing a woman whom he has once loved to confess her past degradation to her own son, is a painful though unsurpassedly vigorous delineation of the ugliness to which anybody can stoop when 'led on through years by the gradual demands of a selfishness which has spread its fibres far and wide through the intricate vanities and sordid cares of an everyday existence.' This is the old strain of *Romola* taken up again. Mr. Jermyn, like Tito, is guilty of a hateful baseness, not because he is a wicked ravening fiend, but because he is weak and mean, and has got to think honour and pity and affection and every other virtue in his relations to another cheaply sacrificed at the price of some gain to himself. 'To such uses may tender relations come when they have ceased to be tender.'

Yet this strong and repeated conviction of how hard or mean or cruel men are to women has not prevented the authoress, here as in other books, from making a man the effective stirrer-up of a pure and lofty enthusiasm in the mind of her heroine. What Savonarola was to Romola, Felix Holt is to Esther. Only the first had the simpler and stronger lever of religion, while Felix Holt elevates Esther to a height as lofty as his own by the subtle force of his own character. It need scarcely be said that the task which the authoress has set herself in the later case is by much the more difficult, and demands a new delicacy and ingenuity. Religious enthusiasm is full of infection, and might have easily grown up under the teaching of Savonarola in a much less noble and less bitterly tried person than Romola was. But enthusiasm for a teacher who brings no pietistic exaltation to his work, and only preaches the doctrine of self-denial from the social point of view and in its least attractive shape, implies a curious and subtle affinity between the teacher and the proselyte. This affinity and its development are very finely brought out. In the mind of a rather dainty heroine, whose taste for the minor graces of life was revolted by ugly and dull sur-roundings, the growth of an appreciation for the mental elevation and robustness which are so much above the minor graces is traced with a singularly supple force. And the study was well worth making, of the impression produced by a robust, self-reliant, undevout, yet thoroughly noble character upon a mind into none of whose moods the doctrines of Calvinistic theology happened to fit. It is a study which suits a time when even the Carlylian gospel of labour, greatly as it needs to be modified for much good to come of it, has done something for people who found that nothing was done for them by formulas about Predestination and Grace and Faith. But in *Felix Holt* the most elevated form of what may without offence be called modern paganism makes way where a dull cut-and-dried theology was worthless, because it was embodied in a vehement and enthusiastic man, who does not shrink from even throwing away a livelihood which he thought involved a trick upon his fellows. The suppleness with which Esther is developed is more than matched in the strong-handed consistency with which the authoress has drawn her hero. It is a pity that the plot of the story, which runs upon the gradual disclosure of a claim to some property, happens to flow from utterly remote and far-off incidents, instead of flowing from the mental movement of the principal actors. Until Esther is taken away in her carriage by Mrs. Transome, the movement of the plot and the movement of character rather jar and clang together. It is true that in the end the possible possession of the property becomes a hinge in the play of character, but meanwhile it has thrown a considerable artificialness over portions of the story. This, however, is only a slight drawback in what is essentially a novel of character, and the figure of Felix Holt stands out with such size and strength, and almost incisive freshness, as to overshadow any minor defect of construction. Behind him there are the other two most conspicuous persons in the book—the sorrowful woman, whose life has been robbed of all its savour and with a terrible secret crushing her heart, and, in effective relief with her, the gentle, ripe-minded, fervent old Dissenting minister, whose views about salvation were barely high enough to please his flock. The authoress's creative energy has never, we think, been so exuberantly exercised before. One group succeeds another, and not a single figure appears in any of them, though it be ever so far in the background, which is not perfectly drawn and perfectly coloured. Even the young ladies at the Manor, who only ask when Dissent began, why Government didn't put a stop to it, and so on, illustrate the intense finish which this accomplished and profound writer puts on every part of her work. Of her exquisite humour, her subtlety and delicacy of analysis, the wide suggestiveness of her bits of 'aside,' and her style which is so fascinating because it is so exact an outward expression of the deep and mellow power with which her mind works and by which it is coloured—of all these we need not speak. They are as perfect and as delightful as they ever were.

40. R. H. Hutton, unsigned review, *Spectator*

23 June 1866, xxxix, 692–3 (see headnote to No. 28).

If there is any fault in this rich and fascinating story, which, like almost all its predecessors from the same hand, will probably live as long as English literature, it is in an overflowing affluence of lively and striking detail, which hardly leaves room for that force, subtlety, and intensity in the carving out of the principal characters, which marked *Adam Bede* and *Romola*. This is the brightest, the least penetrated with inner melancholy, of all George Eliot's stories, and there are wanting in it, perhaps as a consequence, some degrees of that deep-cut purpose graven by a brooding imagination, which gave the former tales so much grandeur of outline. There is no single group here which we shall remember and recur to with the same sense of large accession of intellectual wealth that was conferred on us by the companion pictures of Tito and Tessa in the Florentine story, and of Dinah and Hetty in *Adam Bede*. With very slight exceptions all the sketches in these three volumes, —sketches marvellous in their variety of touch and reality of tone,— are perfect after their sort, and some are drawn with a power that no other living writer has yet displayed. But looking back on the tale, as we lay it down, there seems to be no group in it which towers above the general *personnel* of the story, and lays hold of the imagination with an attraction blended of force and simplicity such as belongs, for instance, to the pictorial effect of Raphael's Cartoons;—and this there certainly was in the greater, though probably less rich and lively, tales by the same author, to which we have alluded. In the present case the central ground of the story is occupied by figures more finished indeed, but scarcely grander and more impressive than the minor characters it contains. *Felix Holt the Radical* is no doubt, himself, a fine picture. Yet the great struggle in his mind between political and moral radicalism which gives the thread of unity to the story is almost past away before it opens; and though it has left behind it a sort of torso enthusiasm which flings itself nobly but half wildly into the social life around, with bare, if any, recognition for that above it, there is no sufficient development in the character, or doubt about its decisions, to make it a really great central interest. There is none of the rapid movement, either upwards or downwards, either of moral gain or tragic deterioration, in him, which made the central interests of *Adam Bede* and *Romola* so profound. And though he is a quite new and perhaps finer type of the same form of merely secular and industrial nobleness which the authoress took so much pains in working out in Adam Bede, the political ferment and agitation of the time in which he lives has taken away all that sobriety and reserve which gives a certain dignity to the self-contained young carpenter, without leading to that other form of dignity proper to enthusiastic characters given by humility and reverence. With all the nobility of Felix Holt's character, there is a certain rudeness and baldness about it, a want of delicate intellectual and moral shades, and something, too, of the awelessness of abrupt passion, which, though highly dramatic, are not features so fascinating as to make up for the absence of development, the absence of any dramatic growth. A man who blurts out abruptly to a stranger, 'You believe in conversion; well, I was converted by six weeks' debauchery,'—is, with all his grandeur of aim, a harsh mutilated sort of figure, that can scarcely occupy the central position of a story without making the story itself take something of the torso effect in the imagination. To our mind, Felix Holt seems a grand *stump* of a character in an impressive but fixed attitude. His radicalism far surpasses the radicalism of the political scribes and pharisees, but has the baldness connected with the *word* 'radicalism' hanging round it still. This no doubt George Eliot's dramatic genius clearly perceived and fully intended. Yet to make nobility of this sort the central power of the story,—subordinating to it almost carefully all the more delicate types of spiritual beauty, such as are so beautifully delineated in Rufus Lyon, the Independent minister, and finely sketched, though only sketched, in Philip Debarry, produces in our mind a certain artistic pain, like that of a piece of sculpture in which an incomplete or mutilated statue of massive mould is the centre of a group of others less grand in build, but finished and of finer symmetry. Next to the sentence we have already quoted, in which Felix Holt, out of mere delight as it were in the nakedness of strong expression, ascribes his 'conversion' to 'six weeks' debauchery,' instead of to the latent faith against the pricks of which he must have been, during the six weeks' debauchery, violently kicking,—the passage most powerfully defining the essence of his character is the following:—

[quotes passage from ch. 27 beginning, 'You seem to care so little about yourself'.]

That is thoroughly dramatic, and very noble of its kind. The deep-lurking scepticism in the sentence, 'It all depends on what a man gets into his consciousness—what life thrusts into his mind, so that it becomes present to him as remorse is present to the guilty, or a mechanical problem to an inventive genius,' is no doubt meant as part of the secret of his power over Esther, whose æsthetic tastes were all of the visible and sensuous kind, and whose conscience is not susceptible to mystical, or even purely spiritual influences. Nothing can be better painted than the relation between the lovers. A sort of brawny nobility and grandeur of purpose, ardent, purely disinterested, yet intelligible, definite, secular, irreverent, was just the sort to break rudely into the equally limited though æsthetic dreams of beauty and luxury,—dreams of an atta-of-roses life,—which are attributed to Esther Lyon. Yet the relation of the two, briefly as it is drawn, does not make a central interest equal to that of George Eliot's greater novels.

Harold Transome, the worldly Radical candidate for Loamshire, seems to us on the whole the most original character in the book,—or at least the most original *now* from our present author, who has more than once given us characters not indeed individually like Rufus Lyon, for the saintly old Independent minister is a new and exquisite sketch,—but of the same general type, as, for instance, in Seth Bede. But Harold Transome, with his keen eye for business, his prompt and cavalier choice of measures for carrying out his own ends, his kindly contempt for views which differ from his own, his half-unconsciousness, half-indifference with respect to the pain he causes in brushing aside the incompatible wishes of others, his sincere wish to give his proud, able, and sensitive mother every comfort and pleasure to which a super-annuated grandmamma is justly entitled and no more, his pride of descent, and Radical impatience with immemorial Tory prejudices, his slightly epicure habits derived from Asiatic life, and his general 'fullness of bread,' is a figure which no one but George Eliot could well have painted. The scene in which his first return to his old home is sketched, when, without knowing it, he rides roughshod over his mother's feelings, dashes at once into business, takes up the *North Loamshire Herald* within the first five minutes, to run his eye down the advertisements, says, 'Gad! what a wreck poor father is!' and insouci-antly drops the fact that he is a Radical without any consciousness of the jar the avowal causes his mother, is one of the most brilliant our author has ever drawn. His mother herself, stately, unreverend, eaten up by pride and self-contempt rather than self-reproach for having lost her good name and her practical power over the estate by a long-extinguished passion for an attorney below her in birth and breeding, as well as essentially selfish, vulgar, and mean at heart, is almost as finely drawn as her son, except in her relations with the attorney himself, which are not adequately 'motived' or imaginatively justified. That a woman so severe in hereditary feeling and so haughty individually, should have sacrificed so much for such a man, is not of course incredible, but, as it is the turning-point of the whole story, should have been made probable and natural. Mrs. Transome and Jermyn, both of them individually finely drawn, are never brought together without a sense on the part of the reader that the key of their past relation to each other is lost, and that it demands therefore the only violent assumption of the story.

There is no limit, except the limit of space, to the wealth of subsidiary observation and humour with which this story is crowded.

[discusses, with lengthy quotation, Mr Lingon, Mrs Holt, and Denner

The vividly intellectual insight and humour which dots the book from beginning to end are, however, its most diffused charm,—the insight and humour, we mean, which mark off the paradoxes of the world in relation to a background of deep and finely traced thought. When we are told of Mrs. Transome that 'she had no ultimate analysis of things which went beyond blood and family,—the Herons of Fanshore or the Badgers of Hillbury,'—and when Esther reflects that a solitary elevation to wealth would look 'as chill and dreary as *the offer of dignities in an unknown country*,' what a world of clear reflection on the phenomena of society and the philosophy of social rank the remarks imply. Then what a charm there is in flashes of humour such as the following, in comparing an inferior public-house at Sproxton, 'The Blue Cow,' with the more prosperous one called 'The Sugar Loaf.' 'It had something of the forlorn air of an abandoned capital; and the company at the Blue Cow was of an inferior kind,—*equal, of course, in the fundamental attributes of humanity, such as desire for beer*, but not equal in ability to pay for it;'—or in this,—where the little boys in seal-skin caps who receive largesse of halfpence scattered by the election agent, Mr. Johnson, on a Sunday morning, are so much astonished at this unprecedented phenomenon that '*they were not without hope that an entirely new order of things had set in;*'—or, again, in the election agent's address to the Sproxton colliers and the interpolated remarks of his audience:—' "What's trade now without steam? and what is steam without coal? And mark you this, gentlemen,—there's no man and no government can make coal." A brief, loud "Haw, haw," showed that this fact was appreciated. "Nor freeston' nayther," said a wide-mouthed, wiry man called Gills, *who wished for an exhaustive treatment of the subject, being a stone-cutter.'* And these are but illustrations of an intellectual insight and humour which sparkle over the whole surface of the story, so that it is scarcely possible to read a page without being struck by the incidental contrast between the gleam of some thought which comes from no superficial stratum, and the reality of some delineation which no mind that does not thoroughly love to play on the surface could have drawn. The same striking depth and beauty of style sparkles, we notice, in all those mottos to the chapters which,—not being quoted from any other author,—are, we conclude, George Eliot's own. If so, we may infer that she must have written poetry and drama of no common order, which at some time or other may be permitted to see the light. We quote the following as a specimen, not of the poetry so much, as of the dramatic play in some of these passages:—

1st Citizen.—Sir, there's a hurry in the veins of youth
    That makes a vice of virtue by excess.
2nd Citizen.—What if the coolness of our tardier veins
    Be loss of virtue?
1st Citizen.—All things cool with time,—
    The sun itself, they say, till heat shall find
    A general level, nowhere in excess.
2nd Citizen.—'Tis a poor climax, to my weaker thought
    That future middlingness.

41. E. S. Dallas, unsigned review, *The Times*

26 June 1866, p. 6

See headnote to No. 8 and Introduction, pp. 26–7.

Hitherto Miss Austen has had the honour of the first place among our lady novelists, but a greater than she has now arisen—a lady who in grasp of thought, in loftiness of feeling, in subtlety of expression, in fineness of humour, in reach of passion, and in all those sympathies which go to form the true artist has never been excelled. In the art of weaving a narrative Miss Austen is still pre-eminent among women. Nothing can be more natural than the way in which she evolves an event, leading up to it with the clearest motives and the most likely accidents, never saying too much, never too little, nothing too soon, nothing too late; sparing of reflection, and letting her characters speak for themselves. George Eliot has not attained this ease of story-telling because she has to deal with subjects far more difficult than Miss Austen ever attempted, with wilder passions, with stronger situations, with higher thoughts. Miss Austen scarcely ever gets out of the humdrum of easy-going respectable life; she can therefore well afford to be calm and neat in arranging every thread of the narrative she has to weave. George Eliot undertakes to set forth the issues of a more tumultuous life, to work out deeper problems, and to play with torrents where Miss Austen played with rills. But if thus dealing with stronger forces she has been as a rule unable to give to her plots the finished ease of movement for which her predecessor is famous, she on the other hand succeeds in veiling any deficiency of story by the wonderous charm of her style. We don't know any Englishwoman who can be placed near her as a writer of prose. There is such a pith in her thinking, such a charm in her writing, such a fresh vigour in the combination of both, that—begin where we will in her volumes—we go on reading, now startled by some strange suggestive thought, now tickled by her humour, now touched by her pathos, and ever fascinated by the results of delicate observation and fine literary polish. Her style is very rich, and not only rich with the palpable meaning which in each individual sentence she has to express, but rich also in those swift, indescribable associations which well chosen words recall, allusions to past reading, the reflected sparkle of past thinking, the fragrance of past feeling.

But, great as the charm of her style is, it is not her most attractive quality. Style will go far to cloak the deficiencies of a story, but it will not account for the strong interest which 'George Eliot' always contrives to awaken. The secret of her power is to be found in the depth and the range of her sympathies. She gets to the heart of her characters, and makes us feel with them, care for them, like to know about them. Even if they are stupid people who lead dull lives, she has the happy art of making us take an interest in their story and wish to hear it out. When we come to care for people—men or women—it really does not much matter what their story is: it fixes our attention. And for the most part we care or don't care for people according as we understand them or not. Dugald Stewart[1] somewhere makes a rather suggestive remark to the effect that many of us are supposed to be wanting in benevolence when we are only wanting in attention or in imagination. The cruelties which we inflict on each other and our indifference to each other's sufferings are the result not of a cruel disposition, but of blindness and thoughtlessness and incapacity of imagination. And so it comes to pass that in most cases, if we can only be made to see people as they are, we learn to care for them. 'Seeing,' says the proverb, 'is believing;' but seeing also is feeling. And this is George Eliot's great gift that she sees and makes her readers see the personages of her tale; and we cannot truly see them, with all the stern conflict of their lives and with all the skeletons which they keep in their closets, without sharing in their hopes and fears, mixing in their griefs, and tasting of their joys. Be the man ever so dull, we become part of him and have a personal interest in his story the moment we can see him and understand him as George Eliot enables us to do. Great is Miss Austen's art of weaving a plot, and great is George Eliot's charm of style; but grandest of all as a means of exciting interest is that sympathy which sets a living character before us, and enables us not merely to see it, but also to feel it.

Felix Holt is certainly a work of rare genius, and worthy of the pen that produced in succession *Adam Bede*, *The Mill on the Floss*, and *Romola*. A critic, if he is in a nibbling mood, may easily pick flaws in it; but what would be the use of such trifling? We could easily show that,

---

[1] Dugald Stewart (1753-1828), Scottish philosopher.

according to the approved methods of handling a plot, George Eliot has made several mistakes, that in some parts of her work there is not sufficient movement, and that in others where the movement is quite sufficient it lacks continuity. But it is to be hoped that true criticism will one day get beyond such cavilling, which reminds one rather vividly of the old paltry squabbles about the unities. Critics have been too much in the habit of insisting that if an author is to please us he shall follow certain rules, and that if he pleases us without following these rules he shall be condemned as an artist. . . .

If George Eliot had the power of inventing situations and of constructing a story as she has that of brilliant writing and of clear and tender characterization, it would be difficult to name any novelist that could be placed before her. And if we were now to complain that some parts of her story are wanting in form, she would have a right to reply that she fulfils every requirement when she has succeeded, as we admit, in thoroughly awakening an interest in her tale. She enlists our sympathies in the lives of her characters—good and bad—with a heartiness which few other living writers can even rival; we care for them as if they were our intimate friends; and we long to know their story.

Felix Holt, the Radical, is not, as its title would lead one to suppose, a political novel, though it necessarily touches on politics—on the politics of a Radical at the time of the passing of the Reform Bill. The progress of the story is made to turn on the incidents of an election in one of the Midland Counties; but the purpose of the author is not, as is usual in a political novel, to advocate or to render palatable any constitutional doctrines—it is rather to exhibit the characters of men as they conduct themselves in a political struggle, here panting after some high ideal of what ought to be, there floundering contented in things as they are, some seeking honestly for the general good, others selfishly grasping at power and pelf. Felix Holt's Radicalism is quite distinct from the common type. He is no democrat thirsting for universal suffrage and mouthing about the rights of man. He sees the degradation of the masses, and he would raise them to their share of power if they deserved it; but he appears to desire far more that they should be raised morally—that they should be educated, that they should learn to be sober, and that the brute element of mere numbers should be made respectable by being combined with intelligence and the love of order. His is not the sort of Radicalism that rages against the superiority of the higher classes—it is the Radicalism that rages against the meanness, the misery, and the ignorance of those who, being of the lower classes, are lower than they need be. The hero of the tale, therefore, is rather a moral and a social than a political reformer. And the great attraction of such a character, for a novelist who can do justice to it, is that it is unconventional—can be set in vivid contrast with the cut and dry characters of every-day life. It is not easy to make a hero of the man who tamely submits to ordinary conventions. He may be strong in many ways—have strength of will, strength of intellect, strength of feeling; but if he submits to the yoke of the society in which he moves, he becomes one of many—he to that extent loses his individuality, and forfeits the exceptional attributes of a hero. And so, as we have no longer demigods like Achilles to worship as heroes, we must find heroes, if we are to find them at all, in men of eccentric ideas and unconventional behaviour—men at least who are to some degree at war with the society to which they belong.

George Eliot is fond of running the contrast between feeling as it flows from the heart and feeling as it is moulded by custom—between the true thinking of minds that judge for themselves and the parrot-thinking of minds that move by rote—between conduct which is perfectly natural and conduct regulated by convention. And we may say of this new novel of hers that the chief characters in it form themselves into two groups which are contrasted somewhat in this fashion. Each group consists of three personages—two men and one woman. That which first claims our attention includes the hero, Felix Holt; his sweetheart, Esther; and her supposed father, the Rev. Rufus Lyon. With these three the author takes infinite pains, and she bestows on them infinite love. Felix Holt, the hero, is the son of a vendor of quack pills and potions, and a great part of his heroism consists in this —that on the death of his father he forbids his mother to have anything more to do with the sale of such medicines. Womanlike, George Eliot has more affection for him than men are ever likely to feel. Men may admire various points in his character—as his honesty, his nobleness of aim, and his strength of purpose; but it is only women who are willing to put up with the arrogance and self-conceit of conscious rectitude. Felix means well and does well, but in his youthful zeal he has such a tendency to be didactic and indignant that we fear if we ever came to know him in the flesh we should vote him a confounded bore. Certain we are that if he belonged to the class of society from which the members of our clubs are chosen there is not a club in London that would not give him blackballs enough to choke off a dozen candidates. He is not a clubbable man. But women sometimes like the man who is arrogant in his goodness, who has all the zeal of a neophyte, who is somewhat of a solemn prig, and who declaims at them till they cry. Men are apt to see what is ridiculous or offensive in such a character; women, especially if the fellow is handsome, are fascinated by his energy, by his courage, and by that concentration which makes him utterly blind to the ridicule he incurs among men. So the concentrated enthusiast Felix Holt is the hero of George Eliot's book, and wins the heart of that lovely girl Esther Lyon.

The character of the girl is very beautiful and wonderfully drawn, and we suppose that if a man, instead of a woman, had written the novel he would have been more proud of Esther than of Felix, and would have named the story after her. In point of fact, it is her story that the novel is chiefly engaged with, and Felix Holt is less interesting in himself than as being interesting to her. The reputed daughter of a humble Dissenting minister, she turns out to be an heiress entitled to 5,000*l.* a year. There is no difficulty as to the proof of the title; but she renounces her inheritance and sacrifices all the luxury and state she might have commanded in order that she may wed the poor watchmaker, Felix Holt. It is not quite clear why she sacrifices her entire estate; she would not have hurt either Felix or herself by keeping one little slice of her own lawful property; but when women are heroic and yield to a sentiment they like to do it thoroughly, they are apt to make no reservations, and they are rather proud of not counting the cost. Whatever we are to think of her sacrifice, which comes upon us at the last as a surprise, there can be no doubt as to the beauty of the maiden's character, and as to the delicacy with which George Eliot has traced its development from the time when she is first lectured and struck dumb by Felix Holt till at length she sacrifices her fortune to become his wife. And the tracing of this progress in the girl's mind is by no means an easy task, for naturally she is very refined and somewhat luxurious in her tastes; therefore naturally unprepared for the uncouthness of her lover's manners and the poverty of his lot. It is probable, indeed, that she would never have thrown in her lot with his, but that his life was in danger—that he was tried for manslaughter—and that she with all his friends became deeply concerned as to his fate. Then comes the crisis which gives George Eliot her grand opportunity —the opportunity of showing how strong feeling works. Here she is in her element, and rises to the occasion. She is not afraid of a passion— she knows its intricacies, and is ever happiest when exhibiting them. And these scenes in the crisis of Esther Lyon's life are set forth with a truth of touch, a subtlety, and a tenderness that are beyond praise. The finest situation in the novel—namely, that in which the girl gets up in court, offers to go into the witness-box to bear her testimony on behalf of Felix Holt, there lets out the secret of her love, and so awakens an interest in herself and in her lover which in the end procures his release from prison, has probably been suggested by a similar situation which Mr. Charles Reade has introduced into his last novel,[1] and which he has handled with exceeding delicacy. But if George Eliot sometimes borrows her best situations, she makes them all her own by the feeling which she imparts to them, the vividness with which she works them out, and the naturalness with which they are introduced.

Nor must we forget here the third personage in this group to which Felix and Esther belong—the Rev. Rufus Lyon, the simple-minded Dissenting minister. Rufus occupies a considerable space in these volumes, and if we judge him merely by his talk we shall scarcely do him justice. He seems to belong to the long-winded, absent sort of characters with which we are sufficiently intimate in Scott's novels—men who are absorbed in their own thoughts, are fond of preaching, and go on talking interminably about abstract doctrines, while their listeners are struggling in vain to change the conversation, and the business to be done is neglected. But the preacher is not merely a preacher; there is a romance in his life which gives a novelty to his character. He is a high Calvinist who has ventured out of the beaten path, who has committed the enormity of losing his heart to a Papist, and who, amid all the pedantry of his calling, cherishes a memory that gives pathos to his life and a peculiar softness to his tone. George Eliot has told his story with all the humour and tenderness of which she is mistress.

The contrasted group of characters comprise Harold Transome, the actual possessor of the estate which of right belongs to Esther—his mother, and the lawyer of the family, Mr. Jermyn—all sharply drawn characters. And as in the one group the world was in error as to the paternity of Esther Lyon, so in this other there is a mistake as to the paternity of Harold Transome, and there is a dark tragedy involved in it which George Eliot works out with great force. But the most striking character of the group,—in some respects, the most striking character of the novel, is Mrs. Transome. She is now in her old age hard and bitter, and in strange contrast to the gentleness of Esther whom she desires to have for a daughter-in-law. There is a curious mixture in

[1] *Griffith Gaunt* (1866).

her of sternness and softness. She has been schooled in adversity, and has learnt to be stern, dictatorial, and unyielding; while in her heart she yearns for the affection of her son, longs in her loveless old age for something to cling to, and trembles over the sins of her youth. She is quite a picture, and George Eliot has produced a wonderfully vivid portrait of a hardened old lady, shaken by remorse and troubled for want of love, but preserving ever an impenetrable silence, a stately reserve, an unbending attitude of almost defiance. The scenes in the third volume, in which, as her secret oozes out, she encounters in succession her ancient lover, her son, and then Esther, are given with remarkable power, and show how perfectly George Eliot can master the difficulties of a strong situation and follow the movements of strong passion. And her companions in this group are worthy of their places beside her—Harold Transome, her son, with all his vigour of decision, and selfishness masked by jollity of manner; Mr. Jermyn, the sleek and supple and handsome lawyer, who plays the villain to his ladylove. These three are more or less people of the world, inured to the world's ways, trained in the world's thinking, and worldly in their aims. They stand, therefore, in contrast to the other trio, who are unworldly in their dispositions and obey the impulses of the heart. And the story consists in bringing the two groups into collision, and exhibiting in the outlines of a tragedy the contrast between natural tenderness and generosity on the one hand and selfishness, hardness, and villainy on the other.

Those we have named are the chief characters of the novel, but we are introduced also to a crowd of minor characters, nearly every one of which is a good study. It would be difficult to name any sketch more perfect than that of the little old waiting woman, Denner—as true and pleasing a bit of portraiture as ever was painted. Then we have a capital group of other servants, and have the conversation of the servants' hall given with much humour. We have groups of miners in a publichouse, and have all their small-beery talk rendered with equal fidelity and sense of humour. Next we have a couple of parsons, each admirable in his way; an electioneering agent, full of bounce and plausibility; a bill sticker, with his wits rather disordered by drinking; the deacons and chosen vessels of a Dissenting chapel who talk in their familiar language; and many more. There is scarcely one of these minor sketches which is not perfect in its way; and they are so numerous that we have no lack of variety in the tale.

While the great charm of the novel depends on the sympathy which the author compels us to feel with these personages and in the interest which she awakens in their doings, we must, in conclusion, recur to that other source of influence which she brings to bear upon her readers in her power of writing. We have stated in general terms that both her thinking and the style in which it finds expression are unusually rich. We may illustrate this by quoting some of the mottoes which she has placed at the head of her chapters, many of which are evidently of her own invention.

[quotes mottoes to chs. 2, 46, 39, and 12, and two short passages]

The novel is full of such mellow wisdom and such sharp incisive remarks. We might cull too from the talk of the characters to whom we are introduced a whole book of proverbs. There is no one personage in the work indeed so witty of speech as good old Mrs. Poyser, with whom we made acquaintance in George Eliot's first novel, but there is abundance of happy sayings throughout the three volumes—sayings which have the inexpressible charm of coming naturally and of seeming to belong rightfully to the people who utter them. It does not matter whether she gives us the talk of peasants or that of ladies and gentlemen; she makes them all talk naturally, and yet like the girl of the fairy tale they talk pearls and diamonds.

42. Frederic Harrison to George Eliot

19 July 1866

The George Eliot Letters, iv, 284–6. Frederic Harrison (1831–1923), barrister and positivist, was a prolific writer on historical and literary subjects. He helped George Eliot with the legal details both in this novel and in *Daniel Deronda*. In the remainder of this lengthy letter, Harrison described the Positivist novel he would have liked George Eliot to write.

Knowing that you were gone to take a complete rest abroad I have waited to thank you for the most welcome and most unexpected copy of *Felix Holt* which I received through your kindness on the morning of publication. I read it all through again just as if it was new to me altogether and I have read it over 4 or 5 times again. I find myself taking it up as I take up Tennyson or Shelley or Browning and thinking out the sequences of thought suggested by the undertones of the thought and the harmony of the lines. Can it be right to put the subtle finish of a poem into the language of a prose narrative? It is not a waste of toil? And yet whilst so many readers must miss all that, most of them even not consciously observing the fact, that they have a really new species of literature before them (a romance constructed in the artistic spirit and aim of a poem) yet is it not all lost. I know whole families where the three volumes have been read chapter by chapter and line by line and reread and recited as are the stanzas of *In Memoriam*. Of course the really worthy readers have taken their feast well and rightly. Indeed I observe that just those whose opinion one most wishes to have have taken the most pains to form it truly and have quite seized the task before them and the standard of thought upon which they have been called. The right people have I think read it in the right way so far as they could.

You will not need me to tell you and will not care to know about the general public or the library world or that sort of thing or what they think or say. The public (poor beast) as you know is greatly delighted and consumes the good thing largely with dim conscious reason to himself why he wags his tail over it. The critics have been too much abashed to commit much folly and some of them have risen into real sense and life. But you know a great deal more of that than you care to know already, I am sure. Enough if I say that public, critics, and people of sense have come to agree (as I ventured to say at first they would) that this is the most complete delightful and abiding thing they have yet had and each party and school are determined to see their own side in it—the religious people, the non-religious people, the various sections of religious people, the educated, the simple, the radicals, the Tories, the socialists, the intellectual reformers, the domestic circle, the critics, the metaphysicians, the artists, the Positivists, the squires, are all quite convinced that it has been conceived from their own point of view.

Not all—I have met a dissentient. At a big house at a big dinner of big people where for my many sins the Devil entrapped me a very beautiful and most stony young lady of fashion—a girl with brains who understood the good and with an ossified heart which just beat strong enough to hate it declared to me with much decision and discrimination that she disliked it all exceedingly. She hated to have such people brought before her or before the world. There might be such people as Felix Holt but they should be put down. It was wrong to encourage their vagaries. It might be natural but not a subject for art. Felix and Esther might have lived and perhaps do but their wrong-headed ways are simply tiresome and disagreeable to men and women of the world. Low rough unregulated natures must be dealt with by schoolmasters parsons and constables, kept out of the way of art and society and beauty—a girl like a block of ice, clear hard and beautiful—a female Lord Cranbourne[1] only beautiful.

Are you sure that your destiny is not to produce a poem—not a poem in prose but in measure—a drama? Is it possible that there is not one yet existing or does it lie like the statue in the marble block? I am no fortune-teller but I believe it is in the Stars.

[1] Sir Robert Cecil (1830–1903) succeeded his brother as Viscount Cranbourne in 1865.

43. Henry James, unsigned review, *Nation*

16 August 1866, iii, 127-8

Henry James wrote in all seven notes and reviews of George
Eliot's novels. His attempts to come to terms with her fiction
throw a great deal of light on his own practice as a novelist.
The best discussion of this is to be found in W. J. Harvey, *The
Art of George Eliot*, 1961. In *The Middle Years* (New York, 1917),
James recalls reading *Felix Holt* for the first time, 'outstretched on
my then too frequently inevitable bed at Swampscott during a
couple of very hot days of the summer of 1866', and then 'sitting
up again, at no great ease, to indite with all promptness a review
of the delightful thing' (pp. 62-3).

Better, perhaps, than any of George Eliot's novels does *Felix Holt*
illustrate her closely wedded talent and foibles. Her plots have always
been artificial—clumsily artificial—the conduct of her story slow, and
her style diffuse. Her conclusions have been signally weak, as the reader
will admit who recalls Hetty's reprieve in *Adam Bede*, the inundation
of the Floss, and, worse than either, the comfortable reconciliation of
Romola and Tessa. The plot of *Felix Holt* is essentially made up, and
its development is forced. The style is the same lingering, slow-moving,
expanding instrument which we already know. The termination is
hasty, inconsiderate, and unsatisfactory—is, in fact, almost an anti-
climax. It is a good instance of a certain sagacious tendency to compromise which pervades the author's spirit, and to which her novels
owe that disproportion between the meagre effect of the whole and the
vigorous character of the different parts, which stamp them as the works
of a secondary thinker and an incomplete artist. But if such are the
faults of *Felix Holt*, or some of them, we hasten to add that its merits
are immense, and that the critic finds it no easy task to disengage
himself from the spell of so much power, so much brilliancy, and so
much discretion. In what other writer than George Eliot could we
forgive so rusty a plot, and such *langueurs* of exposition, such a disparity

GEORGE ELIOT

of outline and detail? or, we may even say, of outline and outline—
of general outline and of particular? so much drawing and so little
composition? In compensation for these defects we have the broad
array of those rich accomplishments to which we owe *Adam Bede* and
Romola. First in order comes the firm and elaborate delineation of
individual character, of which Tito, in *Romola*, is a better example than
the present work affords us. Then comes that extensive human sympathy, that easy understanding of character at large, that familiarity
with man, from which a novelist draws his real inspiration, from which
he borrows all his ideal lines and hues, to which he appeals for a blessing
on his fictitious process, and to which he owes it that, firm locked in the
tissue of the most rigid prose, he is still more or less of a poet. George
Eliot's humanity colors all her other gifts—her humor, her morality,
and her exquisite rhetoric. Of all her qualities her humor is apparently
most generally relished. Its popularity may, perhaps, be partially
accounted for by a natural reaction against the dogma, so long maintained, that a woman has no humor. Still, there is no doubt that what
passes for such among the admirers of Mrs. Poyser and Mrs. Glegg
really rests upon a much broader perception of human incongruities
than belongs to many a masculine humorist. As for our author's
morality, each of our readers has felt its influence for himself. We
hardly know how to qualify it. It is not bold, nor passionate, nor aggres-
sive, nor uncompromising—it is constant, genial, and discreet. It is
apparently the fruit of a great deal of culture, experience, and resignation. It carries with it that charm and that authority which will always
attend the assertions of a mind enriched by researches, when it declares
that wisdom and affection are better than science. We speak of the
author's intellectual culture of course only as we see it reflected in her
style—a style the secret of whose force is in the union of the tenderest
and most abundant sympathies with a body of knowledge so ample and
so active as to be absolutely free from pedantry.

As a story *Felix Holt* is singularly inartistic. The promise of the title
is only half kept. The history of the hero's opinions is made subordinate
to so many other considerations, to so many sketches of secondary
figures, to so many discursive amplifications of incidental points, to so
much that is clear and brilliant and entertaining, but that, compared
with this central object, is not serious, that when the reader finds the
book drawing to a close without having, as it were, brought Felix
Holt's passions to a head, he feels tempted to pronounce it a failure
and a mistake. As a novel with a hero there is no doubt that it *is* a

failure. Felix is a fragment. We find him a Radical and we leave him what?—only 'utterly married;' which is all very well in its place, but which by itself makes no conclusion. He tells his mistress at the outset that he was 'converted by six weeks' debauchery.' These very dramatic antecedents demanded somehow a group of consequents equally dramatic. But that quality of discretion which we have mentioned as belonging to the author, that tendency to avoid extreme deductions which has in some way muffled the crisis in each of her novels, and which, reflected in her style, always mitigates the generosity of her eloquence—these things appear to have shackled the freedom of her hand in drawing a figure which she wished and yet feared to make consistently heroic. It is not that Felix acts at variance with his high principles, but that, considering their importance, he and his principles play so brief a part and are so often absent from the scene. He is distinguished for his excellent good sense. He is uncompromising yet moderate, eager yet patient, earnest yet unimpassioned. He is indeed a thorough young Englishman, and, in spite of his sincerity, his integrity, his intelligence, and his broad shoulders, there is nothing in his figure to *thrill* the reader. There is another great novelist who has often dealt with men and women moved by exceptional opinions. Whatever these opinions may be, the reader shares them for the time with the writer; he is thrilled by the contact of her passionate earnestness, and he is borne rapidly along upon the floods of feeling which rush through her pages. The Radicalism of *Felix Holt* is strangely remote from the reader; we do not say as Radicalism, which we may have overtopped or undermined, but simply as a feeling entertained. In fact, after the singular eclipse or extinction which it appears to undergo on the occasion of his marriage, the reader feels tempted to rejoice that he, personally, has not worked himself nearer to it. There is, to our perception, but little genuine *passion* in George Eliot's men and women. With the exception of Maggie Tulliver in *The Mill on the Floss*, her heroines are all marked by a singular spiritual tenuity. In two of her novels she has introduced seductions; but in both these cases the heroines—Hetty, in *Adam Bede*, and Tessa, in *Romola*—are of so light a character as to reduce to a *minimum* the dramatic interest of the episode. We nevertheless think Hetty the best drawn of her young women. Esther Lyon, the heroine of the present tale, has great merits of intention, but the action subsides without having given her a 'chance.'

It is as a broad picture of midland country life in England, thirty years ago, that *Felix Holt* is, to our taste, most interesting. On this

275

subject the author writes from a full mind, with a wealth of fancy, of suggestion, of illustration, at the command of no other English writer, bearing you along on the broad and placid rises of her speech, with a kind of retarding persuasiveness which allows her conjured images to sink slowly into your very brain. She has written no pages of this kind of discursive, comprehensive, sympathetic description more powerful or exquisite than the introductory chapter of the present work. Against the solid and deep-colored background offered by this chapter, in connection with a hundred other passages and touches, she has placed a vast number of rustic figures. We have no space to discriminate them; we can only say that in their aggregate they leave a vivid sense of that multiplicity of eccentricities, and humors, and quaintnesses, and simple *bizzaries*, which appears to belong of right to old English villages. There are particular scenes here—scenes among common people—miners, tinkers, butchers, saddlers, and undertakers—as good as anything that the author has written. Nothing can be better than the scene in which Felix interrupts Johnson's canvass in the tavern, or that of the speech-making at Duffield. In general, we prefer George Eliot's low-life to her high-life. She seems carefully to have studied the one from without, and the other she seems merely to have glanced at from the midst of it. Mrs. Transome seems to us an unnatural, or rather, we should say, a superfluous figure. Her sorrows and trials occupy a space dispropor-tionate to any part that she plays. She is intensely drawn, and yet dramatically she stands idle. She is, nevertheless, made the occasion, like all of her fellow-actors, however shadowy they may be, of a number of deep and brilliant touches. The character of her son, the well-born, cold-blooded, and moneyed Liberal, who divides the hero-ship with Felix, is delicately and firmly conceived; but like the great Tito even, like Mr. Lyon, the Dissenting preacher in the present work, like Esther Lyon herself, he is too long-drawn, too placid; he lacks dramatic compactness and rapidity. Tito is presented to us with some degree of completeness, only because Romola is very long, and because, for his sake, the reader is very patient.

A great deal of high praise has been given to *Felix Holt*, and a great deal more will be given still; a great many strong words will be used about the author. But we think it of considerable importance that these should at least go no further than they have already gone. It is so new a phenomenon for an English novelist to exhibit mental resources which may avail him in other walks of literature; to have powers of thought at all commensurate with his powers of imagination, that when a writer unites these conditions he is likely to receive excessive homage. There is in George Eliot's writings a tone of sagacity, of easy penetration, which leads us to believe that she would be the last to form a false estimate of her works, together with a serious respect for truth which convinces us that she would lament the publication of such an estimate. In our opinion, then, neither *Felix Holt*, nor *Adam Bede*, nor *Romola*, is a master-piece. They have none of the inspiration, the heat, nor the essential simplicity of such a work. They belong to a kind of writing in which the English tongue has the good fortune to abound—that clever, voluble, bright-colored novel of manners which began with the present century under the auspices of Miss Edgeworth and Miss Austen. George Eliot is stronger in degree than either of these writers, but she is not different in kind. She brings to her task a richer mind, but she uses it in very much the same way. With a certain masculine comprehensiveness which they lack, she is eventually a feminine—a delightfully feminine—writer. She has the microscopic observation, not a myriad of whose keen notations are worth a single one of those great synthetic guesses with which a real master attacks the truth, and which, by their occasional occurrence in the stories of Mr. Charles Reade (the much abused *Griffith Gaunt* included), make him, to our mind, the most readable of living English novelists, and prove him a distant kinsman of Shakespeare. George Eliot has the exquisitely good taste on a small scale, the absence of taste on a large (the vulgar plot of *Felix Holt* exemplifies this deficiency), the unbroken current of feeling and, we may add, of expression, which distinguish the feminine mind. That she should be offered a higher place than she has earned, is easily explained by the charm which such gifts as hers in such abundance are sure to exercise.

44. G. S. Venables, unsigned review, *Edinburgh Review*

October 1866, cxxiv, 435–49

George Stovin Venables (1819–88), a successful parliamentary lawyer, was best known as a prolific leader writer for the *Saturday Review*, and also for *The Times*. He was a close friend of both Thackeray and Tennyson. He broke the nose of the former at Charterhouse and later, it is said, became the model for George Warrington in *Pendennis*. For Tennyson he is reputed to have provided a line of poetry ('If that hypothesis of theirs be sound') at the beginning of the fourth book of *The Princess* (see Introduction, pp. 25–6).

Felix Holt has some of the defects of ordinary novels, but ordinary novels have none of the merits of *Felix Holt*. The great writer who, like Madame Dudevant,[1] adopts the ungraceful disguise of a masculine pseudonym, has, after an excursion into a foreign country and a distant age, happily returned to her own region of provincial English life, in full possession of her former vigour, of her dramatic fidelity to nature, and of her unrivalled humour. Few readers have any knowledge of a state of society which is apparently described from early recollection, aided by local tradition, but a creative imagination spontaneously produces real and living beings. Some of the inhabitants of Treby Magna and its neighbourhood are eccentric and even grotesque, but their language and their modes of thought are so natural and credible that the personages of the story seem to have a real existence. Some justly celebrated humourists produce all their effects by the more or less delicate use of caricature. Wilful exaggeration of oddities may be a legitimate comic method, but an engrained organic absurdity furnishes deeper and more lasting amusement. Mrs. Holt is not less illogical than Mrs. Nickleby, but she is not meant merely to be laughed at. The puzzled and unwilling submission of a commonplace and conceited

[1] George Sand.

278

old woman to a son who has grown out of her comprehension, is not a mere exercise of playful ingenuity, but an illustration of human experience. George Eliot takes almost excessive pleasure in recording the muddle-headed processes of dull and uneducated understandings, but she always enters into the characters which she reproduces, instead of contemplating them as subjects of farce or satire from without. The intelligent reader is conscious that if nature and circumstances had left his mind a blank, he would have thought and talked like the collier at Sproxton, even if he had not 'been obliged to give his wife a black eye, to hinder her from going to the preaching.' Miss Austen was as fond as her more ambitious and powerful successor of incoherent talkers, but, as all her characters occupied the same level of cultivation, she contented herself with studying various forms of intellectual imbecility. Searching deeper into the strata of society, George Eliot finds in the absence or narrowness of education a sufficient explanation of sluggish understandings and of inconsecutive arguments. With scarcely an exception her untaught or half-taught personages set logic at defiance. Her zeal for the elevation of the humbler classes is the more laudable because she has an extraordinary relish for the picturesque results of satisfied ignorance. In her fictions she always recurs by preference to the pre-scientific days, in which conscientious moral agriculturists had not yet learned the duty of extirpating flowering weeds.

[examines the reasons for the failure of *Romola*]

In Loamshire, and at Treby Magna, there are no gorgeous processions, watched by spectators with historical names, requiring each a paragraph of description; but the sporting rector in his velveteen shooting jacket, the pompous butler in the steward's room at the manor, the retired London tradesman who tells his admiring neighbours in the country stories about Mr. Pitt, require no long explanation to make them intelligible and pleasant. The preliminary chapter, which describes a day's journey on a coach, has never been excelled as a sketch of the varieties of English town and country scenery.

George Eliot's power of constructing a fable is not equal to her skill in delineating character. Her shorter tales, as *Silas Marner*, and the *Scenes of Clerical Life* have more unity and rapidity of movement than the *Mill on the Floss*, or *Felix Holt*; yet the celebrated public-house conversation in *Silas Marner* has scarcely any connexion with the principal story. A subtle perception of motives and peculiarities perhaps tends to interrupt the continuous flow of narrative. Scott said that a favourite character, like Dugald Dalgetty,[1] ran away with him, and in the most humorous of fictions, the story of Tristram Shandy never makes the smallest progress. By far the best part of *Adam Bede* consists in the proverb-like sayings of Mrs. Poyser, who has little or nothing to do with the plot. It is not surprising that a writer who has the power of drawing a typical portrait in a few strokes, is tempted to imitate the copious irregularity of Nature, instead of adhering with severe accuracy to a preconceived design. Some of the episodes of *Felix Holt*, after a laboured commencement, end in nothing; and the legal complication which forms the framework of the story is arbitrarily disregarded in the final solution. The doubtful title to the Transome estate, although it is the subject of significant allusion in the introductory chapter, and of incessant anxiety and uncertainty through the entire course of the narrative, exercises no eventual influence on the fortunes of the principal personages. One of the triumphs of English jurisprudence consists in the mixed feeling of curiosity and awe with which it has impressed authors and more especially authoresses of fiction. The law supplies to modern novels the place of that supernatural machinery which was once thought indispensable in epic composition. Like the gods of Olympus, or the Destiny of later times, some entail or settlement operates in its relentless course, impenetrable, inexorable, and sovereignly unjust. The father of Mrs. Browning's Aurora Leigh was prevented by the will of a remote ancestor from leaving not only his landed estate but his large accumulations of personalty to his only child. George Eliot is perhaps a better lawyer than Mrs. Browning, but she appears to be almost equally incapable of understanding that perpetuities are among the few anomalies which are unknown to the law of England.

[discusses, at length, perpetuities and the Transome estate]

The alarm which may have been caused by the description on the title-page of Felix Holt as a Radical is relieved by the discovery that he is neither a popular speaker nor primarily a politician, but a social reformer. The determination of a clever and well-educated son of a tradesman to pass through life as a member of the working class is justly regarded by his neighbours as a crotchet, although the authoress admires his choice and the heroine rewards it with her heart and hand. Sympathy is perhaps less subtle than satirical intuition, for Felix Holt, though his conversation is manly, sensible, and thoughtful, is a less

[1] In *A Legend of Montrose* (1819).

masterly portrait than Tito Melema. The virtue of wearing a cap instead of a hat, and of dispensing with a neckcloth, is rather ostentatious than sublime. If a man who has the power of earning a comfortable income by the exercise of his knowledge and ability, prefers a handicraft and weekly wages, his asceticism is as unprofitable as if it were practised in a Trappist cell, and it involves the non-monastic disadvantage of enforcing useless hardships on the modern saint's wife and children. By a happy instinct George Eliot passes over the sordid incidents which constitute the real sting of poverty. Felix Holt converses in the tone of a gentleman and philosopher with cultivated associates, and although he earns a bare livelihood as a journeyman watchmaker, his time seems to be always at his own disposal. When his mother teazes him with her twaddle, he answers her with a joke about 'the Ciceronian antiphrasis;' and except as a teacher or missionary, he seems to have no social relations with his fellow-workmen or nominal equals. He says, indeed, that he has the stomach of a rhinoceros, so that he can live on porridge, and he even boasts that he is not a mouse to distinguish between a wax and a tallow-candle; but an artisan who can amuse himself with Ciceronian figures of speech, resembles a workman as a shepherd at the opera or in Sèvres china is like a common farm servant. In one of her novels George Eliot compares a feeling of moral repugnance to the dislike of a refined temperament for a coarse odour or a flaring light; yet Felix Holt's contempt for the wax-taper which was necessary to Esther's comfort is represented as a proof of superiority.

If unusual schemes of life are generally fantastic mistakes, self-sacrificing devotion to the supposed good of the community is not the less a respectable rule of conduct. Esther Lyon, cultivating in a humble sphere the tastes of a fine lady, is at first shocked or startled by Felix's paradoxical bluntness, and she has always felt a kindly contempt for the pious orthodoxy of the Independent Minister whom she believes to be her father. If the nature of women is truly delineated by writers of their own sex, an overbearing spirit and a kind of masculine roughness are the qualities which above all others ensure success in love. In ordinary practice reproof and contradiction will be sparingly employed by the judicious suitor; but in novels the incivility of the hero rarely fails of its desired effect. A sensible woman might indeed extract a kind of compliment from the reproof which she has earned by some little burst of nonsense. When Felix Holt reproached Esther for real or affected frivolity, 'she resented his speech, but disliked it less than many Felix had addressed to her.' 'You have enough understanding,' he

GEORGE ELIOT

said, 'to make it wicked that you should add one more to the women who hinder men's lives from having any nobleness in them.' In her anger, slightly modified by a sense of gratification, Esther attempts in vain a pretty and natural diversion.

[quotes episode from ch. 10 beginning, 'What is my horrible guilt?' . . .]

A lovers' quarrel before the conscious beginning of love has never been recorded with more delicate insight. The vigorous and eager *secutor*, with reason and conviction on his side, finds himself constantly hampered by a cast of the net on the part of his fugitive adversary. An argument which includes a French quotation cannot be more effectively parried, than by a complaint that that dreadful accent sets one's teeth on edge. The loose tag or tassel serves for a moment the purpose of turning the tables, but after all the victory remains with the champion of the rightful cause. The number of women 'who hinder men's lives from having any nobleness in them' would be incalculable, if potential nobleness were not almost proportionally rare. Men, however, have generally some employment, if it is only selling tape or drawing pleadings, beyond the limits of home. Too many women cultivate with superfluous care their own original narrowness, by shutting themselves up in a circle of family interests which is but a wider form of selfish isolation. Esther Lyon, like the ordinary reader of her history, fails wholly to understand the principle on which Felix has resolved to belong to the working classes; but after some hesitation, and with a temporary disposition to favour a rival lover, she yields to the logic of personal attachment, and allows his life to be shaped according to his own ideal of nobleness.

Mr. Lyon, the simple-minded Independent Minister, is one of the most agreeable characters in the book; and yet it is a commonplace contrivance to make a modern preacher talk in the long-winded sentences of the seventeenth century. His involuntary contempt for the tradesmen of his congregation, and his preference of the secular reformer Felix Holt to orthodox 'church members,' relieve Mr. Lyon from the imputation of weak and excessive softness. There is a pleasant fallacy in his argument that Wellington and Brougham may be introduced into sermons as properly as Rabshakeh and Balaam; but one of his eccentric proceedings is improbable in itself, and it makes the story run capriciously off on a siding. Mr. Lyon takes advantage of a warm acknowledgment for a trifling service which he had rendered to the

Tory candidate for the county, to ask Mr. Debarry to induce his uncle the rector of Treby Magna to engage in a public discussion on Church-government and the theory of an Establishment. The Reverend Augustus Debarry, in defiance of all probability, accepts the challenge, not for himself but for his curate; and after general expectation has been excited in the town, the curate takes fright, Mr. Lyon is disappointed, and the whole digression ends in nothing. It seems as if the writer had changed her intention at the last moment, on the ground that an ecclesiastical controversy would be an incumbrance on the plot; and it would have been better to pull down the scaffolding when the pro-ject of the building was abandoned. Some such abortive experiments seem to have been tried during the development of organic life by natural selection; but art compensates for its inability to copy the multiplicity of Nature by deliberate attention to unity. Mr. Lyon's desire for a public debate is not inconceivable, but a sensible aristocratic rector would never have indulged his fancy. If the proposal and the subsequent failure were worth describing at all, they ought to have formed a separate sketch in a magazine, and not an episode or excres-cence in a novel.

[describes Mrs Holt]

Like several of George Eliot's favourite female characters, Mrs. Holt is profoundly impressed with her own moral and religious excellence. Mr. Lyon mildly remarks that Felix ought not to be judged rashly.

'Many eminent servants of God have been led by ways as strange.' 'Then I'm sorry for their mothers, that's all, Mr. Lyon, and all the more if they'd been well spoken women. For not my biggest enemy, whether it's he or she, if they'll speak the truth, can turn round and say I've deserved this trouble. And when everybody gets their due, and people's doings are spoken of on the house-tops, as the Bible says they will be, it'll be known what I've gone through with those medicines—the pounding, and the pouring, and the letting stand, and the weighing—up early and down late—there's nobody knows yet but One that's worthy to know; and the pasting o' the printed labels right side upward.'

Such touches as the green-baize Bible, and the merit of letting the medicine stand, and of pasting the labels right side upward are only given by the hand of genius.

The story has the defect of running in two parallel lines with only an occasional and arbitrary connexion. Mrs. Transome and her son know nothing of the world of Independent Ministers, and, if they had heard that the son of a quack-medicine vendor had voluntarily become a journeyman watchmaker, they would scarcely have appreciated so imperceptible a declension in the remoter portion of the social scale. Except in a single interview in matters connected with the election, Felix Holt never speaks to Harold Transome, and to Mrs. Transome his existence is probably unknown. The heroine indeed turns out, as in many other novels, to be the heiress of the estate, and for a time she wavers between the admirer whom she expects to dispossess, and the stern ascetic who requires her to take a non-celibate vow of poverty; yet it is evident that either half of the story would have stood by itself, if Esther Lyon had not been employed as a link between the Minister's little house in Malthouse Yard and the stately park with the bad title.

[summary of the plot, followed by a discussion of Mr Lingon and Rufus Lyon]

The best and wisest inhabitant of Treby on the whole displays the smallest amount of common sense. Felix Holt, who had been endeavouring to persuade the colliers to send their children to school, is indignant at the attempt of his own party to employ his sluggish disciples for purposes of riot. On the election day he takes command of a riot, for the sole purpose of leading the rioters out of mischief, and from the same motive he trips up and accidentally kills a constable who attempts to interfere with the proceedings. He is more fortunate than he deserves in obtaining a pardon on the application of the magistrates headed by the Tory and Radical candidates; but the story was coming to an end; Esther had, after some wavering, determined to refuse Harold Transome; and Felix was required to accept the hand which had long awaited his condescension. It is impossible to judge, from any summary of the plot, of the abundance of thought and humour which more than compensate for any complications or improbabilities in the story. Mrs. Transome's old attendant, with her cynical philosophy of life, forms a life-like and remarkable portrait, although her character is only indicated in one or two short conversations with her mistress; and the farmers and tradesmen who visit the butler at the Manor are each distinguished by some natural and recognisable peculiarity. Less original writers identify their minor characters by some trite or cant saying, but George Eliot always denotes the intellectual or moral differences of the dullest and most commonplace of mankind by some little idiosyncrasy of language or of thought. If *Felix Holt* has none of the tragic depth of *Romola*, it is a truer picture of life, and the changes which have occurred since the date of the story almost give the book a historical value.

MIDDLEMARCH

December 1871–December 1872

45. R. H. Hutton, unsigned reviews, *Spectator*

Several newspapers and weeklies—the *Athenaeum*, the *Examiner*, the *Spectator*, for example—reviewed the separate instalments of *Middlemarch* as they were published in 1871–2. In such a series of articles one can trace the changing attitude of the critic to the novel which is slowly being unfolded before him. R. H. Hutton wrote five reviews in this way of parts 1, 2, 3, 4, and 6 of *Middlemarch* and then he concluded with a review of the whole novel when it was published in four volumes in December 1872 (see Introduction, p. 30).

(a) Review of Book I

Spectator, 16 December 1871, xliv, 1528–9

Whatever the value of 'the higher criticism,' it can hardly be denied that criticism of a mere commencement cannot very easily be criticism of 'the higher' kind,—that it must at least be tentative and provisional, —that the most sharp-sighted critic can hardly be able to see all that a really great author like George Eliot intends by suggestions of which the development is still in reserve, and characters of which only the first outlines are displayed. Yet this volume deserves, if not the full criticism which can only be in place when the work is complete, such notice as may draw the attention of the public to the great wealth of insight and humour which it contains; nor need we hold back such mention of faults of manner as it is impossible that any future development of the tale can turn into beauties. On the character of Miss Brooke, which is the main subject of this introductory part of *Middlemarch*, we shall offer as yet no comment. The first sketch is full of power and original-ity, but so much must depend on the melancholy working-out which George Eliot's not very pleasant, and for her somewhat pedantic, 'prelude' hints at, that it is impossible to say whether it would be most unfair to the author or to the critic to deal with the augury as if it were the event. It seems to us somewhat unnatural that a girl of Dorothea Brooke's depth and enthusiasm of nature should fall in love with a man of so little vital warmth and volume of character as Mr. Casaubon in spite of the twenty-seven years' difference in age, without any apparent reason beyond her thirst for an intellectual and moral teacher. That want is usually very distinctly separable from love, and only glides into it, we should have thought, when there is nature *enough* in the object of reverence to exercise a fascination of a warmer kind. It is true that we are told, by way of explanation, that 'Miss Brooke argued from words and dispositions not less unhesitatingly than other young ladies of her age. Signs are small measurable things, but interpretations are illimitable, and in girls of sweet, ardent nature every sign is apt to conjure up wonder, hope, belief, vast as a sky, and coloured by a diffused thimbleful of matter in the shape of knowledge,' (by the way, should George Eliot assume in the mind of her readers a knowledge of the results of Professor Tyndal's speculations as to the cause of the blueness of the sky?) But we should have said that, liable as all signs are to be interpreted by young and ardent natures into something infinitely larger than they mean, the signs of sufficiency or deficiency of life itself would be particularly easy to interpret truly, and be precisely those which would be most likely to be truly interpreted by 'a girl of sweet ardent nature' like Miss Brooke. However, we freely admit that George Eliot knows a hundred times as much of young ladies as most women or men, the present writer certainly included, and we are therefore disposed to take Miss Brooke's sentiment of love for Mr. Casaubon,—without which such a girl would never have dreamt of marriage,—on her authority, though with some surprise, as a matter of fact. It is, however, hardly adequately accounted for, and certainly leaves the impression of something slightly unnatural and repellent on the reader (who is let into the secret reasons of the matter), no less than on her sister Celia, the lover Sir James Chettam, and the Rector's wife, Mrs. Cadwallader, who are not. Though quite prepared to admire the drawing of Miss Brooke's character as a whole when fully developed, we are sure there is some artistic deficiency in leaving the motive of her engagement and marriage to a dry and formal scholar like Mr. Casaubon so inadequately apprehended by the reader.

The great triumphs of the completed part of *Middlemarch* are the rich and admirable pictures of the bachelor uncle, Mr. Brooke, and the aforesaid Rector's wife, Mrs. Cadwallader. In each there is humour enough as well as truth of drawing enough for a reputation. Mr. Brooke is a perfect type of shambling culture, and of such vagueness of modern enlightenment as is consistent with a country gentleman's position, or as our author describes him, is a man 'of acquiescent temper, miscellaneous opinions, and uncertain vote,' who had travelled in his younger days, and acquired a rambling frame of mind by so doing,—in short, a person of whom it was safe to predict nothing, except that 'he would act with benevolent intentions, and that he would spend as little money as possible in carrying them out.' His good-natured, conversational slouch that is always picking itself up by re-ferring back to his last remark,—'the tendency to say what he had said before,' which our author, with one of her most delicate touches of humour and insight, calls that 'fundamental tendency of human speech,' was, she tells us, 'markedly exhibited in Mr. Brooke,'—his helpless reference to celebrities he had known, as if their mere names were a consolatory *résumé* of interesting ideas; his desultory habit of collecting documents on any interesting point and falling back on them as a kind of strength in reserve, a potential knowledge in some respects less fatiguing than actual knowledge, his easy, slovenly way of broach-ing even serious proposals, are characteristics which make his pleasure in dabbling in great subjects and dread of going too far, which would otherwise be hackneyed features, entirely fresh and vivid. It is hardly possible to draw a character in more distinct relief than Mr. Brooke is drawn, for instance, in the following short passage:—

[quotes passage from ch. 3 beginning, 'He stayed a little longer . . .']

And Mr. Brooke is not only a delicious and perfect sketch in himself,— an exquisite representative of the indolent pleasure in loose culture and the dream of second-hand knowledge, though a country gentleman every inch of him, but his figure is a delightful companion to that of Mrs. Cadwallader, the rector's wife, a woman with a mind 'as active as phosphorus, biting everything that came near into the form that suited it,' as frugal as Mr. Brooke, with more reason for it, of much higher birth, of sharp wit and keen interfering instinct, who furnishes the chief interest of the country-side in which she lives, both by her sarcastic sayings and her vigorous and brilliant strokes of economical policy.

[quotes examples of Mrs Cadwallader's wit]

The characters introduced towards the end of the volume, the Vincys, Mr. Featherstone, and his sister Mrs. Waule, promise almost equally well, but the sketch of them is too unfinished to speak of with any certainty, and we shall therefore conclude with our only complaint of the volume,—the number of rather acrid and, it seems to us, disagreeable and not unfrequently heavy sarcasms which the author introduces, after Thackeray's manner, into her own running comments. Thackeray was a satirist, and it was quite of a piece with his whole style, as a man of the world, to interpose these little sarcasms from time to time, though even he overdid it; but George Eliot's style as a painter of human character and life is a much larger and more sympathetic one than Thackeray's, and it suits that style far better to let human feelings and weaknesses speak for themselves, without a constant run of jarring little laughs at them. Such remarks as the following—and there are plenty more of them—put us out of the mood in which George Eliot's books are enjoyed most:—

Certainly such elements in the character of a marriageable girl tended to interfere with her lot, and hinder it from being decided according to custom, by good looks, vanity, and merely canine affection.

Something certainly gave Celia unusual courage; and she was not sparing the sister of whom she was occasionally in awe. Who can tell what just criticisms Murr the Cat may be passing on us beings of wider speculation?

No speech could have been more thoroughly honest in its intention; the frigid rhetoric at the end was as sincere as the bark of a dog, or the cawing of an amorous rook. Would it not be rash to conclude that there was no passion behind those sonnets to Delia which strike us as the thin music of a mandolin?

Let any lady who is inclined to be hard on Mrs. Cadwallader inquire into the comprehensiveness of her own beautiful views, and be quite sure that they afford accommodation for all the lives which have the honour to co-exist with hers.

To us one of George Eliot's great charms consists in her large friendly way of letting the light fall on human weakness; and these mannered sarcasms—which have always haunted her books—seem altogether out of keeping with that way, seem like broken lancet-points in a living body. Something of the cruelty of vivisection is natural in Thackeray's style, and very unnatural in George Eliot's. She gains her ascendancy over the imagination without inflicting these little superfluous wounds, and they only diminish it. It is the one and almost the only respect in which we prefer her poetry to her prose,—that in her poetry she does not put forth, at least in her own person, the biting power of this acid criticism. For the rest, we shall look to the continuation of this fascinating book with hearty delight.

(b) Review of Book 2

Spectator, 3 February 1872, xlv, 147–8

The second book of *Middlemarch* is very tranquil reading; there is but one interest in it that ever threatens to excite the warmer sympathies, and that is, as yet, but gently strung. Poor Dorothea's woes as the wife of a man who has no place in his nature for the tenderer feelings, and who can neither give nor receive the sort of confidence without which there is no love in such a heart as hers, are commencing, and the picture, like all such pictures in George Eliot's pages, is full of truth and pathos, and all the more original that Dorothea Casaubon has a strong, though utterly unpractised intellect of her own, and is not the mere loving baby without power to see where she has made mistakes and where the weakness of others lies, whom it is usual to sketch in such situations. The most delicate of the touches in this part is the terror which falls upon poor Dorothea on her husband's account when she is told that, from his ignorance of German, he cannot ever know what has been already achieved in reducing comparative mythology to a science, and that he is, in fact, 'groping about in the woods with a pocket-compass,' where the Germans 'have made good roads' of which he knows nothing. The vague dismay with which this careless statement fills her, the dread she begins to feel that he may lose the reward of a life of steady labour from this unfortunate inability to study the best previous works on his own subjects, is the finest element in the disturbed relations between her and her arid husband. The conception of a young wife already travelling, by the aid of quick sympathies and a keen intellect, beyond those artificial limits to the sources of his special knowledge within which a learned student more than twice her age has half-wilfully shut himself up, trembling in her very heart for the disappointment to which he may be exposed after a life's useless labour, and again alarming him by her impatience for some immediate results of his efforts into a painful glimmer of self-consciousness that his ideas are not clear enough, and hardly likely ever to be clear enough, for success, is just such a one as only George Eliot could either conceive or execute, and so far as she deals with it in this volume, the story is both perfectly original and full of pathos. We think, however, that this fine author not unfrequently gives us a rude jar, which diminishes the effect of her own best conceptions by the satiric remarks—made from the external point of view of pure observer—with which she studs her delineations. The following noble passage, for instance, begins with a very fine description of Dorothea's permanently and inexplicably painful associations with Rome where she had first begun to feel the deep want of congeniality between her husband and herself, and it ends with a still finer observation on the tragedies in life of which we are fortunately unable to feel the depth by reason of their frequency; but why is the harshly-expressed and inartistically inserted sentence we have printed in italics put in just to break the beauty and harmony of this very fine piece of writing?—

[quotes the two paragraphs beginning, 'To those who have looked at Rome . . .' from ch. 20. The sentence in italics reads: 'many souls in their young nudity are tumbled out among incongruities and left to "find their feet" among them, while their elders go about their business.']

We suppose the object of that harsh sentence is to carry out the thesis of the 'prelude' that 'these blundering lives are due to the inconvenient indefiniteness with which the Supreme Power has fashioned the natures of women,' a thesis which requires the obtrusion of the notion of mistake and chance throughout the tale. For our own parts, we should have thought the art of this very beautiful passage far more perfect without this bitter parenthetic laugh at the souls in their 'young nudity' 'tumbled out among incongruities.' However, except for one or two apparently intentional sarcasms of this sort, the sketch of Mr. and Mrs. Casaubon and their troubles in Rome is amongst the most beautiful of George Eliot's quieter pictures.

The earlier portion of this part of *Middlemarch*, though quite equal in ability to the Roman episode, is not its equal in interest. The sketch of the Middlemarch banker, Mr. Bulstrode, and his struggle with his trading brother-in-law, Mr. Vincy, the Mayor, is admirable of its kind, as is also the account of the ambitious and able young surgeon,

Mr. Lydgate, his difficulties in choosing between the rival candidates for the hospital chaplaincy, and his succumbing to a political motive in the matter which he knows to be not the highest. But of all this portion of the tale the interest is as yet very mild, and the enjoyment we have in reading it, which is great, is almost purely intellectual; not of that kind which springs from any particular wish to follow the story, as a story, into its developments. Whether Mr. Lydgate is to marry Rosamond Vincy or not, what is the secret object for which the Rev. Camden Farebrother,—admirably painted, by the way,—is so anxious to obtain funds, how far Fred Vincy succeeds in getting his crabbed old uncle, Mr. Featherstone, to leave him his property, are all questions on which the most enthusiastic of readers will be able to bear suspense with perfect equanimity. The pleasure in the earlier portion and, indeed, the greater portion of this volume is rather in the fine drawing than in the flow of the narrative, and this though some of the best of the *Middlemarch* characters do not appear at all. Mrs. Cadwallader, our special favourite, does not once appear on the scene, and Mr. Brooke, our second favourite, only appears for half a page or so to make a short speech on the chaplaincy question, the banker, Mr. Bulstrode, being evidently in possession of the particular wire to which he responds. The smooth, keen, common-place Celia, too, is off the stage. Notwithstanding this absence of several of our favourites, and slight as the interest of this volume to the novel-reader's mind is, the pleasure it has given is not less, perhaps even more, than we received from the first. The thread of criticism on life which always runs through George Eliot's stories is in this portion extremely fine and full of striking points, and these not so often harshly interpolated as they sometimes are, but for the most part natural and effective. Take this, for instance, as a criticism on the deferential mannerism which some men affect or fall into:—'Mr. Bulstrode had also a deferential bending attitude in listening, and an apparently fixed attentiveness in his eyes which made those persons who thought themselves worth hearing infer that he was seeking the utmost improvement from their discourse. Others, who expected to make no great figure, disliked this kind of moral lantern turned on them. If you are not proud of your cellar, there is no thrill of satisfaction in seeing your guest hold up his wine-glass to the light and look judicial. Such joys are reserved for conscious merit.' The implicit flattery of that mannerism has often been remarked upon before, but not the sting it conveys to those who are conscious that their remarks are, as George Eliot elsewhere rather uncomfortably

describes them, 'spotted with commonness.' Or take this description
of the injured vanity of a provincial Mayor,—a politically important
personage,—at his brother-in-law's criticisms:—'To point out other
people's errors was a duty that Mr. Bulstrode rarely shrank from, but
Mr. Vincy was not equally prepared to be patient. When a man has
the immediate prospect of being mayor, and is prepared, in the interests
of commerce, to take up a firm attitude on politics generally, he has
naturally a sense of his importance to the framework of things which
seems to throw questions of private conduct into the background.' Or
again, how good is this remark on the philosophic phrase 'the fitness of
things,' in relation to Fred Vincy's hope that the five notes his uncle
Featherstone had just given him would cover his debts and something
more, for which end they ought to have been five fifty pound notes:—
'Fred was not so happy, however, after he had counted them. For they
actually presented the absurdity of being less than his hopefulness had
decided that they must be. What can the fitness of things mean, if not
their fitness to a man's expectations? Failing this, absurdity and
atheism gape behind him. The collapse for Fred was severe when he
found that he held no more than five twenties, and his share in the
higher education of this country did not seem to help him.' That is
witty and very good, though George Eliot added a somewhat needless
sneer when she said that unless 'fitness of things' means 'fitness to a
man's expectations,' 'absurdity *and atheism*' gape behind him. Why is
she always harping on this discordant string? Another clever, and in its
way quite fair, satirical hit at philosophical controversies rather beyond
the view of most of her readers (though, of course, George Eliot herself
does not mean it to go for anything more than a laugh at the more
extravagant forms of the 'intuitive' philosophy), is contained in the
happy account of the rival systems of the Middlemarch medical
practitioners:—

There was a general impression, however, that Lydgate was not altogether
a common country doctor, and in Middlemarch at that time such an impression
was significant of great things being expected from him. For everybody's family
doctor was remarkably clever, and was understood to have immeasurable skill
in the management and training of the most skittish or vicious diseases. *The
evidence of his cleverness was of the higher intuitive order*, lying in his lady-patients'
immovable conviction, and was unassailable by any objection except that their
intuitions were opposed by others equally strong; each lady who saw medical
truth in Wrench and 'the strengthening treatment' regarding Toller and 'the
lowering system' as medical perdition.

Equally shrewd is the comment on the enhanced medical esteem which Dr. Sprague derived in Middlemarch from the reputation for religious scepticism which he had acquired:—

> The Doctor [Dr. Sprague] was more than suspected of having no religion, but somehow Middlemarch tolerated this deficiency in him as if he had been a Lord Chancellor; indeed it is probable that his professional weight was the more believed in, the world-old association of cleverness with the evil principle being still potent in the minds even of lady-patients who had the strictest ideas of frilling and sentiment. It was perhaps this negation in the Doctor which made his neighbours call him hard-headed and dry-witted; conditions of texture which were also held favourable to the storing of judgments connected with drugs. At all events, it is certain that if any medical man had come to Middlemarch with the reputation of having very definite religious views, of being given to prayer, and of otherwise showing an active piety, there would have been a general presumption against his medical skill.

The whole book is full of running commentary on life of this sharp, sagacious kind,—somewhat more sharp and sagacious than trustful or hopeful, it is true,—but full of noble though too often melancholy sentiment. If all *Middlemarch* is as good as its first two parts, it will be full of a wisdom somewhat too acid at times for our taste, but always truthful, and full also of fine and delicate portraiture. How far the story will weld these elements into any true artistic unity, it would be quite premature as yet even to consider.

(c) Review of Book 3

Spectator, 30 March 1872, xlv, 404–6

Middlemarch improves in interest as it goes on;—in intellectual ability it would be very hard for it to improve; indeed, perhaps, the greatest improvement of which it is susceptible in that direction would be something more of reserve in the display of the authoress's excessive, almost morbid, intellectual ability. As it is, she crowds her books as full of eyes as some of the lower insects are said to be; she dissects her own characters till she spoils the charm of some of them, and makes the humour of others of her conceptions too evident by subtle comment and elaborate analysis. *Middlemarch* is not only a sketch of country life, connected by a story, but a running fire of criticism as well. Sometimes the reader feels that the author is unfairly running down one of her own characters;—that she has conceived in her imagination a much more pleasant character than her party-spirit, as it were, chooses to admit. For instance, it is quite clear that George Eliot decidedly dislikes the type of pretty, attractive, gentle, sensible, limited young ladies so common in modern life, and loses no opportunity of plunging the dissecting-knife into them. Celia Brooke and Rosamond Vincy are the two representatives of this species in the upper and middle spheres of Middlemarch society, and Celia Brooke and Rosamond Vincy are, to use an expressive, though rude, schoolboy phrase, 'always catching it' from the authoress, till we feel decidedly disposed to take their sides. For George Eliot's imagination is too powerful to let her paint these young people exactly as she would (from her own partisan point of view) be inclined to do; she cannot help making us feel, especially of Rosamond Vincy, that however conventional she may be, her's is really a sweet and lovable nature at bottom, and yet she won't let anyone entertain the feeling without an admonitory 'shallow creature that, that you are admiring so,' in his ear. Take the following sentence, for instance, which we entirely object to, as quite beyond the proper duties of a painter of life, who has no right to try and rob her characters of the fair amount of sympathy which would be given to them in real life, except by making her picture more instructive and graphic than real life would ordinarily be. Rosamond is in love, and she has reason to fear that her castle-building has been a mistake:—'Poor Rosamond lost her appetite, and felt as forlorn as Ariadne,—as a charming stage Ariadne left behind with all her boxes full of costumes and no hope of a coach.' Now, that is not an additional touch of the artist's; it is a malicious stab of the critic's, which makes us distrust our author's impartiality, and feel rather more disposed to take Rosamond's part than if the attack had not been made. Sir Walter Scott takes plenty of security that we shall not attach too much value to Rose Bradwardine's tenderness for Waverley, but he never deals these unfeeling blows at her, as it were in the dark. It is Thackeray who has set the example which George Eliot so freely follows of playing unfeeling critic to his own creations, but Thackeray is at least pretty impartial, and criticizes his 'puppets' all round with even satiric indifference. George Eliot has favourites and aversions, and deals very hardly by the latter.

But we are finding too much fault where our own predominant feeling is admiration. This book of *Middlemarch* has certainly as much power in it as either of the others, and more wit. The last scene, the death of Mr. Featherstone, is very finely conceived, and every page in the book is written as no other author in the world could have written it. There is much less of the high-scientific style, which, though it is not pedantry in George Eliot,—who is incapable of pedantry,—has all the effect of it to those who do not know her writings well; and though there is certainly not less of that bitter criticism which, we dislike in George Eliot, whose style is too simple and broad for such needle-pricks of acrid banter, there are more than usual of those exquisite touches of humorous observation which make the pages teem with occasions of silent laughter, without vexing the reader by any trace of bitterness. What can be more perfect than the sketch of the veterinary surgeon, Mr. Horrock, and the horse-dealer, Mr. Bambridge, in whose company Fred Vincy rides to Houndsley horse-fair, bent on selling his own hack to good advantage:—

[quotes at length the scene in ch. 23, beginning 'In Mr Horrock there was certainly . . .' and then a description of Mr Vincy]

As regards the development of the main characters of the story, this new part of *Middlemarch* adds most to the picture of Mary Garth, which promises to be one of the author's best. Dorothea Brooke, now Dorothea Casaubon, and Mary Garth are specimens of the uncon-ventional, warm-hearted girls whom alone George Eliot likes, just as Celia Brooke and Rosamond Vincy are specimens of the 'nice,' super-ficial, conventional young ladies whom she detests, and to whom she is tempted to be more unfair than to any other manner of human creature, even poor Mr. Casaubon (who 'quivers thread-like in small currents of self-preoccupation, or at best of an egoistic scrupulosity') scarcely excepted. The character of Mary Garth, who has had a severer early training than Dorothea Brooke, though she has less of natural sweetness and enthusiasm, is almost brought up in interest to that of Dorothea in this new part of *Middlemarch*. The scene in which she bitterly reproaches Fred for his selfish extravagance, relaxing into kindly raillery when she sees the pain she gives,—and that in which she hands over her earnings to her father to help him to pay the debt which Fred Vincy's extravagance has brought upon him,—when taken together with the last night scene in which she proudly refuses to destroy one of Mr. Featherstone's wills without witnesses lest she be accused of tampering with his property arrangements at the crisis of his weakness, bring before us a very fine and real picture of shrewdness, tenderness, bitterness, and pride. And the glimpse given us in this part of Mary Garth's father and mother adds greatly to the power of this sketch. No one studies more carefully the relations between the characters of parents and their children than George Eliot, or is more successful in showing that difference in likeness which we habitually see in life. Mary Garth resembles her mother,—the shrewd, keen, proud, sensible house-wife,—much more than her father,—the generous, delicate-minded, sensitively honourable, skilful workman, not only inexperienced in human life, but incapable of experience in it, to whom no experience of human untrustworthiness can teach distrust; but she has none of her mother's didactic precision, none of her *governessy* qualities—if we may be permitted to coin a word—and in inheriting something of her father's finer susceptibility of nature, the daughter has inherited what tends to disturb the balance of her judgment, and to complicate her nature with impulses of a softer and finer kind than would seem to belong to her brusque and slightly haughty character. The peremptori-ness with which she keeps down her real affection for Fred Vincy, allowing it only to give her a maternal sort of tenderness in reproving his faults and trying to put him in a better way of living, is drawn with the utmost delicacy; indeed, this part raises a hope that we shall have in Mary Garth a figure at least as powerful as Dorothea Casaubon, whose character gains no absolutely new development in this striking and vigorous instalment of George Eliot's tolerably even and placid, though morbidly intellectual tale.

(d) Review of Book 4

Spectator, 1 June 1872, xlv, 685–7, entitled 'The Melancholy of
Middlemarch'

We all grumble at *Middlemarch*; we all say that the action is slow, that there is too much parade of scientific and especially physiological knowledge in it, that there are turns of phrase which are even pedantic, and that occasionally the bitterness of the commentary on life is almost cynical; but we all read it, and all feel that there is nothing to compare with it appearing at the present moment in the way of English litera-ture, and not a few of us calculate whether we shall get the August number before we go for our autumn holiday, or whether we shall have to wait for it till we return. And yet does it really add to the happiness of its readers or not? We feel that we cannot do without it, that the criticisms on life given by our great novelist, and the pictures of life given by our great critic, are criticisms and pictures such as acquire a double value from the very fact that the criticisms are tested by such an insight and imagination as hers, and the pictures criticised by a judgment so fine and balanced as hers;—but we question whether any one lays the book down without either an extra tinge of melancholy in his feeling, or in its place, a combative disposition to challenge the tendency and dispute the fidelity of tone of the pictures he has been studying. It is not in any degree true that the incidents are specially melancholy. On the contrary, the story is not at all of a gloomy description, and there are characters in it which the reader enjoys as he enjoys a gleam of warm sunshine on a dull October day,—especially that of Caleb Garth, the happy, eager, unworldly land-surveyor. Then, again, there are pictures showing a humour so large and delicate that that laughter which really brightens the spirits breaks out even if we are alone,—especially the picture of the slip-shod-minded bachelor landowner, Mr. Brooke, with his weakness for an economical administration of his estate, his odds and ends of ideas, his desultory 'documents' on all sorts of subjects of which he hopes to see something effective made some day, his disposition to dabble in Liberalism, his easy-going, easily daunted ambition, and his indolent restlessness. Mr. Brooke, and Mrs. Cadwallader,—the crisp-minded, witty, worldly, aristocratic rector's wife,—are enough to cheer the reader of any story, however intellectual, even if we were not always coming in for whiffs of dry humour from other quarters,—from the genial, dubious-minded, whist-playing vicar, for instance, as well as from what George Eliot insists on calling the 'low people' of the story. Still, in spite of these snatches of warm sunshine, and of the frequent springs of delightful humour,— at the end of almost every part and every chapter, if not nearly every page, there comes an involuntary sigh. George Eliot never makes the world worse than it is, but she makes it a shade darker. She paints the confusions of life no worse than they are, but she steadily discourages the hope that there is any light for us behind the cloud. She is large in her justice to the visible elements in human nature, but she throws cold water with a most determined hand on the idealism, as she evidently thinks it, which interprets by faith what cannot be interpreted by sympathy and sight.

For instance, in this new June part,—the ablest yet issued,—nothing can be more melancholy than the language of her final criticism on old Featherstone, not so much for its implied belief that there are plenty of human beings without any good at all left in them, as for the hint she throws out that it is those with the truest and deepest knowledge of man such as she and men of equal endowments possess, who have most reason to believe this, while the opposite belief,—the belief in 'the soul of goodness in things evil,'[1]—is due to the idealism of merely theoretic opinion. 'If any one will here contend,' she says, 'that there must have been traits of goodness in old Featherstone, I will not presume to deny this; but I must observe that goodness is of a modest nature, easily discouraged, and when much elbowed in early life by unabashed vices, is apt to retire into extreme privacy, so that it is more easily believed in by those who construct a selfish old gentleman theoretically, than by those who form the narrower judgments based on his personal acquaintance.' The sneer there against the idealists increases instead of diminishing the melancholy impression produced. It seems to say not merely that the truest insight sees much more of unalloyed evil in the world than the sentimentalism of the day chooses to suppose, but that, after all, it does not very much matter,—that a sarcasm is quite as suitable, by way of attack on such a popular sentimentalism, as a grave and reluctant refutation. From George Eliot such a tone really jars us. Let her say, if she will, what no one has a better right to say with authority, that there are many characters so selfish as not to show a trace of anything good; but she should hardly say it with the taunting air of one who despises the world for its credulity.

Perhaps, however, the deepest symptom of melancholy in this book is the disposition so marked in it to draw the most reflective and most spiritual characters as the least happy. It is not a new thing for George Eliot to draw clergymen of large, tolerant, charitable character, with no great belief in dogma, and not a little secret uneasiness as to their position as spiritual teachers; but she always takes care that the larger the nature and the more spiritual the charity, the less is there any appearance of real rest and satisfaction of spirit. There are two clergymen in this class in *Middlemarch*, Mr. Cadwallader, and Mr. Farebrother, both of them men of large nature and good hearts, but Mr. Farebrother certainly the abler and wiser and more genuinely religious of the two, is certainly also, as the authoress constantly makes you feel, the least happy. She is always touching gently and compassionately Mr. Farebrother's slight moral weaknesses,—his preference for comfortable drawing-rooms and whist, especially whist at which he can make certain small but steady winnings, over the duties of his calling,—his eagerness for the salary of the hospital chaplaincy, for the salary rather than for the work which should earn the salary;—and she takes pains to give the impression of spiritual *wistfulness*, rather than faith as the

[1] *Henry V*, IV, i, 4.

299

hidden centre of the vicar's Christianity. But the most remarkable thread of spiritual melancholy in the book constitutes the real end for which it is written,—the picture of Dorothea's beautiful and noble, but utterly unsatisfied and unresting character, and the illustration of the wreck of happiness which results from her unguided spiritual cravings. In one of the most beautiful, but also one of the most melancholy passages of this new part, Dorothea Casaubon confesses her faith, and how little she can lean on any divine power external to herself for its fulfilment. The private belief, she says, to which she clings as her only comfort, is 'that by desiring what is perfectly good, even when we don't quite know what it is and cannot do what we would, we are part of the divine power against evil,—widening the skirts of light, and making the struggle with darkness narrower.' And she goes on, 'Please not to call it [this faith] by any name. You will say it is Persian, or something else geographical. It is my life. I have found it out, and cannot part with it. I have always been finding out my religion since I was a little girl. I used to pray so much; now I hardly ever pray. I try not to have desires merely for myself, because they may not be good for others, and I have too much already.' That is exquisitely truthful and exquisitely melancholy,—the passion of a soul compelled almost to give up prayer as too exhausting, because it seems the radiation of force into a vacuum, and yet retaining all the passionate love for higher guidance in which prayer finds its source and its justification. And just as Dorothea finds no real access of spiritual strength in the religious life, beyond that which expresses itself in her desire for a religious life, so her unhappy, narrow-hearted husband finds no remedy for his own smallness of life, for his jealousy, in the religious ideas which he accepts. He reflects that his recent seizure—a heart-seizure—might not mean an early death, that he might still have twenty years of work left in him to prove to the critics—Messrs. Carp and Company—who had ridiculed his mighty preparations for small achievements, that they had been mistaken. 'To convince Carp of his mistake,' says our author, 'so that he would have to eat his own words with a good deal of indigestion, would be an agreeable accident of triumphant authorship, which the prospect of living to future ages on earth, and to all eternity in Heaven, could not exclude from contemplation. Since thus the prevision of his own ever-enduring bliss could not nullify the bitter savours of irritated jealousy and vindictiveness, it is the less surprising that the probability of transient earthly bliss for other persons, when he himself should have entered into glory, had not a potently sweetening effect. If the truth should be that some undermining disease was at work within him, there might be large opportunity for some people to be the happier when he was gone; and if one of those people should be Will Ladislaw, Mr. Casaubon objected so strongly, that it seemed as if the annoyance would make part of his disembodied existence.' There you get again, not only the melancholy, but the harsh, caustic tone,—the tone which the author takes when she is disparaging a faith which she thinks vulgar as well as untrue,—the jeering tone in which she says, in describing the creatures of prey who attended old Featherstone's funeral, 'When the animals entered the Ark in pairs, one may imagine that allied species made much private remark on each other, and were tempted to think that so many forms feeding on the same store of fodder were eminently superfluous, as tending to diminish the rations. (I fear that the part played by the vultures on that occasion would be too painful for Art to represent, those birds being disadvantageously naked about the gullet, and apparently without rites and ceremonies.)' Sentences such as these give an occasional impression that George Eliot really likes jeering at human evil, which it is most painful to imagine in one who has so noble and so high a conception of good. One almost gathers that she regards the large speculative power she possesses as itself a source of pure unhappiness. The happiest creatures she draws are those who are most able, like Caleb Garth or Adam Bede, to absorb their whole minds and sink their whole energies in limited but positive duties of visible utility. Go a little higher in the scale to a being like Dorothea, full of nobility of the highest kind, but without a definite practical sphere, and compelled to lavish her life on spiritual efforts to subdue her own enthusiasm, her throbbing, inward yearning for a higher life, and we are in a world of unhappiness where rest is never found. But the height of this unhappiness comes out in the authoress's own comments on the universe and its structure, including in that structure its religions. She takes side gallantly and nobly with the power that wars against evil. The hope that she can do something on that side is part of her life. She has found it out, and cannot part with it. But she has a very poor hope of the issue. She sees evil, and sees it not seldom even unmixed with good in the hearts around her, and scoffs at the attempt to suppose that they are better than they seem. She sees narrowness so oppressive to her that she is constantly laughing a scornful laugh over it, and despairing of any better euthanasia for it than its extinction. And all this makes her bitter. She clings to the nobler course, but she cannot repress discordant cries at the disorder of the universe and the weakness of the painfully struggling principle of good. She is a melancholy teacher,—melancholy because sceptical; and her melancholy scepticism is too apt to degenerate into scorn.

(e) Review of Book 6

Spectator, 5 October 1872, xlv, 1262–4, entitled 'George Eliot's Moral Anatomy'.

Middlemarch bids more than fair to be one of the great books of the world. There are, as we have often noted, tones and undertones in it that are not to our liking, and that to a certain extent jar with the large and genial freedom of delineation that is of the very essence of George Eliot's best manner. But no writer who aims as high as George Eliot, can be free from visible defects,—it is only the well-marked limitations of Miss Austen's aim and field of view which enables her to be in her own way all but absolute perfection,—and when you have, as you have in George Eliot, much more than a dash of the philosophy of character mingled with so wonderful a power of accurate imagination and delineation, when you have so high a moral ideal touching closely the vivid picture of minute practical life, you cannot expect to come off quite without dissonance and inward disappointments. Mr. Trollope scours a still greater surface of modern life with at least equal fidelity, but then how much less is the depth of drawing behind his figures! One would know all his characters if one met them in actual life, and know a great deal more of them than we do of ninety-nine out of every hundred of our actual acquaintances, but then he seldom or never picks out a character that it is not perfectly easy to draw in the light fresco of our modern-society school. He gives you where it is necessary the emotions proper to the situations, but rarely or never the emotions which lie concealed behind the situations and which give a kind of irony to them. His characters are carved out of the materials of ordinary society; George Eliot's include many which make ordinary society seem a sort of satire on the life behind it.

In a word, what gives a great deal of their peculiar stamp, both in the way of fresh interest, and of questionable or even challengeable drift, to George Eliot's pictures, is the theoretic nature of the moral anatomy which she applies to her own creations, subtle and wonderful as its range certainly is. She has a speculative philosophy of character that always runs on in a parallel stream with her picture of character,

sometimes adding to it an extraordinary fascination, sometimes seeming
to distort it by a vein of needless and perhaps unjust suggestion. Her
characters are so real that they have a life and body of their own quite
distinct from her criticisms on them; and one is conscious at times of
taking part with her characters against the author, and of accusing her
of availing herself unfairly of the privilege of author, by adding a trait
that bears out her own *criticism* rather than her own imaginative conception. Thus when she says of Celia, 'Celia, whose mind had never been
thought too powerful, saw the emptiness of other people's pretensions
much more readily' [than Dorothea]; and again, 'to have in general but
little feeling seems to be the only security against feeling too much on
any particular occasion,'—the reader protests vigorously against the
notion that a wide-awake practical mind is necessarily less devoid of
deep feeling than a visionary and idealist mind, though, of course, the
types of feeling are different. Indeed, one is apt to set down that unkind
hit at Celia to personal antipathy on the author's part. So when Celia
subsequently explains, without the least regard to her sister's feelings,
that cruel and ungenerous codicil to Mr. Casaubon's will by which
Dorothea is deprived of her jointure if she marries Will Ladislaw, one is
disposed to attribute this great want of sisterly delicacy more to the
author's prejudice against Celia than to any confidence of the reader in
the asserted fact that this was so. Celia had not only been accused of
want of feeling for seeing through Mr. Casaubon, but her criticisms on
her sister's blind idealism, which were in the main just, had been likened
to those publicly passed by 'Murr the cat' on our human life; and this
certainly looked like an *animus* against Celia, for which the reader was
bound to allow. One knows perfectly well that practical girls of this
far from dreamy type do often exhibit the warmest affections, and so
one is not prepared to accept absolutely George Eliot's rationale of
Celia's clear-sightedness as arising in coldness of heart, and is prepared
to distrust even decidedly asserted facts which appear to be at all
unreasonably depreciative of her.

And so with Rosamond Vincy, against whom also George Eliot, in
her keen exercise of her powers of moral anatomy, appears to make one
of her dead sets. Rosamond Vincy's—or rather, we should say, Rosamond Lydgate's—nature is thin, gently selfish, and obstinate, under a
veil of perfect delicacy and refinement. Nothing can be more marvellously painted than the picture of her irresponsiveness to her husband's
anxieties, fears, and hopes in this new number of *Middlemarch*. It is a
picture such as carries home to those who were previously inclined to

take Rosamond's part against the author, the conviction that they were wrong, and George Eliot right. When her husband warned her not to mention something which he thought would be painful to Will Ladislaw, and she, fully intending to mention it at the next opportunity, 'turned her neck and *patted her hair*, looking the image of placid indifference,' it is impossible to rebel against the force of the picture. You *know* that the girl was what George Eliot is painting her, and this in spite of a certain suspicion of the literary treatment accorded to Rosamond. But then what is it that first inspires this distrust, that induces one to doubt the possible equity of the writer's delineation? It is that apparently malicious bit of moral anatomy in which Rosamond's depression is described when she thinks she is going to lose Lydgate after all,—to get no offer from him:—'Poor Rosamond lost her appetite, and felt as forsaken as Ariadne,—as a charming stage Ariadne left behind with all her boxes full of costumes and no hope of a coach.' Now, that is palpably an unkind author's criticism not founded on truth. Rosamond is thin, and selfish, and self-occupied, but she is not stagey. Her grief, such as it was, though of a feeble and thready kind, was perfectly genuine. That prick of the needle was due to literary malice, a prick that only literary dislike would have given, and hence our early distrust of many of the traits given of Rosamond, until the immense force and power of the picture in the new number conquered us, and we gave in to the general fidelity of the picture. This power of theoretic moral anatomy, considering the liability it involves to the delivery of false thrusts which the picture, even as painted by the author's imaginative genius, does not justify, is a somewhat dangerous one. It often adds greatly to the depth and charm of the drawing. It sometimes shakes one's faith not a little in the impartiality of the author who thus criticises (unfairly) her own creations.

But where the characters are so slightly sketched that there is no possibility of their taking up a distinct life and body of their own independent of their author, where the author's criticism, be it prejudice or be it insight, is an essential part of the sketch, this power of keen moral anatomy adds greatly to the vivacity and humour and life of the picture which is by it compressed into a short space. Compare George Eliot's brief sketches,—such sketches as that of Mr. Trumbull the auctioneer, or Mr. Solomon Featherstone, to neither of which are many lines devoted,—with Mr. Trollope's equally brief sketches, and you will find the difference in vividness immense; and simply for this reason, that one or two touches of keen moral anatomy imply a multitude of traits, which it would take a long and careful delineation to bring out in a full portrait. Here is the first descent of the dissecting-knife into the motives of Solomon Featherstone. 'He was a large-cheeked man, nearly seventy, with small, furtive eyes, and was not only of much blander temper, but thought himself much deeper than his brother Peter; indeed, not likely to be deceived by any of his fellow-men, inasmuch as they could not well be more greedy and deceitful than he suspected them of being. *Even the invisible powers, he thought, were likely to be soothed by a bland parenthesis here and there—coming from a man of property, who might have been as impious as others.*' And again, ' "Might any one ask what their brother has been saying?" said Solomon, *in a soft tone of humility, in which he had a sense of luxurious cunning, he being a rich man and not in need of it.*' Or take the touch in the new number:—'The hour-hand of a clock was quick by comparison with Mr. Solomon, *who had an agreeable sense that he could afford to be slow.* He was in the habit of pausing for a cautious, vaguely designing chat with every hedger or ditcher on his way, *and was especially willing to listen even to news which he had heard before, feeling himself at an advantage over all narrators in partially disbelieving them.*' Without a most delicate and keen divining of motives, it would have taken whole sheets of delineation to have given such a sketch as this of Mr. Solomon.

Again, take the wonderfully skilful anatomy of the auctioneer Mr. Trumbull when suffering under pneumonia.

[quotes several descriptions of Trumbull]

(f) Review of *Middlemarch*, 4 vols, December 1872

Spectator, 7 December 1872, xlv, 1554–6

You hear people say, with a sort of virtuous assumption of artistic feeling, that they will not read novels published in parts;—that they are content to wait till the fragments are pieced into a whole. The present reviewer at least abjures all such æsthetic doctrine. Whether an author who has any claims to such high artistic power as George Eliot should begin to publish till the whole is complete,—and most likely the author of *Middlemarch* did not do so, at least there is no sign of a half-completed or altered design anywhere,—is one question; and whether the reader should study the instalments as they are doled out, is quite another. We are disposed to maintain that no story gets so well apprehended, so completely mastered in all its aspects, as one which, written as a whole, is published in parts. There is, at all events, this to be said in its favour,—that it is the only way in which human life itself, of which fiction is supposed to be the mirror, can be studied. There, you are not allowed to see the beginning, middle, and end at a sitting, like the springing-up, budding, and blowing of a flower beneath the bidding of an Egyptian conjuror, but must usually become perfectly familiar with the human elements of a story before you see them even begin to combine into a plot. And in the case of *Middlemarch*, we are perfectly sure that, other things being equal, those will understand it best and value it most who have made acquaintance slowly during the past year with all its characters, and discussed them eagerly with their friends, in all the various stages of their growth and fortune. The book is called 'A Study of Provincial Life,' and answers to its title. Round the central characters are grouped at greater or less distance all the elements of country society—the country gentry, the surveyor, the clergymen of various types, the country doctors, the banker, the manufacturers, the shopkeepers, the coroner, the auctioneer, the veterinary surgeon, the horse-dealer, the innkeepers, all drawn with a force and yet a perspective which it takes time, and a graduation of feeling not easily commanded in the few hours usually devoted to a novel, to apprehend. Middlemarch and its various sets have now been growing familiar to us for many months, and a large part of the appreciation with which we have read the later chapters, is due to those frequent discussions of the various Middlemarch personages by which their exact social function and position have been fixed in our minds, and the apologies for their various questionable actions have been familiarised. George Eliot has, no doubt, often smiled in reading the criticisms passed on her drift and purpose by those who had but part of her design before them. But so would any one who could see the end from the beginning often smile at the partial and fragmentary criticisms passed on human life. Not the less are such partial and fragmentary criticisms, however false they may prove in the end, of the greatest use in helping those who make them to understand the end in relation to the beginning, when at length the end is attained.

In the only passage throughout the book, which is somewhat artificially, not to say stiltedly written,—and which is accordingly called not a preface, but a 'prelude',—it is hinted that George Eliot's object is to depict the life of a woman of deep and generous enthusiasm, who might have been a St. Theresa if she had been born in an age when society and faith worked together in unison with generous individual aspirations, but whose life is to be actually jarred and spoiled by the incongruity between the spirit within her and the age into which she is born. In the concluding passage of the book, where the same idea is taken up again, George Eliot remarks that the determining acts of her heroine's life 'were not ideally beautiful.' 'They were the mixed result,' she says, 'of young and noble impulse struggling under prosaic conditions,' and to the taint in the social air which her heroine breathed, George Eliot ascribes the cross-purposes of her life, where 'great feelings took the aspect of error and great faith the aspect of illusion.' 'A new Theresa will hardly have the opportunity of reforming a conventual life, any more than a new Antigone will spend her heroic piety in doing all for the sake of a brother's burial; the medium in which these ardent deeds took shape is for ever gone. But we insignificant people, with our daily words and acts, are preparing the lives of many Dorotheas, some of which may present a far sadder sacrifice than that of the Dorothea whose story we know;'—in other words, we are moulding a bad public opinion about women, which must be held responsible for such failures in ideal beauty as the two marriages by which Dorothea showed at once her self-forgetfulness, and her helplessness to work out in practice the high ideal by which she was possessed. If this was really George Eliot's drift, we do not think it particularly well worked out. Dorothea's mistake in devoting herself to Mr. Casaubon,—a clergyman more than double her age, eaten up by unhealthy egoism and a cobwebby kind of intellectual ambition,—may be due to defective education, and the unsatisfactory state of public opinion as to what sacrifices elderly men may legitimately ask of girls, as George Eliot intimates; but there is little or no attempt to trace the connection in this book. In fact the attempt of the 'prelude' and the final chapter to represent the book as an elaborate contribution to the 'Woman's' question, seems to us a mistake, meting out unjust measure to the entirely untrammelled imaginative power which the book displays. The creative power of the author is yoked to no specific doctrine in this, if not her completest, yet in many respects her freest and greatest work, and we re-read both the 'prelude' and the conclusion with a faint surprise when we are familiar with the story. It is true, indeed, that not only is the heroine's (Dorothea) life all but wrecked by a marriage due to misdirected enthusiasm, but the life of the true hero of the story,—though not that of him who eventually gains the heroine, —Lydgate, is still more completely wrecked by his marriage with a shallow-hearted girl of superficial refinement and gentleness, disguising the most absolute selfishness and coldness of heart beneath. But here, again, there is no carefully drawn-out relation between the perverted public opinion of the day about women, and the fatal mistake which Lydgate commits. It is intimated, indeed, that he was misled through sharing the blundering notion of an age in which men and women have few intellectual interests in common,—the notion, namely, that all which intellectual men need in a wife is that softness or feminineness of manner which is supposed to be indicative of pliancy of nature,—a supposition the blunder of which is exposed in *Middlemarch* with the most terrible and almost redundant force. No doubt George Eliot means Lydgate's and Rosamond's history to teach men that if they are to be happy in marriage, they must secure something of positive moral and intellectual sympathy in their wives, and not that mere semblance of tenderness which is called feminine grace. And she does teach us that there is no hardness like the hardness of a narrow mind polished into superficial charm, taught to avoid contentiousness as unfeminine, and hence only the fonder of pursuing its private purposes without the least relation to the reasons and objections of others. But then the type of women represented by Rosamond is far too unique to be much of a contribution towards the 'woman' question. It is her disguised selfishness, not her ignorance, which ruins Lydgate's life. Had she known as little as she does of his intellectual aims, and yet been what Lydgate thought her, a tender, devoted woman, his life would not have been wrecked as it is. Had Rosamond inherited her mother's or her aunt's nature, instead of her father's, there would have been nothing of the tragedy which George Eliot depicts so powerfully in this wonderful book. Rosamond is a most originally-drawn character, but it is not the ignorant admiration which men feel for what she seems to be, but the discrepancy between what she seems to be and what she is, which is chargeable with the wreck of Lydgate's life. Hence we cannot accept George Eliot's apparent wish to make of *Middlemarch* a contribution to the formation of a better opinion as to the education of women, as fairly representing either the actual drift of her story or the scope of the genius it displays.

The real power of *Middlemarch* is, however, no doubt spent on the delineation of two ill-assorted unions, both of them mainly due to the spontaneous preference of the woman for the man,—unions for neither of which, so far as we can see, is a perverted public opinion at all specially responsible. Nothing could be received with less favour by her

friends than Dorothea's resolve to marry Mr. Casaubon, the would-be
author of 'The Key to all Mythologies;' and Rosamond's wish to marry
the ambitious young surgeon, Mr. Lydgate, on account of his distinguished bearing and connection with the Lydgates of Quallingham,
also receives scant favour from her family and friends. But whatever
the motive of George Eliot in choosing these marriages for her theme,
it is impossible to rate too highly the power with which the misery
they cause is delineated. Mr. Casaubon, looking not so much for a wife,
as for a gentle secretary with a melodious voice who will read to him,
write for him, and admire him to his heart's content without expecting
anything from him more than he himself is,—one, in short, who will
'observe his abundant pen-scratches and amplitude of paper with the
uncritical awe of a delicate-minded canary,'—finds himself, instead,
married to a woman of imperious impulses and devoted character,
who craves a part both in his heart and in his aims, making him feel
the former somewhat dry and cold, and the latter obscure and dim.
He finds himself brought to a kind of daily judgment where he expected
only to receive a new and agreeable stimulus to ambition, and withers
rapidly under the demand—to which he is quite unequal—made alike
upon his love and his intellectual life. But that here and there the author
a little caricatures Mr. Casaubon,—the over-pompous letter in which
he makes his offer, for instance, could hardly have been written by a
scholar at all, using as it does the word 'dissimulate' in a sense for which
we can find no sort of apology, and if it had been so written, would
surely have so far disgusted Dorothea as to make her hesitate,—and
that she attributes to him in his last codicil an ungentlemanly act for
which the reader is not prepared,—nothing could be finer than the
account of the unhappiness his marriage causes, and its slow growth.
The painful sense of finding an acute critic instead of a worshipper, the
feverish dread he feels of exciting his wife's pity, the irritable consciousness that he in no way imposes upon her judgment, and the consequent
growth of self-distrust in himself, the soreness and jealousy with which
he notices her tendency to interfere, however delicately, in his family
arrangements, and to take under her protection a young cousin whom
he had never liked, his inability to ask or even accept her sympathy
when his life is threatened, and his wish to dictate her future life to her
even from his grave, are all presented with a clear intellectual outline
and vividness that nothing in any of the author's previous works has
surpassed. Especially the last scenes of Mr. Casaubon's life, where he
shuts himself up in his own wounded sensitiveness so completely as to

repel Dorothea's sympathy for his physical sufferings for fear it should be pity, and where he finally breaks through his reserve only to ask for a pledge that she will govern her life after his death by the wishes he expresses, are painted with a sombre force, and an insight into the bitterness of sore pride, which add some of the greatest of all its treasures to the stores of English literature. And it is impossible to say whether Mr. Casaubon's or his wife's feelings are painted with most power. Dorothea's yearning to devote herself to a great ideal work, and her gradual discovery that in becoming Mr. Casaubon's wife she has entered into no such work, that she has found a dried-up formalist where she expected a loving guide and teacher, that she has devoted herself to a pedant instead of a man of original and masterly intellect, are quite as finely painted as Mr. Casaubon's troubles. The rising, but quickly suppressed scorn with which she observes Mr. Casaubon's distrust both of her and of himself, the generous passion of her sympathy, and the despairing resentment with which she meets the rebuffs inflicted by his proud, thin-skinned reserve, the blundering generosity of her intercessions for the very man whom Mr. Casaubon most dislikes, and the profound dread with which she hears her husband's request that she will take up and pursue after he is gone, the dreary task in which she has lost all faith, are all painted in colours whose glow is all the more striking for the dreary and pallid tone of the wasting and wasted nature with which her lot is linked. A very fine Shelleyan sort of motto (evidently original) prefixed to one of the chapters, which is to describe the tenacious ambition of Mr. Casaubon still clinging eagerly to the hope that his wife will redeem his promises to the world by editing his unfinished work, and the dread with which Dorothea hears the request, runs as follows:—

> Surely the golden hours are turning grey,
> And dance no more and vainly strive to run:
> I see their white locks streaming in the wind—
> Each face is haggard as it looks at me,—

and we cannot give greater praise to the picture which that chapter contains than by saying that it is worthy of the lines prefixed,—that we feel the full haggardness of those hours to both Dorothea and her husband; the recoil of life from life, which ought to be union; the mutual dread and distrust, which ought to be confidence; the tyrannical wish and the instinct of rebellion, which ought to be eagerness on the one side not to impose a yoke, on the other, to accept it by anticipation.

There is hardly a finer touch of genius in English literature than Dorothea's reply, as we may call it, after her husband's death, to his wish that she should complete the confused and pedantic work on which he had built his hopes of fame. 'One little act of hers,' says the author, 'may perhaps be smiled at as a superstition. The *Synoptical Tabulation for the use of Mrs. Casaubon* she carefully enclosed and sealed, writing within the envelope, "*I could not use it. Do you not see now that I could not submit my soul to yours, by working hopelessly at what I have no belief in?*—Dorothea." Then she deposited the paper in her own desk.' Such is the final touch which describes the breaking in pieces of poor Dorothea's effort after an ideal work. We do not think the affection which takes the place of this misdirected one quite worthy of her. Will Ladislaw is altogether uninteresting, and but for very fine fragments of political remark,—which evidently are not his, but the author's,— has nothing but his admiration and his youth to recommend him to Dorothea. He is petulant, small, and made up of spurts of character, without any wholeness and largeness, and except his goodness to little Miss Noble (by the way, is she Miss Winifred or Miss Henrietta Noble? she is called by both names), and his disposition to lie on the hearth-rug, which is certainly praiseworthy, there is not a fascinating touch about him.

The picture of the ambitious and robust-minded Lydgate's complete subjugation by the constant attrition of his wife's soft, selfish obstinacy, of his total inability to govern her, and his utter defeat by her, even when Rosamond is so completely in the wrong that she is detected in all sorts of underhand proceedings—of all responsibility for which she divests herself by simply not feeling it,—is a picture second, of course, in moral and intellectual interest, to the higher picture of Dorothea's shipwreck with Mr. Casaubon, but certainly not second in originality or power. Rosamond, though she is guilty of one deliberate lie,— which is, we fancy, too great a sin against the conventional standard of conduct which she herself admitted to be quite consistent with the idea of the character,—is by far the finest picture of that shallowness which constitutes absolute incapacity for either deep feeling or true morality, we have ever met with in English literature. When she conceals her fixed intentions of deceit and disobedience by a turn of her slender neck, or a gentle patting of her own hair, one turns away from the picture in real dismay, so true is it and so terrible. Nor can anything be more powerful than the picture of the deadening effect produced by her on Lydgate's gusty tenderness and impulsive nobility. In the scene where Dorothea's disinterestedness, force, and depth of feeling carry away even Rosamond for a moment, we are reminded powerfully of some of the great scenes between Dinah and Hetty in *Adam Bede*. It is in kind the same victory won in a different sphere of life and a different plane of feeling, but we are less prepared to believe in Rosamond's capacity for being thus touched than in Hetty's. The author has so steeled us against Rosamond by her previous pictures, that we lay down this fine and moving scene with a certain hesitation as to its fidelity to the character previously sketched, though George Eliot does prepare us for it by suggesting that even Lydgate might have made more impression on his wife, if he had not allowed his nature to be chilled into distrust of itself by her irresponsiveness, but had thrown his whole heart into the effort to take possession of his wife, and infuse a sort of second-nature into her out of the depths of his own earnestness and love.

Such are the main threads of interest in this great book. But the wealth of the secondary life which adds so much to the effect of these great delineations, it is impossible even to indicate in such a review as this. Dorothea's good-natured, slip-shod uncle, Mr. Brooke, whose conversation is so humorous a mosaic of kindliness, scatterbrainedness, niggardliness, and helpless desultory ambition; her good-natured, prosaic brother-in-law, Sir James Chettam, the very incarnation of English high-feeling and narrow, commonplace intellect; her shrewd, commonplace sister Celia, and the exquisitely witty worldly-minded rector's wife, Mrs. Cadwallader, are all figures which bring out the ardent romance and depth of Dorothea's nature in strong relief. The groups of Middlemarch townspeople are not less carefully fitted to bring out in strong relief the pictures of Rosamond and her husband. The tyrannous old miser, Rosamond's uncle, her spendthrift, but warm-hearted brother, her selfish father, her cosy, loving mother; the grim, half-sincere, half-hypocritic evangelical banker Bulstrode, and his ostentation-loving but devoted wife, with the various groups of gossiping townspeople, all serve to throw into relief the thin refinement, the petty vanity, the cold amiability of her nature; and the connection between Lydgate and his unhappy patron Bulstrode is exceedingly finely conceived for the purpose of fully trying the mettle of the former's character. We cannot help thinking that George Eliot makes a mistake in representing a man of Bulstrode's type of mind as entirely unoppressed by the guilt of what he well knew to be, morally, murder, until disgrace comes upon him. The description of the crime itself is wonderfully fine; but the complete equanimity with which he looks back upon it, after the great struggle which preceded it, we cannot accept as true. Of the wonderful humour of the book we must speak on another occasion.

The whole tone of the story is so thoroughly noble, both morally and intellectually, that the care with which George Eliot excludes all real faith in God from the religious side of her religious characters, conveys the same sort of shock with which, during the early days of eclipses, men must have seen the rays of light converging towards a centre of darkness. Mr. Farebrother,—a favourite type with George Eliot, the rector in *Adam Bede* was another variety of him—Caleb Garth, the noble land agent, and Dorothea, are all in the highest sense religious in temperament; two of them go through very keen temptations, and the struggles of one, Dorothea, are minutely and most powerfully described; but in all these cases the province chosen for the religious temperament is solely the discharge of moral duty, and the side of these minds turned towards the divine centre of life, is conspicuous only by its absence, especially in Dorothea's case. In reading the description of the night of Dorothea's darkest trial one feels a positive sense of vacancy; so dramatic a picture of such a one as she is, going through such a struggle without a thought of God, is really unnatural. The omission is owing no doubt to the very natural dislike of the author to attribute, out of pure dramatic instinct, to her highest and noblest character an attitude of spirit with which she could not herself sympathise. The nearest we approach to anything like a positive faith in Dorothea is in the following fine passage:

'Oh! my life is very simple,' said Dorothea, her lips curling with an exquisite smile, which irradiated her melancholy. 'I am always at Lowick.'—'That is a dreadful imprisonment,' said Will, impetuously.—'No, don't think that,' said Dorothea. 'I have no longings.' He did not speak, but she replied to some change in his expression. 'I mean, for myself. Except that I should like not to have so much more than my share without doing anything for others. But I have a belief of my own, and it comforts me.'—'What is that?' said Will, rather jealous of the belief.—'That by desiring what is perfectly good, even when we don't quite know what it is and cannot do what we would, we are part of the divine power against evil—widening the skirts of light and making the struggle with darkness narrow.—'That is a beautiful mysticism—it is a——' —'Please not to call it by any name,' said Dorothea, putting out her hands entreatingly. 'You will say it is Persian, or something else geographical. It is my life. I have found it out, and cannot part with it. I have always been finding out my religion since I was a little girl. I used to pray so much—now I hardly ever pray.

I try not to have desires merely for myself because they may not be good for others, and I have too much already. I only told you, that you might know quite well how my days go at Lowick.'

And there is, it will be observed, a careful vagueness in the phrase 'divine power,' which leaves it quite open to the reader to interpret it as meaning either the collective goodness of the human world, or something higher and better which comes from a purer source. In reading the highest scenes in *Middlemarch* we have a feeling as if the focus of all light and beauty were dark and cold.

Yet, say what we may, it is a great book. Warwickshire has certainly given birth to the greatest forces of English literature, for we are indebted to it not only for by far the greatest of English authors, but also for by far the greatest of English authoresses; and though it would be too much to say that the latter ranks next to the former in our literature, even with a whole firmament of power between, it is not too much to say that George Eliot will take her stand amongst the stars of the second magnitude, with the cluster which contains Scott and Fielding, and indeed all but Shakespeare, on a level of comparative equality with them,—or at least without any distance between her and the greatest of them which can compare for a moment with the distance which divides all of them from Shakespeare.

46. Unsigned review, *Saturday Review*

7 December 1872, xxxiv, 733–4

If we are to call *Middlemarch* a novel at all, we may say that as a didactic novel it has scarcely been equalled. Never before have so keen and varied an observation, so deep an insight into character and motives, so strong a grasp of conceptions, such power of picturesque description, worked together to represent through the agency of fiction an author's moral and social views. But the reservation we have implied is a broad one. No talent, not genius itself, can quite overcome the inherent defect of a conspicuous, constantly prominent lesson, or bridge over the disparity between the storyteller with an ulterior aim ever before his own eyes and the reader's, and the ideal storyteller whose primary impulse is a story to tell, and human nature to portray—not human nature as supporting a theory, but human nature as he sees it. The same reader who gives himself in unreserved trust to the master of humour and pathos whose object is to please him by his art, is justified in suspecting a bias or one-sided estimate of qualities where a moral has to be worked out through human agency. His confidence is disturbed, he is at once put upon his mettle, when the same gifts seem employed to betray him into unconscious, and perhaps unwilling, admissions. Self-respect calls upon him at every turn either to renounce principles and prejudices or to stand up and defend them—attitudes of mind altogether alien from that relaxation which it is the assumed office of fiction to provide for its votaries. Not but that he must be hard to please who cannot, without overtaxing his powers of attention, derive plenty of amusement pure and simple out of *Middlemarch*—all that the ordinary novel-reader reads a novel for; but it would be unjust to so thoughtful, powerful, and earnest a writer to ignore the intention that underlies the whole. And to read such writing and thinking as they ought to be read is a real exercise of mind; especially as we own ourselves, while charmed by inimitable touches of character, and enjoying the author's graces of style and felicity of illustration and allusion, not seldom differing from her views and strictures upon society, and her suggestions for its amendment.

Of course where a moralist and satirist quarrels with society he is very sure to be able to adduce an abundance of facts on his side. The quarrel with humanity in *Middlemarch* is its selfishness, and the quarrel with society is its hollow respectability. Human nature and society are hard things to defend; but care for self up to a point is not identical with selfishness; and respectability which pays its way and conducts itself with external propriety is not hollow in any peculiar sense. And we must say that if our young ladies, repelled by the faint and 'neutral' virtues of Celia on the one hand, and the powerfully drawn worldly Rosamond on the other, take to be Dorotheas, with a vow to dress differently from other women, and to regulate their own conduct on the system of a general disapproval of the state of things into which they are born, the world will be a less comfortable world without being a better one.

Dorothea is so noble and striking a character—her charm growing upon us as the story advances—she is so penetrated by a sense of duty, so ardent in her longing to make the world better and happier, that we would not introduce her as an example unfit for general imitation had the ordinary domestic type of woman with whom she is contrasted been drawn by a more friendly hand. Dorothea is born with the temper and the aspirations of a St. Theresa; to her the destinies of mankind, seen by the light of Christianity, made the solicitudes of feminine fashion appear an occupation for Bedlam. She will not ride, because all people cannot afford a horse. She takes no interest in art, because it is the delight of the few beyond the reach of material want. Her strength of opinions, and her propensity to act on them, thus put her from the first at odds with society, which, we are told, expected women to have weak opinions, 'while still finding its greatest safeguard in the security that opinions were not acted on.' As a foil to these high sentiments, we have her sister Celia, of whom Dorothea says that she never did anything naughty since she was born, and who really never goes contrary to our sense of what is amiable and dutiful in woman; though, not being in the good graces of the author, we are not allowed to find her attractive. Less clever than Dorothea, she has more worldly wisdom, which means perhaps more instinctive perceptions; and not feeling it her duty to subvert the world, she can take her place in it naturally. But surely it is not every girl's duty to refuse the advantages and pleasures of the condition in which she finds herself because all do not share them. She is not selfish because she is serenely happy in a happy home; and if she does her best to help and alleviate the suffering within her reach, she may comfort herself in the belief that the eye of Providence never sleeps.

It is certain that nothing in human nature in the way of a virtue or a grace will stand a strict analysis unshaken. The analytical mind is logically driven into disparagement. Thus Pascal, refining upon the pervading vanity of man, holds it impossible to escape from it. 'Those who write against glory wish for the glory of having written well; those who read it wish for the glory of having read it; and I who write this have perhaps the same longing, and those who read me will have it also.' There is no escape but in the ideal. Perhaps such a state of mind almost leads to hardness where the sympathies are not active—which they are not with our author on first opening her story. Early during its progress we have at times said to ourselves, The subjects and sentiments are tragic, but not the persons; the writer does not identify herself with them. But such a writer too keenly enters into her creations not to become attached to them, and therefore sympathetic; and tenderness for human frailty, and belief in human feeling, with whatever alloy of self, give a pathos to the close which the beginning did not promise.

We have all our especial antipathies among the vices; and the hypocrisy of seeming, the 'dwelling in decencies for ever,'[1] the cant of selfishness, are the antipathies of George Eliot. As one book of this series followed another, each seemed to say, This is your benevolence, this your learning, this your family life, this your religion! The sleek trust in Providence which easy or grasping selfishness makes its boast is the particular subject of warning and contempt. The carefully elaborated character of Bulstrode, no hypocrite of the common type, but one who sincerely hopes to flatter Divine Justice into condoning the wrong done, and permitting ill-gotten gains to prosper on condition of a certain amount of service done, is a leading instance; but most of the selfishness of *Middlemarch* shelters itself under an assumed appeal from conscience to religion. Whether it be poor Celia justifying her girl's love of pretty things under the test that the necklace she longs for won't interfere with her prayers; or Mr. Brooke excusing a political move with one of his favourite summaries—'Religion, properly speaking, is the dread of a Hereafter'; or Mrs. Waule arguing that for her brother Peter to turn his property into Blue-Coat land was flying in the face of the Almighty that had prospered him, the appeal is uniformly a cover to the real thought or motive, and, as such, a fit subject for the satirist's pen. But every man's religion may be vulgarized if the alloy is too curiously sought for. We like things in groups; our preferences and convictions are tied together by association; but it is not always fair to couple the highest of these with the lowest, as though the same amount and quality of thought and conviction went to each. When we are told that Mrs. Bulstrode and Mrs. Pymdale had the same preferences in silks, patterns of underclothing, china ware, and clergymen, it does not prove the religion represented by the clergyman to be superficial and trivial, though it sounds so in such a conjunction. If *Middlemarch* is melancholy, it is due perhaps to its religion being all duty, without a sufficient admixture of hope. We miss the out-look of blue sky which is as essential to the cheerful portraiture of humanity by the moralist as a glimpse into the open is to the portraiture of art.

In so far as *Middlemarch* is an allegory Mr. Casaubon represents learning as opposed to science. Bunyan's Mr. Bat's-eyes is not more a

[1] Pope, *Moral Essays*, Ep. ii, 163.

317

personification of qualities than is Dorothea's first choice, with his lean person, blinking eyes, white moles, and formal phrases; with talents chiefly of the burrowing kind, carrying his taper among the tombs of the past in diligent exploration; his book, the 'Key to all the Mythologies,' itself a tomb. Altogether he is a striking figure, though now and then the author scarcely shows herself as entirely at home in his surroundings—for example, in his college jealousies and sorenesses—as we generally find her. As for Dorothea's sudden choice of him for a husband, it is not without precedent in real life, reminding us at once of Madame de Staël when a prodigy of fifteen gravely proposing to her parents that she should marry Gibbon; as fat a specimen of distinguished middle life as Mr. Casaubon was a lean one. The more a woman has aims of her own, and a sense of power to carry them out, the less is she guided by the common motives and aspirations of her sex. Personally we can acquiesce in her first choice more readily than in her second. There are two views of Ladislaw, who, we scarcely know on what reasonable grounds, is a great favourite with the author. He charms Dorothea by qualities exactly the reverse of her husband's; by his passionate prodigality of statement; by his ready understanding of her thoughts, which Mr. Casaubon always snubbed as long-exploded opinions, if not heresies; by the sunny brightness of his expression and hair, that seemed to shake out light when he moved his head quickly, 'showing poor Mr. Casaubon by contrast altogether rayless'; by his looking an incarnation of the spring which we must suppose he typifies; by his versatility and quick transitions of mood and feeling, being made of such impressionable stuff that the bow of a violin drawn near him cleverly would at one stroke change the aspect of the world for him; by his easy unconventional manners and attitudes, and indifference to the solid goods of life. All these are doubtless attractions. Nature has done much for him, but duty—by which all the other characters of the story are tested—altogether fails in him. He does what he likes, whether right or wrong, to the end of the story; he makes no sacrifices; even his devotion to Dorothea does not preserve him from an unworthy flirtation with his friend Lydgate's wife. He is happy by luck, not desert. Just as devotees of the Virgin are said to be saved at the last moment by a medal worn or a rosary said in her honour, so the chance of his choosing the right woman to worship (though not at the right time) saves him from the consequences of idleness and mere self-pleasing; while poor Lydgate—ten times the better man—suffers not only in happiness, but in his noblest ambitions, and sinks to the lower

level of a good practice and a good income because he marries and is
faithful to the vain selfish creature whom Ladislaw merely flirts with.
We daresay, however, it is inevitable that a grand woman who never
in her life called things by the same name as other people should not
match in her own degree. There is quite enough of the vagabond in
Ladislaw, in spite of his remote kinship with Mr. Casaubon, to make
Mrs. Cadwallader's judgment stick by one, that Dorothea might as
well marry an Italian with white mice; for the author spares us nothing,
and allows his enemies to sum up his genealogy—'the son of a Polish
fiddler, and grandson of a thieving Jew pawnbroker.' It is the man, not
his antecedents, that the ideal woman cares for. But, after all, what is the
example she sets? How does it differ from the ball-room choice of any
ordinary girl who takes the pleasant fellow who pleases her fancy? not
that it is reasonable to require or to expect her to make the same sort
of mistake twice over. This Mrs. Cadwallader—a bright bit of worldly
common sense always welcome in the county circle we get pleasantly
familiar with—is, however, equally caustic upon both objects of
Dorothea's choice. Celia tells her that her sister marries Mr. Casaubon
because he has a great soul. 'With all my heart,' she replies. 'Oh, Mrs.
Cadwallader,' cries Celia, 'I don't think it can be nice to marry a man
with a great soul.' 'Well, my dear, take warning. You know the look of
one now; when the next comes and wants to marry you, don't accept
him.'

We have left ourselves no space for more than recognizing the
immense amount of character described. The book is like a portrait
gallery. From Mr. Brooke with his ingenious summaries, his universal
experience, and never failing reservations—highly amusing to the
reader, but more tolerated in his circle than the ordinary feeling of
human nature towards bores makes quite natural—to the wonderful
group of hungry expectants gathered round the miser's death-bed,
voice, eyes, movement, physiognomy, all are photographed from the
life. Though here we must point out some prejudices, as we would fain
suppose them, which make the author hard upon natural distinctions
of eye and complexion. All her weak and mean and knavish people
are blond, as she calls fair-skinned: and blue eyes are uniformly dis-
ingenuous. The acutest observer is not free from prepossession. But
what a ceaselessly busy observation; what nicety of penetration; what a
tenacity of memory are indicated by these different social pictures! All
the gradations of rank and class, nicely measured and appreciated, even
while the distinctions of rank are represented as provoking the low

ambition of common souls, and therefore things to be overstepped by
natures of higher insight and more universal good will. In such questions
the book is a deliberate challenge to society as at present constituted.
Where we pause to doubt or to dispute we may detect an especial care
and point in the wording, showing the author to be aware of the
reader's arrested attention. As a challenge we have dwelt on the design
of this remarkable book, hoping to return to it on a future occasion[1] as
a novel of character and familiar social life.

47. Edward Dowden: George Eliot's 'second self'

1872

These are the opening paragraphs of Dowden's general essay on
George Eliot, *Contemporary Review* (August 1872), xx, 403–22.

Edward Dowden (1843–1913), the first Professor of English
Literature at Trinity College Dublin, is best known as a Shakespearian scholar, the author of *Shakespeare, his Mind and Art* (1875)
and editor of many of the plays. Lewes told him that he was
'moved to tears' by this essay, and that when he read aloud selected
passages to George Eliot, 'They touched her very much' (*Letters*,
v, 300). At one time, Dowden intended to expand this essay into a
study of the novelist (see Introduction, p. 30 and No. 64).

When we have passed in review the works of that great writer who
calls herself George Eliot, and given for a time our use of sight to her
portraitures of men and women, what form, as we move away,
persists on the field of vision, and remains the chief centre of interest
for the imagination? The form not of Tito, or Maggie, or Dinah, or

[1] See *Saturday Review* (21 December 1872), xxxiv, 794–6.

Silas, but of one who, if not the real George Eliot, is that 'second self' who writes her books, and lives and speaks through them. Such a second self of an author is perhaps more substantial than any mere human personality encumbered with the accidents of flesh and blood and daily living. It stands at some distance from the primary self, and differs considerably from its fellow. It presents its person to us with fewer reserves; it is independent of local and temporary motives of speech or of silence; it knows no man after the flesh; it is more than an individual; it utters secrets, but secrets which all men of all ages are to catch; while, behind it, lurks well pleased the veritable historical self secure from impertinent observation and criticism. With this second self of George Eliot it is, not with the actual historical person, that we have to do. And when, having closed her books, we gaze outward with the mind's eye, the spectacle we see is that most impressive spectacle of a great nature, which has suffered and has now attained, which was perplexed and has now grasped the clue—standing before us not without tokens on lip and brow of the strife and the suffering, but resolute, and henceforth possessed of something which makes self-mastery possible. The strife is not ended, the pain may still be resurgent; but we perceive on which side victory must lie.

This personal accent in the writings of George Eliot does not interfere with their dramatic truthfulness; it adds to the power with which they grasp the heart and conscience of the reader. We cannot say with confidence of any one of her creations that it is a projection of herself; the lines of their movement are not deflected by hidden powers of attraction or repulsion peculiar to the mind of the author; most noteworthy is her impartiality towards the several creatures of her imagination; she condemns but does not hate; she is cold or indifferent to none; each lives his own life, good or bad; but the author is present in the midst of them, indicating, interpreting; and we discern in the moral laws, the operation of which presides over the action of each story, those abstractions from the common fund of truth which the author has found most needful to her own deepest life. We feel in reading these books that we are in the presence of a soul and a soul which has had a history.

At the same time the novels of George Eliot are not didactic treatises. They are primarily works of art, and George Eliot herself is artist as much as she is teacher. Many good things in particular passages of her writings are detachable; admirable sayings can be cleared from their surroundings, and presented by themselves, knocked out clean as we knock out fossils from a piece of limestone. But if we separate the moral soul of any complete work of hers from its artistic medium, if we murder to dissect, we lose far more than we gain. When a work of art can be understood only by enjoying it, the art is of a high kind. The best criticism of Shakspeare is not that which comes out of profound cogitation, but out of immense enjoyment; and the most valuable critic is the critic who communicates sympathy by an exquisite record of his own delights, not the critic who attempts to communicate thought. In a less degree the same is true of George Eliot. There is not a hard kernel of dogma at the centre of her art, and around it a sheath or envelope which we break and throw away; the moral significance coalesces with the narrative, and lives through the characters.

48. H. Lawrenny [Edith Simcox], review, *Academy*

1 January 1873, iv, 1–4

Edith Jemima Simcox (1844–1901) was a learned and gifted writer on a great variety of subjects, and a zealous social reformer. In addition to a great number of articles, she wrote *Natural Law: An Essay in Ethics* (1877), *Episodes in the Lives of Men, Women, and Lovers* (1882), and *Primitive Civilizations* (1894). She was the most embarrassingly passionate of George Eliot's several 'spiritual daughters'. See K. A. McKenzie, *Edith Simcox and George Eliot*, 1961.

Contemporary criticism of great works is apt to prove unsatisfactory, for even when their greatness is recognised at once, the critic labours under a double disadvantage: an unwonted sense of responsibility restrains the free expression of unmotived admiration, and the easy volubility of praise, which is enough for slighter merits, makes way for a guarded tone of respect that looks like coldness on the surface. Nor is this all; for the vocabulary of positive eulogium is soon exhausted; criticism to be significant must be comparative, and there is an obvious difficulty in estimating by old-established standards of excellence a new work that may contain within itself a fresh standard for the guidance and imitation of futurity. For the theory of art is after all only a patchwork of inference from the practice of artists, and, to quit generalities, in one clearly defined and admirable branch of imaginative art—the English novel—our ideal is simply one or other of the masterpieces of one or other of the great novelists between Fielding and George Eliot. *Tom Jones, Clarissa Harlowe, Waverley, Pride and Prejudice, Vanity Fair, Adam Bede*—to which some might wish to add *Eugene Aram, Pickwick,* and *Jane Eyre*—are the sources from whence all theories of the novel, as a prose narrative representation of manners, character and passion, ultimately derive. In truth, variety and intensity, the best of these works left something to be supplied by excellence of a different type: there are stronger as well as more complex passions than Fielding has drawn; Richardson's subtlety works in a narrow field; Miss Austen's knowledge of the world was scanty, and Thackeray's theory of human nature one-sided, while on the other hand it might be argued that an over-systematic plot or too thrilling situations give a *primâ facie* look of unreality to scenes of modern life. No one of course makes it a ground of complaint against these authors that they failed to combine incompatible perfections, but a reference to the natural limitations of the styles in which they severally succeeded may help to show what space was left for a fresh combination of the old ingredients.

Middlemarch marks an epoch in the history of fiction in so far as its incidents are taken from the inner life, as the action is developed by the direct influence of mind on mind and character on character, as the material circumstances of the outer world are made subordinate and accessory to the artistic presentation of a definite passage of mental experience, but chiefly as giving a background of perfect realistic truth to a profoundly imaginative psychological study. The effect is as new as if we could suppose a *Wilhelm Meister* written by Balzac. In *Silas Marner, Romola,* and the author's other works there is the same power, but it does not so completely and exclusively determine the form in which the conception is placed before us. In *Silas Marner* there is a natural and obvious unity in the life of the weaver, but in *Romola*—where alone the interest is at once as varied and as profound as in *Middlemarch*—though the historic glories of Florence, the passions belonging to what, as compared with the nineteenth century, is an heroic age, are in perfect harmony with the grand manner of treating spiritual problems, yet the realism, the positive background of fact, which we can scarcely better bear to miss, has necessarily some of the character of an hypothesis, and does not inspire us with the same confidence as truths we can verify for ourselves. For that reason alone, on the mere point of artistic harmony of construction, we should rate the last work as the greatest; and to say that *Middlemarch* is George Eliot's greatest work is to say that it has scarcely a superior and very few equals in the whole wide range of English fiction.

As 'a study of provincial life,' if it were nothing more, *Middlemarch* would have a lasting charm for students of human nature in its less ephemeral costumes; besides the crowds of men and women whom we have all known in real life, where, however, to our dimmer vision, they seemed less real and life-like than in the book, the relations between the different clusters, the proportions in which the different elements mix, the points of contact and the degree of isolation in the different ranks; the contented coexistence of town and county, the channels of communication between the two always open and yet so rarely used, the effect of class distinctions in varying the mental horizon and obliging the most matter-of-fact observer to see a few things in perspective,— all the subtle factors which make up the character of a definite state of society are given with inimitable accuracy and fulness of insight. The picture in its main outlines is as true of the England of to-day or the England of a hundred years ago as of the England of the Reform agitation. The world as we know it has its wise and good, its fools and hypocrites scattered up and down a neutral-tinted mass in much the same proportion as at Middlemarch. The only difference is that they are not so plainly recognisable, and this is perhaps the reason that a first perusal of the book seems to have an almost oppressive effect on ordinary readers, somewhat as little children are frightened at a live automaton toy. It is not natural to most men to know so much of their fellow-creatures as George Eliot shows them, to penetrate behind the scenes in so many homes, to understand the motives of ambiguous conduct, to watch 'like gods knowing good and evil' the tangled course of intermingled lives, the remote mainsprings of impulse and the wide-eddying effects of action. Even with the author's assistance it is not easy to maintain the same height of observant wisdom for long, and since the intricacy of the subject is real, a feeling of even painful bewilderment in its contemplation is not entirely unbecoming.

But the complicated conditions of so seemingly simple a thing as provincial life are not the main subject of the work. The busy idleness of Middlemarch, its trade, its politics, its vestry meetings, and its neighbouring magnates, only form the background of relief to two or three spiritual conflicts, the scenery amongst which two or three souls spend some eventful years in working out their own salvation and their neighbours', or in effecting, with equal labour, something less than salvation for both. The story of these conflicts and struggles is the thread which unites the whole, and sympathy with its incidents is the force that reconciles the reader to the unwonted strain upon his intellectual faculties already noticed; and to the yet further effort necessary to recognise the fact that the real and the ideal sides of our common nature do coexist in just such relations, and with just such proportionate force as the author reveals. For, without this admission, it is impossible to appreciate the full literary and artistic perfection of the work as a whole; some readers may delight spontaneously in the author's moral earnestness, and only admire her satirical insight, while others delight in her satire and coldly admit the excellence of the moral purpose; but the two are only opposite aspects of the same large theory of the universe, which is at once so charitable and so melancholy that it would be fairly intolerable (although true) without the sauce of an unsparing humour.

Middlemarch is the story of two rather sad fatalities, of two lives which, starting with more than ordinary promise, had to rest content with very ordinary achievement, and could not derive unmixed consolation from the knowledge, which was the chief prize of their struggles, that failure is never altogether undeserved. One of the original mottoes to the first book gives the clue to what follows:

1st Gent. Our deeds are fetters that we forge ourselves.
2nd Gent. Ay, truly; but I think it is the world
That brings the iron:

but as the action proceeds a further consciousness gathers shape: 'It always remains true that if we had been greater, circumstances would have been less strong against us;' which is still more simply expressed in Dorothea's 'feeling that there was always something better which she might have done, if she had only been better and known better.' The two failures, however, have little in common but their irrevocable necessity. From one point of view, Dorothea's is the most tragical, for the fault in her case seems to be altogether in the nature and constitution of the universe; her devotion and purity of intention are altogether beautiful, even when, for lack of knowledge, they are expended in what seems to be the wrong place, but it is a sad reflection that their beauty must always rest on a basis of illusion because there is no right place for their bestowal. Except in the chapter of her marriages Dorothea is a perfect woman, but for a perfect woman any marriage is a *mésalliance*, and as such, 'certainly those determining acts of her life were not ideally beautiful.' But we can as little tell as the Middle-marchers 'what else that was in her power she ought rather to have done.' If she had had no illusions she might have been a useful Lady Bountiful, managing her own affairs like Goethe's Theresa,[1] a personage who inspires but mediocre interest, and might have married Mrs. Cadwallader's philanthropic Lord Triton without suspicion of *mésalliance*: but then she would not have been Dorothea, not the impetuous young woman with 'a heart large enough for the Virgin Mary,' whose sighs, when she thinks her lover is untrue, are breathed for 'all the troubles of all the people on the face of the earth.' The world must be ugly for her power of seeing it as it is not to be beautiful, just as men's lives must be sad and miserable to call for the exercise of her infinite charity. Still the illusions are sweet and the charity beneficent, and since women like Dorothea are content to live only for others, life may offer occasions enough for self-sacrifice to compensate them for the natural impossibility of shaping an ideally perfect course through the multitudinous imperfections of real existence. It would be un-generous to accept such a fate for them without reluctance, and there-fore some sadness must always mix with our thoughts of the historic and unhistoric Dorotheas of the world; but it is also true that the moral force exercised by such characters can no more be wasted than any physical impulse, and that, without the disinterested virtue of the few, the conflicting appetites of a world of Rosamonds would make life impossible. To keep society alive is perhaps a worthier mission than to cheer the declining years of Mr. Casaubon; but to do more than keep it alive, to make it a fit home for future Dorotheas, the present supply of such missionaries would have to be increased; and they are born, not made. Perhaps the strongest example of the author's instinctive truthfulness is that she never loses sight of the limits to the exercise of the power which she represents so vividly and values so highly. A life's growth of empty egotism like Mr. Casaubon's cannot be melted

[1] Characters in George Farquhar's *The Beaux Stratagem*(1707) and Goethe's *Wilhelm Meister* (1796) respectively.

in a year of marriage, even to Dorothea; with a generous example close before her, Rosamond can be almost honest for once at little expense, but she can no more change her character than her complexion or the colour of her eyes, or than she can unmake the whole series of circumstances which have made her life less negatively innocent than Celia's. A little more selfishness, a little more obstinacy, a little less good fortune, and especially life in a just lower moral atmosphere, make all the difference between a pretty, prosaic, kittenish wife and a kind of well-conducted domestic vampire. It is by such contrasts as these that George Eliot contrives to preach tolerance even while showing with grim distinctness the ineffaceableness of moral distinctions and the unrelenting force of moral obligations. If virtue is a matter of capacity, defect only calls for pity; but defects which we do not venture to blame may be none the less fatal to the higher life, while the smallest shoot of virtue, if the heavens and earth chance to be propitious to its growth, may spread into a stately tree.

Such at least is the inference suggested by another contrast, that between Lydgate and Fred, for though marriage appears the 'determining act' in their lives also, it is itself determined by certain essential points of character and disposition. Fred's honest boyish affection for a girl who is a great deal too good for him brings its own reward, as that kind of virtue often will; there was enough self-abandonment in it to deserve a generous answer, and in the long-run people generally get their deserts. The failure of Lydgate's intellectual aspirations, as the consequence of a marriage contracted altogether at the bidding of his lower nature, is of course much more elaborately treated than Fred's simple 'love-problem.' Unlike most of the other characters, Lydgate does not become thoroughly intelligible till the last number of the work has been read in connection with the first: then he appears as a masculine counterpart to Dorothea with the relative proportions of head and heart reversed. But while it was abstractedly impossible for Dorothea to be altogether wise, without detriment to the peculiar and charming character of her goodness, there was nothing but concrete human infirmity to prevent Lydgate from combining the mind of Bichat and the morals of Fred Vincy. Instead of such a compound the actual and very human Lydgate is one of those men whose lives are cut in two, whose intellectual interests have no direct connection with their material selves, and who only discover the impossibility of living according to habit or tradition when brought by accident or their own heedlessness face to face with difficulties that require thought as well as resolution. There was not room in the life he con-templated for a soul much larger than Rosamond's, and it may be doubted whether the Rosamond he wished for would not, by a merely passive influence, have been as obstructive to his wide speculations, for he was just, though not expansive, and the duties entailed by one act of weakness may multiply and branch as much as if they were of a valuable stock. On the other hand, if the scientific ardour had been more absorbing, he might have gone on his own way, crushing all poor Rosamond's little schemes of opposition, and then she would have been the victim instead of the oppressor, but his character would have been as far from ideal excellence as before. The interest culminates when Lydgate, entangled with the consequences of his own and other people's wrongdoing, finds in Dorothea the beneficent influence that spends itself in setting straight whatever is not constitutionally crooked, but he has also of course found out by then that the events which led him to cross her path were the same that had proved fatal to his aspirations; the enlarged sympathies were gathered during the process that paralysed his original activity. The story of a man 'who has not done what he once meant to do' has always a strong element of pathos, but when what he meant to do was not in itself impossible, like the realization of Dorothea's visions, there remains a twofold consolation; if possible in itself, and yet not done as proposed, it must have been impossible to the proposer, and therefore his failure is free from blame, while disappointment of his hopes, though painful, cannot be regarded as an unmitigated evil, since such fallen aspirations as Lydgate's are still something it is better to have had than to be altogether without. Natural fatality and the logic of facts are made to persuade us that all regrets are unpractical except the most unpractical of all—'if we had only known better and been better'—but the first step towards solving a problem is to state it; and one of the many merits of *Middlemarch* is that it shows the inadequacy of all other less arduous short cuts to the reformation of society. Ordinary mortals who are not fatalists have no excuse for calling a book sad which makes the redress of every one's wrongs rest in the last resort with themselves; while people whose idea of the world is already as gloomy as it well can be, cannot fail to derive some consolation from the thought that George Eliot's wider know-ledge and juster perceptions find here and there a little to admire as well as much everywhere to laugh at.

There is no occasion to dwell in detail on the story which every one has read. The studies of Casaubon and Bulstrode would each furnish matter for an ordinary review, though here we have treated them as altogether secondary to the development of the two principal characters. Besides their more direct influence on the action, both serve, with old Featherstone, to illustrate the blindness of selfish calculation. Bulstrode is none the better either for his manslaughter or for his attempt at restitution. If Mr. Casaubon's will had not drawn Dorothea and Ladislaw together, something else would; for the moral forces at work in any direction can only be arrested by other forces of the same kind, while no moral jugglery will ward off the material effects of causes set to work long before. By way of relief from such troublesome spectacles, the Garth household is invaluable, with its common-sense happiness not corrupted by an undue contempt for 'notions.' The choruses of slightly belated popular wisdom, the Featherstone family, Mrs. Dollop's clients, the Middlemarch tea-parties, the dowager Lady Chettam's society, appear from time to time to comment with their usual insight and *à propos* on the doings of their betters. But it is perhaps a mistake to suppose the intention of this class of character to be altogether satirical. The author spends too much invention upon them for them to be quite so stupid as they look. The minds of Mrs. Waule and sister Martha, as of Mrs. Holt and the Tulliver connection move erratically, but their reasoning is often so imaginative that it would be scarcely a compliment to suggest that they only represent, as choruses should, the opinions of the inspired *vox populi* in the process of making: they are an idealization rather than a caricature of the popular sense.

In a work that has scarcely a quality which is not a merit, it is hard to determine what points to leave unnoticed. The gift, shared only, amongst contemporaries by Mr. Browning, of choosing similes and illustrations that do really illustrate the nature of the things compared, is exercised, if anything, more freely than in the author's other works; but her style, always polished and direct, seems to have become still more sharply condensed; the dialogues, always natural, still more simple in their force. This is especially true of the scenes in the last book, where Dorothea probably uses fewer and plainer words than have ever served to express deep feeling before. Mastery like this is the best title to immortality, and posterity will only do the present generation justice if it believes that real emotion speaks so now, if it speaks at all, though in real life it more commonly observes an awkward silence. Many of the less serious conversations have the same classical perfection of finish; one, for instance, between Mary Garth and Rosamond, near the end of part i., will show to those curious in such matters better than all Mr. Trollope's voluminous works, how girls in the nineteenth century discuss the matters in which they are privately interested. The family circle of the Vincys in the chapter before is scarcely inferior, and though we only see in it now a singularly faithful sketch from nature, there can be little doubt of its outliving the nature it represents. It is a little curious that Mr. Brooke, who represents a type, should seem, according to the general experience, to be a commoner acquaintance than Sir James Chettam, who represents a class, which we should be loth to think threatened with extinction. Both are friends of whom one does not soon weary of telling, but if we had indefinite space at command it would be better spent in quoting their sayings or the author's own epigrams. Failing this resource, we can only return to the point from whence we started, the natural incapacity of criticism (or critics— 'the people who have failed in literature and art') to throw much light upon a work like *Middlemarch*. All critics are not like Mr. Borthrop Trumbull, who 'was an admirer by nature, and would have liked to have the universe under his hammer, feeling that it would go at a higher figure for his recommendation.' On the contrary, we hold that an auctioneer's catalogue of the divers and sundry beauties, rarities, and profundities of these admirable volumes, can add nothing to the impression which a leisurely perusal (let no one read them in haste) will leave on the mind of every man and woman whose mental and artistic perceptions are sound and unblunted. And if praise is unnecessary, it is impertinent. Spontaneous admiration is one of the few pleasures of life, but the spurious literary enthusiasm which has to be conjured up with a bede roll of respected adjectives is a caricature of the true feeling. In fact, for the moment, we are of Sir James Chettam's mind. He has just said: 'I don't *like* Casaubon.' (Can anything be more conclusive? if he had said: 'I *like* Middlemarch!') 'He did not usually find it easy to give his reasons; it seemed to him strange that people should not know them without being told, since he only felt what was reasonable.' Except by the amiable baronet, reasons for *disliking* a person—or a book—are easily found; but the best reason for an admiration of *Middlemarch* is—the book itself.

49. Sidney Colvin, review, *Fortnightly Review*

19 January 1873, xiii, 142-7

Sir Sidney Colvin (1845–1927), a Fellow of Trinity College, was Professor of Fine Art at Cambridge (1873–85) and keeper of the prints and drawings at the British Museum (1884–1912). He wrote lives of Landor (1881), and Keats (1887), and edited the letters of Keats (1887) and the Edinburgh edition of R. L. Stevenson's works (1894–7). He was a regular visitor at the Priory.

Fifteen months of pausing and recurring literary excitement are at an end; and *Middlemarch*, the chief English book of the immediate present, lies complete before us. Now that we have the book as a whole, what place does it seem to take among the rest with which its illustrious writer has enriched, I will not say posterity, because for posterity every present is apt in turn to prove itself a shallow judge, but her own generation and us who delight to honour her?

In the sense in which anything is called ripe because of fulness and strength, I think the last of George Eliot's novels is also the ripest. *Middlemarch* is extraordinarily full and strong, even among the company to which it belongs. And though I am not sure that it is the property of George Eliot's writing to satisfy, its property certainly is to rouse and attach, in proportion to its fulness and strength. There is nothing in the literature of the day so rousing—to the mind of the day there is scarcely anything so rousing in all literature—as her writing is. What she writes is so full of her time. It is observation, imagination, pathos, wit and humour, all of a high class in themselves; but what is more, all saturated with modern ideas, and poured into a language of which every word bites home with peculiar sharpness to the contemporary consciousness. That is what makes it less safe than it might seem at first sight to speak for posterity in such a case. We are afraid of exaggerating the meaning such work will have for those who come after us, for the very reason that we feel its meaning so pregnant for ourselves. If, indeed, the ideas of to-day are certain to be the ideas of to-morrow and the day after, if scientific thought and the positive synthesis are indubitably to rule the world, then any one, it should seem, might speak boldly enough to George Eliot's place. For the general definition of her work, I should say, is precisely this—that, among writers of the imagination, she has taken the lead in expressing and discussing the lives and ways of common folks—*votum, timor, ira, voluptas*[1]—in terms of scientific thought and the positive synthesis. She has walked between two epochs, upon the confines of two worlds, and has described the old in terms of the new. To the old world belong the elements of her experience, to the new world the elements of her reflection on experience. The elements of her experience are the 'English Provincial Life' before the Reform Bill—the desires and alarms, indignations and satisfactions, of the human breast in county towns and villages, farms and parsonages, manor-houses, counting-houses, surgeries, streets and lanes, shops and fields, of midlands unshaken in their prejudices and unvisited by the steam-engine. To the new world belong the elements of her reflection; the many-sided culture which looks back upon prejudice with analytical amusement; the philosophy which declares the human family deluded in its higher dreams, dependent upon itself, and bound thereby to a closer if a sadder brotherhood; the habit in regarding and meditating physical laws, and the facts of sense and life, which leads up to that philosophy and belongs to it; the mingled depth of bitterness and tenderness in the human temper of which the philosophy becomes the spring.

Thus there is the most pointed contrast between the matter of these English tales and the manner of their telling. The matter is antiquated in our recollections, the manner seems to anticipate the future of our thoughts. Plenty of other writers have taken humdrum and narrow aspects of English life with which they were familiar, and by delicacy of perception and justness of rendering have put them together into pleasant works of literary art, without running the matter into a manner out of direct correspondence with it. But this procedure of George Eliot's is a newer thing in literature, and infinitely harder to judge of, than the gray and tranquil harmonies of that other mode of art. For no writer uses so many instruments in riveting the interest of the cultivated reader about the characters, and springs of character, which she is exhibiting. First, I say, she has the perpetual application of her own intelligence to the broad problems and conclusions of modern

[1] 'their wishes, fears, anger, pleasures' (Juvenal, *Satire* I, 85).

thought. That, for instance, when Fred Vincy, having brought losses upon the Garth family, feels his own dishonour more than their suffering, brings the reflection how '*we are most of us brought up in the notion that the highest motive for not doing a wrong is something irrespective of the beings who would suffer the wrong.*' That again, a few pages later, brings the humorous allusions to Caleb Garth's classification of human employments, into business, politics, preaching, learning, and amusement, as one which '*like the categories of more celebrated men, would not be acceptable in these more advanced times.*' And that makes it impossible to describe the roguery of a horse-dealer without suggesting that he '*regarded horse-dealing as the finest of the arts, and might have argued plausibly that it had nothing to do with morality.*'

Next, this writer possesses, in her own sympathetic insight into the workings of human nature, a psychological instrument which will be perpetually displaying its power, its subtlety and trenchancy, in passages like this which lays bare the working of poor Mrs. Bulstrode's faithful mind upon the revelation of her husband's guilt: 'Along with her brother's looks and words, there darted into her mind the idea of some guilt in her husband. Then, under the working of terror, came the image of her husband exposed to disgrace; *and then, after an instant of scorching shame in which she only felt the eyes of the world, with one leap of her heart she was at his side in mournful but unreproaching fellowship with shame and isolation.*' Of the same trenchancy and potency, equally subtle and equally sure of themselves, are a hundred other processes of analysis, whether applied to serious crises—like that prolonged one during which Bulstrode wavers before the passive murder which shall rid him of his one obstacle as an efficient servant of God—or to such trivial crises as occur in the experiences of a Mrs. Dollop or a Mrs. Taft, or others who, being their betters, still belong to the class of 'well-meaning women knowing very little of their own motives.' And this powerful knowledge of human nature is still only one of many instruments for exposing a character and turning it about. What the character itself thinks and feels, exposed by this, will receive a simultaneous commentary in what the modern analytic mind has to remark upon such thoughts and feelings: see a good instance in the account . . . of Mr. Casaubon's motives before marriage and experiences after it.

Then, the writer's studies in science and physiology will constantly come in to suggest for the spiritual processes of her personages an explanation here or an illustration there. For a stroke of overwhelming power in this kind, take what is said in one place of Bulstrode—that 'he shrank from a direct lie with an intensity disproportionate to the number of his more indirect misdeeds. *But many of these misdeeds were like the subtle muscular movements which are not taken account of in the consciousness; though they bring about the end that we fix in our minds and desire. And it is only what we are vividly conscious of that we can vividly imagine to be seen by Omniscience.*'

And it is yet another instrument which the writer handles when she seizes on critical points of physical look and gesture in her personages, in a way which is scientific and her own. True, there are many descriptions, and especially of the beauty and gestures of Dorothea—and these are written with a peculiarly loving and as it were watchful exquisiteness—which may be put down as belonging to the ordinary resources of art. But look at Caleb Garth; he is a complete physiognomical study in the sense of Mr. Darwin, with the 'deepened depression in the outer angle of his bushy eyebrows, which gave his face a peculiar mildness;' with his trick of 'broadening himself by putting his thumbs into his arm-holes,' and the rest. Such are Rosamond's ways of turning her neck aside and patting her hair when she is going to be obstinate. So, we are not allowed to forget 'a certain massiveness in Lydgate's manner and tone, corresponding with his physique;' nor indeed, any point of figure and physiognomy which strike the author's imagination as symptomatic. Symptomatic is the best word. There is a medical strain in the tissue of the story. There is a profound sense of the importance of physiological conditions in human life. But further still, I think, there is something like a medical habit in the writer, of examining her own creations for their symptoms, which runs through her descriptive and narrative art and gives it some of its peculiar manner.

So that, apart from the presence of rousing thought in general maxims and allusions, we know now what we mean when we speak of the fulness and strength derived, in the dramatic and narrative part of the work, from the use of so many instruments as we have seen. Then comes the question, do these qualities satisfy us as thoroughly as they rouse and interest? Sometimes I think they do, and sometimes not. Nothing evidently can be more satisfying, more illuminating, than that sentence which explained, by a primitive fact in the experimental relations of mind and body, a peculiar kind of bluntness in the conscience of the religious Bulstrode. And generally, wherever the novelist applies her philosophy or science to serious purposes, even if it may be applied too often, its effect seems to me good. But in lighter applications I doubt if the same kind of thing is not sometimes mistaken. The wit

50. A. V. Dicey, unsigned review, *Nation*

23 January 1873, xvi, 60–2; 30 January 1873, xvi, 76–7

Albert Venn Dicey (1835-1922) was a Vinerian Professor of English Law at Oxford (1882-1909) and Principal of the Working Men's College in London (1899-1912). He wrote extensively on legal and political questions, and was the occasional London correspondent of the *Nation*. His review was published in two parts (see Introduction, p. 29).

I.

There is a well-known remark of Novalis that character is destiny,[1] which George Eliot criticises severely in the *Mill on the Floss*, on the ground that destiny depends rather on circumstances than on disposition. *Middlemarch* might have been written to illustrate at once the truth of the dictum and of the criticism. The main feature of the book is, that it is a history of the development, and generally of the tragic development, of characters which are sometimes noble, sometimes base, and generally neither very noble nor very base, amidst the commonplace circumstances of a country town. That this is the author's theme, as regards Dorothea, is patent. Her outward history, and the moral to be drawn from it, are thus summed up:

She was spoken of (in Middlemarch) to a younger generation as a fine girl who married a sickly clergyman old enough to be her father, and in little more than a year after his death gave up her estate to marry his cousin, young enough to have been his son, with no property and not well-born. Those who had not seen anything of Dorothea observed that she could not have been a 'nice woman,' else she would not have married either the one or the other. Certainly these determining acts of her life were not ideally beautiful; they were the mixed result of a young and noble impulse struggling under prosaic conditions. Among the many remarks made on her mistakes, it was never said in the neighborhood of Middlemarch that such mistakes could not have happened if the society into which she was born had not smiled on propositions of

---

[1] In *Heinrich von Osterdinger* (1802), part II.

fortunes in the book, with laughter or sympathy or pity or indignation or love, there will arise all sorts of questionings, debatings, such as do not arise after a reading which has left the mind satisfied. One calls in question this or that point in the conduct of the story; the attitude which the writer personally assumes towards her own creations; the general lesson which seems to underlie her scheme; above all, the impression which its issue leaves upon oneself.

The questions one asks are such as, within limits like these, it would be idle to attempt to solve, or even to state, except in the most fragmentary way. Are not, for instance, some points in the story a little coarsely invented and handled? At the very outset, is not the hideous nature of Dorothea's blind sacrifice too ruthlessly driven home to us, when it ought to have been allowed to reveal itself by gentler degrees? Is it not too repulsive to talk of the moles on Casaubon's face, and to make us loathe the union from the beginning? Is not the formalism and dryness of Casaubon's nature a little overdone in his first conversation and his letter of courtship? Or again, is not the whole intrigue of Ladislaw's birth and Bulstrode's guilt, the Jew pawnbroker and Raffles, somewhat common and poor? The story is made to hinge twice, at two important junctures, upon the incidents of watching by a deathbed. Is that scant invention, or is it a just device for bringing out, under nearly parallel circumstances, the opposite characters of Mary Garth and of Bulstrode—her untroubled and decisive integrity under difficulties, his wavering conscience, which, when to be passive is already to be a murderer, permits itself at last in something just beyond passiveness? Or, to shift the ground of question, does not the author seem a little unwarrantably hard upon some of her personages and kind to others? Fred and Rosamond Vincy, for instance—one would have said there was not so much to choose. The author, however, is on the whole kind to the brother, showing up his faults but not harshly, and making him in the end an example of how an amiable spendthrift may be redeemed by a good man's help and a good girl's love. While to the sister, within whose mind 'there was not room enough for luxuries to look small in,' she shows a really merciless animosity, and gibbets her as an example of how an unworthy wife may degrade the career of a man of high purposes and capacities. Celia, too, who is not really so very much higher a character, the author makes quite a pet of in comparison, and puts her in situations where all her small virtues tell; and so on. Minute differences of character for better or worse may justly be shown, of course, as producing vast differences of effect under the impulsion of circumstances. Still, I do not think it is altogether fancy to find wanting here the impartiality of the greatest creators towards their mind's offspring.

Then, for the general lesson of the book, it is not easy to feel quite sure what it is, or how much importance the author gives it. In her prelude and conclusion both, she seems to insist upon the design of illustrating the necessary disappointment of a woman's nobler aspirations in a society not made to second noble aspirations in a woman. And that is one of the most burning lessons which any writer could set themselves to illustrate. But then, Dorothea does not suffer in her ideal aspirations from yielding to the pressure of social opinion. She suffers in them from finding that what she has done, in marrying an old scholar in the face of social opinion, was done under a delusion as to the old scholar's character. 'Exactly,' is apparently the author's drift; 'but it is society which so nurtures women that their ideals cannot but be ideals of delusion.' Taking this as the author's main point (and I think prelude and conclusion leave it still ambiguous), there are certainly passages enough in the body of the narrative which point the same remonstrance against what society does for women. 'The shallowness of a water-nixie's soul may have a charm till she becomes didactic:' that describes the worthlessness of what men vulgarly prize in women. 'In the British climate there is no incompatibility between scientific insight and furnished lodgings. The incompatibility is chiefly between scientific ambition and a wife who objects to that kind of residence.' That points to the rarity of a woman, as women are brought up, who prefers the things of the mind to luxury. ' "Of course she is devoted to her husband," said Rosamond, implying a notion of necessary sequence which the scientific man regarded as the prettiest possible for a woman.' That points with poignant irony to the science, as to the realities of society and the heart, of men whose science is solid in other things.

It is perhaps in pursuance of the same idea that Dorothea's destiny, after Casaubon has died, and she is free from the consequences of a first illusory ideal, is not made very brilliant after all. She cannot be an Antigone or a Theresa. She marries the man of her choice, and bears him children; but we have been made to feel all along that he is hardly worthy of her. There is no sense of triumph in it; there is rather a sense of sadness in a subdued and restricted, if not now a thwarted destiny. In this issue there is a deep depression; there is that blending of the author's bitterness with her profound tenderness of which I have already spoken. And upon this depends, or with it hangs together, that feeling of

337

uncertainty and unsatisfiedness as to the whole fable and its impression which remains with the reader when all is done. He could spare the joybells—the vulgar upshot of happiness for ever after—Sophia surrendered to the arms of her enraptured Jones—if he felt quite sure of the moral or intellectual point of view which had dictated so chastened and subdued a conclusion. As it is, he does not feel clear enough about the point of view, the lesson, the main moral and intellectual outcome, to put up with that which he feels to be uncomfortable in the combinations of the story, and flat in the fates of friends and acquaintances who have been brought so marvellously near to him.

That these and such like questionings should remain in the mind, after the reading of a great work of fiction, would in ordinary phrase be said to indicate that, however great the other qualities of the work, it was deficient in qualities of art. The fact is, that this writer brings into her fiction so many new elements, and gives it pregnancy and significance in so many unaccustomed directions, that it is presumptuousness to pronounce in that way as to the question of art. Certainly, it is possible to write with as little illusion, or with forms of disillusion much more cynical, as to society and its dealings and issues, and yet to leave a more harmonious and definite artistic impression than is here left. French writers perpetually do so. But then George Eliot, with her science and her disillusion, has the sense of bad and good as the great French literary artists have not got it, and is taken up, as they are not, with the properly moral elements of human life and struggling. They exceed in all that pertains to the passions of the individual; she cares more than they do for the general beyond the individual. That it is by which she rouses—I say rouses, attaches, and elevates—so much more than they do, even if her combinations satisfy much less. Is it, then, that a harmonious and satisfying literary art is impossible under these conditions? Is it that a literature, which confronts all the problems of life and the world, and recognises all the springs of action, and all that clogs the springs, and all that comes from their smooth or impeded working, and all the importance of one life for the mass,—is it that such a literature must be like life itself, to leave us sad and hungry?

50. A. V. Dicey, unsigned review, *Nation*

23 January 1873, xvi, 60–2; 30 January 1873, xvi, 76–7

Albert Venn Dicey (1835-1922) was a Vinerian Professor of English Law at Oxford (1882-1909) and Principal of the Working Men's College in London (1899-1912). He wrote extensively on legal and political questions, and was the occasional London correspondent of the *Nation*. His review was published in two parts (see Introduction, p. 29).

I.

There is a well-known remark of Novalis that character is destiny,[1] which George Eliot criticises severely in the *Mill on the Floss*, on the ground that destiny depends rather on circumstances than on disposition. *Middlemarch* might have been written to illustrate at once the truth of the dictum and of the criticism. The main feature of the book is, that it is a history of the development, and generally of the tragic development, of characters which are sometimes noble, sometimes base, and generally neither very noble nor very base, amidst the commonplace circumstances of a country town. That this is the author's theme, as regards Dorothea, is patent. Her outward history, and the moral to be drawn from it, are thus summed up:

She was spoken of (in Middlemarch) to a younger generation as a fine girl who married a sickly clergyman old enough to be her father, and in little more than a year after his death gave up her estate to marry his cousin, young enough to have been his son, with no property and not well-born. Those who had not seen anything of Dorothea observed that she could not have been a 'nice woman,' else she would not have married either the one or the other. Certainly these determining acts of her life were not ideally beautiful; they were the mixed result of a young and noble impulse struggling under prosaic conditions. Among the many remarks made on her mistakes, it was never said in the neighborhood of Middlemarch that such mistakes could not have happened if the society into which she was born had not smiled on propositions of

[1] In *Heinrich von Osterdinger* (1802), part II.

339

marriage from a sickly man to a girl less than half his own age, on modes of education which make a woman's knowledge another name for motley ignorance, on rules of conduct which are in flat contradiction with its own loudly asserted beliefs. While this is the social air in which we mortals begin to breathe, there will be collisions such as those in Dorothea's life, when great feelings take the aspect of error and great faith the aspect of illusion.

This passage is remarkable in itself, but its main interest for our present purpose is that, though written of Dorothea, its spirit applies to all the principal personages of the novel. In Lydgate, in Rosamond, in Casaubon, in every other person meant to incite interest, what we are called upon to note is the action of circumstances upon character. 'There is no creature so strong that it is not greatly determined by what lies outside it.' This is the text of the whole work. Like most texts, it sounds at the first hearing like a truism, but it is a truism to which George Eliot's genius has restored all the vividness of a truth.

The main instance, of course, of its application is to be found in the history of Dorothea herself. The actual events of her life are summed up with fairness by Middlemarch gossip. She did marry a clergyman twice her own age, and she committed this folly without anything which, to ordinary persons, would seem a great temptation to the step. She married his cousin shortly after her first husband's death, and again acted free from the stress of any overpowering necessity. Neither act was, as George Eliot admits, 'ideally beautiful,' yet no one can doubt the nobleness of Dorothea's character, and few persons who study *Middlemarch* will long maintain that her actions, blamable or praiseworthy, were not, on the whole, the most natural outcome of her disposition and circumstances. From the first moment you meet her dividing her jewels with Celia, you perceive that she is full of noble aspirations, of life, ignorance, and of impatience. The beauty, and also the defects, of her nature arise from this fulness of life and impatience. She is always trying to escape from little commonplace ways and thoughts, and in the hurry to do so is constantly overlooking things which are commonplace enough, but which, unfortunately, are also true. 'Celia,' said Dorothea with emphatic gravity, 'pray don't make any more observations of that kind.' 'Why not? They are quite true,' returned Celia. . . . 'Many things are true *which only the commonest minds observe.*' 'Then I think the commonest minds must be rather useful. I think it is a pity that Mr. Casaubon's mother had not a commoner mind, she might have taught him better.' The two sisters are discussing Mr. Casaubon's disagreeable manner of eating his soup. He is already, although unknown to Celia, Dorothea's accepted lover. Dorothea had accepted him because she saw he had a 'great soul,' and while dreaming about great souls had neglected to make the observations which occur to commoner minds. The tragedy, in fact, of her life turns on her being so occupied with very noble notions, and so impatient to carry them out, that she failed to notice the commonplace things at her feet. In all her ways, great and small, there is manifest the rush and movement of life. Her delight in riding at a time when she thought the amusement rather worldly, her rapid driving and walking to work off her indignation at her lover's supposed treachery, her sudden, abrupt speeches, are all the outward signs of the same tendency to movement, expression, and action. This tendency is balanced by the keenness of feeling and intensity of sympathy which are sometimes seen in natures overflowing with vigor. The sympathy and the energy combined lead to the noblest act of her career, when, by a gigantic effort of self-sacrifice, she saves her supposed rival, her lover, and herself. But though in the interview with Rosamond you see all the grand side of a noble, impetuous disposition which disdains little things and breaks through petty rules, yet you are never supposed to forget that the same impetuosity is perpetually dragging Dorothea into errors, sometimes of trifling importance, but occasionally of infinite magnitude.

Two curious traits connected with the sympathetic, and at the same time vehement, turn of her mind, are specially worth notice as being true to nature but likely to escape observation. She was interested in intellectual pursuits, and her good uncle, Mr. Brooke, amongst others, obviously believes that she had carried her taste for learning beyond the certain point at which he held that every course of action ought to stop. 'You have not,' he says, 'the same tastes as every young lady; and a clergyman and a scholar who may be a bishop, that kind of thing may suit you better than Chettam. Chettam is a good fellow, a good, sound-hearted fellow, you know, but he does not go much into ideas. I did when I was his age.' But in spite of appearances, and in spite, probably, of Dorothea's own estimate of herself, she has little taste for knowledge. Her admiration for Casaubon's supposed learning really arose, as George Eliot is most careful to point out, from the idea that his wide knowledge would give her an insight into the problems of life which affected her personally. How to make and act up to a noble theory of life for herself was what she thought she wanted to achieve. What she seems truly to have needed was sympathy and a wide field for her power of affection. But for knowledge in itself she cared as little as was possible for any person gifted with keen intelligence. She was again, though some of her ardent admirers may dispute this, deficient in tact. This deficiency did not arise from obtuseness, but was, as it sometimes is, the result of impatience. The same characteristic which led her to rush nobly to Lydgate's defence without considering as accurately as more prudent persons whether his conduct might not turn out indefensible, led her also to press Mr. Casaubon on the two points on which his mind was naturally the most sore—the slow progress of his great work and the way in which he was bound, in Dorothea's view, to make restoration to Will. The latter instance is peculiarly characteristic, because, to give even a pedant his due, as regards the provision for Will, Casaubon was in the right and Dorothea distinctly in the wrong. There is, perhaps, nothing in the whole work better than the way in which the readers see that, while Dorothea had sacrificed herself through mistaking the pettiest and dreariest of pedants for a man like Locke and endowed with a great soul, they are also made to feel that this miserable scholar could hardly have met with a greater calamity than his marriage to Miss Brooke. 'I,' says George Eliot somewhere with the curious irony which distinguishes *Middlemarch*, 'am rather inclined to pity Mr. Casaubon;' and though this sentiment may strike some enthusiastic readers like an expression of compassion for the sufferings of an odious and cold-blooded reptile, yet it is perfectly just. You have in Mr. Casaubon the worst type of that much praised, and at best not very noble character, the gentleman and the scholar. Except in the matter of his will, when jealousy and ill-health had broken down his gentlemanlike habits, he acts as a gentleman. He also shows distinctly enough that he really is a scholar. He has, in fact, developed a kind of dreariness of mind which could be the result of nothing but a life devoted to the cramping pursuit of inner scholarship. But for the rest, he is a man who is always deficient in vitality, eaten up by egotism and jealousy, and by an indistinct consciousness of his own incapacity. His one consolation in marriage would have been a wife stupid enough to admire him, and apathetic enough to leave him to repose. He does marry a wife who, within six months, finds out that he is a sham and suspects 'the reconciliation of the mythologies' to be an imposture, who is prepared for every effort of self-sacrifice, and whose sense of duty and superabundant vitality scarcely leave a moment's true repose either to herself or to her husband. If it is possible for the fate of an utterly mean and contemptible nature to be tragic, the marriage with Miss Brooke makes life as great a tragedy to Casaubon as to his wife. Each of them is, by the irony of circumstances, placed in an utterly false position. Indeed, though Dorothea's life is, in many respects, a failure, still you close the book with a feeling that a noble nature succeeded at last in finding genuine happiness, if not in developing to true greatness. The real tragedy of *Middlemarch*, and by far the most original part of the book, lies in the story of Lydgate, which records the steps by which genius and energy sink at last, overpowered by the force of circumstances, and of circumstances of the pettiest nature.

The flaw in Lydgate's nature, and the ultimate source of his fall, is a certain 'commonness' in his views of everything unconnected with his science. Hence his liking for respectable appearances, hence his original underestimate of Miss Brooke because she was a woman a little out of the common line. Hence his immediate admiration for Rosamond and the marriage which is the bane of his life. The thing to notice is how perfectly natural is this commonness, and how naturally it works out its results. Most readers probably detest Rosamond, principally because of her complete satisfaction with herself, too much to do justice to her victim. But take Rosamond with all her self-satisfaction, pettiness, and duplicity as she is known to the reader, and as, be it remarked, she could be known to nobody else, and she still remains a woman with whom ninety-nine men out of a hundred would most indubitably fall in love. Nor, again, was Lydgate's commonness the only cause of his failure. He fell as men do fall, quite as much by his merits as by his defects. Being a man of genuinely strong affections, he was always in dealing with Rosamond at the untold disadvantage of loving much and scarcely being loved at all. Every pain he gave her was a double pang to himself, whilst her flinty nature was incapable of feeling that she gave pain to others, or of suffering from any pain except mortification to herself. Lydgate's affection, as far as it had any effect on Rosamond, disgusted her, for it deprived him of the kind of calmness which might perhaps have impressed her imagination, or at least cowed her will.

The action and reaction of Lydgate's character upon Rosamond, and Rosamond's upon Lydgate, is merely one example of that power of analyzing the effect of one nature upon another which is one of the most marked features of George Eliot's mind. Contrast her writings, for example, with the works of Thackeray. You will find in the latter a number of characters quite as striking and perhaps more consistent than those painted by the author of *Middlemarch*. But with rare exceptions, the characters of Thackeray each stand out distinct and separate

343

from one another. You know Ethel, and you know Clive. You perfectly understand Becky or Sir Pitt Crawley, but you do not generally see, and Thackeray does not generally care to make you see, the exact influence say of Ethel upon Clive. You do not feel that they, acting together, are something essentially different from what either of them would have been uninfluenced by the other. But throughout *Middlemarch* the influence of mind upon mind is never left out of sight. Dorothea is half-checked, half-irritated by Celia. She is oppressed in the presence of Casaubon, and develops freely under the sunshine of Will's superficial geniality. Casaubon himself is constantly suffering from the consciousness that he is surrounded by unadmiring acquaintance. Lydgate's impatience is brought into play by Rosamond's coldhearted impassibility, and Rosamond herself chills into something slightly more icy than she was by nature under disgust at Lydgate's violence. Take what page you will of the book, and you will find examples of this play of character upon character, and you will also find that, in general, by a strange irony, the inferior character warps and in a sense triumphs over the superior nature.

For, after all, if it were necessary to fix upon any one quality as the characteristic trait of the book, few attentive critics would hesitate to name irony, taking a very extensive sense of the term, as its distinguishing feature. The avowed irony of much of the writing is too obvious to call for much notice. What is better worth observation is the indirect forms in which the same tendency shows itself. There is, for example, a constant irony of situation. Misfortunes befall men just at the moment when they feel the safest from them. Bulstrode buys a charming house, and walks there on a summer evening wrapped in satisfactory religious meditation. He finds in the garden the villain who makes his life a misery. At the cost of something very like murder, he rids himself of his tormentor. He rides home happy after weeks of misery, and almost immediately discovers that the disgrace he had risked his soul to avoid has fallen upon him. This irony of situation often appears in George Eliot's other works, as, for example, where Arthur Donnithorne returns to take possession of his estate, full of good spirits and good intentions, and finds that his intrigue with Hetty has led to all its miserable results. But this contrast between a person's own estimate of his circumstances and his real position is by no means the most subtle way in which George Eliot draws the eternal contrast between what seems and what is. It appears often in the merest turn of a sentence. What, for example, can be a more bitter sarcasm between a man's own feeling of misery and his friend's vapid consolations than Mr. Brooke's advice to Casaubon, broken-hearted with the knowledge that his life would not suffice his work?

'Yes, yes,' said Mr. Brooke, 'get Dorothea to play backgammon with you in the evenings, and shuttlecock. Now I don't know a finer game than shuttlecock for the daytime. . . . But you must unbend, you know. Why, you might take to some light study, conchology, now—I always think that must be a light study—or get Dorothea to read you light things, Smollett, "Roderick Random," "Humphrey Clinker." They are a little broad, but she may read anything now she is married, you know.'

'I never give up anything that I choose to do,' said Rosamond (referring to her engagement). 'God bless you,' said Lydgate, kissing her again. This constancy in the right place was adorable.

These sentences are simple enough; but any one who has followed Lydgate's career to its close will hardly read them without something like a chill of horror, for Lydgate pours blessings upon that wretched constancy of purpose which constitutes his lifelong torture. Exactly the same characteristic appears in the conversations of common people, auctioneers, horse-dealers, and landladies, in which George Eliot delights. They are no doubt amusing and truthful enough in themselves, but they derive a peculiar gusto from their presenting an unconscious parody on the thoughts and language of educated persons. But all the minor forms of irony sink to nothing compared with the irony of the lesson enforced by the conclusion of *Middlemarch* itself. Every one who has commenced life with high aspirations either, like Lydgate, ends in misery, or, like Dorothea, purchases happiness by foregoing all ideal aims. The only persons who prosper are either selfish or commonplace. Fred, who is the very model of an ordinary selfish young man, ends as a prosperous gentleman. Will, who throughout life is and could be nothing but an amateur, gains all his wishes. Rosamond, after causing misery to others which she had not the sense even to perceive, is 'rewarded' by getting rid of her husband, whom she did not like, and keeping his fortune and position, which were sufficient to make her happy. The conclusion of the whole matter is, that happiness depends on the adaptation of character to circumstances, and that, therefore, in a commonplace world, commonplace characters alone have a fair chance of happiness.

II.

Is *Middlemarch* the most successful as it is certainly the most elaborate effort of George Eliot's genius?

Hundreds of critics will answer in the affirmative, and may point to the infinite variety of the persons described, to the exquisite beauty and wit of the remarks and epigrams with which the book teems, in confirmation of their judgment. But though *Middlemarch* has stuff enough in it to fill out four or five ordinary novels, and though it would undoubtedly at once make the reputation of an unknown author, it will not be permanently placed on a level with *Adam Bede*, *Romola*, or with the most exquisite of all George Eliot's works—the *History of Silas Marner*. The defect of the book is, that the parts are much more striking than the whole, and the source of this defect lies in two characteristics, one of which is peculiar to *Middlemarch*, whilst the other, though traceable in all George Eliot's writings, becomes far more prominent in her later than in her earlier works.

What readers care for in *Middlemarch* is the study of character, but the author herself, as she takes pains by the very title to point out, intended it as a study primarily not of character but of provincial life. She in fact aimed at two different objects. Her first aim is to give a picture of existence in an English country town forty years ago; her second, to show how this prosaic life told upon the characters of three or four of the persons born into it. Now, in the attainment of the first object, George Eliot completely succeeds. The novel as a mere rendering of English life rises as much above such works as Mrs. Gaskell's truthful and amusing sketch of *Cranford*, or Miss Austen's truthful but to us, we confess, not very amusing sketches of commonplace people, as a work of genius must always rise above books marked more by grace or cleverness. Looked at in fact as a series of pictures, *Middlemarch* is the most perfect representation of life in an English country town which is to be found in our language. Even the minute details of Fred's petty and somewhat sordid extravagance, and the descriptions of the horse-dealers by whom he is cheated, and of the billiard-room which he frequents, all add something to the picture, and bring before the mind the fearful and oppressive dreariness of a country town. But the very success with which George Eliot has painted *Middlemarch* has been unfavorable to her full attainment of the second, and by far the more important, object of the tale. The form of the story has made it impossible to centre the reader's interest fixedly on any one character.

You can never fully occupy your mind with Dorothea or with Lydgate in the same way in which you can give yourself up unreservedly to the character of Romola or of Silas Marner. Just when you begin to be anxious about Dorothea's fate, you are carried off to Lydgate and Rosamond; and when your whole mind has become filled with the question whether Lydgate's genius will or will not be ruined by Rosamond's pettiness, you are compelled to break away both from Lydgate and Dorothea, and to interest yourself in the fate of Bulstrode or in the happiness of the Garth family. The mere annoyance of being constantly shifted from one scene to another is a trifling consideration. A much more serious evil of this constant shifting is, that it prevents the author from fully elaborating any one character, and from studying the effect of the work as a whole.

It is always an ungraceful and often a foolish thing to complain of a great work because it is not something which it does not profess to be, and there is something specially futile in censuring an author of genius because he has not the peculiar genius of some other writer. There is nothing, for instance, gained by pointing out that *Esmond*, because it is meant for an imitation of a work of the last century, wants the ease of *Pendennis*, or by censuring Dickens because he is not Thackeray, or Thackeray because he is not Dickens. But it is sound criticism to measure an author's productions by the standard of his own greatest works. Now, it is when judged by this criterion that *Middlemarch* will be found defective. The scheme of the book as the picture of a society has, as just pointed out, the inherent defect of making it difficult to fix attention on one or two persons, or to place the minor characters in due subordination to those worth elaborate study. But it happens that George Eliot has herself shown the way in which this difficulty can be met. In her earliest and even now her most striking work you have pictures of society. The *Sketches of Clerical Life* paint perfectly and clearly the social circle in which Janet and Amos Barton move, but you never lose sight of the principal character in the pictures of the minor personages whose figures fill up the canvas. The reason of this certainly is, in part, that the three tales making up the *Sketches of Clerical Life* are kept entirely separate from one another. The wonderful portrait of Janet is not injured by your being called upon to study before you see it complete the picture of Amos Barton's tragic stupidity, and, on the other hand, you can attend to the miseries of the Barton family without having half your mind turned to Mr. Gilfil's romance. If any critic will candidly compare the *Clerical Sketches* and *Middlemarch*, he will admit that the form of the one was planned under a happy, and that of the latter a distinctly unhappy, inspiration. For the one feature which would vindicate the scheme of *Middlemarch* is wanting. At the beginning of the book, every one must have anticipated that the different histories commenced in it will by degrees become so closely interlaced as to form a complete whole. As a matter of fact, though Dorothea's life affects the life of Lydgate, and though there is a link (a very slight one, it may be added) between Fred's marriage and Bulstrode's calamity, still the book consists of at least three perfectly separate tales. A very slight amount of change would make it possible even now to publish separately the history of Dorothea and Casaubon, of Lydgate and Rosamond, and of Fred and Mary, and no one can doubt that the author might originally have produced these histories as three separate tales of life in *Middlemarch*.

'Any one,' writes George Eliot, 'watching keenly the stealthy convergence of human lots, sees a slow preparation of effects from one life to another which tells like a calculated irony on the indifference or the frozen stare with which we look at our unintroduced neighbor. *Destiny stands by sarcastic with dramatis personæ folded in her hand.*' This passage, and especially the last sentence of it, might be taken as a fair description of the attitude occupied by the author towards her own work. To a certain extent in all her books, but to a far greater extent in *Middlemarch* than in any of her other writings, George Eliot performs the part of the 'destiny which stands by sarcastic,' and comments on the fate of the actors whom she brings into existence. A main feature— in short, perhaps the main feature—of *Middlemarch* is the prominence given to what, borrowing a term from Greek tragedy, may be called the 'chorus'. The work begins with a prelude in which the reader is warned that he is to hear the history of a 'St. Theresa, foundress of nothing, whose loving heart-beats and sobs after an unattained goodness tremble off and are dispersed among hindrances instead of centring in some long recognizable deed'; and the work concludes with an epilogue pointing out how the modern Theresa had failed, and the cause of her failure. Throughout the whole course of the story, moreover, the chorus is never long absent. At every turn reflections are introduced upon the characters, upon the events, upon the way the characters and the events work upon one another. No one who admires beautiful writing or can appreciate striking and original thoughts can fail to feel that the chorus or reflective portion of the book is full of beauty and power. To a large class of persons it forms probably the great charm of *Middlemarch*. It certainly constitutes the most peculiar feature of the book. But a critic, even while he admires the reflections themselves, and feels that as moral reflections they possess far greater depth and subtlety than the remarks generally forced upon the world under the guise of moral teaching, can hardly deny that the part taken by George Eliot as the moralizer over her own handiwork, if it gives her novel a peculiar charm, also greatly damages its whole effect. It is a very curious study to observe the results which follow from the characteristic in question. One main and most injurious effect is that some of the characters are never drawn directly. We see not the men themselves, but the personages as they appear in the author's reflections upon them. Take, for example, Bulstrode: an immense amount of skill, pains, and thought has been expended upon him, yet he never becomes a really living character in the sense in which his wife, for example, of whom comparatively little is told us, stands out as a living human being; and the reason of this is obvious. Of Bulstrode's thoughts and motives, of his views of religion, of his ideas of Providence, of his attempt to adjust his actions to principles which he held and yet had not the firmness to practise; of all this we hear a great deal, and a great deal which is very well worth the hearing. As an analysis of a peculiar kind of hypocrisy the account of Bulstrode is perfect, and a reader must be much better or much worse than his neighbors who does not feel many of the reflections on Bulstrode come painfully home to his own conscience. But of Bulstrode himself we know very little. The most marked personal feature about him is that he had a bad digestion, and that painful reflections on the state of his body alternated with anxiety about the state of his soul. All we are told, as far as it goes, is natural enough; but what we maintain is that he is never really painted. We see a reflection of him, but we never see the man.

A somewhat similar defect is traceable in the description of Will. Take him all in all, he is the least satisfactory character in the book. An amateur, who could not work and would not study, who was too proud to propose to a lady whom he thought richer than himself, and not too proud to sneer at and annoy the man on whose charity he lived; who, having apparently a marked distaste for work and a dislike to the serious and prosaic side of life, ends his career as an active member of Parliament somewhere between 1832 and 1840—a follower, we must presume, of the Radicals of that day, that is, men like Joseph Hume—is, we confess, a character which seems to us neither interesting nor consistent. What is most apparent is that Will has a great charm for

George Eliot, and the only conclusion to which one can in fairness come
is that, skilful as she is, she has for once failed to put before the reader
a true picture of the man as he appears to her own mind. Take Will
as the facts of his life paint him, and he appears a feeble, rather well-
disposed Tito, who, late in life, turns into a feeble and less energetic
Felix Holt. Take him as he is spoken of by the author, and you will
suppose him a man of considerable originality, great generosity, and of
a special grace—a person, in short, not absolutely worthy of Dorothea,
yet whom she might marry without sacrificing the lofty greatness of
her nature. The cause of this divergence between the estimate of Will
formed by the author, and the view of him actually taken by the reader,
is, no doubt, that he is not satisfactorily drawn. But the ultimate reason
why the drawing is unsatisfactory is that George Eliot is occasionally
so much occupied in the chorus to her play that she forgets to introduce
us thoroughly to the characters. Will and Bulstrode afford the most
marked instances of this omission; but a careful comparison say of *Silas
Marner* or of 'Janet's Repentance' with *Middlemarch*, is sufficient to prove
to any one but a very fanatical admirer that as the number of George
Eliot's 'wise, witty, and tender' sayings increase, the directness with
which she paints living persons diminishes.

The writer's preoccupation with the reflections which her story is to
suggest injures her actual delineation of even those persons whom
she intends to make prominent by their own acts and speeches. George
Eliot tends, no doubt, unconsciously more and more to make even the
most lively and original characters in the book the representatives of
different aspects of her own thoughts. The tones are very various, but
they all or nearly all seem to be the tones of one voice differently
modulated. Take, for instance, Mrs. Cadwallader. No one is more
amusing and no one more alive, but a great number of her speeches
are really little but the wit of George Eliot thrown into a sharp, rustic,
and caustic form.

Her description of Casaubon's blood, 'somebody put a drop under a
magnifying-glass, and it was all semicolons and parentheses,' is an
exquisite sneer, but it is exactly the kind of sarcasm, dashed with a
flavor of scientific allusion, which comes perfectly naturally into
reflections by George Eliot, but comes far less naturally from the
mouth of the rector's wife. Mrs. Cadwallader, again, tells us how she
had learnt to like her husband's sermons: 'When I married Humphrey I
made up my mind to like sermons, and I set out by liking the end very
much; that soon spread to the middle and the beginning, because I

could not have the end without them.' Here, as elsewhere, the phrases
may be the phrases of Mrs. Cadwallader, but the wit is essentially the
wit of George Eliot. In short, Mrs. Cadwallader, and the same thing is
true of half the secondary characters, is in reality not so much a secondary character as a part of the great chorus of reflection which accom-
panies the tragedy from beginning to end. In general, as we have
said, the reflections, if they somewhat injure the movements of the
drama, are in themselves so beautiful that we should scarcely care to
have them omitted. In one respect, however, they are themselves open
to criticism. They are occasionally injured by what truth compels us
to call scientific conceits. No doubt a time may come when the progress
of knowledge will make metaphors drawn from physical science really
natural as appropriate illustrations, but to such a stage of knowledge
the mass of so-called educated readers have certainly as yet not attained:

Even with a microscope directed on a water-drop we find ourselves making
interpretations which turn out to be rather coarse, for whereas under a weak lens
you may seem to see a creature exhibiting an active voracity, into which other
smaller creatures actively play, as if they were so many animated tax-pennies, a
stronger lens reveals to you tiniest hairlets, which make vortices for these
victims, while the swallower awaits passively at his receipt of custom. In this
way, metaphorically speaking, a strong lens applied to Mrs. Cadwallader's
match-making will show a play of minute causes, producing what may be
called thought and speech vortices to bring her the sort of food she needed.

Now, is there in truth one out of a thousand persons who reads this
passage who finds that the ten lines of scientific metaphor really make
clearer to him the fact, simple enough in itself, that Mrs. Cadwallader
acted under the influence of a number of infinitely small causes? Is there
any one who does not feel that the remark in the *Mill on the Floss*, that
people do not really weave elaborate plots, but live very much from
hand to mouth, is in fact worth all this talk about hairlets, lenses, and
vortices? In truth, throughout *Middlemarch*, we feel inclined more than
half to curse the day when George Eliot began rather to reflect than to
copy. The book is her greatest effort. Its defect is, and this defect places
it to our minds below her most perfect writings, that it is an effort
in a bad as well as in the good sense of the word. The very brilliancy
of the epigrams, the marvellous power of analysis used in tracing the
action of character, the elaborate care given to the separate parts, leaves
in the mind a sense of something like strain, and makes it difficult to look
at the work as a whole. Yet it is impossible to part from a book which
may be said, almost without exaggeration, to have made for many

persons the chief happiness and interest of the last year, with criticisms on defects which, be they real or not, would scarcely deserve notice in another of inferior power. One point which tempts to criticism is that you can easily perceive that when, in the interest of the story, George Eliot forgets theories and has not time to make reflections, the whole power of simple, direct description is still as strong in her as ever. The last number was written under some pressure for space. In one or two points it is certainly less finished than the rest of the book; but just in proportion as the work becomes less elaborate it grows more effective. Harriet Bulstrode is at no time a very prominent person in the story. The reader thinks of her as slightly vulgar and decidedly commonplace. Yet the whole history of her behavior under the most crushing misfortune, when the husband whom she has loved and revered turns out to be certainly a hypocrite and probably an actual murderer, is as pathetic as anything George Eliot has ever written. Mrs. Bulstrode goes down from her room to see her husband, who now knew that she had discovered all:

'Look up, Nicholas.' He raised his eyes with a little start, and looked at her half amazed for a moment. Her pale face, her changed morning dress, the trembling about the mouth, all said 'I know,' and her hands and eyes rested gently on him. He burst out crying, and they cried together, she sitting at his side. They could not yet speak to each other of the shame which she was bearing with him, or of the acts which had brought it down on them. His confession was silent and her promise of faithfulness was silent. Open-minded as she was, she nevertheless shrank from the words which would have expressed their mutual consciousness as she would have shrunk from flakes of fire. She could not say, 'How much is only slander and false suspicion?' and he did not say, 'I am innocent.'

51. Henry James, unsigned review, *Galaxy*

March 1873, xv, 424-8

See Introduction, pp. 31-2.

Middlemarch is at once one of the strongest and one of the weakest of English novels. Its predecessors as they appeared might have been described in the same terms; *Romola*, is especially a rare masterpiece, but the least *entraînant* of masterpieces. *Romola* sins by excess of analysis; there is too much description and too little drama; too much reflection (all certainly of a highly imaginative sort) and too little creation. Movement lingers in the story, and with it attention stands still in the reader. The error in *Middlemarch* is not precisely of a similar kind, but it is equally detrimental to the total aspect of the work. We can well remember how keenly we wondered, while its earlier chapters unfolded themselves, what turn in the way of form the story would take—that of an organized, moulded, balanced composition, gratifying the reader with a sense of design and construction, or a mere chain of episodes, broken into accidental lengths and unconscious of the influence of a plan. We expected the actual result, but for the sake of English imaginative literature which, in this line is rarely in need of examples, we hoped for the other. If it had come we should have had the pleasure of reading, what certainly would have seemed to us in the immediate glow of attention, the first of English novels. But that pleasure has still to hover between prospect and retrospect. *Middlemarch* is a treasure-house of details, but it is an indifferent whole.

Our objection may seem shallow and pedantic, and may even be represented as a complaint that we have had the less given us rather than the more. Certainly the greatest minds have the defects of their qualities, and as George Eliot's mind is preëminently contemplative and analytic, nothing is more natural than that her manner should be discursive and expansive. 'Concentration' would doubtless have deprived us of many of the best things in the book—of Peter Featherstone's grotesquely expectant legatees, of Lydgate's medical rivals, and

of Mary Garth's delightful family. The author's purpose was to be a
generous rural historian, and this very redundancy of touch, born of
abundant reminiscence, is one of the greatest charms of her work. It
is as if her memory was crowded with antique figures, to whom for
very tenderness she must grant an appearance. Her novel is a picture—
vast, swarming, deep-colored, crowded with episodes, with vivid
images, with lurking master-strokes, with brilliant passages of expression; and as such we may freely accept it and enjoy it. It is not compact,
doubtless; but when was a panorama compact? And yet, nominally,
Middlemarch has a definite subject—the subject indicated in the eloquent
preface. An ardent young girl was to have been the central figure, a
young girl framed for a larger moral life than circumstance often
affords, yearning for a motive for sustained spiritual effort and only
wasting her ardor and soiling her wings against the meanness of opportunity. The author, in other words, proposed to depict the career of
an obscure St. Theresa. Her success has been great, in spite of serious
drawbacks. Dorothea Brooks is a genuine creation, and a most remarkable one when we consider the delicate material in which she is wrought.
George Eliot's men are generally so much better than the usual
trowsered off-spring of the female fancy, that their merits have perhaps
overshadowed those of her women. Yet her heroines have always been
of an exquisite quality, and Dorothea is only that perfect flower of
conception of which her predecessors were the less unfolded blossoms.
An indefinable moral elevation is the sign of these admirable creatures;
and of the representation of this quality in its superior degrees the
author seems to have in English fiction a monopoly. To render the
expression of a soul requires a cunning hand; but we seem to look
straight into the unfathomable eyes of the beautiful spirit of Dorothea
Brooks. She exhales a sort of aroma of spiritual sweetness, and we
believe in her as in a woman we might providentially meet some fine
day when we should find ourselves doubting of the immortality of
the soul. By what unerring mechanism this effect is produced—whether
by fine strokes or broad ones, by description or by narration, we can
hardly say; it is certainly the great achievement of the book. Dorothea's
career is, however, but an episode, and though doubtless in intention,
not distinctly enough in fact, the central one. The history of Lydgate's
ménage, which shares honors with it, seems rather to the reader to
carry off the lion's share. This is certainly a very interesting story, but
on the whole it yields in dignity to the record of Dorothea's unresonant
woes. The 'love-problem,' as the author calls it, of Mary Garth, is

placed on a rather higher level than the reader willingly grants it. To the end we care less about Fred Viney than appears to be expected of us. In so far as the writer's design has been to reproduce the total sum of life in an English village forty years ago, this common-place young gentleman, with his somewhat meagre tribulations and his rather neutral egotism, has his proper place in the picture; but the author narrates his fortunes with a fulness of detail which the reader often finds irritating. The reader indeed is sometimes tempted to complain of a tendency which we are at loss exactly to express—a tendency to make light of the serious elements of the story and to sacrifice them to the more trivial ones. Is it an unconscious instinct or is it a deliberate plan? With its abundant and massive ingredients *Middlemarch* ought some-how to have depicted a weightier drama. Dorothea was altogether too superb a heroine to be wasted; yet she plays a narrower part than the imagination of the reader demands. She is of more consequence than the action of which she is the nominal centre. She marries enthusiastic-ally a man whom she fancies a great thinker, and who turns out to be but an arid pedant. Here, indeed, is a disappointment with much of the dignity of tragedy; but the situation seems to us never to expand to its full capacity. It is analyzed with extraordinary penetration, but one may say of it, as of most of the situations in the book, that it is treated with too much refinement and too little breadth. It revolves too con-stantly on the same pivot; it abounds in fine shades, but it lacks, we think, the great dramatic *chiaroscuro*. Mr. Casaubon, Dorothea's husband (of whom more anon) embittered, on his side, by matrimonial disappointment, takes refuge in vain jealousy of his wife's relations with an interesting young cousin of his own and registers this sentiment in a codicil to his will, making the forfeiture of his property the penalty of his widow's marriage with this gentleman. Mr. Casaubon's death befalls about the middle of the story, and from this point to the close our interest in Dorothea is restricted to the question, will she or will she not marry Will Ladislaw? The question is relatively trivial and the implied struggle slightly factitious. The author has depicted the struggle with a sort of elaborate solemnity which in the interviews related in the two last books tends to become almost ludicrously excessive.

The dramatic current stagnates; it runs between hero and heroine almost a game of hair-splitting. Our dissatisfaction here is provoked in a great measure by the insubstantial character of the hero. The figure of Will Ladislaw is a beautiful attempt, with many finely-completed points; but on the whole it seems to us a failure. It is the only eminent failure in the book, and its defects are therefore the more striking. It lacks sharpness of outline and depth of color; we have not found ourselves believing in Ladislaw as we believe in Dorothea, in Mary Garth, in Rosamond, in Lydgate, in Mr. Brooke and Mr. Casaubon. He is meant, indeed, to be a light creature (with a large capacity for gravity, for he finally gets into Parliament), and a light creature certainly should not be heavily drawn. The author, who is evidently very fond of him, has found for him here and there some charming and eloquent touches; but in spite of these he remains vague and impalpable to the end. He is, we may say, the one figure which a masculine intellect of the same power as George Eliot's would not have conceived with the same complacency; he is, in short, roughly speaking, a woman's man. It strikes us as an oddity in the author's scheme that she should have chosen just this figure of Ladislaw as the creature in whom Dorothea was to find her spiritual compensations. He is really, after all, not the ideal foil to Mr. Casaubon which her soul must have imperiously demanded, and if the author of the 'Key to all Mythologies' sinned by lack of order, Ladislaw too has not the concentrated fervor essential in the man chosen by so nobly strenuous a heroine. The impression once given that he is a *dilettante* is never properly removed, and there is slender poetic justice in Dorothea's marrying a *dilettante*. We are doubtless less content with Ladislaw, on account of the noble, almost sculptural, relief of the neighboring figure of Lydgate, the real hero of the story. It is an illustration of the generous scale of the author's picture and of the conscious power of her imagination that she has given us a hero and heroine of broadly distinct interests—erected, as it were, two suns in her firmament, each with its independent solar system. Lydgate is so richly successful a figure that we have regretted strongly at moments, for immediate interests' sake, that the current of his fortunes should not mingle more freely with the occasionally thin-flowing stream of Dorothea's. Toward the close, these two fine characters are brought into momentary contact so effectively as to suggest a wealth of dramatic possibility between them; but if this train had been followed we should have lost Rosamond Viney—a rare psychological study. Lydgate is a really complete portrait of a *man*, which seems to us high praise. It is striking evidence of the altogether superior quality of George Eliot's imagination that, though elaborately represented, Lydgate should be treated so little from what we may roughly (and we trust without offence) call the sexual point of view. Perception charged with feeling has constantly guided the author's hand, and yet her strokes remain as firm, her curves as free, her whole manner as serenely impersonal, as if, on a small scale, she were emulating the creative wisdom itself. Several English romancers—notably Fielding, Thackeray, and Charles Reade—have won great praise for their figures of women: but they owe it, in reversed conditions, to a meaner sort of art, it seems to us, than George Eliot has used in the case of Lydgate; to an indefinable appeal to masculine prejudice—to a sort of titillation of the masculine sense of difference. George Eliot's manner is more philosophic—more broadly intelligent, and yet her result is as concrete or, if you please, as picturesque. We have no space to dwell on Lydgate's character; we can but repeat that he is a vividly consistent, manly figure—powerful, ambitious, sagacious, with the maximum rather than the mimimum of egotism, strenuous, generous, fallible, and altogether human. A work of the liberal scope of *Middlemarch* contains a multitude of artistic intentions, some of the finest of which become clear only in the meditative after-taste of perusal. This is the case with the balanced contrast between the two histories of Lydgate and Dorothea. Each is a tale of matrimonial infelicity, but the conditions in each are so different and the circumstances so broadly opposed that the mind passes from one to the other with that supreme sense of the vastness and variety of human life, under aspects apparently similar, which it belongs only to the greatest novels to produce. The most perfectly successful passages in the book are perhaps those painful fireside scenes between Lydgate and his miserable little wife. The author's rare psychological penetration is lavished upon this veritably mulish domestic flower. There is nothing more powerfully real than these scenes in all English fiction, and nothing certainly more *intelligent*. Their impressiveness, and (as regards Lydgate) their pathos, is deepened by the constantly low key in which they are pitched. It is a tragedy based on unpaid butchers' bills, and the urgent need for small economies. The author has desired to be strictly real and to adhere to the facts of the common lot, and she has given us a powerful version of that typical human drama, the struggles of an ambitious soul with sordid disappointments and vulgar embarrassments. As to her catastrophe we hesitate to pronounce (for Lydgate's ultimate assent to his wife's worldly programme is nothing less than a catastrophe). We almost believe that some terrific explosion would have been more probable than his twenty years of smothered aspiration. Rosamond deserves almost to rank with Tito in *Romola* as a study of a gracefully vicious, or at least of a practically baleful nature. There is one point, however, of which we question the consistency. The author insists on her instincts of coquetry, which seems to us a discordant note. They would have made her better or worse—more generous or more reckless; in either case more manageable. As it is, Rosamond represents, in a measure, the fatality of British decorum.

In reading, we have marked innumerable passages for quotation and comment; but we lack space and the work is so ample that half a dozen extracts would be an ineffective illustration. There would be a great deal to say on the broad array of secondary figures, Mr. Casaubon, Mr. Brooke, Mr. Bulstrode, Mr. Farebrother, Caleb Garth, Mrs. Cadwallader, Celia Brooke. Mr. Casaubon is an excellent invention; as a dusky *repoussoir* to the luminous figure of his wife he could not have been better imagined. There is indeed something very noble in the way in which the author has apprehended his character. To depict hollow pretentiousness and mouldy egotism with so little of narrow sarcasm and so much of philosophic sympathy, is to be a rare moralist as well as a rare story-teller. The whole portrait of Mr. Casaubon has an admirably sustained greyness of tone in which the shadows are never carried to the vulgar black of coarser artists. Every stroke contributes to the unwholesome, helplessly sinister expression. Here and there perhaps (as in his habitual diction), there is a hint of exaggeration; but we confess we like fancy to be fanciful. Mr. Brooke and Mr. Garth are in their different lines supremely genial creations; they are drawn with the touch of a Dickens chastened and intellectualized. Mrs. Cadwallader is, in another walk of life, a match for Mrs. Poyser, and Celia Brooke is as pretty a fool as any of Miss Austen's. Mr. Farebrother and his delightful 'womankind' belong to a large group of figures begotten of the superabundance of the author's creative instinct. At times they seem to encumber the stage and to produce a rather ponderous mass of dialogue; but they add to the reader's impression of having walked in the Middlemarch lanes and listened to the Middlemarch accent. To but one of these accessory episodes—that of Mr. Bulstrode, with its multiplex ramifications—do we take exception. It has a slightly artificial cast, a melodramatic tinge, unfriendly to the richly natural coloring of the whole. Bulstrode himself—with the history of whose troubled conscience the author has taken great pains—is, to our sense, too diffusely treated; he never grasps the reader's attention. But the touch of genius is never idle or vain. The obscure figure of Bulstrode's comely wife emerges at the needful moment, under a few light strokes, into the happiest reality.

All these people, solid and vivid in their varying degrees, are members of a deeply human little world, the full reflection of whose antique image is the great merit of these volumes. How bravely rounded a little world the author has made it—with how dense an atmosphere of interests and passions and loves and enmities and strivings and failings, and how motley a group of great folk and small, all after their kind, she has filled it, the reader must learn for himself. No writer seems to us to have drawn from a richer stock of those long-cherished memories which one's later philsophy makes doubly tender. There are few figures in the book which do not seem to have grown mellow in the author's mind. English readers may fancy they enjoy the 'atmosphere' of *Middlemarch*; but we maintain that to relish its inner essence we must—for reasons too numerous to detail—be an American. The author has commissioned herself to be real, her native tendency being that of an idealist, and the intellectual result is a very fertilizing mixture. The constant presence of thought, of generalizing instinct, of *brain*, in a word, behind her observation, gives the latter its great value and her whole manner its high superiority. It denotes a mind in which imagination is illumined by faculties rarely found in fellowship with it. In this respect—in that broad reach of vision which would make the worthy historian of solemn fact as well as wanton fiction—George Eliot seems to us among English romancers to stand alone. Fielding approaches her, but to our mind, she surpasses Fielding. Fielding was didactic—the author of *Middlemarch* is really philosophic. These great qualities imply corresponding perils. The first is the loss of simplicity. George Eliot lost hers some time since: it lies buried (in a splendid mausoleum) in *Romola*. Many of the discursive portions of *Middlemarch* are, as we may say, too clever by half. The author wishes to say too many things, and to say them too well; to recommend herself to a scientific audience. Her style, rich and flexible as it is, is apt to betray her on these transcendental flights; we find, in our copy, a dozen passages marked 'obscure.' *Silas Marner* has a delightful tinge of Goldsmith—we may almost call it: *Middlemarch* is too often an echo of Messrs. Darwin and Huxley. In spite of these faults—which it seems graceless to indicate with this crude rapidity—it remains a very splendid performance. It sets a limit, we think, to the development of the old-fashioned English novel. Its diffuseness, on which we have touched, makes it too copious a dose of pure fiction. If we write novels so, how shall we write History? But it is nevertheless a contribution of the first importance to the rich imaginative department of our literature.

DANIEL DERONDA

February 1876–September 1876

---

52. Unsigned notice, *Academy*

5 February 1876, ix, 120

The appearance of the first number of *Daniel Deronda* (William Black-wood and Sons) has been looked for the more anxiously because, in spite of the popular impatience of the serial method of publication, the numbers of *Middlemarch* obtained their success *seriatim*. 'The Spoiled Child' is the heroine of the coming romance; its eponymous hero only appears in the first chapter, where he is introduced in the assumption of a silent superiority to the heroine which is not, apparently, intended to have the same peaceable issue as in *Felix Holt*. The story is one of modern life and society. Gwendolen Harleth is a young lady of twenty, beautiful with the *beauté du diable*, but with no more pronounced diabolical propensities than a love of life and luxury and an undefined ambition after some form of superiority or personal ascendancy which should be reconcilable with all the minor good things good society has to offer to brilliant and beautiful girls. In undertaking to represent such a character, and secure attention for the representation, George Eliot is consistent with one of her earliest principles—indifference to the critic saying from his bird's-eye station: 'Not a remarkable specimen; the anatomy and habits of the species have been determined long ago.' George Eliot insists on having the specimen remarked, not because it is rare but because it is real; all the more, indeed, if it is so far from rare that its reality becomes a powerful influence in human life. The representation of this influence of course remains to be developed, and in the meanwhile Gwendolen's individuality is established, like that of Lydgate, by some personal traits that art not commonly supposed to be associated with the general type of character, though a minutely analytical psychology might perhaps show the connexion to have a root in the nature of things. Thus Gwendolen is superstitious, subject to an inexplicable dread of solitude, darkness, and any other physical suggestion of the existence of natural forces inaccessible to the influence of human wills. Again, though possessing all the vanity and coldness of a coquette, 'a certain fierceness of maidenhood' made her object to being directly made love to, and 'the life of passion had begun negatively in her' when a pleasant boy-cousin ventures to offend this instinct; but she has also still enough childish *naïveté* to carry this grievance to her mother, for whom she has a childishly selfish but genuine affection. One or two paragraphs seem to suggest that we are to have in *Daniel Deronda* a treatment (perhaps more full and central than before) of the question presented in some of the writer's other works, namely, by what property of the natural order it comes to pass that the strength of innocent self-regarding desires is a moral snare unless balanced by some sense of external obligation, or in other words, why egotism is a term of re-proach, however fascinating its human habitation. Rex (Gwendolen's cousin) has a vague impression, when he wants to go and bury his dejection in the backwoods, 'that he ought to feel—if he had been a better fellow he should have felt—more about his old ties.' In the *Spanish Gypsy* the 'old ties' of hereditary race-feeling are idealised into a symbol of the strongest bond of human fellowship. In *Middlemarch*, on the other hand, it is noticed as a popular error that 'we are most of us brought up to think that the highest motive for not doing a wrong is something irrespective of the beings who suffer the wrong;' and the reason that the severe morality of the *Mill on the Floss* failed to content some critics seems to have been that there also the ultimate sanction by which right doing was enforced appeared to be only the reluctance to give pain to other persons whose desires were not in any way neces-sarily more moral or exalted than those of the agent. Without wishing the objective vigour of the author's imaginative creations to be clouded by a transparent didactic purpose, her readers may not unnaturally look for an imaged solution of the logical dilemma—If the desires of A are not a trustworthy guide for A's conduct, how can they be a safe moral rule for B; and, conversely, how is A to be more secure in following B's desires than his own? Or, if the strength of moral ties lies rather in their association with the permanent as opposed to the ephemeral experiences of life, than in their association with altruistic as opposed to egoistic impulses, it will still have to be shown—though not of course proved—how and wherein the permanent conditions of life are more respectable than its accidents. Gwendolen is already cast for the *rôle* of demon, but we do not know whether virtue is to be martyred or triumphant—in Rex or in Deronda—or whether George Eliot has yet inclined her ear to the prayer of the novel reader for a 'real hero', one unveraciously ideal, who may be admired without any sense of moral discipline and who will steer his way through the pitfalls of his imaginary career with a confidence the more inspiriting because would-be imitators of his prowess might always find excuse in the obstinate circumstances of actual life for any failure to follow in his footsteps. There is something hopefully unpractical in his returning Gwendolen's necklace, which she has pawned in a gambling freak at Baden, and the first number leaves the reader's mind in an admirable state of suspense as to the 'Meeting of the Streams' of incident indicated in its introductory and concluding chapters.

53. Henry James, unsigned notice, *Nation*

24 February 1876, xxii, 131

In view of the deluge of criticism which is certain to be poured out upon George Eliot's new novel when the publication is completed, it might seem the part of discretion not to open fire upon the first instalment. But this writer's admirers can reconcile themselves to no argument which forbids them to offer the work a welcome, and—putting criticism aside—we must express our pleasure in the prospect of the intellectual luxury of taking up, month after month, the little clear-paged volumes of *Daniel Deronda*. We know of none other at the present time that is at all comparable to it. The quality of George Eliot's work makes acceptable, in this particular case, a manner of publication to which in general we strongly object. It is but just that so fine and rare a pleasure should have a retarding element in it. George Eliot's writing is so full, so charged with reflection and intellectual experience, that there is surely no arrogance in her giving us a month to think over and digest any given portion of it. For almost a year to come the lives of appreci-ative readers will have a sort of lateral extension into another multitu-dinous world—a world ideal only in the soft, clear light under which it lies, and most real in its close appeal to our curiosity. It is too early to take the measure of the elements which the author has in hand, but the imagination has a confident sense of large and complex unfolding. The opening chapters are of course but the narrow end of the wedge. The wedge—as embodied in the person of Gwendolen Harleth—seems perhaps unexpectedly narrow, but we make no doubt that before many weeks have gone by we shall be hanging upon this young lady's entangled destiny with the utmost tension of our highest faculties. Already we are conscious of much acuteness of conjecture as to the balance of her potentialities—as to whether she is to exemplify the harsh or the tender side of tragic interest, whether, as we may say in speaking of a companion work to Middlemarch, the Dorothea element or the Rosamond element is to prevail. A striking figure in these opening chapters is that of Herr Klesmer, a German music-master, who has occasion to denounce an aria of Bellini as expressing 'a puerile state of culture—no sense of the universal.' There could not be a better phrase than this latter one to express the secret of that deep interest with which the reader settles down to George Eliot's widening narra-tive. The 'sense of the universal' is constant, omnipresent. It strikes us sometimes perhaps as rather conscious and over-cultivated; but it gives us the feeling that the threads of the narrative, as we gather them into our hands, are not of the usual commercial measurement, but long electric wires capable of transmitting messages from mysterious regions.

54. Extracts from George Eliot's journal

1875–6

All page references are to *The George Eliot Letters* (see Introduction, p. 33).

25 December 1875.

For the last three weeks, however I have been suffering from a cold and its effects so as to be unable to make any progress. Meanwhile, the 2 first volumes of *Daniel Deronda* are in print and the first Book is to be published on February 1.—I have thought very poorly of it myself throughout, but George and the Blackwoods are full of satisfaction in it. Each part as I see it before me *im Werden*[1] seems less likely to be anything else than a failure, but I see on looking back this morning— Christmas Day—that I really was in worse health and suffered equal depression about *Romola*—and so far as I have recorded, the same thing seems to be true of *Middlemarch*.

I have finished the Vth Book, but am not so far on in the VIth as I hoped to have been, the oppression under which I have been labouring having positively suspended my power of writing anything that I could feel satisfaction in (vi, 200–1).

12 April 1876.

On February 1 began the publication of *Deronda*, and the interest of the public, strong from the first, appears to have increased with Book III. The day before yesterday I sent off Book VII. The success of the work at present is greater than that of *Middlemarch* up to the corresponding point of publication. What will be the feeling of the public as the story advances I am entirely doubtful. The Jewish element seems to me likely to satisfy nobody.—I am in rather better health, having perhaps profited by some eight days' change at Weybridge (vi, 238).

[1] In process of becoming.

3 June 1876.

Book V published a week ago. Growing interest in the public and growing sale, which has from the beginning exceeded that of *Middlemarch*. The Jewish part apparently creating strong interest (vi, 259).

1 December 1876.

Since we came home at the beginning of September I have been made aware of much repugnance or else indifference towards the Jewish part of *Deronda*, and of some hostile as well as adverse reviewing. On the other hand there have been the strongest expressions of interest —some persons adhering to the opinion, started during the early numbers, that the book is my best—delighted letters have here and there been sent to me, and the sale both in America and in England has been an unmistakable guarantee that the public has been touched. Words of gratitude have come from Jews and Jewesses, and there are certain signs that I may have contributed my mite to a good result (vi, 314).

55. R. H. Hutton, unsigned review, *Spectator*

9 September 1876, xliv, 1131-3

Hutton reviewed four of the eight parts of *Daniel Deronda* in the *Spectator* (29 January, 8 April, 10 June, 29 July) as they appeared during 1876. He concluded with this review of the novel when it was published in four volumes (see Introduction, pp. 33-4).

There are both blemishes and beauties in *Daniel Deronda* which belong exclusively to this work of its great author. No book of hers before this has ever appeared so laboured, and sometimes even so forced and feeble, in its incidental remarks. No book of hers before this has ever had so many original mottoes prefixed to the chapters which, instead of increasing our admiration for the book, rather overweight and perplex it. No book of hers before this ever contained so little humour. And no doubt the reader feels the difference in all these respects between *Daniel Deronda* and *Middlemarch*. On the other hand, no book of hers before this, unless, perhaps, we except *Adam Bede*, ever contained so fine a plot, so admirably worked out. No book of hers before this was ever conceived on ideal lines so noble, the whole effect of which, when we look back to the beginning from the end, seems to have been so powerfully given. No book of hers before this has contained so many fine characters, and betrayed so subtle an insight into the modes of growth of a better moral life within the shrivelling buds and blossoms of the selfish life which has been put off and condemned. And last of all, no book of hers before this has breathed so distinctly religious a tone, so much faith in the power which overrules men's destinies for purposes infinitely raised above the motives which actually animate them, and which uses the rebellion, and the self-will, and the petty craft of human unworthiness, only to perfect the execution of His higher ends, and to hasten His day of deliverance. It is true that so far as this book conveys the author's religious creed, it is a purified Judaism,—in other words, a devout Theism, purged of Jewish narrowness, while retaining the intense patriotism which pervades Judaism; and that the hero,—who is intended for an ideal of goodness as perfect as any to which man can reach at present,—evidently sees nothing in the teaching of Christ which raises Christianity above the purified Judaism of Mordecai's vision. But however much we may differ from her here, it is not on such a difference that our estimate of the power or art of this fine tale can turn. So far as its art is concerned, there neither is nor can be any issue of a dogmatic nature embodied in it. But it would be as idle to say that there is no conception of Providence or of supernatural guidance involved in the story, as to say the same of the Œdipean trilogy of Sophocles. The art of this story is essentially religious.

The struggle between evil and good for Gwendolen, her fear of the loneliness and vastness of the universe over which she can exert no influence, and the selfish plunge which she makes, against all her instincts of right and purity, into a marriage in which she fancies she can get her own way, only to find that she has riveted on herself the grasp of an evil nature which she cannot influence at all, though every day makes her fear and hate that nature more; the counteracting influence for good which Deronda gains with her by venturing,—as a mere stranger,

—to warn her and help her against her gambling caprice, and thus identifying himself in her mind with those agencies of the universe beyond the control of her will which 'make for righteousness,' to use Mr. Arnold's phrase; and lastly, that disposal of events which always brings her within reach of Deronda's influence when she most needs it, till good has gained the victory in her, and that influence, too, is withdrawn, to make room for a more spiritual guidance,—all this is told with a power and a confidence in the overshadowing of human lives by a higher control which is of the essence of the art of the story, and essentially religious. And still more essentially religious is that part of the tale which affects Deronda himself. His mother's attempt to separate him in infancy from the Jewish people, whose narrowness, though a Jewess herself, she detested, and to get him the footing of an English gentleman; the effect which this parentless and ambiguous condition of life has in so training Deronda's natural sensitiveness as to make him study the habits, and wants, and feelings of others even before his own; the controlling power which brings him into special relations with his own people, though he does not know them to be his own people; the victory of conscience over his mother when a fatal disease strikes her, and she fulfils her father's wishes, in spite of her own repulsion to them, by revealing to her son to what race he belongs, and what dreams of his future his Jewish grandfather had indulged; and most of all, the effect which human rebelliousness and self-will had in aiding rather than foiling those higher purposes against which they tried to make war,—all this is told with a force that at times resembles that of the Hebrew prophet's belief in the Eternal purposes, and at times that of the Greek tragedian's mysterious trackings of that inscrutable power which now seems to mock us with its irony, and now again to smile on us in compassion. Whatever the blemishes of the story, no one who can appreciate Art of the higher kind will deny that the history of Gwendolen's moral collapse and regeneration, and of Deronda's mother, and her eventual submission to that higher spirit of her father which, by its want of breadth and sympathy with her own individual genius, had utterly alienated her, in the brilliancy of her youth, till she strove with all her might to ignore what was noble and even grand in it, is traced with a sort of power of which George Eliot has never before given us any specimen.

At the same time, it cannot be denied that while there is more which reaches true grandeur in this story than in perhaps any other of the same writer's, there is much less equality of execution and richness of conception. The hero himself is laboured. And though in some of the closing scenes, especially those with his mother and with Gwendolen, we are compelled to admit that the picture is a noble one, so much pains has been expended on *studying* rather than on *painting* him, that throughout (say) three-quarters of the story, we are rather being prepared to make acquaintance with Deronda than actually making acquaintance with him. Again, we are not satisfied with the Jewish heroine, Mirah. After the first scene in which she appears, where in her misery she is contemplating suicide, and, with a minute fore-thought characteristic of times of excitement, takes care to dip her long woollen cloak in the river, in order that she may sink the more easily when she puts it on,—after this scene, we say, Mirah does not gain upon us, but rather irritates us against her by her intolerable habit of crossing her hands on her breast, in sign, we suppose, of the meek-ness and patience of her disposition,—a sign, however, which excites arrogance and impatience in the mind of the readers, and sends a nerve-current through their hands which would be likely to show itself in a sort of action very different from that of Mirah's. The vagueness of the picture of the hero till within a few fine scenes of the end, and this ostentatious humility of the heroine's, seem to us real blots on the higher art of the book.

Then, again, as we have said, the incidental thoughts of the book are in general greatly laboured, and often not only laboured, but feeble. For example, 'A certain aloofness must be allowed to the representative of an old family; you would not expect him to be on intimate terms even with abstractions.' That is forcible-feeble. Or take this, which is still worse—*à propos* of the poverty of the Jewish reformer, Mordecai: —'Such is the irony of earthly mixtures, that the heroes have not always had carpets and teacups of their own; and seen through the open window by the mackerel-vendor, may have been invited with some hopefulness to pay three hundred per cent. in the form of fourpence.' When one realises that all which this laborious sentence means, is that the heroes of the world have often been poor enough to seem fit subjects to be made the prey of grasping costermongers, one is almost bewildered that one of our greatest writers could say anything of so little worth with so elaborate an emphasis. Yet like instances of at once laborious and insignificant remarks are very numerous in *Daniel Deronda*. A similar criticism applies to the original headings prefixed to many of the chapters. Some of them are, as they always used to be, both original and beautiful. But others, again, though even in this book they are certainly the exceptions, are artificial, and even tiresome.

[quotes epigraphs to chs. 1 and 37]

Add to this that the small pedantries, like talking of 'emotive memory' and a 'dynamic' glance, are more numerous than ever, and that perhaps the only sketch of really great humour in the story, is the picture of the composer and pianist Klesmer, and we have shown some reason, we think, for the opinion which is so widely expressed, that at least in some respects *Daniel Deronda* falls far below the level of *Middlemarch*. On the other hand, the cynicism of the incidental irony is certainly much less, and the whole spirit of the book is wider and higher.

But what makes it, after all, uncertain whether, in spite of the much greater inequality of execution and style, *Daniel Deronda* may not rank in the estimate of the critics of the future as a greater work altogether than any which George Eliot has previously written, is the powerful construction of the plot,—almost a new feature in her stories, —and the occasional grandeur of the conceptions which she successfully works out. The whole of the seventh part and the explanation between Gwendolen and Deronda in the last, seem to us to contain perhaps the highest work George Eliot has ever given us. The scene in which Deronda's mother describes the invisible force which is upon her in her pain and weakness to make her,—involuntarily almost, —revoke her own deliberately executed and apparently successfully executed purpose,—the magnificence of the picture of the woman, half-queen, half-actress, and yet wholly real, as she discloses her unmaternal character to the son whom she admires, but neither loves nor cares to have loving her,—the shrinking and yet imploring tenderness which she awakens in her son,—the constraint and yet the passion of their mutual upbraidings, and their efforts to suppress them, —all produce an almost magical effect on the imagination, such as cannot be paralleled, we think, in any former work of this writer's. There is in this interview something of the high scenic imagination of Sir Walter Scott, blended with the greater knowledge of the individual heart possessed by George Eliot. Not so magical in its force,—we might almost say splendour,—but quite as delicate and much more subtly tender, are the later scenes between Gwendolen and Deronda, after the former has lost her husband in the manner which makes her almost accuse herself of his death. It would be hardly possible to exceed the pathos of the parting interview, where Gwendolen suddenly becomes aware that Deronda is not only engaged to another woman, but preparing to leave for the East, to absorb himself in a life in which she has no interest or concern. There is a subtlety in the relations of the two,—relations which have never in any way been those of passion,—and a delicacy in the painting both of her forlorn sinking of the heart and of his natural tenderness for her, which seem to us among the most original conceptions of modern literature. We may, perhaps, extract a part, without destroying the artistic effect on the mind of the reader:—

[quotes at length the scene from ch. 69 beginning, 'What are you going to do?']

We have avoided criticising the no doubt very prominent and important character of Mordecai, the Jewish prophet, simply because we find it very difficult to make up our mind about him. The picture in some respects is a singularly fine one. But the *ideas* and creed of the man, on which, in a case like this, so very much turns, are too indefinitely and vaguely sketched to support the character. Before such a being as Mordecai could seriously have proposed to restore nationality to the Jews, in order that they might resume their proper mission of mediating, as religious teachers at least, between East and West, he must have had a much more defined belief than any which the author chose to communicate to us. And the result is to make us feel that he is rather a fine torso than a perfectly conceived and sculptured figure. We admire him, we revere him, we are touched by him, but we are puzzled by him. He would remind us now and then of Mr. Disraeli and the 'great Asiatic mystery,'[1] if his moral nature were not so much more noble and definite than anything of which Mr. Disraeli ever caught a glimpse. On the whole, Mordecai's influence on Deronda is only half-justified. We cannot dismiss Deronda on his journey to the East without feeling uncomfortably that he is gone on a wild-goose chase,—to preach ideas which have only been hinted, and which must rest on a creed that has hardly been hinted at all. *Daniel Deronda* thus seems to us much more unequal than *Middlemarch*. But it rises at certain points definitely above that great book. Its summits are higher, but its average level of power is very much lower.

[1] The phrase used by Sidonia to describe the hero's quest in *Tancred* (1847), II, xi.

56. George Saintsbury, review, *Academy*

9 September 1876, x, 253-4

George Edward Bateman Saintsbury (1845-1933) was a school teacher, a prolific writer on literary subjects, and in 1895-1915 Professor of Rhetoric and English Literature at Edinburgh University. Some of his best-known works are *A Short History of French Literature* (1882), *Elizabethan Literature* (1887), *A History of Criticism* (1900-4), and *A History of English Prosody* (1906-10). He was a regular contributor to several periodicals, including *Macmillan's Magazine*, *Pall Mall Gazette*, and the *Saturday Review* (see Introduction, p. 33).

Independently of its interest as a mere story and as a vehicle for reflections, *Daniel Deronda* is eminently interesting, because it presents in a fresh and brilliant light the merits as well as the faults of its writer—merits and faults which are here sharply accentuated, and are not, as is too frequently the case, blurred and confused by the wearing of the plate. Both classes of peculiarities should be by this time pretty well known to the student of English letters. On the one hand, we are prepared to find, and we do find, an extraordinarily sustained and competent grasp of certain phases of character; a capacity of rendering minute effects of light and shade, attitudes, transient moods of mind, complex feelings and the like, which is simply unparalleled in any other prose writer; an aptitude for minting sharply ethical maxims; and a wonderful sympathy with humanity, so far, at least, as it is congenial to the writer. On the wrong side of the account must be placed a tendency to talk about personages instead of allowing them to develop themselves, a somewhat lavish profusion of sententious utterance, a preference for technical terms in lieu of the common dialect which is the fitter language of the novelist, and a proneness to rank certain debateable positions and one-sided points of view among the truths to which it is safe to demand universal assent. To this black list must be added some decided faults in style. In discussing a book which is in everybody's hands, it will be well to show how the above points are brought out, and how they affect the general merit of the book, rather than to indulge in superfluous description of the plot.

In the matter of character, then, we find two signal triumphs of portraiture. The part of Gwendolen Harleth is throughout an overwhelming success: and the minutest and least friendly examination will hardly discover a false note or a dropped stitch. Her self-willed youth; the curious counterfeit of superiority in intellect and character, which her self-confidence and her ignorance of control temporarily give her; her instant surrender at the touch of material discomfort; the collapse of her confidence in the presence of a stronger spirit; the helpless outbursts of self-pity, of rage, of supplication, which follow that collapse; the struggle between blind hatred and almost equally blind glimmerings of conscience; the torrent of remorse and final prostration of will—are all imagined with a firmness, and succeed each other with an undoubted right of sequence, which cannot but command admiration. The husband is almost equally admirable; indeed, one's admiration is here increased by the perception that the hand which is so faithful is distinctly unfriendly, and that the author would like us to detest Grandcourt. Yet there is not the slightest exaggeration in the portrait, as he appears before us, acting with strict politeness to his wife, in no way violent towards her (if we except the occasional use of somewhat forcible language), and employing, for the purposes of his refined tyranny, nothing stronger than the methods of 'awful rule and right supremacy.' If he should appear to anyone all the more detestable, it may be suggested that it is difficult for any husband to extricate himself handsomely from the position of being hated by his wife and having that hatred confided to a bewitching rival.

The more study we give to these wonderful creations the better we like them, and an additional interest is imparted by the discovery that Gwendolen is at heart a counterfoil of Dorothea, animated by an undisciplined egotism instead of an undisciplined altruism, and by the fanaticism of enjoyment instead of the fanaticism of sympathy. It might even suggest itself to a symmetrical imagination that the soul of Casaubon clothed with the circumstances and temperament of a fine gentleman would animate just such a personage as Grandcourt. But these are fancies. The point of present importance is that the interest of the story undoubtedly tends to centre in these two admirable characters and is unfortunately not allowed to do so. Of the third (according to the author's design, the first) personage we cannot speak as we have just spoken. The blameless young man of faultless feature who clutches his coat-collar continually; who at the age of some twenty years wished 'to get rid of a merely English attitude in studies;' who, in the words of his best friend, was disposed 'to take an antediluvian point of view lest he should do injustice to the megatherium;' of whom it was impossible to believe, in the still more graphic words of the friend's sister, 'that he had a tailor's bill and used boot-hooks;' who never does a wicked thing, and never says one that is not priggish—is a person so intolerably dreadful that we not only dislike, but refuse to admit him as possible. Only once, perhaps, is he human—when he persuades himself on all sorts of ethico-physico-historical grounds that he should like to be a Jew, solely because (as that very sensible woman his mother, the Princess, discovers at once) he wishes to marry a fascinating Jewess. We cannot accept as an excuse for the selection of this 'faultless monster' as hero the pleas put forward in the book that it is only the 'average man' and the 'dull man' that will not understand him, and that the average man is not very clear about the 'structure of his own retina,' and the dull man's 'dulness subsists, notwithstanding his lack of belief in it.' In the first place, the cases are not parallel: for, though the average man may know very little about the structure of his retina, he can tell a real eye from a glass one well enough. And, in the second place, the dull man may fairly retort, 'If you are a great novelist, *make* me believe in your characters.'

In this dearth, or rather distortion, of central interest, the minor characters do not help us much. They are far less individual, and far less elaborate than is usual with George Eliot. *Daniel Deronda* does not supply a fifth to join the noble quartette of Mdmes. Holt and Cadwallader, Poyser and Glegg. Sir Hugo Mallinger, with Hans Meyrick and his sister Mab, makes a shift to fill up the gap, but it is but a shift. Lapidoth, the unwelcome father, is chiefly welcome to us, the readers, because of the happy boldness of the incident which finally unites the lovers. Mordecai we must not, we suppose, call a minor character, but of him more hereafter.

There is no lack in these volumes of the exquisite cabinet pictures to which George Eliot has accustomed us. The account of Gwendolen's 'grounds of confidence;' the charming etching of the waggon passing Pennicote Rectory; the scene of the first ride with Grandcourt; Gwendolen, after Klesmer has crushed her hopes of artistic success, and again immediately before she at last accepts her lover; the wonderful sketch of Grandcourt 'sitting meditatively on a sofa and abstaining from literature;' Deronda in the synagogue; the stables at the Abbey; the waiting at Genoa for the Princess; and lastly, Gwendolen's retrospect of Offendene—are all effects of the finest in this kind. But this good gift and other good gifts have been somewhat repressed, as it seems to us, in order that certain tendencies not so excellent in themselves, and very much the reverse of excellent when inordinately indulged, might have freer play. No one can read *Daniel Deronda* without perceiving and regretting the singular way in which the characters are incessantly pushed back in order that the author may talk about them and about everything in heaven and earth while the action stands still. Very sparingly used this practice is not ineffective, but the unsparing use of it is certainly bad, especially when we consider in what kind of language these parabases or excursus are expressed. We cannot away (in a novel) with 'emotive memory' and 'dynamic quality,' with 'hymning of cancerous vices' and 'keenly perceptive sympathetic emotiveness,' with 'coercive types' and 'spiritual perpetuation,' still less with hundreds of phrases less quotable because bulkier. No doubt many of these expressions are appropriate enough, and they are all more or less intelligible to decently-educated people. No doubt the truths of science, mental and physical, are here, as elsewhere in our author's works, rendered with astonishing correctness and facility. But it appears to us that the technical language of psychology is as much out of place in prose fiction as illustration of its facts is appropriate. In philosophy, in politics, in religion, in art, a novelist, when he speaks in his own person, should have no opinion, should be of no sect, should indulge in no *argot*.

If we are dissatisfied with the Jewish episode which is so remarkable in this book, it is not merely because it has supplied temptations to indulge in psychological disquisition. We do not in the slightest degree feel 'imperfect sympathy' with Jews, and we hold that Shylock had the best of the argument. But the question here is whether the phase of Judaism now exhibited, the mystical enthusiasm for race and nation, has sufficient connexion with broad human feeling to be stuff for prose fiction to handle. We think that it has not, and we are not to be converted by references to the 'average man.' The average man has never experienced the passion of Hamlet, of Othello, or of Lear; he is not capable of the chivalry of Esmond, of the devotion of Des Grieux,[1] of the charity of the Vicar of Wakefield. But he has experienced, and he is capable of, something of which all these sublime instances are merely

[1] The hero of *Manon Lescaut* (1731) by Abbé Prévost.

exalted forms. Now the 'Samothracian mysteries of bottled moon-shine' (to borrow a phrase from *Alton Locke*) into which Mordecai initiates Deronda are not thus connected with anything broadly human. They are not only 'will-worship,' but they have a provincial character which excludes fellow feeling. Poetry could legitimately treat them; indeed, many of Mordecai's traits may be recognised,—as we think, more happily placed—in the Sephardo of *The Spanish Gypsy*. They are, no doubt, interesting historically; they throw light on the character and aspirations of a curious people, and supply an admirable subject for a scientific monograph. But for all this they are not the stuff of which the main interest or even a prominent interest, or anything but a very carefully reduced side interest, of prose novels should be wrought. It is hardly necessary to say that this dissatisfaction with the manner and scale of his appearances does not blind us to the skill applied in the construction of Mordecai. Probably no other living writer is capable of the patient care with which these intricate and unfamiliar paths are followed; certainly no other is master of the pathos which half reconciles the reluctant critic. If the thing was to be done, it could hardly have been done better, assuredly it could not have been done with greater cunning of analysis or in a manner more suggestive.

We should have no right to complain that to the simplicity and passion which characterise the subjects and situations of the author's earlier books there has succeeded something more complex and analytic in the present: it is a time-honoured transition, and one which has before now yielded excellent results. But in reality the transition is not in this case great, because the subject-matter really remains the same although there may be somewhat less directness of treatment. The book is little more than a fresh variation on the theme which has informed so much of George Eliot's work, which lurks even in the *Scenes of Clerical Life*, which is hardly in abeyance in *Adam Bede*, which is the professed motive of *The Mill on the Floss*, of *The Spanish Gypsy*, and of *Romola*, which gives charm to the slightness of *Silas Marner*—to wit, the excellence of obeying the instigations of kinship and duty rather than the opposing instinct, 'All for Love and the World well Lost.' Perhaps the motive has hardly depth and volume enough to bear such constant application. But this is matter of opinion. The matter of fact remains, that we have once more presented to us in the contrast between Gwendolen's misery and the prosperity of the sleek Deronda the same moral as we had in Hetty's catastrophe, in the fate which punished Maggie Tulliver's partial declension from the standard,

GEORGE ELIOT

in the ruin and disgrace that sprang from Duke Silva's passion, in the
degradation and death of Tito Melema; the same theories which led to
the sympathetic selection of Felix Holt for a hero and of Dorothea
Brooke for a heroine. The moral, and the standard, and the theories
are doubtless of a fine severity, and deal deserved rebuke to the lax
pleasure-seeking which has been considered a vice at all times, and is
not openly considered a virtue even yet. In the illustrations of these
doctrines the author has again given us admirable portraits, and much
exquisitely-drawn surrounding. But perhaps she has also once more
illustrated the immutable law that no perfect novel can ever be written
in designed illustration of a theory, whether moral or immoral, and
that art, like Atticus and the Turk, will bear no rival near the throne.

57. Unsigned review, *Saturday Review*

16 September 1876, xlii, 356–8

This review, one of the most unsympathetic towards the Jewish
part of the novel, was continued on 23 September 1876 (see
Introduction, p. 33).

The reader, in closing the last book of *Daniel Deronda*, can hardly be
certain to what cause is due the impression that the present work is a
falling off from *Adam Bede*, and *Middlemarch*, and a whole train of
favourites. He knows very distinctly what his feeling in the matter is,
but he has to ask himself whether the conviction that the author has
fallen below her usual height is owing to any failure of power in herself, or to the utter want of sympathy which exists between her and her
readers in the motive and leading idea of the story. This is a question
which can hardly be settled. Some resolute admirers may indeed
endeavour to adjust their sympathies to this supreme effort, but there
can be no class of sympathizers. Jew and Christian must feel equally
at fault; and those who are neither one nor the other are very unlikely

376

to throw themselves with any fervour into the mazes of Mordecai's mystic utterances. Yet we recognize George Eliot's distinctive excellences all through; we never detect a flat or trivial mood of mind; if anything, the style is more weighty and pregnant than ever, we may even say loaded with thought. Nobody can resort to the time-honoured criticism that the work would have been better for more pains, for labour and care are conspicuous throughout, and labour and care which always produce suitable fruit; but the fact is that the reader never —or so rarely as not to affect his general posture of mind—feels at home. The author is ever driving at something foreign to his habits of thought. The leading persons—those with whom her sympathies lie— are guided by interests and motives with which he has never come in contact, and seem to his perception to belong to the stage once tersely described as peopled by 'such characters as were never seen, conversing in a language which was never heard, upon topics which will never arise in the commerce of mankind.'

And not only are these personages outside our interests, but the author seems to go out with them into a world completely foreign to us. What can be the design of this ostentatious separation from the universal instinct of Christendom, this subsidence into Jewish hopes and aims? We are perpetually called away from the action of the persons of the drama to investigate the motive for such a choice of theme. It might be explained if it were the work of a convert, but *Daniel Deronda* may be defined as a religious novel without a religion and might have been composed in the state of mind attributed to the hero when 'he felt like one who has renounced one creed before embracing another.' We are at sea throughout. Nobody seems to believe in anything in particular. Nobody has any prejudices. If it were not for the last page, we should be utterly at a loss to know what is the hero's aim in life, to what purpose he is going to devote it. Nobody expects a novel to contain a religious confession, and the reader of strictest personal faith may pass over latitude in this matter in an author whose legitimate work of delineating human nature is well executed; but when a young man of English training and Eton and University education, and, up to manhood, of assumed English birth, so obliging also as to entertain Christian sympathies, finishes off with his wedding in a Jewish synagogue, on the discovery that his father was a Jew, the most confiding reader leaves off with a sense of bewilderment and affront—so much does definite action affect the imagination, and we will add the temper, more than any implication or expression of mere opinion. It is impossible to ignore differences which lead to such a conclusion. It is true that everything has its turn, and it may perhaps be regarded as significant that the turn of Judaism has come at last; that almost simultaneously with the last book of *Daniel Deronda* there has appeared the first of a series of papers 'On the Liturgy of the Jews, by a Jew,' in a popular contemporary,[1] where, to the uninitiated, the subject seems most curiously incongruous. We gather from it that party spirit runs high between Hebrew Conservatives and Liberals, or the writer would not have exposed to the ridicule of the Gentile world certain portions of the 'Liturgy' recited in the synagogues every Sabbath from the Piyutim; and hence that there may be Jews willing to accept the aid of auxiliaries who regard them, not on the side of their faith but of their race, which we need not say is the point of sympathy and attraction with the present author.

Force of imagination this writer certainly possesses; but a fertile imagination is not one of her distinctive gifts. To one class of her admirers the stores of her exact memory, treasured by the keenest observation, and set off by a humour especially rare in women, and a power of analysis rare in all writers, have supplied one main charm of her novels. The scenes and persons which strike them as a sort of glorified, harmonized, poetized reproduction come most readily to their recollection in recalling her masterpieces; but such stores must necessarily come to an end. No experience holds inexhaustible examples of mother wit and wisdom, of quaint rustic ignorance and cunning, of strong prejudice which has never felt the breath of cultivated opinion. Each work hitherto has been enriched by some lifelike portrait drawn from this source, but with sign of more and more effort. At first these resuscitations from a vivid past mix themselves with the body of the story, act in it, and assist its development. We cannot think of *Adam Bede* without Mrs. Poyser, or of the *Mill on the Floss* without Mrs. Tulliver and the wonderful group of aunts and their husbands, or of *Silas Marner* without Dolly Winthrop and the company so ensnaring to her husband at the 'Rainbow.' But this transfusion of the characters derived from memory into the very heart and substance of the story, so that they have entered into the first plan and conception of it, necessarily gives place in time to another use of these diminished stores, when they are brought in for the purpose of enlivening a narrative to which they are not essential; as we see in *Felix Holt*, where the hero's mother says strange things to show herself off and amuse the reader, not

[1] *Pall Mall Gazette* (18 August 1876), xxiv, 653.

to advance the plot, outside of which she stands. The same may be said of the group of 'waiters for death' in *Middlemarch*. The present story has no representatives of this class. We recognize no figure as certainly a portrait drawn out of the past. The Jew pawnbroker and his family fill the place of these recollections, but they are clearly a study of more recent date; a study, the reader suspects, made with a purpose, and not from the simple early instinct of observation to which we have assumed the others to be due. The failure of one source of supply must necessarily induce more labour. To reproduce, to revivify a cherished memory is a more loving and congenial task than to educe from inner consciousness the personages fitted to illustrate certain views and theories. We feel that the writer's earlier works must have flowed more easily from her pen and been a more invigorating effort than to personify an idea in the person of Mordecai; because, for one reason, the labour of composition, never slight in work of so high a standard as hers, must have been cheered by confidence in the sympathy of her readers, by notes of approval sounding in her ears; but what security of that kind, what echo of wide sympathy, can have encouraged the unwinding of Mordecai's mazy, husky sentences, with their false air of prophecy without foretelling anything? She must know her public too well to have allowed herself any delusion here, and must have been fully aware that Mordecai would be caviare to the multitude, an unintelligible idea to all but an inner circle. The mystery lies, not so much in himself, for this readers would not care to unravel, but in the question as to what reason the author can have had for thrusting him on their unwilling attention. The ordinary reader indeed ignores these mystic persons, and in family circles Gwendolen has been as much the heroine—if we may so term the central and most prominent female figure—as if there were no Mirah.

Of course in the design of *Daniel Deronda* we are reminded of the part played by Fedalma in the *Spanish Gipsy*. Fidelity to race stands with this author as the first of duties and virtues, nor does it seem material what the character of the race is. Fedalma feels her gipsy blood, as soon as she is made aware of her origin, to be as strong and imperious a chain as his Jewish descent is with Deronda. In each, race, as linking past and future together, is the idea of an earthly perpetuity. In obedience to this sentiment, the one throws over faith and lover and takes ship with her people; the other, except that he is lucky in a Mirah, follows the same course, throws over every previous association, and takes ship to the vague East.

It is not often that the poet or novelist sets himself to draw a perfect man. The effort is commendable, for it is mostly its own reward. True it is that the low light in most hands gives the colour. Tennyson's *King Arthur* and Wordsworth's *Happy Warrior* have perpetuated some grand ideas with this aim, but the latest prose image of perfection that occurs to us in our own tongue is *Sir Charles Grandison*. There are certain conditions from which no invention can escape. Thus, perfection must extend to person as well as mind, and beauty and charm must work their usual effects on imperfect people; that is, the perfect hero must be fallen in love with by more women than he can oblige by a return of affection, and the manner of tender, gentle suppression cannot escape a touch of the Grandisonian. Personal characteristics, however, may vary with the age. It fits with the eighteenth century to impute to its model man an air of vivacity and intrepidity, and an intelligence as penetrating as a sunbeam, which only served to quicken our un-doubting faith. In the ideal portrait of our own day gravity, thought, and doubt predominate. The perfect man takes nothing for granted, and is deciding for himself all day long on the most fundamental questions. People who will take nothing on trust are not commonly the most interesting and pleasant to meet with; but Deronda is so far successful as a portrait that we believe no other writer of our day, inspired by the same intention, could have imparted the degree of amiability, life, and reality which our author has infused into her ideal. It has evidently been a labour of love to apply her special talents to the embodiment of cherished ideas in an external form; to dramatize them, as it were, and make them speak for themselves, through the person and action of her hero; and no one is more successful in helping her readers to realize, not through elaborate and ineffective description, but by conveying an image through its effect on others. Deronda does nothing, but he has a curious influence.

[quotes several descriptions of Deronda's sympathetic nature]

But what is wanting in himself Deronda yet seems to supply to others. The author invests him with many spiritual functions, not scrupling to add certain adjuncts impressive to the imagination, as where it is noted, in Gwendolen's confession in the library, that a joint fragrance of Russian leather and burning wood gave the idea of incense, 'of a chapel in which censers have been swinging.' Not only is he Gwendolen's preacher, confessor, and director, but he is her conscience, and in this capacity she calls his eye dreadful. There are

occasions even when he arrives at an elevation higher than this; when
he suggests the idea of a Providence, when he is a Being with a capital
B, and is foretold by his grandfather as Deliverer with a capital D, and
finally he represents to Mordecai, whose inward need of a prolonged
self had been dwelt on, something beyond even this. The dying Jew
commits his soul into his charge. 'Where thou goest, Daniel, I shall go.
Is it not begun? Have I not breathed my soul into you? We shall live
together.' It is not easy to reconcile these qualities, functions, or
attributes—whatever we may call them—with the costume of the
day, whether evening full dress, which he sets off so well, or that
morning drab suit which sets off him. The task which the author has
set herself to accomplish in these volumes is to bring together past and
present; to modify, by certain explanatory analogies, ancient beliefs into
modern doubt, and in her own case to show how the keenest insight
into the world's doings may work side by side with a vein of speculation far removed and alien from ordinary sympathies. We have left
ourselves no room for the story proper, or for the characters who work
it out; these we must reserve for another occasion.

58. R. E. Francillon, review, *Gentleman's Magazine*

October 1876, xvii, 411–27

Robert Edward Francillon (1841–1919) was on the staff of the *Globe* (1872–94) and wrote many novels, some of whose titles were: *Olympia: A Romance*, *Zelda's Fortune*, *Pearl and Emerald*, and *Streaked with Gold*. In 1868, George Eliot read the first two numbers of his novel *Madame Aurelia* in *Blackwood's* and 'thought them promising' (*Letters*, iv, 481). This review, entitled 'George Eliot's First Romance', is one of the most perceptive and sympathetic attempts to come to terms with *Daniel Deronda* (see Introduction, pp. 34–5).

When a great artist, whose very name has become a sure note of excellence, produces a work that the great fame-giving majority refuses to accept on the sole ground that it is his, or hers, there is a matter for dull congratulation. Such an event shows that past triumphs have been neither decreed blindly on the one hand, nor on the other accepted as a dispensation from the duty of making every new work a new and original title to future laurels. And such an event is the production of *Daniel Deronda*.

The author herself can have looked for no immediate fortune but that of battle. The very merits of the book are precisely the reverse of those to which the wide part of her fame is due. Not a few critics have already said that *Daniel Deronda* is not likely to extend George Eliot's reputation. That is unquestionably true—the sympathies to which it appeals are not, as in the case of *Adam Bede*, the common sympathies of all the world. But whether *Daniel Deronda* is not likely to *heighten* her reputation is an entirely different question, and will, I firmly believe, meet with a very different answer when certain natural and perhaps inevitable feelings of disappointment have passed away, and her two generations of admirers have reconciled themselves to seeing in her not only the natural historian of real life, whom we know and have known for twenty years, but also a great adept in the larger and fuller truth of romance, whom as yet we have only just begun to know.

Daniel Deronda is essentially, both in conception and in form, a Romance: and George Eliot has not only never written a romance before, but is herself, by the uncompromising realism of her former works, a main cause for the disesteem into which romantic fiction has fallen—a disesteem that has even turned the tea-cup into a heroine and the tea-spoon into a hero. George Eliot should be the last to complain that the inimitable realism of *Middlemarch* has thrown a cold shade over the truth and wisdom that borrow the form of less probable fiction in *Daniel Deronda*. She is in the position of every great artist who having achieved glory in one field sets out to conquer another. The world is not prone to believe in many-sided genius: one supremacy is enough for one man.

In short, I cannot help thinking that George Eliot's new novel has caused some passing disappointment because it is not another *Adam Bede* or *Middlemarch*, and not because it is *Daniel Deronda*. The first criticism of a book is sure to be founded on a comparison with others. Fortunately, *Daniel Deronda* lies so far outside George Eliot's other works in every important respect as to make direct comparison impossible. It cannot be classed as first, or second, or third, or last—that favourite but feeble make-shift for criticism, as if any book, or picture, or song could be called worse in itself because another is better, or better because another is worse. I believe that *Daniel Deronda* is absolutely good—and the whole language of criticism contains no stronger form of literary creed. Not only so, but I believe that it promises to secure for its author a more slowly growing, perhaps less universal, but deeper and higher fame than the works with which it does not enter into rivalry. In any case it marks an era in the career of the greatest English novelist of our time. It is as much a first novel, from a fresh hand and mind, as if no scene of clerical life had ever been penned. And, as such, it calls for more special criticism even than *Middlemarch*— the crown and climax of the series that began with the sad fortunes of the Reverend Amos Barton. It is not even to be compared with *Romola* —that was no romance in the sense that the term must be applied to *Daniel Deronda* as the key to its place and nature.

However much we may divide and subdivide, there are in reality only two distinct orders of fiction. Unfortunately, while we have a distinctive name for the one, we have none for the other. Perhaps the difference between the fiction which deals with ordinary or actual things and people and that which deals with extraordinary things and people is so marked and obvious that no names are wanted to express it any more than a scientific term is needed to express the difference between an eagle and a phœnix. The important point is that *Daniel Deronda* is very broadly distinguishable from all its predecessors by not dealing with types—with the ordinary people who make up the actual world, and with the circumstances, events, characteristics, and passions that are common to us all. We have all been so accustomed to see ourselves and all our relations and friends mirrored and dissected that we naturally expected to find the same familiar looking-glass or microscope in *Daniel Deronda*. It is small consolation to a plain man, who looks forward to the ever-new pleasure of examining his own photograph, to be presented with the portrait of a stranger, though the stranger may be handsomer and less common than he. Nevertheless it may well be that he will prize the picture most when he is in the mood to remember that the world does not consist wholly of types, and that the artist who ignores the existence of even improbable exceptions gives a very inadequate, nay, a very false representation of the *comédie humaine*. If George Eliot can be said to have shown any serious fault as an artist, it is that she has hitherto almost timidly kept to the safe ground of probability. Of course the law on this subject is well understood, and has been clearly laid down a hundred times. Fiction is bound by certain rules of probability: fact by none. But this is only sound law where what is called realistic fiction—the novel of types and manners—is concerned. Applied to the Romance, it is not sound law. Romance is the form of fiction which grapples with fact upon its whole ground, and deals with the higher and wider truths— the more occult wisdom—that is not to be picked up by the side of the highway. 'This, too, is probable, according to that saying of Agathon: "it is a part of probability that many improbable things will happen," ' says George Eliot herself, quoting from Aristotle. 'It is easier to know mankind than to know a man,' she quotes from Rochefoucauld. And, as she herself says, 'Many well-proved facts are dark to the average man, even concerning the action of his own heart and the structure of his own retina.' But this is not the line upon which she has hitherto proceeded. Her practice is best described in her own words—'Perhaps poetry and romance are as plentiful as ever in the world except for those phlegmatic natures who I suspect would in any age have regarded them as a dull form of erroneous thinking. They exist very easily in the same room with the microscope and even in railway carriages: what banishes them is the vacuum in gentlemen and lady passengers.' That vacuum she has hitherto done her best to supply, and has supplied it so far as such a thing is possible. We have learned—and we are apt to forget how ill we knew the lesson before *Adam Bede* made its mark upon the literature of the century—that poetry and romance are among the chippings of a carpenter's workshop, are even hovering about the whist-tables of a Middlemarch drawing-room, and are not strangers to the shops of Holborn pawnbrokers. But are poetry and romance, any more than wit and wisdom, to be looked for only in studies and railway trains? We shall find plenty of all by taking the train for St. Oggs, or Treby Magna, or paying a visit to Mrs. Poyser of Dale Farm, or, for that matter, by staying at home among our own relations and friends. But we may travel far before we make the acquaintance of a complete Gwendolen Harleth or an entire Henleigh Mallinger Grandcourt in the flesh, though we may come here and there upon scraps and fragments of them—farther still before meeting a Hebrew prophet in a second-hand book-stall, or hearing from a Frankfort banker the legacies of wisdom bequeathed by a Daniel Charisi. And why should we not, for once in a way, travel away from ourselves? By risking the immediate disappointment of a large number of her most ardent admirers, George Eliot has paid us a higher compliment than if she had given us another Silas Marner. She has practically refused to believe the common libel, upon us who read fiction, that we only care to look at our own photographs and to be told what we already know.

Gwendolen Harleth is as much a romance heroine as Undine. When we are first introduced to her across the green table at Leubrunn we are not, like Deronda himself, puzzled by the question whether the good or the evil genius was dominant in her eyes. She is so far from being a 'She-Tito,' as one excellent critic, showing less discrimination than usual, has called her, as to be his very opposite—Tito Melema not only had a soul, but was an absolutely soul-haunted man. In Gwendolen we see at once not a soul, but only the possibility of a soul—not an actual, but only possible battle-field for the good genius and the evil. The faun in broadcloth, in Hawthorne's 'Transformation,' is more than matched by this nymph with the *ensemble du serpent* in sea-green and silver. Of course thus far Gwendolen Harleth is obviously typical: just as there are many Maggie Tullivers with grand ready-made souls all at sea among mean, narrow, and vulgar surroundings, so, by way of

contrast, are there many Rosamond Vincys and Gwendolen Harleths.
The bitter tragedy of Rosamond and Lydgate tells how one of these
soulless creatures can act as the basil plant to which the Middlemarch
surgeon likened his wife in after times—'a flower that flourished
wonderfully on a murdered man's brains.' That story demands for its
development nothing but the plainest and simplest realism and the closest
and most exclusive connection with every-day things—the smaller and
commoner the better. But, suppose it had been part of George Eliot's
plan to endow Rosamond Vincy or Hetty Sorrel with a soul—the
realistic, every-day machinery of *Adam Bede* and *Middlemarch* must
have ignominiously broken down. It would have been as adequate
to endow Aunt Pullet herself with one. The seeming transformation of
which we may fairly and without fear of being misunderstood—at
least by any reader of *Daniel Deronda*—speak as the birth of a human
soul is a possible thing in every case, but, in any given case, absolutely
unlikely. It must depend upon outward circumstances, and the circumstances must necessarily be of an exceptional kind—either unlikely
in themselves, or so intensified as to seem unlikely. That is to say, it
demands the unbounded, open air of Romance for its representation,
where Nature may be seen at work in her rarer aspects: where things
are not as we all see them every day, but as some few people may see
them once in a lifetime, and thus become exceptionally wise themselves,
and, if they impart their rare experience, make others wiser. Gwendolen
in St. Oggs, Gwendolen in Treby, Gwendolen in Middlemarch, *must*
have lived and died 'with her gunpowder hidden,' as Sir Hugo
Mullinger would say: with her goodness always at that stage of harvest
when 'it lies all underground, with an indeterminate future . . . and
may have the healthy life choked out of it by a particular action of the
foul land which rears or neighbours it.' To make the original situation
more striking, the difficulties of transformation more insuperable, the
creator of Gwendolen Harleth has shown remorseless cruelty in depriv-
ing the possible, invisible harvest of every chance of showing a single
blade. She is not only 'the spoiled child,' but is narrowed and grooved
by spoiling. 'To be protected and petted, and to have her susceptibilities
consulted in every detail, had gone along with her food and clothing
as matters of course in her life.' She was not high enough placed to
dream of playing a part in the great world, or low enough to have a
share in the battles of the wide one. She had no exceptional powers or
affections or passions or ambitions. Her only talents were an eccentric
sort of beauty that was not likely to prove marketable, and a cold sharp

tongue, pointed by a scornful wit of the sort that frightens men and repels women. She is only a bright ripple upon a dead background. Not one of her surroundings can possibly, except in a negative way, have the smallest influence upon her for good or evil. When by accident she comes in contact with great things, as in the person of Herr Klesmer, her thin nature shrivels up: she is nothing, and nowhere. The lively impertinences with which she amused herself at the expense of Tasso and Mrs. Arrowpoint, Jennings and young Clintock, turn into mere shafts of ill-temper when let fly in a broader horizon. She is a real woman: and her blank horizon is more hopelessly, even more tragically, real than the indefinite tragedy which opens in prospect when she is made to faint, with a presentiment of conscience, at a sudden sight of the picture behind the panel at Offendene. It is more pathetic even than the gross and vulgar surroundings of Maggie Tulliver. She could not have found openings and revelations in chance looks and chance words like the miller's daughter. Poor Maggie's soul was above circumstance: circumstance stood to poorer Gwendolen in the place of a soul. George Eliot, who is never weary of dwelling upon the all-importance of early associations in developing character, and of showing how 'what we have been makes us what we are,' has carefully and explicitly denied her even the remembrance of a fixed dwelling. 'Pity,' she says, 'that Offendene was not the home of Miss Harleth's childhood, or endeared to her by family memories! A human life, I think, should be well rooted in some spot of a native land . . . a spot where the definiteness of early memories may be inwrought with affection. . . . At five years old mortals are not prepared to be citizens of the world, to be stimulated by abstract nouns, to soar above preference into impartiality. . . . The best introduction to astronomy is to think of the nightly heavens as a little lot of stars belonging to one's own homestead.' Gwendolen knew but of one star: and that was Gwendolen.

The whole of the first book is devoted to this portrait of Gwendolen —it is a masterly picture, and, in spite of the careful and even exaggerated extraction from her life of all positive circumstance, in spite of the extraordinary difficulty of giving life to a character with no more tangible consistency than a moonbeam, we soon grow to know her as well as her familiar contrast, Maggie Tulliver. I feel tempted to say as well as we know the blacksmith's boy who set Rex Gascoigne's shoulder, for the sake of dwelling upon the marvellous skill with which George Eliot has more than once compressed a whole character, which suggests a whole history apart from events, into a sentence or two. He comes and goes, and we feel as if he had set our shoulder, instead of Rex Gascoigne's. But even before we can guess at the nature of the story, beyond a suspicion that exceptional sin, or exceptional sorrow, beyond common experience, is needed to transform the young lady of Offendene into a woman, the shadow of Grandcourt appears. The manner of his entry is striking and artistic. He, also, at first sight, resembles one of Gwendolen's surrounding *vacua*—the addition of a cypher to a line of cyphers. It is only by degrees that he assumes the rank of the integer before them that gives them value. And, as he develops, he also develops the significance of Deronda. Passages from George Eliot's works could easily be multiplied to show how intensely she regards our active personal influence upon one another from without, the blows, so to speak, given and taken in the battle of life, rather than self-consciousness or self-culture, as the machinery for growth and change. She believes in the mesmeric effect of personality. Nearly every one of her novels contains an influencing character, in a greater or less degree—Dinah Morris, Edgar Tryan, Felix Holt, Dorothea Brooke, Savonarola are only more strongly marked instances. Naturally, in novels of types and manners, such personal influence mostly takes a large religious or social form. But to bring Gwendolen Harleth into relation with such men and women as these—the experiment would be absurd. That 'utterly frustrated look, as if some confusing potion were creeping through her system,' still repeats itself, I am sure, though she is married to Rex and corresponds with Deronda, whenever she feels herself standing on the edge of an idea—though she has no doubt given up the childish experiment of trying to read learned books in order to make herself wise. Her experiences were bound to be special and peculiarly her own: 'Souls,' said Dorothea Brooke to her sister, 'have complexions too: what will suit one will not suit another.' And so happened to her what is utterly unlikely, and therefore utterly inadmissible in representations of typical life and character such as all George Eliot's former works have been: perfectly necessary for the complete study of Gwendolen's transformation, and therefore perfectly legitimate in Romance, which studies human nature in its seeming exceptions, and not in its rules. The end is exceptional: the machinery must be exceptional also. And so the life of Gwendolen Harleth became bound up with that of Henleigh Grandcourt on the one hand and with that of Daniel Deronda on the other.

No doubt the main interest attaching to Deronda and Grandcourt is their relation to Gwendolen. Taken apart from her, and from the romance of her destiny, their intensity would savour of exaggeration. But nobody would dream of talking about exaggeration in connection with the fiend and the angel who, in the well-known picture, are playing at chess for a human soul. There are many men more or less like Grandcourt, or rather like parts of Grandcourt: but he, taken as a whole, is a cunning combination of all the qualities, positive and negative, fit—to refer again to the harvest simile—to choke out the germ 'by damage brought from foulness afar,' just as her earlier life represented the evil action of the rearing and neighbouring land. George Eliot has shown the force of her genius by turning this necessary *dysdæmon* into an actual man, and by bringing him into relation with Gwendolen in a simple and natural way, that serves to illustrate both his character—apart from his intended use—and hers. His original conception seems to belong to a speech of Mrs. Transome in *Felix Holt*, 'A woman's love is always freezing into fear.. She wants everything, she is secure of nothing. This girl has a fine spirit—plenty of fire and pride and wit. Men like such captives, as they like horses that champ the bit and paw the ground: they feel more triumph in their mastery. What is the use of a woman's will?—if she tries, she doesn't get it, and she ceases to be loved. God was cruel when he made women.' This one-sided, poetical outburst is translated for Gwendolen into plain and bitter prose. She required to be crushed out of her very small self before she could expand into a self that was larger: and as such a preliminary process was a labour of Hercules we have a Grandcourt to fulfil the labour. One of the many passages to which I have already referred as illustrating George Eliot's stress upon personal influence is quite as applicable to her relations with her husband as to her feelings about Deronda: 'It is one of the secrets in that change of mental poise which has been fitly named conversion that to many among us neither heaven nor earth has any revelation till some personality touches theirs with a peculiar influence, subduing them into receptiveness. It had been Gwendolen's habit to think of the persons around her as stale books, too familiar to be interesting.' Had she been left to Grandcourt alone, only half the process of transformation could have been possible: she would have undergone all the grinding sorrow, all the heart-breaking self-contempt, and all the longing to destroy life so that she might destroy her bonds; but she would have escaped from all this in time—her soul would have been strangled in its birth: she would have ended by becoming assimilated more and more to her tyrant, and would have been worse than at first because, instead of having no soul at all, she would have had the soul of a slave. That would not have been transformation, but degradation. It is at this point we see the full force of the title-page motto,

Let thy chief terror be of thine own soul—

For the soulless nymph is growing a soul now, and it is a soul to be feared. When she saw Mrs. Glasher riding in the park, unrecognised by Grandcourt, 'What possible release could there be for her from this hated vantage-ground, which yet she dared not quit, any more than if fire had been raining outside it? What release, but death? Not her own death. Gwendolen was not a woman who could easily think of her own death as a near reality, or front for herself the dark entrance on the untried and invisible. It seemed more possible that Grandcourt should die: and yet not likely. The power of tyranny in him seemed a power of living in the presence of any wish that he should die. The thought that his death was the only possible deliverance for her was one with the thought that deliverance would never come; the double deliverance from the injury with which other beings might reproach her, and from the yoke she had brought on her own neck. No! She foresaw him always living, and her own life dominated by him; the "always" of her young experience not stretching beyond the few immediate years that seemed immeasurably long with her passionate weariness. The thought of his dying would not subsist: it turned as with a dream-change into the terror that she should die with his throttling fingers on her neck avenging that thought. Fantasies moved within her like ghosts, *making no break in her more acknowledged consciousness and finding no obstruction in it: dark rays doing their work invisibly in the broad light.*' I have emphasised these last words because they express directly, and not merely suggest, the part that Grandcourt is intended to play in what promises to be her soul's tragedy.

Of course Deronda's part, if we remember the depth and subtlety of the drama that is being played, is obvious. It was necessary that we should perceive the action of the good as distinctly and intensely as that of the evil. And in incarnating the good influence, so to speak, I do not think that George Eliot has altogether succeeded so completely in enlisting our sympathies as usual. It is true the difficulties of the task were almost insurmountable. We know what men in general are apt to call men in particular who talk with never failing wisdom, and in whose armour of virtue there is no flaw. We know also what women for the most part think of such men, and therefore we know what novel readers in general will say and think of Gwendolen's good angel. I must own to a feeling of relief when Deronda was conscious of a wish to horsewhip Grandcourt; it was a touch of good warm-blooded sympathetic humanity. However, the sneer is a very cheap and not very effective form of criticism. Nobody dreams of sneering at the Red Cross Knight, in another romance, or at Bayard, *sans peur et sans reproche*, in romantic history.[1] Nobody has ever suggested that ideal beauty of soul differs from ideal beauty of face in not being worth painting. It is one of the highest privileges of the romance to idealise: to show what, under intensely favouring circumstances of nature or culture, may be the best goodness as well as the worst wickedness of a man. If it is true that we needs must love the highest when we see it, it is well that we should have an opportunity of seeing the highest from time to time. In relation to Gwendolen, it is not so much with Deronda himself as with the wisdom and the goodness of Deronda that we are concerned. But he justly gives his name to the novel in so far as he, if not the principal actor in any drama, is a moving influence in three dramas which are only very subtly and indirectly connected—the stories of Gwendolen, of Mirah, and Mordecai.

Deronda is certainly not one of those who find nothing but barrenness from Dan to Beersheba. There are persons in real life who cannot walk from Charing Cross to Temple Bar and not meet with an adventure for every flag-stone: and he is one of these people. If Gwendolen is a nineteenth century nymph, he is a nineteenth century knight errant, and a fortunate one. He is not, however, unique or even very exceptional thus far, and there is a passage in Chapter XXXII.—too long for quoting at length, and too complete for spoiling by mutilation —which paints him in detail, and which ought to place him at once and for all in sympathetic *rapport* with us, if there be any power in words to keep our attention fixed to anything but incidents and conversations. At any rate, the remarkable circumstances of his birth and bringing up, his harmonious nature, his unbounded and all-sided sympathies, and by no means least, his wonderful talent for finding adventures at every turning, from his cradle to his marriage, qualify him to serve as the conductor whom we need to lead us, by natural steps, into the wide air of romance which Gwendolen must breathe if she is not to die. Through his eyes, which do not look upon common things commonly, we see that romance, the natural history of exceptions and intensities, is as true as reality, and more true than much that seems real. It is very

[1] Pierre du Terrail, Seigneur de Bayard (c. 1473–1524), famous French knight.

remarkable that, in dealing with him, George Eliot has not only
adopted the spirit of romance but its forms—nay, often its common and
conventional forms, and that with deliberate preference and intention.
Many of her novels contain a romantic incident, and some introduce
many, but that is a different thing. Here we have the romantic framework made up of separate incidents not very unlikely in themselves,
but which when added or rather multiplied together make up a very
unlikely whole. What is the 'plot' of Daniel Deronda's history, if it is
condensed after the manner of hurried reviewers? A foreign Jewish
singer wishes that her only child may be spared what she considers the
miseries of his race and become an English gentleman. He is brought
up in luxury and kindness, but in ignorance of his race and parentage,
by a baronet who is his mother's rejected lover. He saves from suicide
a beautiful young girl—herself a Jewess, which is a rather strong
concidence—whom he afterwards marries. He—another strong
coincidence—meets with the most untypical of all untypical Jews, a
poor workman in London with the brain of a scholar, the heart of a
poet, and the soul of a prophet, who by sheer force of enthusiasm
inspires, and naturally inspires, the young man of thought and culture
with a Quixotic purpose that is to absorb all his years and powers.
Meanwhile he has been recognised at Frankfort, a little mysteriously,
by a Jew banker as the grandson of his bosom friend, Daniel Charisi;
and Deronda's mother, from some motive that I will not call insufficient
only because I cannot understand it, sends for him, tells him his family
history, and then passes out from his life again for ever. Thus set out
like a pile of dry bones, and covering mysteries and family puzzles to
which it is not George Eliot's ordinary habit to give more importance
then they are worth, which is at best very little, the events of Deronda's
life look like the skeleton of a pre-arranged dream. The effect is even
carefully enhanced by such a coincidence as that between Mordecai's
second-sighted vision of the manner in which his completer soul was to
appear to him, 'distantly approaching or turning his back towards him,
darkly painted against a golden sky . . . mentally seen darkened by the
excess of light on the aërial background,' and the way in which
Deronda actually approached him along the river, dark in face and
dress, and as 'from the golden background' of a glorious sunset. But let
us at once put all these things, these wonders let us call them, in sharp,
immediate contrast with the story of Gwendolen. The contrast is extreme—all the better. It is not more extreme, in truth, than the contrast
between life's limits and conditions as dimly guessed by Gwendolen and

its unconditioned boundlessness through Art as felt by Klasmer. We need to feel strongly all the difference between her original soullessness and the largeness of an idealised world. It is a strange sensation to go straight from Gwendolen, who needs a revelation to learn that the world is larger than one of her whims, to Mordecai the prophet, to Jacob—not the less a prophet because Jacob is only little Jacob Cohen, the pawnbroker's son. I think one is not obliged to take any profound interest in the Hebrew politics of the future to appreciate Mordecai, so far as we are capable of extending our sympathies in an upward direction. In any case he amply fulfils a sufficient mission by keeping well before our eyes the existence of an ideal world, where all things, though but in dreams and visions, may seem possible, while we are watching Gwendolen's attempts to see beyond the edge of her gown. The Cohens are a foil to him that he may be the more forcible contrast to her, just as the picture of a Dutch kitchen is the most telling preparation for the study of a picture of saints and angels, and that, in its turn, for sympathy with one of human life or history.

There is no reason to fear that the adoption of the common forms of the romance shows poverty or carelessness in invention, or indeed that it shows anything at all except that there is a limit to the permissible length of a novel which the most popular of writers must not exceed. In the novel of types and manners situations are not more important than the way we arrive at them. In the romance—still using the word in its special and contrasted sense—the effects and situations are all-important, and the artist will not spoil his climax by elaborating preliminary details that are, except in their result, of no importance at all. It is not inartistic to use the romance-framework that comes readiest to hand, just as a musician would be very ill-advised who wasted power in inventing a new form for every new sonata. He would set people thinking about his forms too much, and about his effects too little. The direct, uncompromising adaptation of the spirit and form of the romance to a novel of our own time by the author of *Middlemarch* is in itself a striking and daring, perhaps hazardous, experiment in the art of fiction, and certainly the experiment is the more complete, and its effect the stronger, by using forms which held the same good wine of romance that was drunk by our less exigent fathers. If they are but a ready machinery for saving time that can be used for better purpose, they serve their turn. The mere story of *Daniel Deronda* may not be a particularly good one; but then few people have ever read a novel by George Eliot, unless it was *Silas Marner*, merely, if at all, for the sake of the story. It is more important to note whether she displays the qualities—apart from the close realism she does not affect—for which they are read like the lives of old friends that are always new. And in this respect one striking feature of *Daniel Deronda* is that it is not only George Eliot's first romance, but the first novel in which she has either taken our own day for her date, or the class of whom novel readers in general have most personal experience—excluding prophets and pawn-brokers—for her *dramatis personæ*.

In the very first page of the very first of her published works the authoress of 'The Sad Fortunes of the Reverend Amos Barton' affects to complain that 'Mine, I fear, is not a well-regulated mind: it has an occasional tenderness for old abuses; it lingers with a certain fondness over the days of nasal clerks and top-booted parsons, and has a sigh for the departed shades of vulgar errors.' And these words were written when a great many things were in full force and vigour that have since joined those departed shades. If *Adam Bede* and *The Mill on the Floss* were old world pictures when they were published, what are they now? They have almost fallen back into idylls, so far as that indefinite word implies any idea of obsolete antiquity. They already illustrate history, and—as somebody once suggested in the case of Dickens—will soon require an archæological museum for their illustration, including, for example, a parish clerk, a parson's top-boots, and Master Marner's loom. The brass bands and ribbons of the North Loamshire election will stir no corresponding chord in the breasts of our grandchildren, who never saw the member chaired, or spent at least eight exciting hours in feeling that the welfare of creation depended on the difference between orange and blue. George Eliot's works are more full of such matters than even of advanced scientific allusions; she has the air at times of looking upon the present only as a link between the past that we love and regret and the future that we love and hope for. And, in so far as she is thus historical, the outward, circumstantial aspects of her novels must inevitably lose some amount of living interest as time goes on. Even so, we cannot read *Waverly* or *Redgauntlet* quite in the same personally sympathetic spirit as men who still numbered among them Jacobites in heart and, like the father of British romance himself, had talked with those who remembered the '45. For our own immediate selves, there is all the difference between *Daniel Deronda* and *The Mill on the Floss* that lies between Now and Once upon a Time. But there is a greater difference still. Each and all her works may be very easily separated into its accidents of period and circumstance and its essentials of what is true and human always, under all circumstances, and every-where. I will say nothing about Shakespeare, but she certainly has a share in the genius and therefore probably in the fortunes of Chaucer, who is as great as he is obsolete in small things, as enduring as he is great in large. It is precisely in the detailed elaboration of the little, characteristic, everyday things which procure universal acceptation for a book at once that we are most conscious of an unusual want in *Daniel Deronda*. In this respect also it is distinctively of the nature of the Romance, which tends to bring universal and essential things into prominence, and to leave accidental and transitory things on one side. It will never require a department in the museum, at least until the peculiarities of Jews are merged in the yet greater oddities of Gentiles, and that time looks too far off to be worth considering. Its drawing-room atmosphere is only a roughly washed-in background: and then the atmosphere of the drawing-room is not likely to be changed, any more than that of the studio. Whatever of truth, wisdom, and human nature it contains is *absolutely* independent of circumstances and back-grounds. So far as Deronda and Mordecai are unlikely now, they will always be unlikely: but their creation will always be of equal value, because they are not men of this time in particular, but bring out into idealised prominence the history of the birth of Gwendolen's soul, which is a woman's soul. It would be surprising indeed if *Daniel Deronda* achieved at once the public triumph of *Adam Bede*—it is a novel professedly treating of our own day, and of the novel-reading class, and yet does not base its interest upon the afternoon tea-table. But it is one of the few books that can afford to wait for a long and quiet triumph with patient security. That also is one of the privileges of Romance: and of all books that recognise and reveal the truth that lies in the well of dreams.

It is of course tempting to dwell upon the various characters, sub-ordinate as well as principal, in detail, and to indulge in the pleasure of marking what has struck oneself more particularly in the course of two careful readings. Mirah Cohen, the ostensible heroine of the romance as Gwendolen is of the reality; Klesmer, the latest type of musician; Mrs. Davilow, the innocent cause of Gwendolen; the honest, almost simple-hearted, worldly wisdom of the Rector of Pennicote, and the complicated unworldly humour of Hans Meyrick the painter, and some score of minor sketches, seem to call for more or less unlimited space in their due degree. Nobody, alas, has taken up the mantle of

Mrs. Poyser. There is altogether less epigram and more serious, sub-humorous reflection than usual, as befits an age when mother-wits have also gone over to the majority and joined the ghosts of vulgar errors. But there is no lack of sayings, though couched in less homely language than hers, that might grow into proverbs—usefully I would say if proverbs were ever useful. 'Those who trust us, educate us.' 'The dullness of things is a disease in ourselves.' But I assume that my readers are also already my fellow-readers, and these and many similar sentences are easily known and easily recalled. What I wish to dwell upon mainly is that the comparative method of criticism, unsatisfactory always, is extraordinarily inapplicable to *Daniel Deronda*. It cannot be said to differ from *dam Bede*, or *The Mill on the Floss*, or *Silas Marner*, or *Middlemarch*, or *Felix Holt*, or even from *Romola* in degree, because it differs from them all in kind—in conception, scope, circumstance, and form. They deal with men and women in the aggregate, as they are or have been: this with individual men and women as they may be or can be. They treat prominently of manners: this leaves manners out of the question. They have to do with the broad passions and emotions common to us all: this with exceptional moods and passions, brought out by exceptional circumstances, special to individuals. They develop the study of healthy anatomy: this of pathology. They exclude, this includes, the unlikely. They reflect, this magnifies. They teach us to know ourselves, this helps us to guess at others. They appeal straight to the heart, this takes the road of the mind. They combine facts, this expands them into fancies. In a word, *Daniel Deronda* differs from them in being a Romance—and that of the highest kind—and moves upon different though converging lines according to different laws. Thus considered, it is practically a first book by a new author, and must be judged accordingly. We are not justified in saying whether we prefer this to any other novel or any other to this: we can go no farther than preferring one kind of novel to another. So far as truth to human nature is concerned, both forms are of equal virtue, and indeed supply each other's deficiencies. It would be a 'poor tale,' as George Eliot's midland farmers say, if any form or feature or guess at truth of any kind were to be left hidden because some kind of machinery for extracting them is forbidden by critical laws. A certain kind of fiction, which simply reflects faithfully, must of course be bound to accurate, typical fidelity by the strictest laws. But fiction at large, which has as much to do with unlikely things as Nature herself, has only one law, and that is the complete attainment of its end by any means, by the sacrifice of anything but possibility—and what is not possible, where human nature is concerned, is proverbially hard to say. If the machinery of the Arabian Nights were necessary for extracting an additional scrap of human nature worth having out of the mine, then let it be used by all means, and gratefully. Fortunately we need not fear being driven to any such desperate resource when we see how powerful the ordinary forms of the Romance are in the hands of a great artist for depicting what surely cannot be shown by painting everyday types and everyday manners: the invisible transformation of a germ into a soul. No mere naturalist, who only knows what he sees, could describe the birth of the moth from the worm. 'Deronda laughed, but defended the myth. "It is like a passionate word," he said; "the exaggeration is a flash of fervour. It is an extreme image of what is happening every day." ' Such is not the mere apology for the romance—it is its more than sufficient reason for being.

It is, of course, idle to speculate whether *Daniel Deronda* marks the beginning of a new manner, as musical biographers say, on the part of its author. In its romance aspect it may be simply a parenthesis, a brilliant display of strength in a foreign field. But it would be pleasant to regard it as the forerunner of a line of fiction that will immediately concern ourselves and our children who live in the England of to-day. We cannot help envying the England of yesterday the painter it has found. As she says of Deronda, 'To glory in a prophetic vision . . . is an easier exercise of believing imagination than to see its beginning in newspaper placards, staring at you from a bridge beyond the corn fields: and it might well happen to most of us dainty people that we were in the thick of the battle of Armageddon without being aware of anything more than the annoyance of a little explosive smoke and struggling on the ground immediately about us.' George Eliot has hitherto too much neglected the newspaper placards upon the railway bridges and thought—I dare not add the words 'too much'—of the cornfields. She has abandoned the houses, not of St. Oggs or Middlemarch, but of London, too freely to those who try to copy the close realism that she herself popularised among us without 'the force of imagination that pierces or exalts the solid fact, instead of floating among cloud-pictures.' After all, there is something better than pleasure and vanity in our wishing to see our own selves as we are, and we have a right to complain that we have been neglected—until to-day. Our afternoon tea-tables have been photographed *ad nauseam*: it is time for the cover to be removed, that we may see underneath them. We welcome *Daniel Deronda* not only as a grand romance of a woman's soul, in the highest sense of the word, but also the first novel that gives us the hope of studying ourselves in the same spirit with which we have been able to study mankind at large as typified by our fathers. There are incomplete Grandcourts and imperfect Derondas who will repay study as fully as the more picturesque class of country-town people and Loamshire farmers, and no less for their own sakes than as means to an end. Gwendolen Harleth alone is enough to show how closely and deeply she can study our drawing-room Undines, if such there be. And *Daniel Deronda* alone (the book, not the man) is proof enough that its author has the courage to enter upon the surest road to the highest kind of popularity—that which apparently leads above it. There is not a sentence, scarcely a character, in *Daniel Deronda* that reads or looks as if she were thinking of her critics before her readers at large, or of her readers at large before the best she could give them. She has often marred a stronger and more telling effect for the sake of a truer and deeper—and this belongs to a kind of courage which most artists will be inclined to envy her. But her processes of construction open another question, too long to speak of in a few words. Apart from all considerations of such processes in detail, *Daniel Deronda* is a probably unique example of the application of the forms of romance to a rare and difficult problem in human nature, by first stating the problem—(the transformation of Gwendolen)—in its extremest form, and then, with something like scientific precision as well as philosophic insight, arranging circumstance so as to throw upon it the fullest light possible. From this point of view even the objects of Mordecai's enthusiasm have their place in the drama as supplying the strongest contrast to common lives and thoughts obtainable in these days, and Deronda's perfection as affording the ideal we must keep in our minds in order to study whatever falls short of it. Less even in its intrinsic merits, with all their greatness, than in the promise it gives of doing tardy justice to the profounder poetry of our own immediate day, lies the highest value of this true Romance of Gwendolen Harleth and Daniel Deronda.

59. A. V. Dicey, unsigned review, *Nation*

19 October 1876, xxiii, 245-6

The first half of this two-part review appeared in the *Nation* on 12 October 1876 (see Introduction, p. 34, and headnote to No. 50).

The sense of dissatisfaction with the result of *Daniel Deronda* has its source in something deeper than any of the peculiarities of the story. The reader feels that there is something disappointing in the development of George Eliot's own genius. The power, the humor, and the deep moral insight which were revealed to the public in *Adam Bede* and *Scenes of Clerical Life* are all to be found in *Deronda*. The genius is still there, but the proportions of the qualities which make up the genius have, it is felt, gradually changed. Reflection prevails over description, and the moral purpose always discernible in George Eliot's works threatens to throw into the shade the author's creative power. For observation and painting are substituted analysis and reflection, and instead of the action of a drama telling its own tale, you have the reflective comment of a chorus of moralists.

The predominance of what may be fairly termed the chorus is the main characteristic by which George Eliot's earlier and later works are distinguished from one another. This chorus, it is true, is a feature of every novel which George Eliot has produced. The author at times directly, at times through the mouths of villagers or artisans, constantly reflects on the progress of the drama, notes the development of the character of heroes or heroines, and points the moral of their conduct. To object to this is futile, for to object is in effect to admit that you do not appreciate George Eliot's whole mode of thought and writing. That Mr. Main should, apparently with the author's sanction, collect together 'wise, witty, and tender sayings' from George Eliot's writings may be open to remark, and certainly suggests that George Eliot thinks more of the duties of a teacher than of the reputation of an author. But any one who does not appreciate the wisdom and wit to be found in all the novels published by the author of *Adam Bede* had better at once lay these novels aside. What we note is not the moral aim of the works but the mode in which the moral instruction they contain is now enforced. In George Eliot's earlier works the chorus kept in the background, the tale told its own moral. In *Middlemarch*, and still more in *Daniel Deronda*, the chorus becomes obtrusive. The aphorisms which head the chapters are long, though often impressive, texts, suggestive of a sermon, and the chorus is not kept outside the narrative, but delays the action of the piece to press home truths which intelligent readers might in many cases discover for themselves. Occasionally the result of superfluous moralizing is to produce a painful jar. Compare the following two passages from the works of the same writer, each of which deals with a somewhat similar situation.

The first describes Gwendolen's arrival at her husband's home, and the sudden revulsion of feeling produced by Mrs. Glasher's letter:

Grandcourt entered, dressed for dinner. The sight of him brought a new nervous shock, and Gwendolen screamed again and again with hysterical violence. He had expected to see her dressed and smiling, ready to be led down. He saw her pallid, shrieking, as it seemed with terror, the jewels scattered around her on the floor. Was it a fit of madness?

In some form or other the Furies had crossed his threshold.

The second describes the shock to Arthur Donnithorne when he returned home elated with the sense of actual heirship and future good intentions to find the letter announcing: 'Hetty Sorrell is in prison, and will be tried on Friday for the crime of child-murder.'

Arthur read no more. He started from his chair, and stood for a single minute with a sense of violent convulsion in his whole frame, as if the life were going out of him with horrible throbs. But the next minute he rushed out of the room, still clutching the letter. He was hurrying along the corridor and down the stairs into the hall. Mills was still there, but Arthur did not see him as he passed like a hunted man across the hall and out along the gravel. . . . When Mills got to the stables the horse was being saddled, and Arthur was forcing himself to read the remaining words of the letter. . . .

'Tell them I'm gone—gone to Stoniton,' he said, in a muffled tone of agitation, sprang into the saddle and set off at a gallop.

Who can read the passages side by side without seeing that in each case the horror of the situation tells its own tale, that all moralizing is out of place, and that the misplaced reference to the 'Furies' risks the descent from the height of tragedy to the bathos of a sermon?

The remarks, further, of the chorus, though often striking, are some-times more strained than impressive. A long passage which contrasts the pettiness of Gwendolen's hopes and fears with the greatness of the issues and interests raised by the war of Secession, supposed to be waged at the time of Grandcourt's courtship, concludes in these words: 'What, in the midst of that mighty drama, are girls and their blind visions? They are the Yea and Nay of that good for which men are enduring and fighting. In these delicate vessels is borne onward through the ages the treasure of human affections.' Here one may legitimately ponder over the precise meaning of an enigmatic sentence. When we are told that Deronda's mind 'glanced over the girl tragedies that are going on in the world hidden, unheeded, like the tragedies of the copse or the hedgerow, where the helpless drag wounded wings for-sakenly and streak the shadowed moss with the red moment-hand of their own death,' we know well enough what is meant, and that the meaning is only too weighty; but we may reasonably suspect that the desire to give force to the author's meaning is gradually overreach-ing itself, and leading George Eliot to pass from the eloquence of sim-plicity to the affectation of conceits. The narrative of Hetty Sorrell's tragedy contains no reference to 'red moment-hands.'

The impression of a want of simplicity is increased by a study of the mottoes which adorn or deface each chapter. They are often effective: a stanza which forms the motto of the second volume compresses into seven striking lines the moral of the whole book. But any one who doubts that the long-winded reflections taken from the commonplace-book or the unpublished works of George Eliot afford examples of the way in which a statement that has a meaning may be overloaded by the conceits in which it is expressed, should examine carefully the motto to the first chapter, and consider honestly whether a rather commonplace sentiment is not beaten out into an inordinate number of words.

But to criticise the minor defects of a great writer is poor work, and it would not be worth while to notice strained expressions did they not afford a sign of the transition from description to analysis, which is the characteristic and, in our judgment, the defect of our author's later works. The tendency to over-analysis produces its most disastrous effect when George Eliot places before the reader a character such as that of Deronda, on which has been expended an infinity of thought and labor. There is something absolutely painful in the kind of vivi-section to which his physical and moral qualities are subjected. Of his eyes, his voice, his complexion, the expressiveness of his countenance, and his perfect beauty we hear more than enough. The unravelling of his moral nature gives rise, no doubt, to suggestions which are in themselves full of instruction. 'His plenteous, flexible sympathy had ended by falling into one current with that reflective analysis which tends to neutralize sympathy. Few men were able to keep themselves clearer of vices than he, yet he hated vices mildly, being used to think of them less in the abstract than as a part of mixed human natures which it was the bent of his mind to trace with understanding and pity.' In these sentences is contained a profound explanation of that strange combination, which in modern days is often found to exist, of moral purity with the absence of indignation at vice. If you seek for an explanation of the fact that men who are virtuous and love virtue yet scarcely know the feeling which theologians call an abhorrence of sin, you cannot do better than study the passage we have quoted. But as page after page is filled with reflection of a similar kind, the reader feels that he is studying an instructive essay on human nature, but is not obtaining a picture of Deronda. The author, too, is dissatisfied, and, returning again and again to the hero's character, retouches a portrait which the very painter seems hardly to consider a likeness. When dealing with minor characters or carried away by the stress of the drama, George Eliot falls back on artistic instinct and paints with a bold hand. Hence Sir Hugh, Klesmer, Miss Arrowpoint, the Princess, and Joseph Kalonymos are full of life, whilst Deronda, and even to a certain extent Gwendolen, are bundles of qualities.

The deficiency, however, in the portrait of Gwendolen is only an indirect result of George Eliot's passion for reflection and analysis. Her character is rather incomplete than indistinct. The author has expended so much space on the elucidation of the play of varying motive and sentiment which decides Deronda's conduct, that she seems to have wanted the space needed to fill in the outlines even of her most important characters. Gwendolen's selfishness, waywardness, and caprice are made clearly apparent. Why a girl so selfish should have felt as many much better women would not have felt the wrong done to Mrs. Glasher, is never made really clear. The process of her 'conversion,' for no other term describes the awakening of her conscience, is itself rather hinted at than explained. The horror of something like the guilt of murder is intelligible enough. The sensitiveness of conscience which kept Gwendolen miserable in the midst of prosperity, before the commission of what the world would have held a great crime, needs more explanation than it receives. The grandest tale George Eliot has written has for its theme a woman's salvation from sin and misery under the influence of a man better than herself. No one ever felt they needed further explanation either of the repentance of Janet or of the influence of Mr. Tryan. Gwendolen's conversion will always remain a but half-explained enigma. Something the same may be said of Grandcourt's character. A motto to one of the chapters hints that Grandcourt exhibited the complete development of selfishness. His soul had morally died before his physical death. Such things may be, but one feels that some of the reflections lavished on the character of Deronda might have been well employed in drawing out with more clearness the steps by which Grandcourt had sunk from a man into a mere incarnation of joyless selfishness.

Another result of George Eliot's habit of analysis is that there exists occasionally a great difference between the portrait of a hero which George Eliot presents to the public and the effect which the hero's character makes on the author's own mind. This was conspicuously apparent in the case of Will Ladislaw. The same thing is true of Deronda. We can scarcely be mistaken in supposing that Daniel is meant to portray a character coming near to human perfection, in which all the strength and energy of a man are blended with the sensitive tenderness and keen personal sympathies of a woman. It is at bottom his perfect goodness which appears to have roused the conscience of Gwendolen. His exquisitely sensitive conscience enabled him to save Gwendolen when many men in his position would have been false to her or to themselves. Yet, despite the art used to make Deronda's virtues apparent to the reader, it may well be doubted whether the man, as actually drawn, will kindle much admiration even amongst those who most highly admire George Eliot's genius. He is incurably weak. He is at every stage of his life a slave to circumstances. He never ventures to ask Sir Hugh whether he is the baronet's son, and through life was thus oppressed by an unfounded belief in his own illegitimacy. He can determine on no career till fate or the influence of Mordecai forces him to take up a pursuit in life. A question from his mother reveals to him that he is in love. A question from a stranger determines him to devote himself to the service of his countrymen. Accident and the suggestion of a friend lead him to propose to Mirah. No doubt he is full of kindliness and sympathy, but his character has a painful touch of what may fairly be called 'priestly,' though not in the worst sense of that word. He has a genuine concern for the souls of his neighbors,

especially when these neighbors are pretty women. He sermonizes and
flirts at the same time, though both the flirtation and the sermonizing
are unconscious. His mixed weakness and sympathy lead, as is natural,
to cruelty. He puts off revealing to Gwendolen his marriage and his
plans till that revelation becomes the hardest of blows to the woman
whom his influence had aroused to goodness. He has, it is true, a charm.
His mother calls him a 'beautiful creature,' and throughout the whole
description of the interview between son and mother you feel it difficult
to think she is not addressing a daughter. The interview is perfectly
true to nature. Here as elsewhere George Eliot's drawing is truer than
George Eliot's reflections on the character drawn. Daniel remains
morally as well as physically a 'beautiful creature.' It is not of such stuff
that reformers are made. When Deronda wanders off to the East we
feel sure that he will travel about year after year doing deeds of kindness and cherishing noble aspirations, but further removed than even a
passionate dreamer like Mordecai from working out any deliverance
either for his people or for mankind. George Eliot might urge that our
estimate of Deronda is unjust. We doubt not that in a sense this is so.
Our very point is that from some cause or other Deronda is so drawn as
not to produce the intended impression on the reader. That this failure
to ensure an intended effect is closely connected with George Eliot's
increasing tendency to analysis is at least highly probable. This tendency is at any rate the real cause of all the legitimate dissatisfaction
which many of those who most keenly appreciate *Adam Bede*, *Romola*,
Silas Marner, or *Middlemarch* feel with regard to *Daniel Deronda*. The
book is a marvellous production. It exhibits all and perhaps more than
all the power of George Eliot's earlier works, but as you read it you
feel that throughout reflection predominates over spontaneous creation,
and that the chorus usurps the place of the actors. Admiration for the
result of labor and meditation cannot banish regret for the abundant
life of *Adam Bede* or the unbroken harmony of *Silas Marner*.

60. George Eliot to Harriet Beecher Stowe

29 October 1876

The George Eliot Letters, vi, 301–2.

As to the Jewish element in *Deronda*, I expected from first to last in writing it, that it would create much stronger resistance and even repulsion than it has actually met with. But precisely because I felt that the usual attitudes of Christians towards Jews is—I hardly know whether to say more impious or more stupid when viewed in the light of their professed principles, I therefore felt urged to treat Jews with such sympathy and understanding as my nature and knowledge could attain to. Moreover, not only towards the Jews, but towards all oriental peoples with whom we English come in contact, a spirit of arrogance and contemptuous dictatorialness is observable which has become a national disgrace to us. There is nothing I should care more to do, if it were possible, than to rouse the imagination of men and women to a vision of human claims in those races of their fellow-men who most differ from them in customs and beliefs. But towards the Hebrews we western people who have been reared in Christianity, have a peculiar debt and, whether we acknowledge it or not, a peculiar thoroughness of fellowship in religious and moral sentiment. Can anything be more disgusting than to hear people called 'educated' making small jokes about eating ham, and showing themselves empty of any real knowledge as to the relation of their own social and religious life to the history of the people they think themselves witty in insulting? They hardly know that Christ was a Jew. And I find men educated at Rugby supposing that Christ spoke Greek. To my feeling, this deadness to the history which has prepared half our world for us, this inability to find interest in any form of life that is not clad in the same coat-tails and flounces as our own lies very close to the worst kind of irreligion. The best that can be said of it is, that it is a sign of the intellectual narrowness—in plain English, the stupidity, which is still the average mark of our culture.

Yes, I expected more aversion than I have found. But I was happily independent in material things and felt no temptation to accommodate my writing to any standard except that of trying to do my best in what seemed to me most needful to be done, and I sum up with the writer of the Book of Maccabees—'if I have done well, and as befits the subject, it is what I desired, but if I have done ill, it is what I could attain unto.'[1]

61. James Picciotto, review, *Gentleman's Magazine*

November 1876, xvii, 593–603

Picciotto (1830–97) was a historian, the author of *Sketches of Anglo-Jewish History*. This review, entitled 'Deronda the Jew', is characteristic of the Jewish defence of the neglected half of the novel (see Introduction, p. 34).

Formerly the Israelite in novels was as accurate a representative of his race, as was the frog-eating French dancing master or the howling wild Irishman of ancient farces. He was a coiner, a buyer of stolen goods, a trainer of young thieves, a pettifogging attorney, a sheriff's officer, a money-lender, a swindling financier. He was a Jew, a man with no other thought than greed for money, no other sense of honour than that which is said to exist among the class to which he was compared, and with scarcely a soul to save. If old, he was hawk-eyed, hook-nosed, or with ferrety eyes. If young, he was red-lipped, with greasy ringlets, and wore showy jewellery. But young or old he was coarse, vulgar, the embodiment of covetousness and rapacity, with seldom one ennobling trait to redeem the repulsive picture. The delineation was as truthful as if a Whitechapel costermonger had been held out as the type of British merchants. To make a Jew the hero of a story, or even

[1] *II Maccabees* xv, 38.

to endeavour to enlist the sympathies of the reader in his favour, was contrary to the canons of fiction.

The noble example of Sir Walter Scott has been forgotten by more recent novelists. Thackeray seldom had a kindly word for the Hebrew, though I believe that private representations made to him induced him to refrain from continuing to caricature the Jews in a story which he was publishing at the time in the pages of *Fraser's Magazine*.[1] Charles Dickens, it is true, made *amende honorable* before the world for the villanies of Fagin, in the virtues of Riah;[2] but the wrong he had committed was serious, and the effect of twenty years of misrepresentation by the most popular novelist of the day could be wiped out by no retractation.

The race is accustomed to hard knocks. It is difficult to know whether to admire most the tender feeling and good taste which induce Miss Rhoda Broughton[3] to regret that 'those oily, greasy Jews' can no longer be beaten to death with impunity, or the mental constitution of 'Ouida,'[4] according to whom a Jew who claimed payment for a bill he had discounted, was only spared from instant death for his presumption, by the rare magnanimity of the hero.

At the same time, in some few instances, the Jew in fiction was a being endowed with almost supernatural gifts, an intellectual hero, a transcendent genius. Mr. Disraeli in his earlier works glorified beyond all things the Semitic race. A love for his lineage and a romantic disposition betrayed him occasionally into extravagance and exaggeration. The supremacy of the world belonged to the Jews, who reigned paramount everywhere by their wealth and intellect. The author of *Lothair*, however, seems to have modified his opinions, since in that work it is the Aryan race which contains the salt of the earth.

Alroy and *Tancred* were followed by some imitators, who ended by throwing ridicule upon the cause they intended to advance. No Erckmann-Chatrian[5] arose in England, like the Alsatian pair, to draw the foibles of the Jewish character, to delineate its virtues and faults with delicate humour and with deep pathos, with a keen and masterly

[1] Two of the sketches which formed part of the 'Confessions of George Fitz-Boodle' in *Fraser's Magazine*: 'Miss Lowe' (October 1842), xxvi, 395–405, and 'Dorothea' (January 1843), xxvii, 76–84.
[2] In *Our Mutual Friend* (1864–5).
[3] Rhoda Broughton (1840–1920), novelist.
[4] Pseudonym of Marie Louise de la Ramée (1839–1908), romantic novelist.
[5] Compound name of two French writers: Émile Erckmann (1822–99) and Alexandre Chatrian (1826–90).

pen freely wielded by a friendly hand. Nevertheless much has been written of late concerning the Jews, and a truer estimate is being formed of the Hebrew mind. The Jew is perceived to be neither a Sidonia[1] nor a Fagin; neither a Shylock nor a Riah. The mission of the Israelite is neither to govern the universe nor to discount suspicious little bills at 60 per cent. All the celebrated personages in the world are not Jews, nor all the millionaires; neither does the race absorb every old clothes-man or money-lender or rogue.

A great novelist of non-Jewish extraction has now turned towards the comparatively uncultivated field. The first living artist in fiction in the English language has thought the modern Jews worthy of special study, the results of which have been given to the world in a highly-interesting form. Here we have what goes a considerable way towards filling an intellectual void—faithful pictures of modern Anglo-Jewish domestic life. But the author in some respects proceeds further, and evidently possesses loftier and wider aims than the mere exercise of the romance-writer's skill among new scenes. George Eliot has thrown no hasty or superficial glance over the externals of Judaism. She has acquired an extended and profound knowledge of the rites, aspirations, hopes, fears, and desires of the Israelites of the day. She has read their books, inquired into their modes of thought, searched their traditions, accompanied them to the synagogue; nay, she has taken their very words from their lips, and, like Asmodeus,[2] has unroofed their houses. To say that some slight errors have crept into *Daniel Deronda* is to say that no human work is perfect; and these inaccuracies are singularly few and unimportant. To Christians it is really of no consequence to know that the *kaddish* or prayer for the dead is recited by children only for their parents, and for the period of eleven months, and not eleven years, as Daniel Deronda's mother believes. Nor does it signify much that men repeat daily their thanks to God for not having been created females, instead of on the Sabbath only, as it is stated in the book. The author must have devoted much time and labour to the acquisition of the particular knowledge she has mastered; and these trifling blemishes do not detract from the general marvellous accuracy and vividness of the scenes depicted.

Curiously enough the Jewish episodes in *Daniel Deronda* have been barely adverted to by the reviewers. Most of these gentlemen have slurred over some of the finest and most characteristic passages in the

[1] Character in Disraeli's novels, *Coningsby* (1844) and *Tancred* (1847).
[2] *Tobit*, iii, 8.

book, with the remark that they possessed no general interest. Possibly the critics were unable to appreciate the beauty of the scenes they deemed unworthy of attention, or perhaps they considered the Jewish body too insignificant to be worth much discussion. However, it appears that the general public is not so indifferent to Jewish affairs as it is represented; and the periodical press of late has entered keenly enough into many details of Hebrew life and customs. Jewish thought is not entirely without influence in Gentile circles; and though the Hebrew personages in *Daniel Deronda* more immediately concern Israelites, yet there are several points and issues raised which more or less directly affect Christians and Christianity.

The aspirations of the hero of the book, it must be admitted, can scarcely enlist the warm sympathy of the general reader. Few of the novel-reading public are likely to have thought much about the restoration of Israel or to be aroused to any especial enthusiasm in its favour. Nevertheless many persons in all probability will peruse with curiosity descriptions of the habits and mode of life of the Jews. George Eliot's works are intended for people who possess intellectual faculties and know how to exercise them, and this class will find food for reflection in following the career of Daniel Deronda. The hero is seen under different lights, as various phases of his character are rendered apparent. At first we meet Deronda as one of those ideal men, drawn by feminine hands, who are happily impossible in real life, and whose very perfections would render them almost intolerable bores. In the hands of a less consummate artist he would have been one of those impeccable youths whose mission is to set himself up above the rest of mankind, and to preach morals by the yard, until his best friends must secretly dread his advent. In French novels this type of hero ordinarily becomes a mentor to beautiful young married women, whose education he completes by leading them into an infraction of the Seventh Commandment.

Fortunately, Daniel Deronda soon emerges from his shadowy superiority to show himself not absolutely above human weaknesses. He is fond of boating and cricketing, and his temper is not always angelic. He is a warm-hearted, romantic young man, with a feeling of intense sympathy for all kinds of suffering. His mental disposition inclines him to take up passionately the cause of wronged individuals as of oppressed races. Many of his actions are the result of pure impulse. He interferes to save from a dangerous indulgence in gambling propensities a young woman he had never seen before, and for whom he certainly felt no admiration; and he rescues another from drowning—

a complete stranger—of whom he constitutes himself the guardian. In early youth all his associations were Christian, and his knowledge of Jews and Judaism must have been derived from books or hearsay. Nevertheless he enthusiastically accepts the mission bequeathed to him by Mordecai, however incongruous it may appear to an individual brought up in fashionable circles. How singular are, or at least were, popular notions on these subjects the reader can judge for himself. Mirah's question to Daniel, when she announces her faith—'Do you despise me for it?'—is a good test of the estimation in which her people were held.

How far a young man of good social position is likely to break with his former ties to embrace ancient religious forms which must, to say the least, expose him to the ridicule of his late companions, and cause him considerable embarrassment, must be determined by the amount of sacrifice each person is disposed to make on behalf of his convictions.

There is nothing inherently improbable in the fact of any given individual returning to the creed of his ancestors, especially in the case of descendants of a race who cling obstinately to their traditions. Moreover, with regard to Daniel Deronda, the impulses of his conscience are quickened by the contagious enthusiasm of a poetical dreamer, and by the love of a tender, bright pure face. In recent years, the well-known case has occurred in the Jewish community of an officer in the army, the grandson of an Israelite, albeit himself born a Christian, who returned spontaneously to the religion of his ancestors. In this instance no worldly circumstances to influence his conduct were visible, and certainly the change of faith of the convert could not have rendered his regimental position more agreeable.

The transformation of the *fat* Deronda, as Grandcourt calls him, into Deronda the Jew, is not then an astonishing event. The readiness of the supposed son of Sir Hugo Mallinger to undertake a national mission of the most improbable realisation, only proves an amount of belief in possibilities which all great men who have achieved difficult enterprises must have shared. The unity of Italy half a century since appeared as idle a dream as may now seem the reassembling of Israel in its own kingdom. Garibaldi and Mazzini were regarded as fanatics and visionaries, yet the leader of the thousand of Marsala has sat in the Parliament of United Italy which holds its meetings in the Eternal City. Daniel Deronda has never breathed, and may never live, but Jews have arisen and will again rise, who, if not resembling him in his perfections, will at least equal him in love of race and in ardour for the national cause.

The book is a romance. Artistic truth in literature, as in painting, is always sought for by great workmen in preference to mere realistic truth. In Daniel Deronda, George Eliot has created a type which, though scarcely likely to appeal to the masses, ought to teach more than one lesson to serious thinkers. Here is a man who lays aside entirely all purely personal considerations, all feelings of ambition or aggrandisement, to devote the best years of his existence to the loftiest national aims. True the Jews of England now possess a splendid example of high philanthropism in the person of a well-known benefactor of his race, who has repeatedly undertaken distant and perilous expeditions merely to help distressed mankind. Unfortunately illustrations derived from actual life frequently exercise little influence. It is possible that parallels drawn from fiction may prove more impressive.

The Pricesss Halm-Eberstein forms a complete contrast to her son Daniel. He is emotional, sympathetic, affectionate, and tender-hearted. She is cold, calculating, ambitious, and of an unloving disposition. A mother who entrusts her only child to strangers for questionable reasons, is scarcely likely to inspire much sympathy or attachment. After remaining for nearly a quarter of a century without seeing her offspring, she might very well have gone to the end of her days without embracing a son for whom she did not pretend to feel any great solicitude. Why, indeed, she met him at that particular juncture is not explained. The secret of his birth might have been communicated by Sir Hugo Mallinger, and any one year would have served the purpose as well as another. In religious matters, too, the contrast between mother and son is very marked. While he is imbued with sincere belief in the principles of Judaism, she denounces that faith as too narrow, formal, and rigid; as a creed which places woman in an inferior position and limits her sphere to her domestic duties. The truth is the Princess is a bold ambitious woman who declines to be bound by the trammels of religion, just as she despises family ties. However, when she deserted her son she did not rob him of his due. She carefully placed his father's fortune under the guardianship of Sir Hugo Mallinger, who had formerly been an admirer of the lady, and who fulfils his trust with considerable kindness. Having once parted from her son and deprived him of maternal love, the Princess doubtless thought sincerely that she acted for his interest when she caused him to be brought up in ignorance of his origin, as a Christian gentleman. If in a particular country red-haired men laboured under any especial disqualification, a mother might be justified in having the hair of her child dyed of the hue affected by the inhabitants. Many others besides Princess Halm-Eberstein have preferred expediency to principle; and the forms of a religion which hangs rather loosely round the wearer may be easily thrown aside altogether in obedience to worldly considerations.

The sneers of the Princess with reference to the facility with which some Jews change their family names as they would an old garment, are not entirely undeserved. There is a growing tendency in this country among a certain class of the Jewish community to adopt strange patronymics as if they were desirous of concealing their Semitic origin. It must be stated at the same time that the Israelites of Spanish and Portuguese descent are above this weakness; they have carefully preserved through generations and ages their ancient family names, and are proud of them.

The Princess feels evident twinges of conscience concerning her conduct towards Daniel Deronda, and her misgivings and doubts are finely expressed. The Alcharisi, the greatest singer of the day, is no common personage. She is endowed with a strong masculine mind and with the musical genius undoubtedly possessed by the Hebrew race; and she displays acuteness of perception in resigning her stage royalty when she foresees the impending loss of her supremacy. It is to be regretted that she disappears as fitfully as she appears, and that a character which might have served as an interesting study, slips away from the reader and melts into thin air.

Had not Daniel Deronda formed casually an acquaintance with Mirah and Mordecai, it is very questionable whether his Jewish aspirations would ever have been developed. Of course chance is a most important element in human combinations, especially in fiction. His mother's revelations, but for his preceding adventures, might not altogether have delighted him. At the same time it is singular that he should never have suspected his origin, which ought to have left visible traces.

The influence exercised by Mirah seems to steal gradually and gently upon him, and, as usually happens in the case of women of her type, the power she acquires proves irresistible. Mirah is not a favourite character with the reviewers, who, whilst busy in following the fortunes of the grand Gwendolen and in attentively watching the evolution of her soul, lose sight of the unpretending little Jewess. Mirah is a typical daughter of Israel, simple and childlike, unambitious and unpretending, undervaluing her own talents, warm in affections, and above all profoundly attached to her family and race. It is astonishing of what deep heroism those quiet little women are capable. The serpent-like beauty of Gwendolen, her grand airs, her sharp tongue, would probably cause men to flock to her side in a drawing-room, leaving Mirah scarcely noticed until she began to discourse divine music. Nevertheless Mirah Cohen, with a San Benito over her lovely head, standing in the midst of roaring flames lighted by fierce fanaticism, would sing a hymn to the Lord of Israel; whilst in all human probability Gwendolen Harleth would readily embrace any faith that offered her wealth and a well-appointed establishment. Some critics cannot forgive the author for having made Daniel Deronda prefer the 'insignificant' Mirah to the stately and chastened Gwendolen. It may be suspected that some of the dissatisfaction expressed by those gentlemen arises from the fact that Daniel Deronda has become Deronda the Jew. Gwendolen Harleth, thoroughly selfish and detestable as she appears in the beginning of the book, succeeds by her misfortunes and by the better feelings which are evidently aroused in her, in enlisting the full sympathy of the reader. But a man in England is not yet permitted to marry two wives at the same time, and had Daniel Deronda selected Gwendolen, the author would have assuredly committed an artistic error. We must lament Gwendolen Grandcourt's trials, and regret to leave her a disconsolate widow. She is still young, and it is reasonable to suppose that she will find some heart-free individual who can make her drink the waters of Lethe.

Lapidoth forms a foil to the virtues of his daughter, and the author skilfully introduces the gambler and reprobate by the side of the pure-minded child. Lapidoth is a thief, Mirah is the soul of honour. George Eliot has studied nature too well not to divide her lights and shadows. No race monopolises moral excellence or villany, and unprincipled scoundrels unfortunately flourish among all nations and religions.

In addition to a wide range of reading in Jewish books, the author of *Daniel Deronda* must have had especial opportunities of personally observing Hebrew customs and manners and of speaking with intelligent Israelites. The portrait of the Cohen family is a photographic likeness which has probably been taken from life. Ezra Cohen is a pawnbroker in Holborn, a real embodiment of the qualities, good and indifferent, that make up the Jewish tradesman. The business of a pawnbroker is certainly not ennobling, but it may be carried on as honestly as any other. The small Jewish tradesman, keen as he usually is in the pursuit of gain, hard as he may seem in driving a bargain, is ordinarily an excellent father and husband and a strict follower of the practices of his faith. It is only some of the great families that find it convenient to drop troublesome ceremonies. Daniel Deronda's visit to the pawnbroker on imaginary business naturally affords an occasion for an insight into the ways of the family. Here we may admire the business aptitude of the youthful Jacob and the mixture of childish vanity and adult carefulness of his youngest sister when she asks whether she should wear her 'Shabbesfyock' before the strange gentleman. The shrewdness, vulgarity, and kindness of heart which combine to constitute the man Ezra Cohen are amusingly illustrated in his parting speech to Mordecai, which is an odd compound of calculation and sentiment. It seems singular, however, that the cautious pawnbroker should at first sight ask a complete stranger to share the Sabbath evening meal with his own family; and it is even more astonishing that Ezra Cohen, who is intended to be a strict Jew, should be described as transacting business on Friday evening, a proceeding which according to Jewish ideas would be deemed a desecration of the Sabbath.

The dreams and inspirations of Mordecai naturally chiefly concern Israelites. He is a prophet, a seer, but far from being the absolutely impossible character he has been considered by some critics. Anciently the most eloquent and learned rabbis among the Jews practised trades or handicrafts. Who shall say that among the immigrants from distant climes or among the Jews of Great Britain there is no workman whose whole heart is wrapped up in visions of the future greatness of his race? Indeed, it appears that Mr. G. H. Lewes, in an article on Spinoza, published in the *Fortnightly Review* of the 1st April, 1866, described a club which was wont to meet at a tavern in Red Lion Square about a generation since, and wherein the discussion of philosophical topics was carried on. The president of this club was a highly intelligent German named Kohn, Cohn, or Cohen, and probably he was the prototype of Mordecai.

The Jews, notwithstanding their ardour in mercantile pursuits, have always produced thinkers and philosophers.

Mordecai had long been seeking a co-religionist to whom he could confide the mission which fate would not permit him even to attempt to accomplish himself. He introduces Daniel Deronda to the philosopher's club, and the arguments therein brought to light, though possibly uninteresting to general readers, are deserving of close attention by Israelites. On the one hand, we have Gideon and Pash, who desire that the Jews should merge into the Christian population in the midst of which they dwell; and their opinion will be echoed by not a few of their co-religionists who care for naught but ease and self-indulgence.

On the other hand, Mordecai, with a loftier vision, expounds the mission of Israel. The poetry of Mordecai will prove *caviare* to the multitude. He is one of those pure abstractions such as all nations have produced—a man of dreams rather than a man of actions—and yet what could a poor Jew have accomplished? Even had the 'Ruach Hakodesh,' the breath of divine thought, entered that poor diseased body of his, not even his own co-religionists would have listened to its manifestations. George Eliot has studied Hebrew poetry, and the touching verses which she places in Mordecai's lips are not unlike those Hebrew poems recited by the Ashkenazim, and called 'Peyutim.' When Mordecai goes to his long sleep he is at all events happy, for he has bequeathed his mission to a trusty successor, and ere his breath leaves him the start is already made towards the East.

The author does not enter into the nice distinctions between the Sephardim or Spanish and Portuguese Jews, and the Ashkenazim or German and Polish Jews. Daniel Deronda appertains to the former class, which once contained the *sangre azul*[1] of the nation; whilst Mirah Cohen or Lapidoth, as coming from Poland, would naturally belong to the latter. To the present day these sections of the Hebrew race form in England and in most other countries distinct communities; but practically all difference between them has ceased to exist.

It is not necessary here to express any opinion on the merits of *Daniel Deronda* in its entirety as a work of fiction. George Eliot has passed from the realism of *Middlemarch* to the idealism of her present work. We cannot judge of Daniel Deronda and of Mordecai from the matter-of-fact surroundings of prosaic every-day life—albeit neither of these two characters is so totally imaginary and so far removed from actual truth as has been asserted. *Daniel Deronda* is no light novel to while away idle hours. It is a book full of deep thoughts, seeking to convey high lessons. It is scarcely a story in the ordinary sense of the word; the thread of the narrative is frequently disconnected and inter-rupted by reflections and disquisitions revealing a thinker and student of psychology of unusual faculties. The analysis of a difficult problem in human nature, the transformation of Gwendolen, is undoubtedly one of the aims of the book. But there is a far greater purpose in *Daniel Deronda* than the tale of a woman's life and the development of her soul.

[1] The 'blue blood', nobility.

It is the vindication of a long maligned race against ignorant misrepresentation or wilful aspersion, the defence of Jews and Judaism against fanaticism and prejudice. George Eliot has laid open before a larger audience than had ever before been summoned for a similar purpose, the aims and scope and innermost thoughts of Judaism, and she has accomplished more for the cause of toleration and enlightenment than could have been achieved by any amount of legislation.

Two questions are raised in *Daniel Deronda* which concern principally, but not exclusively, the Jewish race. The object of Deronda, expressed in his own words, 'To bind our race together in spite of heresy,' is one of the aspirations that must be felt by every Israelite whilst admitting the difficulty of the solution. To bring the Judaism that was regarded 'as a sort of eccentric fossilised form which an accomplished man might dispense with studying and leave to specialists,' into consonance with modern ideas, is a task which only Daniel Deronda can effect. To maintain intact the spirit of Judaism, to preserve in pristine purity the faith and traditions of Israel, without keeping up the inflexible rigidity which opposes every improvement, and which drove out of the community an Isaac Disraeli, forms one of those problems which are still awaiting a satisfactory solution.

The political future of the Hebrew race may become more important to the world at large than its religious future. The reassembling of the Jews into a separate State, if such an event ever happen, must obviously affect more or less all Europe in addition to the provinces occupied. The influence possessed by the Jews in the financial world would certainly make itself felt on their withdrawal to distant lands. However, the dreams of Mordecai and Daniel Deronda are likely to remain dreams for the present. Not only are there no signs of their speedy realisation, but it is not at all sure that such a consummation is desired by the bulk of the Hebrew nation. The Israelites have become too firmly attached to the countries of western Europe, which have given them shelter, to be easily induced to abandon them *en masse*, and their magnates are scarcely likely to exchange the splendour and luxury they enjoy in the European capitals, for a residence in an arid and semi-civilised land. It is to be feared that notwithstanding all the efforts of Daniel Deronda and of real living philanthropists, it will be long before Palestine will cease to be, in the passionate language of Mordecai, 'a place for saintly beggary to await death in loathsome idleness.'

To have broached these questions before the popular mind is already to have obtained a great gain, and George Eliot has thus earned the gratitude, not only of her countrymen of the Jewish race, but of all thinkers and friends of progress.

62. Henry James: 'Daniel Deronda: A Conversation'

Atlantic Monthly (December 1876), xxxviii, 684–94

James's brilliantly witty and argumentative conversation between the hostile Pulcheria, the enthusiastic Theodora, and the middle-of-the-road Constantius captures vividly not only the critical conflict over *Daniel Deronda*, but also reflects James's own ambiguous estimate of George Eliot (see Introduction, p. 33).

Theodora, one day early in the autumn, sat on her piazza with a piece of embroidery, the design of which she invented as she proceeded, being careful, however, to have a Japanese screen before her, to keep her inspiration at the proper altitude. Pulcheria, who was paying her a visit, sat near her with a closed book, in a paper cover, in her lap. Pulcheria was playing with the little dog, rather idly, but Theodora was stitching, steadily and meditatively. 'Well,' said Theodora, at last, 'I wonder what he accomplished in the East.' Pulcheria took the little dog into her lap and made him sit on the book. 'Oh,' she replied, 'they had tea-parties at Jerusalem,—exclusively of ladies,—and he sat in the midst and stirred his tea and made high-toned remarks. And then Mirah sang a little, just a little, on account of her voice being so weak. Sit still, Fido,' she continued, addressing the little dog, 'and keep your nose out of my face. But it's a nice little nose, all the same,' she pursued, 'a nice little short snub nose, and not a horrid big Jewish nose. Oh, my dear, when I think what a collection of noses there must have been at that wedding!' At this moment Constantius steps out upon the piazza from the long parlor window, hat and stick in hand and his shoes a trifle dusty. He has some steps to take before he reaches the end of the piazza where the ladies are sitting, and this gives Pulcheria time to murmur, 'Talk of snub noses!' Constantius is presented by Theodora to Pulcheria, and he sits down and exclaims upon the admirable blueness of the sea, which lies in a straight band across the green of the little lawn; comments too upon the pleasure of having one side of one's piazza in the shade. Soon Fido, the little dog, still restless, jumps off Pulcheria's lap and reveals the book, which lies title upward. 'Oh,' says Constantius, 'you have been finishing *Daniel Deronda*?' Then follows a conversation which it will be more convenient to present in another form.

Theodora. Yes, Pulcheria has been reading aloud the last chapters to me. They are wonderfully beautiful.

Constantius (after a moment's hesitation). Yes, they are very beautiful. I am sure you read well, Pulcheria, to give the fine passages their full value.

Theodora. She reads well when she chooses, but I am sorry to say that in some of the fine passages of this last book she took quite a false tone. I could n't have read them aloud, myself; I should have broken down. But Pulcheria,—would you really believe it?—when she could n't go on, it was not for tears, but for—the contrary.

Constantius. For smiles? Did you really find it comical? One of my objections to *Daniel Deronda* is the absence of those delightfully humorous passages which enlivened the author's former works.

Pulcheria. Oh, I think there are some places as amusing as anything in *Adam Bede* or *The Mill on the Floss*: for instance, where, at the last, Deronda wipes Gwendolen's tears and Gwendolen wipes his.

Constantius. Yes, I know what you mean. I can understand that situation presenting a slightly ridiculous image; that is, if the current of the story does not swiftly carry you past that idea.

Pulcheria. What do you mean by the current of the story? I never read a story with less current. It is not a river; it is a series of lakes. I once read of a group of little uneven ponds resembling, from a bird's-eye view, a looking-glass which had fallen upon the floor and broken, and was lying in fragments. That is what *Daniel Deronda* would look like, on a bird's-eye view.

Theodora. Pulcheria found that comparison in a French novel. She is always reading French novels.

Constantius. Ah, there are some very good ones.

Pulcheria (perversely). I don't know; I think there are some very poor ones.

Constantius. The comparison is not bad, at any rate. I know what you mean by *Daniel Deronda* lacking current. It has almost as little as *Romola.*

Pulcheria. Oh, *Romola* is unpardonably slow; it absolutely stagnates.

Constantius. Yes, I know what you mean by that. But I am afraid you are not friendly to our great novelist.

Theodora. She likes Balzac and George Sand and other impure writers.

Constantius. Well, I must say I understand that.

Pulcheria. My favorite novelist is Thackeray, and I am extremely fond of Miss Austen.

Constantius. I understand that, too. You read over *The Newcomes* and *Pride and Prejudice.*

Pulcheria. No, I don't read them over, now; I think them over. I have been making visits for a long time past to a series of friends, and I have spent the last six months in reading *Daniel Deronda* aloud. Fortune would have it that I should always arrive by the same train as the new number. I am considered a frivolous, idle creature; I am not a disciple in the new school of embroidery, like Theodora; so I was immediately pushed into a chair and the book thrust into my hand, that I might lift up my voice and make peace between all the impatiences that were snatching at it. So I may claim at least that I have read every word of the work. I never skipped.

Theodora. I should hope not, indeed!

Constantius. And do you mean that you really didn't enjoy it?

Pulcheria. I found it protracted, pretentious, pedantic.

Constantius. I see; I can understand that.

Theodora. Oh, you understand too much! Here is the twentieth time you have used that formula.

Constantius. What will you have? You know I must try to understand, it's my trade.

Theodora. He means he writes reviews. Trying *not* to understand is what I call that trade!

Constantius. Say, then, I take it the wrong way; that is why it has never made my fortune. But I do try to understand; it is my—my— (He pauses.)

Theodora. I know what you want to say. Your strong side.

Pulcheria. And what is his weak side?

Theodora. He writes novels.

Constantius. I have written *one*. You can't call that a side.

Pulcheria. I should like to read it,—not aloud!

Constantius. You can't read it softly enough. But you, Theodora, you did n't find our book too 'protracted'?

Theodora. I should have liked it to continue indefinitely, to keep coming out always, to be one of the regular things of life.

Pulcheria. Oh, come here, little dog! To think that *Daniel Deronda* might be perpetual when you, little short-nosed darling, can't last at the most more than eight or nine years!

Theodora. A book like *Daniel Deronda* becomes part of one's life; one lives in it or alongside of it. I don't hesitate to say that I have been living in this one for the last eight months. It is such a complete world George Eliot builds up; it is so vast, so much-embracing! It has such a firm earth and such an ethereal sky. You can turn into it and lose yourself in it.

Pulcheria. Oh, easily, and die of cold and starvation!

Theodora. I have been very near to poor Gwendolen and very near to dear little Mirah. And the dear little Meyricks, also; I know them intimately well.

Pulcheria. The Meyricks, I grant you, are the best thing in the book.

Theodora. They are a delicious family; I wish they lived in Boston. I consider Herr Klesmer almost Shakespearian, and his wife is almost as good. I have been near to poor, grand Mordecai—

Pulcheria. Oh, reflect, my dear; not too near.

Theodora. And as for Deronda himself, I freely confess that I am consumed with a hopeless passion for him. He is the most irresistible man in the literature of fiction.

Pulcheria. He is not a man at all!

Theodora. I remember nothing more beautiful than the description of his childhood, and that picture of his lying on the grass in the abbey cloister, a beautiful seraph-faced boy, with a lovely voice, reading history and asking his Scotch tutor why the Popes had so many nephews. He must have been delightfully handsome.

Pulcheria. Never, my dear, with that nose! I am sure he had a nose, and I hold that the author has shown great pusillanimity in her treatment of it. She has quite shirked it. The picture you speak of is very pretty, but a picture is not a person. And why is he always grasping his coat-collar, as if he wished to hang himself up? The author had an uncomfortable feeling that she must make him do something real, something visible and sensible, and she hit upon that awkward device.

I don't see what you mean by saying you have been *near* those people; that is just what one is not. They produce no illusion. They are described and analyzed to death, but we don't see them or hear them or touch them. Deronda clutches his coat-collar, Mirah crosses her feet, and Mordecai talks like the Bible; but that does n't make real figures of them. They have no existence outside of the author's study.

Theodora. If you mean that they are nobly imginative, I quite agree with you; and if they say nothing to your own imagination, the fault is yours, not theirs.

Pulcheria. Pray don't say they are Shakespearian again. Shakespeare went to work another way.

Constantius. I think you are both in a measure right; there is a distinction to be drawn. There are in *Daniel Deronda* the figures based upon observation and the figures based upon invention. This distinction, I know, is rather a rough one. There are no figures in any novel that are pure observation and none that are pure invention. But either element may preponderate, and in those cases in which invention has preponderated George Eliot seems to me to have achieved at the best but so many brilliant failures.

Theodora. And are *you* turning severe? I thought you admired her so much.

Constantius. I defy any one to admire her more, but one must discriminate. Speaking brutally, I consider *Daniel Deronda* the weakest of her books. It strikes me as very sensibly inferior to *Middlemarch.* I have an immense opinion of *Middlemarch.*

Pulcheria. Not having been obliged by circumstances to read *Middlemarch* to other people, I did n't read it at all. I could n't read it to myself. I tried, but I broke down. I appreciated Rosamond, but I couldn't believe in Dorothea.

Theodora (very gravely). So much the worse for you, Pulcheria. I have enjoyed *Daniel Deronda because* I had enjoyed *Middlemarch.* Why should you throw *Middlemarch* up against her? It seems to me that if a book is fine it is fine. I have enjoyed *Deronda* deeply, from beginning to end.

Constantius. I assure you, so have I. I can read nothing of George Eliot's without enjoyment. I even enjoy her poetry, though I don't approve of it. In whatever she writes I enjoy her mind—her large, luminous, airy mind. The intellectual brilliancy of *Daniel Deronda* strikes me as very great, in excess of anything the author had done. In the first couple of numbers of the book this ravished me. I delighted in its tone, its deep, rich English tone, in which so many notes seemed melted together.

Pulcheria. The tone is not English, it is German.

Constantius. I understand that—if Theodora will allow me to say so. Little by little I began to feel that I cared less for certain notes than for others. I say it under my breath—I began to feel an occasional temptation to skip. Roughly speaking, all the Jewish burden of the story tended to weary me; it is this part that produces the small illusion which I agree with Pulcheria in finding. Gwendolen and Grandcourt are admirable. Gwendolen is a masterpiece. She is known, felt, and presented, psychologically, altogether in the grand manner. Beside her and beside her husband—a consummate picture of English brutality refined and distilled (for Grandcourt is before all things brutal)—Deronda, Mordecai, and Mirah are hardly more than shadows. They and their fortunes are all improvisation. I don't say anything against improvisation. When it succeeds it has a surpassing charm. But it must succeed. With George Eliot it seems to me to succeed only partially, less than one would expect of her talent. The story of Deronda's life, his mother's story, Mirah's story, are quite the sort of thing one finds in George Sand. But they are really not so good as they would be in George Sand. George Sand would have carried it off with a lighter hand.

Theodora. Oh, Constantius, how can you compare George Eliot's novels to that woman's? It is sunlight and moonshine.

Pulcheria. I really think the two writers are very much alike. They are both very voluble, both addicted to moralizing and philosophizing *à tout bout de champ*, both inartistic!

Constantius. I see what you mean. But George Eliot is solid and George Sand is liquid. When occasionally George Eliot liquefies,—as in the history of Deronda's birth, and in that of Mirah,—it is not to as crystalline a clearness as the author of *Conseulo* and *André*. Take Mirah's long narrative of her adventures, when she unfolds them to Mrs. Meyrick. It is arranged, it is artificial, old-fashioned, quite in the George Sand manner. But George Sand would have done it better. The false tone would have remained, but it would have been more persuasive. It would have been a fib, but the fib would have been neater.

Theodora. I don't think fibbing neatly a merit; and I don't see what is to be gained by such comparisons. George Eliot is pure and George Sand is impure; how can you compare them? As for the Jewish element in *Deronda*, I think it a very fine idea; it 's a noble subject.

Wilkie Collins and Miss Braddon[1] would not have thought of it, but that does not condemn it. It shows a large conception of what one may do in a novel. I heard you say, the other day, that most novels were so trivial—that they had no general ideas. Here is a general idea, the idea interpreted by *Deronda*. I have never disliked the Jews, as some people do; I am not like Pulcheria, who sees a Jew in every bush. I wish there were one; I would cultivate shrubbery! I have known too many clever and charming Jews; I have known none that were not clever.

Pulcheria. Clever, but not charming!

Constantius. I quite agree with you as to Deronda's going in for the Jews and turning out a Jew himself being a fine subject, and this quite apart from the fact of whether such a thing as a Jewish revival is at all a possibility. If it is a possibility, so much the better—so much the better for the subject, I mean.

Pulcheria. A la bonne heure!

Constantius. I rather suspect it is not a possibility; that the Jews in general take themselves much less seriously than that. They have other fish to fry! George Eliot takes them as a person outside of Judaism—picturesquely. I don't believe that is the way they take themselves.

Pulcheria. They have the less excuse, then, for keeping themselves so dirty.

Theodora. George Eliot must have known some delightful Jews!

Constantius. Very likely; but I should n't wonder if the most delightful of them had smiled a trifle, here and there, over her book. But that makes nothing, as Herr Klesmer would say. The subject is a noble one. The idea of depicting a nature able to feel and worthy to feel the sort of inspiration that takes possession of Deronda, of depicting it sympathetically, minutely, and intimately—such an idea has great elevation. There is something very fascinating in the mission that Deronda takes upon himself. I don't quite know what it means, I don't understand more than half of Mordecai's rhapsodies, and I don't perceive exactly what practical steps could be taken. Deronda could go about and talk with clever Jews—not an unpleasant life.

Pulcheria. All that seems to me so unreal that when at the end the author finds herself confronted with the necessity of making him start for the East by the train, and announces that Sir Hugo and Lady Mallinger have given his wife 'a complete Eastern outfit,' I descend to the ground with a ludicrous jump.

[1] Mary Elizabeth Braddon (1837-1915), the novelist.

Constantius. Unreal if you please; that is no objection to it; it greatly
tickles my imagination. I like extremely the idea of Mordecai believing, without ground of belief, that if he only waits, a young man on
whom nature and society have centred all their gifts will come to
him and receive from his hands the precious vessel of his hopes. It is
romantic, but it is not vulgar romance; it is finely romantic. And there
is something very fine in the author's own feeling about Deronda. He
is a very generous creation. He is, I think, a failure—a brilliant failure;
if he had been a success I would call him a splendid creation. The
author meant to do things very handsomely for him; she meant,
apparently, to make a faultless human being.

Pulcheria. She made a dreadful prig.

Constantius. He *is* rather priggish, and one wonders that so clever a
woman as George Eliot should n't see it.

Pulcheria. He has no blood in his body. His attitude at moments
absolutely trenches on the farcical.

Theodora. Pulcheria likes the little gentlemen in the French novels
who take good care of their attitudes, which are always the same
attitude, the attitude of 'conquest,' and of a conquest that tickles their
vanity. Deronda has a contour that cuts straight through the middle
of all that. He is made of a stuff that is n't dreamt of in their philosophy.

Pulcheria. Pulcheria likes very much a novel which she read three
or four years ago, but which she has not forgotten. It was by Ivan
Tourguéneff, and it was called *On the Eve.* Theodora has read it, I
know, because she admires Tourguéneff, and Constantius has read it
I suppose, because he has read everything.

Constantius. If I had no reason but that for my reading, it would be
small. But Tourguéneff is my man.

Pulcheria. You were just now praising George Eliot's general ideas.
The tale of which I speak contains in the portrait of the hero very much
such a general idea as you find in the portrait of Deronda. Don't you
remember the young Bulgarian student, Inssaroff, who gives himself
the mission of rescuing his country from its subjection to the Turks?
Poor man, if he had foreseen the horrible summer of 1876! His
character is the picture of a race-passion, of patriotic hopes and dreams.
But what a difference in the vividness of the two figures. Inssaroff is a
man; he stands up on his feet; we see him, hear him, and touch him.
And it has taken the author but a couple of hundred pages—not eight
volumes—to do it!

Theodora. I don't remember Inssaroff at all, but I perfectly remember the heroine, Elena. She is certainly most remarkable, but, remarkable as she is, I should never dream of calling her so wonderful as Gwendolen.

Constantius. Tourguéneff is a magician, which I don't think I should call George Eliot. One is a poet, the other is a philosopher. One cares for the reason of things and the other cares for the aspect of things. George Eliot, in embarking with Deronda, took aboard, as it were, a far heavier cargo than Tourguéneff with his Inssaroff. She proposed, consciously, to strike more notes.

Pulcheria. Oh, consciously, yes!

Constantius. George Eliot wished to show the possible picturesqueness—the romance, as it were—of a high moral tone. Deronda is a moralist, a moralist with a rich complexion.

Theodora. It is a most beautiful nature. I don't know anywhere a more complete, a more deeply analyzed portrait of a great nature. We praise novelists for wandering and creeping so into the small corners of the mind. That is what we praise Balzac for when he gets down upon all fours to crawl through the *Père Goriot* or the *Parents Pauvres*. But I must say I think it a finer thing to unlock with as firm a hand as George Eliot some of the greater chambers of human character. Deronda is in a manner an ideal character, if you will, but he seems to me triumphantly married to reality. There are some admirable things said about him; nothing can be finer than those pages of description of his moral temperament in the fourth book—his elevated way of looking at things, his impartiality, his universal sympathy, and at the same time his fear of their turning into mere irresponsible indifference. I remember some of it verbally: 'He was ceasing to care for knowledge—he had no ambition for practice—unless they could be gathered up into one current with his emotions.'

Pulcheria. Oh, there is plenty about his emotions. Everything about him is 'emotive.' That bad word occurs on every fifth page.

Theodora. I don't see that it is a bad word.

Pulcheria. It may be good German, but it is poor English.

Theodora. It is not German at all; it is Latin. So, my dear!

Pulcheria. As I say, then, it is not English.

Theodora. This is the first time I ever heard that George Eliot's style was bad!

Constantius. It is admirable; it has the most delightful and the most intellectually comfortable suggestions. But it is occasionally a little too long-sleeved, as I may say. It is sometimes too loose a fit for the thought, a little baggy.

Theodora. And the advice he gives Gwendolen, the things he says to her, they are the very essence of wisdom, of warm human wisdom, knowing life and feeling it. 'Keep your fear as a safeguard, it may make consequences passionately present to you.' What can be better than that?

Pulcheria. Nothing, perhaps. But what can be drearier than a novel in which the function of the hero—young, handsome, and brilliant— is to give didactic advice, in a proverbial form, to the young, beautiful, and brilliant heroine?

Constantius. That is not putting it quite fairly. The function of Deronda is to have Gwendolen fall in love with him, to say nothing of falling in love himself with Mirah.

Pulcheria. Yes, the less said about that the better. All we know about Mirah is that she has delicate rings of hair, sits with her feet crossed, and talks like a book.

Constantius. Deronda's function of adviser to Gwendolen does not strike me as so ridiculous. He is not nearly so ridiculous as if he were lovesick. It is a very interesting situation—that of a man with whom a beautiful woman in trouble falls in love, and yet whose affections are so preoccupied that the most he can do for her in return is to enter kindly and sympathetically into her position, pity her, and talk to her. George Eliot always gives us something that is strikingly and ironically characteristic of human life; and what savors more of the essential crookedness of human fortune than the sad cross-purposes of these two young people? Poor Gwendolen's falling in love with Deronda is part of her own luckless history, not of his.

Theodora. I do think he takes it to himself rather too little. No man had ever so little vanity.

Pulcheria. It is very inconsistent, therefore, as well as being extremely impertinent and ill-mannered, his buying back and sending to her her necklace at Leubronn.

Constantius. Oh, you must concede that; without it there would have been no story. A man writing of him, however, would certainly have made him more peccable. As George Eliot lets herself go about him she becomes delightfully, almost touchingly feminine. It is like her making Romola go to housekeeping with Tessa, after Tito Melema's death; like her making Dorothea marry Will Ladislaw. If Dorothea had married any one after her misadventure with Casaubon, she would have married a hussar!

Theodora. Perhaps some day Gwendolen will marry Rex.

Pulcheria. Pray, who is Rex?

Theodora. Why, Pulcheria, how can you forget?

Pulcheria. Nay, how can I remember? But I recall such a name in the dim antiquity of the first or second book. Yes, and then he is pushed to the front again at the last, just in time not to miss the falling of the curtain. Gwendolen will certainly not have the audacity to marry any one we know so little about.

Constantius. I have been wanting to say that there seems to me to be two very distinct elements in George Eliot—a spontaneous one and an artificial one. There is what she is by inspiration, and what she is because it is expected of her. These two heads have been very perceptible in her recent writings; they are much less noticeable in her early ones.

Theodora. You mean that she is too scientific? So long as she remains the great literary genius that she is, how can she be too scientific? She is simply permeated with the highest culture of the age.

Pulcheria. She talks too much about the 'dynamic quality' of people's eyes. When she uses such a phrase as that in the first sentence in her book she is not a great literary genius, because she shows a want of tact. There can't be a worse limitation.

Constantius (laughing). The 'dynamic quality' of Gwendolen's glance has made the tour of the world.

Theodora. It shows a very low level of culture on the world's part to be agitated by a term perfectly familiar to all decently-educated people.

Pulcheria. I don't pretend to be decently educated; pray tell me what it means.

Constantius (promptly). I think Pulcheria has hit it in speaking of a want of tact. In the manner of *Daniel Deronda*, throughout, there is something that one may call a want of tact. The epigraphs in verse are a want of tact; they are sometimes, I think, a trifle more pretentious than really pregnant; the importunity of the moral reflections is a want of tact; the very diffuseness of the book is a want of tact. But it comes back to what I said just now about one's sense of the author writing under a sort of external pressure. I began to notice it in *Felix Holt*; I don't think I had before. She strikes me as a person who certainly has naturally a taste for general considerations, but who has fallen upon an age and a circle which have compelled her to give them an exaggerated attention. She does not strike me as naturally a critic, less still as naturally a skeptic; her spontaneous part is to observe life and to

427

feel it, to feel it with admirable depth. Contemplation, sympathy, and faith,—something like that, I should say, would have been her natural scale. If she had fallen upon an age of enthusiastic assent to old articles of faith, it seems to me possible that she would have had a more perfect, a more consistent and graceful development, than she has actually had. If she had cast herself into such a current,—her genius being equal, —it might have carried her to splendid distances. But she has chosen to go into criticism, and to the critics she addresses her work; I mean the critics of the universe. Instead of feeling life itself, it is 'views' upon life that she tries to feel.

Pulcheria. Pray, how can you feel a 'view'?

Constantius. I don't think you can; you had better give up trying.

Pulcheria. She is the victim of a first-class education. I am so glad!

Constantius. Thanks to her admirable intellect she philosophizes very sufficiently; but meanwhile she has given a chill to her genius. She has come near spoiling an artist.

Pulcheria. She has quite spoiled one. Or rather I should n't say that, because there was no artist to spoil. I maintain that she is not an artist. An artist could never have put a story together so monstrously ill. She has no sense of form.

Theodora. Pray, what could be more artistic than the way that Deronda's paternity is concealed till almost the end, and the way we are made to suppose Sir Hugo is his father?

Pulcheria. And Mirah his sister. How does that fit together? I was as little made to suppose he was not a Jew as I cared when I found out he was. And his mother popping up through a trap-door and popping down again, at the last, in that scrambling fashion! His mother is very bad.

Constantius. I think Deronda's mother is one of the unvivified characters; she belongs to the cold half of the book. All the Jewish part is at bottom cold; that is my only objection. I have enjoyed it because my fancy often warms cold things; but beside Gwendolen's history it is like the full half of the lunar disk beside the empty one. It is admirably studied, it is imagined, it is understood; but it is not realized. One feels this strongly in just those scenes between Deronda and his mother; one feels that one has been appealed to on rather an artificial ground of interest. To make Deronda's reversion to his native faith more dramatic and profound, the author has given him a mother who on very arbitrary grounds, apparently, has separated herself from this same faith, and who has been kept waiting in the wing, as it were, for many acts, to come on and make her speech and say so. This moral situation of hers we are invited retrospectively to appreciate. But we hardly care to do so.

Pulcheria. I don't *see* the princess, in spite of her flame-colored robe. Why should an actress and prima-donna care so much about religious matters?

Theodora. It was not only that; it was the Jewish race she hated, Jewish manners and looks. You, my dear, ought to understand that.

Pulcheria. I do, but I am not a Jewish actress of genius; I am not what Rachel was. If I were, I should have other things to think about.

Constantius. Think now a little about poor Gwendolen.

Pulcheria. I don't care to think about her. She was a second-rate English girl who spoke of her mother as 'my mamma,' and got into a flutter about a lord.

Theodora. I don't see that she is worse than if she were a first-rate American girl, who should speak of her female parent as 'mother,' and get into exactly the same flutter.

Pulcheria. It would n't be the same flutter, at all; it would n't be any flutter. She would n't be afraid of the lord.

Theodora. I am sure I don't perceive whom Gwendolen was afraid of. She was afraid of her misdeed,—her broken promise,—after she had committed it, and through that fear she was afraid of her husband. Well she might be! I can imagine nothing more vivid than the sense we get of his absolutely *clammy* selfishness.

Pulcheria. She was not afraid of Deronda when, immediately after her marriage, and without any but the most casual acquaintance with him, she begins to hover about him at the Mallingers', and to drop little confidences about her conjugal woes. That seems to me very indelicate; ask any woman.

Constantius. The very purpose of the author is to give us an idea of the sort of confidence that Deronda inspired—its irresistible potency!

Pulcheria. A lay father-confessor. Dreadful!

Constantius. And to give us an idea also of the acuteness of Gwendolen's depression, of her haunting sense of impending trouble.

Theodora. It must be remembered that Gwendolen was in love with Deronda from the first, long before she knew it. She did n't know it, poor girl, but that was it.

Pulcheria. That makes the matter worse. It is very disagreeable to have her rustling about a man who is indifferent to her, in that fashion.

Theodora. He was not indifferent to her, since he sent her back her necklace.

Pulcheria. Of all the delicate attention to a charming girl that I ever heard of, that little pecuniary transaction is the most felicitous.

Constantius. You must remember that he had been *en rapport* with her at the gaming table. She had been playing in defiance of his observation, and he, continuing to observe her, had been in a measure responsible for her loss. There was a tacit consciousness of this between them. You may contest the possibility of tacit consciousness going so far, but that is not a serious objection. You may point out two or three weak spots in detail; the fact remains that Gwendolen's whole history is superbly told. And see how the girl is known, inside out, how thoroughly she is felt and understood! It is the most *intelligent* thing in all George Eliot's writing, and that is saying much. It is so deep, so true, so complete, it holds such a wealth of psychological detail, it is more than masterly.

Theodora. I don't know where the perception of character has sailed closer to the wind.

Pulcheria. The portrait may be admirable, but it has one little fault. You don't care a straw for the original. Gwendolen is not an interesting girl, and when the author tries to invest her with a deep tragic interest she does so at the expense of consistency. She has made her at the outset too light, too flimsy; tragedy has no hold on such a girl.

Theodora. You are hard to satisfy. You said this morning that Dorothea was too heavy, and now you find Gwendolen too light. George Eliot wished to give us the perfect counterpart of Dorothea. Having made one portrait she was worthy to make the other.

Pulcheria. She has committed the fatal error of making Gwendolen vulgarly, pettily, dryly selfish. She was *personally* selfish.

Theodora. I know nothing more personal than selfishness.

Pulcheria. I am selfish, but I don't go about with my chin out like that; at least I hope I don't. She was an odious young woman, and one can't care what becomes of her. When her marriage turned out ill she would have become still more hard and positive; to make her soft and appealing is very bad logic. The second Gwendolen does n't belong to the first.

Constantius. She is perhaps at the first a little childish for the weight of interest she has to carry, a little too much after the pattern of the unconscientious young ladies of Miss Yonge and Miss Sewell.[1]

[1] The novelists Charlotte Yonge (1823-1901) and Anna Sewell (1820-78).

Theodora. Since when is it forbidden to make one's heroine young? Gwendolen is a perfect picture of youthfulness—its eagerness, its presumption, its preoccupation with itself, its vanity and silliness, its sense of its own absoluteness. But she is extremely intelligent and clever, and therefore tragedy *can* have a hold upon her. Her conscience does n't make the tragedy; that is an old story, and, I think, a secondary form of suffering. It is the tragedy that makes her conscience, which then reacts upon it; and I can think of nothing more powerful than the way in which the growth of her conscience is traced, nothing more touching than the picture of its helpless maturity.

Constantius. That is perfectly true. Gwendolen's history is admirably typical—as most things are with George Eliot; it is the very stuff that human life is made of. What is it made of but the discovery by each of us that we are at the best but a rather ridiculous fifth wheel to the coach, after we have sat cracking our whip and believing that we are at least the coachman in person? We think we are the main hoop to the barrel, and we turn out to be but a very incidental splinter in one of the staves. The universe, forcing itself with a slow, inexorable pressure into a narrow, complacent, and yet after all extremely sensitive mind, and making it ache with the pain of the process—that is Gwendolen's story. And it becomes completely characteristic in that her supreme perception of the fact that the world is whirling past her is in the disappointment not of a base, but of an exalted passion. The very chance to embrace what the author is so fond of calling a 'larger life' seems refused to her. She is punished for being narrow and she is not allowed a chance to expand. Her finding Deronda preëngaged to go to the East and stir up the race-feeling of the Jews strikes one as a wonderfully happy invention. The irony of the situation, for poor Gwendolen, is almost grotesque, and it makes one wonder whether the whole heavy structure of the Jewish question in the story was not built up by the author for the express purpose of giving its proper force to this particular stroke.

Theodora. George Eliot's intentions are extremely complex. The mass is for each detail and each detail is for the mass.

Pulcheria. She is very fond of deaths by drowning. Maggie Tulliver and her brother are drowned, Tito Melema is drowned, Mr. Grandcourt is drowned. It is extremely unlikely that Grandcourt should not have known how to swim.

Constantius. He did, of course, but he had a cramp. It served him right. I can't imagine a more consummate representation of the most detestable kind of Englishman—the Englishman who thinks it low to articulate. And in Grandcourt the type and the individual are so happily met: the type with its sense of the proprieties, and the individual with his absense of all sense. He is the apotheosis of dryness, a human expression of the simple idea of the perpendicular.

Theodora. Mr. Casaubon in *Middlemarch* was very dry, too; and yet what a genius it is that can give us two disagreeable husbands who are so utterly different.

Pulcheria. You must count the two disagreeable wives, too—Rosamond Vincy and Gwendolen. They are very much alike. I know the author did n't mean it; it proves how common a type the worldly, *pincée*, illiberal young Englishwoman is. They are both disagreeable; you can't get over that.

Constantius. There is something in that, perhaps. I think, at any rate, that the secondary people here are less delightful than in *Middlemarch*; there is nothing so good as Mary Garth and her father, or the little old lady who steals sugar, or the parson who is in love with Mary, or the country relatives of old Mr. Featherstone. Rex Gascoigne is not so good as Fred Vincy.

Theodora. Mr. Gascoigne is admirable, and Mrs. Davilow is charming.

Pulcheria. And you must not forget that you think Herr Klesmer 'Shakespearian.' Would n't 'Wagnerian' be high enough praise?

Constantius. Yes, one must make an exception with regard to the Klesmers and the Meyricks. They are delightful, and as for Klesmer himself, and Hans Meyrick, Theodora may maintain her epithet. Shakespearian characters are characters that are born out of the *overflow* of observation, characters that make the drama seem multitudinous, like life. Klesmer comes in with a sort of Shakespearian 'value,' as a painter would say, and so, in a different tone, does Hans Meyrick. They spring from a much-peopled mind.

Theodora. I think Gwendolen's confrontation with Klesmer one of the finest things in the book.

Constantius. It is like everything in George Eliot, it will bear thinking of.

Pulcheria. All that is very fine, but you cannot persuade me that *Deronda* is not a very awkward and ill-made story. It has nothing that one can call a subject. A silly young girl and a heavy, overwise young man who *don't* fall in love with her! That is the *donnée* of eight monthly volumes. I call it very flat. Is that what the exquisite art of Thackeray and Miss Austen and Hawthorne has come to? I would as soon read a German novel outright.

Theodora. There is something higher than form—there is spirit.

Constantius. I am afraid Pulcheria is sadly æsthetic. She had better cònfine herself to Mérimée.

Pulcheria. I shall certainly to-day read over the 'Double Méprise'.[1]

Theodora. Oh, my dear, don't!

Constantius. Yes, I think there is little art in *Deronda*, but I think there is a vast amount of life. In life without art you can find your account; but art without life is a poor affair. The book is full of the world.

Theodora. It is full of beauty and sagacity, and there is quite art enough for me.

Pulcheria (to the little dog). We are silenced, darling, but we are not convinced, are we? (The dog begins to bark.) No, we are not even silenced. It's a young woman with two band-boxes.

Theodora. Oh, it must be our muslins.

Constantius (rising to go). I see what you mean!

[1] A story by Prosper Mérimée, 1833.

63. R. R. Bowker, unsigned review, *International Review*

January 1877, iv, 68–76

Richard Rogers Bowker (1848–1938) was an American publisher, bibliographer, and author. He was literary editor of the *New York Evening Mail* (1869–75), then joined the staff of the *New York Tribune*, and in 1876 helped to found the *Library Journal*. This is an extract from his review of *Daniel Deronda* (see Introduction, p. 35).

Considering then that a novel with a purpose and with a personality may still be recognized as a novel and as a work of art, we may take it as a chief element of George Eliot's greatness that her books are so persistently occupied with the greatest of problems—the problem, old as humanity, that must forever be set before each man as his question of life or death. As unreligious in the personality of her novels as Shakespeare the dramatist, George Eliot is always dealing with the most profound of practical religious questions. That truceless conflict which the Persians deified into alternating gods of Light and of Darkness; which Protestantism has philosophized into the problem of free-will *vs.* predestination; which is presented in history by the sustaining faith of the Jew on the one hand and the disintegrating fatalism of the Turk on the other; which in the experience of the individual is figured by the immortal parable of St. Anthony's strugglings between the spirit and the flesh—this clashing of the universe, one through its many phases, fought out now with the world for its battle-field, but oftenest in the inmost recesses of the human heart, presents itself to the rationalistic mind of George Eliot as the conflict between character and circumstance. Through all the full harmony of her writings is heard this theme.

Daniel Deronda not only treats of this question; it is built up upon it. The novel has two centres, Gwendolen and Mordecai, between whose circles the author's hero is the connecting link. The evident difference of opinion between the author and her readers, as to which is the leading person of the story, grows out of the conditions of this pervasive problem. She concentrates her attention upon Deronda because he represents character, force—originative in its relations to Gwendolen, transmissive in its relations with Mordecai. The reader looks upon him more as a force than as a person. On the other hand, the reader's attention is concentrated upon Gwendolen, this throbbing, bleeding heart, torn by the thwarting circumstance we all know to our pain, herself the product of circumstance and the battle-field of opposing character—because this is human and near to us. On either hand are the angel and the demon—not above, shadowy in the clouds, but called Deronda and Grandcourt. The one is indeed αγγελος, the messenger of life, the quickener; the other, the mocking spirit of negation which Goethe pictures as truly devil. Both of these men are evidently intended to represent 'character' in Emerson's sense. 'This is that which we call Character,' says this seer, 'a reserved force which acts directly by presence and without means.'[1] Tito Melema, the antipodes of Deronda, we know through his deeds, but neither Deronda nor Grandcourt *do* any thing. George Eliot has thus set to herself the most difficult task before creative art. There is more in these men than can be told of them, even in real life, and in endeavoring to give to the reader her own impression of Deronda she has returned again and again to the picture, only to find that, with all her pains, the reader must take something for granted. The reader who will take nothing for granted—in the heavens or under them, who, in a word, has no sense of spiritual force—finds Deronda a nonentity and Grandcourt an impossibility. Gwendolen knew, and we know, that this is not true; these men are those who are able to successfully oppose circumstance, and get the better of events. Perhaps if George Eliot had been content just to give us her word for Deronda, to elaborate him less, she would have accomplished more. We might then have seen him through the eyes of Gwendolen.

There are other readers who pronounce Grandcourt a living realization, but Deronda an unreal and objectionable prig. But Deronda is neither unreal nor a prig. There may be some to whom George Eliot has not made him evident, partly because literary art fails her to paint the real being she knows; partly because they could not, by their nature, know this real being in actual life. We can not make a photograph of a sunbeam, because it is the sunbeam which makes the photograph; we can not make any photograph evident to

[1] In his essay 'Character' (1844).

the blind. But some of us have known these Messianic men—we speak reverently—of whom Deronda is a type: strong with man's strength, tender with the tenderness of woman, touching no life that they did not lighten and inspire. Yet what could we tell of them that should make our friends know them as we know them? It is Deronda's literary misfortune that he is placed in conditions which in many minds attribute to him effeminacy: it doesn't look very manly to treat a woman as if she were in love with you. It is provoking also to poor humanity to gaze long upon too near an approach to unstained goodness, nor do men take kindly to that unpartisan catholicity which, seeing good on both sides as well as ill on both, seems to each party a defender of the other. Thus Deronda arouses manifold prejudices, but they are prejudices and not judgments. His character is justified as the book reaches its real climax and conclusion in that touching sentence of Gwendolen, the noblest testimony a noble soul can have: 'It is better—it shall be better with me—because I have known you.'

To most readers it goes without saying that this problem of character and circumstance is the mainspring of the Gwendolen side of Daniel Deronda's double history; it will be seen also that what is commonly known as 'the Jewish business' no less grows out of it, while even in a side personage like Klesmer we are shown the triumph of character over social circumstance. The history of the Jews appealed powerfully to the imagination of George Eliot, because it presented at once the most remarkable proof of the abidingness of character, in its broader relations, and the most striking illustration of that contact of ideal character and every-day circumstance which, as in the frequent suggestion that Deronda has a modern tailor, she is so fond of pointing out. The Jewish is so far the one race in history that can lay claim to immortality—because the earlier Ezras founded its national life upon a Rock. It was these Prophets of Judea, strong in faith, and defying circumstance, who, with that fire of soul that blazed into the most splendid and fervent oratory the world has known, gave to their petty state that principle of life which could never be quenched by the whole power of the magnificent empires that one after another fell to pieces around it. And it is this people, the chosen of God, who time and time again have turned aside, betrayed by the lusts of the flesh, into the entanglement of circumstance—who, to-day, leave the ancient and splendid ritual of their synagogues, to cheat Jehovah and the Gentiles on the street. 'Seest thou,' says Mordecai, in one of the great passages of the book, 'our lot is the lot of Israel. The grief and the glory are mingled as the smoke and the flame.' The very name of Mordecai and his contrasting fellow-Cohens itself tells the story. Associated in our minds with a common order of people, Cohen is (כהן) the Hebrew word for priest. Always, as in *The Spanish Gypsy*, emphasizing the idea of race, the thought of Judaism came also personally home to George Eliot, not so much in the influence of her husband, as has been suggested, as in that of her friend Emanuel Deutsch,[1] whose *Literary Remains* have shown to the world one whose kindling enthusiasm, thwarted aspirations, and gentle, pathetic life bring to mind both Deronda and Mordecai. For the latter, the direct suggestion came of course from that Cohen who was the leader of the philosophical club described in Lewes's *Fortnightly* article on 'Spinoza,'[2] but it is doubtless the life of Deutsch that has given life to Mordecai. In his influence upon George Eliot, as in that of Mordecai upon Deronda, is seen that transmissive inspiration and 'apostolic succession' of character that is a chief factor and proof of greatness. It is perhaps his enthusiasm for the East, also, that unfortunately started off Deronda upon a mission, of the geographical reunion of the Jews, which, in the light of modern relations, seems useless and absurd, as well as chimerical, and runs counter not least to the usual philosophy of George Eliot herself.

Of the minor characters it must suffice to say that the general voice has acknowledged in most of them new proofs of that masterly power of genius, so evident in *Romola*, through which by a few strokes a great canvas is filled in with individual creations. Whether any one character is real and living is much the same question as whether, to most of his readers—readers of his proper circle—an author has succeeded in making the character seem real and living, and judged by this test of literary *vox populi*, a foretaste of the verdict of posterity, Mirah, as well as Deronda himself, is not the person George Eliot meant her to be. Scarcely enough stress has been laid upon that superb portrait of Lapidoth, absolutely true to life, and the swift analysis of the disintegration of his moral fibre into absolute rottenness. This must take rank close to Tito Melema.

Having asserted that a novel may properly, by reason of its difference from the drama, have purpose and personality, and having endeavored to discover the *motif* and purpose of George Eliot's work, it is now time to ask whether in *Daniel Deronda* she has fulfilled, not the rigid canons of a too narrow criticism, but the conditions she has set for herself. It

[1] Emanuel Deutsch (1829–73), Jewish orientalist and friend of George Eliot.
[2] *Fortnightly Review* (1 April 1866), iv, 395–406.

can not be denied that as a writer, as well as artist, she has seriously lapsed. Some indications of this have already been pointed out. The plan of the book is not as diffusive as that of *Middlemarch*, and to many readers the interest is more concentrated and continuous, but it oscillates between two plots, neither of which can be considered a sub-plot. This lapse of continuity is not lessened by the frequency with which the chorus occupies so large a portion of the stage, or by the literary fault in which George Eliot unfortunately indorses Browning's worst tendencies. An author may fairly be called upon to give good reason for distracting the reader from his continuity of thought and feeling by sending him to the dictionary for the meaning of a word not generally known, or by calling his attention to a word or phrase so novel or peculiar as to stand out from the text. We don't go to George Eliot as to Sir Thomas Browne, and she herself plans for a wider circle of readers. That the words she uses are pregnant with meaning is not enough; dictionaries of science and of positivism ought not to be the necessary vestibule to a book meant for general reading. Nor is it healthful for a writer to depart far from the usual speech of his day and generation: he is instantly in danger of being led away into affectations which separate him from a wide sympathy with the heart and life of the people. This has wrecked many poets and, despite Miss Evans, some novelists.

64. Edward Dowden, review, *Contemporary Review*

February 1877, xxix, 348–69

Extracts from Dowden's essay entitled '*Middlemarch* and *Daniel Deronda*', which at one time he intended to be part of a critical study of the novelist (See No. 47). Lewes thanked Dowden for his open-minded and perceptive treatment of the novel: 'The deep insight, and that upon which all might is founded, the sympathy, expressed in your article has therefore been peculiarly grateful both to her and me . . .' (*Letters*, vi, 336) (see Introduction, p. 35).

To discover the central motive of *Daniel Deronda* it should be studied in connection with its immediate predecessor, *Middlemarch*. In externals the contrast is striking. In *Middlemarch* the prosaic or realistic element occupies a much larger place; a great proportion of the book is only not a satire because with the word satire we are accustomed to associate the idea of exaggeration and malicious purpose. The chief figures—Lydgate, Dorothea—are enveloped by a swarm of subordinate characters, each admirably real, and to whom we are compelled to give away a share of our interest, a share of our admiration or our detestation. In *Daniel Deronda* the poetical or ideal element as decidedly preponderates. We should feel the needle-pricks of Mrs. Cadwallader's epigrams an irritating impertinence. Our emotions are strung too tensely to permit us to yield an amused tolerance to the fine dispersion of idea in Mr. Brooke's discourse. In place of a background of ugliness,—the Middlemarch streets, the hospital, the billiard-room, the death-chamber of Peter Featherstone, his funeral procession attended by Christian carnivora,—we have backgrounds of beauty, the grassy court of the abbey enclosed by a Gothic cloister, its July sunshine, and blown roses; Cardell Chase, and the changing scenery of the forest from roofed grove to open glade; evening on the Thames at Richmond with the lengthening shadows and the mellowing light, its darkening masses of tree and building between the double glow of the sky and the river; the Turneresque splendour of sunset in a great city, while the lit, expectant face is gazing from Blackfriars Bridge westward, where the grey day is dying gloriously; the Mediterranean, its shores gemlike with purple shadows, a sea where one may float between blue and blue in an open-eyed dream that the world has done with sorrow.

These differences in externals correspond with the essential inward difference between the two works,—the one, *Middlemarch*, is critical, while its successor aims at being in a certain sense constructive.

[discussion of *Middlemarch* follows]

But *Middlemarch* is not the final word of our great imaginative teacher. Whether consciously so designed or not, *Daniel Deronda* comes to us as a counterpoise or a correlative of the work which immediately preceded it. There we saw how two natures framed for large disinterested services to humanity can be narrowed—the one into the round of the duteous sweet observances of domestic life—the other into the servitude,

Eyeless, in Gaza, at the mill, with slaves,[1]

which the world imposes upon those who accept its base terms and degrading compensations. Here we are shown how two natures can be ennobled and enlarged: the one rescued through anguish and remorse, and by the grace, human if also divine, which the soul of man has power to bestow upon the soul of man, from self-centered insolence of youth, the crude egoism of a spoiled child; and rendered up, first a crushed penitent to sorrow, then weak as a new-yeaned lamb to the simplicity of a mother's love, and at last plunged into a purgatory of fire, consuming and quickening and seven times heated, until the precious soul is released from bond and forfeiture, and reclaimed for places consecrated by love and duty: the other, a nature of finer mould and temper than that of Lydgate, with none of the spots of commonness in it which produced a disintegrating effect on Lydgate's action, but exposed through its very plenteousness and flexibility of sympathy to peculiar dangers—the danger of neutrality in the struggle between common things and high which fills the world, the danger of wandering energy and wasted ardours; and from these dangers Deronda is delivered, he is incorporated into a great ideal life, made one with his nation and race, and there is confided to him the heritage

---

[1] *Samson Agonistes*, 41.

of duty bound with love which was his forefathers', and of which it had been sought to deprive him.

Such are the spiritual histories of Gwendolen Harleth and of Daniel Deronda, told in the briefest summary. When we speak of *Middlemarch* as more realistic, and the later novel as more ideal, it is not meant that the one is true to the facts of life and the other untrue; it is rather meant that in the one the facts are taken more in the gross, and in the other there is a passionate selection of those facts that are representative of the highest (and also of the lowest) things. The Dresden Madonna, with awed rapture, a sacred joy and terror, in her eyes, bearing the divine Child, is not less true to the essential facts of womanhood than is a plain grandmother of Gerard Dow[1] shredding carrots into her pot. That some clever critics should find the hero of George Eliot's last novel detestable is easily understood; that some should find him incredible proves no more than that clever critics in walking from their lodgings to their club, and from their club to their lodgings, have not exhausted the geography of the habitable globe. If 'knowledge of the world' consist chiefly in a power of estimating the average force of men's vulgar or selfish appetites, instincts, and interests, it must be admitted that in such knowledge the author of *Middlemarch* and of *Felix Holt* is not deficient; but there is another knowledge of the world which she also possesses, a knowledge which does not exclude from recognition the martyr, the hero, and the saint.

Daniel Deronda, however, as we meet him in the novel, has not attained to be any of these: with all the endowments needed for an eminent benefactor of men, we yet perceive how he might have failed of his true direction and function. To some readers he has seemed no thin shadow, no pallid projection from the author's imagination, but a veritable creature of flesh and blood, and his trials and dangers have seemed most real and worthy of the closest scrutiny. Here and there, if we have but eyes framed for moral discovery, we may still discern some well-begotten son or daughter of whom the father or mother declares with a little quiver of loving pride in the voice, 'He has never given me an hour's trouble since he was born,' one who in the venerable Christian words has been 'filled with the Holy Ghost from his mother's womb.'[2] The speciality of Deronda among the *dramatis personæ* of George Eliot's art is that a pure sympathetic nature is with him innate; his freedom from egoism is a possession which has come to him without a struggle. Maggie Tulliver is tempted with a fierce

---

[1] Gerard Dou (1613–75), Dutch painter. [2] *Luke*, i, 15.

temptation to sacrifice the happiness of another to her own. It is through an agony that Fedalma becomes able to slay the life within her of personal joy. Even Dorothea has a great discovery of the heart to make; she had early emerged from the moral stupidity of taking the world 'as an udder to feed her supreme self; yet it had been easier to her to imagine how she would devote herself to Mr. Casaubon, and become wise and strong in his strength and wisdom, than to conceive with that distinctness which is no longer reflection but feeling . . . that he had an equivalent centre of self, whence the lights and shadows must always fall with a certain difference.' Deronda even in childhood is sensible of the existence of independent centres of self outside himself, and can transfer his own consciousness into theirs. He is thus predestined to be a saviour and redeemer. And however incredulous critics of culture, with extensive knowledge of the world, may be as to the existence of this type among men, the heart of humanity in all ages, alike in the mystic East and the scientific West, has clung to belief in its existence as to the most precious of man's spiritual possessions. From the very fact that such persons are free from an absorbing egoism it becomes difficult to determine the precise outline of their personality. We can more easily describe the character of Mohammed than that of Jesus, if for no other reason than that the one had a pride and lust of power and personal pleasure of which we find no trace in the other. When a man diffuses himself, as the sun diffuses warmth and light, the force which communicates itself so generously seems to be alienated from its original owner. A Grandcourt whose nature is one main trunk of barren egoism from which all the branches of fresh desire have withered off, is recognized forthwith to be human. But Deronda, sensitive at every point with life which flows into him and throughout him, and streams forth from him in beneficent energy,—Deronda is a pallid shadow rather than a man! . . . And at this point it may be worth while to notice two counter-objections which are alleged against George Eliot's work. To some readers the whole story of Mordecai and of his relation to Deronda appears fantastic and unreal—a piece of workmanship all carved out of the carver's brain, or even something less solid and substantial than this—a mere luminous vapour, or a phantom of the mind, which science cannot justify or even recognize. On the other hand, able critics lament over the growth, in George Eliot's writings, of scientific habits of thought and expression, and in a style of warning 'eäsy and freeä,' which seems to combine the authorities of 'godamoighty' and 'parson,' bid our great thinker and artist expect the extinction of her genius. She has actually employed in a work of fiction such words as 'dynamic' and 'natural selection,' at which the critic pricks up his delicate ears and shies. If the thorough-bred critic could only be led close up to 'dynamic,' he would find that 'dynamic' will not bite. A protest is really called for against the affectation which professes to find obscurity in words because they are trisyllabic or because they carry with them scientific associations. Language, the instrument of literary art, is an instrument of ever-extending range, and the truest pedantry, in an age when the air is saturated with scientific thought, would be to reject those accessions to language which are the special gain of the time. Insensibility to the contemporary movement in science is itself essentially unliterary, for literature with its far-reaching sensibilities should be touched, thrilled, and quickened by every vital influence of the period; and indeed it is not alone the intellect which recognizes the accuracy and effectiveness of such scientific illustration as George Eliot occasionally employs; the cultured imagination is affected by it, as the imagination of the men of Spenser's time was affected by his use of the neo-classical mythology of the Renaissance.

But there is graver reason which justifies an artist of the present day in drawing near to science, and receiving all it has to bestow of ascertained truth and enlightened impulse. The normal action of the reason upon the imagination has been happily described by Comte,—'Elle la stimule en la réglant.'[1] This expresses with accuracy the relation of these faculties in the nature of our English novelist,—reason is to her imagination both law and impulse. And therefore her art is not a mere luxury for the senses, not a mere æsthetic delicacy or dainty. It has chosen for its part to be founded in truth, to nourish the affections, to quicken the conscience, to reinforce and purify the will. In her art the artist lives,

> Breathing as beauteous order that controls
> With growing sway the growing life of man.

Art dissociated from the reason and the conscience becomes before long a finely distilled poison; while considered merely as art it has thus declined—in however exquisite little phials it may be presented—from its chief functions. It no longer sways or controls our being; it painfully seeks to titillate a special sense. An indifference arises as to what is called the substance or 'content' of works of art, and the form is spoken

[1] 'It stimulates as it controls' (*Discours sur l'Ensemble du Positivisme* (1848), ch. 5).

of as if that had a separate and independent existence. There follows, as Comte has again observed, 'the inevitable triumph of mediocrities;' executive or technical skill, of the kind which commands admiration in a period devoid of noble motive and large ideas, being attainable by persons of mere talent. The artificial refinements of a coterie are held to constitute the beautiful in art, and these can be endlessly repeated. 'A deplorable aptitude in expressing what they neither believe nor feel,' continues the great thinker whose words have just been quoted, 'gains in the present day an ephemeral ascendency for talents as incapable of an æsthetic creation as of a scientific conception.' And George Eliot has herself alluded in a passing way to the presence of the same vice in our contemporary literature: 'Rex's love had been of that sudden, penetrating, clinging sort which the ancients knew and sung, and in singing made a fashion of talk for many moderns whose experience has been by no means of a fiery dæmonic character.' The largeness and veracity of George Eliot's own art proceed from the same qualities which make truth-seeking a passion of her nature; and a truth-seeker at the present day will do ill to turn a deaf ear to the teachings of science. As little as Dante need George Eliot fear to enter into possession of the fullest body of fact which the age can deliver to her; nay, it is essential to the highest characteristics of her art that she should not isolate herself from the chief intellectual movement of her time. If in the objection which has been brought against her recent style there be any portion of truth, it will be found in the circumstance that an occasional sentence becomes laboured, and perhaps overloaded in her effort to charge it fully and accurately with its freight of meaning. The manner of few great artists—if any—becomes simpler as they advance in their career, that is, as their ideas multiply, as their emotions receive more numerous affluents from the other parts of their being, and as the vital play of their faculties with one another becomes swifter and more intricate. The later sonatas of Beethoven still perplex facile and superficial musicians. The later landscapes of Turner bewilder and amaze the profane. The difference between the languid and limpid fluency of the style of *The Two Gentlemen of Verona* and the style of Shakspere's later plays, so compressed, so complex, so live with breeding imagery, is great. Something is lost but more has been gained. When the sustained *largo* of the sentences of *Daniel Deronda* is felt after the crude epigrammatic smartnesses of much of the writing in *Scenes of Clerical Life* we perceive as great a difference and as decided a preponderance of gain over loss.

But what renders singular the warning addressed to George Eliot that her work is undergoing a 'scientific depravation' is that the whole of her last book is a homage to the emotions rather than to the intellect of man. Her feeling finds expression not only in occasional gnomic utterances in which sentiments are declared to be the best part of the world's wealth, and love is spoken of as deeper than reason, and the intellect is pronounced incapable of ascertaining the validity of claims which rest upon loving instincts of the heart, or else are baseless. The entire work possesses an impassioned aspect, an air of spiritual prescience, far more than the exactitude of science. The main forces which operate in it are sympathies, aspirations, ardours, and ideas chiefly as associated with these. From his meditative numbness Deronda is roused, his diffused mass of feeling is rendered definite, and is impelled in a given direction, his days become an ordered sequence bound together by love and duty, his life is made one with the life of humanity. How is this change brought about? And how is that other change effected by which Gwendolen is checked in her career of victorious self-pleasing, is delivered from her habits of a spoiled child, and is made—she also—a portion of the better life of man? Does Deronda take counsel with a Lydgate, and learn by the microscope the secrets of moral energy and resolved submission to spiritual motive? Or does some theory of ethics make the moral world new for him? Neither of these. It is the discovery of his parentage and his people which creates claims to which his heart consents with joy, and Deronda's life takes its new direction not from the inductions of a savant of the West, but from the inspirations of a Hebrew prophet with whom the inferences of what Coleridge would have named the prudential understanding are wholly overshadowed by the faith of what he would have named the imaginative reason.

. . . We owe to the author of *Daniel Deronda* the gratitude due to one who enriches human life for her discovery in Ram's bookshop, and among the kindly-hearted mercenary Cohens, of a prophet of the Exile. To feel that intense spiritual forces lie concealed under the heaped *débris* of follies, and fashions, and worldliness which accumulates around us, makes our existence one of more awed responsibility, and of quicker hopes and fears. There are powers in our midst of which we are not aware; the electric charge of the spirit may play upon us at any moment, we know not from what point; material interests and machinery are not yet, and never will be, supreme; still from the spirit of man to the spirit of man flow forth the issues of life and death. 'This consumptive Jewish workman in threadbare clothing, lodged by charity, delivering himself to hearers who took his thoughts without attaching more consequences to them than the Flemings to the ethereal chimes ringing above their market-places, had the chief elements of human greatness: a mind consciously, energetically moving with the larger march of human destinies, but not the less full of conscience and tender heart for the footsteps that tread near and need a leaning-place; capable of conceiving and choosing a life's task with far-off issues, yet capable of the unapplauded heroism which turns off the road of achievement at the call of the nearer duty whose effect lies within the beatings of the hearts that are close to us, as the hunger of the unfledged bird to the breast of its parent.'

To understand aright the Jewish idea of Mordecai we should approach it through the wider human idea of George Eliot. It might indeed be contended that at a period when on the continent of Europe the idea of nationality—unity of Italy, pan-Teutonism, pan-Slavism—has played and is playing so important a part, there were a historical justification and a historical propriety in its employment as a poetical motive in a work of art. If the political imagination of the English nation is seldom assailed by great principles or ideas, their force upon the history of the world has not therefore been small; lives have been spent for them, and blood has been gladly offered up. Probably none but English readers in our day would refuse to accept as deserving of imaginative credence such an idea as that which inspires Mordecai. That an ancient people, who under every battering shock of doom have preserved their faith and their traditions, should resume their place in the community of nations, could be hardly more wonderful than that they exist at all. A French philosopher conceived a polity of Western nations, with France as the presiding power; there is grandeur (and grandeur is a quality of thought by no means necessarily implying something unreal or theatrical) in the conception of a future which shall include an organization of the East as well as of the West, and which places at the head of Eastern civilization the greatest and most spiritual of Shemitic races.

But the central conception of *Daniel Deronda* is religious, and not political: religious, not in the sense which implies faith in a personal providence superintending the lives of men, or faith in the intervention of the miraculous and the supernatural, or faith in a life for each man and woman beyond the grave in other worlds than ours. No miraculous apparition of a Holy Grail in the mediæval romance is bright with more mysterious glory, and solemn with more transcendent awe, than the meeting of the Jewish workman and Deronda in the splendour of sunset, and in the gloom of the little second-hand bookshop, while the soul of one transfuses itself into the soul of the other. But the miracles are wrought by the spirit of man; human life itself is shown to be sacred, a temple with its shrines for devout humility and aspiration, its arches and vaults for praise, its altar for highest sacrifice. 'The refuge you are needing from personal trouble,' declares Deronda to Gwendolen, 'is the higher, the religious life, which holds an enthusiasm for something more than our own appetites and vanities.' The religious conception of *Daniel Deronda*, as of the other writings of George Eliot, is that of a life of mankind over, above, and around the life of the individual man or woman, and to which the individual owes his loyalty and devotion, the passion of his heart, and the utmost labour of his hand. 'Thou hast beset me behind and before, and laid thine hand upon me. . . . Thine eyes did see my substance, yet being unperfect. How precious are thy thoughts unto me! how great is the sum of them!' Of this religion—a religion by which a man's life may become a noble self-surrender whether it contain but a portion of truth or contain the whole—Mordecai is a prophet, and Deronda is a chosen and anointed priest. The Judaic element comes second in the book—the human element first.

65. W. H. Mallock on George Eliot

1879

This is the first half of an unsigned review of *Impressions of Theophrastus Such* (1879), *Edinburgh Review* (October 1879), cl, 557–86.

William Hurrell Mallock (1849–1923), political philosopher and satirist, is best known as the author of *The New Republic* (1877), a satire on contemporary English society and ideas, in which Jowett, Arnold, Pater, Huxley, etc. appear thinly disguised. George Eliot considered that the book's cheap ridicule made it 'one of the most condemnable of the day' (*Letters*, vi, 406) (see Introduction, p. 36).

A distinguished living author once observed in our hearing, that there was a time when George Eliot's genius seemed to him to be of almost boundless promise. 'I even thought,' he proceeded, 'that some day she might perhaps have equalled Miss Austen.' There are few, we conceive, amongst George Eliot's admirers who would either thank our critic for these liberal hopes, or sympathise with him in his implied disappointment; nor do we ourselves share in the temper of his criticism. We disagree with him, however, not because his judgment was entirely false, but because it was only very partially true. So far as he had viewed the matter, his view was accurate. It is misleading only because its scope was limited. There are few minds which have accomplished much, that to observant eyes have at one time not promised more. Even the most many-sided genius must have given hints, at the outset, of the possession of many powers it could never bring to perfection; and we shall often best estimate a writer's chief achievements by examining first the extent and the nature of his partial failures. When, therefore, it is said that George Eliot might have been a second Miss Austen, and has failed to be so, we need not, in assenting to this, be passing a degrading judgment. We advance instantly from

448

our notice of the success she has foregone, to inquiring what other success she has tried to achieve instead of it—what greater birthright she has bought by the sacrifice of her mess of pottage. This inquiry is not altogether an easy one; and a more significant homage could not be paid to the authoress than to say that it is worth our while, in her case, to make it with all care and seriousness. Her present volume is especially welcome, not only because it suggests such a task to us, but also because it will assist us in attempting it.

The most obvious aspect under which we look at her is that simply of a novelist—as a dramatic artist in prose. It is not here that her real pre-eminence lies; but we will confine ourselves at first to this very restricted view of her, and regard her as though she were simply a novelist among novelists.

Now, the qualities that a novelist most requires are, in their own degree, the same as those required by a dramatist. A novel, like a drama, is a work of art, and must, like a drama, conform to certain artistic laws, and present certain artistic qualities. The most prominent of these have their close analogies in painting. The first requirements in a picture are that it conform to certain rules of composition, grouping, chiaro-oscuro, and perspective. In like manner we require first of all in a novel or a drama that there be a certain method, grace, and unity in the plot. The various incidents must be presented to us in their due proportion. The attention must not be distracted by unnecessary figures or events. Everything must be properly subordinate to some central interest; and form parts of a single organic whole. When the novelist or the dramatist fulfils these requirements, we may say, in painters' language, that the *composition* of his piece is perfect. As equally apposite examples of this kind of perfection, we may cite two works, which, in other ways, are of a widely different character— *Tom Jones*, and the *Œdipus Tyrannus* of Sophocles. But *composition* is not all. We require moral perspective and moral chiaro-oscuro as well. What is trivial and incidental must not be drawn too large. What is important must not be drawn too small. And further, the lights and shades, or, if we like to add a new metaphor, the colours, must be properly harmonised and distributed. Everything must not be made an unrelieved darkness by vice or sorrow, or a flat and even brightness by joy or virtue. The novelist and the painter have each of them a kindred artistic effect to produce with shine and shadow, and with various combinations of colour.

Further, there is a second class of requirements needful for a novelist,

449

which might also, were there occasion for it, be illustrated by a reference to painting; and this is an insight into the human heart which is not only profound, but at the same time wide and impartial; and a power, not alone of describing character, but still more of presenting it in action.

If we judge George Eliot's work by the tests above suggested, there is scarcely one adverse criticism to which it is not open. The *composition* of her stories is to the utmost rude and faulty; or rather, in the artistic sense of the word, there is no composition in them at all. In *Middlemarch*, for instance, we have not one plot, but two, and these joined together in the clumsiest and most unskilful fashion. Elsewhere, it is true, her designs may have more unity; but the unity, even where most traceable, is obscured or quite distorted by masses of irrelevant detail. Every stone in her building may be of marble, and of marble finely cut: but the building as a whole is not fitly framed together; and many of the blocks which exhibit the finest carving are not only not needed by the structure, but they overload it, and destroy its symmetry. She recognises the time-worn truth that a story must have a beginning, a middle, and an end; but between these three parts she observes no just proportion. Her action moves onwards by fits and starts. She hurries when we would have her linger: she lingers when we would have her hurry: and her pace seems to depend not so much on the nature of the road, as on the flowers she desires to pluck by the side of it, or the views of distant scenery which she leans over gates to contemplate.

But there is a greater defect still to notice. In dealing with her principal characters she does not, as a general rule, so much *present* them, as *describe* them to us. And we are made all the more keenly conscious of this, because with her minor characters her procedure is exactly opposite. Mrs. Tulliver and Aunt Pullet, discussing a bonnet, are presented to us. Maggie and Stephen Guest, in their love scenes, are described to us. The former group is a painting left to speak for itself. The latter is a charcoal sketch, with a long explanation under it. We are not saying that the sketch may not show higher powers than the painting: but they are not powers of the same order; they are not the powers we expect to find in an artist. And so far as artistic success—the success of the true novelist—goes, it is not too much to say that with George Eliot this varies in an inverse ratio to the importance which she herself attaches to her subjects.

It will be recollected that in making these remarks we are purposely narrowing our view. We are regarding the authoress under only one aspect. And if our judgment should seem to be somewhat too severe, it is she herself who is responsible for the severity. We are trying her by standards that she has herself suggested; and those standards are the highest. We are condemning the faults of what she has done by the perfection of what she shows us she might have done. She might have been a second Miss Austen: and that within its limits is no small praise; for it means at any rate that she might have been a consummate artist. And it is only because we see her to have been capable of perfect art, that we are forced to note the imperfections of the art she has actually given us.

But if she has failed as a novelist where novelists of less genius have succeeded, she exhibits powers to which, amongst other novelists, we can hardly find a parallel, and which only very rarely have expressed themselves in prose fiction at all. She may be less than Miss Austen in art, but she is greater than Scott in insight. Indeed, to compare her even to Scott is an unfairness to her. We must go for our parallel yet a stage higher; and we must not stop short of the world's greatest poets. The art of the novelist, and presumably his vision also, rests on the surface of life and of society. His eyes, so far as he can use them, may be as keen and piercing as the poet's; but he uses them from a different point of view. The varied human landscape lies before him, and he paints what he sees of it; but he is not, like the poet, at a sufficient height above it, to see to the bottom of its deep ravines and valleys, or to the summits of its lofty mountains. That it has deep valleys and that it has mountain peaks, he presumes; but he has neither descended to the one, nor scaled the other. With George Eliot, however, the case is different. She, like the poet, takes a more commanding standpoint. Her eyes are occupied with the high and deep places of the human spirit, and the larger and profounder questions of human destiny. For her, as for the poet, life is, as it were, transparent; and she sees the mightiest issues hiding under the most trivial. Her materials for excitement and interest are not the excitements of adventure, with their varieties of surface incident; her materials for tragedy are not murders or escapes from murder, with the manœuvres of criminals and detectives: but they are the inner spiritual events that take place beneath the surface, and of which the outer events are for her the signs merely. Her works partake thus of the quality that separates the poetry of a great drama from the prose of a great novel. The essential difference, for instance, between *Hamlet* and *Pendennis* lies in the different level in human life to which the two works pierce. The one reaches to the poetry of life; the other only presumes it, or at best points to it from a distance. But the vision of George Eliot goes straight to it, and encounters it face to face. She has seen and has felt like Sophocles, that

> Full many things are wonderful, but none
> More fearful and more wonderful than man;[1]

and she has seen and felt this with something of the emotion that is common and almost peculiar to the greatest tragic poets.

And yet with all this George Eliot is not a poet; and putting form altogether out of the question, her works are not poetry. They bear the same relation to poems that a chrysalis does to a butterfly, just before the change. We feel them to be quivering with a life that demands some further development. We feel that something is on the ground that requires to fly, and that is every moment on the point of soaring. But the wings never unfold themselves. The strength is wanting somewhere by which the prison is to be broken.

Thus, to pass on her work any general literary judgment is a somewhat puzzling task. But going again for assistance to a simile drawn from painting, we may compare her work, not so much to so many separate pictures, as to so many separate canvases, each covered with a number of pictorial fragments—fragments connected together indeed by some thread, inward or outward, of thought or meaning; but neither in conception nor execution fused together into coherent artistic wholes. We have studies for some heroic subject—some great and solemn action—which are instinct with power and genius, but in which the figures are grouped ill, and often only partly outlined; and we have this heroic group broken or surrounded by a number of semi-serious figures—not in outline, but painted in solid colour, and with the most masterly and complete finish. Such at least is the impression which her earlier works have made on us. Her manner latterly, it is true, has grown in some ways more congruous; but this is not because she has learnt to finish the whole of her pictures as she once did their secondary parts; but because she has ceased to use her brush at all, and has left the whole in the condition of shadowy sketches.

To the eye, therefore, of purely artistic criticism, George Eliot's work, even at its highest, is full of flaws and blemishes. The world, however, is not made up entirely of artistic critics; and the common sense of the public, with its wise want of fastidiousness, often detects

[1] *Antigone*, 333.

in a writer what there is of genius, the better for not detecting what there is lacking in art and skill. And such is the case with George Eliot. She sees truths about life which vast numbers of men and women feel to be true, and which they are grateful to her for having expressed and set before them. She has given definiteness to views which before were dim and vague to them; she has given voice to thoughts and feelings which before were inarticulate. They feel that she has done this for them *somehow*; and *how*, they neither know nor care to criticise. Her books are more to them like Bibles than books of mere amusement; and they have been treated and read with a reverence that was perhaps never before accorded to any works of fiction.

Her position is thus sufficiently remarkable; but there is a point about it beyond any we have yet touched upon, which makes it more remarkable still; and this is a point, probably, that is little suspected by the larger part of her most earnest and most reverent students. She is the first great *godless* writer of fiction that has appeared in England; perhaps, in the sense in which we use the expression, the first that has appeared in Europe. To say this may sound a paradox or an insult; but it is neither. And this will appear presently, when we have explained the meaning which we attach to the obnoxious word *godless*.

We must remember that generally, up to the present time, human conduct was, amongst serious people, supposed to bear reference, before all things, to some power above ourselves, and of a different nature, to whom our souls belonged, and for whose sake we were bound to keep them pure. And this conception has so penetrated our modern civilisation, that it has been implied in the entire lives and thoughts of numbers who not only never thought of affirming it, but who even posed as deniers of the belief upon which it rested. Shakespeare, for instance, may or may not have been a religious man; he may or may not have been a Catholic, or a Protestant. But whatever his personal views or feelings may have been, the light by which he viewed life was the light of Christianity. The shine, the shadow, and the colours of the moral world he looked upon, were all caused or cast by the Christian Sun of Righteousness. But now amongst the vast changes that human thought has been undergoing, the sun that we once all walked by has for many eyes become extinguished; and every energy has been bent upon supplying man with a substitute, which shall have, if possible, an equal illuminating power, and at any rate the same power of moral actinism. This substitute at present is, it is true, somewhat nebulous; but the substance it is composed of is already sufficiently plain. The new object of our duty is not our Father which is in Heaven, but our brothers and our children who are on earth. It is to these alone, according to the new gospel, that our piety is due; it is indeed to these that all true piety has, in all ages, been ignorantly paid. It is needless to dwell upon this conception longer. Whether we think it sound or hollow, its general character is familiar enough to all of us; and we know that a growing number of men and women around us are adopting it. But it is one thing to adopt a belief in theory—another thing to put it in practice; and again another thing, to receive it, as it were in solution, into our daily thoughts and feelings, so that we not only act and think by it, but also instinctively judge and feel by it. This third stage is the one that is reached latest, and we doubt whether as yet any considerable body of men and women have attained to it. The nearest approach to it, so far as we know, is to be found in the novels of George Eliot: only there even it is not reached perfectly; for the moral standard of the novelist, and the rational justification of her own judgments and sympathies, are not present to her mind instinctively, and as matters of course; but they are for ever being consciously emphasised by herself, and for ever being pointed out, more or less directly, to the reader. At any rate, in the world of earnest art, she is the first legitimate fruit of our modern atheistic pietism; and as such, she is an object of extreme interest, if not to artistic epicures, at any rate to all anxious inquirers into human destiny. For in her writings we have some sort of presentation of a world of high endeavour, pure morality, and strong enthusiasm, existing and in full work, without any reference to, or help from, the thought of God. *Godless* in its literal sense, and divested of all vindictive meaning, exactly describes her writings. They are without God, not against Him. They do not deny, but they silently and skilfully ignore Him. We have the same old liturgies of human faith and action, only they are intercepted and appropriated by a new object, when they seemed to be on their way to the old. The glory and the devotion that was once given to God is transferred silently to man.

The way in which this feat is performed is very remarkable; for the characters she presents us with are suffered rarely, if ever, to hold opinions that are consciously to themselves at all akin to the author's. On the contrary, they are most of them Christian people, with the love of God and the fear of hell presumably before their eyes. But in all their more vital struggles after God, the supernatural element in their beliefs is represented as having no effect on them. It is treated as a husk

454

or shell, concealing, or perhaps sheltering, something more precious than itself; or at best conveying a truth in metaphor through the channel of a sacramental lie. Mr. Tryan, in 'Janet's Repentance', and Savonarola in *Romola*, are both of them marked instances of this; and the author's dealing with these characters is exceedingly skilful. Mr. Tryan is a clergyman, passionately devoted to his sacred calling, an ardent disciple of a special school of divinity, and eaten up with the sincerest zeal for souls. And yet the writer contrives to exhibit all that she wishes us to admire in him as resting on a basis with which his religious beliefs have nothing at all to do. In her portrait of Savonarola this treatment is yet more distinguishable and yet more significant. His chief connexion with the story in which she introduces him, is his conversion of the heroine, from the neo-paganism of the Renaissance, to the precepts of Christ, and to a humble acceptance of sorrow. But in all his exhortations to her, and they are some of them singularly beautiful, there is hardly one appeal to Christianity on its supernatural side. Savonarola is the spokesman of Humanity made divine, not of Deity made human. In so far as he is not this, but the reverse of this, there, according to George Eliot, lies his weakness and not his strength. The 'higher life,' the withdrawal from man for the sake of communion with God, is for her a diseased weakness, if not a wickedness. The Christ of the Christian Church says, 'If a man love father and mother more than me, he is not worthy of me.' The Christ of George Eliot says the exact opposite: 'A man is not worthy of me unless he love me less than father or mother.' With her, as she says often and explicitly, the 'transcendent morality' is to share willingly in the 'common lot,' and not to seek escape from ties 'after those ties have ceased to be pleasant.' She urges with a solemn eloquence, she seems to see in a solemn ecstasy, that a man's highest life is to be found in sorrow, borne for the sake of others; and that all seeming miseries may be turned to blessings, by making an offering of them to something beyond ourselves. But an offering to what? To the God who has made us, loved us, and suffered for us, and into whose presence we may one day win admission? To no such God; but to some impersonal cause, some force of human progress. 'Make your marriage-sorrows,' says Savonarola to Romola, 'an offering, too, my daughter: an offering to *the great work* by which sin and sorrow are to be made to cease.' This is the one teaching of all her novels; and its fundamental difference from the highest Christian teaching lies in this, that it asserts the part to be greater and more complete than the whole; that it asserts those human hopes, and loves, and enthusiasms which Christianity has developed for us, and bequeathed to us, to be in reality complete in themselves, and clogged and weighted only, not supported by, what were once supposed to be their divine foundations.

This fact, as we have said before, is probably little suspected by the majority of George Eliot's readers. These carry with them the lamp of their own religion into that tender but gloomy world into which the author leads them; and do not perceive what the only light is, with which it would be else provided. They have themselves supplied what is wanting before they have felt the want. And they have imagined that the beliefs which they do not find dwelt upon, have been presupposed as true, instead of being studiously ignored as false. But if we would really see George Eliot in all her full significance, we must not close our eyes thus. If we do, we shall not only miss the one thing which she has renounced much to teach us; but we shall miss something that is of an importance far more general. We shall miss the first concrete examples of the workings of the new religion of humanity; and the only means as yet offered us by which to test the results of it, as seen or anticipated by one of its own apostles. Further, if we look at her in this way, and with this intention, her work, which seems so chaotic when judged by any mere artistic tests, becomes congruous and intelligible. It is not so much a series of novels, interspersed with philosophical reflections; it is a gradual setting forth of a philosophy and religion of life, illustrated by a continuous succession of diagrams. That this is the true view of the matter has been getting more and more evident as the career of the author has proceeded. How far this line of development has been conscious and intentional, with herself, it is not ours to inquire. But, consciously or unconsciously, the main stream of her powers has drifted into the philosophic channel, and has left her artistic powers as a mere auxiliary to these, although from the very nature of the case closely connected with them. It is, therefore, by her philosophy that she has the strongest claim to be judged.

Now, it is not our intention here (for neither place nor space permit of it) to discuss that philosophy with reference to its truth or permanent value. But for reasons that will appear presently it will be well to glance at certain salient features of it. The first article of her creed is—I believe in Humanity as the embracer of every moral end that is possible for man; as the only and sufficient object of his highest hopes, and his truest religious emotions. And it is her aim, conscious or unconscious, through-out all her writings to exhibit to us the highest lives directed and nourished only by motives that are purely human. One thing therefore is at once evident. She does not, if we recollect rightly, profess herself to be an optimist. We think indeed she has expressed her convictions somewhere as a creed of '*meliorism*.' But at any rate the whole fabric of her system and her emotions rests, for its one foundation, on a profound satisfaction in the fact of the human race existing, and an earnest hope and expectation of a blessed, if not of a quite perfect, future for it. It is an unspeakable good that it exists now; it will be a yet more unspeakable good that it exists by-and-by. We need not, however, seek to define her hopes too exactly. It is sufficient that her entire philosophy is an impassioned protest against pessimism, and that it presents the human life and the human lot to us as worthy of all our piety—all our love and reverence. The question that at once arises is, how far does this Deity, as she presents it to us, justify or excite the adoration that she is so pressing we should accord to it? And the answer to this question is somewhat startling. George Eliot, as we have said, is theoretically no pessimist; and yet the picture she presents to us of the world we live in almost exactly answers to the description given of it by Schopenhauer, as nothing better than a 'penal settlement.' It might at first sight seem hard to account for this inconsistency. It might seem that her philosophic theories and her true natural vision were at hopeless war with one another; and that her diagrams refuted instead of illustrating the text of her proposition. Or we might figure her as labouring under a destiny the exact reverse of Balaam's; and having resolved to bless the human destiny, finding herself constrained by the power of truth to curse it.

For in what light is it that she exhibits men to us? She exhibits them as, first and before all things, beings who are not isolated, but linked together by countless ties of duty and affection; and the essence of all right conduct, and the moral *raison d'être* of existence, consists, according to her, in our willingly keeping these ties inviolate. Thus far the matter does not sound unpromising. But if we go farther, it will appear that the race of beings that are thus linked together, form no happy and rejoicing brotherhood, finding each a glad reward in the sense that the rest are helped by him; but a sad and labouring race of chained convicts, whose highest glory it is not to attempt escaping. We are all born, she teaches, with bonds about us, and we inevitably increase their number, prompted by our own cravings, as we live on. And, says George Eliot, every such bond 'is a debt: the right lies in the payment of that debt; *it can lie nowhere else. In vain will you wander* over the earth; you will be wandering away for ever from the right.'

Now 'the right,' according to her teaching, has two distinct characteristics: in the first place, it is the hardest thing of all to attain; and in the next place, it is the only thing that is worth attaining. But when it is attained it seems, as she describes it, little better, at the best, from the human stand-point, than a choice between evils. 'Renunciation,' she says explicitly, 'does not cease to be a sorrow; but it is a sorrow borne willingly.' And again she says in another place, 'the highest happiness . . . often brings so much pain with it that we can only tell it from pain by its being what we would choose before everything else, because our souls see it is good.' But thus far clearly she must be doing it some injustice. For elsewhere a sense of positive rapture is supposed to be a part of its content; and despite all its anguish, it is supposed to admit us to some 'vision, that makes all life below it dross for ever.' The matter is a mystery, and is seen by herself to be so; so much so, indeed, that the illustration and simplification of it is really the one purpose that runs through all her novels. The central action of all of them—at least of all the later ones—is transparently the same. It is the choice or the refusal of some person or persons of this highest happiness, which can hardly be told from pain, but which, when once chosen, is to make all else dross for ever. And by these examples she seeks to convince us of three things: firstly, that the *right*, for its own sake, and resting on a strictly human basis, does practically bring its own reward with it, in the way her system requires of it; secondly, that men and women will recognize this truth, without any bias derived from supernatural hopes or affections; and, lastly, we gather her to imply that though the number of these loftier natures be but small, they yet impart a kind of vicarious value and sanctity to the entire race they belong to; and thus give ground to the philosopher for a solemn piety towards that race as it is, and a sure if anxious hope for it as it will be.

Now, as this philosophy of George Eliot's is the most rational and moving statement of all that, according to many modern thinkers, the salvation of man depends on, it becomes a matter of no small interest to inquire what basis of fact it rests upon. It certainly does not rest— and this is the grand point in its favour—on an ignorance or careless observation of life's meanness, sins, and miseries. She does not underestimate the causes for despair. The question is, does she over-estimate the causes for hope? In other words, how far does this prophetess of humanity understand and present correctly the realities of human nature?

The answer to this question is, we fear, not reassuring. We have already pointed out in her work certain artistic anomalies which are fatal to it from the point of view of the artist; and chief amongst these was the strange want of unity in her manner, which we compared to a mixing together of finished figures in oil with shadowy charcoal outlines. Looking at her simply as a novelist, this phenomenon was puzzling. Looking at her as a philosopher, it becomes, we conceive, sufficiently explicable. In her side characters we see her genuine artistic vision, her genuine artistic powers. We see living men and women presented to us with all the power of a dramatist. But when we pass from her side characters to her principal ones, the whole spectacle changes. We have not what the artist discovers as existing, but what the theorist dreams of as that which ought to exist. We have the phantoms of the philosopher projected into the world of reality. In other words, her higher characters, which she holds up to us as the salt of the earth and the examples of right action, are hardly, as she presents them to us, human characters at all. They are principles, not incarnate in so many different bodies, but dressed up in different suits of clothes, and set working under different circumstances. Romola, except in externals, is the same as Dorothea; so too, towards the end of her history, is Maggie Tulliver. This last character, by the way, is in one respect a very curious one. She is a composite product of both of the author's methods. She is begun according to one, she is finished according to the other. She is begun as a little flesh-and-blood girl; she is gradually sublimated into a great philosophy in action. And amongst such shadowy presences, which alone are to be our models and our en- couragements, Aunt Glegg moves as Dante did through the world of spirits—a solid body and casting a human shadow, and which we feel at once to belong to quite a different order of beings.

The treatment by George Eliot of her own genius may be compared to her treatment, just noticed, of the character of Maggie Tulliver. There were two tendencies always visible in her—that of the artist, and that of the philosopher. Could the first of these have absorbed and employed the second, the highest artistic work might doubtless have been the result. As a matter of fact, the philosophy has gained the day; and as the philosophy has grown, the art has dwindled. But, like Pharaoh's lean kine, it has not fattened by what it has fed upon. Her view of human nature as a philosopher has grown wider than it would have been as an artist; but as it has grown wider it has grown less accurate; and as her inductions have grown more confident, the basis on which she rests them has become less reliable. To make such systems as hers of any practical value, two things are needed. One is a knowledge of the great general principles of human impulse; the other is a knowledge of the various complex circumstances under which these impulses act upon us, and by which their power is profoundly modified. It is this latter sort of knowledge in which George Eliot appears to us to be so deficient. She reminds us of an engineer or a shipwright, who may be deeply versed, to a certain extent, in the laws of motion, but who knows little of the practical difficulties caused by friction, or of the various strengths and consistencies of the only materials in which his designs can be carried out. And the shadowy and unreal impression which her typical characters convey to us, we take to be but the outward sign of a fundamental unreality in her conception of them.

66. Lord Acton on George Eliot

1880, 1881, 1885

The first two extracts are from the *Letters of Lord Acton to Mary, Daughter of the Right Hon. W. E. Gladstone*, ed. Herbert Paul, 1904; the third is the conclusion to Acton's review of Cross's *Life* in *Nineteenth Century* (March 1885), xvii, 464–85.

Sir John Emerich Edward Dalberg Acton (1834–1902), politician and famous historian, was the leader of the Liberal Catholics in England and edited their two most influential journals, the *Rambler* and the *Home and Foreign Review*. In 1895, he became Regius Professor of Modern History at Cambridge and subsequently planned the *Cambridge Modern History* (1899–1912).

(a) 27 December 1880

But when I speak of Shakespeare the news of last Wednesday [George Eliot's death] comes back to me, and it seems as if the sun had gone out. You cannot think how much I owed her. Of eighteen or twenty writers by whom I am conscious that my mind has been formed, she was one. Of course I mean ways, not conclusions. In problems of life and thought, which baffled Shakespeare disgracefully, her touch was unfailing. No writer ever lived who had anything like her power of manifold, but disinterested and impartially observant sympathy. If Sophocles or Cervantes had lived in the light of our culture, if Dante had prospered like Manzoni, George Eliot might have had a rival (p. 57).

(b) 21 January 1881

It is hard to say why I rate *Middlemarch* so high. There was a touch of failure in the two preceding books, in *Felix Holt*, and even in *Romola*. And it was *Middlemarch* that revealed to me not only her grand serenity, but her superiority to some of the greatest writers. My life is spent in endless striving to make out the inner point of view, the *raison d'être*, the secret of fascination for powerful minds, of systems of religion and philosophy, and of politics, the offspring of the others, and one finds that the deepest historians know how to display their origin and their defects, but do not know how to think or to feel as men do who live in the grasp of the various systems. And if they sometimes do, it is from a sort of sympathy with the one or the other, which creates partiality and exclusiveness and antipathies. Poets are no better. Hugo, who tries so hard to do justice to the Bishop and the Conventionnel, to the nuns and the Jacobinical priest, fails from want of contact with the royalist nobleman and the revolutionary triumvirate, as Shakespeare fails ignobly with the Roman Plebs. George Eliot seemed to me capable not only of reading the diverse hearts of men, but of creeping into their skin, watching the world through their eyes, feeling their latent background of conviction, discerning theory and habit, influences of thought and knowledge, of life and of descent, and having obtained this experience, recovering her independence, stripping off the borrowed shell, and exposing scientifically and indifferently the soul of a Vestal, a Crusader, an Anabaptist, an Inquisitor, a Dervish, a Nihilist, or a Cavalier without attraction, preference, or caricature. And each of them should say that she displayed him in his strength, that she gave rational form to motives he had imperfectly analysed, that she laid bare features in his character he had never realised (pp. 60–1).

(c) March 1885

George Eliot did not believe in the finality of her system, and, near the close of her life, she became uneasy as to the future of her fame. True to the law that the highest merit escapes reward, she had fixed her hope on unborn generations, and she feared to make sure of their gratitude. Though very conscious of power and no longer prone to self-disparagement, she grew less satisfied with the execution of her designs, and when comparing the idea before her with her work in the past, her mind misgave her. She was disconcerted by ignorant applause, and she had not yet poured her full soul. Having seen the four most eloquent French writers of the century outlive their works, and disprove the axiom that style confers immortality, she might well doubt whether writings inspired by distinct views and dedicated to a cause could survive by artistic qualities alone. If the mist that shrouded her horizon should ever rise over definite visions of accepted truth, her doctrine might embarrass her renown. She never attained to the popular pre-eminence of Goethe, or even of Victor Hugo. The name of George Eliot was nearly unknown in France; she had lost ground in America; and at home her triumph did not pass unchallenged, when men like Beaconsfield, Ruskin, Arnold, Swinburne denied her claims. Lewes himself doubted the final estimate, for he announced with some excitement that she had been compared to Wordsworth, and that somebody thought the comparison inadequate. Men very far asunder —the two Scherers, Montégut, Mr. Spencer and Mr. Hutton, Professor Tyndall and Mr. Myers[1]—have declared with singular unanimity that she possessed a union of qualities seldom, if ever, exceeded by man, and not likely to be seen again on earth; that her works are a highwater-mark of feminine achievement; that she was as certainly the greatest genius among women known to history as Shakespeare among men. But George Eliot did not live to recognise, in the tribute of admiring friends, the judgment of history.

She has said of herself that her function is that of the æsthetic, not the doctrinal teacher—the rousing of the nobler emotions which make mankind desire the social right, not the prescribing of special measures. The supreme purpose of all her work is ethical. Literary talent did not manifest itself until she was thirty-seven. In her later books the wit and the descriptive power diminish visibly, and the bare didactic granite shows through the cultivated surface. She began as an essayist, and ended as she had begun, having employed meanwhile the channel of fiction to enforce that which, propounded as philosophy, failed to convince. If the doctrine, separate from the art, had no vitality, the art without the doctrine had no significance. There will be more per-fect novels and truer systems. But she has little rivalry to apprehend until philosophy inspires finer novels, or novelists teach nobler lessons of duty to the masses of men. If ever science or religion reigns alone over an undivided empire, the books of George Eliot might lose their central and unique importance, but as the emblem of a generation distracted between the intense need of believing and the difficulty of belief, they will live to the last syllable of recorded time. Proceeding from a system which had neglected Morals, she became the pioneer in that movement which has produced the *Data of Ethics* and the *Phänomenologie*.[2] Her teaching was the highest within the resources

[1] Edmond Scherer (1815–89), Wilhelm Scherer (1841–86), Émile Montégut (1825–95), Herbert Spencer (1820–1903), R. H. Hutton (1826–97), John Tyndall (1820–93), and F. W. H. Myers (1843–1901).
[2] By Herbert Spencer, 1879, and Hegel, 1807, respectively.

to which Atheism is restricted, as the teaching of the *Fioretti*[1] is the highest within the Christian limits. In spite of all that is omitted, and of specific differences regarding the solemn questions of Conscience, Humility, and Death, there are few works in literature whose influence is so ennobling; and there were people divided from her in politics and religion by the widest chasm that exists on earth, who felt at her death what was said of the Greek whom she had most deeply studied —σκότον εἶναι τεθνηκότος.[2]

67. Leslie Stephen on George Eliot

1881

Unsigned obituary article, *Cornhill* (February 1881), xliii, 152–68.

Sir Leslie Stephen (1832–1904), critic, biographer, moral philosopher, mountaineer, agnostic, and father of Virginia Woolf, wrote several biographies for the 'English Men of Letters' series, including that of George Eliot (1902). He edited both the *Cornhill* (1871–82) and the first twenty-six volumes of the *Dictionary of National Biography*. The novelist consulted him on Cambridge life while she was writing *Daniel Deronda*, and he was an occasional visitor at the Priory. In this essay, Stephen makes an authoritative distinction between George Eliot's early and late phase, the division which was to affect her reputation profoundly (see Introduction, pp. 37–8).

Had we been asked, a few weeks ago, to name the greatest living writer of English fiction, the answer would have been unanimous. No one— whatever might be his special personal predilections—would have refused that title to George Eliot. To ask the same question now would be to suggest some measure of our loss. In losing George Eliot we have

[1] A fourteenth-century collection of stories about St Francis and his followers.
[2] Aristophanes' comment on Aeschylus: 'there was darkness when he died' (*Fragment 643*).

probably lost the greatest woman who ever won literary fame, and one of the very few writers of our day to whom the name 'great' could be conceded with any plausibility. We are not at a sufficient distance from the object of our admiration to measure its true elevation. We are liable to a double illusion on the morrow of such events. In political life we fancy that all heroism is extinct with the dead leader, whilst there are within the realm five hundred good as he. Yet the most daring optimist can hardly suppose that consolatory creed to be generally true in literature. If contemporaries sometimes exaggerate, they not unfrequently underestimate their loss. When Shakespeare died, nobody imagined—we may suspect—that the English drama had touched its highest point. When men are crossing the lines which divide one of the fruitful from one of the barren epochs in literature, they are often but faintly conscious of the change. It would require no paradoxical ingenuity to maintain that we are even now going through such a transition. The works of George Eliot may hereafter appear as marking the termination of the great period of English fiction which began with Scott. She may hereafter be regarded as the last great sovereign of a literary dynasty, who had to bequeath her sceptre to a comparatively petty line of successors: though—for anything that we can say to the contrary—it may also be true that the successor may appear to-morrow, or may even be now amongst us in the shape of some writer who is struggling against a general want of recognition.

Ephemeral critics must not pretend to pronounce too confidently upon such questions. They can only try to say, in Mr. Browning's phrase, how it strikes a contemporary. And a contemporary is prompted by the natural regret to stray into irrelevant reflections, and dwell needlessly in the region of might-have-beens. Had George Eliot lived a little longer, or begun to write a little earlier, or been endowed with some additional quality which she did not in fact possess, she might have done greater things still. It is very true, and true of others besides George Eliot. It often seems as if even the greatest works of the greatest writers were but fragmentary waifs and strays—mere indications of more splendid achievements which would have been within their grasp, had they not been forced, like weaker people, to feel out the way to success through comparative failure, or to bend their genius to unworthy tasks. So, of the great writers in her own special department, Fielding wasted his powers in writing third-rate plays till he was five-and-thirty, and died a broken-down man at forty-seven. Scott did not appear in the field of his greatest victories till he was forty-three, and all his really first-rate work was done within the next ten years. George Eliot's period of full activity, the time during which she was conscientiously doing her best under the stimulus of high reputation, lasted some twenty years; and so long a space is fully up to the average of the time allowed to most great writers. If not a voluminous writer, according to the standard of recent novelists, she has left enough work, representative of her powers at their best, to give a full impress of her mind.

So far, I think, we have little reason for regret. When once a writer has managed to express the best that was in him to say, the question of absolute mass is trifling. Though some very great have also been very voluminous writers, the immortal part of their achievement bears a slight proportion to the whole. Goethe lived to a good old age, and never lapsed into indolence: yet all of Goethe that is really of the highest excellence will go into some half-dozen volumes. Putting aside Scott, hardly any great English writer has left a greater quantity of work representing the highest level of the author's capacity than is equivalent to the *Scenes of Clerical Life*, *Adam Bede*, the *Mill on the Floss*, *Silas Marner*, *Romola*, and *Middlemarch*. Certainly, she might have done more. She did not begin to write novels till a period at which many popular authors are already showing symptoms of exhaustion, and indulging in the perilous practice of self-imitation. Why, it may be said, did not George Eliot write immortal works in her youth, instead of translating German authors of a heterodox tendency? If we could arrange all such things to our taste, and could foresee a writer's powers from the beginning, we might have ordered matters differently. Yet one may observe that there is another side to the question. Imaginative minds often ripen quickly; and much of the finest poetry in the language derives its charm from the freshness of youth. But writers of the contemplative order—those whose best works represent the general experience of a rich and thoughtful nature—may be expected to come later to their maturity. The phenomenon of early exhaustion is too common in these days to allow us to regret an occasional exception. If during her youth George Eliot was storing the thoughts and emotions which afterwards shaped themselves into the *Scenes of Clerical Life*, we need not suppose that the time was wasted. Certainly, I do not think that any one who has had a little experience in such matters would regard it as otherwise than dangerous for a powerful mind to be precipitated into public utterance. The Pythagorean probation of silence may be protracted too long; but it may afford a most useful discipline:

and I think that there is nothing preposterous in the supposition that George Eliot's work was all the more powerful because it came from a novelist who had lain fallow through a longer period than ordinary.

If it is rather idle to pursue such speculations, it is still more idle to indulge in that kind of criticism which virtually comes to saying that George Eliot ought to have been Walter Scott or Charlotte Brontë. You may think her inferior to those writers; you may dislike her philosophy or her character; and you are fully justified in expressing your dislike. But it is only fair to ask whether the qualities which you disapprove were mere external and adventitious familiarities or the inseparable adjunct of those which you admire. It is important to remember this in considering some of the common criticisms. The poor woman was not content simply to write amusing stories. She is convicted upon conclusive evidence of having indulged in ideas; she ventured to speculate upon human life and its meaning, and still worse, she endeavoured to embody her convictions in imaginative shapes, and probably wished to infect her readers with them. This was, according to some people, highly unbecoming in a woman and very inartistic in a novelist. I confess that, for my part, I am rather glad to find ideas anywhere. They are not very common; and there are a vast number of excellent fictions which these sensitive critics may study without the least danger of a shock to their artistic sensibilities by anything of the kind. But if you will permit a poor novelist to indulge in such awkward possessions, I cannot see why he or she should not be allowed occasionally to interweave them in her narrative, taking care of course to keep them in their proper place. Some of that mannerism which offends many critics represents in fact simply George Eliot's way of using this privilege. We are indeed told dogmatically that a novelist should never indulge in little asides to the reader. Why not? One main advantage of a novel, as it seems to me, is precisely that it leaves room for a freedom in such matters which is incompatible with the requirements, for example, of dramatic writing. I can enjoy Scott's downright story-telling, which never reminds you obtrusively of the presence of the author; but with all respect for Scott, I do not see why his manner should be the sole type and model for all his successors. I like to read about Tom Jones or Colonel Newcome; but I am also very glad when Fielding or Thackeray puts his puppets aside for the moment and talks to me in his own person. A child, it is true, dislikes to have the illusion broken, and is angry if you try to persuade him that Giant Despair was not a real personage like his favourite Blunderbore.[1] But the attempt to produce such illusions is really unworthy of work intended for full-grown readers. The humorist in particular knows that you will not mistake his puppet-show for reality, nor does he wish you to do so. He is rather of opinion that the world itself is a greater puppet-show, not to be taken in too desperate earnest. It is congenial to his whole mode of thought tó act occasionally as chorus, and dwell upon some incidental suggestion. The solemn critic may step forward, like the physician who attended Sancho Panza's meal, and waive aside the condiment which gives a peculiar relish to the feast. It is not prepared according to his recipe. But till he gives me some better reason for obedience than his *ipse dixit*, I shall refuse to respect what would destroy many charming passages and obliterate touches which clearly contribute to the general effect of George Eliot's work.

Were it not indeed that some critics in authority have dwelt upon this supposed defect, I should be disposed simply to plead 'not guilty,' for I think that any one who reads the earlier books with the criticism in his mind, and notes the passages which are really obnoxious upon this ground, will be surprised at the rarity of the passages to which it applies. One cannot help suspecting that what is really offensive is not so much the method itself as the substance of the reflections introduced, and occasionally the cumbrous style in which they are expressed. And upon these points there is more to be said. But it is more desirable, if one can do it, to say what George Eliot was than what she was not; and to try to catch the secret of her unique power rather than to dwell upon shortcomings, some of which, to say the truth, are so obvious that it requires little critical acumen to discover them, and a decided tinge of antipathy to dwell upon them at length.

What is it, in fact, which makes us conscious that George Eliot had a position apart; that, in a field where she had so many competitors of no mean capacity, she stands out as superior to all her rivals; or that, whilst we can easily imagine that many other reputations will fade with a change of fashion, there is something in George Eliot which we are confident will give delight to our grandchildren as it has to ourselves? To such questions there is one obvious answer at hand. There is one part of her writings upon which every competent reader has dwelt with delight, and which seems fresher and more charming whenever we come back to it. There is no danger of arousing any controversy in saying that the works of her first period, the *Scenes of Clerical Life*,

[1] The giants in *The Pilgrim's Progress* (1678) and 'Jack the Giant-killer'.

Adam Bede, *Silas Marner*, and the *Mill on the Floss*, have the unmistakable mark of high genius. They are something for which it is simply out of the question to find any substitute. Strike them out of English literature, and we feel that there would be a gap not to be filled up; a distinct vein of thought and feeling unrepresented; a characteristic and delightful type of social development left without any adequate interpreter. A second-rate writer can be more or less replaced. When you have read Shakespeare, you can do very well without Beaumont and Fletcher, and a study of the satires of Pope makes it unnecessary to plod through the many volumes filled by his imitators. But we feel that, however much we may admire the other great English novelists, there is none who would make the study of George Eliot superfluous. The sphere which she has made specially her own is that quiet English country life which she knew in early youth. It has been described with more or less vivacity and sympathy by many observers. Nobody has approached George Eliot in the power of seizing its essential characteristics and exhibiting its real charm. She has done for it what Scott did for the Scotch peasantry, or Fielding for the eighteenth century Englishman, or Thackeray for the higher social stratum of his time. Its last traces are vanishing so rapidly amidst the changes of modern revolution, that its picture could hardly be drawn again, even if there were an artist of equal skill and penetration. And thus, when the name of George Eliot is mentioned, it calls up, to me at least, and, I suspect, to most readers, not so much her later and more ambitious works, as the exquisite series of scenes so lovingly and vividly presented in the earlier stage: snuffy old Mr. Gilfil, drinking his gin-and-water in his lonely parlour, with his faithful Ponto snoring on the rug and dreaming of the early romance of his life; and the inimitable Mrs. Poyser in her exquisite dairy, delivering her soul in a series of pithy aphorisms, bright as the little flames in Mr. Biglow's pastoral, that 'danced about the chaney on the dresser;'[1] and the party in the parlour of the 'Rainbow' discussing the evidences for 'ghos'es;' or the family conclaves in which the affairs of the Tulliver family were discussed from so many and such admirably contrasted points of view. Where shall we find a more delightful circle, or quainter manifestations of human character, in beings grotesque, misshapen, and swathed in old prejudices, like the mossy trees in an old-fashioned orchard, which, for all their vagaries of growth, are yet full of sap and capable of bearing mellow and

[1] James Russell Lowell, *The Biglow Papers* (Second series, 1867), Introduction: 'The Courtin'', 15–16.

toothsome fruit? 'It was pleasant to Mr. Tryan,' as we are told in 'Janet's Repentance', 'to listen to the simple chat of the old man—to walk in the shade of the incomparable orchard and hear the story of the crops yielded by the red-streaked apple-tree, and the quite embarrassing plentifulness of the summer pears—to drink in the sweet evening breath of the garden as they sat in the alcove—and so, for a short interval, to feel the strain of his pastoral task relaxed.' Our enjoyment is analogous to Mr. Tryan's. We are soothed by the atmosphere of the old-world country life, where people, no doubt, had as many troubles as ours, but troubles which, because they were different, seem more bearable to our imagination. We half wish that we could go back to the old days of stage-coaches and wagons and shambling old curates in 'Brutus wigs,' preaching to slumberous congregations enshrouded in high-backed pews, contemplating as little the advent of railways as of a race of clergymen capable of going to prison upon a question of ritual.

So far, indeed, it can hardly be said that George Eliot is unique. She has been approached, if she has not been surpassed, by other writers in her idyllic effects. But there is something less easily paralleled in the peculiar vein of humour which is the essential complement of the more tender passages. Mrs. Poyser is necessary to balance the solemnity of Dinah Morris. Silas Marner would lose half his impressiveness if he were not in contrast with the inimitable party in the 'Rainbow' parlour. Omit the few pages in which their admirable conversation is reported, and the whole harmony of the book would be altered. The change would be as fatal as to strike out a figure in some perfect composition, where the most trifling accessory may really be an essential part of the whole design. It might throw some light upon George Eliot's peculiar power if we could fairly analyse the charm of that little masterpiece. Psychologists are very fond of attempting to define the nature of wit and humour. Hitherto they have not been very successful, though, of course, their failure cannot be due to any want of personal appreciation of those qualities. But I should certainly despair of giving any account of the pleasure which one receives from that famous conflict of rustic wits. Why are we charmed by Ben Winthrop's retort to the parish clerk: 'It's your inside as isn't right made for music; it's no better nor a hollow stalk;' and the statement that this 'unflinching frankness was regarded by the company as the most piquant form of joke;' or by the landlord's ingenious remarks upon the analogy between a power of smelling cheeses and perceiving the supernatural; or by that quaint stumble into something surprising to the speaker himself by its apparent resemblance to witty repartee, when the same person says to the farrier: 'You're a doctor, I reckon, though you're only a cow-doctor; for a fly's a fly, though it may be a horse-fly'? One can understand at a proper distance how a clever man comes to say a brilliant thing, and it is still more easy to understand how he can say a thoroughly silly thing, and, therefore, how he can simulate stupidity. But there is something mysterious in the power possessed by a few great humorists of converting themselves for the nonce into that peculiar condition of muddle-headedness dashed with grotesque flashes of common-sense which is natural to a half-educated mind. It is less difficult to draw either a perfect circle or a purely arbitrary line than to see what will be the proportion of the regular figure on some queer, lop-sided, and imperfectly-reflecting surface. And these quaint freaks of rustic intelligence seem to be rags and tatters of what would make wit and reason in a cultivated mind, but when put together in this grotesque kaleidoscopic confusion suggests, not simple nonsense, but a ludicrous parody of sense. To reproduce the effect, you have not simply to lower the activity of the reasoning machine, but to put it together on some essential plan, so as to bring out a new set of combinations distantly recalling the correct order. We require not a new defect of logic, but a new logical structure.

There is no answer to this as to any other such problems. It is enough to take note of the fact that George Eliot possessed a vein of humour, of which it is little to say that it is incomparably superior, in depth if not in delicacy, to that of any feminine writer. It is the humour of a calm contemplative mind, familiar with wide fields of knowledge, and capable of observing the little dramas of rustic life from a higher standing-point. It is not—in these earlier books at any rate—that she obtrudes her acquirements upon us; for if here and there we find some of those scientific allusions which afterwards became a kind of mannerism, they are introduced without any appearance of forcing. It is simply that she is awake to those quaint aspects of the little world before her which only show their quaintness to the cultivated intellect. We feel that there must be a silent guest in the chimney-corner of the 'Rainbow,' so thoroughly at home with the natives as to put no stress upon their behaviour, and yet one who has travelled out of sight of the village spire, and known the thoughts and feelings which are stirring in the great world outside. The guest can at once sympathise and silently criticise; or rather, in the process of observation, carries on the two processes simultaneously by recognising at once the little oddities of the microcosm, and yet seeing them as merely one embodiment of the same thoughts and passions which present themselves on a larger scale elsewhere. It is in this happy combination of two characteristics often disjoined that we have one secret of George Eliot's power. There is the breadth of touch, the large-minded equable spirit of loving contemplative thought, which is fully conscious of the narrow limitations of the actor's thoughts and habits, but does not cease on that account to sympathise with his joys and sorrows. We are on a petty stage, but not in a stifling atmosphere, and we are not called upon to accept the prejudices of the actors or to be angry with them, but simply to understand and be tolerant. We have neither the country idyl of the sentimentalist which charms us in some of George Sand's stories of French life, but in which our enjoyment is checked by the inevitable sense of unreality, nor the caricature of the satirist who is anxious to proclaim the truth that base passions and grovelling instincts are as common in country towns as in court and city. Everything is quietly set before us with a fine sense of its wider relations, and yet with a loving touch, significant of a pathetic yearning for the past, which makes the whole picture artistically charming. We are reminded in Mr. Gilfil's love-story how, whilst poor little Tina was fretting over her wrongs, the 'stream of human thought and deed was hurrying and broadening around.' 'What were our little Tina and her trouble in this mighty torrent, rushing from one awful unknown to another? Lighter than the smallest centre of quivering life in the water-drop—hidden and uncared for as the pulse of anguish in the breast of the tiniest bird that has fluttered down to its nest with the long-sought food, and has found the nest torn and empty.' It is this constant reference, tacit or express, suggested by pathetic touches, and by humorous exhibition of the incongruities and contrasts of the little drama of village life to the outer world beyond, and to the wider universe in which it too is an atom, that distinctly raises George Eliot above the level of many merely picturesque descriptions of similar scenes. We feel that the artist is at an intellectual elevation high enough to be beyond the illusions of the city fashion; but the singular charm springs out of the tender affection which reproduces the little world left so far behind and hallowed by the romance of early association.

George Eliot's own view of the matter is given in more than one of these objectionable 'asides' of which we have had to speak. She entreats us to try to see the poetry and the pathos, the tragedy and the comedy, to be found in the experience of poor dingy Amos Barton. She rarely looks, she says, at 'a bent old man or a wizened old woman' without

seeing 'the past of which they are the shrunken remnant; and the unfinished romance of rosy cheeks and bright eyes seems sometimes of
feeble interest and significance compared with that drama of hope and
love which has long ago reached its catastrophe, and left the poor soul,
like a dim and dusty stage, with all its sweet garden scenes and fair
perspectives overturned and thrust out of sight.' To reflect that we
ought to see wizened old men and women with such eyes is of course
easy enough; to have such eyes—really to see what we know that we
ought to see—is to possess true genius. George Eliot is not laying down
a philosophical maxim to be proved and illustrated, but is attempting
to express the animating principle of a labour of love. Mr. Gilfil, the
person who suggests this remark, is the embodiment of the abstract
principle, and makes us feel that it is no empty profession. Everybody
has noticed how admirably George Eliot has portrayed certain phases of
religious feeling with which, in one sense, she had long ceased to sympathise. Amongst the subsidiary actors in her stories, none are more tenderly and lovingly touched than the old-fashioned parsons and dissenting preachers—Barton and Gilfil and Tryan, and Irwin and Dinah Morris
in *Adam Bede*, and Mr. Lyon in *Felix Holt*. I do not know that they or
their successors would have much call to be grateful. For, in truth, it is
plain enough that the interest is in the kindly old-fashioned parson,
considered as a valuable factor in the social system, and that his creed
is not taken to be the source of his strength; whilst the few Methodists
and the brethren in Lantern Yard are regarded as attaining a very
imperfect and stammering version of truths capable of being very
completely dissevered from their dogmatic teaching. In any case, her
breach with the creed of her youth involved no breach of the ties formed
by early reverence for its representatives. The change involved none
of the bitterness which is sometimes generated by a spiritual revolt.
Dickens—who is sometimes supposed to represent the version of
modern Christianity—could apparently see nothing in a dissenting
preacher but an unctuous and sensual hypocrite—a vulgarised Tartuffe
such as Stiggins and Chadband.[1] If George Eliot had been the mere
didactic preacher of mere critics, she might have set before us mere
portraits of spiritual pride or clerical charlatanism. But, whatever her
creed, she was too deep a humorist, too thoughtful and too tender, to
fall into such an error. She never sinned against the 'natural piety' which
should bind our days together. The tender regard which she had
retained for all the surroundings of her youth did not fail towards

[1] Clergymen in *The Pickwick Papers* (1836-7) and *Bleak House* (1852-3).

those whose teaching had once roused her reverence, and which could never become the objects of indiscriminate antipathy.

In this one may perhaps say George Eliot was a true woman. Women, indeed, can be fully as bitter in their resentment as the harsher sex; but their bitterness seems to be generated in the attempt to outdo their masculine rivals, and to imply perverted rather than deficient sensibility. They seldom exhibit pachydermatous indifference to their neighbour's emotions. The so-called masculine quality in George Eliot—her wide and calm intelligence—was certainly combined with a thoroughly feminine nature; and the more one reads her books and notes her real triumphs, the more strongly this comes out. The poetry and pathos which she seeks to reveal under commonplace surroundings is found chiefly in feminine hearts. Each of the early books is the record of an ordeal endured by some suffering woman. In the *Scenes of Clerical Life* the interest really centres in the women whose fate is bound up with the acts of the clerical heroes; it is Janet and Molly Barton in whom we are really interested; and if poor little Tina is too weak to be a heroine, her vigorous struggle against the destinies is the pivot of the story. That George Eliot succeeded remarkably in some male portraits, and notably in Tom Tulliver, is undeniable. Yet the men were often simply women in disguise. The piquancy, for example, of the famous character of Tito is greatly due to the fact that he is the voluptuous, selfish, but sensitive character, not unfamiliar in the fiction which deals with social intrigues, but generally presented to us in feminine costume. We are told of Daniel Deronda, upon whose character an extraordinary amount of analysis is expended, that he combined a feminine affectionateness with masculine inflexibility. To our perceptions, the feminine vein becomes decidedly the most prominent; and this is equally true of such characters as Philip Wakem and Mr. Lyon. Adam Bede, indeed, to mention no one else, is a thorough man. He represents, it would seem, that ideal of masculine strength which Miss Brontë used with curious want of success to depict in Louis Moore[1]—the firm arm, the offer of which (as we are told *à propos* of Maggie Tulliver and the offensive Stephen Guest) has in it 'something strangely winning to most women.' Yet if Adam Bede had shown less Christian forbearance to young Squire Donnithorne, we should have been more convinced that he was of masculine fibre throughout.

Here we approach more disputable matters. George Eliot's early

[1] In *Shirley* (1849).

books owe their charm to the exquisite painting of the old country-life
—an achievement made possible by a tender imagination brooding
over a vanishing past—but, if we may make the distinction, they owe
their greatness to the insight into passions not confined to one race or
period. Janet Dempster would lose much of her charm if she were
transplanted from Milby to London; but she would still be profoundly
interesting as representing a marked type of feminine character. Balzac
—or somebody else—said, or is said to have said—that there were only
seven possible plots in fiction. Without pledging oneself to the particular number, one may admit that the number of radically different
motives is remarkably small. It may be added that even great writers
rarely show their highest capacity in more than one of these typical
situations. It is not hard to say which is George Eliot's favourite theme.
We may call it—speaking with proper reserve—the woman in need of a
confessor. We may have the comparatively shallow nature, the poor
wilful little Tina, or Hetty or Tessa—the mere plaything of fate, whom
we pity because in her childish ignorance she is apt, like little Red
Ridinghood, to mistake the wolf for a friend, though not exactly to take
him for a grandmother. Or we have the woman with noble aspirations
—Janet, or Dinah, or Maggie, or Romola, or Dorothea, or, may we
add, Daniel Deronda—who recognises more clearly her own need of
guidance, and even in failure has the lofty air of martyrdom. It is in the
setting such characters before us that George Eliot has achieved her
highest triumphs, and made some of her most unmistakable failures.
It is here that we meet the complaint that she is too analytic; that she
takes the point of view of the confessor rather than the artist; and is
more anxious to probe the condition of her heroines' souls, to give us
an accurate diagnosis of their spiritual complaints, and an account of
their moral evolution, than to show us the character in action. If I
must give my own view, I must venture a distinction. To say that
George Eliot's stories are interesting as studies of human nature, is
really to say little more than that they deserve serious attention. There
are stories—and very excellent and amusing stories—which have
comparatively little to do with character; histories of wondrous and
moving events, where you are fascinated by the vivacity of the narrator
without caring much for the passions of the actors—such stories, in
fact, as compose the Arabian Nights, or the voluminous works of the
admirable Alexandre Dumas. We do not care to understand Aladdin's
sentiments, or to say how far he differed from Sinbad and Camaralza-
man. The famous musketeers have different parts to play, and so far

different characters; but one does not care very much for their psychology. Still, every serious writer must derive his power from his insight into men and women. A Cervantes or Shakespeare, a Scott, a Fielding, a Richardson or Thackeray, command our attention by forcible presentation of certain types of character; and, so far, George Eliot's does not differ from her predecessors'. Nor, again, would any truly imaginative writer give us mere abstract analyses of character, instead of showing us the concrete person in action. If George Eliot has a tendency to this error it does not appear in her early period. We can see any of her best characters as distinctly, we know them by direct vision as intimately, as we know any personage in real or fictitious history. We are not put off with the formulæ of their conduct, but persons are themselves revealed to us. Yet it is, I think, true that her stories are preeminently studies of character in this sense, that her main and conscious purpose is to set before us the living beings in what may be called, with due apology, their statical relations—to show them, that is, in their quiet and normal state, not under the stress of exceptional events. When we once know Adam Bede or Dinah Morris, we care comparatively little for the development of the plot. Compare, for example, *Adam Bede* with the *Heart of Midlothian*, the first half of which seems to me to be one of the very noblest of all fictions, though the latter part suffers from the conventional madwoman and the bit of commonplace intrigue which Scott fancied himself bound to introduce. Jeanie Deans is, to my mind, a more powerfully drawn and altogether a more substantial and satisfactory young woman than Dinah Morris, who, with all her merits, seems to me, I will confess, to be a bit of a prig. The contrast, however, to which I refer is in the method rather than in the characters or the situation. Scott wishes to interest us in the magnificent trial scene, for which all the preceding narrative is a preparation; he is content to set the Deans family before us with a few amazingly vigorous touches, so that we may thoroughly enter into the spirit of the tremendous ordeal through which poor Jeanie Deans is to pass in the conflict between affection and duty. We first learn to know her thoroughly by her behaviour under that overpowering strain. But in *Adam Bede* we learn first to know the main actors by their conduct in a number of little scenes, most admirably devised and drawn, and serving to bring out, if not a more powerful, a more elaborate and minute manifestation of their inmost feelings. When we come to the critical parts in the story, and the final catastrophe, they are less interesting and vivid than the preliminary detail of apparently insignificant events. The trial and the arrival of the reprieve are probably the weakest and most commonplace passages; and what we really remember and enjoy are the little scenes on the village green, in Mrs. Poyser's dairy, and Adam Bede's workshop. We have there learnt to know the people themselves, and we scarcely care for what happens to them. The method is natural to a feminine observer who has learnt to interpret character by watching its manifestations in little every-day incidents, and feels comparatively at a loss when having to deal with the more exciting struggles and calamities which make a noise in the world. And therefore, as I think, George Eliot is always more admirable in careful exposition—in setting her personages before us—than in dealing with her catastrophes, where, to say the truth, she sometimes seems to become weak just when we expect her full powers to be exerted.

This is true, for example, of *Silas Marner*, where the inimitable opening is very superior to the sequel. It is still more conspicuously true of the *Mill on the Floss*. The first part of that novel appears to me to mark the culmination of her genius. So far, it is one of the rare books which it is difficult to praise in adequate language. We may naturally suspect that part of the singular vividness is due to some admixture of an autobiographical element. The sonnets called *Brother and Sister*— perhaps her most successful poetical effort—suggest that the adventures of Tom and Maggie had some counterpart in personal experience. In any case, the whole account of Maggie's childhood, the admirable pathos of the childish yearnings, and the quaint chorus of uncles and aunts, the adventure with the gipsies, the wanderings by the Floss, the visit to Tom in his school, have a freshness and brilliance of colouring showing that the workmanship is as perfect as the sentiment is tender. But when Maggie ceases to be the most fascinating child in fiction, and becomes the heroine of a novel, the falling off is grievous. The unlucky affair with Stephen Guest is simply indefensible. It may, indeed, be urged—and urged with plausibility—that it is true to nature; it is true, that is, that women of genius—and, indeed, other women—do not always show that taste in the selection of lovers which commends itself to the masculine mind. There is nothing contrary to experience in the supposition that the imagination of an impulsive girl may transfigure a very second-rate young tradesman into a lover worthy of her; but this does not excuse the author for sharing the illusion. It is painfully true that some women, otherwise excellent, may be tempted, like Janet Dempster, to take to stimulants. But we should not have been satisfied if her weakness had been represented as a creditable or venial peculiarity, or without a sense of the degradation. So it would, in any case, be hardly pleasant to make our charming Maggie the means of illustrating the doctrine that a woman of high qualities may throw herself away upon a low creature; but when she is made to act in this way, and the weakness is not duly emphasised, we are forced to suppose that George Eliot did not see what a poor creature she has really drawn. Perhaps this is characteristic of a certain feminine incapacity for drawing really masculine heroes, which is exemplified, not quite so disagreeably, in the case of Dorothea and Ladislaw. But it is a misfortune, and all the more so because the error seems to be gratuitous. If it was necessary to introduce a new lover, he should have been endowed with some qualities likely to attract Maggie's higher nature, instead of betraying his second-rate dandyism in every feature. But the engagement to Philip Wakem, who is at least a lovable character, might surely have supplied enough tragical motive for a catastrophe which would not degrade poor Maggie to common clay. As it is, what promises to be the most perfect story of its kind ends most pathetically indeed, but yet with a strain which jars most painfully upon the general harmony.

The line so sharply drawn in the *Mill on the Floss* is also the boundary between two provinces of the whole region. With Maggie's visit to St. Ogg's, we take leave of that part of George Eliot's work which can be praised without important qualification—of work so admirable in its kind that we have a sense of complete achievement. In the later stories we come upon debatable ground: we have to recognise distinct failure in hitting the mark, and to strike a balance between the good and bad qualities, instead of simply recognising the thorough harmony of a finished whole. What is the nature of the change? The shortcomings are, as I have said, obvious enough. We have, for example, the growing tendency to substitute elaborate analysis for direct presentation; there are such passages, as one to which I have referred, where we are told that it is necessary to understand Deronda's character at five-and-twenty in order to appreciate the effect of after-events; and where we have an elaborate discussion which would be perfectly admissible in the discussion of some historical character, but which, in a writer who has the privilege of creating history, strikes us as an evasion of a difficulty. When we are limited to certain facts, we are forced to theorise as to the qualities which they indicate. Real people do not always get into situations which speak for themselves. But when we can make such facts as will reveal character, we have no right to give the abstract theory for the concrete embodiment. We perceive when this is done that the reflective faculties have been growing at the expense of the imagination, and that, instead of simply enriching and extending the field of interest, they are coming into the foreground and usurping functions for which they are unfitted. The fault is palpable in *Romola*. The remarkable power not only of many passages but of the general conception of the book is unable to blind us to the fact that, after all, it is a magnificent piece of cram. The masses of information have not been fused by a glowing imagination. The fuel has put out the fire. If we fail to perceive this in the more serious passages, it is painfully evident in those which are meant to be humorous or playful. People often impose upon themselves when they are listening to solemn rhetoric, perhaps because, when we have got into a reverential frame of mind, our critical instincts are in abeyance. But it is not so easy to simulate amusement. And if anybody, with the mimicry of Mrs. Poyser or Bob Jakin in his mind, can get through the chapter called 'A Florentine Joke' without coming to the conclusion that the jokes of that period were oppressive and wearisome ghosts of the facetious, he must be one of those people who take in jokes by the same faculty as scientific theorems. If we are indulgent, it must be on the ground that the historical novel proper is after all an elaborate blunder. It is really analogous to, and shows the weakness of, the various attempts at the revival of extinct phases of art with which we have been overpowered in these days. It almost inevitably falls into Scylla or Charybdis; it is either a heavy mass of information striving to be lively, or it is really lively at the price of being thoroughly shallow, and giving us the merely pretty and picturesque in place of the really impressive. If any one has succeeded in avoiding the horns of this dilemma, it is certainly not George Eliot. She had certainly very imposing authorities on her side; but I imagine that *Romola* gives unqualified satisfaction only to people who hold that academical correctness of design can supply the place of vivid directness of intuitive vision.

Yet the situation was not so much the cause as the symptom of a change. When George Eliot returned to her proper ground, she did not regain the old magic. *Middlemarch* is undoubtedly a powerful book, but to many readers it is a rather painful book, and it can hardly be called a charming book to any one. The light of common day has most unmistakably superseded the indescribable glow which illuminated the earlier writings.

The change, so far as we need consider it, is sufficiently indicated by one circumstance. The 'prelude' invites us to remember Saint Theresa.

Her passionate nature, we are told, demanded a consecration of life to some object of unselfish devotion. She found it in the reform of a religious order. But there are many modern Theresas who, with equally noble aspirations, can find no worthy object for their energies. They have found 'no coherent social faith and order,' no sufficient guidance for their ardent souls. And thus we have now and then a Saint Theresa, 'foundress of nothing, whose loving heart-beats and sobs after an unattained goodness tremble off and are dispersed among hindrances instead of centering in some long recognisable deed.' This, then, is the keynote of *Middlemarch*. We are to have one more variation on the theme already treated in various form; and Dorothea Brooke is to be the Saint Theresa with lofty aspirations to pass through a searching ordeal, and, if she fails in outward results, yet to win additional nobility from failure. And yet, if this be the design, it almost seems as if the book were intended for elaborate irony. Dorothea starts with some admirable, though not very novel, aspirations of the social kind, with a desire to improve drainage and provide better cottages for the poor. She meets a consummate pedant, who is pitilessly ridiculed for his petty and hidebound intellect, and immediately takes him to be her hero and guide to lofty endeavour. She fancies, as we are told, that her spiritual difficulties will be solved by the help of a little Latin and Greek. 'Perhaps even Hebrew might be necessary—at least the alphabet and a few roots—in order to arrive at the core of things and judge soundly on the social duties of the Christian.' She marries Mr. Casaubon, and of course is speedily undeceived. But, curiously enough, the process of enlightenment seems to be very partial. Her faith in her husband receives its death-blow as soon as she finds out—not that he is a wretched pedant, but that he is a pedant of the wrong kind. Will Ladislaw points out to her that Mr. Casaubon is throwing away his labour because he does not know German, and is therefore only abreast of poor old Jacob Bryant in the last century, instead of being a worthy contemporary of Prof. Max Müller. Surely Dorothea's error is almost as deep as ever. Casaubon is a wretched being because he has neither heart nor brains—not because his reading has been confined to the wrong set of books. Surely a man may be a prig and a pedant, though he is familiar with the very last researches of German professors. The latest theories about comparative mythology may be familiar to a man with a soul comparable only to a dry pea in a bladder. If Casaubon had been all that Dorothea fancied, if his knowledge had been thoroughly up to the mark, we should still have pitied her for her not knowing the difference between a man and a stick. Unluckily, she never seems to find out that in this stupendous blunder, and not in the pardonable ignorance as to the true value of his literary labours, is the real source of her misfortune. In fact, she hardly seems to grow wiser even at the end; for when poor Casaubon is as dead as his writings, she takes up with a young gentleman, who appears to have some good feeling, but is conspicuously unworthy of the affections of a Saint Theresa. Had *Middlemarch* been intended for a cutting satire upon the aspirations of young ladies, who wish to learn Latin and Greek, when they ought to be nursing babies and supporting hospitals, these developments of affairs would have been in perfect congruity with the design. As it is, we are left with the feeling that aspirations of this kind scarcely deserve a better fate than they meet, and that Dorothea was all the better for getting the romantic aspirations out of her head. Have not the commonplace people the best of the argument?

It would be very untrue to say that the later books show any defect of general power. I do not think, for example, that there are many passages in modern fiction so vigorous as the description of poor Lydgate, whose higher aspirations are dashed with a comparatively vulgar desire for worldly success, gradually engulfed by the selfish persistence of his wife, like a swimmer sucked down by an octopus. On the contrary, the picture is so forcible and so lifelike that one reads it with a sense of actual bitterness. And as in *Daniel Deronda*, though I am ready to confess that Mordecai and Daniel are to my mind intolerable bores, I hold the story of Grandecourt and Gwendolen to be, though not a pleasant, a singularly powerful study of the somewhat repulsive kind. And it may certainly be said both of *Romola* and of *Middlemarch*, that they have some merits of so high an order that the defects upon which I have dwelt are felt as blemishes, not as fatal errors. If there is some misunderstanding of the limits of her own powers, or some misconception of true artistic conditions, nobody can read them without the sense of having been in contact with a comprehensive and vigorous intellect, with high feeling and keen powers of observation. Only one cannot help regretting the loss of that early charm. In reading *Adam Bede*, we feel first the magic, and afterwards we recognise the power which it implies. But in *Middlemarch* we feel the power, but we ask in vain for the charm. Some such change passes over any great mind which goes through a genuine process of development. It is not surprising that the reflective powers should become more predominant in later years; that reasoning should to some extent take the place of intuitive perception; and that experience of life should give a sterner and sadder tone to the implied criticism of human nature. We are prepared to find less spontaneity, less freshness of interest in the little incidents of life, and we are not surprised that a mind so reflective and richly stored should try to get beyond the charmed circle of its early successes, and to give us a picture of wider and less picturesque aspects of human life. But this does not seem to account sufficiently for the presence of something jarring and depressing in the later work.

Without going into the question fully, one thing may be said: the modern Theresa, whether she is called Dorothea, or Maggie, or Dinah, or Janet, is the central figure in the world of George Eliot's imagination. We are to be brought to sympathise with the noble aspirations of a loving and unselfish spirit, conscious that it cannot receive any full satisfaction within the commonplace conditions of this prosaic world. How women are to find a worthier sphere of action than the mere suckling of babes and chronicling of small beer is a question for the Social Science Associations. Some people answer it by proposing to give women votes or degrees, and others would tell us that such problems can only be answered by reverting to Saint Theresa's method. The solution in terms of actual conduct lies beyond the proper province of the novelist. She has done all that she can do if she has revealed the intrinsic beauty of such a character, and its proper function in life. She should make us fall in love with Romola and Maggie, and convert us to the belief that they are the true salt of the earth.

Up to a certain point her success is complete, and it is won by high moral feeling and quick sympathy with true nobility of character. We pay willing homage to these pure and lofty feminine types, and we may get some measure of the success by comparing them with other dissatisfied heroines whose aspirations are by no means so lofty or so compatible with delicate moral sentiment. But the triumph has its limits. In the sweet old-world country life a Janet or a Dinah can find some sort of satisfaction from an evangelical preacher, or within the limits of the Methodist church. If the thoughts and ways of her circle are narrow, it is in harmony with itself, and we may feel its beauty without asking awkward questions. But as soon as Maggie has left her quiet fields and reached even such a centre of civilisation as St. Ogg's, there is a jar and a discord. *Romola* is in presence of a great spiritual disturbance where the highest aspirations are doomed to the saddest failure; and when we get to *Middlemarch* we feel that the charm has somehow vanished. Even in the early period, Mrs. Poyser's bright common-sense has some advantages over Dinah Morris's high-wrought sentiment. And in *Middlemarch* we feel more decidedly that high aspirations are doubtful qualifications; that the ambitious young devotee of science has to compound with the quarrelling world, and the brilliant young Dorothea to submit to a decided clipping of her wings. Is it worth while to have a lofty nature in such surroundings? The very bitterness with which the triumph of the lower characters is set forth seems to betray a kind of misgiving. And it is the presence of this feeling, as well as the absence of the old picturesque scenery, that gives a tone of melancholy to the later books. Some readers are disposed to sneer, and to look upon the heroes and heroines as male and female prigs, who are ridiculous if they persist and contemptible when they fail. Others are disposed to infer that the philosophy which they represent is radically unsatisfactory. And some may say that, after all, the picture is true, however sad, and that, in all ages, people who try to lift their heads above the crowd must lay their account with martyrdom and be content to be uncomfortable. The moral, accepted by George Eliot herself, is indicated at the end of *Middlemarch*. A new Theresa, she tells us, will not have the old opportunity any more than a new Antigone would 'spend heroic piety in daring all for the sake of a brother's funeral; the medium in which these ardent deeds took shape is for ever gone.' There will be many Dorotheas, and some of them doomed to worse sacrifices than the Dorothea of *Middlemarch*, and we must be content to think that her influence spent itself through many invisible channels, but was not the less potent because unseen.

Perhaps that is not a very satisfactory conclusion. I cannot here ask why it should not have been more satisfactory. We must admit that there is something rather depressing in the thought of these anonymous Dorotheas feeling about vaguely for some worthy outlet of their energies, taking up with a man of science and discovering him to be an effete pedant, wishing ardently to reform the world, but quite unable to specify the steps to be taken, and condescending to put up with a very commonplace life in a vague hope that somehow or other they will do some good. Undoubtedly we must admit that, wherever the fault lies, our Theresas have some difficulty in fully manifesting their excellence. But with all their faults, we feel that they embody the imperfect influence of a nature so lofty in its sentiment, so wide in its sympathies, and so keen in its perceptions, that we may wait long before it will be adequately replaced. The imperfections belong in great measure to a time of vast revolutions in thought which produce artistic discords as well as philosophic anarchy. Lower minds escape the difficulty because they are lower; and even to be fully sensitive to the deepest searchings of heart of the time is to possess a high claim on our respect. At lowest, however we may differ from George Eliot's teaching on many points, we feel her to be one who, in the midst of great perplexities, has brought great intellectual powers to setting before us a lofty moral ideal, and, in spite of manifest shortcomings, has shown certain aspects of a vanishing social phase with a power and delicacy unsurpassed in her own sphere.

68. A too serious life, unsigned review of Cross's *Life*, *Saturday Review*

(7 February 1885), lix, 181–2

This unsympathetic review expresses the impatience and disappointment which so many contemporaries felt with the biography. Cross's George Eliot did not conform to their idea of a novelist (see Introduction, pp. 38–40).

There are some books the total impression of which on minds even in a moderate degree accomplished and competent must be of necessity almost identical, and of such books Mr. Cross's *Life of George Eliot* seems to be an eminent example. There is much, no doubt, to be said against the practice—now an established one—of hurrying reviews of important books into daily newspapers at the very moment of their appearance. But it has this advantage, that the impression given to the public is of necessity to a great extent genuine and *prime-sautier*; there is no time for second thoughts, for comparison with other people, for hedging and harmonizing. George Eliot herself, who hated reviewers (with an energy which may or may not have been due to the facts that, to borrow a pleasant jest from Mr. Punch, 'she once kep'' a table herself'), would, we fear, scarcely have been reconciled to them by their reception of her Life. We who have read the book at leisure, and have approached it with, perhaps, less *parti-pris* than some of its other readers, frankly admit that there are few books in which one cast of the reviewer's office is less necessary. It needs hardly any interpretation; the general meaning and conclusion of it jump to the eyes.

Mr. Cross has been complimented and reproached by turns for having exercised on his wife's papers the censorship which Mr. Froude refused to exercise on Mr. Carlyle's. We have his own word that he has omitted much; but that that much would have satisfied lovers of scandal and ill-nature, or that it would have exhibited George Eliot in any other light than that in which the actual book exhibits her, we do not for a moment believe. The fact is that, short of positive garbling by insertion, by twisting, or by omission of contexts, it is impossible to publish three volumes almost entirely composed as these are of autobiographic matter not originally intended for the general eye, and yet to disguise the writer's faults. The documents speak too clearly, and whatever Mr. Cross may have left out, or whatever he may have 'edited,' it is perfectly certain that these volumes give to any competent student of human nature George Eliot as she was. Of the *facture* of the book we need say but little. It is, as has been said, almost exclusively composed of letters and journals tied together by a sufficient but very sparingly used thread of editorial comment. As a matter of practical convenience, it is a pity that Mr. Cross has used the same type for comment and text, the effect, despite a slight indenting of the comment, being occasionally, and indeed frequently, misleading. As for his judgment as editor, he has sinned rather by insertion than omission. It surely must have been a trial, and we think an unnecessary trial, to him to print his wife's expression of satisfaction at 'feeling daily the loveliness of his [Mr. Cross's] nature close to her.' A very high testimonial to Mr. Cross's nature, no doubt; but editorial modesty and general *respect humain* surely called for the postponement of its publication, at least to Mr. Cross's, let us hope, long-distant tombstone. Yet it must be admitted that the phrase is the keynote to a great deal of personal utterance which can only be called gush, and which, though it will be highly distasteful to some readers and perhaps not quite intelligible to others, is one of the most noteworthy things in the book. One other not very pleasant subject we may as well mention at once and get over. For Mr. Cross's treatment of the connexion between

Mary Ann Evans and George Henry Lewes we have no blame, and indeed very little comment; he has got himself out of a difficult situation very well. George Eliot's own attitude towards her conduct is briefly but significantly exhibited here, and simply condenses into little the curious paradox (some cynical people say the amusing inconsistency) of a woman who for years inculcated the sternest submission of inclination to duty in her books, and practically illustrated her principles by living all the time with another woman's husband. For ourselves, we like no part so little as that of the 'unco guid.'[1] George Eliot stood or fell to her own master, not to us. But we shall only say that, when third persons speak of 'Mrs. Lewes,' of 'husband,' or 'wife,' and so forth, in reference to this connexion, they not only debase the moral currency, but, taking the matter out of debatable points, endorse a deliberate literary and historical falsification. It is no more true that the author of *Adam Bede* was Mrs. Lewes than it is true that the author of *Adam Bede* was Mr. Liggins.

Of the actual events of George Eliot's not very eventful life these volumes tell little that was not known before, but as a commentary on her works they are simply invaluable. They contain, perhaps, no information which a literary critic of the first class could not get out of those works themselves with the aid of the clue afforded by the antecedent knowledge of the general facts of her life. But they confirm, supplement, and illuminate that information in a most remarkable degree. The motto and moral of the whole Mr. Cross has himself given, quite unawares, in a chance phrase relating to his wife's conduct in society. 'She took things,' he says, 'too seriously.' That is exactly what she did all through, if we may be permitted a vernacular idiom in speaking of a mistress of the idiomatic vernacular. It may seem a wild absurdity to say that George Eliot's fault was lack of humour in presence of the abundance of that quality which floods her works from *Adam Bede* to *Theophrastus Such*, illuminating and relieving even the lifeless bulk of *Daniel Deronda*. But we must be permitted to fall back on the memorable answer of Mr. Jolliffe when he arbitrated on the dispute between Mr. Midshipman Easy and the gunner. 'These things,' said that good and wise master's mate, were 'parallels and not parallels.'[2] So, also, the humourist of the Poysers and the Gleggs, of Mr. Brooke and Mrs. Holt, of the man-servant in *Theophrastus*, and the character-description of Grandcourt in *Deronda*, was George Eliot

[1] See Burns' poem, 'Address to the Unco Guid, or the Rigidly Righteous' (1784).
[2] Frederick Marryat, *Mr Midshipman Easy* (1836), II, ii.

and not George Eliot. The theory of the double essence—of the attendant *lutin*, as Molière put it, if anybody likes that better—has never been illustrated so thoroughly. The George Eliot of the better part of the novels knew 'the humour cure that saves the life of man' well and wisely. The George Eliot of the rest of the novels, and, as far as we can make out, of the whole actual life, except at the rarest intervals, seems to have been as ignorant of humour as the typical Dissenting class-leader, whom in her letters and part of her published writings she resembles in every point except that her kirk was of the other complexion. The way in which these volumes are saturated with what may be called the cant of Freethinking, the goody-goodiness of irreligion, the unction of the anti-supernatural, the gush of Positivism and Nihilism, might be disagreeable if it were not so extremely interesting. The moral and intellectual atmosphere is that of the class-room and the tea-party, only that the experiences are anti-Christian and the proceedings are opened with a chapter of Strauss instead of a chapter of the Bible. A very curious incident noticed here is that Miss Evans translated the Crucifixion and Resurrection part of the *Leben Jesu* with a crucifix before her as a relief to the disgust of her subject—an instance of feminine logic which is probably unparalleled. Indeed, the whole book shows how impressionable, how emotional, how illogical, how feminine she was. In an Evangelical *milieu* she was strongly Evangelical. Transferred to the little Freethinking coterie of Hennells, Brays, Brabants, &c., she exchanged the matter of her evangelicism for unbelief, retaining its manner. It will probably provoke screams from her admirers, but we say hardily that if at the time when she fell under Lewes's male influence she had fallen under the male influence of an orthodox Churchman she would probably have been a pillar of the faith and a brand plucked from the burning. The person whom superficial critics long took to be the most masculine of her sex was a very woman.

Of her literary life many curious glimpses are here given. Many things have been said of Mr. Lewes's cleverness, but there is perhaps hardly anything in which he showed so much of that quality as in his training of George Eliot. We mean nothing derogatory. His affection for her is not questionable, and there is something very creditable in the way in which, after being an independent man of letters patronizing a promising literary aspirant, he accepted the position of literary assistant and man of business to a writer of genius. But, as we have said, he did train his distinguished companion, not at all in the sense of educating her, but in the sense of arranging her circumstances so as best to suit the production of her novels. The hothouse kind of life which she preferred and which he enabled her to enjoy, the fending off of adverse and distasteful criticism, the submission (which to a man of decidedly sociable and rather Bohemian tastes like Lewes must have been a real sacrifice) to long periods of solitude *à deux*, formed, as far as we can judge, the only course of treatment which could have enabled this nervous, delicate, and curiously constituted competitor to win the Novel Stakes time after time as she did. With another course of treatment she might have been a healthier-minded woman, and her books, if they had appeared, might have been healthier books; but it may be very strongly doubted whether they would have appeared at all.

Of the peculiarities which Lewes had to consider, the already referred to hatred of reviewers and reviewing is perhaps the most remarkable. Most writers, no doubt, have felt towards our mystery (the fact that they have generally themselves belonged to it making no difference) after the fashion expressed pleasantly enough by a late member of the University of Oxford when he was asked to subscribe to the establishment of a new critical journal. 'This,' he said, 'is rather too like the practice of Marshal Haynau,[1] who used to flog women and send in a bill for the expenses of the proceeding to their relations.' Not ours is it to discuss the reasonableness of the attitude in general. But in very few writers was it ever so pronounced and so systematic as in George Eliot. Despite her companion's care to keep the accursed thing away from her, or only to give access to laudatory notices acceptable in manner (for George Eliot, like another distinguished writer, 'could not forgive the praise'[2] when it was not the particular praise she wanted), she never seems to have got over her criticophobia. Probably, indeed, her ignorance of what critics did actually say made her more fearful of the divers and disgusting things which she imagined them to be saying. But it is clear that the secret of her objection was not mere *amour propre*, or, to speak more correctly, was not *amour propre* only. It was the fatal and feminine idea of a mission which pursued her, and which made her look at adverse critics not as at possibly mistaken tasters of a work of art, but as good or bad men who sympathized or did not sympathize with her gospel. She was constantly expostulating directly or indirectly with the 'average man' and the 'dull man' who would not understand, and it is characteristic enough to find her praising an industrious

[1] Marshal Haynau (1786-1853), Austrian soldier, the 'Hyaena of Brescia'.
[2] Tennyson, 'To Christopher North' (1832).

compiler of a Book of Beauties[1] from her work as having taken the 'right' passages and the 'right' ideas 'in relation to the author's feeling and purpose.' A less immediately explicable and less agreeable feature (for critic-hating is even to critics a human and pardonable weakness) is her complaints of readers who borrow her books instead of buying them. She, at least, had surely no reason to complain of insufficient pecuniary rewards. But here, no doubt, it is the same curious *amour propre* of a peculiar kind that is wounded, and not a mere desire of gain.

We have left unnoticed some traits of the book which would need long comment, such as the singular unhappiness, not wholly or even mainly explicable by bad health, which seems to have haunted George Eliot in the midst of immense reputation, of ample means, of the society of the man she loved, of a life entirely *à sa guise*. This unhappiness seems to have been positively greater than Carlyle's, though it is less abundantly and in a less stentorian fashion bewailed to gods and men. But, as we began, so we may end by remarking that the morals of this interesting and singular biography are written so that he who runs may read. The reader for the story will not get far; the reader in search of a curious literary and psychological study partly divined already, and now fully unfolded, will not miss a word.

[1] Alexander Main, *Wise, Witty, and Tender Sayings in Prose and Verse Selected from the Works of George Eliot* (1872).

69. Henry James on George Eliot

1885

Review of Cross's *Life*, *Atlantic Monthly* (May 1885), lv, 668–78.

This essay, the last of his many discussions of George Eliot, shows that James shared many of the contemporary reservations about the novelist's career. But his praise of 'the magnificent mind, vigorous, luminous, and eminently sane' looks ahead to Virginia Woolf's essay in 1919 and the subsequent rescue of George Eliot's works from the formidable *Life* (see Introduction, pp. 39, 43).

The writer of these pages has observed that the first question usually asked in relation to Mr. Cross's long-expected biography is whether the reader has not been disappointed in it. The inquirer is apt to be disappointed if the question is answered in the negative. It may as well be said, therefore, at the threshold of the following remarks, that such is not the feeling with which this particular reader laid down the book. The general feeling touching the work will depend very much on what has been looked for: there was probably, in advance, a considerable belief that we were to be treated to 'revelations.' I know not, exactly, why it should have been, but certain it is that the announcement of a biography of George Eliot has been construed more or less as a promise that we were to be admitted behind the scenes, as it were, of her life. No such result has taken place. We look at the drama from the point of view usually allotted to the public, and the curtain is lowered whenever it suits the biographer. The most 'intimate' pages in the book are those in which the great novelist notes her derangements of health and depression of spirits. This history, to my sense, is quite as interesting as it might have been; that is, it is of the deepest interest, and can miss nothing that is characteristic or involved in the subject, except, perhaps, a few more examples of the *vis comica* which made half the fortune of *Adam Bede* and *Silas Marner*. There is little that is absent that it would have been in Mr. Cross's power to give us. George Eliot's letters and

journals are only a partial expression of her spirit, but they are evidently
as full an expression as it was capable of giving itself when she was not
wound up to the epic pitch. They do not explain her novels; they reflect
in a singularly limited degree the process of growth of these great
works; but it must be added that even a superficial acquaintance with
the author was sufficient to assure one that her rich and complicated
mind did not overflow in idle confidences. It was benignant and recep-
tive in the highest degree, and nothing could have been more gracious
than the manner of its intercourse; but it was deeply reserved, and
very far from egotistical, and nothing could have been less easy or
agreeable to it, I surmise, than to attempt to tell people how, for
instance, the plot of *Romola* got itself constructed, or the character of
Grandcourt got itself observed. There are critics who refuse to the
delineator of this gentleman the title of a genius; who say that she
had only a great talent, overloaded with a great store of knowledge.
The label, the epithet, matters little, but it is certain that George Eliot
had this characteristic of the mind *possessed*; that the creations which
brought her renown were of the incalculable kind, shaped themselves
in mystery, in some intellectual back shop or secret crucible, and were
as little as possible implied in the aspect of her life. There is nothing
more singular or striking in Mr. Cross's volumes than the absence of
any indication, up to the time the *Scenes from Clerical Life* were published, that Miss Evans was a likely person to have written them; unless
it be the absence of any indication, after they were published, that the
deeply-studious, concentrated, home-keeping Mrs. Lewes was a likely
person to have produced their successes. I know very well that there
is no such thing, in general, as the air of the novelist, which it behooves
those who practice this art to put on, so that they may be recognized
in public places; but there is such a thing as the air of the sage, the
scholar, the philosopher, the votary of abstractions and of the lore of
the ages, and in this pale but rich Life that is the face that is presented.

The plan on which it is composed is, so far as I know, without
precedent, but it is a plan that could have occurred only to an 'outsider'
in literature, if I may venture to apply this term to one who has
executed a literary task with such tact and success. The regular *littérateur*,
hampered by tradition, would, I think, have lacked the boldness, the
artless artfulness, of conjoining in the same text selected morsels of
letters and journals, so as to form a continuous and multifarious *talk*,
on the writer's part, punctuated only by marginal names and dates and
divisions into chapters. There is something a little violent in the system,

in spite of our feeling that it has been applied with a gentle hand; but it was probably the best that Mr. Cross could have adopted, and it served especially well his purpose of appearing only as an arranger, or rather of not appearing at all. The modesty, the good taste, the self-effacement, of the editorial element in the book are, in a word, complete, and the clearness and care of arrangement, the accuracy of reference, leave nothing to be desired. The form Mr. Cross has chosen, or invented, becomes, in the application, highly agreeable, and his rule of omission (for we have, almost always, only parts and passages of letters) has not prevented his volumes from being as copious as we could wish. George Eliot was not a great letter-writer, either in quantity or quality; she had neither the spirit, the leisure, nor the lightness of mind to conjure with the epistolary pen, and after her union with George Henry Lewes her disposition to play with it was farther restricted by his quick activity in her service. Letter-writing was part of the trouble he saved her; in this, as in other ways, he interposed between the world and his sensitive companion. The difference is striking between her habits in this respect and those of Madame George Sand, whose correspondence has lately been collected into six closely printed volumes, which testify afresh to her extraordinary energy and facility. Madame Sand, however, indefatigable producer as she was, was not a woman of study; she lived from day to day, from hand to mouth (intellectually), as it were, and had no general plan of life and culture. Her English compeer took work more seriously, and distilled her very substance into the things she gave the world. There was, therefore, so much the less of it left for her casual writing.

It was not till Marian Evans was past thirty, indeed, that she became an author by profession, and it may accordingly be supposed that her early letters are those which take us most into her confidence. This is true of those written when she was on the threshold of womanhood, which form a very full expression of her feelings at the time. The drawback here is that the feelings themselves are rather wanting in interest— one may almost say in amiability. At the age of twenty Marian Evans was a deeply religious young woman, whose faith took the form of a narrow evangelicism. Religious, in a manner, she remained to the end of her life, in spite of her adoption of a scientific explanation of things; but in the year 1839 she thought it ungodly to go to concerts and to read novels. She writes to her former governess that she can 'only sigh' when she hears of the 'marrying and giving in marriage that is constantly transacted;' expresses enjoyment of Hannah More's letters ('the contemplation of so blessed a character as hers is very salutary'); wishes that she 'might be more useful in her own obscure and lowly station' ('I feel myself to be a mere cumberer of the ground'), that she 'might seek to be sanctified wholly.' These first fragments of her correspondence, first glimpses of her mind, are very curious; they have nothing in common with the later ones but the deep seriousness of the tone. Serious, of course, George Eliot continued to be to the end; the sense of moral responsibility, of the sadness and difficulty of life, was the most inveterate part of her nature. But the provincial strain in the letters from which I have quoted is very marked: they reflect a meagreness and grayness of outward circumstance; have a tinge as of Dissent in a small English town, where there are brick chapels in back streets. This was only a moment in her development; but there is something touching in the contrast between such a state of mind and that of the woman before whom, at middle age, all the culture of the world unrolled itself, and towards whom fame and fortune and an activity which at the earlier period she would have thought very profane pressed with rapidity. In 1839, as I have said, she thought very meanly of the art in which she was to attain such distinction. 'I venture to believe that the same causes which exist in my own breast to render novels and romances pernicious have their counterpart in every fellow creature. . . . The weapons of Christian warfare were never sharpened at the forge of romance.' The style of these pietistic utterances is singularly strenuous and heavy; the light and familiar are absent from them, and I think it is not too much to say that they show scarcely a single premonitory ray of the genius which had *Silas Marner* in reserve. This dryness was only a phase, indeed; it was speedily dispelled by more abundant showers of mental experience. Premonitory rays are still absent, however, after her first asceticism passes away—a change apparently coincident with her removal from the country to the pleasant old town of Coventry, where all American pilgrims to midland shrines go to-day to look at the 'three tall spires' commemorated in Tennyson's *Godiva*. After the evangelical note began to fade, it was still the desire for faith (a faith which could reconcile human affection with some of the unamiable truths of science), still the religious idea, that colored her thought; not the love of human life as a spectacle, nor the desire to do something in art. It must be remembered, though, that during these years, if she were not stimulating prophecy in any definite form, she was inhaling those impressions which were to make her first books so full of the delightful midland quality, the air of old-fashioned provincialism. The first piece of literary work she attempted (and she brought it to the best conclusion) was a translation of Strauss's *Life of Jesus*, which she began in 1844, when she was not yet twenty-five years of age; a task which indicates not only the persistence of her religious preoccupations, as well as the higher form they took, but the fact that, with the limited facilities afforded by her life at that time, she had mastered one of the most difficult of foreign languages and the vocabulary of a German exegetist. In 1841 she thought it wrong to encourage novels, but in 1847 she confesses to reading George Sand with great delight. There is no exhibition in Mr. Cross's pages of the steps by which she passed over to a position of tolerant skepticism: but the details of the process are after all of minor importance; the essential fact is that the change was pre-determined by the nature of her mind.

The great event of her life was, of course, her acquaintance with George Henry Lewes. I say 'of course,' because this relation had an importance even more controlling than the publication and success of her first attempt at fiction, inasmuch as it was in consequence of Mr. Lewes's friendly urgency that she wrote the *Scenes of Clerical Life*. She met him for the first time in London, in the autumn of 1851; but it was not till the summer of 1854 that the connection with him began (it was marked to the world by their going to spend together several months in Germany, where he was bent on researches for his *Life of Goethe*) which was to become so much closer than many formal marriages, and to last till his death in 1878. The episode of Miss Evans's life in London during these three years was already tolerably well known. She had become by this time a professional literary woman, and had regular work as assistant editor of the *Westminster Review*, to which she gave her most conscientious attention. Her accomplishments now were wide. She was a linguist, a copious reader, an earnest student of history and philosophy. She wrote much for the *Westminster*, as well as solicited articles from others, and several of her contributions are contained in the volume of essays published after her death,—essays of which it is fair to say that they give but a faint intimation of her latent powers. George Henry Lewes was a versatile, hard-working journalist, with a tendency, apparently, of the drifting sort; and after having been made acquainted with each other by Mr. Herbert Spencer the pair commingled their sympathies and their work. Her letters, at this season, contain constant mention of Lewes (one allusion to the effect that he 'has quite won my regard, after having had a good deal of my vituperation'); she takes an interest in his health, and corrects his proofs for him when he is absent. It was impossible for Mr. Lewes to marry, as he had a wife living, from whom he was separated. He had also three children, of whom the care did not devolve upon their mother. The union Miss Evans formed with him was a deliberate step, of which she accepted all the consequences. These consequences were excellent, so far as the world is at liberty to judge, save in an important particular. This particular is the fact that her false position, as we may call it, produced upon George Eliot's life a certain effect of sequestration, which was not favorable to social freedom, and which excited on the part of her companion a certain protecting, sheltering, fostering, precautionary attitude,—the assumption that they lived in special, in abnormal conditions. It would be too much to say that George Eliot had not the courage of the situation she had embraced, but she had, at least, not the indifference; she was unable, in the premises, to be sufficiently superficial. Her deep, strenuous, much-considering mind, of which the leading mark is the capacity for a sort of luminous brooding, fed upon the idea of her irregularity with an intensity which doubtless only her magnificent intellectual activity and Lewes's brilliancy and ingenuity kept from being morbid. The fault of most of her work is the absence of spontaneity, the excess of reflection; and by her action in 1854 (which seemed, superficially, to be of the sort usually termed reckless) she committed herself to being nothing if not reflective, to cultivating a kind of compensatory earnestness. Her earnestness, her refined conscience, her exalted sense of responsibility, were colored by her peculiar position; they committed her to a plan of life, of study, in which the accidental, the unexpected, were too little allowed for, and this is what I mean by speaking of her sequestration. If her relations with the world had been easier, in a word, her books would have been less difficult. Mr. Cross, very justly, merely touches upon this question of her forming a tie which was deprived of the sanction of the law; but he gives a portion of a letter written to Mrs. Bray more than a year after it had begun, which sufficiently indicates the serenity of her resolution. Repentance, of course, she never had,—the success of her experiment was too rare and complete for that; and I do not mean that her attitude was ever for a moment apologetic. On the contrary, it was only too superabundantly confirmatory. Her effort was to pitch her life ever in the key of the superior wisdom that made her say to Mrs. Bray, in the letter of September, 1855, 'That any unworldly, unsuperstitious person who is sufficiently acquainted with the realities of life can pronounce my relation to Mr.

Lewes immoral I can only understand when I remember how subtle and complex are the influences that mould opinion.' I need not attempt to project the light of criticism on this particular case of conscience; there remains ever, in the mutual relations of respectable men and women, an element which is for themselves alone to consider. One reflection, however, forces itself upon the mind: if the connection had not taken place, we should have lost the spectacle and influence of one of the most complete and tender unions presented to us in the history of literature. There has been much talk about George Eliot's 'example,' which is not to be deprecated so long as it is remembered that in speaking of the example of a woman of such rare nobleness of mind we can only mean example for good. Exemplary indeed, in her long connection with George Henry Lewes, were her sympathy, appreciation, affection, constancy.

She was thirty-seven years old when the *Scenes from Clerical Life* were published, but this work opened wide for her the door of success, and fame and fortune came to her rapidly. Her union with Lewes had been a union of poverty: there is a sentence in her journal, of the year 1856, which speaks of their ascending certain cliffs called the Tors, at Ilfracombe, 'only twice; for a tax of 3*d*. per head was demanded for this luxury, and we could not afford a sixpenny walk very frequently.' The incentive to writing *Amos Barton* seems to have been mainly pecuniary. There was an urgent need to make money, and it appears to have been agreed between the pair that there was at least no harm in the lady's trying her hand at a story. Lewes professed a belief that she would really do something in this line, while she, more skeptical, reserved her judgment till after the test. The *Scenes from Clerical Life* were therefore pre-eminently an empirical work of fiction. With the sending of the first episode to the late Mr. John Blackwood for approval, there opened a relation between publisher and author which lasted to the end, and which was probably more genial and unclouded than any in the annals of literature, as well as almost unprecedentedly lucrative to both parties. This first book of George Eliot's has little of the usual air of a first book, none of the crudity of an early attempt; it was not the work of a youthful person, and one sees that the material had been long in her mind. The ripeness, the pathos, a sort of considered quality, are as striking to-day as when 'Amos Barton' and 'Janet's Repentance' were published, and enable us to understand that people should have asked themselves with surprise, at that time, who it was, in the midst of them that had been taking notes so long and so wisely without giving a sign. *Adam Bede*, written rapidly, appeared in 1859, and George Eliot found herself a consummate novelist without having suspected it. The book was an immense, a brilliant success, and from this moment the author's life took its definite and final direction. She accepted the great obligations which to her mind belonged to a person who had the ear of the public, and her whole effort thenceforth was highly to respond to them,—to respond to them by teaching, by vivid moral illustration, and even by direct exhortation. It is striking that from the first her conception of the novelist's task is never in the least as the game of art. The most interesting passage in Mr. Cross's volumes is, to my sense, a simple sentence in a short entry in her journal in the year 1859, just after she had finished the first volume of *The Mill on the Floss* (the original title of which, by the way, had been *Sister Maggie*): 'We have just finished reading aloud *Père Goriot*, a hateful book.' That Balzac's masterpiece should have elicited from her only this remark, at a time, too, when her mind might have been opened to it by her own activity of composition, is significant of so many things that the few words are, in the whole *Life*, those I should have been most sorry to lose. Of course they are not all George Eliot would have had to say about Balzac, if some other occasion than a simple jotting in a diary had presented itself. Still, what even a jotting may *not* have said after a first perusal of *Le Père Goriot* is eloquent; it illuminates the author's general attitude with regard to the novel, which, for her, was not primarily a picture of life, capable of deriving a high value from its form, but a moralized fable, the last word of a philosophy endeavoring to teach by example.

This is a very noble and defensible view, and one must speak respectfully of any theory of work which would produce such fruit as *Romola* and *Middlemarch*. But it testifies to that side of George Eliot's nature which was weakest—the absence of free æsthetic life (I venture this remark in the face of a passage quoted from one of her letters in Mr. Cross's third volume); it gives the hand, as it were, to several other instances that may be found in the same pages. 'My function is that of the *æsthetic*, not the doctrinal teacher; the rousing of the nobler emotions, which make mankind desire the social right, not the prescribing of special measures, concerning which the artistic mind, however strongly moved by social sympathy, is often not the best judge.' That is the passage referred to in my parenthetic allusion, and it is a good general description of the manner in which George Eliot may be said to have acted on her generation; but the 'artistic mind,' the possession of which it implies, existed in her with limitations remarkable in a writer whose imagination was so rich. We feel in her, always, that she proceeds from the abstract to the concrete; that her figures and situations are evolved, as the phrase is, from her moral consciousness, and are only indirectly the products of observations. They are deeply studied and elaborately justified, but they are not *seen* in the irresponsible plastic way. The world was, first and foremost, for George Eliot, the moral, the intellectual world; the personal spectacle came after; and lovingly, humanly, as she regarded it, we constantly feel that she cares for the things she finds in it only so far as they are types. The philosophic door is always open, on her stage, and we are aware that the somewhat cooling draught of ethical purpose draws across it. This constitutes half the beauty of her work; the constant reference to ideas may be an excellent source of one kind of reality—for, after all, the secret of seeing a thing well is not necessarily that you see nothing else. Her preoccupation with the universe helped to make her characters strike you as also belonging to it; it raised the roof, widened the area, of her æsthetic structure. Nothing is finer, in her genius, than the combination of her love of general truth and love of the special case; without this, indeed, we should not have heard of her as a novelist, for the passion of the special case is surely the basis of the storyteller's art. All the same, that little sign of all that Balzac failed to suggest to her showed at what perils the special case got itself considered. Such dangers increased as her activity proceeded, and many judges perhaps hold that in her ultimate work, in *Middlemarch* and *Deronda* (especially the latter), it ceased to be considered at all. Such critics assure us that Gwendolen and Grandcourt, Deronda and Myra, are not concrete images, but disembodied types, pale abstractions, signs and symbols of a 'great lesson.' I give up Deronda and Myra to the objector, but Grandcourt and Gwendolen seem to me to have a kind of superior reality; to be, in a high degree, what one demands of a figure in a novel, planted on their legs and complete.

The truth is, perception and reflection, at the outset, divided George Eliot's great talent between them; but, as time went on, circumstances led the latter to develop itself at the expense of the former—one of these circumstances being apparently the influence of George Henry Lewes. Lewes was interested in science, in cosmic problems; and though his companion, thanks to the original bent of her versatile, powerful mind, needed no impulse from without to turn herself to speculation, yet the contagion of his studies pushed her further than she would otherwise have gone in the direction of *scientific* observation, which is but another form of what I have called reflection. Her early novels are full of natural as distinguished from systematic observation, though even in them it is less the dominant will, I think, than the love of the 'moral,' the reaction of thought in the face of the human comedy. They had observation sufficient, at any rate, to make their fortune, and it may well be said that that is enough for any novel. In *Silas Marner*, in *Adam Bede*, the quality seems gilded by a sort of autumn haze, an afternoon light, of meditation, which mitigates the sharpness of portraiture. I doubt very much whether the author herself had a clear vision, for instance, of the marriage of Dinah Morris to Adam, or of the rescue of Hetty from the scaffold at the eleventh hour. The reason of this may be, indeed, that her perception was a perception of nature much more than of art, and that these particular incidents do not belong to nature (to my sense, at least); by which I do not mean that they belong to a very happy art. I cite them, on the contrary, as an evidence of artistic weakness; they are a very good example of the view in which a story must have marriages and rescues in the nick of time as a matter of course. I must add, in fairness to George Eliot, that the marriage of the nun-like Dinah, which shocks the reader, who sees in it a base concession, was a *trouvaille* of Lewes's, and is a small sign of that same faulty judgment in literary things which led him to throw his influence on the side of her writing verse—verse which is *all* reflection, with direct, vivifying vision remarkably absent.

It is a part of this same limitation of the pleasure she was capable of taking in the fact of representation for itself that the various journals and notes of her visits to the Continent are, though by no means destitute of the tempered enjoyment of foreign sights, which was as near as she ever came to rapture, singularly vague in expression on the subject of the general and particular spectacle—the life and manners, the works of art. She enumerates diligently all the pictures and statues she sees, and the way she does so is a proof of her active, earnest intellectual habits; but it is rarely apparent that they have, as the phrase is, said much to her, or that what they have said is one of their deeper secrets. She is capable of writing, after coming out of the great chapel of San Lorenzo, in Florence, that 'the world-famous statues of Michael Angelo on the tombs . . . remained to us as affected and exaggerated in the original as in copies and casts.' That sentence startles one, on the part of the author of *Romola*, and that Mr. Cross should have printed it is a commendable proof of his impartiality.

It was in *Romola*, precisely, that the equilibrium I spoke of just now was lost, and that reflection began to weigh down the scale. *Romola* is preëminently a study of the human conscience in an historical setting which is studied almost as much, and few passages in Mr. Cross's volumes are more interesting than those relating to the production of this magnificent romance. George Eliot took all her work with a noble seriousness, but into none of it did she throw herself with more passion. It drained from her as much as she gave to it, and none of her writing ploughed into her, to use her biographer's expression, so deeply. She told him that she began it as a young woman, and finished it as an old one. More than any of her novels, it was evolved, as I have said, from her moral consciousness—a moral consciousness encircled by a prodigious amount of literary research. Her literary ideal was at all times of the highest, but in the preparation of *Romola* it placed her under a control absolutely religious. She read innumerable books, some of them bearing only remotely on her subject, and consulted without stint contemporary records and documents. She neglected nothing that would enable her to live, intellectually, in the period she had undertaken to describe. We know, for the most part, I think, the result. *Romola* is on the whole the finest thing she wrote, but its defects are almost on the scale of its beauties. The great defect is that, except in the person of Tito Melema, it does not seem positively to live. It is overladen with learning, it smells of the lamp, it tastes just perceptibly of pedantry. In spite of its incomplete animation, however, it assuredly will survive in men's remembrance, for the finest pages in it belong to the finest part of our literature. It is on the whole a failure, but such a failure as only a great talent can produce; and one may say of it that there are many great 'hits' far less interesting than such a mistake. A twentieth part of the erudition would have sufficed, would have given us the feeling and color of the time, if there had been more of the breath of the Florentine streets, more of the faculty of optical evocation, a greater saturation of the senses with the elements of the adorable little city. The difficulty with the book, for the most part, is that it is not Italian; it has always seemed to me the most Germanic of the author's productions. I cannot imagine a German writing (in the way of a novel) anything half so good; but if I could imagine it, I should suppose *Romola* to be very much the sort of picture he would achieve—the sort of medium through which he would show us how, by the Arno-side, the fifteenth century came to an end. One of the sources of interest in the book is that, more than any of its companions, it indicates how much George Eliot proceeded by reflection and research; how little important, comparatively, she thought that same breath of the streets. It carries to a maximum the in-door quality.

The most definite impression produced, perhaps, by Mr. Cross's volumes (by the second and third) is that of simple success—success which had been the result of no external accidents (unless her union with Lewes be so denominated), but was involved in the very faculties nature had given her. All the elements of an eventual happy fortune met in her constitution. The great foundation, to begin with, was there —the magnificent mind, vigorous, luminous, and eminently sane. To her intellectual vigor, her immense facility, her exemption from cerebral lassitude, her letters and journals bear the most copious testimony. Her daily stint of arduous reading and writing was of the largest. Her *ability*, as one may express it in the most general way, was astonishing, and it belonged to every season of her long and fruitful career. Her passion for study encountered no impediment, but was able to make everything feed and support it. The extent and variety of her knowledge is by itself a *résumé* of an existence which triumphed wherever it wished. Add to this an immense special talent, which, as soon as it tries its wings, is found to be capable of the highest, longest flights, and brings back great material rewards. George Eliot of course had drawbacks and difficulties, physical infirmities, constant liabilities to headache, dyspepsia, and other illness, to deep depression, to despair about her work; but these jolts of the chariot were small in proportion to the impetus acquired, and were hardly greater than was necessary for reminding her of the secret of all ambitious workers in the field of art —that effort, effort, always effort, is the only key of success. Her great furtherance was that, intensely intellectual being as she was, the life of affection and emotion was also widely open to her. She had all the initiation of knowledge and none of its dryness, all the advantages of judgment and all the luxuries of feeling. She had an imagination which enabled her to sit at home with book and pen, and yet enter into the life of other generations; project herself into Warwickshire ale-houses and Florentine symposia, reconstitute conditions utterly different from her own. Toward the end she triumphed over the great impossible; she reconciled the greatest sensibility with the highest serenity. She succeeded in guarding her pursuits from intrusion; in carrying out her habits; in sacrificing her work as little as possible; in leading, in the midst of a society united in conspiracies to interrupt and demoralize, an independent, strenuously personal life. People who had the honor of penetrating into the sequestered precinct of the Priory—the house in London, in which she lived from 1863 to 1880—remember well a kind of sanctity in the place, an atmosphere of stillness and concentration, something that suggested a literary temple.

It was part of the good fortune of which I speak that in Mr. Lewes she had found the most devoted of caretakers, the most jealous of ministers, a companion through whom all business was transacted. The one drawback of this relation was that, considering what she attempted, it limited her experience too much to itself, but for the rest it helped her in a hundred ways; it saved her nerves, it fortified her privacy, it protected her leisure, it diminished the friction of living. His admiration of her work was of the largest, though not always, I think, truly discriminating, and he surrounded her with a sort of temperate zone of independence—independence of everything except him and her own standards. Nervous, sensitive, delicate in every way in which genius is delicate (except, indeed, that she had a robust reason), it was a great thing for her to have accident made rare and exposure mitigated; and to this result Lewes, as the administrator of her fame, admirably contributed. He filtered the stream, and gave her only the clearer water. The accident of reading reviews of one's productions, especially when they are bad, is, for the artist of our day, one of the most frequent; and Mr. Lewes, by keeping these things out of her way, enabled her to achieve what was perhaps the highest form of her success—an inaccessibility to the newspaper. 'It is remarkable to me,' she writes in 1876, 'that I have entirely lost my *personal* melancholy. I often, of course, have melancholy thoughts about the destinies of my fellow creatures, but I am never in that *mood* of sadness which used to be my frequent visitant even in the midst of external happiness.' Her later years, colored by this accumulated wisdom, when she had taken her final form before the world, and had come to be regarded more and more as a teacher and philosopher, are full of suggestion to the critic, but I have exhausted my limited space. There is a certain coldness in them, perhaps—the coldness that results from most of one's opinions being formed, one's mind made up, on many great subjects; from the degree, in a word, to which 'culture' had taken the place of the more primitive processes of experience.

'Ah, les livres, ils nous débordent, ils nous étouffent—nous périssons par les livres!'[1] That cry of a distinguished French novelist (there is no harm in mentioning M. Alphonse Daudet), which fell upon the ear of

---

[1] 'Ah, books, they overwhelm and stifle us—we are being destroyed by books.'

the present writer some time ago, represents as little as possible the emotion of George Eliot, confronted with literatures and sciences. M. Alphonse Daudet went on to say that, to his mind, the personal impression, the effort of direct observation, was the most precious source of information for the novelist; that nothing could take its place; that the effect of books was constantly to check and pervert this effort; that a second-hand, third-hand, tenth-hand, impression was constantly tending to substitute itself for a fresh perception; that we were ending by seeing everything through literature instead of through our own senses; and that, in short, literature was rapidly killing literature. This view has immense truth on its side, but the case would be too simple if, on one side or the other, there were only one way of finding out. The effort of the novelist is to find out, to know, or at least to see and no one, in the nature of things, can afford to be less indifferent to side-lights. Books are themselves, unfortunately, an expression of human passions. George Eliot had no doubts, at any rate; if impressionism, before she laid down her pen, had already begun to be talked about, it would have made no difference with her—she would have had no desire to pass for an impressionist.

There is one question we cannot help asking ourselves as we close this record of her life; it is impossible not to let our imagination wander in the direction of what turn her mind or her fortune might have taken if she had never met George Henry Lewes, or never cast her lot with his. It is safe to say that, in one way or another, in the long run, her novels would have got themselves written, and it is possible they would have been more natural, as one may call it, more familiarly and casually human. Would her development have been less systematic, more irresponsible, more personal, and should we have had more of *Adam Bede* and *Silas Marner*, and less of *Romola* and *Middlemarch*? The question, after all, cannot be answered, and I do not push it, being myself very grateful for *Middlemarch* and *Romola*. It is as George Eliot does actually present herself that we must judge her—a condition that will not prevent her from striking us as one of the noblest, most beautiful minds of our time. This impression bears the reader company throughout these letters and notes. It is impossible not to feel, as we close them, that she was an admirable being. They are less brilliant, less entertaining, than we might have hoped; they contain fewer 'good things,' and have even a certain grayness of tone, something measured and subdued, as of a person talking without ever raising her voice. But there rises from them a kind of fragrance of moral elevation; a love of justice, truth, and light; a large, generous way of looking at things; and a constant effort to hold high the torch in the dusky spaces of man's conscience. That is how we see her during the latter years of her life: frail, delicate, shivering a little, much fatigued and considerably spent, but still meditating on what could be acquired and imparted; still living, in the intelligence, a freer, larger life than probably had ever been the portion of any woman. To her own sex her memory, her example, will remain of the highest value; those of them for whom the 'development' of woman is the hope of the future ought to erect a monument to George Eliot. She helped on the cause more than any one, in proving how few limitations are of necessity implied in the feminine organism. She went so far that such a distance seems enough, and in her effort she sacrificed no tenderness, no grace. There is much talk to-day about things being 'open to women;' but George Eliot showed that there is nothing that is closed. If we criticise her novels, we must remember that her nature came first and her work afterwards, and that it is not remarkable that they should not resemble the productions, say, of Alexandre Dumas. What *is* remarkable, extraordinary— and the process remains inscrutable and mysterious—is that this quiet, anxious, sedentary, serious, invalidical English lady, without animal spirits, without adventures, without extravagance, assumption, or bravado, should have made us believe that nothing in the world was alien to her; should have produced such rich, deep, masterly pictures of the multifold life of man.

Bibliography

Select bibliography of works listing or describing the nineteenth-century criticism of George Eliot's novels.

ANDERSON, J. P., Bibliography in Oscar Browning's *Life of George Eliot*, 1892.

BARRY, J. D. 'The Literary Reputation of George Eliot', unpublished dissertation, Northwestern University, Evanston, 1955. A survey covering both the nineteenth and twentieth centuries.

BARRY, J. D. 'The Literary Reputation of George Eliot's Fiction: A Supplementary Bibliography', *Bulletin of Bibliography*, (January–April 1959), xxii, 176–82. A very useful supplement which brings the bibliographies of Anderson, Cooke, and Waldo up to 1957.

COOKE, G. W., Bibliography in *George Eliot: A Critical Study of Her Life, Writings and Philosophy*, 1883.

COUCH, J. P., *George Eliot in France: A French Appraisal of George Eliot's Writings, 1858–1960*, Chapel Hill, 1967. Valuable survey of a large quantity of periodical criticism.

HAIGHT, G. S., *A Century of George Eliot Criticism*, Boston, 1965. Selected reviews and critical extracts; particularly valuable for the criticism of the novels since George Eliot's death.

HARVEY, W. J., 'George Eliot', *Victorian Fiction: A Guide to Research*, ed. Lionel Stevenson, Cambridge, Mass., 1964, pp. 294–323. Focuses on modern criticism, but also theorises suggestively on George Eliot's reputation in general.

HARVEY, W. J., 'Criticism of the Novel: Contemporary Reception', *Middlemarch. Critical Approaches to the Novel*, ed. Barbara Hardy, 1967, pp. 125–47. An excellent analysis of the contemporary reception of *Middlemarch*.

HOLMSTROM, J. and L. LERNER, *George Eliot and Her Readers: A Selection of Contemporary Reviews*, 1966.

PARLETT, M., 'The Influence of Contemporary Criticism on George Eliot', *Studies in Philology*, (January 1933), xxx, 103–32. Suggests that periodical criticism of the early novels prompted changes in George Eliot's later writing.

WALDO, F. and G. A. TURKINGTON, Bibliography in Mathilde Blind's *George Eliot*, new ed., Boston, 1904.

Index